Noticing and Second Language Acquisition: Studies in Honor of Richard Schmidt

NFLRC
monographs

NFLRC Monographs is a refereed series sponsored by the National Foreign Language Resource Center at the University of Hawai'i which presents the findings of recent work in applied linguistics that is of relevance to language teaching and learning, with a focus on the less commonly-taught languages of Asia and the Pacific.

New perspectives on Japanese language learning, linguistics, and culture
Kimi Kondo-Brown, Yoshiko Saito-Abbott, Shingo Satsutani, Michio Tsutsui, & Ann Wehmeyer (Editors), 2013
ISBN 978–0–9835816–3–5

Developing, using, and analyzing rubrics in language assessment with case studies in Asian and Pacific languages
James Dean Brown (Editor), 2012
ISBN 978–0–9835816–1–1

Research among learners of Chinese as a foreign language
Michael E. Everson & Helen H. Shen (Editors), 2010
ISBN 978–0–9800459–4–9

Toward useful program evaluation in college foreign language education
John M. Norris, John McE. Davis, Castle Sinicrope, & Yukiko Watanabe (Editors), 2009
ISBN 978–0–9800459–3–2

Second language teaching and learning in the Net Generation
Raquel Oxford & Jeffrey Oxford (Editors), 2009
ISBN 978–0–9800459–2–5

Case studies in foreign language placement: Practices and possibilities
Thom Hudson & Martyn Clark (Editors), 2008
ISBN 978–0–9800459–0–1

Chinese as a heritage language: Fostering rooted world citizenry
Agnes Weiyun He & Yun Xiao (Editors), 2008
ISBN 978–0–8248328–6–5

Perspectives on teaching connected speech to second language speakers
James Dean Brown & Kimi Kondo-Brown (Editors), 2006
ISBN 978–0–8248313–6–3

ordering information at nflrc.hawaii.edu

Noticing and Second Language Acquisition: Studies in Honor of Richard Schmidt

edited by

Joara M. Bergsleithner
Sylvia Nagem Frota
Jim K. Yoshioka

National Foreign Language Resource Center
University of Hawai'i at Mānoa

Manufactured in the United States of America.

The contents of this publication were developed in part under a grant from the U.S. Department of Education (CFDA 84.229, P229A100001). However, the contents do not necessarily represent the policy of the Department of Education, and one should not assume endorsement by the Federal Government.

ISBN: 978–0–9835816–6–6

Library of Congress Control Number: 9780983581666

book design by Deborah Masterson | *cover photo ©2012 Jennifer Crites*

distributed by

National Foreign Language Resource Center
University of Hawai'i
1859 East-West Road #106
Honolulu HI 96822–2322
nflrc.hawaii.edu

NFLRC
monographs

About the National Foreign Language Resource Center

The National Foreign Language Resource Center, located in the College of Languages, Linguistics, & Literature at the University of Hawai'i at Mānoa, has conducted research, developed materials, and trained language professionals since 1990 under a series of grants from the U.S. Department of Education (Language Resource Centers Program). A national advisory board sets the general direction of the resource center. With the goal of improving foreign language instruction in the United States, the center publishes research reports and teaching materials that focus primarily on the languages of Asia and the Pacific. The center also sponsors summer intensive teacher training institutes and other professional development opportunities. For additional information about center programs, contact us.

Janes Dean Brown, Director
National Foreign Language Resource Center
University of Hawai'i at Mānoa
1859 East-West Road #106
Honolulu, HI 96822–2322

email: nflrc@hawaii.edu
website: nflrc.hawaii.edu

NFLRC Advisory Board 2010–2014

Contents

Preface ix

Part One: Situating the Noticing Hypothesis in SLA

1 Noticing and Dick Schmidt's Personal and Academic History: An Introduction
Jim K. Yoshioka, Sylvia Nagem Frota, & Joara M. Bergsleithner ... 1

2 Schmidt's Noticing Hypothesis: More Than Two Decades After
Ronald P. Leow 11

3 Noticing and L2 Development: Theoretical, Empirical, and Pedagogical Issues
Shinichi Izumi 25

4 Attention, Awareness, and Noticing in Language Processing and Learning
John N. Williams 39

Part Two: Observing and Enhancing Noticing

5 Recasts, Uptake, and Noticing
Rod Ellis & Nadia Mifka-Profozic 61

6 Is Metalinguistic Stimulated Recall Reactive in Second Language Learning?
Takako Egi, Rebecca J. Adams, & Ana-María Nuevo 81

7 The Effects of L2 Learner Proficiency on Depth of Processing, Levels of Awareness, and Intake
Anne M. Calderón 103

8 The Effects of Aural Input Enhancement on L2 Acquisition
Minyoung Cho & Hayo Reinders 123

9 Instruction in Support of Noticing: An Empirical Study of EFL in Brazil
Sylvia Nagem Frota & Joara M. Bergsleithner 139

10 **Investigating Relationships Among Noticing, Working Memory Capacity, and Accuracy in L2 Oral Performance**
Joara M. Bergsleithner & Mailce Borges Mota 151

11 **Nurturing Noticing**
Peter Skehan 169

Part Three: Keeping a Close Eye on Noticing

12 **What Do Eye Movements Tell Us About Awareness? A Triangulation of Eye-Movement Data, Verbal Reports, and Vocabulary Learning Scores**
Aline Godfroid & Jens Schmidtke 183

13 **Observing Noticing While Reading in L2**
Daphnée Simard & Denis Foucambert 207

14 **Coming Eye-to-Eye With Noticing**
Patti Spinner, Susan Gass, & Jennifer Behney 227

Part Four: Beyond Noticing

15 **Implicit and Explicit Knowledge of Form-Meaning Connections: Evidence From Subjective Measures of Awareness**
Patrick Rebuschat, Phillip Hamrick, Rebecca Sachs, Kate Riestenberg, & Nicole Ziegler 249

16 **Implicit Second Language Learning and Individual Differences**
Daniel O. Jackson 271

17 **A Cognitive Neuroscientific Approach to Studying the Role of Awareness in L2 Learning**
Lester C. Loschky & Michael Harrington 289

18 **The Task at Hand: Noticing as a Mind–Body–World Phenomenon**
Christine M. Jacknick & Scott Thornbury 309

19 **Noticing and Mediation: A Sociocultural Perspective**
Riikka Alanen 331

About the Contributors 343

Preface

As editors, we are deeply pleased to organize this volume in honor of Dick Schmidt and pay him the unquestionable and long-deserved tribute for his immense and brilliant contributions to the field of applied linguistics throughout the years. In particular, it is our hope that this book will help illuminate and spur on future research into noticing and attention in L2 studies. It is with great satisfaction that we present these 19 chapters to the SLA community.

The nineteen contributions assembled in this volume comprise a compilation of works on noticing, particularly on issues related to attention, awareness, different measurements of noticing, L2 development, L2 learning, language processing, working memory capacity, individual differences, and so forth. Together they expand, fine tune, confirm, challenge, and take Schmidt's seminal research and ideas into exciting future directions.

The book is divided into four parts. Part One—*Situating the Noticing Hypothesis in SLA*—includes four chapters that situate the noticing hypothesis and its contribution to language development and pedagogical issues in SLA. Based on an interview conducted in the summer of 2012 and written by the editors of this volume, Chapter 1 opens up a personal and professional history of Dr. Schmidt, the inquisitive and perceptive mind and man behind the hypothesis. Part One then continues with theoretical chapters on noticing and related issues, which contribute to the discussion of the construct of noticing. In Chapter 2, "Schmidt's Noticing Hypothesis: More Than Two Decades After," Leow presents a theoretical and methodological review of the noticing hypothesis. In Chapter 3, "Noticing and L2 Development: Theoretical, Empirical, and Pedagogical Issues," Izumi illuminates a discussion on different types of noticing and its relationship with SLA processes, and to close this section, in Chapter 4, "Attention, Awareness, and Noticing in Language

Processing and Learning," Williams provides an update on psychological issues concerning the noticing hypothesis.

Part Two—*Observing and Enhancing Noticing*—consists of seven chapters that propose to observe and to enhance noticing by conducting mostly empirical studies, which use different methods to assess noticing. In Chapter 5, "Recasts, Uptake, and Noticing," Ellis and Mifka-Profozic examine to what extent uptake following a recast can be evidence of noticing. In Chapter 6, "Is Metalinguistic Stimulated Recall Reactive in Second Language Learning?", Egi, Adams, and Nuevo use retrospective verbalizations to look into whether metalinguistic stimulated recall may affect learning outcomes. In Chapter 7, "The Effects of L2 Learner Proficiency on Depth of Processing, Levels of Awareness, and Intake," Calderón supports Schmidt's hypothesis on the role of awareness and levels of awareness in L2 intake. In Chapter 8, "The Effects of Aural Input Enhancement on L2 Acquisition," Cho and Reinders explore the effects of aural input enhancement and its types in SLA. In Chapter 9, "Instruction in Support of Noticing: An Empirical Study of EFL in Brazil," Frota and Bergsleithner investigate whether instruction can support noticing in subsequent input. In Chapter 10, "Investigating the Relationship Among Noticing, Working Memory Capacity, and L2 Oral Performance," Bergsleithner and Mota examine whether there is a relationship between noticing and working memory capacity and how these two cognitive constructs can relate to L2 oral performance, and, to conclude the second section of this volume, in Chapter 11, "Nurturing Noticing," Skehan reviews tasks and neatly presents ideas and evidence that, although they are not often acknowledged in SLA work, directly bear on the noticing hypothesis.

Part Three of the book—*Keeping a Close Eye on Noticing*—involves studies on eye-tracking measurement investigations. In Chapter 12, "What Do Eye Movements Tell Us About Awareness? A Triangulation of Eye-Movement Data, Verbal Reports, and Vocabulary Learning Scores," Godfroid and Schmidtke provide a concise summary of research investigating L2 learners' attention and awareness, which attempts to improve construct specification and measurement of noticing. In Chapter 13, "Observing Noticing While Reading in L2," Simard and Foucambert investigate the effect of textual enhancement on noticing, taking some individual differences into consideration linking directly to the noticing hypothesis as currently formulated by Schmidt (2012), and, to finish the third section of this volume, in Chapter 14, "Coming Eye-to-Eye with Noticing," Spinner, Gass, and Behney look at noticing of morphophonology and syntax in order to understand what exactly learners attend to as they sort out issues of gender agreement.

Last but certainly not least, Part Four of the book—*Beyond Noticing*—entails a different and instigative view of noticing for L2 studies. In Chapter 15, "Implicit and Explicit Knowledge of Form-Meaning Connections: Evidence from Subjective Measures of Awareness," Rebuschat, Hamrick, Sachs, Riestenberg, and Ziegler replicate two studies and clarify the differences in their results by adding subjective measures of awareness, namely confidence ratings and source attributions. In Chapter 16, "Implicit Second Language Learning and Individual Differences," Jackson reviews literature on L2 learning in the absence of awareness and explores evidence as regards the roles of cognitive, experiential, and affective differences in language learning. In Chapter 17, "A Cognitive Neuroscientific Approach to Studying the Role of Awareness in L2 Learning," Loschky and Harrington review some studies about online L2 processing of grammatical violations using ERPs and reveal evidence for both conscious and unconscious processing. In Chapter 18, "The Task at Hand: Noticing as a Mind–Body–World Phenomenon," Jacknick and Thornbury scrutinize the role that gesture plays in visual and cognitive attention when co-constructing opportunities for learning, and finally in Chapter 19, "Noticing and Mediation: A Sociocultural Perspective," Alanen discusses the role of consciousness in SLA and approaches noticing within a sociocultural perspective.

We would not have been able to put together this book without the wonderful contributions from our authors and without the expert help and guidance of the following individuals: Lourdes Ortega, Daniel O. Jackson, Munehiko Miyata, Douglas Margolis, Peter Robinson, Deborah Masterson, James Dean Brown, and, of course, Dick Schmidt. We owe them a debt of gratitude.

On a personal note, the editors would each like to offer their thanks to Dick Schmidt. Joara M. Bergsleithner wishes to thank Dick for being an inspiring and supportive mentor during her Ph.D. dissertation research and analysis when she was a visiting scholar in Hawai'i. In addition, his talent, intelligence, friendship, patience, and humanity have had a profound influence on her growth as both a researcher and person. Sylvia Nagem Frota wishes to express her very special thanks to Dick for inviting her as his co-author for their Schmidt and Frota (1986) paper, undoubtedly the greatest honor and a landmark in her academic career, forever raising her academic appetite. His insightful, wise, and brilliant teachings and guidance have been, are, and will always be crucial for her. She also wishes to thank Dick for his generous, warm, and personal friendship throughout the years. Jim Kei Yoshioka wishes to thank Dick for his excellent leadership and guidance as director of the National Foreign Language Resource Center at the University of Hawai'i, their many collaborative projects together (like AAAL 2003), his great and funny stories, his generosity, and his friendship.

May 23, 2013

Joara Martin Bergsleithner, *University of Brasília, Brazil*

Sylvia Nagem Frota, *Federal University of Rio de Janeiro, Brazil*

Jim Kei Yoshioka, *University of Hawai'i at Mānoa*

Part One:
Situating the Noticing Hypothesis in SLA

Noticing and Dick Schmidt's Personal and Academic History: An Introduction

Jim K. Yoshioka
University of Hawai'i at Mānoa

Sylvia Nagem Frota
Federal University of Rio de Janeiro, Brazil

Joara M. Bergsleithner
University of Brasília, Brazil

Based on an interview conducted in 2012, this chapter provides a brief overview of the education and major life and professional experiences of Dick Schmidt, from his years studying Arabic and working in the Middle East to his groundbreaking research at the University of Hawai'i at Mānoa to his learning of Portuguese in Rio de Janeiro. They would spur and illuminate his subsequent critical inquiries into noticing, attention and awareness, motivation, individual differences, and other areas, which have continued to enrich the field of second language acquisition.

Personal background and interest in language

Dick Schmidt is one of the most well-known and respected linguists in the second language acquisition (SLA) community and has influenced multitudes of researchers with his groundbreaking ideas and studies (see subsequent chapters in this volume for just a sample). From his widely cited noticing hypothesis to his subsequent research into cognitive and affective factors, such as attention, awareness, and motivation, influencing adult second and foreign language learning, his contributions continue to stimulate critical discussions and expansions in the field and illuminate our understanding of the beautiful, complex, and often thorny nature of language.

Yoshioka, J. K., Frota, S. N., & Bergsleithner, J. M. (2013). Noticing and Dick Schmidt's personal and academic history: An introduction. In J. M. Bergsleithner, S. N. Frota, & J. K. Yoshioka (Eds.), *Noticing and second language acquisition: Studies in honor of Richard Schmidt* (pp. 1–9). Honolulu: University of Hawai'i, National Foreign Language Resource Center.

Given all that, it may come as a surprise that when Dick Schmidt[1] was growing up, he was not particularly interested in foreign languages. He lived in a very monolingual town in Massachusetts, near Boston, where the only immigrants were mostly native-English speakers. He recounted that he never knew anyone at that time who spoke other languages. And although he did take some French classes in high school and university and got high marks, he didn't learn to speak the language, and to him, it was just another school subject like math or science. His appreciation and interest in languages would not take hold until he was out in the real world.

In 1963, Dick graduated from Harvard University, with a BA in social relations (a combination of sociology, psychology, and cultural anthropology), and soon afterwards, he decided to apply for and join the U.S. Foreign Service. Under the auspices of the U.S. Department of State, the Foreign Service sends officers out to work in American embassies, consulates, and other diplomatic missions in countries around the world. It was at this time that he first experienced living in foreign cultures and took a keen interest in language.

His first assignment was to the U.S. Embassy in Egypt in 1964, and in order to prepare for it, he was sent to study Arabic for six months, about eight hours a day, following a strict audiolingual drill approach, the method of the time:

> It was okay. I felt, when I was taking that class, it was very small. There were only six people, I think, in the class and one instructor and one linguist who supervised. I didn't really know if anybody outside of my teacher spoke that language. It's not like now. I would have internet. People didn't have the idea that language learning would take place outside the classroom. So, you know, we're just in there getting drilled all day long, and then we go home and speak English.

As it turned out, the variety of Arabic he was learning was Palestinian Arabic, so when he arrived in Egypt, he ended up having to re-learn much of his vocabulary for the Egyptian dialect all over again.

After his one-year training assignment in Egypt, the Foreign Service sent him to Lebanon where he stayed for five years. During his stay in Lebanon, he became fascinated with Arabic:

> I really like the language. I like the sound of it. I like the feeling of it. I liked learning a language that's got very few cognates with English. That made it hard but interesting… It's got its own genius. It's very subtle and amazingly regular in some areas and other areas not. But, I really got into it.

At this point, the development of his Arabic came about primarily through his interactions with people outside of work. "The only reason I succeeded at Arabic, better than most Americans at least, is I found friends, made close relationships with people who didn't speak English, so it was really important for me to communicate with them. And I was going to do it by learning their language, not by teaching them English."

In addition to being able to better carry out the daily activities of life, he also had another strong motivation for continuing to learn Arabic. Given the geopolitical situation of this era, the better his Arabic, the more likely he would be labeled as essential personnel by the U.S. government. With this designation, he could potentially avoid being shipped off to Vietnam,

1 This chapter is based on an interview with Dick Schmidt, conducted by Jim K. Yoshioka, on July 6, 2012. The authors are grateful for Professor Schmidt's time, generosity, and input into this account of some of the major events of his professional life.

which at the time was a very plausible reality. Of course, things were not quiet in the Middle East either. Lebanon was not a direct protagonist in the Arabic-Israeli war of 1967 but was seriously affected by it, exacerbating internal and external stresses that would lead to civil war a few years later.

In Beirut Dick was the director of the American cultural center, which had an affiliated language school, which he was nominally the boss of. As such, he felt he should educate himself appropriately, so he took classes in English linguistics and teaching English as a Foreign Language (TEFL) at the American University of Beirut, which he enjoyed. He also volunteered to teach EFL courses at the language school. His interest in languages had grown substantially by then. At the same time, he knew that the BA he had was not enough to get by in life, so he set his sights on furthering his education in the direction of linguistics.

As he came to the close of his Foreign Service years, he had the opportunity to take a year's leave of absence to pursue a Master's degree. He also applied for and received a National Defense Education Act scholarship, the predecessor to the modern day Foreign Language and Area Studies (FLAS) grants, which would cover up to four years of funding, as long as his studies included further study on Arabic. He completed his MA in linguistics at Brown University in 1971, in a year as planned. But, since he already had additional funding available and had been accepted into the Ph.D. program, he decided to quit the Foreign Service and continue at Brown. He carried on with his graduate work in Arabic linguistics, and in preparation for his Ph.D. dissertation focusing on sociolinguistics, he returned to Egypt to collect data. His research, based on the work of William Labov, especially Labov (1966, 1972), focused on examining how people shift registers in different environments. In particular, he examined shifts between colloquial and standard varieties of Egyptian Arabic and the social class dimensions that affected them. His doctoral dissertation was entitled "Socio-Stylistic Variation in Spoken Egyptian Arabic: A Re-Examination of the Concept Diglossia," and he graduated from Brown in 1974.

After finishing his Ph.D., he went back to Egypt for two and a half years and taught as an assistant professor at the American University in Cairo in its MA in TEFL program, which he really enjoyed. One highlight of those years was teaching a course on Arabic sociolinguistics as an adjunct (visiting) professor at Al-Azhar University, including a field trip with graduate students to undertake work on a dialect survey of the province of Qena in Upper Egypt. During that period he maintained his interest in Arabic but also became much more interested in English teaching and applied linguistics, and some of his students from those days at AUC later became co-authors and co-researchers in studies carried out in later years, especially studies of motivation in language learning (Schmidt, Boraie, & Kassabgy, 1996).

Soon he decided he wanted to return to the States, but not many institutions had a prominent MA ESL/EFL program like the American University in Cairo, known to people in the Middle East—perhaps just UCLA, the University of Hawai'i (UH), the University of Illinois, and a few others—at the time. He gravitated toward Hawai'i because he didn't want to go back to the East Coast, a colleague in Egypt was taking up a post at the East-West Center near the UH campus, Hawai'i seemed like an interesting place to live, and the ESL curriculum at UH was quite similar to the American University in Cairo's.

So in 1976, he applied for and accepted a position as an assistant professor in the Department of English as a Second Language (now called the Department of Second

Language Studies) at the University of Hawai'i at Mānoa (UHM). He had never been to Hawai'i previously and found it a beautiful and wonderful place to live and work.

He served as professor for 35 years at the University of Hawai'i until his retirement in December 2011. During that period, the reputation of the Department of Second Language Studies (SLS) grew enormously due to the acclaimed research and important hypotheses in the field of applied linguistics contributed by Dick Schmidt and many other renowned faculty members. Today, it is considered one of the premiere programs in second language studies internationally.

Besides being a professor in the SLS Department, he was also the second and longest-serving director of the National Foreign Language Resource Center (NFLRC) at the University of Hawai'i at Mānoa, a total of 16 years, starting in 1995. The NFLRC is one of fifteen Title VI national Language Resource Centers, which serve to promote the learning and teaching of less commonly taught languages (LCTLs) in the United States. In particular, the NFLRC focuses on LCTLs of Asia and the Pacific. He regards the Center as having both internal and external benefits. Internally, it promotes interdepartmental collaboration within the UHM College of Languages, Linguistics, and Literature on research and materials development projects as well as through professional development opportunities. Externally, he sees the Center as continuing to be helpful to the foreign language community in the U.S. through the synergy achieved by bringing together people from different fields and different interdisciplinary backgrounds and by providing a wealth of publications, including an excellent series of monographs and three online refereed journals, as well as annual offerings of teacher/researcher training events (conferences, summer institutes, workshops).

The seeds—Two seminal studies

Dick Schmidt is primarily recognized for two well-known studies that eventually provided the seeds and framework for the development of his noticing hypothesis. The first of these was a case study on "Wes," an adult Japanese male ESL learner. Dick met Wes in 1978 when he barely spoke English. Dick was interested in working with Wes because Wes had not studied English in Japan before moving to Hawai'i. He wanted to learn English but did not want to take classes because he had never liked school. Wes believed that the only way to learn a language was to meet and interact with native speakers, listen to what they say, and basically say the same thing. Personality-wise, Wes was strongly motivated to learn, outgoing, and funny, a risk-taker.

Dick was particularly keen to study Wes, because, at that time, he was very interested in John Schumann's acculturation theory (1978), which claims that the degree to which you acquire a language is a function of the degree to which you acquire the culture. Since Wes seemed to be a person who would acculturate quickly and had the personality characteristics Schumann listed as ideal, Dick thought this would be a good test of the theory. Also, in terms of social characteristics, Schumann's acculturation theory asserts that if the two cultures involved are unequally valued, the study will likely run into complications. For example, conquerors do not learn the language of the defeated, and oppressed people tend to resist learning the language of their conquerors. In Wes's case, however, Japan and the U.S. are two cultures that generally respect each other, which is felt even more tangibly in Hawai'i where Japanese culture has a strong presence. Dick thought this would make an interesting, fun, theory-oriented case study, and he was looking forward to seeing what could be observed. Wes was also quite receptive to participating in the study.

The Wes study (Schmidt, 1983) was carried out over 4–5 years (1978–83), amassing 30 hours of naturalistic recordings. As Wes progressed in his learning of English, the process became more and more mysterious to Dick, who was intrigued about the complexity of language learning and all the issues regarding why people succeed and why they don't and where it goes right and where it goes wrong during the second language acquisition process.

The Wes study may have had the impact it did because it pointed out that the acculturation theory needed to be reformulated. Schumann's theory was originally phrased in terms of the acquisition of grammar, so if a person were strongly motivated and acculturated, he should acquire the grammar. But Wes pretty much learned how to communicate without much morphology or grammar, which changed very little throughout the years. When Wes spoke to people, they frequently commented on how communicative and how good his English was, often due to his good pronunciation, stress, and intonation. However, he could go for long stretches without using articles, plurals, or past tense markers, again speaking without grammar or morphology. Conclusions from this case study were not decisive, and Dick admits Wes's case is still a puzzlement to him in many ways.

The Wes study did, however, spur him to begin focusing on the role of noticing in language learning:

> I started thinking, 'Why do people think his English is good when, if I take a transcript and analyze it linguistically, in that sense, it's not?' See, I don't think he's a failure at all. I don't. People think I portray him as a deficient learner, but that's not really it. He's got strengths and weak points. But why do people think his English is so good when he doesn't use prepositions, articles, plurals, and tense? I think it's because when people talk to him and listen to him, *they don't notice* that he doesn't use them. So maybe the problem of his non-acquisition of them is when people use them to him, *he doesn't notice.* So I had that idea. I don't think I expressed it quite that succinctly from that study of Wes, but that was kind of the germ of the noticing hypothesis...was trying to figure out what was going on in Wes's mind and what the psychological part of it was like. And then right after that, I went to Brazil.

The second case study, Schmidt and Frota (1986), was carried out in Rio de Janeiro, Brazil, his first time there, where Dick was a visiting Fulbright lecturer for five months in 1983, and it centered on his own learning of Portuguese:

> I went there with the intention of answering some of the questions from the Wes study. I thought, 'I can't read his mind, but I can read my own.'... I could give a first-person account of what it's like to learn a second language like that. But even before I got there, I knew that idea would be challenged. Because, right after I got the letter saying you've got this Fulbright award to Brazil, I spoke to a well-known linguist... and he said, 'Are you going to do any research when you're there?' And I said, 'Yeah, I'm going to try to learn Portuguese and keep a journal and study my own acquisition of Portuguese.' To which he replied, 'Rubbish! You cannot do that. Language learning is a completely unconscious process, and learners know nothing about it.' Wow, that's very challenging. That's a very strong statement. But, you know, I can see, he's an extreme Chomsky type, interested in deep principles of grammar that are not introspectable but sharing this presumption that many people had, which was very strong at that time, I would say, in the early 80s, mid 80s, which is that language acquisition is unconscious... Some little invisible language acquisition device is doing the work. So, that's why, as soon as I got to Brazil, I had to start looking and try to find somebody who would cooperate with me. And enter into a joint project where I'm

> trying to keep a record of my learning in Portuguese but somebody else, who's a native speaker of Portuguese and a trained linguist, is looking at it independently, separately, looking at it from their point of view.

While in Brazil, Dick taught a class on second language acquisition at the Catholic University of Rio de Janeiro and took a five-week intensive course in Portuguese (2 hours a day, five days a week), again still primarily audiolingual in approach. As with Arabic, his main language learning, however, was through interaction with native speakers, taking place outside of work, and in this case with friends and a late night theatre/restaurant crowd he hung out with, including media personalities, some of them quite famous. Language learning wasn't always an easy process, especially due to his shorter stay (five months total, compared to nine years in Arabic-speaking countries) and other factors:

> Brazil is very interesting this way, at least Rio—I don't want to generalize to a whole country...you don't find a lot of people who want to practice their English with you. They assume that you can learn Portuguese, and they'd like you to do it, and do it quickly please. So I had a lot of pressure to speak Portuguese better and learn faster. I used to go to this restaurant almost every night, and the proprietress said, 'You're getting a little better, but you know, when I moved here from Italy, I learned Portuguese perfectly in three weeks! What's wrong with you?'

In addition,

> With Portuguese, one of the hard things for me was the phonology, the listening of it. It's very hard. I found that after spending five months in Brazil, honest truth, I think I can understand Spanish better than Portuguese!... Spoken Portuguese, it's very hard to match it to the written form. Really hard.

Getting back to the study, it was based on two data sources: a journal Dick kept, recording his experiences learning Brazilian Portuguese, and more objective data collected from a series of tape-recorded conversations in Brazilian Portuguese between Dick and Brazilian linguist Sylvia Nagem Frota (co-author of this chapter and co-editor of the volume).

The main focus of the study reflected a single question: Is language picked up unconsciously or was Dick noticing what people said and consciously registering that? After the compilation of data, the results supported the idea that people consciously register aspects of a second language while learning it. Based on an analysis of his own production data, Schmidt noted that, other than words he had been taught explicitly, he only produced forms that he noticed people saying to him:

> There were just so many cases where something shows up in my speech and I check my diary and the week before someone came over and said it, and I wrote it down and started using it. So there was a really close connection between what I was able to notice people use... I think all the way through people are noticing things, all the time, all the time.

The results then indicated that classroom instruction was very useful, but presence and frequency in communicative input were more important. Based on comparisons among the notes on Dick's journal and the tape-recordings of his developing L2 production and interaction abilities, the study also found that some forms that were frequent in input were still not acquired until they were consciously noticed in the input.

In addition, a slightly different hypothesis called *noticing the gap* was suggested in the same study. It was found that although Dick was frequently corrected for his grammatical errors in conversation with native speakers, in many cases this had no effect because he was unaware that he was being corrected. This suggested the idea that in order to overcome errors, learners must make conscious comparisons between their own output and target language input.

Dick argues that the subjective experiences that people phenomenologically are aware of as they are learning a language are what drive language learning. It is not some little hidden language acquisition device deep in the recesses of their brains that is doing the work for them. This was the origin of the noticing hypothesis.

The noticing hypothesis

The noticing hypothesis is mainly based on the claim that learners must attend to and notice linguistic features of the input that they are exposed to if those forms are to become intake for learning.

Following the publication of Schmidt and Frota (1986), Dick undertook an extensive reading of the psychology literature on conscious and unconscious learning and concluded that, although earlier traditions in language teaching had over-emphasized the importance of conscious study and learning, SLA theory and some applied linguistics practices (such as extreme versions of communicative language teaching) in the mid to late 80s hugely over-valued the extent to which unconscious processes can guarantee successful adult learning. In Schmidt (1990), he presents a review of that literature on consciousness and argues that, although subconscious processes are important for and common in language comprehension and production, subliminal language learning is impossible and noticing is the necessary and sufficient condition for input to become intake. He believes that mere exposure to input and subconscious processing are not enough to trigger language development.

Later, he turned the focus of his interest from noticing to, more specifically, the role of attention and awareness in second language acquisition (Schmidt, 1995, 2001), for which he is probably best known, among other valuable contributions to the field:

> I like to talk more nowadays about attention. Attention is kind of the basic concept, and it's where lots of elements come together. And it's got a lot of practical value too. In one sense, one of the things that language teachers do is focus the attention of students on things that need to be attended to and help them become aware of things they wouldn't discover by themselves. One of the things that happens when people learn through conversational interaction is that they jointly construct the focus of the attention.

This discussion is crucial to many theoretical and practical controversies in the field, such as language acquisition mechanisms, interlanguage development and second language fluency, existence of implicit learning, and foreign language pedagogy. Dick argues that all learning requires attention and a lower level of awareness (which he calls *noticing*) but not necessarily an intention to learn. He also argues that awareness at the level of understanding is needed for explicit learning but not for implicit learning. The noticing hypothesis (Schmidt, 1990, 1992, 1994, 1995) has been very influential, and it is now regarded as a mainstream SLA construct.

Other areas of research

Another topic that Dick Schmidt has been interested in for a long time is the role of socio-affective factors such as individual differences and motivation (Schmidt, 2001, 2012). These also have their connections to attention and awareness:

> We think of noticing as a psychological phenomenon, a personal subjective phenomenon. It's clearly related to the construct of attention. Basically, we're aware of

> whatever we're paying attention to at the moment. So, that's a key construct, but also, if you think about something like motivation and think about the idea of 'Why do people who are strongly motivated learn more? What's the mechanism?', one view is that motivation is part of the affective filter, a metaphorical concept, some kind of a mental block. You think of it as some kind of screen that can go up and down. If it's low, then the input goes through to the place in the brain where the language acquisition device is located, wherever that may be. But that's a fairly passive view of language learning, right? It's just saying, 'As long as you don't have a mental block and you've got a nice attitude and you're exposed to input, it'll just go in.' I don't think so. I think motivated learners learn more because they pay attention. They pay attention, they notice things, and they try to figure them out. If they don't succeed, they try harder. So persistence comes in. So there's a connection there.

The same argument can be made about aptitude and individual differences because some people are better at noticing than others. Other individual differences that play a role in second/foreign language learning are also closely related to attention, such as working memory capacity, which can just as easily be viewed as working attention.

A distinguished career and new frontiers

From a youth who had no particular interest in languages to an inquisitive and insightful scholar whose ideas and investigations have become an integral part of the fabric of the second language acquisition literature, Dick can look proudly back on a distinguished career full of pivotal studies, presentations, and publications, among them the recent 4th edition of the *Longman dictionary of language teaching and applied linguistics* (2010), which he co-wrote with Jack C. Richards, a former colleague and longtime friend. He is among the most cited researchers in the field of applied linguistics, and his many honors and awards include the Distinguished Service & Scholarship Award (2009) from the American Association for Applied Linguistics (AAAL) (which he served as President of in 2003–04), Special Service Awards from the Center for Asia-Pacific Exchange in 1990 and 2010, and honorary membership in the Japanese Association of College English Teachers (JACET).

Now as professor emeritus, Dick has been enjoying the less busy, more relaxed nature of retirement but is looking, as ever, for new avenues to spark his curiosity and keen intellect. We are always the richer for it.

To Dick, our gratitude, our best wishes, and our aloha!

References

Labov, W. (1966). *The social stratification of English in New York City*. Washington, DC: Center for Applied Linguistics.

Labov, W. (1972). *Sociolinguistic patterns*. Philadelphia, PA: University of Pennsylvania Press.

Schmidt, R. (1983). Interaction, acculturation, and the acquisition of communicative competence. In N. Wolfson & E. Judd (Eds.), *Sociolinguistics and language acquisition* (pp. 137–174). Rowley, MA: Newbury House.

Schmidt, R. (1990). The role of consciousness in second language learning. *Applied Linguistics, 11*, 129–158.

Schmidt, R. (1992). Psychological mechanisms underlying second language fluency. *Studies in Second Language Acquisition, 14*, 357–385.

Schmidt, R. (1994). Deconstructing consciousness in search of useful definitions for applied linguistics. In J. H. Hulstijn & R. Schmidt (Eds.), *Consciousness and second language learning: Conceptual, methodological, and practical issues in language learning and teaching. Thematic issue of AILA Review—Revue de l'AILA, 11*, 11–26.

Schmidt, R. (1995). Consciousness and foreign language learning: A tutorial on attention and awareness in learning. In R. Schmidt (Ed.), *Attention and awareness in foreign language learning* (pp. 1–63). Honolulu, HI: University of Hawai'i, National Foreign Language Resource Center.

Schmidt, R. (2001). Attention. In P. Robinson (Ed.), *Cognition and second language instruction* (pp. 3–32). Cambridge University Press.

Schmidt, R. (2012). Attention, awareness, and individual differences in language learning. In W. M. Chan, K. N. Chin, S. K. Bhatt, & I. Walker (Eds.), *Perspectives on individual characteristics and foreign language education* (pp. 27–50). Boston/Berlin, De Gruyter Mouton.

Schmidt, R., Boraie, D., & Kassabgy, O. (1996). Foreign language motivation: Internal structure and external connections. In R. Oxford (Ed.), *Language learning motivation: Pathways to the new century* (pp. 9–70). Honolulu, HI: University of Hawai'i, National Foreign Language Resource Center.

Schmidt, R., & Frota, S. (1986). Developing basic conversational ability in a second language: A case study of an adult learner of Portuguese. In R. R. Day (Ed.), *Talking to learn: Conversation in second language acquisition* (pp. 237–326). Rowley, MA: Newbury House.

Schumann, J. (1978). The acculturation model for second-language acquisition. In R. Gringas (Ed.), *Second language acquisition and foreign language teaching* (pp. 27–50). Washington, DC: Center for Applied Linguistics.

NFLRC
monographs

Schmidt's Noticing Hypothesis: More Than Two Decades After

Ronald P. Leow
Georgetown University

This chapter succinctly and critically traces some major research trajectories that originated with Schmidt's (1990) noticing hypothesis, from its theoretical underpinnings to empirical findings from several strands of research premised upon it, to the thorny issue of the operationalization and measurement of attention and (levels of) awareness (together with the accompanying methodological issue of reactivity), to the role of unawareness in SLA. The chapter provides some reflections on Schmidt's noticing hypothesis from theoretical, methodological, and terminological perspectives.

Introduction

Schmidt's noticing hypothesis (1990 and elsewhere) is arguably the most influential theoretical underpinning in SLA over the last two decades and has contributed tremendously to the centralization of both the roles of attention and awareness in the process of acquiring or learning a second or foreign language (L2). Indeed, his hypothesis has been, with or without researchers' awareness, adopted in several major strands of research that include input enhancement, learning conditions, interaction, feedback, and instruction. In addition, his seminal 1990 article has propelled several researchers to probe more deeply into the operationalization and measurement of the constructs of attention and awareness in an effort to understand better the cognitive processes involved during the early stages of SLA, and more specifically, intake[1]. This chapter succinctly and critically traces—from theoretical, empirical, and methodological perspectives—some major research trajectories that originated with Schmidt's (1990) noticing hypothesis, namely, from its theoretical

1 Leow's (1993) definition of intake is "that part of the input that has been attended to by the second language learners while processing the input. Intake represents stored linguistic data which may be used for immediate recognition and does not imply language acquisition" (p. 334). See Leow (2012) for a further elaboration of the concept of intake in SLA.

Leow, R. P. (2013). Schmidt's noticing hypothesis: More than two decades after. In J. M. Bergsleithner, S. N. Frota, & J. K. Yoshioka (Eds.), *Noticing and second language acquisition: Studies in honor of Richard Schmidt* (pp. 11–23). Honolulu: University of Hawai'i, National Foreign Language Resource Center.

underpinnings to empirical findings from several strands of research premised upon it to the thorny issue of the operationalization and measurement of attention and (levels of) awareness (together with the accompanying methodological issue of reactivity) to the role of unawareness in SLA.

The first decade: 1990–1999

The first half of this decade witnessed the seminal publication of Schmidt's noticing hypothesis (1990) followed by a series of publications that elaborated on his hypothesis (1993, 1994a, 1994b, 1995) and early empirical studies that attempted to address the effects of noticing on L2 development from an off-line/non-concurrent methodological approach. The second half of the decade saw a move toward employing a pure use of a concurrent data elicitation procedure (think aloud (TA) protocols) to operationalize and measure not only the process of noticing but also to probe deeper into the construct of awareness before statistical analyses were performed to address their effects on L2 development.

Schmidt's (1990) noticing hypothesis

Schmidt's (1990, 2001) noticing hypothesis[2] is the first theoretical postulation in the SLA field to address the role of attention in direct relation to the construct of awareness in L2 input processing. Drawing from works in cognitive psychology (e.g., Bowers, 1984), his own personal experience while learning Portuguese (Schmidt & Frota, 1986), and other studies that did not methodologically address the role noticing played in the research designs (e.g., Bardovi-Harlig, 1987), Schmidt's noticing hypothesis postulates that attention controls access to awareness and is responsible for the subjective experience of noticing, which is "the necessary and sufficient condition for the conversion of input to intake" (1993, p. 209). Schmidt (1994a) defines noticing as "the registration of the occurrence of a stimulus event in conscious awareness and its subsequent storage in long-term memory" (p. 166). According to Schmidt, to learn any linguistic feature of the L2, for example, sounds, words, grammar, pragmatics, etc., this feature in the L2 input must be noticed with minimally a low level of awareness by learners, even though they may lack understanding of the underlying rule associated with this linguistic feature. Given that attention, according to Schmidt, is isomorphic with awareness, he strongly argues against the possibility of implicit learning when this term is understood as an abstraction that takes place outside of awareness and without the help of conscious processes such as hypothesis formation and testing (1994b, p. 18). He operationalizes noticing as availability for self-report either during or immediately after exposure to the input. However, Schmidt cautions that lack of self-report does not necessarily imply lack of awareness, since certain subjective experiences may be difficult to verbalize due to memory limitations and/or lack of meta-language.

In addition, Schmidt proposes a level of awareness that is higher than awareness at the level of noticing, namely, awareness at the level of understanding. Whereas awareness at the level of noticing leads to mere intake or item learning, this higher level of awareness promotes deeper learning marked by restructuring and system learning and is underscored by learners' ability to analyze, compare, and test hypotheses about the linguistic input at this level (1990, p. 132–133).

Given the methodological problem of establishing zero awareness at the point of noticing or processing, Schmidt has withdrawn from his original postulation of noticing as "the

2 It is of interest to note that Schmidt (1990) originally postulated three levels of consciousness as awareness: (1) perception, (2) noticing, and (3) understanding. However, Schmidt did not elaborate on the level of perception viewed as perceptual processing below the "subjective threshold" of awareness only (Schmidt, 2001, p. 20).

necessary and sufficient condition for the conversion of input into intake" (Schmidt, 1993, p. 209) to one of "more noticing leads to more learning" (Schmidt, 1994a, p. 129), underscoring the facilitative nature of noticing in the early stages of the learning process.

The key features of this hypothesis are the following: (1) the relatively strong argument that intake does not take place without some level of awareness associated with such a process at the preliminary stage of learning, (2) the claim that what is noticed becomes intake (and is available to be processed further or internalized), (3) the claim that more noticing leads to more learning, and (4) the claim that while not necessary for subsequent processing of the input, there is also a higher level of awareness involved during the learning process.

Operationalizing and measuring noticing in SLA: An off-line/non-concurrent approach

Early studies within the noticing hypothesis strand that attempted to operationalize and measure the process of noticing employed a non-concurrent or off-line data elicitation procedure following the classic design of pretest–experimental exposure–posttest. Off-line or non-concurrent operationalization occurs at the stage of retrieval or reconstruction, that is, *after* the data have been processed (cf. Leow, Johnson, & Zárate-Sández, 2011, for further discussion on construction vs. reconstruction stages in relation to the learning process), and the measures employed included, for example, underlining, circling, or checking targeted linguistic structures in written text (e.g., Fotos, 1993) or off-line questionnaires (e.g., Robinson, 1996).

During this period, Tomlin and Villa (1994) published a model of input processing in SLA that, while concurring with Schmidt's noticing hypothesis on the important role of attention in learning, theoretically contradicted his noticing hypothesis regarding the role of awareness at the input-to-intake stage of the L2 learning process. Drawing on work in cognitive science (e.g., Posner & Peterson, 1990), Tomlin and Villa propose a functionally-based, fine-grained analysis of attention for input processing in SLA. In their model, they posit that attention has three components, all of which have neurological correlates: (1) alertness (an overall readiness to deal with incoming stimuli), (2) orientation (the direction of attentional resources to a certain type of stimuli), and (3) detection (the cognitive registration of stimuli). According to Tomlin and Villa, it is detection alone that is necessary for further processing of input and subsequent learning to take place. The other two components can enhance the chances that detection will occur, but neither is necessary.

1995–1999: Operationalizing and measuring attention and awareness in SLA: An online/concurrent approach

The role attention plays in the learning process was almost always assumed in the earliest studies in the field of SLA. Any kind of exposure (aural or written, manipulated or authentic) to the L2 is arguably premised on the learner minimally paying attention to the input. The SLA field up to the mid 1990s had generally assumed that experimental conditions elicited the required attention paid to the targeted items in the second language input, as evidenced in the type of research design employed in the studies. Schmidt's noticing hypothesis, Tomlin and Villa's critique of its coarse-grained concept of the process of attention, and their proposed fine-grained attentional functions literally attracted attention to the methodological limitation of previous studies that were premised explicitly or implicitly on the role of attention in L2 development. The experimental design of these studies was usually the classical pretest–experimental exposure/treatment–posttest design. However, off-line measures at the stage of the posttest can only make inferences as to whether learners paid attention to or noticed targeted forms in the input during the experimental exposure phase and, consequently, did constitute in itself a coarse-grained measurement of attention (cf. Leow, 1999, for a critical evaluation of the methodological adequacy of SLA studies conducted within an attentional framework in the 1990s). To address this methodological limitation that is closely tied to the issue of level of internal validity (i.e., whether the findings faithfully reflect what the study set out to investigate), Leow (1998a) employed concurrent measures of attention in SLA where attention is operationalized at the stage of encoding or construction, that is, *while* learners are processing the incoming data. The intention of this study was to first attempt to establish the process of attention via concurrent online data elicitation procedures (think aloud protocols, that is, asking participants to think aloud as they perform an experimental task without any need to explain or elaborate on what they are thinking) before statistically addressing whether attention had an effect on adult learners' subsequent performance or behavior.[3] The research design was a hybrid design that employed both qualitative (based on online think aloud protocols data) and quantitative (based on off-line procedures data) analyses to triangulate the data collected in order to address effectively the constructs under investigation. This hybrid methodological approach was subsequently employed by several studies in the SLA literature (Leow, 1997, 1998a, 1998b, 2000, 2001a, 2001b; Leow, Egi, Nuevo, & Tsai, 2003; Leow, Hsieh, & Moreno, 2008; Martínez-Fernández, 2008; Rosa & O'Neill, 1999; Rosa & Leow, 2004a, 2004b; Sachs & Suh, 2007) and has led to a closer look at several strands of SLA research (e.g., input or textual enhancement, learning conditions, processing instruction, interaction/feedback) that are premised on the role of attention but, due to the research design (pretest–exposure without concurrent data collected–posttest) employed in the published studies, are unable to definitively attribute the results to the role of attention.

The benefits of gathering concurrent data were immediate. In addition to (1) providing empirical support for potential alternative interpretations made in several previous studies that did not employ concurrent data elicitation procedures, namely, the role of prior knowledge, (Leeman, Arteagoitia, Fridman, & Doughty, 1995), the representative nature of participants' performances in experimental groups (Williams & Evans, 1998), and additional exposure to the targeted linguistic form or structure (White, 1998), and (2) raising the internal validity of the study, the data provided insights into learner processes while they were exposed to and/or interacting with the L2 data. The next section looks closely at the construct of awareness, which plays a crucial role in Schmidt's noticing hypothesis.

Awareness

While the role of attention in L2 learning is not controversial and relatively accepted in the SLA field and others such as cognitive psychology and cognitive science, there is quite a contention regarding the other construct embedded in Schmidt's noticing hypothesis, namely, whether awareness in addition to attention is indeed important for intake to take place and, subsequently, L2 learning. As Leow et al. (2011) pointed out, the multifaceted nature of the construct of awareness makes it undoubtedly one of the slipperiest to operationalize and measure in both SLA and non-SLA fields of research.

One early study to address empirically the construct of awareness in L2 development was Leow (1997 and updated in 2001a), who reported on the role of awareness in SLA together with potential levels of awareness and their correlations with amount of L2 development. More specifically, the results of this study provided empirical support for Schmidt's noticing

3 Within the attentional framework in SLA, arguably the first published empirical study in this strand to employ concurrent think aloud protocols was Alanen (1995) who employed a combination of online, concurrent think-aloud protocols, a grammaticality judgment task, and a rule statement test to compare explicit information versus implicit textual enhancement.

hypothesis in relation to his proposed levels of awareness (at the levels of noticing and understanding) in addition to the potential of more than two levels of awareness. Several studies followed addressing not only the construct of awareness and its purported levels in SLA but also extending the targeted forms in the original study to other linguistic structures and language levels (Martínez-Fernández, 2008; Rosa & O'Neill, 1999; Rosa & Leow, 2004a, 2004b; Sachs & Suh, 2007).

The second decade: 2000–2009

The first decade of this millennium witnessed studies probing deeper into the roles of both constructs of awareness and unawareness in L2 development leading to two different definitions and operationalizations of what comprises implicit learning, that is, learning without awareness, in SLA. Conflicting findings have subsequently made this issue as controversial in SLA as it is in other non-SLA fields, for example, cognitive psychology and cognitive science. In addition, a new strand of research began to address the role of reactivity in SLA research designs, employing concurrent data elicitation procedures to investigate cognitive processes employed by L2 learners as they process the L2 data. The issues of unawareness in L2 learning and reactivity are highlighted below.

2000–2004: Unawareness

Conflicting findings were reported in the three published studies investigating this construct during the first half of this decade. Leow (2000) reported that learning did not appear to occur among unaware learners for his particular population, which provided empirical support for Schmidt's noticing hypothesis. On the other hand, Williams (2004, 2005) reported findings to the contrary. Given that the issue of the role of awareness during the initial stage of the L2 learning process, that is, the input-to-intake stage, is fundamental to Schmidt's noticing hypothesis, these early studies that have empirically investigated the role of unawareness in L2 learning are elaborated a bit below.

Leow (2000) addressed the effect of awareness or lack thereof on L2 learners' subsequent intake and written production of L2 morphological forms. The targeted forms were the third persons of Spanish irregular preterit verbs (ending in either *–er* or *–ir*) that have a stem change in this tense (e.g., **morió* but *murió* 'he died'). Thirty-two English-speaking adults, learning Spanish as a foreign language at the college level, participated in a problem-solving task (crossword puzzle) in which they were exposed to ten incomplete exemplars of the targeted forms among fifteen clues. The crossword puzzle was designed to require learners to fill in the correct endings of the irregular verbs without the need to pay attention to the stem-change present in the incomplete targeted verb form (e.g., *mur—*).

Pretests and posttests comprised a four-option MC recognition assessment task with items that were identical to those in the crossword clues and a written production assessment task (a fill-in-the-blank). To operationalize the construct of awareness, participants were instructed to think aloud non-metacognitively while completing the crossword puzzle and also during the post-exposure assessment tasks. The verbal reports from the think-aloud protocols were then coded to establish whether a participant was either aware or unaware, based on the criteria posited in Leow (1997) for levels of awareness. Interestingly, even though exposed to the same L2 data and task, the think aloud protocols provided data that revealed participants' behavior evenly split into two groups: aware and unaware. Participants were assigned to the aware group if they "provided a report of being aware of the target forms [a simple reference to the target forms which does not require mentioning of rules] or some form of metalinguistic description of the underlying rule" (p. 564) and others to the unaware group (their unawareness level was also cross-checked with off-line awareness measures via post-exposure questions and an interview). While aware learners improved significantly from pretest to posttest and also in comparison to unaware learners, the latter did not statistically improve from pretest to posttest. Leow concluded that "no disassociation between awareness and learning was found in this study" (p. 573) and cautioned that the findings reported were only directed to his sample of "adult beginning learners of Spanish" (p. 573).

These findings were contradicted by Williams' (2004) study that reported evidence of learning without awareness. Given that Williams (2005) is a methodological improvement of Williams (2004), the former study is reported. Williams (2005) conducted two experiments to test whether participants were able to learn miniature noun class systems without awareness. While his 41 participants were informed that of the four novel determiners (*gi*, *ro*, *ul*, *ne*), the first two meant *near* and the latter two *far*, they were not informed that these determiners also carried animacy values: *gi* and *ul* were animate, and *ro* and *ne* were inanimate.

During the training phase, the participants were presented aurally with individual sentences with noun phrases that comprised a novel determiner and an English noun (e.g., *gi* dog, 'near dog'). For each sentence, they a) listened to a sentence, b) indicated if the novel word meant *near* or *far*, c) repeated the sentence aloud, and d) were requested to create a mental image of the situation described by the sentence.

After the training phase, to test participants' learning of the animacy rules, participants were instructed to select in a two-option MC assessment task one of two noun phrases (old and new) that "seemed 'more familiar, better, or more appropriate' on the basis of what they had heard during the training task" (pp. 282–283). Unlike Leow (2000), operationalization of awareness was via an off-line questionnaire in which participants were asked what criteria (or explicit knowledge) they had used to make these choices. If they did not mention "any references to living or nonliving, moves or does-not-move, and so forth" (p. 283) as a reason for their choice, they were classified as unaware. According to the author, the results showed "that, at least for some individuals, it is possible to learn form-meaning connections without awareness of what those connections are" (p. 293).

This controversy regarding whether learning can take place among unaware learners will be revisited once more in the next decade.

To think aloud or not to think aloud: The issue of reactivity

The second prominent feature of the first part of the second decade was the new strand of research that began to address empirically the methodological use of concurrent data elicitation procedures, namely, think aloud protocols, in SLA research designs. This new strand was based on the inevitable question regarding the potential of reactivity, that is, whether thinking aloud could have affected participants' cognitive processes while engaging with the L2. To empirically address this methodological issue in SLA (it has been of great interest in other non-SLA fields), Leow and Morgan-Short (2004) reported the failure to find a reactive effect on participants' performances after a reading exposure when compared to a control group. It is noteworthy that they also cautioned readers that "given the many variables that potentially impact the issue of reactivity in SLA research methodology, it is suggested that studies employing concurrent data-elicitation procedures include a control group that does not perform verbal reports as one way of addressing this issue" (p. 50).

2005–2009

The reactivity strand of research grew exponentially in this second part of the decade with several studies (Bowles, 2008; Bowles & Leow, 2005; Egi, 2008; Rossomondo, 2007; Sachs &

Polio, 2007; Sachs & Suh, 2007; Sanz, Lin, Lado, Bowden, & Stafford, 2009; Yoshida, 2008) addressing the issue of reactivity in relation to various variables. While a cursory glance at the eight studies (with a total of 10 experiments) published in this period would reveal one study reporting positive (Sanz et al., 2009) and one reporting negative (Sachs & Polio, 2007, in which the protocols were produced in the L2) effects in one of two experiments and another reporting positive effects (Rossomondo, 2007), a recent meta-analysis (Bowles, 2010) has reported an effect size value that "is not significantly different from zero" (p. 138); that is, it is not a reliable effect. A more recent empirical study (Morgan-Short, Heil, Botero-Moriarty, & Ebert, 2012) reported similar findings while another study (Stafford, Bowden, & Sanz, 2012) contradicts Sanz et al.'s (2009) reactive findings. At the same time, Goo (2010), not included in the meta-analysis, reported negative reactivity for comprehension based on a trend toward statistical significance ($p = .054$) with a medium effect size ($d = .62$). Currently, the standard methodological practice in research designs employing concurrent TAs is to include a control group to control for any potential reactive effect that could contaminate the data collected.

2010–2012

The issue of implicit learning, that is, whether one can learn the L2 without awareness, began to heat up at the beginning of this decade, two decades after Schmidt's postulation that only L2 information that is attended to with a low level of awareness can be taken in by the L2 learner. A series of empirical studies addressing implicit learning were published early in this decade and once again the findings are conflicting and clearly based on *how* implicit learning is defined, whether it is a process (operationalized concurrently while occurring at the point of encoding or during the input-to-intake stage) or a product (operationalized non-concurrently as knowledge) after the experimental exposure (cf. Leow, forthcoming, for further elaboration). The next section takes a closer look at these two competing approaches to the study of unawareness in SLA.

Learning (as a product) without awareness: Empirical non-concurrent evidence in SLA

Extending Williams' (2005) research design by employing the novel determiners (*gi*, *ro*, *ul* and *ne*) in the L1 with different embedded features in their respective studies, Leung and Williams (2011, 2012) reported that unaware learners can provide evidence of learning form-meaning connections without awareness of what those connections are. In these studies, participants' attention was generally focused on the relationship of a given form-meaning connection with the targeted connections embedded in the same forms. Like Williams (2005), operationalization of awareness was via an off-line questionnaire in which participants were asked whether they had any feelings about, for example, when *gi* versus *ro* and *ul* versus *ne* were used (Leung & Williams, 2011). If they did not mention any references to the targeted connection, they were classified as unaware. However, unlike the original study, in these two studies learning of the mapping between thematic roles and a set of novel determiners was measured by participants' performances on a reaction time test. On this task, participants demonstrated their comprehension or interpretation of a stimulus by hitting corresponding response keys.

Chen, Guo, Tang, Zhu, Yang, and Dienes (2011), a conceptual replication of Williams (2005), reported similar evidence of learning without awareness among their participants, providing empirical support for the external validity of the findings reported in Williams' (2005) original study.

Learning (as a process) without awareness: Empirical concurrent evidence in SLA

The research designs of the product-based implicit learning studies have been methodologically challenged in the SLA literature. Hama and Leow (2010) extended Williams (2005) by addressing several methodological issues of Williams' research design, namely (1) employing a hybrid design to gather data at the concurrent stage of encoding, during the testing phase, and after the experimental exposure, (2) increasing the number of items (four instead of two) on his two-option multiple-choice test to include the presence of distance in learners' selection of options (i.e., animacy *plus* distance) in order to replicate the training context and a more normal learning context, (3) including a production test in addition to the MC test to address participant performance after the internalization stage (cf. Leow, 1998b, for the need to employ several assessment tasks), and (4) providing the same modality for both the learning and testing phases to address the potential impact of this variable not addressed in the original study (cf. Leow, 1995).

The think aloud protocols served to eliminate participants who demonstrated awareness of the animacy rule, employed a non-animacy-based strategy, or became aware of the rule while performing the post-exposure assessment task. A critical statistical analysis (chance correction formula, p. 488) was then performed to align the study's four-option MC test to the original two-option one employed in Williams (2005) to ensure statistical comparability in behavior between the current and original studies. Contrary to Williams (2005), the findings revealed that "unaware learners, at the stage of encoding, did not appear to demonstrate any significant animacy bias in either their selection or production of the trained or new determiner-noun combinations" (p. 482). One critique of this study may be the failure to control for reactivity.

Similarly, Faretta-Stutenberg and Morgan-Short (2011), a conceptual replication of Williams (2005), reported no evidence of learning without awareness among their participants, failing to provide empirical support for the external validity of the findings reported in Williams' (2005) original study. In addition, Leow and Hama (in press) question Leung and Williams' (2011) (and indirectly Leung and Williams, 2012) level of internal validity mainly due to three major limitations, namely, the stage of operationalization and measurement of the construct of awareness, which was off-line, the provision of implicit feedback during the treatment phase, and additional exposure to trained items during the post-exposure phase of the study. As can be clearly seen, the theoretical and methodological debate on the role of unawareness in L2 development in the SLA field is beginning to parallel other non-SLA fields of inquiry and clearly constitutes a worthy strand for future research.

Some reflections on the noticing hypothesis

I would like to reflect on the noticing hypothesis from three perspectives, namely, theoretical, methodological, and terminological. Theoretically, the noticing hypothesis is relatively coarse-grained; that is, it does not appear to acknowledge that there may be several other variables that may be potentially associated with the process of noticing. Think aloud data appear to reveal that the process of noticing may be associated with higher levels of cognitive effort and processing when compared to, for example, detection or peripheral attention paid to selected data in the L2 input. It is also noted that while noticing is empirically supported to be facilitative of subsequent intake and potential learning, there is no hard evidence that all such noticed intake is logically processed further and, indeed, learned or internalized in the internal system. In addition, the construct of intake is clearly in need of further elaboration in the field. As Truscott and Sharwood (2011) point out, what specifically comprises intake? Indeed, concurrent data appear to suggest that there may be different types or levels of intake dependent upon the levels of processing or amount of cognitive effort involved while attending to L2 input. A more fine-grained model of the L2 learning process in SLA in which noticed intake is associated with features that differentiate it from detected intake (without awareness) and attended intake (peripheral attention paid) may be warranted in future research.

Methodologically, Schmidt's notion of attention being isomorphic with awareness, the two constructs comprising the two sides of noticing, is currently raising the issue of whether it is possible to separate these two constructs. I have personally employed think aloud protocols to operationalize and measure both attention and awareness with the premise that whatever is verbalized necessarily needed to be paid attention to. At the same time, it is well accepted that not everything that has been attended to is verbalized. One current proposal (Godfroid, Boers, & Housen, in press) is to operationalize and measure the constructs of attention and awareness at two different stages (concurrent for attention via eye-tracking and non-concurrent for awareness via stimulated recalls) due to an apparent fear of reactivity. Perhaps employing concurrently *both* eye-tracking measures and think aloud protocols simultaneously while controlling for reactivity would appear at this point in time to be the more appropriate methodological procedure to minimally establish the process of attention (via eye-tracking) and (levels of) awareness (via think alouds). In this way, the internal validity of the study is promoted, and the strengths and limitations of the two procedures are addressed while investigating the process of noticing at exactly the stage at which it is occurring, namely, the input-to-intake stage.

Finally, it is interesting to note at what stage of the learning process the original noticing hypothesis (as postulated by Schmidt in 1990) was targeting. His hypothesis was clearly premised on the input-to-intake stage of the learning process. In other words, if we were to use a coarse-grained framework of the learning process in SLA such as

input⇒intake⇒internal system⇒output

the learning process can be viewed as comprising several stages beginning with the input-to-intake stage in which some of the L2 data in the L2 input are taken in by the learner (Intake), a subset of which may be further processed and become L2 knowledge in the Internal system, which may then be produced as Output. Viewed within this framework, the original postulation of the noticing hypothesis is very basic, namely, whether the role of awareness at the input-to-intake stage of the learning process is necessary or facilitative of L2 data being *taken in*, not learned. Consequently, any reference associating noticing with any process (e.g., intake processing) or product (e.g., knowledge) beyond the input-to-intake stage did not appear to be an issue in the hypothesis.

Interestingly, this terminological confusion was perhaps promoted by Schmidt himself as he elaborated his noticing hypothesis in many instances in terms of *learning* that is beyond the input-to-intake stage ("more noticing leads to more learning," Schmidt, 1994a, p. 129) and an indirect postulation that whatever data were noticed were subsequently processed ("the registration of the occurrence of a stimulus event in conscious awareness and its subsequent storage in long-term memory," Schmidt, 1994a, p. 166), most likely not paying attention to the stage of the learning process originally postulated in his hypothesis. In addition, concurrent data gathered also indicate that noticed intake may or may not be further processed and what appears to account for this is whether *further* processing of such intake does take place.

Conclusion

Schmidt's (1990) seminal article on his noticing hypothesis brought into the SLA field a theoretical postulation that the roles of attention and awareness were isomorphic (two sides of the same coin) and crucial in any L2 development, and more specifically, during the early stage of the learning process, namely, the input-to-intake stage. It is indeed remarkable that after two decades, the noticing hypothesis not only dominates the theoretical underpinning of many studies but also continues to stimulate further empirical investigation in the SLA field, be it from a theoretical or methodological perspective. I personally view Schmidt's noticing hypothesis in the SLA field as the second milestone along the route to current (un) awareness studies, the first being Krashen's (1981) monitor model where the focus was on consciousness versus subconscious processes and products. There is no doubt that Schmidt's theoretical contribution to the SLA field via his noticing hypothesis warrants the highest respect from SLA researchers. There is also no doubt that my personal research agenda is strongly tied to his noticing hypothesis. Consequently, I owe quite a lot to Dick Schmidt, and for this I am eternally and academically grateful.

References

Alanen, R. (1995). Input enhancement and rule presentation in second language acquisition. In R. W. Schmidt (Ed.), *Attention and awareness in foreign language learning* (pp. 259–302). Honolulu, HI: University of Hawai'i, National Foreign Language Resource Center.

Bardovi-Harlig, K. (1987). Markedness and salience in second language acquisition. *Language Learning, 37,* 385–407.

Bowers, K. (1984). On being unconsciously influenced and informed. In K. Bowers & D. Meichenbaum (Eds.), *The unconscious reconsidered* (pp. 227–272). New York: Wiley.

Bowles, M. A. (2008). Task type and reactivity of verbal reports in SLA: A first look at an L2 task other than reading. *Studies in Second Language Acquisition, 30,* 359–387.

Bowles, M. (2010). *The think-aloud controversy in second language research.* New York: Routledge.

Bowles, M., & Leow, R. P. (2005). Reactivity and type of verbal report in SLA research methodology: Expanding the scope of investigation. *Studies in Second Language Acquisition, 27,* 415–440.

Chen, W., Guo, X., Tang, J., Zhu, L., Yang, Z., & Dienes, Z. (2011). Unconscious structural knowledge of form–meaning connections. *Consciousness and Cognition, 20,* 1751–1760.

Egi, T. (2008). Investigating stimulated recall as a cognitive measure: Reactivity and verbal reports in SLA research methodology. *Language Awareness, 17,* 212–228.

Faretta-Stutenberg, M., & Morgan-Short, K. (2011). Learning without awareness reconsidered: A replication of Williams (2005). In G. Granena, J. Koeth, S. Lee-Ellis, A. Lukyanchenko, G. Prieto Botana, & E. Rhoades (Eds.), *Selected proceedings of the 2010 Second Language Research Forum* (pp. 18–28). Somerville, MA: Cascadilla Proceedings Project.

Fotos, S. (1993). Consciousness-raising and noticing through focus on form: Grammar task performance vs. formal instruction. *Applied Linguistics, 14,* 385–407.

Godfroid, A., Boers, F., & Housen, A. (in press). An eye for words: Gauging the role of attention in L2 vocabulary acquisition by means of eye-tracking. To appear in *Studies in Second Language Acquisition, 35*(3).

Goo, J. (2010). Working memory and reactivity. *Language Learning, 60,* 1–41.

Hama, M., & Leow, R. P. (2010). Learning without awareness revisited: Extending Williams (2005). *Studies in Second Language Acquisition, 32*, 465–491.

Krashen, S. D. (1981). *Second language acquisition and second language learning*. Oxford: Pergamon Press.

Leeman, J., Arteagoitia, I., Fridman, B., & Doughty, C. (1995). Integrating attention to form with meaning: Focus on form in content-based Spanish instruction. In R. W. Schmidt (Ed.), *Attention and awareness in foreign language learning* (pp. 217–258). Honolulu, HI: University of Hawai'i, National Foreign Language Resource Center.

Leow, R. P. (1993). To simplify or not to simplify: A look at intake. *Studies in Second Language Acquisition, 15*, 333–355.

Leow, R. P. (1995). Modality and intake in SLA. *Studies in Second Language Acquisition, 17*, 79–89.

Leow, R. P. (1997). Attention, awareness, and foreign language behavior. *Language Learning, 47*, 467–506.

Leow, R. P. (1998a). Toward operationalizing the process of attention in second language acquisition: Evidence for Tomlin and Villa's (1994) fine-grained analysis of attention. *Applied Psycholinguistics, 19*, 133–159.

Leow, R. P. (1998b). The effects of amount and type of exposure on adult learners' L2 development in SLA. *Modern Language Journal, 82*, 49–68.

Leow, R. P. (1999). The role of attention in second/foreign language classroom research: Methodological issues. In J. Gutiérrez-Rexach & F. Martínez-Gil (Eds.), *Advances in Hispanic Linguistics: Papers from the 2nd Hispanic Linguistics Symposium* (pp. 60–71). Somerville, MA: Cascadilla Press.

Leow, R. P. (2000). A study of the role of awareness in foreign language behavior: Aware vs. unaware learners. *Studies in Second Language Acquisition, 22*, 557–584.

Leow, R. P. (2001a). Attention, awareness, and foreign language behavior. *Language Learning, 51*, 113–155.

Leow, R. P. (2001b). Do learners notice enhanced forms while interacting with the L2?: An online and off-line study of the role of written input enhancement in L2 reading. *Hispania, 84*, 496–509.

Leow, R. P. (2012). Intake. In P. Robinson (Ed.), *The Rutledge encyclopedia of second language acquisition* (pp. 327–329). New York, NY: Taylor & Francis.

Leow, R. P. (forthcoming). Implicit learning in SLA: Of processes and products. In P. Rebuschat (Ed.), *Implicit and explicit learning of languages*. John Benjamins.

Leow, R. P., Egi, T., Nuevo, A.-M., & Tsai, Y. (2003). The roles of textual enhancement and type of linguistic item in adult L2 learners' comprehension and intake. *Applied Language Learning, 13*, 93–108.

Leow, R. P., & Hama, M. (in press). Implicit learning in SLA and the issue of internal validity: A response to Leung and Williams' "The implicit learning of mappings between forms and contextually derived meanings." To appear in *Studies in Second Language Acquisition, 35 (3)*.

Leow, R. P., Hsieh, H., & Moreno, N. (2008). Attention to form and meaning revisited. *Language Learning, 58*, 665–695.

Leow, R. P., Johnson, E., & Zárate-Sández, G. (2011). Getting a grip on the slippery construct of awareness: Toward a finer-grained methodological perspective. In C. Sanz

& R. P. Leow (Eds.), *Implicit and explicit conditions, processes, and knowledge in SLA and bilingualism* (pp. 61–72). Washington, DC.: Georgetown University Press.

Leow, R. P., & Morgan-Short, K. (2004). To think aloud or not to think aloud: The issue of reactivity in SLA research methodology. *Studies in Second Language Acquisition, 26*, 35–57.

Leung, J. H. C., & Williams, J. N. (2011). The implicit learning of mappings between forms and contextually derived meanings. *Studies in Second Language Acquisition, 33*, 33–55.

Leung, J. H. C., & Williams, J. N. (2012). Constraints on implicit learning of grammatical form-meaning connections. *Language Learning, 62*, 634–662.

Martínez-Fernández, A. (2008). Revisiting the involvement load hypothesis: Awareness, type of task, and type of item. In M. Bowles, R. Foote, S. Perpiñán, & R. Bhatt (Eds.), *Selected proceedings of the 2007 Second Language Research Forum* (pp. 210–228). Somerville, MA: Cascadilla Proceedings Project.

Morgan-Short, K., Heil, J., Botero-Moriarty, A., & Ebert, S. (2012). Allocation of attention to second language form and meaning: Issues of think alouds and depth of processing. *Studies in Second Language Acquisition, 34*, 659–685.

Posner, M. I., & Petersen, S. E. (1990). The attention system of the human brain. *Annual Review of Neuroscience, 13*, 25–42.

Robinson, P. (1996). Learning simple and complex second language rules under implicit, incidental, rule-search, and instructed conditions. *Studies in Second Language Acquisition, 18*, 27–68.

Rosa, E., & O'Neill, M. D. (1999). Explicitness, intake, and the issue of awareness. *Studies in Second Language Acquisition, 21*, 511–556.

Rosa, E. M., & Leow, R. P. (2004a). Computerized task-based exposure, explicitness, and type of feedback on Spanish L2 development. *Modern Language Journal, 88*, 192–216.

Rosa, E. M., & Leow, R. P. (2004b). Awareness, different learning conditions, and second language development. *Applied Psycholinguistics, 25*, 269–292.

Rossomondo, A. E. (2007). The role of lexical temporal indicators and text interaction format in the incidental acquisition of the Spanish future tense. *Studies in Second Language Acquisition, 29*, 39–66.

Sachs, R., & Polio, C. (2007). Learners' uses of two types of written feedback on an L2 writing revision task. *Studies in Second Language Acquisition, 29*, 67–100.

Sachs, R., & Suh, B.-R. (2007). Textually enhanced recasts, learner awareness, and L2 outcomes in synchronous computer-mediated interaction. In A. Mackey (Ed.), *Conversational interaction in second-language acquisition: A series of empirical studies* (pp. 197–227). Oxford: Oxford University Press.

Sanz, C., Lin, H.-J., Lado, B., Bowden, H. W., & Stafford, C. A. (2009). Concurrent verbalizations, pedagogical conditions, and reactivity: Two CALL studies. *Language Learning, 59*, 33–71.

Schmidt, R. (1990). The role of consciousness in second language learning. *Applied Linguistics, 11*, 129–158.

Schmidt, R. W. (1993). Awareness and second language acquisition. *Annual Review of Applied Linguistics, 13*, 206–226.

Schmidt, R. W. (1994a). Implicit learning and the cognitive unconscious: Of artificial grammars and SLA. In N. Ellis (Ed.), *Implicit and explicit learning of languages* (pp. 165–209). London: Academic Press.

Schmidt, R. W. (1994b). Deconstructing consciousness in search of useful definitions for applied linguistics. In J. H. Hulstijn & R. W. Schmidt (Eds.), *AILA Review: Consciousness and second language learning: Conceptual, methodological, and practical issues in language learning and teaching, 11*, 11–26.

Schmidt, R. (1995). Consciousness and foreign language learning: A tutorial on the role of attention and awareness in learning. In R. W. Schmidt (Ed.), *Attention and awareness in foreign language learning* (pp. 1–63). Honolulu, HI: University of Hawai'i, National Foreign Language Resource Center.

Schmidt, R. (2001). Attention. In P. Robinson (Ed.), *Cognition and second language instruction* (pp. 3–32). Cambridge: Cambridge University Press.

Schmidt, R., & Frota, S. (1986). Developing basic conversational ability in a second language: A case study of an adult learner of Portuguese. In R. R. Day (Ed.), *Talking to learn: Conversation in second language acquisition* (pp. 237–326). Rowley, MA: Newbury House.

Stafford, C., Bowden, H., & Sanz, C. (2012). Optimizing language instruction: Matters of explicitness, practice, and cue learning. To appear in *Language Learning, 62*, 741–768.

Tomlin, R. S., & Villa, V. (1994). Attention in cognitive science and second language acquisition. *Studies in Second Language Acquisition, 16*, 183–203.

Truscott, J., & Sharwood Smith, M. (2011). Input, intake, and consciousness: The quest for a theoretical foundation. *Studies in Second Language Acquisition, 33*, 497–528.

White, J. (1998). Getting the learners' attention: A typographical input enhancement study. In C. Doughty & J. Williams (Eds.), *Focus on form in classroom second language acquisition* (pp. 85–113). Cambridge: Cambridge University Press.

Williams, J., & Evans, J. (1998). What kind of focus and on which forms? In C. Doughty & J. Williams (Eds.), *Focus on form in classroom second language acquisition* (pp. 139–155). Cambridge: Cambridge University Press.

Williams, J. N. (2004). Implicit learning of form-meaning connections. In B. VanPatten, J. Williams, S. Rott, & M. Overstreet (Eds.), *Form meaning connections in second language acquisition* (pp. 203–218). Mahwah, NJ : Erlbaum.

Williams, J. N. (2005). Learning without awareness. *Studies in Second Language Acquisition, 27*, 269–304.

Yoshida, M. (2008). Think-aloud protocols and type of reading task: The issue of reactivity in L2 reading research. In M. Bowles, R. Foote, S. Perpiñán, & R. Bhatt (Eds.), *Selected proceedings of the 2007 Second Language Research Forum* (pp. 199–209). Somerville, MA: Cascadilla Proceedings Project.

NFLRC *monographs*

3

Noticing and L2 Development: Theoretical, Empirical, and Pedagogical Issues

Shinichi Izumi
Sophia University

Noticing is claimed to be an important psychological process by which second language (L2) learners convert input into intake for second language acquisition (SLA). Since Schmidt and Frota's (1986) seminal paper in which the noticing hypothesis was first proposed, many empirical and theoretical papers have been published, all based on the assumption that noticing plays a central role in driving L2 development forward. Admitting the importance of noticing in SLA, however, what remains underexplored are the issues concerning how noticing may be related to overall SLA processes, beyond simply converting input into intake, which, as crucial as it may be, is no more than an initial step in the long process of L2 learning. To illuminate this area of SLA research, this paper first reexamines the notion of noticing in terms of different types of noticing and their relationships to overall SLA processes. It then takes up, by way of example, two key theoretical constructs proposed in the SLA literature—the U-shaped learning curve and developmental sequences—and examines how noticing may play differential roles at different points in IL development. By so doing, I hope to highlight some areas in need of further research on the relationship between noticing and long-term L2 development.

Introduction

Noticing is claimed to be an important psychological process by which second language (L2) learners convert input into intake for second language acquisition (SLA). Since Schmidt and Frota's (1986) seminal paper in which the noticing hypothesis was first proposed, many empirical and theoretical papers have been published, all based on the assumption that noticing plays a central role in driving L2 development forward. Admitting the importance of noticing in SLA, however, what remains underexplored are the issues concerning how noticing may be related to overall SLA processes, beyond simply converting input into intake, which, as crucial as it may be, is no more than an initial step in the long process of

Izumi, S. (2013). Noticing and L2 development: Theoretical, empirical, and pedagogical issues. In J. M. Bergsleithner, S. N. Frota, & J. K. Yoshioka (Eds.), *Noticing and second language acquisition: Studies in honor of Richard Schmidt* (pp. 25–38). Honolulu: University of Hawai'i, National Foreign Language Resource Center.

L2 learning. To illuminate this area of SLA research, this paper first reexamines the notion of noticing in terms of different types of noticing and their relationships to overall SLA processes. It then takes up some developmental patterns found in previous SLA research and examines how noticing may be relevant in these processes.

To begin with, let us first examine Schmidt's idea to clarify what he means by noticing in SLA. Schmidt's main contention is that attention and awareness play key roles in propelling L2 development. In his words:

> [t]he concept of attention is necessary in order to understand virtually every aspect of second language acquisition (SLA), including the development of interlanguages (ILs) over time, variation within IL at particular points in time, the development of L2 fluency, the role of individual differences such as motivation, aptitude, and learning strategies, and the ways in which interaction, negotiation for meaning, and all forms of instruction contribute to language learning... There is no doubt that attended learning is far superior [to unattended learning], and for all practical purposes, attention is necessary for all aspects of L2 learning. (Schmidt, 2001, p. 3)

Noticing, in Schmidt's sense, is a concrete outcome of a person paying focal attention to something, and it requires a subjective sense of awareness on the part of the learner at the point of learning if it is to exert any substantial impact on learning. Schmidt also separates noticing from *metalinguistic awareness* or *understanding*, by stating that "the objects of attention and noticing are elements of the surface structure of utterances in the input—instances of language, rather than any abstract rules or principles of which such instances may be exemplars" (Schmidt, 2001, p. 5).

The distinction between noticing and understanding, however, may not be as clear as Schmidt makes it sound. As Truscott and Sharwood Smith (2011) argue, "[t]here is no sense in the idea of recognizing that something is relevant to a particular aspect of the language system while having absolutely no understanding of it. The process presupposes some degree of understanding of the form" (p. 503). Debate also continues regarding the possibility of learning without awareness. However, given the practical difficulty in establishing empirically instances of learning without awareness, Schmidt's (2001, 2012) current contention is that more noticing leads to more learning and that noticing, therefore, is at least facilitative, if not necessary and sufficient, for L2 learning. Taking this stance on noticing as a promoter for L2 development, this paper starts by first clarifying arguments for different types of noticing thus far introduced in the SLA literature.

Different types of noticing

Schmidt's idea of noticing has been interpreted in various ways and given rise to discussion of different types of noticing in the SLA literature, which include the following:

Noticing a form(-meaning-function) relationship

This may be the most basic idea proposed in the original postulation of noticing by Schmidt and Frota (1986). That is, learners' IL competence develops when they notice how a particular form is used in the input they receive. What needs to be emphasized is that noticing here refers not just to noticing form alone, but noticing form *in relation to* the meaning it conveys and the context in which it is used (Schmidt, 2001). In other words, the noticing in this sense entails noticing form-meaning-function relationships. This, in my view, is an important point to underscore because one may notice only form without necessarily connecting it with meaning or function. Noticing only form may be sufficient for learning perceptual aspects of novel words, but not for learning to use the form for communication, in which, naturally, meaning and function become equally important.

When EFL learners in Japan, for instance, are taught the *be* verb in grammar-focused instruction, their attention may be drawn to the conjugation rule with the use of example sentences like *I am a student* and *You are a teacher.* In such cases, meaning, while being there at least superficially, may not and often does not need to be attended to; as a result, these learners often fail to use the form in communication. In another instance, noticing form may occur in relation to only one function when the same form may have multiple functions. Sugaya and Shirai (2007), for instance, showed that L2 Japanese learners use the form *te i-ru* with progressive meaning, as in *Ken-ga odot-te i-ru* ('Ken is dancing'), but not with resultative meaning (as in *Gomi-ga ochi-te i-ru*, 'The trash has fallen'), even though the latter use occurs more frequently in the input. It is argued that functional, rather than perceptual, salience affects this learning bias in that *te i-ru* is a form uniquely used for progressive meaning, but other forms can convey the resultative meaning. It is only when learners notice the connection between a particular form and a particular meaning in relation to a particular function that they learn to use the form for practical communicative purposes.

Noticing the gap between IL and TL

Initial noticing of form may often be only partial, as learners may process only part of what is relevant to acquire the form. This results in incomplete learning. Another sense of noticing, therefore, is also discussed in the literature as playing an important role in L2 learning—noticing the gap. The gap here refers to the difference between how the learner uses a language form and how a more proficient user uses it to convey the same idea. For example, upon hearing an expression containing the past hypothetical conditional such as *I should have been more careful*, a learner may notice the word *should* being used as a way to show one's regret. She may later start to use it, producing sentences like *I should ask you* when referring to something that should have happened in the past but did not. When the learner uses this expression in different occasions, she may notice something different in the way she uses it and the way other people say it, as when given a corrective recast in conversation (e.g., A: *I should ask you.* B: *Yeah, you should have asked me*). In such a case, initial noticing of form is followed by noticing of the gap, which functions to fine-tune the learner's knowledge as she makes a *cognitive comparison* in her head (Doughty, 2001).

Hanaoka (2007) reports that in a multi-stage writing task where Japanese EFL learners were told to compose a story based on a picture strip and later shown model essays written by native speakers, a learner noticed the form *traffic jam* to express a situation depicted in one of the pictures but did not notice the collocation used with it, *was caught in a traffic jam.* As a result, this learner only incorporated the noun phrase and used it simply as *it is traffic jam.* On the other hand, another learner who already knew the expression *traffic jam* noticed in the input that it is used together with the verb *catch*; later she wrote *She didn't catch in the traffic jam.* Still another learner who already knew the expression *be in a traffic jam* noticed that it is used with *catch* in the passive voice; this learner then revised her original essay by writing *He was caught in a traffic jam.* Hanaoka argues that the *scope of noticing*—a notion not yet widely discussed in the literature—is closely related to the learner's current L2 knowledge and may be an important element to consider in our discussion of the importance of noticing in SLA. For learners who do not possess any knowledge of the form, noticing form may take place initially. For other learners who have some knowledge of the form, they may go on to notice the gap between their version and the use of the form in the surrounding input. Noticing the gap, therefore, entails noticing the form and may thus be considered a more advanced process than simple noticing of the form.

Noticing holes in IL

Noticing a hole was first discussed by Swain (1998), who argued for the role of output in language learning. Her argument was that when learners try to express an idea in their output, they may notice that they do not have the means to express it, whether the problem relates to vocabulary or grammar. This sense of noticing is clearly different from the preceding ideas of noticing, as the learner in this case notices the absence of a form in his/her IL, not the presence of it in the target language (TL) input. Such noticing, by itself, does not promote language acquisition, but it can prompt the learner to search for what is missing when receiving input, and this is expected to promote noticing the form. This idea, known as the noticing function of output, posits that the need to produce output triggers noticing in ways that a simple requirement for general comprehension of the input would not. Swain (1998) argues that noticing a hole may be a prerequisite to noticing a form. Some empirical support to this hypothesis was provided by a series of studies by Izumi (Izumi, 2002; Izumi & Bigelow, 2000; Izumi, Bigelow, Fujiwara, & Fearnow, 1999), where learners who had opportunities to produce output before receiving input outperformed learners who only engaged in a comprehension task in learning the targeted grammatical form (see also Hanaoka, 2007, 2012; Toth, 2006).

Noticing the gap in one's ability

Related to the notion of noticing the hole is the idea of noticing the gap between what one wants to say and what one can actually say using one's current IL repertoire. The gap here is different from the gap discussed above, which is the gap between IL and TL forms. Noticing the IL-TL gap leads to identification of IL solutions ("This is how I said it, but that's how others say it"). On the other hand, noticing the gap in one's ability results from the comparison being made inside the learner when she tries to express an idea and notices that she does not have the means to say it as exactly as she wants it, which leads to identification of IL problems ("This is what I want to say, but I don't know how to say it precisely/correctly/appropriately"). The difference between the two kinds of gap here is related to when noticing takes place during the course of message production. In the case of noticing the gap in one's ability, the learner compares her intended message to the formulated IL message and finds a gap. In the case of noticing the IL-TL gap, noticing occurs later, after the message is produced and upon exposure to relevant input, at which point IL production is compared to TL input and the learner finds a gap.

Because noticing the gap in one's ability occurs learner-internally, it may be conceived similarly to the notion of noticing the hole, and some researchers indeed use the *gap* and *hole* in almost identical ways (e.g., Doughty & Williams, 1998; Swain, 1998). However, the subtle difference may be that while noticing a hole indicates a complete absence of the form in question (thus termed a *hole*, not the *gap* or *crack*), the gap here could suggest that the learner is at least partially able to express the given concept but not as precisely or as adequately as she may want it. For instance, using the above example of *the traffic jam*, in trying to use this form, a learner may notice that she does not know what verb to use with it and thus may end up using a generic verb such as *is* or *has*. The learner may feel somewhat funny about this use of the phrase, which leads her to notice the gap between her available means of expression in her IL and the precise intention of the message to be conveyed. It is possible that noticing a hole may be more likely to result in covert problems in which production problems do not become manifest in the learner's output (as any relevant knowledge of the form is missing), while noticing the gap in one's ability may be more likely to result in overt problems that leave observable traces in the resultant learner output (see Hanaoka & Izumi, 2012, for an empirical study on this issue).

What needs to be highlighted here is the fact the while noticing the hole and noticing the gap in one's ability occur essentially within the learners (though they may be prompted by the task setup), noticing form and noticing the gap between IL and TL take place in interaction between the learner and the surrounding input. Going along with the time course of the production and interaction processes involved, the former two types of noticing may predispose the learners to experience the latter two types of noticing, which then is expected to drive their IL development forward. It may be hypothesized that noticing a hole is closely related to noticing a form, and that noticing the gap in one's ability is closely related to noticing the gap between IL and TL.

Noticing in relation to overall SLA processes and influencing factors

As important as noticing may be in L2 development, it is only "the first step in language building, not the end of the process" (Schmidt, 2001, p. 31). If so, it would be important to examine the role of noticing from a longer-term developmental perspective. To this end, it will be useful to capture the different types of noticing by using a commonly accepted model of SLA processes in the literature (e.g., Ellis, 2008; Gass & Selinker, 2008; Izumi, 2003; VanPatten, 2004). Figure 1 shows the model in relation to different types of noticing.

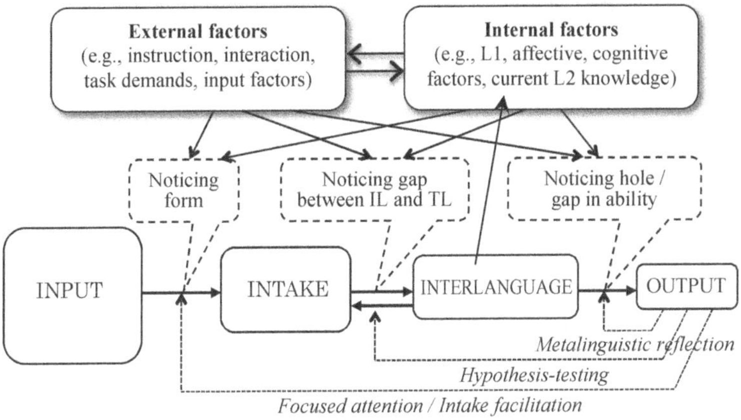

Figure 1. Noticing of different types in relation to overall SLA processes and affecting factors

The solid arrows connecting input through output depict the main SLA processes whereby, based on input, learners incorporate noticed language features into their IL, which they use to produce output. The arrows connecting intake and interlanguage are bidirectional because working memory (a site for intake) and long-term-memory (a site for IL knowledge) closely interact with each other (cf. Ortega, 2009b). The dotted arrows connecting output to other processes indicate how output affects overall SLA processes in dynamic ways as proposed by the output hypothesis (Swain, 1985, 1998, 2005). The figure also depicts a number of factors—both learner-internal and -external factors—that are hypothesized to affect learners' noticing of different types at different stages of language development. The external factors include instruction, feedback, interaction, and task demands, as well as various input factors (e.g., frequency, perceptual saliency, communicative value of the form). The internal factors, on the other hand, include learner's L1, their current IL state, affective factors such as motivation, cognitive factors such as developmental readiness, and aptitude. All these factors also likely interact with each other to determine the outcome of noticing. Given the multitude of factors involved, it is not a simple matter to determine whether, when, what kind of, and to what degree and scope of noticing may occur in the course of L2 development.

Note that any of the proposed external or internal factors may promote or inhibit learner noticing, so their effects are not necessarily positive for L2 development. Instruction, for instance, is often believed to exert positive influence in promoting learner noticing (e.g., Ellis, 1997; Fotos, 1993). Anecdotally, a student of mine once told me that she learned in an EFL class in Japan the pattern *want+somebody+to do* using example sentences like *I want you to be punctual*, but she never actually used it in real life. Later, when she had a chance to study in the U.S., she noticed that English native speakers often used this structure as a way to make offerings to other people, as in *Do you want me to get you anything?* or *Do you want me to give you a ride home?* This is when she learned the form in connection with its new function, which then prompted her to start using it in similar contexts as she noticed it. She recalls that it was thanks to the instruction she had received earlier that she was able to comprehend the meaning and connect it with the new function with relative ease.

On the other hand, noticing may also be discouraged at least temporarily because of instruction. For example, in a study on the use of tense backshifting in English indirect reported speech, Charkova and Halliday (2011) showed that Bosnian and Bulgarian EFL learners tended to backshift the tenses significantly more frequently than did native English speakers. For example, while native speakers would normally say, "Two weeks ago, I met Marian and she told me that Shawn *was arrested* for underage drinking. She said that he actually *tried* to bite the cop when they *handcuffed* him and that he *spent* the night in jail for that," the EFL learners were much more likely to use *had been arrested, had tried, had handcuffed*, and *had spent* for the italicized parts of the above sentences. The learners, therefore, ended up producing stilted reports that failed to convey their point of view as reporters vis-à-vis the original utterance. Since tense backshifting is not a feature of indirect speech in the learners' L1s, it was argued that the reason for the EFL participants' overuse of backshifting was a result of the special emphasis put on it during their English classes, where backshifting is treated as an automatically applicable grammatical rule without any consideration of pragmatic and semantic factors. As a result of such treatment in teaching, EFL learners may become oblivious to the contradictory evidence contained in the natural input. Such a possibility is supported by the argument and evidence put forth for learned attention effects in L2 learning, whereby prior learning blocks attention to new cues by lowering their psychological salience (Ellis & Sagarra, 2011).

It is possible, however, that such negative instructional influence on learner noticing may later be overridden if the learners continue to receive naturalistic input for an extended period of time. In fact, it was also found in the same study (Charkova & Halliday, 2011) that ESL participants performed differently from their EFL counterparts, in that the more time ESL speakers had spent in the U.S., the more selectively they employed backshifting. Especially those who had spent more than two years in the U.S. defied the backshift rule the most, thus closely resembling the performance of the NSs. The authors speculate that the fact that both the ESL and EFL groups in their study were composed of in-service teachers with relatively high metalinguistic understanding of English grammar might have affected the results. Whether their possession of metalinguistic knowledge worked negatively or positively, in the short term or long term, however, is a matter not settled in this research. It would be interesting to continue to investigate whether and how instruction of different types promotes or inhibits learner noticing.

Noticing and some commonly observed SLA developmental phenomena

Having reviewed different types of noticing and situated them in overall SLA processes, in what follows, I will discuss some cases of patterned L2 development in stages that have often been discussed in the SLA literature and examine how noticing may be relevant in these learning processes. By so doing, I hope to highlight some areas in need of further research on the relationship between noticing and long-term L2 development. For reasons of space, I will focus on only two cases below, the U-shaped learning curve and developmental sequences.

U-shaped learning curve

Contrary to the popular belief that learners make more errors at the initial stages and make fewer errors at later stages of L2 development, it is often observed that learners in fact do not make many errors at the beginning, but instead the error rate increases as they progress in their IL development and decreases at still later stages. This three-stage developmental phenomenon has been observed to occur in both first and second language acquisition and is known as the U-shaped learning curve. Figure 2 depicts this developmental pattern.

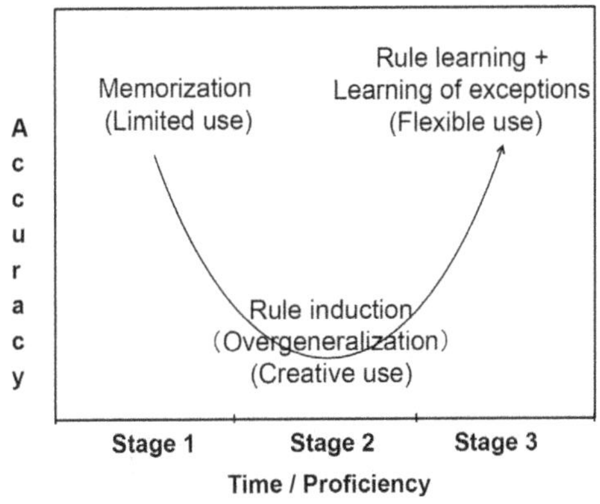

Figure 2. U-shaped learning curve (adapted from Kellerman, 1985)

In the case of L2 acquisition of English, the U-shaped learning curve has been observed to occur for the acquisition of such structures as the regular past tense, plural marking of nouns, hypothetical conditionals, verb transitivity, and passivization, to name a few. For example, Kellerman (1985) illustrates how Dutch learners of L2 English sometimes use expressions like *If he would come, we would go out*, where the modal auxiliary *would* is double marked in both *if* and main clauses. Interestingly, this kind of error does not seem to occur much among lower-proficiency learners. It occurs more frequently among higher-proficiency learners and starts to disappear among still higher-proficiency learners. Kellerman explains that the use of *would* in both clauses is motivated by the fact that learners wish to express the notion of hypotheticalness but feel it awkward to mark it with a past tense form when they do not mean to refer to the past event. This desire to mark hypotheticalness by means other than the target-like form apparently seems to occur when the learners progress in their IL development, when they become increasingly keen on the concept of realis vs. irrealis and tense uses in English.

For another example, in a partial replication study of Izumi and Lakshmanan (1998), Inagaki, Katsurahara, Yamashita, Kusrini, and Dohi (2009) investigated the acquisition of the English passive voice by Japanese EFL learners. Japanese has two different types of passives, direct and indirect. Direct passives are similar to English passives, as seen in sentences like *Taro was kissed by Hanako.* Indirect passives, on the other hand, are unique to Japanese and some Asian languages in that the subject of the sentence can be other than the object of its active counterpart. For instance, in a direct translation from Japanese, one can say something like *Taro was eaten his cake by Hanako*, by which it means that Taro was inconvenienced because Hanako ate his cake. Likewise, when one says *Taro was cried by Hanako*, it means that Taro was embarrassed or troubled when Hanako cried. In both of these cases, the subject of the sentence is somehow adversely affected by the action taken by somebody else, the connotation of which is expressed by means of the passive-like structure. In the grammaticality judgment task used in the study, Inagaki et al. found that while the error rate continually decreased in the case of the indirect passives involving intransitive verbs from junior high school, to high school, and to university students, such was not the case for the indirect passives containing transitive verbs. In other words, high school students accepted more such sentences than did junior high school or university students. The data, thus, seems to follow the U-shaped learning curve for the indirect passive with transitive verbs.

Various reasons have been suggested for why the U-shaped learning curve occurs in language acquisition. In the case of over-regularization errors of past tense and plural marking (where learners use forms like *breaked* and *researches*), it is the consolidation of the learning of regularization rules (i.e., add *-ed* at the end of the verb to mark past and *-s* to mark plural) that prompts the learners to use them beyond their limit. The more instances of regularly changed forms they learn, the more likely they will apply the rules not just to regular but also to irregular cases. In this sense, it is more learning, not less learning or less consolidation, that causes more errors. In the case of the Dutch learners' overuse of *would* in hypothetical conditional sentences (which, incidentally, is also a common mistake made by Japanese EFL learners and also appears as a nonstandard form in NS English), as explained earlier, it is essentially the sophistication in learners' metalinguistic sensitivity that seems to cause it. Likewise, Japanese EFL learners' errors with the passive voice appear to occur as a result of strong L1 influence, which, importantly, interacts with a learner-internal developmental factor, that is, their increasing sensitivity to the transitive-intransitive distinction. (This is reminiscent of Kellerman's 1985 well-known example of Dutch EFL learners' rejection of the grammatical sentence *The cup broke.* The sentence was rejected more by intermediate-level learners than by beginning or advanced learners in a grammaticality judgment task, due arguably to the seemingly odd use of the verb *break* with a non-agentive subject.)

In all cases, the reason for more errors exists learner-internally. Learners ignore input evidence, so to speak, for the sake of internal organization and reorganization of their IL. When learners are obedient and faithfully compliant with the forms used in the input or the classroom instruction, they may simply use the form in the way they heard or learned it, sometimes as a memorized chunk, so their error rate is, not surprisingly, low. It is when they start to truly internalize the form and use it creatively beyond simple memorization that they begin to make more IL errors. This apparently is caused not by input or instruction but by changes in the learners' internal IL state, as is reflected in their increasing sophistication in their IL grammar formation. Given this understanding, then, how does noticing, as a site for and a concrete outcome of the interface between learner internal factors and external factors, play a role in creating the U-shaped learning curve?

It is hypothesized that noticing plays a vital role in some stages but not in all. Noticing, in other words, may play a key role in the first stage when learners notice the form and make the initial form-meaning mapping. However, noticing presumably has little role to play in stage 2, where learners are driven more by their internal forces (e.g., L1, internal analysis, need to impose regularity, developmental constraints) at the expense of input evidence. It is especially at this point that "learners build mental representations that are rather different from what the input in their surrounding environment looks like" (Ortega, 2009a, p. 82). And then once again, noticing may play a role to move the learners to stage 3, this time arguably in the form of noticing the gap between their IL and the TL. Noticing of different types, therefore, may be operative at different stages of IL development.

Our theoretical discussion so far raises many issues for future empirical research. One issue concerns the kind of noticing that takes place at each stage of development. What exactly do learners pay attention to at stage 1? What prompts the noticing at this stage of development? What role, if any, is there for noticing to play at stage 2? Are learners really ignoring input evidence (i.e., not noticing anything relevant at all) at this stage? What is the nature of the attentional bias here? Another issue relates to how learners recover from stage 2 to move up to stage 3. If learners are more or less impervious to external influences at stage 2, what prompts them to change to go beyond it? If noticing the gap between IL and TL may play a role here, what prompts this shift in noticing? Can learners notice the gap at stage 1, or do they have to wait till they get to stage 2? Does noticing the gap need to involve overt output and feedback to it so that learners can make an effective cognitive comparison? In terms of pedagogy, what role does instruction play in this process? What kind of instruction is beneficial for what stage of learning? How should the teachers vary the type of instruction to give for learners at different stages of learning? Given that not all learners may progress all the way through to the complete mastery of the L2 (many may be stuck at stage 2), answering these questions is of obvious importance for both theory development and practical applications to language pedagogy.

Developmental sequences

Let us now take a look at another well-known phenomenon in L2 development, that of developmental sequences. This is another area of research with robust findings, which indicate that L2 learners follow developmental patterns for the acquisition of certain structures more or less similarly, regardless of age, learning context, or L1 background. One case is question formation in L2 English. As shown in Table 1, learners' ways of asking questions in English change as they increase their capacity to manipulate and control syntactic operations in real-time language use. Even if learners possess a large amount of metalinguistic knowledge about English grammar, they may not be able to use higher stage forms unless their real-time processing capacity has already reached the point that allows them to use the syntactic operation in question. Note that increase in stage is not necessarily reflected in increase in accuracy, as for example, developmentally more advanced stage 3 questions, asked with the question words fronted in the sentence without concomitant subject-verb inversion, are less accurate than stage 2 questions, asked in a declarative form with rising intonation.

Table 1. Developmental sequence for question formation in L2 English (adapted from Pienemann, Johnston, & Brindley, 1988)

stage	description	example
1	single words, formulae, or sentence fragments	Four children? A dog?
2	rising intonation	It's a monster in the right corner? The boys throw the shoes?
3	fronting	Where the little children are? Does in this picture there is four dogs? Is the picture has two planets on top?
4	inversion in wh- + copula and 'yes/no' questions	Where is the sun? Is there a fish in the water?
5	inversion in wh- questions	How do you say it? What's the boy doing?
6	complex questions	It's better, isn't it? Why can't you go? Can you tell me what the date is today?

It is also important to bear in mind that movement of stages is identified by the frequency of use, especially by noting the emergence of the given structure in multiple *creative* contexts. Another important point to mention is the common observation in SLA research that the developmental sequences are strongly resistant to change by instruction or any other external influences. Instruction, if successful, can help accelerate the speed of learning (the learners' traversing of the stages), but it may not allow them to skip the stages (e.g., Ellis, 2008; Lightbown & Spada, 2006; Ortega, 2009a, 2009b). Pienemann (e.g., 1984, 1989, 1998) proposed the teachability hypothesis, which claims that instruction does not enable the learners to move up the stage in the sequence unless it matches the learners' developmental readiness, defined in terms of steady and gradual development of the learners' syntactic processing abilities. Thus, learners at stage 2 may likely benefit from the instruction targeting stage 3 forms by moving up to stage 3; the stage 1 learners receiving the same instruction may either stay at stage 1 or move up to stage 2, but not skip over to stage 3 (Mackey, 1999; Spada & Lightbown, 1999). Alternatively, an undesirable consequence may result if unready learners avoid using the structure altogether, thinking, quite reasonably in light of research evidence, that it is beyond their capacity (Pienemann, 1984, 1998).

What role, if any, does noticing play in the face of the powerful internal cognitive mechanism that regulates this aspect of IL development? To move up to stage 2, for instance, learners presumably have to notice the fact that English users ask questions with rising intonation. The relative salience in this aspect of English phonology, together with no need for any syntactic movement operation at this stage, make it easier for learners to reach this stage relatively quickly. To move up to stage 3, learners may need to notice the presence of such question words as *wh*-words, *do*, *are*, and *is* in the input. Again, the perceptual salience of the initial positioning of these words in the sentence eases the learners' burden for their noticing and processing. Thinking in this way, noticing does seem to play a crucial role in enabling learners to move along these stages, even though it alone may not be powerful enough to permit skipping of the stages. The same line of argument may also apply to other stages too, in that for each stage, learners have to notice in the input how questions of different types are formed, for example, by noting the co-occurrence of *wh*-fronting and subject-verb inversion for stage 5 and the cancelation of inversion in embedded questions in stage 6.

Several questions may be raised that warrant further research here. What is the relationship between developmental readiness and noticing? Can learners notice form in the input only if they are developmentally ready to process it? Is processing in this case limited to production, or does it apply equally to receptive use of language? Is it possible for learners to notice the form in the input, yet be unable to move up to the next stage in their production due to developmental constraints, in which case noticing may have a delayed effect on L2 development? How and at what point does the type of noticing change in the course of acquisition? It may be that simple noticing of form (e.g., *wh*-words in the sentence-initial position) may suffice at initial stages, but more detailed noticing, that of the gap between IL and TL, may be needed for the learners to advance to higher stages. If this is the case, does it help the learners to engage in output processing for them to notice the gap? Or does input processing suffice to move up to higher stages? Is there any difference between noticing preceded by output attempt (experiencing production problems, i.e., noticing holes or gap in ability) and that not preceded by it?

On a more pedagogical side, what kind of input and/or output opportunities should be provided to learners to help speed up their traversal of the stages? To what aspect of the input should the teacher draw the learners' attention, and how might it differ for learners at different stages? If it is not global attention but specifically focused attention that is needed for noticing (Schmidt, 2001), it will be helpful for the teacher to be informed of what learners should pay attention to at different stages of development. Another question is whether and how metalinguistic awareness brought about from explicit instruction may help learners to notice aspects of input and help them traverse through the developmental stages. In all cases, it would be wise to take into account the learners' developmental patterns identified in SLA research in our investigation of both other-directed (e.g., teacher-induced) and self-initiated (e.g., task-induced) noticing, so that we can work with, not blindly and needlessly fight against, natural and powerful developmental processes.

Conclusion

Learners are not free to notice anything and everything they wish to notice. Our limited processing capacity necessitates that attention and noticing be selective and should be strategically allocated and managed. Noticing is not always voluntarily controlled, either. It is constrained and regulated by many properties in the input, as well as many factors internal to the learners. If this is the case, we need to understand the role of noticing by situating it in the complex interplay of many factors at play in SLA. In this paper I took two examples of SLA processes in an effort to find the relevance of noticing in a larger framework of L2 development. There are, however, obviously many other important processes discussed in SLA literature that I was not able to deal with in this paper, including such well-attested phenomena as the morpheme accuracy order, implicational hierarchies, and sequenced development of temporal expressions. The significance of knowing such processes for the sake of language teaching is succinctly and aptly summarized by Ortega (2009a):

> [k]nowledge about the sequences and processes of interlanguage development can inform good teaching by helping teachers (and their students) cultivate a different attitude toward 'errors,' and more enlightened expectations for 'progress.' It can help them recognize that many so-called errors are a healthy sign of learning, that timing is

> hugely important in language teaching, and that not all that can be logically taught can be learned if learners are not developmentally ready. (p. 101)

Knowledge about SLA processes helps us not only to develop reasonable expectations for language learning and teaching, but also to situate the role of noticing in a broader perspective. If research on noticing is to develop further and to be of practical use for language teaching, it is imperative that researchers delve into the investigation of the relationship between noticing and L2 development by taking a long-term, developmental perspective, not a short-term, single-shot, hit-or-miss perspective in our thinking of SLA processes.

References

Charkova, K. D., & Halliday, L. J. (2011). Second- and foreign-language variation in tense backshifting in indirect reported speech. *Studies in Second Language Acquisition, 33*, 1–32.

Doughty, C. (2001). Cognitive underpinnings of focus on form. In P. Robinson (Ed.), *Cognition and second language instruction* (pp. 206–257). Cambridge: Cambridge University Press.

Doughty, C., & Williams, J. (1998). Pedagogical choices in focus on form. In C. Doughty & J. Williams (Eds.), *Focus on form in classroom second language acquisition* (pp. 197–261). New York: Cambridge University Press.

Ellis, N., & Sagarra, N. (2011). Learned attention in adult language acquisition: A replication and generalization study and meta-analysis. *Studies in Second Language Acquisition, 33*, 589–624.

Ellis, R. (1997). *SLA research and language teaching.* Oxford: Oxford University Press.

Ellis, R. (2008). *The study of second language acquisition.* Oxford: Oxford University Press.

Fotos, S. (1993). Consciousness raising and noticing through focus on form: Grammar task performance versus formal instruction. *Applied Linguistics, 14*, 385–407.

Gass, S., & Selinker, L. (2008). *Second language acquisition: An introductory course (3rd Edition).* New York: Routledge/Taylor Francis.

Hanaoka, O. (2007). Output, noticing, and learning: An investigation into the role of spontaneous attention to form in a four-stage writing task. *Language Teaching Research, 11*, 459–479.

Hanaoka, O. (2012). *Spontaneous attention to form in EFL writing: The role of output and feedback texts*. Unpublished Ph.D. dissertation, Sophia University, Tokyo, Japan.

Hanaoka, O., & Izumi, S. (2012). Noticing and uptake: Addressing pre-articulated covert problems in L2 writing. *Journal of Second Language Writing, 21*, 332–347.

Inagaki, S., Katsurahara, M., Yamashita, G., Kusrini, D., & Dohi, M. (2009, May). *Why can't you "be eaten your cake"? Overgeneralizations of the passive by Japanese EFL learners at different proficiency levels.* Paper session presented at the 9th annual conference of the Japan Second Language Association, Tokyo, Japan.

Izumi, S. (2002). Output, input enhancement, and the noticing hypothesis: An experimental study on ESL relativization. *Studies in Second Language Acquisition, 24*, 541–577.

Izumi, S. (2003). Comprehension and production processes in second language learning: In search of the psycholinguistic rationale of the output hypothesis. *Applied Linguistics, 24*, 168–196.

Izumi, S., & Bigelow, M. (2000). Does output promote noticing and second language acquisition? *TESOL Quarterly, 34*, 239–278.

Izumi, S., Bigelow, M., Fujiwara, M., & Fearnow, S. (1999). Testing the output hypothesis: Effects of output on noticing and second language acquisition. *Studies in Second Language Acquisition, 21*, 421–452.

Izumi, S., & Lakshmanan, U. (1998). Learnability, negative evidence, and the L2 acquisition of the English passive. *Second Language Research, 14*, 62–101.

Kellerman, E. (1985). If at first you do succeed.... In S. Gass & C. Madden (Eds.), *Input in second language acquisition* (pp. 345–353). Boston, MA: Heinle and Heinle.

Lightbown, P., & Spada, N. (2006). *How languages are learned.* New York: Oxford University Press.

Mackey, A. (1999). Input, interaction, and second language development: An empirical study of question formation in ESL. *Studies in Second Language Acquisition, 21*, 557–587.

Ortega, L. (2009a). Sequences and processes in language learning. In M. H. Long & C. J. Doughty (Eds.), *Handbook of language teaching* (pp. 81–105). Malden, MA: Wiley-Blackwell.

Ortega, L. (2009b). *Understanding second language acquisition.* London: Edward Arnold.

Pienemann, M. (1984). Psychological constraints on the teachability of languages. *Studies in Second Language Acquisition, 6*, 186–214.

Pienemann, M. (1989). Is language teachable? Psycholinguistic experiments and hypotheses. *Applied Linguistics, 10*, 52–79.

Pienemann, M. (1998). *Language processing and second language development: Processability theory.* Amsterdam: Benjamins.

Pienemann, M., Johnston, M., & Brindley, G. (1988). Constructing an acquisition-based procedure for second language assessment. *Studies in Second Language Acquisition, 10*, 217–243.

Schmidt, R. (2001). Attention. In P. Robinson (Ed.), *Cognition and second language instruction* (pp. 3–32). Cambridge: Cambridge University Press.

Schmidt, R. (2012). Attention, awareness, and individual differences in language learning. In W. M. Chan, K. N. Chin, S. K. Bhatt, & I. Walker (Eds.), *Perspectives on individual characteristics and foreign language education* (pp. 27–50). Boston/Berlin: De Gruyter Mouton.

Schmidt, R., & Frota, S. (1986). Developing basic conversational ability in a second language: A case study of an adult learner of Portuguese. In R. R. Day (Ed.), *Talking to learn: Conversation in second language acquisition* (pp. 237–326). Rowley, MA: Newbury House.

Spada, N., & Lightbown, P. (1999). Instruction, first language influence, and developmental readiness in second language acquisition. *Modern Language Journal, 83*, 1–22.

Sugaya, N., & Shirai, Y. (2007). The acquisition of progressive and resultative meanings of the imperfective aspect marker by L2 learners of Japanese: Transfer, universals, or multiple factors. *Studies in Second Language Acquisition, 29*, 1–38.

Swain, M. (1985). Communicative competence: Some roles of comprehensible input and comprehensible output in its development. In S. Gass & C. Madden (Eds.), *Input in second language acquisition* (pp. 235–253). Rowley, Mass.: Newbury House.

Swain, M. (1998). Focus on form through conscious reflection. In C. Doughty & J. Williams (Eds.), *Focus on form in classroom second language acquisition* (pp. 64–81). New York: Cambridge University Press.

Swain, M. (2005). The output hypothesis: Theory and research. In E. Hinkel (Ed.), *Handbook of research in second language teaching and learning* (pp. 471–483). Mahwah, NJ: Laurence Erlbaum.

Toth, P. D. (2006). Processing instruction and a role for output in second language acquisition. *Language Learning, 56*, 319–385.

Truscott, J., & Sharwood Smith, M. (2011). Input, intake, and consciousness: The quest for a theoretical foundation. *Studies in Second Language Acquisition, 33*, 497–528.

VanPatten, B. (Ed.) (2004). *Processing instruction: Theory, research, and commentary.* Mahwah, NJ: Lawrence Erlbaum.

NFLRC monographs

Attention, Awareness, and Noticing in Language Processing and Learning

John N. Williams
University of Cambridge

This chapter reviews current psychological and applied linguistic research that is relevant to Schmidt's landmark theoretical analysis of the concepts of attention, conscious awareness, and noticing. Recent evidence that attention and awareness are dissociable makes it possible to ask which of these constructs is required for either processing familiar stimuli or learning novel associations. There is good evidence for processing familiar stimuli without conscious awareness and even without attention. There is mounting evidence for learning without awareness at the level of understanding regularities, particularly when meaning is involved (semantic implicit learning). There is even some recent evidence for learning without awareness at the level of noticing form, for example, learning associations between subliminal and liminal words. Thus, whilst attention does appear to be necessary for learning, awareness might not be. It is suggested that future research should probe the types of regularity that can be learned without awareness and that this will shed more light on the nature of the underlying learning mechanism and permit an evaluation of its relevance to SLA.

Richard Schmidt's noticing hypothesis has been hugely influential in the field of SLA. Prompted by case studies of second language learners (Schmidt, 1983; Schmidt & Frota, 1986), Schmidt questioned what was then the dominant view of second language development as an unconscious, implicit process. He noted that the presence of a form in the input did not guarantee acquisition even after many years of exposure. A detailed analysis of his own output as a learner of Portuguese, the input he had received in the classroom, and the instances of language that he had noted in his diary showed that "R learned and used what he was taught if he subsequently heard it and if he noticed it" (Schmidt & Frota, 1986, p. 279). In other words, being taught a form was not sufficient nor was exposure to it in the input; he also had to notice the form in order for it to appear in his production. The term *notice* was used in its everyday meaning: "...a second language learner

Williams, J. N. (2013). Attention, awareness, and noticing in language processing and learning. In J. M. Bergsleithner, S. N. Frota, & J. K. Yoshioka (Eds.), *Noticing and second language acquisition: Studies in honor of Richard Schmidt* (pp. 39–57). Honolulu: University of Hawai'i, National Foreign Language Resource Center.

will begin to acquire the targetlike form if and only if it is present in comprehended input and *noticed* in the normal sense of the word, that is, consciously" (p. 311). In subsequent publications he backed up this intuitive idea with thorough reviews of the psychological literature on attention and learning (Schmidt, 1990, 1994, 2001), concluding that there is no evidence for learning forms without conscious attention. The attentional system filters the input and determines what becomes intake. However, he distinguished another sense in which awareness may be involved in learning—what he called *awareness at the level of understanding*—which relates not to whether learners are aware of forms as such but whether they are aware of the rules that govern the distribution of those forms. He was open to the idea that this level of awareness may not be necessary for learning, although, again on the basis of the psychological literature of the time, remained sceptical about its contribution to adult second language acquisition.

Schmidt's ideas, his detailed analysis of the concept of attention, and his appeal to mainstream cognitive psychological research represents landmark work in the field of SLA. The noticing hypothesis fed into the development of pedagogic approaches that attempt to stimulate learning by encouraging an appropriate orientation of attention (Long & Robinson, 1988; VanPatten, 1996). He inspired researchers, including myself, to make direct connections between experimental work on cognitive learning processes and SLA. The noticing hypothesis constituted a clear, falsifiable proposition that was open to empirical investigation using experimental methods.

In this chapter I will provide an update on the psychological background to the concepts underlying the noticing hypothesis. The theoretical concepts of attention and consciousness continue to be refined as more phenomena are explored experimentally, advancing our understanding of learning processes. Once we have characterised the learning processes, then perhaps we will be in a position to evaluate their potential contribution to SLA.

What is attention? Dissociating attention and conscious awareness

William James (1890) is often cited as expressing a common-sense view of attention: "Everyone knows what attention is. It is the taking possession of the mind, in clear and vivid form, of one out of what seem several simultaneously possible objects or trains of thought. Focalisation, concentration, of consciousness are of its essence. It implies withdrawal from some things in order to deal effectively with others." Our intuition tells us that we are aware of what we pay attention to, "My experience is what I agree to attend to" (James, 1890, p. 403). When we say we have not been paying attention to something, we essentially mean that we have not been aware of it. We also intuitively identify the contents of awareness with *working memory* (Baars, 1988; Cowan, 1999) and consciousness as a *workspace* in which information from different sources can be integrated (Baars, 1988; Dehaene & Naccache, 2001). Schmidt (2001) concurs with this common-sense identification of attention and awareness.

Attention without awareness

In fact, recent research suggests that attention and awareness are separate and potentially dissociable. Consider subliminal priming. If a stimulus is flashed very briefly and followed immediately by a masking pattern, then under the right conditions an experimental participant will be unaware of what the stimulus was. Yet responses to a subsequent stimulus will be affected (Marcel, 1983; Perea, Dunabeitia, & Carreiras, 2008). This demonstrates processing without awareness. But does it show processing without attention? From the common-sense perspective we might think that it does; if the prime was not in awareness, then it was not attended. However, there are now numerous demonstrations that top-down attentional factors affect processing of unconscious stimuli. Subliminal priming effects depend on attention being directed to the right moment in time when the prime is presented (Naccache, Blandin, & Dehaene, 2002) or to relevant kinds of information for supporting priming effects (Kunde, Kiesel, & Hoffmann, 2003; Spruyt, De Houwer, Everaert, & Hermans, 2012). A similar phenomenon has been found in studies of blindsight[1] (Kentridge, Heywood, & Weiskrantz, 2004). Despite claiming not to consciously see anything in their blind field, blindsight patients are able to make visual discriminations at above chance levels (e.g., indicate whether a bar in the blind field is horizontal or vertical). Just as for subliminal priming, this shows processing without awareness. However, it has also been shown that when provided with a valid spatial cue, which they are aware of (e.g., an arrow pointing to a location in the blind field), their discrimination performance is enhanced in the blind field. So conscious attention can affect processing of an unconscious stimulus.

Consider how we orient attention. Clearly we are pre-programmed to attend to sudden and unexpected changes in the environment. The elephant crashing through the jungle will attract our attention as will the police siren. In these cases we would say that we are aware of the stimulus, orient our attention to it, engage in deeper processing, and decide what action to take. From the common-sense view it would seem to be impossible to orient our attention to something that we are not even aware of. Yet this seems to be the case. In one study (Jiang, Costello, Fang, Huang, & He, 2006) arousing images were masked so as to make them completely invisible. Nevertheless, an image of a naked woman would be more likely to attract spatial attention than an image of a man but only for heterosexual males (and the opposite for heterosexual females). This shows that quite fine distinctions can be computed for stimuli that are not conscious or focally attended and that unconscious stimuli can direct conscious attention.

It seems from these examples that attention and consciousness should be thought of as different things (Dehaene, Changeux, Naccache, Sackur, & Sergent, 2006; Koch & Tsuchiya, 2007). It is therefore more precise to think of attention as a (limited) cognitive resource that when applied to a representation results in deeper and more elaborate processing. But just because something is attended does not mean that we are necessarily aware of it (as in the case of subliminal priming), and the attentional system can orient to stimuli that are not consciously perceived.

Awareness without focal attention

If awareness and attention can be dissociated, then it becomes possible to conceive of forms of awareness that depend minimally on attention. After all, focal attention is highly limited in capacity, and if we were only aware of the contents of focal attention, then we would have a blinkered view of the world, a kind of tunnel vision. Yet our conscious experience seems to be much broader than this, as if it overflows the restrictions of focal attention. Driven by this intuition, Block (2007) has argued for a distinction between two forms of awareness. *Access awareness* corresponds to the contents of focal attention and is reportable. *Phenomenal awareness* extends beyond access awareness, is fleeting, and is not reportable. The concept of access awareness appears to correspond to Schmidt's notion of noticing as being the reportable contents of focal attention. The intuition that there is more to our conscious experience than this perhaps gives rise to the idea that there might be forms of processing and learning that can occur outside of this narrow focus. But what is the evidence for phenomenal awareness?

1 Blindsight patients are cortically blind, which is to say that the eyes and optic nerves are intact but there is damage to striate cortex (area V1). In some cases they can be blind on one side of the visual field and see normally on the other.

In an experiment by Sperling (1960), people were briefly shown an array of 16 alphanumeric characters in a 4 by 4 grid. After it disappeared, they could only report about 4 characters, yet they had the impression of seeing around 8. Thus, the contents of access awareness could be described as 4 recognised characters plus more items that were only processed to the level of being recognised as characters but not identified. As one would expect from the common-sense view, only a limited number of items receive sufficient attention to be processed to the level of recognition, and there is minimal processing of the remaining items in the array. What is intriguing, though, is that if after the display disappears, people are cued to report a specific line of the grid, then they can do so with high accuracy (see also Landman, Spekreijse, & Lamme, 2003). This might be taken to imply that people are actually momentarily and *phenomenally* aware of the identity of all of the characters in the display. But only a subset can receive sufficient attention to enter access awareness.

Not unsurprisingly, the claim that people are aware of (and identify) more than they can report is contentious, not least because it is difficult to prove (see the commentaries on Block, 2007). A simpler and more traditional explanation would be that the entire array is held in iconic memory and that there is sufficient raw stimulus information to enable identification when cued. In this view the contents of phenomenal awareness are fleeting and unreportable because they are unanalysed. But we can still retain the idea that consciousness overflows focal attention, consistent with our subjective experience.

Other experiments on visual perception have claimed that it is possible to achieve access awareness for objects outside of focal attention. For example, people can indicate whether complex pictures of natural scenes contain animals (Li, VanRullen, Koch, & Perona, 2002) or they can discriminate famous and non-famous faces (Reddy, Reddy, & Koch, 2006). However, they cannot make what might appear to be simpler discriminations such as between large Ts and Ls or red-green discs from green-red ones. Thus, there are clearly limitations on processing of non-attended stimuli, but at least in the case of vision, high-level semantic descriptions of scenes (*gist*) appear to be available to access awareness. However, it is debatable whether such findings demonstrate awareness without attention. Cohen, Alvarez, and Nakayama (2011) suggest that in these experiments focal attention was not sufficiently taxed to deprive resources from the critical stimuli. They show that the ability to report natural scenes is drastically reduced when a highly demanding distracting task is employed. Interestingly, though, it is still not entirely eliminated, suggesting that a low level of access awareness for unattended stimuli is possible (or that no distracting task is completely distracting). See Cohen, Cavannagh, Chun, and Nakayama (2012) for an argument that there is no double dissociation between attention and awareness.

The above studies attempt to explore awareness outside the focus of attention. The least radical interpretation of the findings is that there are iconic forms of memory that retain stimulus information in a relatively raw form, requiring minimal attention but supporting conscious experience (phenomenal awareness). For certain classes of stimuli there can be access awareness outside of focal attention, but processing is not entirely attention-independent. After all it would be surprising if there were a complete firewall between information that is in focal attention and information that lies outside it.

All of this raises the possibility that there might be not only processing, but also learning, of stimuli outside of the attentional focus, that is, learning without noticing. Let's first consider processing.

Can there be processing without attention or awareness?

As mentioned above, Naccache et al. (2002) showed that subliminal semantic priming depends upon attention. If the participant's attention is directed to a moment in time different from when the prime is flashed, then no semantic priming effect is obtained. This would appear to show that there is no processing without attention (although, as traditional subliminal priming experiments show, there can be processing without awareness). However, this is a case where the stimulus is presented extremely briefly and followed, or preceded, by a pattern mask, so there is limited information entering the system from the bottom up. But what about situations where the stimulus is not masked and under normal conditions it would be easily perceptible, but we have no access awareness of it because our attention is occupied elsewhere? This is the kind of situation that might arise during language learning. For example, the relevant form is clearly present in the input, but the learner does not notice it because their attention is focused elsewhere, perhaps on the meaning of the message.

The everyday experience of mind-wandering provides a case in point. For example, whilst reading, it sometimes happens that we start thinking about something that might (or might not) be totally irrelevant to the text. We become absorbed in our thoughts, yet our eyes continue to traverse the page. At some point we realise that our attention has wandered, a special state of consciousness that Schooler, Smallwood, Christoff, Handy, Reichle, and Sayette (2011) refer to as *meta-awareness* (the state of being aware that we are aware, or in this case, not aware). Our attention snaps back to the text, and perhaps we try to find the point where we lost track. Studies have shown that when mind-wandering during reading, there are reduced event related potential[2] (ERP) effects, and eye movements lose their normal sensitivity to lexical variables such as frequency (Reichle, Reineberg, & Schooler, 2010). Clearly, when attention is occupied elsewhere, the degree of processing of the text is drastically reduced, and we have no access awareness of what the text was about, although we appear to have phenomenal awareness of the physical words on the page.

Similarly, in dichotic listening experiments people have to perform an attention-demanding task on the stimulus stream in one channel while ignoring the material in the other channel. Early research showed that participants were oblivious to even the most basic characteristics of the unattended channel, such as whether it was in a known language or played forwards or backwards. Later studies showed that there may be some processing in the unattended channel, but it was difficult to rule out the possibility that these effects were caused by momentary switches of attention (Holender, 1986).

Although studies of mind-wandering and dichotic listening show that we have no memory for unattended material, there still might be local processing effects that we are not aware of (and that might support some form of learning). Using dichotic listening, Dupoux, Kouider, and Mehler (2003) looked for repetition priming effects from words in the unattended channel to lexical decisions on words in the attended channel. Under conditions when participants claimed not to have been aware of the words in the unattended channel, there were no priming effects suggesting that there is no lexical access from unattended words. However, Dupoux et al. embedded the prime words in time-compressed *babble noise* with no pause before or after the prime. Whilst segmentation of the words was possible under full attention, it is possible that the bottom-up stimulus information was insufficient for recognition without attention (akin to the situation under masking in the case of Naccache et al., 2002). In a similar paradigm but using normal speech, Rivenez, Darwin, and

2 Event related potentials are brain responses to specific events and are measured using electroencephalography (EEG).

Guillaume (2006) showed that there is no priming when the stimuli in the two channels have the same fundamental frequency (as was the case in Dupoux et al., 2003), but effects can be obtained when the frequencies are different. Most impressively of all, priming effects can be obtained when the participants have detected a target word in the attended channel that is coincident with the prime word in the unattended channel making it extremely unlikely that the prime was attended. Therefore, using natural speech that is perceptually distinguishable from the attended channel but a task that makes attention-switching extremely unlikely, momentary lexical access from unattended words appears to be possible.

Studies of the attentional blink (AB) provide evidence for semantic processing of unattended words. The AB refers to the fact that after detecting one target in a very rapid stream of stimuli, there is a momentary lapse of attention, making it difficult to detect another target in the next 500 milliseconds or so, even though that target would ordinarily be perfectly visible (Luck, Vogel, & Shapiro, 1996). The question is what kind of processing do *blinked* words receive? Numerous studies have provided evidence for semantic processing of words that are not detected during the AB (Frings, Bermeitinger, & Wentura, 2011; Luck et al., 1996; Martens, Wolters, & van Raamsdonk, 2002) and even for distracters that occur during the AB, which is surprising because they would be even less likely to be attended than targets (Harris & Little, 2010). Thus, there seems to be quite deep processing of stimuli that are not noticed and are not even attended during the AB, even though they could cross the threshold into consciousness if attention were not occupied elsewhere. Dehaene et al. (2006) refer to such stimuli as *pre-conscious* and suggest that because they produce relatively strong bottom-up activation, they can attain deep levels of processing despite the absence of top-down attention.

To return to the language learning situation, just because the learner apparently has no access awareness, say, of a form and their attention does not appear to have been directed towards it, this does not mean that they have not processed it to some level. Of course, the above studies employed familiar words in the participants' native language. It is a different matter whether there can be learning of new forms or novel associations between known forms without access awareness or focal attention.

Can there be learning without attention?

It is one thing to show short-term priming effects from unattended stimuli; it is another to show longer-term effects, that is, learning. The most basic form of learning is memory for a stimulus. Obviously, if an attentional manipulation has been successful, participants will have little conscious, explicit memory for unattended stimuli. And indeed research has consistently shown that conscious recognition memory is far superior for attended than unattended items, a phenomenon that has been referred to as *inattentional amnesia* (Rees, Russell, Frith, & Driver, 1999; Ruz, Worden, Tudela, & McCandliss, 2005). But as is the case in actual amnesia, might implicit memory be revealed if indirect memory measures are used? Indeed, there is some evidence for this. Using a dichotic listening paradigm, Bentin, Kutas, and Hillyard (1995) showed the usual substantial recognition memory advantage for attended over unattended words. However, of more interest were the responses to new words. Some of these were semantically related to *old* words that had occurred in the dichotic listening task, and some were unrelated. The rate of false alarms (incorrectly judging as old) was higher for new words that were semantically related to words that had occurred in the dichotic listening task. Critically, this effect was as large when the new word was related to an unattended old word as an attended old word. They also found that facilitation of lexical decisions was as large for repetitions of unattended as unattended old words (repetition priming). These results suggest that the participants had equally strong implicit memory for unattended as attended words, despite having far superior explicit memory for the latter.

One study has even claimed that explicit memory for unattended words can be demonstrated, provided that the memory test is sufficiently sensitive. In Hoffman, Bein, and Maril (2011) exposure to attended and unattended words was followed by a recognition memory task. As expected, there was absolutely no discrimination between new words and unattended old words, apparently showing no conscious memory for unattended words. However, the participants were also required to rate their confidence as *high* or *low* for each decision. It was found that high confidence *no* responses were more likely for new words than unattended old words, and conversely, low confidence *no* responses were more likely for unattended old words than new words. Assuming that confidence ratings reflect conscious judgement knowledge (Dienes, 2008), then this study suggests that there can be conscious effects from memory traces left by unattended words, even if participants are unable to translate these into reliable recognition memory judgements.[3]

Both of the above examples only show *learning* in the sense of long-term representational changes as a result of processing a known, but unattended, word. This form of learning is the basis for frequency effects, for the strengthening of representations through exposure, and as such is an important aspect of learning a language (Ellis, 2002). But in language learning we are also, and primarily, concerned with learning new associations—either between existing phonological and orthographic representations to learn new word forms, between forms and meanings, or between forms and forms. Is there any evidence for this kind of learning without attention?

Experiments by Logan and Etherton (1994) show how attention affects learning of novel associations between known words. Participants were presented with pairs of words (one above the other but both recognisable in a single fixation) and had to indicate if one of them belonged to a pre-specified semantic category. Some word pairs were periodically repeated, and the question was whether decision times would become faster for targets in repeated pairings than novel pairings. This was indeed the case, demonstrating incidental learning of the word pairs. However, in another condition an arrow oriented attention to the target just before the word pair appeared, meaning that participants never had to attend to the distracter word. Now the learning effect disappeared, even though the distracter word was presented close enough to fixation to be recognised. Presumably with no prior cue both words had to be attended in order to determine which one belonged to the pre-specified category. But with prior orientation of attention, there was no learning of the association between attended words and unattended distracters.

Other experiments suggest that learning novel associations does not depend simply on whether a stimulus is attended but on whether the appropriate dimension is attended. One has to pay attention in the right way for learning to occur. Jiménez and Méndez (1999) conducted a sequence learning experiment in which a stimulus moved around four positions on the screen and participants simply had to indicate its position by tapping corresponding keys. The stimulus appeared to be randomly one of * ? ! or x. In fact, its identity predicted the position of the next stimulus (e.g., a ! might predict that the next stimulus would occur in the right-most screen position). When participants only had to respond according to the

3 In this and the previous case, it is tempting to attribute the findings to attention-switching during the learning phase. However, this cannot explain the results because in Hoffman et al. (2011) there was no evidence for actual recognition of unattended words and in Bentin et al. (1995) performance on implicit tests was equally strong for unattended and attended words despite far superior recognition memory for the latter.

position of the stimulus on the screen, there was no learning of this regularity. Learning was only obtained when they had to also keep a running count of, for example, how many times either x or * appeared. Thus, learning the association between character identity and screen position only occurred when character identity was *noticed*, in Schmidt's sense. In fact, one can be even more specific because further analyses showed that what participants actually learned was a relationship between being counted or not and the following possible screen positions; the specific associations between characters and screen positions were not learned. This is not to say that they did not also notice the identity of the stimulus, but the act of noticing whether the stimulus was counted was closer in time to the predicted event (the position of the stimulus on the next trial) than the act of noticing the identity of the character. This experiment provides a particularly good example of the relationship between noticing and learning and how the timing of noticing events can be critical to learning.

Finally, in a more linguistically relevant context, Toro, Sinnett, and Soto-Faraco (2005) studied the human ability to segment words from meaningless strings of syllables by tracking transition probabilities (e.g., the stream *tu-pi-ro-go-la-bu-bi-da-ku-pa-do-ti-go-la-bu-pa-do-ti-tu-pi-ro-bi-da-ku* is composed of the non-words *tupiro, golabu, bidaku, padoti*). It had originally been claimed that this form of statistical learning does not require attention (Saffran, Newport, Aslin, Tunick, & Barrueco, 1997). However, Toro et al. showed that learning was drastically reduced under dual task conditions. For example, the pitch of some of the syllables was randomly increased by 20 Hz above the baseline frequency of 200 Hz, and participants were required to press a button when they detected a pitch change. After 7 minutes of exposure, performance on the word segmentation test was only 55%, not significantly different from the chance level of 50% and significantly worse than the 64% achieved by participants who listened passively to the same stream. Even though the participants in the tone monitoring condition were attending closely to the input, they were attending to, and noticed, pitch and not syllables, and so they did not learn the transitional probabilities between them.

These experiments convincingly demonstrate the importance of attention for learning. In all cases there is a stimulus, or a stimulus dimension, that is clearly present, providing ample bottom-up stimulus information, but it is not receiving top-down attention. It is hard to believe that participants are not phenomenally aware of these unattended stimuli or stimulus dimensions. For example, in Toro et al. participants would presumably notice if the stimuli switched from syllables to simple tones of the same pitch. Information is present in phenomenal awareness, as a form of echoic memory, but it is not being attentionally selected for further processing and decision making because of the nature of the task that is set.

How do we square this with the evidence that there can be quite deep processing without attention, for example, lexical access from unattended words in dichotic listening or semantic processing during the attentional blink? If there can be deep processing and implicit memory without attention, why can there be no learning without attention? An obvious possibility is that activating existing representations in memory is one thing whereas forming new connections in memory is another (Cowan, 1999). So in the Logan and Etherton (1994) experiment, under advance cue conditions, a distracter word may well activate its lexical representation and meaning, but for some reason this cannot form a lasting association with the focally attended word. Both need to be simultaneously attended for this to happen—or at least nearly simultaneously attended as when in Jiménez and Méndez (1999) people learn the association between *counted* and the next screen position. Attention appears to provide a kind of *glue* for bonding stimuli together in memory.

Pacton and Perruchet (2008) provide a good example of this principle in the context of learning sequential dependencies. Previous research had shown that whereas people can track the dependencies between adjacent syllables (as in the example from Toro et al. above), they have trouble doing so when the dependent syllables are separated by a random syllable (Newport & Aslin, 2004). Pacton and Perruchet (2008) showed that associations between stimuli that are non-adjacent in the input stream can be learned if the learner's task requires them to attend to these stimuli at the same time (for example, in the case of digit sequences because they have to perform a calculation upon them). Unitization in the attentional focus does not have to be a response to specific task instructions. Gestalt principles of perceptual organisation can have a similar effect, as when the stimuli to be associated are similar and the intervening one is dissimilar, e.g., because they are consonants and the intervening item is a vowel (Newport & Aslin, 2004). As Pacton and Perruchet (2008) put it, "associative learning is an automatic process that links together all the components that are present in the attentional focus at a given point" (p. 82). But whilst attention is clearly required for learning, what is the role of awareness?

Can there be learning without awareness?

Given that awareness and attention are dissociable, just because there can be no learning without attention does not mean that there can be no learning without awareness. Can people learn associations between stimuli without being aware of those associations? Or, as a more extreme scenario, can they learn novel associations between stimuli when they are not even aware of one of them (even though unconscious attention might be allocated to them)?

Schmidt (2001) made an extremely useful distinction between awareness at the level of noticing, which is having access awareness for forms in the input, and awareness at the level of understanding, which is having a conscious understanding of the relationships between forms. On the basis of a review of artificial grammar learning (AGL) research at the time, Schmidt (1995) concluded that there was no evidence for learning without awareness at the level of understanding because such experiments actually provide no evidence for learning abstract rules, contrary to the original claims made by Reber (1993). People might learn fragmentary chunks and recurring sequences of letters at salient positions, but they do not learn the underlying grammar as such. Whilst Schmidt recognised that there may be forms of simple associative learning that can lead to learning without awareness at the level of understanding, he was sceptical about the possibility of learning the kind of complex rule-based generalisations that underlie language.

Research in this area continues to support Schmidt's view. Even when AGL experiments appear to demonstrate acquisition of abstract knowledge through transfer (Altmann, Dienes, & Goode, 1995), this still does not demonstrate learning of the abstract grammar. What people appear to learn is the *repetition structure* of the training items, that is, salient patterns of alternation and doubling in the strings (Tunney & Altmann, 2001). Whilst this knowledge is abstract, it does not correspond to knowledge of the grammar as such. Nevertheless there is good evidence that whatever non-rule-based knowledge is being acquired in AG experiments is unconscious as assessed through subjective measures (Dienes & Scott, 2005; Scott & Dienes, 2010). Serial reaction time experiments also provide good evidence of sensitivity to sequential regularities without awareness of what those regularities are (Jiménez & Méndez, 1999, is a good example). These all constitute examples of learning without awareness at the level of understanding but at a level below abstract generalisations.

In visual perception the contextual cuing paradigm reveals the ability to learn associations between targets and contexts without conscious understanding (Chun, 2000). People are required to locate a pre-specified target in a visual array containing what appear to be many randomly distributed distracters. For example, they might have to locate a rotated letter T in an array of randomly rotated Ls. In fact, some of the displays are repeated, and the remainder are random. As the task progresses, people become faster at locating targets in repeated as opposed to unrepeated displays, showing that they have learned the spatial context for these targets. Just as in Logan and Etherton's (1994) experiment with word pairs, there is incidental learning of arbitrary associations provided that attention is at least momentarily allocated to the context (Jiang & Chun, 2002). The difference here is that learning was shown to be implicit because people had no conscious memory for the repeating displays; in a subsequent recognition test, participants were unable to distinguish repeating displays from new displays. In another experiment people appeared to learn the association between the shapes of the distracters and the shape of the target, regardless of position (Chun, 2000). People implicitly learned which shapes went together, despite not being able to discriminate consistent from inconsistent pairings in a follow-up test. Thus, there is good evidence for learning associations between forms without awareness of what those associations are.

All of these experiments examine what are essentially form-level associations. Implicit learning at this level is presumably relevant to learning word forms and multi-word units. From a statistical learning perspective, co-occurrences at the form level might correlate with, and bootstrap the acquisition of, higher-level grammatical distinctions (Saffran, 2003). But what about implicit learning beyond the form level and involving meaning? This is particularly important for functional and usage-based perspectives that emphasise the acquisition of form-function mappings (Ellis, 1998; MacWhinney, 1997; Tomasello, 2000).

Learning without awareness of meaning: Semantic implicit learning

Within experimental psychology there is growing evidence for meaning-based implicit learning, a phenomenon that one might refer to as *semantic implicit learning*. In a variant of the sequence learning paradigm, Goschke and Bolte (2007) showed that people can become sensitive to recurring semantic category sequences, for example, that a picture of an animal will follow a picture of a body part, without any awareness of the regularity. Variants of the contextual cuing paradigm have been developed in which target position is predicted by the semantic properties of the distracters—the oddness or evenness of digits (Goujon, Didierjean, & Marmeche, 2007), the semantic category of words (Goujon, Didierjean, & Marmeche, 2009), or which kind of scene the target appeared in (bedroom, kitchen, etc.) (Goujon, 2011). These phenomena present a challenge to a strong form of the noticing hypothesis because generalisations are formed without awareness at the level of understanding and at a level that goes beyond simple chunking of surface forms (see Paciorek & Williams, forthcoming, for further discussion of semantic implicit learning experiments).

There is also more direct evidence for semantic-based implicit learning effects within the domain of language. In Williams (2005) four novel determiners were injected into standard English. The participants were told that *gi* and *ro* were used with objects that were near to the speaker and *ul* and *ne* with objects that were far. They then heard sentences such as "I was terrified when I turned around and saw *gi* lion right behind me," "The children threw sticks at *ul* monkey in the tree," "I knocked over *ro* cup and the coffee spilled on my book," "I couldn't read the title of *ne* book that was on the top shelf." What the participants were not told was that there was an additional regularity governing use of the novel determiners: *gi* and *ul* were used with living things and *ro* and *ne* with non-living things (see Rebuschat, Hamrick, Sachs, Riestenberg, & Ziegler, this volume, for further procedural details). Participants who claimed to have been unaware of this regularity were nevertheless significantly above chance at choosing the correct determiner to use in novel article-noun combinations (generalisation items). The participants appeared to have developed some sensitivity to the correlation between the determiners and animacy without being aware of what that correlation was.

Of course, any claim for learning without awareness can only be as convincing as the means used to measure awareness. Post-experiment debriefing may be not the most sensitive measure as it is separated from the moment at which knowledge was used in actual test performance. Subsequent conceptual replications of the Williams (2005) study have addressed this issue. Chen, Guo, Tang, Zhu, Yang, and Dienes (2011) assessed awareness by requiring the participants to indicate whether each decision in the test phase was based on guess, intuition, memory, or rule. Across two experiments responses to generalisation items that were based on guess and intuition combined were significantly above chance (and were 55% and 58% correct, respectively). In contrast, in a conceptual replication that introduced many procedural changes, Hama and Leow (2010) asked participants to think aloud during both the training and test phases. There was no evidence of learning the animacy rule amongst unaware participants. However, results of another replication study by Rebuschat et al. (this volume) suggest that think aloud obliterates learning in this paradigm.

The above studies used judgement tasks in the test phase, and these might have invited participants to draw on explicit knowledge. If veridical and unreported, this will lead to spurious claims of learning without awareness; if erroneous, it will reduce the observed learning effect. It is therefore better to use test tasks that reduce the potential contribution of conscious knowledge. To this end Leung and Williams (2012) adapted the Williams (2005) animacy system for a reaction time task. Essentially, on hearing a noun phrase (e.g., "*ul* monkey"), participants had to indicate as quickly as possible by a button press whether the object being referred to is living or not. At the end of the experiment a block of violation trials were included in which the animacy rule was reversed. Participants who in a post-experiment questionnaire claimed not to be aware of the correlation between determiners and animacy were still slower in the Violation block than the preceding Control block, suggesting sensitivity to animacy without awareness.[4]

Apart from animacy, other types of semantic distinction have been shown to support implicit learning. Using a reaction time methodology, Leung and Williams (2011) showed implicit learning of a correlation between novel determiners and the thematic role of the following noun, this time in a task that did not require an explicit decision based on the hidden regularity. Using a method based on Williams (2005), Guo, Zheng, Zhu, Yang, Chen, Zhang, Ma, and Dienes (2011) showed implicit learning of semantic prosody, the tendency for some words to take collocates with a positive or negative connotation (e.g., *cause* tends to take negative collocates whereas *promote* tends to take positive ones).

The methodology used in all of these semantic implicit learning studies draws participants' attention to the relevant forms. In most of them their attention is not explicitly drawn to the relevant aspects of meaning, although in some cases it is (the reasons for this variation are presently unclear). What is critical, though, is that the participants do not appear to be aware of the correlation between forms and certain aspects of meaning, and yet this affects their performance in detectable ways. Thus, there is learning at the level of understanding

4 Interestingly, the participants who reported awareness of the rule showed a distinctive reaction time profile in that they were able to make their animacy decisions before the noun had been heard (there was a one-second interval between determiner onset and noun onset). This pattern was not observed in any of the *unaware* participants, suggesting that what people reported in the post-experiment questionnaire reflected their use of conscious knowledge in the task.

but without awareness. This contrasts with the general outcome of research within the AGL tradition where it has been very difficult to show that participants implicitly learn much by way of the underlying abstract structure of the grammar. Maybe, though, there is something more *natural* about forming generalisations over form-meaning correlations than over, for example, sequences of letters generated by a finite state grammar. The issue of naturalness will be revisited in the Conclusion.

Learning associations without awareness at the level of noticing

Finally, we return to experimental psychology research to consider what appears to be a case of learning without awareness at the level of form or, in Schmidt's terms, without awareness at the level of noticing. Participants in Alonso, Fuentes, and Hommel (2006) saw target words on a screen and had to indicate whether they were animals or items of furniture. Each word was preceded by a subliminal, masked prime word, which was one of two category labels—all animals were preceded by the word BODY and all items of furniture by the word PLANT (e.g., BODY–dog, PLANT–chair). The question was whether participants would learn the association between the categories (body part–animal, plant–furniture). This was tested in a subsequent lexical decision task, again using subliminal primes, in which the order of the categories was reversed. The prime ANIMAL was followed by exemplars of body parts (e.g., ANIMAL–hand), and FURNITURE was followed by exemplars of plants (e.g., FURNITURE–rose). Facilitation was obtained relative to the opposite pairings (e.g., ANIMAL–rose, FURNITURE–hand). So people had learned an arbitrary bidirectional association between the categories (BODY–ANIMAL, PLANT–FURNITURE) that generalised to words not encountered in training. This occurred without awareness at the level of noticing one of the words during either the learning or testing phases. This effect has subsequently been replicated (Custers & Aarts, 2011). Using a different methodology, Schlaghecken, Blagrove, and Maylor (2007) also showed that the predictiveness of masked cues can be learned without awareness of what those cues are.

On the face of it, these results appear to challenge the idea that attention is required for learning novel associations. Crucially, though, note that the claim here is not that learning occurred without attention, merely that it occurred without awareness at the level of noticing form. Novel associations can be learned even when one of the relevant forms is not consciously perceived, but an appropriate attentional orientation is still necessary (Custers & Aarts, 2011).

Finally, these studies revealed evidence of an interesting qualitative difference between learning with and without awareness. In another of Alonso et al.'s (2006) experiments, no masking was used and all words were clearly visible. Although all of the participants would have had awareness at the level of noticing the primes, it was found that about half of them were aware of the regular relationship between primes and targets (e.g., that BODY was always followed by an animal). Interestingly, it was this aware group, who had achieved awareness at the level of understanding, who did *not* show a priming effect when the order of the categories was reversed in the lexical decision test phase. This effect was only obtained for the unaware group. Aware participants appear to learn unidirectional associations whereas unaware participants learn bidirectional associations. Custers and Arts (2011) showed that even participants who were unaware because primes were masked would only learn unidirectional associations after their attention had been *tuned* to process pre-target events as predictive. They argue that it is not awareness, but attention, that plays a causal role in learning.

Why were bidirectional associations only learned without awareness? Alonso et al. (2006) suggest that aware participants learn that BODY *predicts* animals. But this does not mean that ANIMAL will predict body parts; hence, there is no priming when the direction of the association is reversed in the test phase. On the other hand, unaware participants merely learn that BODY and ANIMAL words *go together*, and so presentation of either one will activate the other and produce priming. One could regard the first kind of learning as cognitive and inferential and the second as associative. Learning with and without awareness might lead to qualitatively different kinds of knowledge (Jiménez, Vaquero, & Lupianez, 2006).

Conclusion

The common-sense view of attention, expressed, for example, by James (1890), accords with our everyday experience; we are aware of what we attend to. What we attend to is processed deeply and is learned, and what we do not attend to is not. However, psychological research suggests that things are not so simple. Attention and awareness can be dissociated: Attention affects processing of stimuli that we are not aware of, and there may be forms of awareness that depend minimally on attention (phenomenal awareness). Attention does not determine all that is processed; there can be recognition, and even semantic processing, of stimuli that are not even attended, let alone conscious. There is even some evidence for implicit memory for non-attended words, demonstrating a form of learning without attention that could support the reinforcement of representations with repetition. However, in the SLA context we must bear in mind that many of these phenomena concern words in the native language. Perhaps then they tell us more about the automaticity of processing than the non-selectivity of attention, and we may wonder at what level of fluency such effects could be detected in the L2. But in principle, it does appear that non-attended stimuli can lead to lasting changes in representations.

When it comes to learning new associations, rather than reinforcing existing representations, then, there is ample evidence that attention to the relevant forms, or more specifically the relevant dimensions of forms, is necessary. But is awareness, or what Schmidt referred to as *awareness at the level of noticing*, also necessary? Whilst the assumption within psychology and SLA appears to be that it is, some recent evidence suggests that new associations might be formed even when one of the stimuli to be associated is not consciously recognised. Although this may challenge the idea that awareness is necessary for learning, it does not diminish the role of attention (as dissociable from awareness). Note also that the effects again relate to native language words for which lexical access can be assumed to be highly automatic.

What about awareness of associations, as opposed to the stimuli themselves, what Schmidt referred to as *awareness at the level of understanding*? At the level of learning associations between forms, as chunks or sequences, the psychological literature on implicit learning provides numerous examples of learning simple regularities without awareness of what they are. Implicit learning of this type underpins statistical learning more generally. However, Schmidt's scepticism was directed more at learning generalizable rules. In the area of ordering rules underlying artificial or semi-artificial languages, evidence for learning without awareness remains elusive. However, there is mounting evidence from a variety of paradigms that people can show sensitivity to meaning-based generalisations without awareness of what those generalisations are, although attention to the relevant stimuli during learning is clearly necessary.

A central observation in Schmidt's diary study was that "R subjectively felt as he was going through the learning process that conscious awareness of what was present in the input was causal" (Schmidt & Frota, 1986, p. 281). The experimental evidence reviewed here suggests that learning is still possible without conscious awareness, at least of regularities, and possibly of forms themselves. Of course, processing is deeper and more sustained with awareness, and learning effects are much larger. The resultant knowledge can be intentionally controlled and used flexibly. In contrast, even though effects of learning without awareness are detectable, the effects tend to be small. They produce unconscious biases in performance: for example, slightly faster times to locate a target in a display (Chun, 2000), a slight bias towards accepting items that respect a semantic regularity (Chen et al., 2011), or slightly slower semantic decision times when a regularity is violated (Leung & Williams, 2012). It is no surprise then that in comparisons of broadly *implicit* and explicit teaching methods that do not employ sensitive performance measures the explicit methods appear to be more effective (Norris & Ortega, 2000; Spada & Tomita, 2010). At the present time, though, the main motivation for examining learning without awareness is theoretical and through that to understand the contribution that it could make to learning problems such as SLA that are of a scale that cannot be investigated in the lab.

Of course, the question whether there can be learning without awareness continues to be debated within both psychology and applied linguistics (Hama & Leow, 2010). Some psychologists continue to deny the possibility, essentially on the grounds that learning consists, minimally, in the association of ideas (Shanks, 2007), and in the extreme, even simple associations are not mere mechanical connections but have propositional content and attitudes (Mitchell, De Houwer, & Lovibond, 2009). In this view even something as simple as classical conditioning requires awareness of the relevant predictive relationships (Lovibond & Shanks, 2002). Note, however, that such research examines completely novel and arbitrary associations, such as pairings of a tone and puff of air, which do not make contact with prior knowledge structures. In contrast, most of the examples of learning without awareness described above involve meaningful material, stimuli that automatically activate representations in a rich knowledge base. This is particularly true of the cases of semantic implicit learning. Thus, it is important to investigate the relationship between learning and awareness in environments that are more naturalistic than those typically studied in psychology experiments.

Once we accept the relevance of existing knowledge structures, then we need to explore how they constrain the learning process. For example, there is evidence that not all semantic distinctions are equally learnable. Leung and Williams (2012) found no implicit learning of a correlation between determiners and the relative size of two objects (e.g., *gi* would occur with the smaller object, regardless of its absolute size). And using the judgement task based on Williams (2005), Chen et al. (2011) found no learning of a correlation between determiners and the size of the object relative to a dog. Both of these systems are linguistically unnatural, suggesting that, within language at least, semantic implicit learning is constrained. The constraints may derive from prior knowledge of universally encodable semantic distinctions (Bickerton, 2001) or from general, and still potentially universal, cognitive factors such as concept availability. Thus, we move away from the question of whether implicit learning occurs at all to a more theoretically interesting one of whether there are innate or more general cognitive predispositions for learning certain patterns within language. Clearly, if we are interested in why some linguistic correlations are spontaneously absorbed by the mind and others not, then we are going to have to employ paradigms that tap into implicit, as opposed to explicit, learning processes. When we know more about the areas of language that appear amenable to implicit learning, then we will know where to look for its effects in real world language learning situations.

References

Alonso, D., Fuentes, L. J., & Hommel, B. (2006). Unconscious symmetrical inferences: A role of consciousness in event integration. *Consciousness and Cognition, 15*, 386–396.

Altmann, G. T. M., Dienes, Z., & Goode, A. (1995). Modality independence of implicitly learned grammatical knowledge. *Journal of Experimental Psychology: Learning Memory and Cognition, 21*, 899–912.

Baars, B. J. (1988). *A cognitive theory of consciousness*. Cambridge: Cambridge University Press.

Bentin, S., Kutas, M., & Hillyard, S. A. (1995). Semantic processing and memory for attended and unattended words in dichotic-listening: Behavioral and electrophysiological evidence. *Journal of Experimental Psychology: Human Perception and Performance, 21*, 54–67.

Bickerton, D. (2001). Okay for content words, but what about functional items? Commentary on Bloom: How children learn the meanings of words. *Behavioral and Brain Sciences, 24*, 1104–1105.

Block, N. (2007). Consciousness, accessibility, and the mesh between psychology and neuroscience. *Behavioral and Brain Sciences, 30*, 481–548.

Chen, W. W., Guo, X. Y., Tang, J. H., Zhu, L., Yang, Z. L., & Dienes, Z. (2011). Unconscious structural knowledge of form-meaning connections. *Consciousness and Cognition, 20*, 1751–1760.

Chun, M. M. (2000). Contextual cueing of visual attention. *Trends in Cognitive Sciences, 4*, 170–178.

Cohen, M. A., Alvarez, G. A., & Nakayama, K. (2011). Natural-scene perception requires attention. *Psychological Science, 22*, 1165–1172.

Cohen, M. A., Cavanagh, P., Chun, M. M., & Nakayama, K. (2012). The attentional requirements of consciousness. *Trends in Cognitive Sciences, 16*, 411–417.

Cowan, N. (1999). An embedded-processes model of working memory. In A. Miyake & P. Shah (Eds.), *Models of working memory: Mechanisms of active maintenance and executive control* (pp. 62–101). Cambridge: Cambridge University Press.

Custers, R., & Aarts, H. (2011). Learning of predictive relations between events depends on attention, not on awareness. *Consciousness and Cognition, 20*, 368–378.

Dehaene, S., Changeux, J. P., Naccache, L., Sackur, J., & Sergent, C. (2006). Conscious, preconscious, and subliminal processing: A testable taxonomy. *Trends in Cognitive Sciences, 10*, 204–211.

Dehaene, S., & Naccache, L. (2001). Towards a cognitive neuroscience of consciousness: Basic evidence and a workspace framework. *Cognition, 79*, 1–37.

Dienes, Z. (2008). Subjective measures of unconscious knowledge. *Progress in Brain Research, 168*, 49–64.

Dienes, Z., & Scott, R. (2005). Measuring unconscious knowledge: Distinguishing structural knowledge and judgment knowledge. *Psychological Research, 69*, 338–351.

Dupoux, E., Kouider, S., & Mehler, J. (2003). Lexical access without attention? Explorations using dichotic priming. *Journal of Experimental Psychology: Human Perception & Performance, 29*, 172–184.

Ellis, N. C. (1998). Emergentism, connectionism, and language learning. *Language Learning, 48*, 631–664.

Ellis, N. C. (2002). Frequency effects in language processing: A review with implications for theories of implicit and explicit language acquisition. *Studies in Second Language Acquisition, 24*, 143–188.

Frings, C., Bermeitinger, C., & Wentura, D. (2011). Inhibition from blinked category labels: Combining the attentional blink and the semantic priming paradigm. *Journal of Cognitive Psychology, 23*, 514–521.

Goschke, T., & Bolte, A. (2007). Implicit learning of semantic category sequences: Response-independent acquisition of abstract sequential regularities. *Journal of Experimental Psychology: Learning, Memory, and Cognition, 33*, 394–406.

Goujon, A. (2011). Categorical implicit learning in real-world scenes: Evidence from contextual cueing. *Quarterly Journal of Experimental Psychology, 64*, 920–941.

Goujon, A., Didierjean, A., & Marmeche, E. (2007). Contextual cueing based on specific and categorical properties of the environment. *Visual Cognition, 15*, 257–275.

Goujon, A., Didierjean, A., & Marmeche, E. (2009). Semantic contextual cuing and visual attention. *Journal of Experimental Psychology: Human Perception and Performance, 35*, 50–71.

Guo, X., Zheng, L., Zhu, L., Yang, Z., Chen, C., Zhang, L., Ma, W., & Dienes, Z. (2011). Acquisition of conscious and unconscious knowledge of semantic prosody. *Consciousness and Cognition, 20*, 417–425.

Hama, M., & Leow, R. P. (2010). Learning without awareness revisited. *Studies in Second Language Acquisition, 32*, 465–491.

Harris, I. M., & Little, M. J. J. (2010). Priming the semantic neighbourhood during the attentional blink. *Plos One, 5*.

Hoffman, Y., Bein, O., & Maril, A. (2011). Explicit memory for unattended words. *Psychological Science, 22*, 1490–1493.

Holender, D. (1986). Semantic activation without conscious identification in dichotic-listening, parafoveal vision, and visual masking—a survey and appraisal. *Behavioral and Brain Sciences, 9*, 1–23.

James, W. (1890). *The principles of psychology*. New York: Holt.

Jiang, Y., & Chun, M. M. (2002). Contextual cueing: Reciprocal influences between attention and implicit learning. In L. Jiménez (Ed.), *Attention and implicit learning* (pp. 277–296). Amsterdam: Bejamins.

Jiang, Y., Costello, P., Fang, F., Huang, M., & He, S. (2006). A gender- and sexual orientation-dependent spatial attentional effect of invisible images. *Proceedings of the National Academy of Sciences, 103*, 17048–17052.

Jiménez, L., & Méndez, C. (1999). Which attention is needed for implicit sequence learning? *Journal of Experimental Psychology: Learning, Memory, and Cognition, 25*, 236–259.

Jiménez, L., Vaquero, J. M. K., & Lupianez, J. (2006). Qualitative differences between implicit and explicit sequence learning. *Journal of Experimental Psychology: Learning, Memory, and Cognition, 32*, 475–490.

Kentridge, R. W., Heywood, C. A., & Weiskrantz, L. (2004). Spatial attention speeds discrimination without awareness in blindsight. *Neuropsychologia, 42*, 831–835.

Koch, C., & Tsuchiya, N. (2007). Attention and consciousness: Two distinct brain processes. *Trends in Cognitive Sciences, 11*, 16–22.

Kunde, W., Kiesel, A., & Hoffmann, J. (2003). Conscious control over the content of unconscious cognition. *Cognition, 88*, 223–242.

Landman, R., Spekreijse, H., & Lamme, V. A. F. (2003). Large capacity storage of integrated objects before change blindness. *Vision Research, 43*, 149–164.

Leung, J. H. C., & Williams, J. N. (2011). The implicit learning of mappings between forms and contextually derived meanings. *Studies in Second Language Acquisition, 33*, 33–55.

Leung, J. H. C., & Williams, J. N. (2012). Constraints on implicit learning of grammatical form-meaning connections. *Language Learning, 62*, 634–662.

Li, F. F., VanRullen, R., Koch, C., & Perona, P. (2002). Rapid natural scene categorization in the near absence of attention. *Proceedings of the National Academy of Sciences, 99*, 9596–9601.

Logan, G. D., & Etherton, J. L. (1994). What is learned during automatization? The role of attention in constructing an instance. *Journal of Experimental Psychology: Learning, Memory, and Cognition, 20*, 1022–1050.

Long, M. H., & Robinson, P. (1988). Focus on form: Theory, research, and practice. In C. Doughty & J. Williams (Eds.), *Focus on form in classroom second language acquisition* (pp. 15–41). Cambridge: Cambridge University Press.

Lovibond, P. F., & Shanks, D. R. (2002). The role of awareness in Pavlovian conditioning: Empirical evidence and theoretical implications. *Journal of Experimental Psychology: Animal Behavior Processes, 28*, 3–26.

Luck, S. J., Vogel, E. K., & Shapiro, K. L. (1996). Word meanings can be accessed but not reported during the attentional blink. *Nature, 383*, 616–618.

MacWhinney, B. (1997). Second language acquisition and the competition model. In A. M. B. de Groot & J. F. Kroll (Eds.), *Tutorials in bilingualism* (pp. 113–142). Mahwah, New Jersey: Lawrence Erlbaum Associates.

Marcel, A. J. (1983). Conscious and unconscious perception: Experiments on visual masking and word recognition. *Cognitive Psychology, 15*, 197–237.

Martens, S., Wolters, G., & van Raamsdonk, M. (2002). Blinks of the mind: Memory effects of attentional processes. *Journal of Experimental Psychology: Human Perception and Performance, 28*, 1275–1287.

Mitchell, C. J., De Houwer, J., & Lovibond, P. F. (2009). The propositional nature of human associative learning. *Behavioral and Brain Sciences, 32*, 183–246.

Naccache, L., Blandin, E., & Dehaene, S. (2002). Unconscious masked priming depends on temporal attention. *Psychological Science, 13*, 416–424.

Newport, E. L., & Aslin, R. N. (2004). Learning at a distance I. Statistical learning of non-adjacent dependencies. *Cognitive Psychology, 48*, 127–162.

Norris, J. M., & Ortega, L. (2000). Effectiveness of L2 instruction: A research synthesis and quantitative meta-analysis. *Language Learning, 50*, 417–528.

Paciorek, A. W., & Williams, J. N. (forthcoming). Semantic implicit learning. In P. Rebuschat (Ed.), *Implicit and explicit learning of languages*.

Pacton, S., & Perruchet, P. (2008). An attention-based associative account of adjacent and nonadjacent dependency learning. *Journal of Experimental Psychology: Learning, Memory, and Cognition, 34*, 80–96.

Perea, M., Dunabeitia, J. A., & Carreiras, M. (2008). Masked associative/semantic priming effects across languages with highly proficient bilinguals. *Journal of Memory and Language, 58*, 916–930.

Reber, A. S. (1993). *Implicit learning and tacit knowledge*. Oxford: Oxford University Press.

Reddy, L., Reddy, L., & Koch, C. (2006). Face identification in the near-absence of focal attention. *Vision Research, 46*, 2336–2343.

Rees, G., Russell, C., Frith, C. D., & Driver, J. (1999). Inattentional blindness versus inattentional amnesia for fixated but ignored words. *Science, 286*, 2504–2507.

Reichle, E. D., Reineberg, A. E., & Schooler, J. W. (2010). Eye movements during mindless reading. *Psychological Science, 21*, 1300–1310.

Rivenez, M., Darwin, C. J., & Guillaume, A. (2006). Processing unattended speech. *Journal of the Acoustical Society of America, 119*, 4027–4040.

Ruz, M., Worden, M. S., Tudela, P., & McCandliss, B. D. (2005). Inattentional amnesia to words in a high attentional load task. *Journal of Cognitive Neuroscience, 17*, 768–776.

Saffran, J. R. (2003). Statistical language learning: Mechanisms and constraints. *Current Directions in Psychological Science, 12*, 110–114.

Saffran, J. R., Newport, E. L., Aslin, R. N., Tunick, R. A., & Barrueco, S. (1997). Incidental language learning: Listening (and learning) out of the corner of your ear. *Psychological Science, 8*, 101–105.

Schlaghecken, F., Blagrove, E., & Maylor, E. A. (2007). Incidental learning of S-R contingencies in the masked prime task. *Journal of Experimental Psychology: Human Perception and Performance, 33*, 1177–1188.

Schmidt, R. (1983). Interaction, acculturation, and the acquisition of communicative competence. In N. Wolfson & E. Judd (Eds.), *Sociolinguistics and language acquisition* (pp. 137–174). Rowley, MA: Newbury House.

Schmidt, R. (1990). The role of consciousness in second language learning. *Applied Linguistics, 11*, 129–158.

Schmidt, R. (1994). Implicit learning and the cognitive unconscious: Of artificial grammars and SLA. In N. C. Ellis (Ed.), *Implicit and explicit learning of languages* (pp. 165–209). London: Academic Press.

Schmidt, R. (1995). Consciousness and foreign language learning: A tutorial on the role of attention and awareness in learning. In R. Schmidt (Ed.), *Attention and awareness in foreign language learning* (pp. 1–63). Honolulu: Hawai'i: National Foreign Language Resource Center.

Schmidt, R. (2001). Attention. In P. Robinson (Ed.), *Cognition and second language instruction* (pp. 3–32). Cambridge: Cambridge University Press.

Schmidt, R., & Frota, S. (1986). Developing basic conversational ability in a second language: A case study of an adult learner of Portuguese. In R. R. Day (Ed.), *Talking to learn: Conversation in second language acquisition* (pp. 237–326). Rowley, MA: Newbury House.

Schooler, J. W., Smallwood, J., Christoff, K., Handy, T. C., Reichle, E. D., & Sayette, M. A. (2011). Meta-awareness, perceptual decoupling, and the wandering mind. *Trends in Cognitive Sciences, 15*, 319–326.

Scott, R. B., & Dienes, Z. (2010). Knowledge applied to new domains: The unconscious succeeds where the conscious fails. *Consciousness and Cognition, 19*, 391–398.

Shanks, D. R. (2007). Associationism and cognition: Human contingency learning at 25. *Quarterly Journal of Experimental Psychology, 60*, 291–309.

Spada, N., & Tomita, Y. (2010). Interactions between type of instruction and type of language feature: A meta-analysis. *Language Learning, 60*, 263–308.

Sperling, G. (1960). The information available in brief visual presentations. *Psychological Monographs: General and Applied, 74*, 1–29.

Spruyt, A., De Houwer, J., Everaert, T., & Hermans, D. (2012). Unconscious semantic activation depends on feature-specific attention allocation. *Cognition, 122*, 91–95.

Tomasello, M. (2000). The item-based nature of children's early syntactic development. *Trends in Cognitive Sciences, 4*, 156–163.

Toro, J. M., Sinnett, S., & Soto-Faraco, S. (2005). Speech segmentation by statistical learning depends on attention. *Cognition, 97*, B25–B34.

Tunney, R. J., & Altmann, G. T. M. (2001). Two modes of transfer in artificial grammar learning. *Journal of Experimental Psychology: Learning, Memory, and Cognition, 27*, 614–639.

VanPatten, B. (1996). *Input processing and grammar instruction: Theory and research.* Norwood, New Jersey: Ablex Publishing Corporation.

Williams, J. N. (2005). Learning without awareness. *Studies in Second Language Acquisition, 27*, 269–304.

Part Two:
Observing and Enhancing Noticing

NFLRC
monographs

Recasts, Uptake, and Noticing

Rod Ellis
Nadia Mifka-Profozic
University of Auckland

A key issue in the debate surrounding the effectiveness of recasts as a corrective feedback strategy concerns the extent to which learners (a) notice them, (b) identify them as corrective, and (c) pay attention to the specific forms that have been corrected. This chapter examines the extent to which uptake following a recast can be taken as evidence of noticing. It reports a study that investigated the effects of two types of implicit corrective feedback (recasts and clarification requests) on both uptake with repair and acquisition of a French verb tense (passé composé). The main findings were (a) 84.5% of the recasts were followed by uptake with repair, (b) there was no evidence that repairing errors was related to acquisition, (c) there was only limited evidence that learners who had the opportunity to repair their errors following recasts benefited more than those who just audited the recasts, and (d) those learners who produced uptake with repair following recasts outperformed those learners who produced uptake with repair following clarification requests. Overall, these findings suggest that it is the noticing of the target feature in the input provided by recasts rather than self-correction that is important for learning. It is suggested that in the instructional context investigated (French as a foreign language in high school) the recasts were highly salient to the learners and that the corrections of their passé composé errors were consistently noticed.

Introduction

Recasts reformulate erroneous utterances, providing learners with both negative and positive evidence regarding the correctness of linguistic features. A key issue in the debate surrounding the effectiveness of recasts as a corrective feedback strategy concerns the extent to which they are salient to learners, i.e., whether learners in fact recognize that they are *corrective* and are able to *notice the gap* (Schmidt & Frota, 1986) between their initial erroneous utterance and the recast. In accordance with Schmidt's noticing hypothesis, it can

Ellis, R., & Mifka-Profozic, N. (2013). Recasts, uptake, and noticing. In J. M. Bergsleithner, S. N. Frota, & J. K. Yoshioka (Eds.), *Noticing and second language acquisition: Studies in honor of Richard Schmidt* (pp. 61–79). Honolulu: University of Hawai'i, National Foreign Language Resource Center.

be hypothesized that recasts will assist L2 acquisition when noticing occurs but may not do so if it does not occur. One way of investigating whether noticing does occur is by inspecting the learner uptake move that follows a recast. Lyster and Ranta (1997) distinguish uptake in terms of *repair* and *no repair*. Although *no repair* cannot be assumed to indicate that no noticing has occurred, uptake that repairs the initial error constitutes evidence that noticing at some level has taken place. Thus, it can be hypothesized that uptake with repair will be positively associated with L2 acquisition. The purpose of this contribution to the festschrift for Dick Schmidt is to explore to what extent uptake with repair contributes to L2 learning.

The noticing hypothesis

Over time Schmidt has slightly modified his noticing hypothesis. The earlier version (Schmidt 1990, 1993, 1994, 1995) claimed that noticing is a necessary condition for learning. That is, no noticing, no learning. Subsequently, however, Schmidt (2001) acknowledged that some subliminal learning might be possible and thus modified the claim by proposing that the more learners notice, the more they can learn. As he put it "attended learning is far superior" (p. 3). Thus, the essential claim has remained the same: "for all practical purposes, attention is necessary for all aspects of learning" (p. 4). Schmidt has also been careful to explain what he means by conscious attention to linguistic form. It does not mean that learners notice *rules* (for example, the word order in embedded questions in English); it means only that they pay conscious attention to exemplars of a rule (for example, they notice that in a sentence like *Sam asked who Mary loves*, *loves* follows *Mary*). Noticing an exemplar of a grammatical feature may or may not result in acquisition. The feature may just be noticed and then forgotten. Alternatively, it may lead to some change in the learners' long-term memory. The more often an exemplar of the same feature is noticed, the more likely it is to affect a change in the underlying system. Schmidt was also careful to distinguish consciousness at the level of noticing from consciousness at the level of understanding. Thus, noticing an exemplar of a rule in the input is very different from and does not entail a conscious representation of the underlying rule. Noticing does not guarantee learning no matter whether this is defined as involving explicit or implicit knowledge.

There are also two kinds of noticing in Schmidt's hypothesis, both of which were first introduced in Schmidt's account of his experience of learning Portuguese in Brazil (Schmidt & Frota, 1986). First, there is the noticing of instances of features in the input (or in the learner's output), as described in the paragraph above. Second, there is *noticing the gap*. This occurs when learners conduct cognitive comparisons of their own output and the input and detect a difference between them. For example, if a learner happens to say *Sam asked me who does Mary love?* and then receives as a response *Did Sam really ask you who Mary loves?*, an opportunity arises for the learner to notice the difference between *who does Mary love* and *who Mary loves*. This noticing the gap is an important part of the noticing hypothesis because it indicates a role for learner output in acquisition. Acquisition is input-driven[1], but some of the best input arises in response to what a learner has said. This is one reason why researchers have become interested in corrective feedback as it provides learners with opportunities to notice the gap.

Truscott (1998) pointed to a number of problems with the noticing hypothesis, one of which was that "one must still explain exactly what must be noticed" (p. 115) for learning to take place. Truscott claimed that the noticing hypothesis had not done this. However,

1 Not all SLA researchers view learning as *input-driven*. Such a claim derives from a computational model of L2 acquisition of the kind that Schmidt himself worked with. Sociocultural theorists (e.g., Lantolf, 2000) would consider that learning can be output-driven (i.e., it originates in other-assisted production).

this point has been addressed. According to the connectionist model of learning that underlies Schmidt's claims about noticing, conscious attention to *tokens* in the input cumulatively contributes to the representation of underlying *types*. That is, learners do not notice grammatical categories but rather bootstrap their way to these features as a result of repeated attention to the linguistic tokens that realise them (N. Ellis, 1996). Truscott also claimed that the hypothesis "defies direct testing" and that, therefore, "one must rely on indirect evidence" (p. 116). In this he is entirely correct. It is impossible to observe whether a learner is consciously attending to a linguistic feature in input or output. The indirect evidence that Truscott then evaluated was that provided by form-focused instruction (FFI) studies. He argued that the majority of the studies that demonstrated a positive effect for FFI on acquisition were flawed because (1) they only measured learning by means of tests that were likely to tap into metalinguistic knowledge and (2) they failed to demonstrate that any effect was long-lived (i.e., they did not include a delayed posttest). Thus, he argued that the FFI studies had failed to provide any evidence in support of the noticing hypothesis. Such a claim is less tenable these days. Norris and Ortega's (2000) meta-analysis of FFI studies showed that FFI does have a positive effect even when acquisition is measured in terms of free production. Ellis (2002) likewise produced evidence to suggest that FFI results in implicit knowledge (what Truscott would call *real competence*). However, simply showing that FFI benefits acquisition, while compatible with the noticing hypothesis, does not really constitute clear support for it. FFI, more often than not, involves intentional learning rather than the kind of incidental learning[2] that the hypothesis was intended to address. That is, FFI caters not just to *noticing* but also to *understanding*, making it impossible to determine which of these cognitive processes is responsible for learning. Clearly, then, other kinds of evidence—still indirect—are needed. In particular, it is important to try to show (1) that noticing has taken place and then (2) that as a result, some learning has occurred.

Using stimulated recall to investigate noticing

A number of studies have examined whether noticing occurs as a result of the corrective feedback that learners receive on their erroneous utterances. These studies have made use of stimulated recall (i.e., they have replayed extracts of interactions containing corrective feedback and asked learners to comment on their perceptions of what took place).

Mackey, Gass, and McDonough (2000) used stimulated recall to investigate L2 learners' perceptions of feedback moves. The results showed that "whereas the feedback episodes primarily concerned morphosyntax and phonology, the learners' stimulated-recall comments were more widely distributed across all six category types, with the greatest percentages occurring in phonology, lexis, and semantics" (p. 484). In fact, the ESL learners in this study only perceived that the feedback was directed at morphosyntactical features 13% of the time and the FL learners only 24%.

Egi (2007) also used stimulated recall to investigate whether a particular type of corrective feedback—recasts (i.e., utterances that reformulate learners' erroneous utterances by correcting their errors)—led to noticing. Her study is interesting because she developed a more delicate coding system for the learners' comments. She coded the learners' recalls in terms of whether they reported attending to the recasts or not. If they reported noticing them, she then distinguished recall responses in terms of whether the learners reported interpreting a recast as relating to semantic or pragmatic content or as a correction of their

2 Krashen (1981) used the term *acquisition* to refer to incidental learning and the term *learning* to refer to *intentional learning*. However, in this chapter, we will use the terms *acquisition* and *learning* interchangeably as is now current practice in SLA, but when necessary, we will specify which type of learning/acquisition we are referring to.

error. In the case of the latter, Egi distinguished interpretations of a recast as (1) negative evidence (i.e., the learner showed awareness that an error had been made but no awareness of the target-like form in the recast), (2) positive evidence (i.e., the learner showed awareness of the target-like model but had not indicated awareness that the original utterance was problematic), and (3) as both negative and positive evidence (i.e., the learner was both aware an error had been committed and that the target-like model had been provided). For morphosyntax, Egi reported that 18.7% of the learners' comments demonstrated awareness of positive evidence and a further 26.05% awareness of both negative and positive evidence. One interpretation of these results is that learners sometimes noticed the target-like form and on other occasions noticed the gap. However, as in Mackey et al.'s study, most of the time no noticing was reported.

Neither of these studies demonstrated that noticing is more likely to occur following corrective feedback than in interactions where there is no correction. However, a small-scale study by Sakai (2011) indicates that this is indeed the case. Sakai asked learners who performed a communicative task and received recasts on their past tense errors to complete a stimulated recall and then compared their comments with those of an equivalent group that performed the same task without any recasts. Learners in the recast group reported noticing the target form in the recasts 21.6% of the time whereas those in the no-feedback group reported noticing the same form only rarely.

These studies suggest that noticing of morphosyntatic corrections in the context of communicative interactions is not common. More often than not, learners either fail to notice they have been corrected or do not attend to the specific form being corrected. This is true of all three studies although, as Sakai's study shows, noticing is more common following corrective feedback. It is also possible that stimulated recall leads to an overestimate of the amount of noticing that takes place as learners may not be recalling what transpired during the original interaction but rather commenting on what they were attending to at the time of the stimulated recall. It should also be noted that Mackey et al. and Egi's studies took place in laboratory settings and involved one-on-one interactions between a learner and a native speaker. Noticing is perhaps more likely to occur in such a setting than in a classroom context.

Uptake as an indicator of noticing

Another possible way of investigating noticing is by examining *uptake*. This is the term used to refer to the move that follows a corrective feedback move. Thus, in the following exchange, the final utterance constitutes the uptake move. The learner mistakenly uses *what* instead of *how* but, as a result of the teacher's corrective feedback, is able to eventually produce the correct WH pronoun.

Extract (1)

S1: What do you spend with your wife?

T: What? (clarification request)

S1: What do you spend your extra time with your wife?

T: Ah, how do you spend? (recast)

S1: how do you spend

Lyster and Ranta (1997) distinguished two types of uptake: uptake with repair and uptake with no repair. The exchange above illustrates uptake with repair. The following exchange illustrates uptake with no repair:

Extract (2)

S: I went there two times.

T: You've been. You've been there twice as a group?

S: Yeah.

In this example the teacher corrects the learner's misuse of the past tense, but the learner fails to correct her error in the uptake move. Instead she simply acknowledges the teacher's confirmation request.

Now, it would seem reasonable to assume that uptake with repair provides clear evidence of noticing. The learner in extract (1) would not have been able to produce the correct WH pronoun if he had not noticed the teacher's use of it in the corrective feedback move. However, it is not possible to assume that uptake with no repair is indicative of a failure to attend to the correct form. It is possible that the learner in extract (2) did notice the teacher's correction but opted for a pragmatic response to the teacher's utterance rather than repairing the error. Nevertheless, it would seem likely that, on the whole, noticing is more likely to have occurred when there is uptake with repair than when the uptake does not repair the error. But does uptake with repair constitute evidence of noticing the gap? Possibly not as the learner in extract (1) may be simply repeating what the teacher has said and may not have carried out the cognitive comparison between the teacher's utterance and his own initial erroneous utterance.[3] Thus, we might tentatively propose the following:

- Uptake with repair demonstrates that some noticing has taken place.
- However, uptake with no repair does not necessarily mean that no noticing has occurred.
- Uptake with repair indicates that noticing the gap may have occurred but does not constitute conclusive evidence.

There is some support for (2) in Mackey et al.'s study considered above. They reported that the "learners' stimulated recall reports generally revealed accurate perceptions about feedback for which they had uptake at the time of the interaction" (p. 492). In other words, the learners were much more likely to report noticing if they had produced uptake than if they hadn't. However, Mackey et al. did not distinguish between uptake with repair and uptake without repair.

Recasts, uptake, and noticing

Of all the corrective feedback strategies, recasts have received the most attention from researchers (see, for example, Ellis & Sheen (2006), Long (2007), and Nicholas, Lightbown, & Spada (2001) for reviews of the literature on recasts). There are good reasons for this attention. First, a number of studies have shown that recasts constitute the most common type of corrective feedback in classroom contexts. Sheen (2004) examined the frequency of recasts in four different instructional contexts. She reported that 54.7% of all feedback moves were recasts in Canadian immersion classrooms, 54.9% in a Canadian ESL classroom, 68.3% in adult ESL classrooms in New Zealand, and 82.8% in adult Korean EFL classrooms. No other type of corrective feedback strategy came anywhere near these levels. Seedhouse (1997) suggested that recasts are so prevalent because they are non-face-threatening (e.g., the

3 McDonough and Mackey (2006) reported a laboratory-based study that showed that productive use of a form a short time after hearing it, rather than just repeating or mimicking it immediately after hearing, was more beneficial for learning. In other words, this study suggested that uptake with repair immediately following a recast contributes little to learning.

corrective force of a recast is hidden if the recast takes the form of a confirmation check). There is another possible reason why teachers prefer recasts; they are input-providing (i.e., they actually provide a target-like model). In this respect they differ from *prompts* (Lyster, 2004), which indicate an error has been committed but require the learner to self-correct.

The noticing hypothesis predicts that recasts will be effective in promoting learning if learners notice the correction. As Egi's study suggests, this involves recognizing the corrective force of the recast, noticing the target form in the recast, and noticing the gap between the learner's erroneous utterance and the recast. As mentioned above, her study suggests that learners often fail to perceive a recast as corrective and that, even if they do, they often fail to notice the form that has been corrected. Further evidence for this comes from studies that have investigated whether recasts elicit uptake and, in particular, uptake with repair. Lyster and Ranta (1997) reported a relatively low level of uptake—only 54.8% of recasts were followed by uptake—in comparison to prompts (e.g., *elicitation* resulted in uptake 100% of the time) by Grade 6 children in French immersion classrooms. They also noted that only 48.9% of the uptake moves involved repair. In other words, only about 25% of the recasts led to uptake with repair. This would suggest a fairly low level of noticing and noticing the gap. However, Sheen's (2004) study suggests that levels of uptake (and therefore of noticing) are much higher in other instructional contexts. For example, in New Zealand adult ESL classes, 80.4% of the recasts were followed by uptake, and 69.1% of this involved repair. This would suggest that the extent to which noticing occurs depends on the learners' orientation (i.e., whether they see themselves as *content learners* or *language learners*) and, perhaps, also their age.

Schmidt (1990) suggested that the following factors are likely to trigger noticing: instruction that primes learners to notice features by establishing expectations about language, frequency, the learner's skill level, perceptual salience, and task demands. Other researchers have investigated the factors that influence the level of uptake following recasts. Learners are not always given the opportunity to uptake. Oliver (2000), for example, reported that one reason for the low level of uptake following recasts in her study of ESL classrooms was that the teachers often continued their turns without giving the students a chance to respond. She noted that if the *no chance* exchanges were excluded, the rate of uptake was much higher. In this case, then, uptake cannot constitute a reliable measure of noticing. The presence of another corrective feedback strategy may also enhance the salience of a recast and lead to uptake. Doughty and Varela (1998) investigated *corrective recasting*, which consisted of two moves—(1) a teacher repetition of a learner's error, with emphasis placed on the erroneous word(s) and (2) a reformulation of the complete learner utterance, as in Extract 3:

Extract (3)

L: I think that the worm will go under the soil.

T: I *think* that the worm *will* go under the soil?

L: (no response)

T: I *thought* that the worm *would* go under the soil.

L: I *thought* that the worm *would* go under the soil. (p. 124)

As this example illustrates, uptake with repair is more likely when the recast is supported in this way.

Other factors have to do with the nature of the recasts. Recasts come in many different forms, and some types have been found to be more likely to lead to uptake than others.

Sheen (2006) distinguished single-move recasts in terms of mode (i.e., whether the recast is declarative in form or interrogative), scope (i.e., whether the recast just reformulates the learner utterance or incorporates new semantic content), reduction (i.e., whether the recast formulates all or just part of the learner utterance), length (i.e., the number of words in the recast), the number of changes made to the learner's utterance, and the type of change (i.e., whether it involves addition, substitution, or reordering). Length (i.e., single word recasts) and type of change (i.e., substitution as opposed to addition) were associated with higher levels of uptake. Length, type of change (i.e., a single change), mode (i.e., declarative), reduction, and number of changes (i.e., one as opposed to many) were associated with higher levels of uptake with repair. Sheen concluded that recasts were more likely to result in uptake and uptake with repair if they were of the more explicit kind.

If uptake with repair is taken as a measure of noticing, it is clear that learners are more likely to pay attention to the target feature in some kinds of recasts than in others. Philp (2003) examined learners' ability to recall recasts immediately after hearing them. She found that short recasts were recalled better than long recasts, especially by the less proficient learners, and recasts with just one or two changes were recalled more accurately by all learners, irrespective of proficiency. Egi's (2007) study also shows that the type of recast influences uptake. She found that learners reported noticing the target feature more frequently if the recast was short and included fewer changes. In contrast, longer recasts involving multiple changes were more likely to be perceived as responses to the content of their utterances (i.e., the learners failed to notice their corrective force).

In short, the research indicates:

- Recasts constitute the primary means by which teachers respond to learners' errors.
- They do not constitute a homogeneous construct; they exist in many different forms.
- Recasts have been considered a type of implicit corrective feedback, but in fact, many recasts make the corrective force quite transparent.
- The characteristics of the recasts themselves (e.g., the length and number of changes made in the recast) influence whether recasts result in uptake with repair.
- When the corrective force of a recast is made explicit and when teachers allow time for the learner to respond, uptake with repair is likely.

In short, recasts afford ample opportunities for learners to notice that they have made an error and how to correct it. The key question, however, is whether such noticing facilitates acquisition.

Recasts, noticing, and L2 learning

Recasts can assist learning in three ways:

- By directing learners' attention to the target form that they have erroneously produced (i.e., inducing noticing).
- By facilitating noticing of the difference between their form and the target form (i.e., noticing the gap).
- By providing learners with an opportunity to repair their own error (i.e., helping learners to produce the correct form).

In the case of (1), recasts are seen as facilitative of learning through the input they provide; in the case of (2) and (3), they are seen as facilitative because of the *pushed output* that results in uptake with repair and because they lead to noticing the gap. The noticing hypothesis would seem to allow for both possibilities. However, there are a number of controversial issues.

As Ellis and Sheen (2006) noted, the key question is whether repair contributes to acquisition. There are differing theoretical positions here. For Long (2007) it is the positive evidence that recasts afford rather than the opportunity for learners to repair their errors that is important. An input-driven view of L2 acquisition views output only as a means of increasing control over knowledge derived initially from input. According to this view, the acquisition of new linguistic forms is dependent entirely on input. However, Swain's (1985) output hypothesis claims that output serves as a means by which learners can develop greater metalinguistic awareness and fill in the gaps in their interlanguages. A skill-learning view of recasts would also lend support to an important role for output. Lyster (2004), for example, has argued that when learners repair their errors following corrective feedback, they are able to gain greater control over grammatical forms that have been partially acquired. Lyster proposed that, for this reason, prompts constitute a more effective type of corrective feedback than recasts because they are more likely to result in uptake with repair. Thus, there is no agreement among SLA theorists whether it is the noticing that recasts can trigger or the actual repair that can follow recasts that is important for acquisition.

To resolve this debate, it is necessary to investigate the relationship between recasts and uptake, on the one hand, and L2 learning, on the other. Unfortunately, there are still relatively few studies that have attempted this. The research that has investigated the relationship between uptake and L2 learning has produced very mixed results. Mackey and Philp (1998) reported that successful uptake (i.e., repair) was not a significant factor in acquisition, although only 5% of the recasts resulted in uptake with repair in this study. However, Loewen (2005) found that both uptake in general and uptake with repair predicted the scores on posttests, but this was for corrective feedback in general. Loewen and Philp (2006) focused specifically on recasts and reported that those recasts with explicit linguistic characteristics were more likely to result in both uptake and learning.

Two other studies have examined the relationship between uptake and learning. Havranek and Cesnik (2001) compared the effects of feedback with and without uptake on learning by both those learners who had committed specific errors (i.e., the perpetrators) and on the other students in the class (i.e., the auditors). Havranek and Cesnik reported that the auditors were more likely to make correct use of the structures they had received feedback on than the perpetrators (i.e., 61% as opposed to 51.4% of the time). They also noted that corrective feedback was most effective when the perpetrators were able to successfully uptake the correction. However, of the types of corrective feedback they examined, recasts were the least successful in this respect. In other words, uptake with repair was related to learning but only to a very limited extent for recasts. Mackey (2006) was interested in the relationships between implicit corrective feedback, noticing, and acquisition. She investigated the effects of two implicit types of corrective feedback—recasts and clarification requests—on noticing and the acquisition of three different grammatical structures. She obtained data on the learners' noticing from their stimulated recall protocols, reporting that the level of noticing varied according to the target structure. Only in the case of one of the target structures—questions—was there a relationship between noticing and L2 development. However, Mackey did not report separate results for recasts and clarification requests and did not investigate whether uptake following these two types of corrective feedback had any effect on either noticing or learning.

It is difficult to reach clear conclusions about the effect that repairing errors following recasts has on learning. The results of the above studies show that uptake with repair following recasts has been found to be related to learning in some studies (e.g., Loewen & Philp, 2006) but only weakly or not at all in others (e.g., Havranek & Cesnik, 2001; Mackey & Philp, 1998). It should be noted that these and other studies varied in how they measured learning. In some cases it was measured by means of group-administered posttests, in others by tailor-made tests administered to individual learners, and in others by examining subsequent use of the features that had been corrected in classroom discourse.

Based on the results of the research to date, we see a need for studies that investigate issues such as the following:

- Whether the effect of uptake with repair on learning depends on how explicit the recasts are.
- Whether the extent to which uptake with repair occurs and has an effect on learning depends on the specific grammatical feature that was corrected by the recasts.
- Whether there is a difference in the effect that uptake with repair following recasts has on learning for learners who perform the repairs and for those who just audit the repairs.
- Whether there is a difference in the effect that uptake with repair has on learning depending on the type of corrective feedback (e.g., recasts versus clarification requests).

The study reported below was designed to investigate some of these issues.

Research questions

- To what extent do learners repair their errors following recasts?
- Is there any difference in learning between learners who repair their errors following recasts and those who do not?
- Is there any difference in learning between learners who carry out repairs as opposed to those who simply audit other learners' repairs?
- Is there any difference in learning between those learners who repair their errors following recasts and those who repair errors following clarification requests?

Method

Participants

The 36 participants were secondary school students learning French as a foreign language in two secondary schools in Auckland. There were a total of 22 females and 14 males. They belonged to two intact Year 11 and Year 12 classes. Their average age was 16–17 years. They had been learning French for three years, with 6 hours of instruction per week. They also received about 20 minutes of conversation with a native-speaker French assistant each week. The students' proficiency can be described as low to high intermediate. The students were studying for the National Certificate in Education and were strongly motivated to learn French.

Design

The quasi-experimental study involved two groups of learners (*n*=18 in both) who completed a pretest, engaged in an instructional treatment involving corrective feedback, and then took an oral production test immediately after the instruction was completed and a delayed posttest approximately two weeks later. The focus of the instructional treatment was passé composé. One group received corrective feedback on their errors in the form of recasts and the other in the form of clarification requests. Both types of feedback can be considered *implicit*[4] but differed in terms of whether it was input-providing (i.e., recasts) or output-prompting (i.e., clarification requests).

Target structure

Passé composé poses learning difficulty for L2 learners of French (Harley, 1989). It is formally complex as it employs two different auxiliaries (*avoir* and *être*) and the past participle, which requires agreement with the subject according to relatively complex grammar rules. It is also functionally problematic even though it has only one basic meaning—perfective or completed action. This is because English-speaking learners typically find it difficult to distinguish between passé composé and imparfait given that the functions performed by these two tenses do not match those of the corresponding English tenses. That is, whereas the French language distinguishes perfective and imperfective aspect, English distinguishes simple and progressive aspect.

Instructional treatments

Both groups of students completed three narrative tasks in a whole-class context. Each task consisted of six pictures. The students were given three of the pictures while the teacher kept the other three pictures. Task 1 involved a story about two boys who started fighting over a bottle of coke, and one of them ended up in hospital when hit by a car. Task 2 involved a story about a family of five who went camping. Unfortunately, their holidays were spoilt by an accident in which their car fell into a lake. Task 3 involved a story about a brother and sister who went on a day excursion but had a problem with the tyre on their motorbike and so had to return home. The students were told to elicit the information they needed to tell a story from the teacher and when they had done so, take it in turn to tell the story. Each narrative task took approximately 25 minutes.

When the students made errors in the use of the passé composé and imparfait tenses, they received corrective feedback. Recasts consisted of reformulations of a learner's erroneous utterance that provided the learner with the correct verb form while preserving the meaning of the utterance (Long, 1996):

Example

S2: ummm les deux garçons un garcon acheté et

T: ils ont acheté? (=recast)

S2: ils ont acheté une coca

T: bien bien

S2: et et ils ont acheté seulement un coca

Requests for clarification indicated that an utterance had been misunderstood by the teacher or that the utterance was ill-formed and that a repetition or a reformulation was required (Lyster & Ranta, 1997):

---

4 As pointed out earlier, recasts can be more or less implicit/explicit. The recasts in this study were relatively explicit. They were partial and involved only changes in the target structure (passé composé). However, there was no overt marker of the corrective force of the recasts. The clarification requests were more clearly implicit.

Example

S34: très soif…et ils a acheté..

T: hmmm tu peux répeter? (CR 1st time)

S34: ils ssssssssss..sont ils sont

T: hmmm? (CR 2nd time)

S34: ils ont acheté

T: bien

Thus, recasts provided the learners with input consisting of the correct target language form whereas clarification requests provided an opportunity for learners to self-correct their own errors. The performance of the tasks was audio-recorded and transcriptions prepared.

Oral production tests

Three oral production tests were used to measure the level of learners' acquisition of the target verb structures. The immediate posttest took place immediately after the completion of the treatment. The delayed posttest was administered four weeks later. The test materials consisted of picture-based narrative tasks. A short one-sentence introduction was provided as a context for the use of past tense. The participants performed the tasks individually and were audio-recorded. Task 1 comprised six pictures showing a teacher who overslept in the morning and was late at school while students were waiting for him in the classroom. Task 2 was about a young man who was dreaming of going on holiday with his girlfriend, but his plans fell through. Task 3 involved a story about a house painter who fell from the ladder while looking at a lady walking along the street. The three tasks were counterbalanced so that each student told a different story for the pretest, immediate posttest, and delayed posttest.

Analysis

The following measures were obtained from the treatment data and the oral production tests:

- The number of recasts and clarification requests received by each learner in the treatment groups.
- The frequency of each learner's uptake (i.e., the learners' responses to the corrective feedback). Uptake was classified into *uptake with repair* and *uptake with no repair.* The number of times that no uptake occurred was also recorded.
- Gains in accuracy for passé composé between the pretest and the immediate posttest (Gain 1) and between the pretest and the delayed posttest (Gain 2). Accuracy was measured in terms of target-like use (Pica, 1984). That is, obligatory occasions for use of the tense were identified in the oral narratives that served as the pre- and post-tests and the number of times each learner supplied the correct form of the tense calculated. However, as the passé composé consists of an auxiliary and a past participle, 2 points were given for the use of the correct auxiliary and the past participle and 1 point for the use of an incorrect auxiliary and a verb form. If no auxiliary was used, no points were awarded even if the correct past participle was used. The final score also took account of overuse of the passé composé in accordance with Pica's formula for target-like use.

The gain scores were found to be normally distributed. *t*-tests for independent samples were computed to compare the gain scores of those learners who received recasts and repaired their error and those learners who did not receive any recasts (i.e., auditors) and also to compare the gain scores of those learners who repaired their errors in the recasts and clarification requests group. As multiple tests were conducted, the Bonferroni correction was applied setting the alpha level for statistical significance at .025.

Results

The frequency of the two types of corrective feedback moves and the extent to which learners repaired their errors in the use of passé composé following the recasts and the clarification requests is shown in Table 1. There was a total of 33 recasts provided by the teacher out of which 28 (85%) resulted in uptake with repair. There were fewer clarification requests (only 17). The level of uptake with repair was also less than for recasts (i.e., 11 or 65%).

Table 1. Uptake following corrective feedback

	recasts (*n*=18)	**clarification requests (*n*=18)**
number of cf moves	33	17
uptake with repair	28 (84.8%)	11 (64.7%)
uptake–no repair	3 (9.1 %)	6 (35.3%)
no uptake	2 (6.1 %)	0 (0 %)

Not all the learners in the two groups received corrective feedback. In the recast group 12 learners received feedback (see Table 2). Thus, six learners only audited the feedback received by the others and had no chance for uptake. Table 2 also shows that the number of recasts received by the individual learners varied considerably, from a high of 9 (Learner 6) to a low of just 1 (Learners 3, 4, 12, 16, and 17). The auditors in this group received 0 recasts. However, all the learners exposed to recasts, except Learner 12, produced uptake with repair at least once. Table 3 shows the number of clarification requests received by the individual learners. 11 learners received feedback, leaving seven learners who were just auditors. Tables 2 and 3 also show the gains in accuracy for Gain 1 (pretest to immediate posttest) and Gain 2 (pretest to delayed posttest).

Table 2. Frequency of recasts and uptake for the individual learners

number	**number of recasts**	**uptake with repair**	**uptake – no repair**	**no uptake**	**gain 1**	**gain 2**
L 1	4	4	0	0	8.02	13.85
L 2	4	3	0	1	33.34	27.92
L 3	1	1	0	0	13.18	17.73
L 4	1	1	0	0	36.60	33.75
L 6	9	6	2	1	39.58	20.67
L 7	5	5	0	0	23.08	22.22
L 8	2	2	0	0	8.33	15.00
L 11	2	2	0	0	23.62	19.45
L 12	1	0	1	0	0.84	0.00
L 14	2	2	0	0	0.00	14.36
L 16	1	1	0	0	32.91	27.78
L 17	1	1	0	0	–2.78	28.89

Table 3. Frequency of clarification requests and uptake for the individual learners

number	number of clarification requests	uptake with repair	uptake – no repair	no uptake	gain 1	gain 2
L 19	1	1	0	0	–6.25	–25.00
L 20	4	3	1	0	10.72	14.29
L 21	1	1	0	0	–10.41	–13.72
L 22	2	0	2	0	–24.11	–37.92
L 23	2	0	2	0	47.50	69.64
L 27	1	1	0	0	–30.52	–21.43
L 28	1	1	0	0	–9.72	–13.13
L 32	1	0	1	0	0.00	10.00
L 34	1	1	0	0	31.25	24.05
L 35	1	1	0	0	–37.35	19.64
L 36	2	2	0	0	–	–

Table 4 shows the mean gain scores for those learners in the recast group who successfully repaired at least one of their passé composé errors and those learners who did not receive any recasts and thus were only auditors of the recasts directed at others[5]. In Gain 1 scores, those learners who were only auditors outscored the recasters. However, the difference was not statistically significant (t=.559; *ns*) and the effect size was small (d=–.28). The repairers achieved higher Gain 2 scores than the auditors, and in this case the difference was statistically significant (t=2.54; p=.022) and the effect size large (d=1.14). It should be noted, however, that there was no relationship between the number of times a learner who received a recast and repaired the error and either Gain 1 score or Gain 2 score ($r(s)$=.333, p=.290; $r(s)$=.03, p=.938).

Table 4. Mean passé composé gain scores of repairers and auditors in the recast group

	gain 1		gain 2	
	Mean	*SD*	*Mean*	*SD*
recasters with repair (*n*=11)	19.62	15.1	24.0	7.5
auditors (*n*=7)	24.37	18.5	11.54	13.4

Finally, Table 5 compares the gain scores for those learners in the recast and clarification request groups who repaired their passé composé errors. The repairers in the recast group outperformed those in the clarification group, and the differences were statistically significant for both Gain 1 (t=3.01; p=.008) with a large effect size (d=1.38) and Gain 2 (t=3.86; p=.001) also with a large effect size (d=1.68).

5 A reviewer of this chapter noted that the recasters were also auditors of the recasts received by other learners. In effect then, the comparison being made here is between those learners who received a recast and thus had the opportunity for uptake and those learners who had no such chance (i.e., were only auditors).

Table 5. Mean passé composé scores of repairers in the recast and clarification request groups

	gain 1		gain 2	
	Mean	*SD*	*Mean*	*SD*
recasts (repair) (*n*=11)	19.62	15.1	24.0	7.5
clarification request (repair) (*n*=8)	–7.5	23.4	–2.2	20.7

Discussion

The first research question asked "To what extent do learners repair their errors following recasts?" This question was motivated by the assumption that if learners repair their errors following a recast, they must have noticed the target form in the recast. Table 1 shows that 84.5% of the recasts resulted in uptake with repair. Thus, it would seem that in this classroom context the learners (1) identified the corrective force of the recasts and (2) paid attention to the target form. The level of uptake with repair was much higher than that reported for immersion classrooms by Lyster and Ranta (1997) and also somewhat higher than that reported for adult ESL and EFL classrooms by Sheen (2004). The explanation that Sheen provided for the difference between the immersion and EFL/ESL classrooms was that the learners in the latter were more likely to function as language learners and focus on form. Requests for clarification resulted in a much lower level of uptake with repair (64.7%), suggesting that the learners in this study were often either unable to identify the error in their original utterances or incapable of correcting it.

The second research question asked "Is there any difference in learning between learners who repair their errors following recasts and those who do not?" This question could not be addressed effectively as, out of the 12 learners who received recasts, all but one of them repaired their errors on at least one occasion. The one learner (L 12) who failed to repair did not demonstrate any gains in accuracy in either the short or longer term. Another way of examining the relationship between repair and learning is to examine whether the number of repairs a learner made correlates with the gains he/she made. However, correlation coefficients were both low and statistically non-significant. Thus, there is no evidence to show that repairing errors is related to learning. Other studies (e.g., Mackey & Philp, 1998) have also found no relationship between uptake and learning.

The third research question asked "Is there any difference in learning between learners who carry out repairs as opposed to those who simply audit other learners' repairs?" There were eleven learners who received recasts (i.e., the *recasters*) and successfully repaired their errors. There were seven learners who received no recasts and thus functioned as auditors. There was no statistically significant difference between the recasters' and the auditors' Gain 1 scores, but there was for the Gain 2 scores. Thus, the recasters demonstrated greater improvement in the use of passé composé than the auditors over time. There are a number of possible explanations for this. One is that the recasters engaged in more noticing of the target feature than the auditors—both during the instructional treatment and subsequently. Another is that the repairers benefited from correcting their errors following the recasts. A third possibility is that the recasters were simply more motivated or more proficient than the auditors and thus participated more actively in the communicative task and improved more. The fact that the relationship was only evident for the Gain 2 scores echoes previous findings (e.g., Ellis, Loewen, & Erlam, 2006; Li, 2010) that have shown the effect of corrective feedback to be stronger in delayed than in immediate tests.

The final research question asked "Is there any difference in learning between those learners who repair their errors following recasts and those who repair their errors following clarification requests?" Table 5 shows that those learners who produced uptake with repair following recasts outperformed those learners who produced uptake with repair following clarification requests in both the short and long term. Repair following recasts is indicative that (1) noticing of the target feature has occurred and (2) the learner is able to self-correct. Repair following clarification requests is indicative of only (2). Thus, a possible interpretation of these results is that it is the noticing of the target feature in the input rather than self-correction that is important for learning.

To summarise:

- The learners who received recasts were very likely to repair their errors.
- The relationship between the number of times a student repaired an error following a recast and learning gains was weak and statistically non-significant.
- Learners who received recasts and repaired their errors demonstrated greater long-term improvement in accuracy in passé composé than learners who simply audited the recasts.
- Learners who produced uptake with repair following recasts showed greater long-term gains in accuracy than learners who produced uptake with repair following clarification requests.

What then can be said about whether uptake with repair provides evidence of learner noticing? This study indicates that in a foreign language classroom where learners were used to paying attention to form, uptake with repair was common, indicating that learners did notice the corrections of their passé composé errors. The extract below illustrates the learners' responses to the teacher's recasts. It demonstrates clearly the attention the learners paid to the corrections. This learner repeatedly uses *est*+past participle, failing to ensure agreement between the subject and the auxiliary in the first and third errors and using *etre* instead of *avoir* in the second. The teacher's recasts were didactic rather than communicative (i.e., they involved the negotiation of form rather than meaning—see Ellis, Basturkmen, & Loewen, 2001), and they were also short and involved a single change. As suggested by previous research (Philp, 2003; Egi, 2007), such corrections are salient to learners and appear to have been so for this learner. In each case he successfully repaired his error. While this does not demonstrate that noticing the gap had occurred, it indicates evidence that the learner had noticed the auxiliary employed in the recast. This learner demonstrated substantial gains in accuracy in both the immediate oral production test (39.58%) and the delayed test (20.67%).

Extract (4)

S6: ...boisson et les deux garcons <u>s'est disputé</u>

T: <u>ils se sont disputés</u>?

S6: oui <u>ils se sont disputés</u> ummmm parce que le garçon n'est umm <u>n'est donné</u>

T: <u>n'a pas donné</u>?

S6: <u>n'a pas donné</u> la bouteille à à le autre garçon uhmmm <u>ils s'est battre</u>

T: <u>ils se sont battus</u>?

S6: <u>ils se sont battus</u> ummm et...je sais pas ooh ah

The question of whether it is the noticing or the production of the correct form that is important for learning remains unsettled, however. The fact that those learners who received recasts and repaired their errors demonstrated greater gains in accuracy than those who simply audited the recasts might suggest that it is the production of the correct form that facilitates learning, but this may not be the case. It is quite possible that the difference is due to the fact that an individual learner is more likely to pay attention to a recast if it is directed at the learner him/herself. This may be especially the case if the recasts take the form of confirmation checks, which require some kind of response. The auditors were free to ignore the recasts if they wished. Likewise those learners who received recasts were free to ignore the recasts when they were not directed specifically at them. The fact that the learners in the recast group demonstrated stronger gains in accuracy than those in the clarification request group might suggest that it is the noticing rather than the production of the correct forms that promotes learning, as the difference between these two groups lies in whether or not they were exposed to input containing the passé composé. But an alternative explanation is possible. The recast group experienced substantially more corrective feedback moves than the clarification request group. So it is possible that it was the amount rather than the type of corrective feedback that was responsible for the difference in the two groups' learning. Such an interpretation, however, is not supported by the finding that there was no relationship between the number of repairs made by individual students in the recast group and learning gains. It would seem that it is not the frequency of repair that is important for learning. On balance, then, the evidence supports Long's (2007) claim that recasts promote learning because they induce noticing of target language forms rather than because of the repair that learners carry out when they uptake recasts. There is, in fact, nothing in this study to support Lyster's (2004) claims regarding the superiority of output-prompting corrective feedback over recasts[6] in the foreign language context this study investigated.

Conclusion

The results of this study do not match those of Havranek and Cesnik (2001). Havranek and Cesnik found that auditors benefited more from corrective feedback than perpetrators of errors. They also reported that repair was related to learning. However, Havranek and Cesnik also found that recasts were the least successful of the types of corrective feedback they investigated. In contrast, the recasts in this study were effective in promoting learning, and repair was not related to learning. The explanation for the difference in findings probably lies in the extent to which recasts are salient to learners and thus noticed by them. As other researchers (e.g., Nicholas, Lightbown, & Spada, 2001) have noted, the corrective force of recasts can be more or less implicit/explicit. Arguably, for recasts to be effective, they need to be explicit—as, arguably, they were in this study—so that learners can notice the corrections of their errors. Indeed, this is exactly what the noticing hypothesis would predict. The study of corrective feedback—and recasts in particular—affords an excellent means of investigating how noticing mediates language learning and, also, of the factors that influence whether and when noticing takes place.

The study reported in this chapter has a number of limitations. Noticing was investigated only in terms of learner uptake. Ideally, additional evidence is needed, for example, by means of stimulated recall. However, this was not possible in this study. The sample size was

6 Lyster (2004) compared the effect of recasts and prompts. The latter consisted of a variety of different corrective feedback strategies (e.g., elicitations as well as clarification requests), some of which were highly explicit. Thus, one reason for the greater effect for prompts that he found may have been their explicitness. This study just compared the effect of recasts and clarifications requests.

relatively small (only 12 students received recasts and only 11 clarification requests). The total number of recasts and clarification requests was also small—only 33 and 17. Some of the learners only received a single recast or a single clarification request. In particular, it might be argued that for clarification requests to have an effect on learning, they need to be much more intensive than in this study. Also, in a classroom study such as this, it was not possible to make a clear distinction between repairers and auditors as the repairers were also auditors of the recasts directed at other learners. To investigate the effect of just hearing a recast as opposed to repairing an error following a recast would require a laboratory-based study where the two conditions were carefully controlled. This might be a direction future research could take although such a study would lack ecological validity as, in a lockstep classroom setting, learners inevitably function as both repairers and auditors.

References

Doughty, C. J., & Varela, E. (1998). Communicative focus on form. In C. Doughty & J. Williams (Eds.), *Focus on form in classroom second language acquisition* (pp. 114–138). Cambridge: Cambridge University Press.

Egi, T. (2007). Interpreting recasts as linguistic evidence: The role of linguistic target, length, and degree of change. *Studies in Second Language Acquisition, 29*, 511–538.

Ellis, N. (1996). Sequencing in SLA: Phonological memory, chunking, and points of order. *Studies in Second Language Acquisition, 18*, 91–126.

Ellis, R. (2002). Does form-focused instruction affect the acquisition of implicit knowledge? A review of the research. *Studies in Second Language Acquisition, 24*, 223–36.

Ellis, R., Basturkmen, H., & Loewen, S. (2001). Learner uptake in communicative ESL lessons. *Language Learning, 51*, 281–318.

Ellis, R., Loewen, S., & Erlam, R. (2006). Implicit and explicit corrective feedback and the acquisition of L2 grammar. *Studies in Second Language Acquisition, 28*, 339–68.

Ellis, R., & Sheen, Y. (2006). Re-examining the role of recasts in SLA. *Studies in Second Language Acquisition, 28*, 575–600.

Harley, B. (1989). Functional grammar in French immersion: A classroom experiment. *Applied Linguistics, 19*, 331–59.

Havranek, G., & Cesnik, H. (2001). Factors affecting the success of corrective feedback. In S. H. Foster-Cohen & A. Nizegorodzew (Eds.), *EUROSLA Yearbook, Volume 1* (pp. 99–122). Amsterdam: Benjamins.

Krashen, S. D. (1981). *Second language acquisition and second language learning.* Oxford: Pergamon.

Lantolf, J. (2000). Introducing sociocultural theory. In J. Lantolf (Ed.), *Sociocultural theory and second language learning* (pp. 1–26). Oxford: Oxford University Press.

Li, S. (2010). The effectiveness of corrective feedback in SLA: A meta-analysis. *Language Learning, 60*, 309–365.

Loewen, S. (2005). Incidental focus on form and second language learning. *Studies in Second Language Acquisition, 27*, 361–86.

Loewen, S., & Philp, J. (2006). Recasts in the adult English L2 classroom: Characteristics, explicitness, and effectiveness. *Modern Language Journal, 90*, 536–56.

Long, M. (1996). The role of the linguistic environment in second language acquisition. In W. R. Ritchie & T. J. Bhatia (Eds.), *Handbook of second language acquisition* (pp. 413–68). San Diego: Academic Press.

Long, M. (2007). Chapter 5: Recasts in SLA: The story so far. In M. Long, *Problems in SLA* (pp. 75–116). Mahwah, NJ: Lawrence Erlbaum.

Lyster, R. (2004). Differential effects of prompts and recasts in form-focused instruction. *Studies in Second Language Acquisition, 26*, 399–432.

Lyster, R., & Ranta, L. (1997). Corrective feedback and learner uptake: Negotiation of form in communicative classrooms. *Studies in Second Language Acquisition, 19*, 37–66.

Mackey, A. (2006). Feedback, noticing, and instructed second language learning. *Applied Linguistics, 27*, 405–430.

Mackey, A., Gass, S., & McDonough, K. (2000). How do learners perceive interactional feedback? *Studies in Second Language Acquisition, 22*, 471–97.

Mackey, A., & Philp, J. (1998). Conversational interaction and second language development: Recasts, responses, and red herrings? *Modern Language Journal, 82*, 338–56.

McDonough, K., & Mackey, A. (2006). Responses to recasts: Repetitions, primed production, and linguistic development. *Language Learning, 56*, 693–720.

Nicholas, H., Lightbown, P. M., & Spada, N. (2001). Recasts as feedback to language learners. *Language Learning, 51*, 719–758.

Norris, J., & Ortega, L. (2000). Effectiveness of L2 instruction: A research synthesis and quantitative meta-analysis. *Language Learning, 50*, 417–528.

Oliver, R. (2000). Age differences in negotiation and feedback in classroom and pairwork. *Language Learning, 50*, 119–151.

Philp, J. (2003). Constraints on "noticing the gap": Non-native speakers' noticing of recasts in NS-NNS interaction. *Studies in Second Language Acquisition, 25*, 99–126.

Pica, T. (1984). Methods of morpheme quantification: Their effect on the interpretation of second language data. *Studies in Second Language Acquisition*, 6, 69–78.

Sakai, H. (2011). Do recasts prompt noticing the gap in L2 learning? *Asian EFL Journal, 12*, 357–385.

Schmidt, R. (1990). The role of consciousness in second language learning. *Applied Linguistics, 11*, 129–58.

Schmidt, R. (1993). Consciousness, learning, and interlanguage pragmatics. In G. Kasper and S. Blum-Kulka (Eds.), *Interlanguage pragmatics* (pp. 21–42). Oxford: Oxford University Press.

Schmidt, R. (1994). Deconstructing consciousness in search of useful definitions for applied linguistics. *AILA Review, 11*, 11–26.

Schmidt, R. (1995). Consciousness and foreign language learning: A tutorial on the role of attention and awareness in learning. In R. Schmidt (Ed.), *Attention and awareness in foreign language learning* (pp. 1–63). Honolulu, HI: University of Hawai'i, National Foreign Language Resource Center.

Schmidt, R. (2001). Attention. In P. Robinson (Ed.), *Cognition and second language instruction* (pp. 3–32). Cambridge: Cambridge University Press.

Schmidt, R., & Frota, S. (1986). Developing basic conversational ability in a second language: A case study of an adult learner of Portuguese. In R. R. Day (Ed.), *Talking to learn: Conversation in second language acquisition* (pp. 237–326). Rowley, MA: Newbury House.

Seedhouse, P. (1997). The case of the missing "no": The relationship between pedagogy and interaction. *Language Learning, 47*, 547–83.

Sheen, Y. (2004). Corrective feedback and learner uptake in communicative classrooms across instructional settings. *Language Teaching Research, 8*, 263–300.

Sheen, Y. (2006). Exploring the relationship between characteristics of recasts and learner uptake. *Language Teaching Research, 10*, 361–92.

Swain, M. (1985). Communicative competence: Some roles of comprehensible input and comprehensible output in its development. In S. M. Gass & C. Madden (Eds.), *Input in second language acquisition* (pp. 235–53). Rowley, MA: Newbury House.

Truscott, J. (1998). Noticing in second language acquisition: A critical review. *Second Language Research, 14*, 103–135.

NFLRC monographs

Is Metalinguistic Stimulated Recall Reactive in Second Language Learning?

Takako Egi
University of Kentucky

Rebecca J. Adams
Northcentral University

Ana-María Nuevo
American University

While the use of retrospective verbalizations has increased in second language interaction research (e.g., Egi, 2010; Kim & Han, 2007; Mackey, 2006; Tocalli-Beller & Swain, 2007), limited evidence exists about their reactivity (Egi, 2008; Lindgren & Sullivan, 2003) and in particular about metalinguistic verbalizations, which may lead to deeper processing that can enhance learning (Ericsson & Simon, 1993; Schmidt, 1995; Swain, 2005). The current study sought to clarify whether metalinguistic stimulated recall affected learning outcomes. Twenty-seven Japanese learners participated in a pretest/posttest study with three groups: non-metalinguistic stimulated recall, metalinguistic stimulated recall, and control. The results indicated non-significant differences among the groups, suggesting non-reactivity of metalinguistic and non-metalinguistic retrospective verbalizations.

Introduction

Increased interest in cognitive factors such as attention and awareness in second language (L2) learning has led to a greater use of introspective data collection methods (Bowles & Leow, 2005). Because cognitive processes occur internally, in many cases they can only be measured and analyzed through what learners can report to researchers about their processing. Data collection techniques that require learners to verbally report on their internal thoughts are collectively known as *verbalizations* or *verbal reports*. Schmidt (1990) defined noticing as availability for verbal reports, and these reports have become one of

Egi, T., Adams, R. J., & Nuevo, A.-M. (2013). Is metalinguistic stimulated recall reactive in second language learning? In J. M. Bergsleithner, S. N. Frota, & J. K. Yoshioka (Eds.), *Noticing and second language acquisition: Studies in honor of Richard Schmidt* (pp. 81–102). Honolulu: University of Hawai'i, National Foreign Language Resource Center.

the standard measures in research on attention and awareness (Leow, Johnson, & Zárate-Sández, 2011). As verbalization becomes more common as a data collection technique, it is increasingly important for researchers to understand how the use of this technique may influence empirical findings. The purpose of the current study is to examine the validity of metalinguistic retrospective verbalizations as a research tool.

Verbalization as an introspective methodological tool

Verbalizations were first used as a means of data collection in cognitive science (Hafner, 1957; Marks, 1951) but have now been adopted in research in fields ranging from accounting (Anderson, 1985) to mathematical cognition (Geary, Frensch, & Wiley, 1993; Siegler, 1989) to marketing research (Biehal & Chakravarti, 1989). This diverse range of research foci reflects the usefulness of verbal reports. In language research they have been applied to understand first language (L1) and L2 reading processes (Farrington-Flint & Wood, 2007; Nassaji, 2006; Yang, 2006), L1 and L2 writing processes (Cavalcanti & Cohen, 1990; Chenoweth & Hayes, 2001; Qi & Lapkin, 2001), the development of interlanguage pragmatics (Kasper, 1999; Taguchi, 2008), the role of attention and awareness in learning (Bowles, 2003; Hama & Leow, 2010; Leow, 1997, 2000; Rosa & Leow, 2004), and cognitive processing during communicative interaction (Bao, Egi, & Han, 2011; Egi, 2010; Mackey, Gass, & McDonough, 2000; R. Yoshida, 2010). As Robinson (2001) points out, because verbal reports yield both evidence that participants are engaged in cognitive processing and information about these processes, they provide insights to researchers that are otherwise inaccessible and are a fruitful source of new theory (Green, 1995). However, the use of verbal reports has been repeatedly questioned on the grounds of concerns about veridicality and reactivity.

Veridicality refers to the extent to which a verbal report forms a valid representation of cognitive processing. Veridicality issues include concerns about both the veracity of the reports (i.e., are cognitive processes accurately reported?) and the completeness of the reports (i.e., how fully do subjects report their experience?) (Leow & Morgan-Short, 2004). Nisbett and Wilson (1977) suggested that some aspects of cognitive processing may not be fully accessible to participants, and therefore, they may not be able to provide complete reports, a point echoed by Lyons (1986). For instance, in Nisbett and Wilson (1977), participants were asked to memorize word pairs, some of which would semantically cue a target answer on a word association task conducted later in the experiment. Although the word pair cues doubled the frequency of the target responses, participants almost never mentioned word pair cues when discussing why they gave each of their responses on the word association task. This suggests that some aspects of processing are not available for verbal report, compromising veridicality. Other work on verbal reports has indicated that information reported may vary according to the instructions given and the type of materials used, suggesting that reports may be more or less valid under different conditions (Egi, 2008; Olson, Duffy, & Mack, 1984).

Reactivity, the focus of the current study, refers to the possibility that the act of reporting influences participants' cognitive processes during a task (for concurrent reports) or their post-task behaviors (for retrospective reports). Russo, Johnson, and Stephens (1989) have pointed out that reactivity is the primary concern for verbal reports, arguing that if verbalization changes the nature of the processing involved in task performance, it is irrelevant whether the altered processing was accurately reported or not. In examining questions of reactivity in verbalizations, it is important to consider the timing of reporting. While for concurrent verbal reports (such as think-aloud protocols) cognitive processing and reporting occur simultaneously, for retrospective reports (such as stimulated recall protocols) reporting occurs sometime after processing ends. In concurrent protocols reactivity occurs if the act of reporting influences the way learners process and complete the task (Ericsson & Simon, 1993). Although reactivity is a concern primarily to concurrent reports, Russo et al. states, "however paradoxical it may seem, reactivity can occur in retrospective as well as concurrent protocols" (p. 765). In retrospective protocols, reactivity occurs if "verbalizing information (even retrospectively) may change and deform it, and hence affect subsequent task behavior" (Ericsson & Simon, 1993, p. 102; see also Russo et al., 1989). Reactivity may also occur if the opportunity to review or report on earlier processing that had occurred during the research task influences learning from the task (cf. Ericsson & Simon, 1993; Gass & Mackey, 2000).

Concurrent verbal reporting can cause reactivity for several reasons. It impacts on task latency, extending the time participants spend on a task and potentially allowing participants to attend to additional information that may not otherwise have been processed (Berardi-Coletta, Dominowski, Buyer, & Rellinger, 1995; Craik & Tulving, 1975). It may also allow for rehearsal of stimulus information (Jacoby, 1973) that may strengthen memory traces and make information from earlier processing available for later processing (Biehal & Chakravarti, 1989). Biehal and Chakravarti (1989) also suggest that concurrent verbalization may also encourage participants to use more systematic processing, rendering information that was processed and verbalized more easily retrievable at a later stage.

Retrospective verbalization, on the other hand, will not influence cognitive processing during a task. In psychological and cognitive science studies that involve non-linguistic tasks (e.g., mathematical tasks), retrospective reports are generally elicited after each trial or in preselected point(s) within a task session consisting of a series of trials. In some cases, verbalizations are gathered between task sessions, with a much longer time interval between the primary task and recall (e.g., 2 days delayed recall in Schooler & Engstler-Schooler, 1990). These types of retrospection may influence participants' performance on subsequent trials (see Ericsson & Simon, 1993, for a comprehensive review). Retrospective verbalization may also have an impact on how much information is retained from a task and therefore on estimates of the effectiveness of the task for learning purposes. This reactivity effect is particularly relevant for L2 tasks designed to promote language learning. Also, this effect may be pronounced in stimulus-cued retrospective verbalizations, such as stimulated recall, in which after task completion participants are exposed to task-related stimuli a second time (to aid their recall). As Adams (2003) suggests, such a stimulus presentation may give participants a *second pass* through the task and a chance to process information they may not have been able to process with one attempt alone.

Early psychological studies of the reactivity for both concurrent and retrospective verbalizations found mixed results. Concurrent verbalization has been found to influence performance in problem-solving tasks (Short, Schatschneider, Cuddy, Evans, Dellick, & Basili, 1991), decision-making tasks (Biehal & Chakravarti, 1989), and mathematical reasoning tasks (Russo et al., 1989). However, other studies of verbalization in various tasks found little or no effect on performance (Carroll & Payne, 1977; Fernandez-Ballesteros & Manning, 1984; Henry, LeBreck, & Holzemer, 1989; Norris, 1990). Similarly, findings on the reactivity of retrospective reports have also been mixed, with some finding reactivity (Berry, 1983; Russo et al., 1989; Schooler & Engstler-Schooler, 1990; Schooler, Ohlsson, & Brooks, 1993; Stanley, Mathews, Buss, & Kolter-Cope, 1989; Wilson & Schooler, 1991) and some finding no effects of verbalization (Bowers & Snyder, 1990; Brinkman, 1993; Henry et al., 1989; Norris, 1990; Robinson, 2001; Sowder, 1974).

In a comprehensive review of verbalizations, Ericsson and Simon (1993) pointed out that the different results on the reactivity of concurrent and retrospective verbalizations might be related to the nature of the verbalizations. They distinguished among three levels of cognitive processing that are associated with different types of verbalizations. At one end of the scale are Level 1 verbalizations that make overt already occurring covert linguistic encodings associated with task performance. In Level 1 verbalizations, participants simply verbalize information that was heeded. Because no further immediate processing, such as reasoning and explanation, is required, Ericsson and Simon hypothesized that Level 1 verbalizations would not interfere with processing. At the opposite end of the scale are Level 3 verbalizations, which require participants to explain their underlying reasoning as they work through a task. Ericsson and Simon explained that these higher-level verbalizations require additional interpretive processing and as such are likely to influence the way that learners process information as they work through a task. Other additional intermediate processes involved in Level 3 verbalizations include filtering processes. When participants are asked to report only selected information, they are required to judge whether the heeded information is the requested type. Level 3 verbalizations may also occur when participants are asked to verbalize information that they would not ordinarily attend to. Several recent second language acquisition (SLA) studies on verbal reporting have labeled Level 1 verbalizations as *non-metalinguistic* and Level 3 verbalizations (particularly those requiring justification and reasoning) as *metalinguistic* (Bowles, 2008; Bowles & Leow, 2005; Leow & Morgan-Short, 2004).

Further research on verbalizations has lent support to Ericsson and Simon (1993). For concurrent verbalizations, many studies have indicated that non-metalinguistic verbalizations did not influence task performance, while metalinguistic verbalizations significantly affected task performance (Ahlum-Heath & Di Vesta, 1986; Allwood, 1990; Berardi-Coletta et al., 1995; Berry, 1983; McGeorge & Burton, 1989; Rhenius & Heydemann, 1984), particularly when participants are under time pressure and when the range of response options is relatively open (Dickson, McLennan, & Omodei, 2000).

A similar trend has been reported for retrospective metalinguistic verbalization (Berry, 1983; Russo et al., 1989; Schooler et al., 1993; Stanley et al., 1989; Wilson & Schooler, 1991). For example, Stanley et al. (1989) found reactivity of metalinguistic reports in an experiment where participants were asked to give instructions on a simulated process control task to an imaginary partner. After every 10 trials, they were instructed to explain in detail how they made their choices during the task so that the imaginary partner could perform the same task later using their instructions. Their task performance was significantly more accurate than control groups who remained silent during the task. Similarly, Schooler et al. (1993) found reactivity of retrospective verbalizations when participants were asked to report their approach, strategies, and any solutions they tried while performing six problem-solving tasks. One-third of the way through the allotted time for solving each problem, participants were interrupted for verbalization for 1.5 minutes and then resumed working on the problem. Their task performance was significantly less accurate than the control group, who were also interrupted but not asked to report their processing. Berry (1983) contrasted the effects of metalinguistic concurrent and retrospective verbalizations on the transfer of logical processes across tasks. Concurrent and retrospective groups were asked to elaborate on the logic behind their performance on problem-solving tasks either during or following the task, respectively. Both groups' performance on a subsequence task was significantly more accurate than silent groups. Berry suggested that the production of metacognitive verbalizations may have allowed participants to pinpoint aspects of reasoning necessary for success. Russo et al.

(1989) pointed out that the effects of verbalization on task performance are not general but depend on the demands of the task. They found reactivity of metalinguistic retrospective reports on two of the four experimental tasks of varying cognitive demands, suggesting that verbalization may be reactive when participants' processing capacity exceeds the demands of the task. These studies provide evidence that metalinguistic verbal reports can be reactive regardless of the timing of verbalizations, corroborating Ericsson and Simon's prediction.

Verbalizations in L2 research

Several recent studies have tackled the question of the reactivity of concurrent verbalizations in L2 tasks. For example, Leow and Morgan-Short (2004) examined the effects of non-metalinguistic thinking aloud on the learning of the Spanish impersonal imperative from reading texts that contained multiple uses of the form. Concurrent verbalizations in this study did not influence comprehension, recognition of the form after the treatment, or the ability to correctly produce the form in a controlled writing task following the treatment. The authors conclude that non-metalinguistic verbalizations were not reactive for either comprehension or learning in this task. Similar findings were reported by Sachs and Suh (2007) in a study of learning from feedback in computer-mediated communication, where no reactivity of non-metalinguistic thinking aloud was found.

However, results on the reactivity of non-metalinguistic thinking aloud in L2 research are not so clear-cut. For example, Sachs and Polio (2007) found reactivity of non-metalinguistic thinking aloud in a repeated-measures study using a three-stage composition-comparison-revision task. When adult learners of English wrote a story and compared it to a reformulated version by a native speaker while thinking aloud, they were significantly less accurate in a subsequent revision of the original text.[1] Goo (2010) suggests that these discrepancies may be related to individual differences among learners. He found reactivity for non-metalinguistic concurrent verbalizations on L2 reading comprehension but only among learners with high working memory capacities as measured by an operation span test.

Several studies extended this line of research by investigating the reactivity of metalinguistic thinking aloud. For example, Bowles and Leow (2005) contrasted the effects of metalinguistic and non-metalinguistic verbalizations during reading of texts that contained multiple examples of the Spanish pluperfect subjunctive. They measured reactivity in terms of text comprehension, ability to use exemplars of the target form found in the text, ability to use new exemplars of the target form, and task latency. In this study, participants who produced metalinguistic verbalizations demonstrated significantly lower comprehension than those who provided non-metalinguistic verbalizations (although neither was significantly different from the silent control group). Importantly, however, learning of the form was not related to the type of verbalization given. Other research suggests that instructional conditions may influence the reactivity of metalinguistic concurrent verbalizations. Sanz, Lin, Lado, Bowden, and Stafford (2009) studied the learning of Latin semantic functions under two learning conditions. Though the study was designed to examine non-metalinguistic thinking aloud, qualitative analyses of the protocols indicated that most of them were metalinguistic in nature under both conditions. While thinking aloud during computerized explicit instruction was not reactive, thinking aloud during less explicit instruction improved learners' performance on two of the three post-treatment measures. Furthermore, M. Yoshida (2008) cautions that tasks used to measure performance may also influence whether or not the reactivity of metalinguistic concurrent verbalizations is found. In a study of L2 reading comprehension, she found no reactivity when comprehension was

1 However, a second experiment without repeated measures did not uncover reactivity.

measured by post-reading questions but uncovered evidence of reactivity when in-reading measurements, such as outlining, were used.

While studies involving reading and other silent activities are appropriate for concurrent verbal reports, much of L2 research focuses on language use through oral activities. Because it is not possible to complete an oral task and concurrently verbalize thought processes, many researchers have instead chosen to use retrospective verbalization, such as stimulated recall (Gass & Mackey, 2000). As Leow and Morgan-Short (2004) point out, the distinction between concurrent and retrospective verbalizations may be equally important in terms of reactivity as the distinction between metalinguistic and non-metalinguistic verbalizations. As noted above, reactivity of retrospective verbalizations in L2 contexts refers not to an influence on how the primary task is carried out but rather to whether verbalizations provide an extra learning opportunity, potentially inflating the measured learning effects of treatments they were designed to investigate. Gass and Mackey (2000) point out the need to conduct retrospective verbalizations as soon as possible following an experimental treatment, as memory traces decay exponentially over time. In longitudinal research this often necessitates the inclusion of verbal protocols between treatments and posttests. In such contexts the question for retrospective verbalizations is whether their inclusion in a study design will be reactive to learning overall.

Despite the common use of stimulated recall in research on interactional feedback (Bao et al., 2011; Egi, 2007b, 2010; Kim & Han, 2007; R. Yoshida, 2010), classroom dyadic interactions (Adams, 2003; Swain & Lapkin, 2002; Tocalli-Beller & Swain, 2007), and learner noticing and L2 development (Egi, 2007a; Mackey, 2006; Nabei & Swain, 2002), very little research has investigated the reactivity of stimulated recall verbalizations. While not separately investigated, the reactivity of stimulated recall has been assumed by Swain and Lapkin and their colleagues in a series of studies on learner processing of form when engaged in collaborative work (Lapkin, Swain, & Smith, 2002; Qi & Lapkin, 2001; Swain & Lapkin, 2002; Tocalli-Beller & Swain, 2007). In these studies, stimulated recall has been considered to be part of the learning process.

Adams (2003) sought to empirically separate the effects of non-metalinguistic stimulated recall from the effects of feedback and found that learners who participated in stimulated recall after receiving feedback on collaborative written work were more likely to produce corrected forms in subsequent writing. Adams discusses benefits of retrospective reports in comparison with concurrent reports, noting that the reactivity of concurrent verbalizations may lead to inhibited performance because the dual task of engaging in processing and reporting might overtax working memory. In contrast, with retrospective protocols, reactivity may be more likely to lead to greater learning opportunities, as participants do not have the dual burden imposed by concurrent verbalizations. Adams additionally points out that the stimulus used to redirect participants to their prior cognitive processing (e.g., audio- or video-recording of task performance) may give learners a second chance to acquire linguistic information from the task. Thus, stimulated recall may be reactive because of the stimulus and also because verbalization may reorganize prior cognitive processing.

Egi (2008) sought to determine whether non-metalinguistic stimulated recall was reactive and if so, whether the reactivity was related to the stimulus or to the effects of verbalization. In the study three groups of learners of Japanese completed a pretest on two pre-selected Japanese morphological target forms. Following the pretest, they participated in teacher-fronted interactive tasks designed to elicit the use of the forms and were provided with corrective feedback. One group then participated in stimulated recall based on video clips of interactions involving the target forms from their class. The second group reviewed similar clips from their classrooms, but they were not asked to verbalize their processing either overtly or covertly. The third group was a control group that participated only in tasks without recall or stimulus viewing. Analysis of a posttest administered following these sessions indicated that the three groups experienced similar gains on the pre-selected targets, indicating that neither the verbalization nor the stimulus was reactive. However, Egi (2008) points out that the stimuli from classroom interactions may have limited opportunities for learning, as each clip was based on only one learner's or a few learners' experience, which may not have been cognitively engaging nor at an appropriate developmental level for other learners who were not part of the interactions.

To date, very few studies (Bowles, 2008; Bowles & Leow, 2005) have contrasted the reactivity of metalinguistic and non-metalinguistic verbalizations. These studies, however, examined concurrent verbalizations, and the reactivity of retrospective metalinguistic verbalizations has been relatively unexplored despite their prevalence in L2 research. Lindgren and Sullivan (2003) is one of the few studies that investigated retrospective metalinguistic verbalizations. They addressed the effect of metalinguistic stimulated recall in a study where two EFL learners repeated a two-stage writing activity (first, writing a letter, then revising the letter) on similar topics twice, the first time without metalinguistic stimulated recall and the second time with it. Specifically, they were asked to explain why they had made revisions while watching a recording of their keystrokes on the computer. The recall session was also complemented by focus-on-form instruction. Both learners made more revisions in the second activity, which the authors attributed to their heightened awareness via the metalinguistic stimulated recall. Lindgren and Sullivan claim that their findings point to the reactivity of metalinguistic stimulated recall. This claim, however, may be compromised by their operationalization of metalinguistic stimulated recall, which conflated at least three variables: verbalization, task repetition, and focus-on-form instruction. That is, because the recall was the second writing activity on a topic similar to the one for the first activity and because they received focus-on-form instruction during recall, the improvement is not necessarily solely attributable to the metalinguistic stimulated recall.

While Lindgren and Sullivan (2003) provide preliminary evidence that metalinguistic stimulated recall may be reactive, more research is needed to understand how the use of stimulated recall may influence results in studies that examine cognitive processing in L2 learning. The goal of the current study is to fill this gap by examining the reactivity of metalinguistic and non-metalinguistic stimulated recall, as stated in the research question: "Is metalinguistic stimulated recall reactive in subsequent L2 learning?" Our hypothesis was that learners who participated in metalinguistic stimulated recall would be reactive, or in other words, they would show greater development than those who participated in non-metalinguistic stimulated recall and those who were not engaged in any recall.

Method

Participants

Participants were 29 (12 male, 17 female) beginning adult learners of Japanese as a foreign language. They were recruited from three intact sections of a second-semester intensive Japanese course at a university.[2] The class met five times a week for 50 minutes each time and included form-focused instruction and conversational activities similar to those used in this study. On average, learners had received formal instruction in Japanese for 12 months.

2 The current study utilized a subset of data gathered for a previous study by one of the authors (non-metalinguistic stimulated recall and silent groups).

Their ages ranged from 18 to 23 (M=20). All learners were native speakers of English, except one learner whose L1 was Chinese.

The recall stimuli used in this study were video clips of teacher-fronted classroom activities. Each clip captured interactions between the teacher and one or several learners (discussed below). As Egi (2008) pointed out, recall stimuli of this sort might not be cognitively engaging to learners who were not part of the interactions. Therefore, of the 39 learners in the original participant pool, five learners who were not involved in any of the interactions shown in the video were excluded from the study. Additionally, another five learners who failed to complete all treatment sessions were eliminated, leaving 29 learners in the final participant pool.

Teacher participants were the two experienced Japanese instructors for the three sections of the course and led the communicative activities for the study. Before the experiment they met with one of the researchers and received training in using the communicative tasks and providing corrective feedback. The teachers took part in role-plays in which they played the role of learners and received corrective feedback, such as recasts and negotiation, from the researcher. Then, they switched their roles, and the teachers practiced giving feedback to a wide array of learner errors modeled by the researcher.

Linguistic targets

The linguistic targets for the study were the morpheme *-te* and numeral classifiers. The morpheme *-te* is a bound morpheme that attaches to verbs and expresses various grammatical functions. This study examined the imperative function of the morpheme attached to Japanese regular verbs (i.e., verbs with consonant-final root) in the polite imperative construction (verb-*te kudasai*, 'please verb'). When the morpheme attaches to regular verbs, *te*-formation involves morphological as well as phonological changes, which Tsujimura refers to as *morphophonological change* (2007, p. 37) (e.g., *isog-u+te kudasai=isoide kudasai*, 'please hurry'). Numeral classifiers are bound morphemes that attach to numeral expressions, which specify the quantity of the noun they modify. Of the wide range of numeral classifiers found in Japanese, the study examined classifiers for long, cylindrical objects (*-hon*), books (*-satsu*), and small animals (*-hiki*). As with the *te*-formation of regular verbs, these numerical classifiers also involve morphological and phonological changes when attached to certain numbers (e.g., *ichi+hon=ippon*; 'one'+*hon*=a long cylindrical object).

Although learners in the current study had previously received formal instruction on the forms, their production involved frequent errors, and this created a context for corrective feedback to naturally occur. To minimize ceiling effects, two learners who scored more than 50% on the pretest of numeral classifiers (one from each non-metalinguistic stimulated recall and control group) were excluded from the analysis of numeral classifiers, leaving 27 learners for this target.

Design

Figure 1 summarizes the design of the study. The three intact classes were randomly assigned to one of the two recall groups (non-metalinguistic and metalinguistic stimulated recall) and one control group. First, all groups completed a background questionnaire and took the pretest in a language laboratory. One week later, they participated in two communicative activities conducted over the course of two consecutive classes. On the following day, the two recall groups participated in a stimulated recall session and took the immediate posttest in the laboratory. The control group only took the immediate posttest without participating in recall. One week after the immediate posttest, all groups took the delayed posttest. Each experimental instrument is described below.

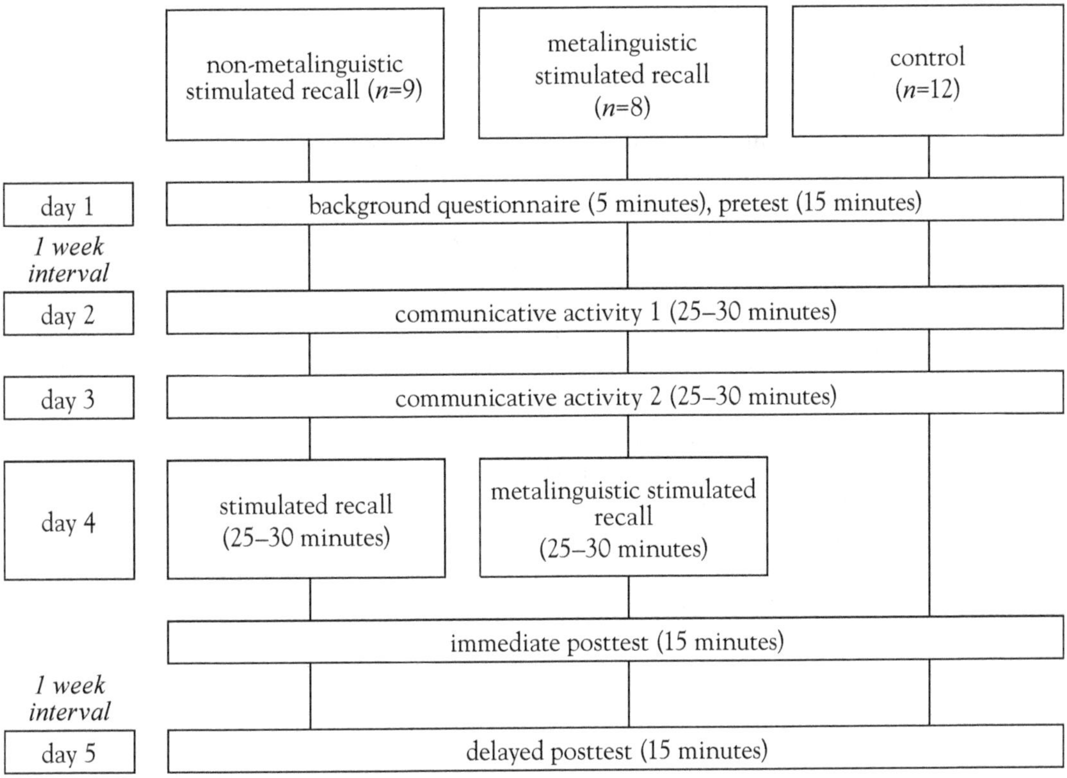

Figure 1. Experimental procedure and approximate times

Pre- and post-tests

Pre- and post-tests were picture-cued oral production tasks that involved 15 pictures designed to elicit the use of numeral classifiers and the morpheme *-te*. There were 10 production opportunities for each target. The tests were administered using a tape-mediated format in the laboratory, which was equipped with individual carrels with a noise cancellation headset and microphone. At each testing session, learners received one of the three versions of the test. Both the number of learners who received each version at each session and the order of the versions were counterbalanced. Learners first listened to prerecorded task instructions and worked on two practice items. Following this, they were prompted to describe each of the 15 pictures; 25 seconds were provided for each picture to digitally record their responses. The pretest took approximately 15 minutes.

Communicative activities

All groups participated in teacher-led information-gap activities during a class period on two consecutive days. In each session, learners first engaged in a picture placement task and then a spot-the-difference task. Two versions of each task were created, one for the first session and another for the second. The tasks were designed to elicit the use of the two target structures in communicative contexts. During the tasks learners received corrective feedback (recasts and negotiation) on their errors with the target structures and some of the other linguistic items. Corrective feedback of this sort has been found to promote L2 acquisition (see Mackey & Gass, 2006, for a discussion).

The picture placement tasks depicted scenes where people were making various requests at a restaurant or stores (e.g., a restaurant manager asking an employee to take out the trash). These requests were shown in callouts using pictures and key words (e.g., a picture of a person taking out the trash and 'please' in a callout above the manager). In addition, various objects in different quantities were shown in the pictures. From both the teacher's and students' pictures, some items in the callouts and scene were erased and moved to the margin of the task sheet (e.g., the picture of a person taking out the trash was moved to the margin, leaving only 'please' in the callout). Some items that were not part of the original pictures were also included as distracters. The items removed from the students' picture appeared in their original locations in the teacher's picture, and those removed from the teacher's picture appeared in their original locations in the learners' picture. The task goal was for the teacher and learners to ask one another questions and to move the removed items in the margin back to their original positions.

The spot-the-difference tasks consisted of two sets of similar pictures that also showed people making requests to each other. The pictures also showed various objects in different quantities. The teacher received one picture, and learners received the other. Each party took turns describing their pictures in order to identify 15 differences between them. At the end of each task, the teacher showed the class her task sheet using an overhead projector to confirm that the task was successfully completed. The classes took approximately 25–30 minutes to complete the two tasks on each day. One of the researchers videotaped the task interactions from a back corner of the classroom on both days.

Stimulated recall

The non-metalinguistic and metalinguistic stimulated recall groups participated separately in stimulated recall conducted by one of the researchers in the laboratory. Learners first read the instructions as they listened to the prerecorded instructions. Both groups were asked to recall their thoughts in English at the time of task interaction, but not at the time of video viewing. If thoughts at the time of interaction could not be clearly recalled, learners were given an option to withhold reporting. They were also asked not to write down anything during recall. In addition, learners were told that their teachers would not listen to their reports; this was to encourage learners to express their thoughts freely without concerns for negative evaluations by their teachers. Both groups were given an opportunity to clarify any questions about the procedure before viewing the video.

In addition to these general directions, the two groups received group-specific instructions. The non-metalinguistic stimulated recall group was requested to simply "recall in English what you were thinking at the time the video was taken (NOT what you are thinking about now as you watch the video)." While these instructions did not direct the non-metalinguistic learners' attention to any particular aspects of the interactions, the metalinguistic learners were specifically oriented to "recall whatever you noticed about the language (e.g., words, grammar, pronunciations), the language that was new to you, and/or how your teacher corrected you/your classmates (if any) at the time the video was taken." They were also given two examples of such recall comments:

> "I did not know that a chicken in Japanese was NIWATORI. I thought it was TORINIKU ('chicken meat'). I guess TORINIKU is for chicken meat;"

"my classmate said 'INU GA ARIMASU' ('there is [inanimate] a dog') and the teacher corrected him, 'INU GA IMASU' ('there is [animate] a dog'). Yeah, for animate things, we should use IMASU, not ARIMASU."

For each group, two enlarged copies of the group-specific instructions above were posted on the whiteboard. After receiving the instructions, each group was shown 10 video clips taken from their second activity session on large wall-mounted televisions. The second activity was chosen because the temporal proximity between the second activity and recall was thought to enhance the accuracy and completeness of recall (Gass & Mackey, 2000). The clips included both feedback and non-feedback (distractor) episodes involving the target as well as other linguistic items. As mentioned earlier, because the activities were conducted in the teacher-fronted format with about 13 students in class, each clip showed interactions between the teacher and one learner or several learners. Thus, learners viewed not only their own but also their classmates' performances. The researcher paused the video after each clip and prompted the class to recall their thoughts. In order to help learners recall their thoughts about the task interactions, two enlarged copies of the learner's task sheet were posted under the televisions and on the whiteboard. For each clip, the researcher pointed to the part of the picture that was being discussed in the video. Both groups were given 45 seconds to record their recall comments about each clip on individual microphones. The recall sessions lasted approximately 25–30 minutes.

Test scoring and inter-rater reliability

On all tests two points were awarded to correct responses, one point for partially correct responses, and zero points for incorrect responses. For each linguistic target the scoring range was zero to 20, and raw scores were submitted to statistical analyses. Two independent raters scored all tests and reached high inter-rater agreement, as measured by simple agreement (99%) and Pearson's correlation ($r=.99$, $p<.01$).

Results

Research question: Is metalinguistic stimulated recall reactive in subsequent L2 learning?

For both numeral classifiers and *te*-form, the three groups performed similarly on the pretest, as demonstrated by non-significant results of one-way analysis of variance (ANOVA) ($F(2, 24)=.758$, $p=.479$ for classifiers, $F(2, 26)=.242$, $p=.787$ for *te*-form). Their immediate and delayed posttest scores were separately submitted to one-way ANOVA to examine possible effects of metalinguistic and non-metalinguistic stimulated recall on learners' post-recall performance. In addition, an effect size, which shows the magnitude of effects independently of sample size (Cohen, 1969), was calculated to minimize the possible misinterpretation of the results due to a Type 2 error. Descriptive and inferential statistics will be reported first for numeral classifiers and then for *te*-form.

Numeral classifiers

Table 1 summarizes descriptive statistics, and Figure 2 graphically shows the pattern. The one-way ANOVA indicated non-significant differences between the three groups on both immediate and delayed posttests, $F(2, 23)=.072$, $p=.931$, $\eta 2=.006$, and $F(2, 24)=.387$, $p=.683$, $\eta 2=.031$, respectively.[3] An effect size analysis indicated that when compared to the control group, the effect of non-metalinguistic stimulated recall was almost non-existent ($d=-0.08$)

3 Because of the small sample size, a non-parametric Kruskal-Wallis test was also performed to complement the parametric analysis. It also yielded non-significant results for both linguistic targets.

and relatively small (d=–0.34) on the immediate and delayed posttests, respectively.[4] The effect of metalinguistic stimulated recall was also very small on both immediate (d=–0.17) and delayed (d=0.10) posttests. The ANOVA results and effect size analysis together suggest that neither non-metalinguistic nor metalinguistic stimulated recall affected learners' posttest performance, or in other words, they were non-reactive.

Table 1. Numeral classifiers: Mean test scores

	non-metalinguistic SR				metalinguistic SR				control		
	n	M	*SD*	*d* (vs. control)	*n*	M	*SD*	*d* (vs. control)	*n*	M	*SD*
pretest	8	2.38	3.20	– –	8	0.88	1.64	– –	11	2.18	2.89
immediate	8	11.25	4.89	–0.08	8	10.75	4.23	–0.17	10*	11.70	6.24
delayed	8	8.13	5.28	–0.34	8	10.50	6.70	0.10	11	9.91	5.13

note: *One student was absent from the immediate posttest session. SR=stimulated recall.

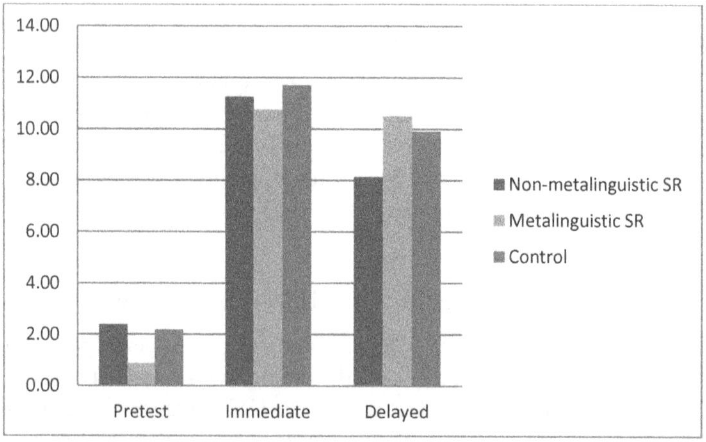

Figure 2. Numeral classifiers: Mean test scores

Te-form

As shown in Table 2 and Figure 3, the three groups performed similarly on all tests. One-way ANOVA did not find significant between-group differences on any of the tests (posttest: $F(2, 25)$=.283, p=.756, $\eta 2$=.022; delayed posttest: $F(2, 26)$=.032, p=.969, $\eta 2$=.002). Effect sizes indicate very small effects of non-metalinguistic stimulated recall on learners' immediate and delayed posttest scores (d=0.10 for both tests). The effects of metalinguistic stimulated recall were relatively small (d=0.38) and negligible (d=0.02) on immediate and delayed posttests, respectively. These findings suggest that both metalinguistic and non-metalinguistic stimulated recall were non-reactive.

4 Following Cohen (1969), effect sizes were interpreted as follows: small ($0.2<d<0.5$), medium ($0.5<d<0.8$), and large ($0.8<d$)

Table 2. *Te*-form: Mean test scores

	non-metalinguistic SR				metalinguistic SR				control		
	n	*M*	*SD*	*d* (vs. control)	*n*	*M*	*SD*	*d* (vs. control)	*n*	*M*	*SD*
pretest	9	4.56	2.30	– –	8	4.88	2.17	– –	12	4.08	2.94
immediate	9	9.78	5.76	0.10	8	11.00	4.11	0.38	11*	9.27	4.90
delayed	9	9.22	6.26	0.10	8	8.75	4.23	0.02	12	8.67	4.94

note: *One student was absent from the immediate posttest session. SR=stimulated recall.

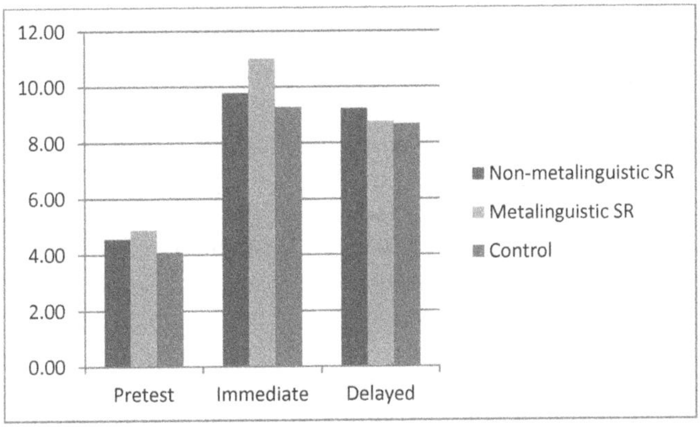

Figure 3. *Te*-form: Mean test scores

Discussion

The research question asked whether metalinguistic stimulated recall would be reactive. The hypothesis was that the metalinguistic stimulated recall group would show greater development than the non-metalinguistic stimulated recall and no recall groups. However, contrary to the prediction, the metalinguistic group did not significantly differ from the non-metalinguistic group or the control group on either the immediate or delayed posttest of either linguistic target. The effect size analyses also indicated negligible to very small effects of metalinguistic verbalization. These findings collectively suggest the non-reactivity of the retrospective metalinguistic verbalizations.

The findings of the current study contrast with Lindgren and Sullivan (2003) who found metalinguistic stimulated recall to be reactive. This contradiction may be explained by the conflation of independent variables in their study. As discussed earlier, the variables of metalinguistic verbalization, task repetition, and focus-on-form instruction were not empirically separated, and this made it difficult to attribute the observed reactivity solely to metalinguistic verbalization. A similar argument may be made for studies by Swain and her colleagues who generally found the benefits of collaborative work involving stimulated recall (Lapkin et al., 2002; Qi & Lapkin, 2001; Swain & Lapkin, 2002; Tocalli-Beller & Swain, 2007). Because these studies were not intended to investigate reactivity of stimulated recall, the variable of verbalization was not empirically isolated, again making it implausible to attribute the learning benefits solely to stimulated recall.

Another reason for the absence of reactivity in this study might lie in the recall instructions for metalinguistic verbalizations. Ericsson and Simon (1993) hypothesize that Level 3 verbalizations, which require participants to explain their underlying reasoning, will be reactive, and this is the type of metalinguistic verbalizations examined in most SLA and non-SLA studies. However, participants in the current study were not asked to report justifications or reasoning. Instead, they were asked to recall whatever they noticed about the language (e.g., words, grammar, pronunciations), the language that was new to them, and/or how their teacher corrected their classmates. These instructions were thought to cause reactivity because Ericsson and Simon predict that requests to verbalize particular information add a filtering requirement and causes reactivity. However, it is possible that they did not influence the learners' processing in the way instructions requesting reasoning and justification do. Continued research may employ the latter type of instructions to examine the effect of retrospective verbalizations of reasoning and justifications on L2 learning.

Although the metalinguistic instructions in this study did not cause reactivity in terms of L2 learning, they did influence what learners reported, corroborating the argument that recall instructions could significantly affect the content of verbalizations (Bowles & Leow, 2005; Ericsson & Simon, 1993; Lapierre, 1994, cited in Swain, 1998). For example, Lapierre investigated the effects of different recall instructions on learner-learner dialogues about the L2 (metatalk). Forty-eight child French immersion students were assigned to a metalinguistic or comparison group and participated in pair activities after watching a model of metatalk. The metatalk modeled for the metalinguistic group involved abundant grammatical terms and explanations, whereas the one modeled for the comparison group did not include such metalinguistic cues. The metalinguistic group produced language-related episodes almost three times more than the comparison group, suggesting that the instructions could significantly influence what learners report. Similarly, in Bowles and Leow (2005), the metalinguistic group generally demonstrated meta-awareness of the target structure when verbalizing justifications and reasoning for their answers on the production posttests. They stated, "the requirement to verbalize justifications for all answers on the production tasks pushed the participants to have a certain level of awareness" (p. 433).

Following Lapierre (1994, cited in Swain, 1998) and Bowles and Leow (2005), a post hoc analysis was conducted on learners' awareness of the target structures. As Schmidt (1990, 1993, 1995) has argued, the quality of learner awareness may range from a broad awareness of discrete L2 exemplars (awareness at the level of noticing), to an awareness of the discrepancies between interlanguage and L2 form (noticing the gap), to an awareness of the rules underlying the form (awareness at the level of understanding). An awareness at the level of understanding indicates the deepest processing, setting itself apart from broader awareness represented by awareness at the level of noticing and noticing the gap. Thus, learner commentaries were divided into two major categories, *noticing* and *understanding*. The former was operationalized as the learner's commentaries on discrete examples of the target structures or those on differences between his own or classmates' error of the target form and the correct form. The latter was operationalized as the learner's comment on grammatical rule(s) underlying the target forms.

Example 1a. Noticing.
...Umm...I was recalling the new verb *sosoiru*, *sosoi..*, I'm not sure of the verb, but the *te*-form is *sosoide* ('to pour'), umm...that I had never heard prior to this experiment. (Participant #2, non-metalinguistic group)

Example 1b. Noticing.
Sensei ('teacher') corrected X-*san* ('Mr. X') that *isogu*'s ('hurry') *te*-form is *isoide* not **isonde*. (Participant #34, metalinguistic group)

Example 2. Understanding.
I noticed that he said **gobiki* ('five animals') instead of *gohiki*, and, so I realized that one could use the counter when it starts with an H, and you say *nan* ('wh-'), like the B kind of form of the word, so *nanbiki* ('how many animals'), but like when you have the number like *go* ('five'), you say *gohiki* ('five animals'), which makes sense. (Understanding of a rule governing the phonological changes involved in the suffixation of the numeral classifier *-hiki* [used to count small animals] to numbers.[5]) (Participant #32, metalinguistic group)

Each learner's protocols were examined for the highest level of awareness they demonstrated about each linguistic target, and the results are summarized in Table 3.

Table 3. Reported levels of awareness

	n	**no reported noticing**	**noticing**	**understanding**
numeral classifiers				
non-metalinguistic SR	8	4	4	0
metalinguistic SR	8	0	4	4
***te*-form**				
non-metalinguistic SR	9	2	7	0
metalinguistic SR	8	0	6	2

note. SR=stimulated recall.

Roughly the same number of non-metalinguistic and metalinguistic learners reported their awareness at the level of noticing for both targets. However, while four (numeral classifiers) and two (*te*-form) metalinguistic learners demonstrated awareness at the level of understanding, none of the non-metalinguistic learners indicated this high level of awareness. Furthermore, several non-metalinguistic learners did not report noticing the form all together. Consistent with Bowles and Leow (2005) and Lapierre (1994, cited in Swain, 1998), many of the metalinguistic learners were influenced by the recall instructions that oriented their attention to grammatical aspects of the input and corrective feedback.

A further post hoc analysis was conducted on the reactivity of metalinguistic verbalization based on what learners actually reported rather than on what they were requested to report. This analysis focused on metalinguistic learners who reported awareness at the level of understanding (four learners for numeral classifiers and two for *te*-form) and contrasted their performance with non-metalinguistic learners who did not report this high level of awareness. Because of the small sample size, only descriptive statistics will be reported (see Table 4). For numeral classifiers all groups performed similarly on the immediate posttest. However, while the non-metalinguistic and control groups showed a decline in scores at

5 The classifier *-hiki* changes to *-biki* when it is followed by the word 'what' or the number 3. It changes to *-piki* when followed by the numbers 1, 6, and 8. At other times, *-hiki* remains as is.

delayed post-testing, the metalinguistic group showed slight improvement. For *te*-form, while the metalinguistic group performed a little better than the other groups on the immediate posttest, the differences diminished by the time of delayed post-testing. However, the small sample size of the study made the finding inconclusive. A larger study would allow a more effective post hoc grouping of learners according to the content of their reports, enabling researchers to examine reactivity effects of metalinguistic retrospective verbalizations in a more definite term.

Table 4. Mean test scores

	non-metalinguistic			metalinguistic			control		
	n	M	*SD*	*n*	M	*SD*	*n*	M	*SD*
classifiers									
pretest	8	2.38	3.20	4	1.00	2.00	11	2.18	2.89
posttest	8	11.25	4.89	4	11.25	4.50	10*	11.70	6.24
delayed	8	8.13	5.28	4	13.75	4.72	11	9.91	5.13
***te*-form**									
pretest	9	4.56	2.30	2	5.00	1.41	12	4.08	2.94
posttest	9	9.78	5.76	2	12.50	6.36	11*	9.27	4.90
delayed	9	9.22	6.26	2	9.00	7.07	12	8.67	4.94

note. *One student was absent from the immediate posttest session. SR: stimulated recall.

A large number of studies have found facilitative effects of noticing, particularly awareness at the level of understanding (Leow, 1997, 2000; Mackey, 2006; Rosa & Leow, 2004; Rosa & O'Neill, 1999). This would naturally lead to a question of why the metalinguistic group did not perform significantly better than the non-metalinguistic and control groups. Several methodological issues may account for this. First, this study measured learning only in terms of learners' oral production, and the results could have been different with written tests where learners have more time to consult their explicit knowledge. There is increasing awareness that different types of assessments measure different types of knowledge, such as explicit and implicit knowledge (Ellis, Loewen, & Erlam, 2006). Reactivity, therefore, may be observed on one assessment measure but not on another, depending on the type of knowledge learners developed through treatments and verbalizations (Sanz et al., 2009; M. Yoshida, 2008). Future research could employ a range of assessment measures to better understand the reactivity of metalinguistic retrospective verbalizations.

Second, the observed dissociation between reported awareness and learning may in part be explained by the type of recall stimuli used in this study. While recall stimuli in most of the earlier studies were based on individuals' performances, those in the current study were classroom interactions. Because Egi (2008), which also used classroom data, suggested that learners were more engaged in recall stimuli when they were directly involved in the interactions, the current analysis excluded learners who did not participate in any of the interactions selected for the group recall sessions. However, while each learner appeared in several of the video clips, they did not appear in *all* of them. Thus, it is possible that linguistic issues discussed in a given interaction were not always problematic or new to those who were not directly involved in this particular interaction. Such linguistic information might consolidate their L2 knowledge yet contribute little to interlanguage changes. Recall comments did not always clearly indicate whether the information was new or old to the learner. For example, whereas comments like Example 1a above clearly show that the information was new to the learner, a neutral description of an event like Example 1b did not allow the researchers to clearly gauge the newness of the information to the learner. Nonetheless, the speculation that linguistic problems discussed in an interaction were not always useful for those who merely observed the interaction is consistent with earlier findings that active participants in interactions improved more than observers (Mackey, 1999). This could potentially explain why the metalinguistic group did not show superior post-treatment performance. This also suggests a possibility that stimulated recall is reactive when recall stimuli focus on individuals' performances, and the use of stimulated recall in such context may require more care.

In summary, reactivity may not be an effect of a single factor, but concerted effects of multiple factors, including but not limited to recall instructions, measures of reactivity, type of recall stimuli, and new versus known information. These factors may individually and collectively account for the current findings that contradicted Ericsson and Simon's (1993) predictions and earlier studies (Lindgren & Sullivan, 2003; Russo et al., 1989; Schooler et al., 1993). The insights obtained from the current investigation could help refine the design of future research. Also, future studies could be conducted with a larger sample size and different learner populations for greater generalizability. Continued research should also provide learners with recall training, which could not be given in the current study for logistical reasons, to raise the internal validity of the study. Additionally, compared to concurrent reports, the veracity and completeness of stimulated recall comments tends to be compromised (i.e., non-veridical) due to the larger temporal distance between thought processes and verbalizations, and this needs to be acknowledged as an inherent limitation of retrospective reports. Also, in cued-retrospective reports, such as stimulated recall, in addition to reporting on earlier processing, participants are exposed to the L2 input once again. Although Egi (2008) found non-reactivity of recall stimuli alone, further investigation is warranted on the possibility that a second pass through the original task may enhance learning independently of verbalizations.

It is important to underscore that implications of this study are not intended to apply to all retrospective techniques that fall under the name of stimulated recall. A wide variation exists among cued-retrospective reports (Ericsson & Simon, 1993; Gass & Mackey, 2000). For example, the timing of recall may range from immediately to weeks after the event to be recalled. The recall stimuli may take a variety of formats: video, audio, written, or other materials. The interview can take place individually, in pairs, or in groups. The procedure adopted in this study represents only one possible form of stimulated recall, and the results need to be contextualized within the current study. We do not claim that stimulated recall is non-reactive in absolute terms.

Conclusion

The current study investigated the reactivity of metalinguistic stimulated recall on the learning of two Japanese structures by contrasting metalinguistic stimulated recall, non-metalinguistic stimulated recall, and no recall groups to determine whether stimulated recall increases noticing, facilitating learning. Contrary to the hypothesis, the results indicated non-significant differences between the groups, lending support for the non-reactivity of metalinguistic stimulated recall. However, the post hoc analysis of recall protocols indicated that some of the metalinguistic learners reported a high level of awareness of the target forms. However, interestingly, these qualitative differences did not translate to noticeable differences in learners' posttest performances. Various factors, including recall instructions, measures of reactivity, type of recall stimuli, and new versus known information, may have individually and collectively contributed to this result. Given an increasing number of L2 studies that draw insight from learners' stimulated recall protocols to measure cognitive processes like noticing, future research can investigate the reactivity of stimulated recall with careful consideration to the factors discussed above. Such continued efforts will bolster researchers' rationale for using stimulated recall to access information on learner cognitive processing.

References

Adams, R. (2003). L2 output, reformulation, and noticing: Implications for IL development. *Language Teaching Research, 7*, 347–376.

Ahlum-Heath, M. E., & Di Vesta, F. J. (1986). The effect of conscious controlled verbalization of a cognitive strategy on transfer in problem solving. *Memory and Cognition, 14*, 281–285.

Allwood, C. M. (1990). On the relation between justification of solution method and correctness of solution in statistical problem solving. *Scandinavian Journal of Psychology, 31*, 181–190.

Anderson, M. (1985). Some evidence on the effect of verbalization on process: A methodological note. *Journal of Accounting Research, 23*, 843–852.

Bao, M., Egi, T., & Han, Y. (2011). Classroom study on noticing and recast features: Capturing learner noticing with uptake and stimulated recall. *System, 39*, 215–228.

Berardi-Coletta, B., Dominowski, R. L., Buyer, L. S., & Rellinger, E. R. (1995). Metacognition and problem solving: A process-oriented approach. *Journal of Experimental Psychology, 21*, 205–223.

Berry, D. C. (1983). Metacognitive experience and transfer of logical reasoning. *Quarterly Journal of Experimental Psychology, 35*, 39–49.

Biehal, G., & Chakravarti, D. (1989). The effects of concurrent verbalization on choice processing. *Journal of Marketing Research, 26*, 84–96.

Bowers, V. A., & Snyder, H. L. (1990). Concurrent versus retrospective verbal protocol for comparing window usability. *Proceedings of the 34th Annual Meeting of the Human Factors and Ergonomics Society, 34*, 1270–1274.

Bowles, M. (2003). The effects of textual input enhancement on language learning: An online/offline study of fourth-semester Spanish students. In P. Kempchinsky & C. E. Piñeros (Eds.), *Theory, practice, and acquisition: Papers from the 6th Hispanic Linguistics Symposium and the 5th Conference on the Acquisition of Spanish and Portuguese* (pp. 395–411). Somerville, MA: Cascadilla Press.

Bowles, M. (2008). Task type and reactivity of verbal reports in SLA: A first look at a L2 task other than reading. *Studies in Second Language Acquisition, 30*, 359–387.

Bowles, M. A., & Leow, R. (2005). Reactivity and type of verbal report in SLA research methodology: Expanding the scope of investigation. *Studies in Second Language Acquisition, 27*, 415–440.

Brinkman, J. (1993). Verbal protocol accuracy in fault diagnosis. *Ergonomics, 36*, 1381–1397.

Carroll, J. S., & Payne, J. M. (1977). Judgments about crime and the criminal: A model and a method for investigating parole decisions. In B. D. Sales (Ed.), *Perspectives in law and psychology: The criminal justice system* (pp. 191–239). New York: Plenum.

Cavalcanti, M. C., & Cohen, A. D. (1990). Comentarios em composições: Uma comparação dos pontos de vista do professor e do aluno [Comments on compositions: A comparison of the professor's and student's points of view]. *Trabalhos em Lingüística Aplicada, 15,* 7–23.

Chenoweth, N. A., & Hayes, J. R. (2001). Fluency in writing: Generating text in L1 and L2. *Written Communication, 18,* 80–98.

Cohen, J. (1969). *Statistical power analysis for the behavioral sciences.* New York, NY: Academic Press Inc.

Craik, F., & Tulving, E. (1975). Depth of processing and the retention of words in episodic memory. *Journal of Experimental Psychology: General, 104,* 268–294.

Dickson, J., McLennan, J., & Omodei, M. M. (2000). Effects of concurrent verbalization on a time-critical, dynamic decision-making task. *The Journal of General Psychology, 127,* 217–228.

Egi, T. (2007a). Recasts, learners' perceptions, and L2 development. In A. Mackey (Ed.), *Conversational interaction in second language acquisition: A series of empirical studies* (pp. 249–267). Oxford: Oxford University Press.

Egi, T. (2007b). Interpreting recasts as linguistic evidence: The roles of length and degree of change. *Studies in Second Language Acquisition, 29,* 511–537.

Egi, T. (2008). Investigating stimulated recall as a cognitive measure: Reactivity and verbal reports in SLA research methodology. *Language Awareness, 17,* 212–228.

Egi, T. (2010). Uptake, modified output, and learner perceptions of recasts: Learner responses as language awareness. *The Modern Language Journal, 94,* 1–21.

Ellis, R., Loewen, S., & Erlam, R. (2006). Implicit and explicit corrective feedback and the acquisition of L2 grammar. *Studies in Second Language Acquisition, 28,* 339–368.

Ericsson, K., & Simon, H. (1993). *Protocol analysis: Verbal reports as data* (2nd ed.). Boston: MIT Press.

Farrington-Flint, L., & Wood, C. (2007). The role of lexical analogies in beginning reading: Insights from children's self reports. *Journal of Educational Psychology, 99,* 326–338.

Fernandez-Ballesteros, R., & Manning, L. (1984). Rod and frame test scores and verbalized strategies. *Perceptual and Motor Skills, 58,* 255–258.

Gass, S., & Mackey, A. (2000). *Stimulated recall methodology in second language research.* Mahwah, NJ: Lawrence Erlbaum Associates.

Geary, D. C., Frensch, P. A., & Wiley, J. G. (1993). Simple and complex mental subtraction: Strategy choice and speed-of-processing differences in young and elderly adults. *Psychology and Aging, 8,* 242–256.

Goo, J. (2010). Working memory and reactivity. *Language Learning, 60,* 712–752.

Green, A. J. (1995). Verbal protocol analysis. *The Psychologist, 8,* 126–129.

Hafner, J. (1957). Influence of verbalization on problem solving. *Psychological Reports, 3,* 360.

Hama, M., & Leow, R. (2010). Learning without awareness revisited. *Studies in Second Language Acquisition, 32,* 465–491.

Henry, S. B., LeBreck, D. B., & Holzemer, W. L. (1989). The effect of verbalization on cognitive processes on clinical decision making. *Research in Nursing and Health, 12,* 187–193.

Jacoby, L. (1973). Encoding processes, rehearsal, and recall requirements. *Journal of Verbal Learning and Verbal Behavior, 12,* 302–310.

Kasper, G. (1999). Data collection in pragmatics research. *University of Hawai'i Working Papers in ESL, 18*, 71–107.

Kim, J., & Han, Z. (2007). Recasts in communicative EFL classes: Do teacher intent and learner interpretation overlap? In A. Mackey (Ed.), *Conversational interaction in second language acquisition: A series of empirical studies* (pp. 269–297). Oxford: Oxford University Press.

Lapkin, S., Swain, M., & Smith, M. (2002). Reformulation and the learning of French pronominal verbs in a Canadian French immersion context. *The Modern Language Journal, 86*, 485–507.

Leow, R. (1997). Attention, awareness, and foreign language behavior. *Language Learning, 47*, 467–505.

Leow, R. (2000). A study of the role of awareness in foreign language behavior: Aware versus unaware learners. *Studies in Second Language Acquisition, 22*, 557–584.

Leow, R., Johnson, E., & Zárate-Sández, G. (2011). Getting a grip on the slippery concept of awareness: Toward a finer-grained methodological perspective. In C. Sanz & R. Leow (Eds.), *Implicit and explicit language learning* (pp. 61–72). Washington, DC: Georgetown University Press.

Leow, R., & Morgan-Short, K. (2004). To think aloud or not to think aloud. *Studies in Second Language Acquisition, 26*, 35–57.

Lindgren, E., & Sullivan, K. P. H. (2003). Stimulated recall as a trigger for increasing noticing and language awareness in the L2 writing classroom: A case study of two young female writers. *Language Awareness, 12*, 172–186.

Lyons, W. (1986). *The disappearance of introspection*. Cambridge, MA: MIT Press.

Mackey, A. (1999). Input, interaction, and second language development: An empirical study of question formation in ESL. *Studies in Second Language Acquisition, 21*, 557–587.

Mackey, A. (2006). Feedback, noticing, and instructed second language learning. *Applied Linguistics, 27*, 405–430.

Mackey, A., & Gass, S. (2006). Introduction. *Studies in Second Language Acquisition, 28*, 169–178.

Mackey, A., Gass, S. M., & McDonough, K. (2000). How do learners perceive interactional feedback? *Studies in Second Language Acquisition, 22*, 471–497.

Marks, M. R. (1951). Problem solving as a function of the situation. *Journal of Experimental Psychology, 41*, 74–80.

McGeorge, P., & Burton, A. M. (1989). The effects of concurrent verbalization on performance in a dynamic systems task. *British Journal of Psychology, 80*, 455–465.

Nabei, T., & Swain, M. (2002). Learning awareness of recasts in classroom interaction: A case study of an adult EFL student's second language learning. *Language Awareness, 11*, 43–63.

Nassaji, H. (2006). The relationship between depth of vocabulary knowledge and L2 learners' lexical inferencing strategy use and success. *The Modern Language Journal, 90*, 387–401.

Nisbett, R. E., & Wilson, T. D. (1977). Telling more than we can know: Verbal reports on mental processes. *Psychological Review, 84*, 231–259.

Norris, S. P. (1990). Effect of eliciting verbal reports of thinking on critical thinking test performance. *Journal of Educational Measurement, 27*, 41–58.

Olson, G., Duffy, S., & Mack, R. (1984). Thinking-out-loud as a method for studying real-time comprehension processes. In D. Kieras & M. Just (Eds.), *New methods in reading comprehension research* (pp. 253–286). Hillsdale, NJ: Erlbaum.

Qi, D. S., & Lapkin, S. (2001). Exploring the role of noticing in a three-stage second language writing task. *Journal of Second Language Writing, 10*, 277–303.

Rhenius, D., & Heydemann, M. (1984). Lautes Denken beim Bearbeiten von RAVEN-Aufgaben [Thinking aloud while processing Raven's matrices]. *Zeitschrift für Experimentelle und Angewandte Psychologie, 31*, 308–327.

Robinson, K. M. (2001). The validity of verbal reports in children's subtraction. *Journal of Educational Psychology, 93*, 211–222.

Rosa, E., & Leow, R. (2004). Awareness, different learning conditions, and second language development. *Applied Psycholinguistics, 25*, 269–292.

Rosa, E., & O'Neill, M. D. (1999). Explicitness, intake, and the issue of awareness: Another piece to the puzzle. *Studies in Second Language Acquisition, 21*, 511–556.

Russo, J. E., Johnson, E. J., & Stephens, D. L. (1989). The validity of verbal protocols. *Memory and Cognition, 17*, 759–769.

Sachs, R., & Polio, C. (2007). Learners' uses of two types of written feedback on a L2 writing revision task. *Studies in Second Language Acquisition, 29*, 67–100.

Sachs, R., & Suh, B. R. (2007). Textually enhanced recasts, learner awareness, and L2 outcomes in synchronous computer-mediated interaction. In A. Mackey (Ed.), *Conversational interaction in second language acquisition: A collection of empirical studies* (pp. 197–227). Oxford: Oxford University Press.

Sanz, C., Lin, H., Lado, B., Bowden, H. W., & Stafford, C. A. (2009). Concurrent verbalizations, pedagogical conditions, and reactivity: Two CALL studies. *Language Learning, 59*, 33–71.

Schmidt, R. (1990). The role of consciousness in second language learning. *Applied Linguistics, 11*, 129–158.

Schmidt, R. (1993). Awareness and second language acquisition. *Annual Review of Applied Linguistics, 13*, 206–226.

Schmidt, R. (1995). Consciousness and foreign language learning: A tutorial on the role of attention and awareness in learning. In R. Schmidt (Ed.), *Attention and awareness in foreign language learning* (pp. 1–63). Honolulu, HI: University of Hawai'i, National Foreign Language Resource Center.

Schooler, J. W., & Engstler-Schooler, T. Y. (1990). Verbal overshadowing of visual memories: Some things are better left unsaid. *Cognitive Psychology, 22*, 36–71.

Schooler, J. W., Ohlsson, S., & Brooks, K. (1993). Thoughts beyond words: When language overshadows insight. *Journal of Experimental Psychology: General, 122*, 166–183.

Short, E. J., Schatschneider, C., Cuddy, C. L., Evans, S. W., Dellick, D. M., & Basili, L. A. (1991). The effect of thinking aloud on the problem-solving performance of bright, average, learning disabled, and developmentally handicapped students. *Contemporary Educational Psychology, 16*, 139–153.

Siegler, R. S. (1989). Hazards of mental chronometry: An example from children's subtraction. *Journal of Educational Psychology, 81*, 497–506.

Sowder, L. (1974). The influence of verbalization of discovered numerical- or sorting-task generalizations on short-term retention in connection with the Hendrix hypothesis. *Journal for Research in Mathematics Education, 5*, 167–176.

Stanley, W. B., Mathews, R. C., Buss, R. R., & Kolter-Cope, S. (1989). Insight without awareness: On the interaction of verbalization, instruction, and practice in a stimulated process control task. *The Quarterly Journal of Experimental Psychology, 41*, 553–577.

Swain, M. (1998). Focus on form through conscious reflection. In C. Doughty & J. Williams (Eds.), *Focus on form in classroom second language acquisition* (pp. 64–81). Cambridge, UK: Cambridge University Press.

Swain, M. (2005). The output hypothesis: Theory and research. In E. Hinkel (Ed.), *Handbook of research in second language teaching and learning* (pp. 471–483). Mahwah: Lawrence Erlbaum Associates.

Swain, M., & Lapkin, S. (2002). Talking it through: Two French immersion learners' response to reformulation. *International Journal of Educational Research, 37*, 285–304.

Taguchi, N. (2008). Pragmatic comprehension in Japanese as a foreign language. *The Modern Language Journal, 92*, 558–576.

Tocalli-Beller, A., & Swain, M. (2007). Riddles and puns in the ESL classroom: Adults talk to learn. In A. Mackey (Ed.), *Conversational interaction in second language acquisition: A series of empirical studies* (pp. 143–167). Oxford: Oxford University Press.

Tsujimura, N. (2007). *An introduction to Japanese linguistics*. Malden, MA: Blackwell.

Wilson, T. D., & Schooler, J. W. (1991). Thinking too much: Introspection can reduce the quality of preferences and decisions. *Journal of Personality and Social Psychology*, 60, 181–92.

Yang, Y. F. (2006). Reading strategies or comprehension monitoring strategies? *Reading Psychology, 27*, 313–343.

Yoshida, M. (2008). Think-aloud protocols and type of reading activity: The issue of reactivity in L2 reading research. In M. Bowles, R. Foote, S. Perpinan, & R. Bhatt (Eds.), *Selected proceedings of the 2007 Second Language Research Forum* (pp. 199–209). Somerville, MA: Cascadilla Proceedings Project.

Yoshida, R. (2010). How do teachers and learners perceive corrective feedback in the Japanese language classroom? *The Modern Language Journal, 94*, 293–314.

NFLRC
monographs

The Effects of L2 Learner Proficiency on Depth of Processing, Levels of Awareness, and Intake

Anne M. Calderón
Georgetown University

Research probing deeper into Schmidt's (1990) noticing hypothesis has not only empirically supported his postulation of different levels of awareness but also reported that higher levels of awareness appear correlated with higher amounts of intake (e.g., Leow, 1997; Rosa & Leow, 2004; Rosa & O'Neill, 1999). While previous studies have reported positive effects of learner proficiency on intake (Leow, 1993, 1995), only a handful of researchers have reported on the concept of depth of processing (e.g., Gass, Svetics, & Lemelin, 2003; Qi & Lapkin, 2001; Shook, 1994), and there have been no definitive findings. Whether learner proficiency plays a role in depth of processing, level of awareness, and amount of intake clearly warrants further investigation. To this end, the current study investigated the relationships between learner proficiency, depth of processing, levels of awareness, and learners' intake of linguistic items contained in aural input. Participants were 24 L1 English learners of university-level first- and third-semester Spanish who were exposed to an aural passage in Spanish and then performed off-line concurrent verbal reports during a multiple-choice sentence completion immediate posttest. The verbal reports measured depth of processing and levels of awareness while the multiple-choice sentence completion posttest measured intake. Although results of a repeated measures ANOVA revealed that there were no significant main effects for proficiency, intermediate participants showed more awareness at both levels of awareness than did low proficiency participants, and the intermediate group also had significantly lower depth of processing. Furthermore, there were positive relationships in the low proficiency group between high depth of processing and not only both levels of awareness but also intake. In the intermediate group there were significant positive relationships between high depth of processing and both awareness at the level of noticing and intake. Results of the current study support Schmidt's postulation regarding the role of awareness and levels of awareness in L2 intake. Findings

Calderón, A. M. (2013). The effects of L2 learner proficiency on depth of processing, levels of awareness, and intake. In J. M. Bergsleithner, S. N. Frota, & J. K. Yoshioka (Eds.), *Noticing and second language acquisition: Studies in honor of Richard Schmidt* (pp. 103–121). Honolulu: University of Hawai'i, National Foreign Language Resource Center.

also suggest that depth of processing is facilitative at the intake stage of L2 Spanish development but that awareness is even more important. The roles that these two variables play seem to depend on learner proficiency.

Depth of processing, levels of awareness, and intake: Does learner proficiency make a difference?

There is an overall consensus in the fields of second language acquisition (SLA) and cognitive science that learners need to minimally pay attention to input before formal features may be learned (Schmidt, 2001; Tomlin & Villa, 1994). The generally accepted assumption regarding attention is that it is selective, limited, and essential for long-term memory storage (Broadbent, 1958; Deutsch & Deutsch, 1963; McLaughlin, 1987; Schmidt, 2001; Tomlin & Villa, 1994; Whittlesea & Dorken, 1993; Wickens, 1989). Within SLA, Schmidt's (1990, 1993, 1994, 1995, 2001) framework of attention in the L2 learning process represents the most common view in SLA: that without awareness, processing input beyond short-term memory cannot occur.

Theoretical background and empirical studies

Schmidt (1993) originally defines noticing as "the necessary and sufficient condition for the conversion of input into intake" (p. 209) and maintains that noticing can be operationalized as the availability for either a concurrent or a retrospective self-report. Likewise, his noticing hypothesis (Schmidt, 1990) proposes that attention controls access to awareness and is responsible for noticing. In his view, focal attention and awareness are isomorphic. However, Schmidt has withdrawn from his original postulation of noticing to one of "more noticing leads to more learning" (Schmidt, 1994, p. 129). Schmidt's noticing hypothesis posits two levels of awareness: awareness at the level of noticing and awareness at the level of understanding. While awareness at the level of noticing leads to mere intake, awareness at the level of understanding is a higher level and involves the ability to analyze, compare, and test hypotheses about input. Several researchers have reported empirical support for Schmidt's two levels of awareness and their effects on both intake and written production of target items in the input (e.g., Leow, 1997; Martínez-Fernández, 2008; Rosa & Leow, 2004; Rosa & O'Neill, 1999; Sachs & Suh, 2007). Leow, Johnson, and Zárate-Sández (2010) provide a review of awareness studies.

Schmidt's framework also specifically addresses the early stages of the learning process: he argues that "intake is that part of the input that the learner notices" (Schmidt, 1990, p. 139). In other words, something must be noticed for it to become intake.

Along with Schmidt's noticing hypothesis, Tomlin and Villa (1994) and Robinson (1995) also provide attentional frameworks that together serve as the cornerstone for a theoretical account of SLA. Tomlin and Villa (1994) propose that it is the attentional function of detection that is necessary for second language (L2) acquisition. A key component to their framework is the non-essential role of awareness at the level of detection. Robinson (1995) reconciles the differing views of Schmidt (1990) and Tomlin and Villa when he postulates that noticing includes detection plus rehearsal in short-term memory; a certain threshold must be reached before an activation can become a part of awareness. By placing noticing farther along the acquisitional processing timeline than detection, Robinson concurs with Schmidt that lack of awareness precludes learning.

Introspective methods and verbal reports

SLA research has incorporated introspective methods of data elicitation for at least three decades now (cf. Cohen, 1996, 1998; Ericsson & Simon, 1993; also see Faerch & Kasper, 1987). This use of introspective methods is premised on the assumption that a person can observe what takes place in their consciousness just as they can describe events in the external world (Gass & Mackey, 2000). Introspective methods include both online and off-line reporting: whereas the concurrent (online) stage of construction involves the encoding and accessing of incoming experimental information and includes verbal reports, the retrospective (off-line) stage of reconstruction involves the retrieval of stored knowledge after it has been initially processed and includes off-line verbal reports and oral interviews (Ericsson & Simon, 1984, 1993; Litman & Reber, 2005).

Verbal reports have become a standard research tool in the field of SLA: introspective comments have been used to explain learners' developmental changes in many attentional studies (Egi, 2007, 2008; Mackey, 2006; Rosa & Leow, 2004; Swain & Lapkin, 2002). However, the possible effects of both reactivity and veridicality must be taken into consideration (Bowles, 2010). While reactivity refers to the idea that the act of thinking aloud (providing a verbal report) might alter cognitive processes, veridicality questions whether the information in verbal reports accurately represents the thought process it is designed to capture. Bowles' meta-analysis showed that, overall, thinking aloud while performing a verbal task has only a small effect on post-task performance and mainly for metalinguistic verbal reports. Regarding veridicality, Ericsson and Simon's (1984) model predicts that off-line reports performed immediately after the experimental task, in contrast to delayed off-line reports, still allow the participant to have the necessary retrieval cues in short-term memory and retrospections and should still provide a close approximation to actual memory structures from the stages of encoding. Regardless, Ericsson and Simon do recommend that concurrent (online) verbal reports be used whenever possible; this has much to do with attempting to access information at two different times and the possibility of memory decay.

Depth of processing

Craik and Lockhart (1972) first made mention of the construct *levels of processing* in the field of cognitive psychology: they purported that remembered information depends not only on attending to it during its occurrence and rehearsing it afterward but also on how deeply it is processed. The concept of depth of processing has slowly been refined over the last several years (e.g., Baddeley & Wilson, 2002; Craik, 2002). Many of the frameworks that describe the initial stages of L2 learning also assign a role to depth of processing. In Tomlin and Villa's (1994) view, enhanced processing can result from awareness. Similarly, Schmidt's (2001) concept of detection is proposed to enable further processing of a stimulus at higher levels. Also, Gass (1988) argues that her concept of *level of analysis* affects intake: the level of analysis of the input that a learner reaches determines whether a particular instance of comprehended input will become intake. More recently, Craik (2002) relates depth of processing to elaboration and a high degree of consciousness. Table 1 provides a summary of studies that have addressed the notion of depth of processing in L2 development.

Table 1. Summary of studies investigating the concept of depth of processing

study	participants & proficiency	tasks	levels of processing	results
Craik & Tulving (1975)	between 12 and 36 in several L1 experiments	question asked to induce processing the word to one of three levels of analysis; visual word exposure; retention test	analysis of the word's physical structure (lower level of processing), phonemic level (medium), or semantic category (higher)	deeper level questions resulted in enhanced retention
Shook (1994)	125 1st and 2nd year L2 Spanish	2 reading passages, production and recognition assessments	no attention drawn, attention drawn, and attention drawn plus forming grammatical rules	drawing attention = more information gained; type of attention was not significant; only production depended on L2 experience
Qi & Lapkin (2001)	1 advanced L2 English learner, 1 low-intermediate L2 English learner	think-aloud while writing, compared draft with reformulation, and revising	noticing with/without understanding	higher quality and quantity of noticing for higher proficiency participant
Gass, Svetics, & Lemelin (2003)	34 L1 English learners in 1st, 2nd, or 3rd year Italian class	reading a story, written tasks	+/– focused attention groups: +focused attention group drew attention to target through underlining and instructions	except in syntax, learning occurred regardless; focused attention had greatest effect among lower proficiency
Leow, Hsieh, & Moreno (2008)	72 2nd semester L2 Spanish learners	read passage with think-aloud, multiple-choice comprehension test	circle target (level 1), verbal report of having attended to target (level 2), interpreting or translating target (level 3)	deeper processing did not negatively affect processing for meaning
Morgan-Short, Heil, Botero-Moriarty, & Ebert (2012)	308 3rd semester L2 Spanish learners	(same as Leow et al., 2008)	(same as Leow et al., 2008)	positive relationship between level of processing and comprehension

As seen in Table 1, the preliminary evidence suggests that depth of processing has a facilitative effect on L2 learning as measured by a variety of comprehension, retention, and production tasks. However, further research needs to examine this more closely. Morgan-Short, Heil, Botero-Moriarty, and Ebert (2012) reported a small but reliable positive relationship between level of processing and comprehension; results from Craik and Tulving's (1975) native language (L1) study on levels of processing and memory also showed enhanced retention with deeper levels of processing. Qi and Lapkin (2001) reported facilitative effects for what they called *quality of noticing* on written production. Findings from Shook (1994) show that higher *attentional level* resulted in more information gained. On the contrary, Gass et al. (2003) reported that except in the area of syntax, *learning* (as operationalized by performance on grammaticality judgment and translation tasks) occurred regardless of *focused attention*; they suggest that focused attention may be better used in more complex linguistic areas. Leow et al. (2008) reported that deeper processing did not positively or negatively affect processing for meaning.

The limited results of the influence of L2 proficiency on depth of processing are mixed. Qi and Lapkin (2001) reported that the quantity of noticing during the composing stage and the quality of noticing during the composing and reformulation stages increased with proficiency. They conclude that quality of noticing may be positively related to L2 proficiency. Nonetheless, Gass et al. (2003) reported that focused attention had a diminishing effect in the learning of three linguistic areas: it seemed to be greatest in the early periods of learning and the least during later stages.

Levels of awareness and intake

Numerous empirical studies employing online data elicitation procedures have documented the existence of distinct levels of awareness in L2 development and also their facilitative effect on L2 development (Leow, 1997, 2001; Martínez-Fernández, 2008; Rosa & Leow, 2004; Rosa & O'Neill, 1999; Sachs & Suh, 2007). Many of these studies have linked levels of awareness to intake: Leow (1997) and Rosa and O'Neill (1999) both found that awareness at the level of noticing and understanding resulted in significant increases in learners' ability to take in a targeted form or structure. Furthermore, awareness at the level of understanding has been shown to lead to significantly more intake (Leow, 1997, 2001; Rosa & O'Neill, 1999) when compared to awareness at the level of noticing. In addition, Leow and Rosa and O'Neill reported correlations between awareness at the level of understanding and the use of high-order skills such as hypothesis testing and rule formation. However, no study has investigated the role that learner L2 proficiency plays in levels of awareness.

In addition, intake has been linked to learner L2 proficiency; it has also been shown to be affected by levels of awareness. In a study of two different proficiency levels of Spanish learners, Leow (1993) hypothesized that learners exposed to simplified written input would take in significantly more linguistic items contained in the input than learners not exposed to simplified input. A total of 137 first- and fourth-semester undergraduate students of Spanish comprised the subject group; the former had not yet been formally exposed to either of the target linguistic forms (present subjunctive or present perfect), while the later already had been. Subjects completed a pretest three weeks prior to the study and then read one of four written passages varying in text simplification (+/- simplified) and target form (present perfect tense or present subjunctive). The multiple-choice sentence completion task was comprised of the same questions as the pretest and measured intake. Results indicated that participants with more language experience took in significantly more linguistic items from written input. Leow suggested that future studies should examine other variables that may affect L2 learners' intake and concluded that learners' relative performance may vary depending on several factors, one of which is tasks that demand different processing strategies. A similar study (Leow, 1995) reported the same findings for aural input; Leow concluded that these results indicate that regardless of mode, beginner and intermediate students may be regulated by distinct cognitive processes throughout the processing of input.

In summary, Schmidt's (1990) noticing hypothesis, purporting that conscious attention is required for learning, provides a solid theoretical foundation for many empirical studies examining variables such as depth of processing, levels of awareness, intake, and learner L2 proficiency. Several preliminary studies (Craik & Tulving, 1975; Morgan-Short et al., 2012; Qi & Lapkin, 2001; Shook, 1994) on the concept known as depth of processing have shown that it has a facilitative effect on L2 comprehension, retention, and production. Furthermore, previous studies have linked intake to levels of awareness (Leow, 1997, 2001; Rosa & Leow, 2004; Rosa & O'Neill, 1999) and also to L2 proficiency (Leow 1993, 1995). In addition, no decisive conclusions can be made regarding the effects of L2 proficiency on depth of processing.

These previous studies have limitations, however, that serve to direct future studies. Regarding depth of processing, one serious limitation of previous studies is the terminology. Several researchers have conflated the terms (level of) attention with (level of) processing. Shook (1994) referred to *attentional levels*, Gass et al. (2003) used the term *focused attention*, and Qi and Lapkin (2001) discussed *quality of noticing*. More recently, Leow et al. (2008) and Morgan-Short et al. (2012) used data from concurrent verbal reports to operationalize depth of processing according to three levels of processing. It appears that all of these researchers are actually referring to processing instead of mere attention. Specifically, one can pay attention to an item in the input, but this does not always translate to it being further processed. Instead of mere attention, it appears that the additional processing is what the previously mentioned studies all attempt to address. While attention is what controls access to awareness and is responsible for noticing (Schmidt, 1990), depth of processing can be envisioned as cognitive effort with the possibility for making a form/meaning connection at higher levels. In other words, depth of processing may or may not lead the learner to a correct hypothesis.

Critically, the only aforementioned study to present the experimental input in the aural mode was Leow (1995); all others presented in the written mode. Since Leow (1995) did not employ introspective reports, there is no published study in the field of SLA that uses verbal reports to investigate constructs such as depth of processing and awareness of certain features of aural input. This concept creates a conundrum, however, because it is inherently difficult, if not impossible, to provide a concurrent verbal report while attending to aural input. Therefore, although the preferred method to collect introspective data is through online verbal reports (Ericsson & Simon, 1987), it appears that the best alternative for collecting introspective data on aural input is through what can be termed *off-line concurrent verbal reports*, or verbal reports which are collected after the encoding stage (therefore, off-line), but still reflect concurrent verbalizations of the task used to provide the stimulus to the recall.

Overall, there is little doubt that attention plays an important role in L2 learning. Empirical research in the attentional strand of SLA maintains that variables such as depth of processing, levels of awareness, intake, and L2 proficiency are all important factors in the learning process. While empirical studies have addressed a combination of some of these variables to some extent, research still needs to better operationalize and define them in order to more clearly determine the role they play in the early stages of SLA.

Given the theoretical foundation of Schmidt's noticing hypothesis and the several accounts of attention in SLA that hint at the existence of levels of processing (Gass, 1988; Schmidt, 2001; Tomlin & Villa, 1994), in addition to the need for a more thorough empirical investigation of several variables influencing the early stages of learning, the current study aims to investigate the effects of L2 proficiency on depth of processing, levels of awareness, and intake. In particular, this study is guided by the following research questions:

What are the effects of level of L2 learner proficiency (low vs. intermediate) on learners' a) intake, b) levels of awareness, and c) depth of processing of a grammatical target form contained in aural input?

Are there any significant relationships between depth of processing and a) levels of awareness and b) intake?

Methodology

Participants

Participants were 24 college-level L2 Spanish learners enrolled in either second- or fourth-semester Spanish classes at a mid-Atlantic university. The original participant pool consisted of 69 learners, 45 of whom were eliminated due to the following reasons: (1) they indicated familiarity with the target form on the off-line concurrent reports and/or the debriefing questionnaire, (2) they did not complete both sessions of the experiment, (3) they scored higher than 25% on the pretest, (4) they did not think aloud, (5) they were not native speakers of English, and (6) they indicated more than two years' study of another Romance language on the debriefing questionnaire. This resulted in a carefully selected total of 24 participants: 18 in second-semester Spanish (*low proficiency*) and six in fourth-semester Spanish (*intermediate proficiency*). There were fewer fourth-semester participants because they were more likely to be eliminated from the study due to demonstrated or stated prior knowledge of the target structure.

Experimental text

The aural input passage used in this study was a modified version of the simplified text used in Leow (1993, 1995). The original version was taken from *Hombre de Mundo*, a monthly Mexican magazine, and the topic is the purchase of computers by business owners. The input passage was 304 words long and was modified to accommodate the target structure. The recording that participants heard lasted two minutes and twenty seconds.

Target structure

The past perfect subjunctive was the target structure and appears eight times throughout the aural input passage. There were several motivations behind the use of the past perfect subjunctive *-ese* form (*hubiese comparado*) as the target structure. First, it is introduced fairly late in the Spanish program, thus allowing almost all second-semester and some fourth-semester learners to claim no knowledge of this form. Second, it is a grammatically complex structure that encodes the subjunctive, an aspect that is not explicitly expressed in English. Third, the *hubiese* form of the past perfect subjunctive, although in free variation with the *hubiera* form, is not as frequently used as the *hubiera* form. This lowers the probability that any participant may have had prior exposure to it, especially at the earlier levels of the language curriculum.

Assessment tasks

The same multiple-choice sentence completion task was used for the pretest as for the posttest and was presented via computer. The pretest/posttest consisted of 16 sentence completion multiple-choice items, eight of which were distracters. The eight experimental questions were instances of exact phrases from the aural input in which the participant was given the beginning of a phrase and had to choose the correct completion of the phrase according to how it appeared in the aural input. There were four options for each item: one grammatically correct option and three grammatically incorrect options. Each item appeared on a different screen and had four options: one correct and three grammatically incorrect. Item randomization was not necessary given that there was a period of three weeks between the pretest and the posttest. The multiple-choice format was chosen because it facilitates various important characteristics: a single and final answer, the administration of an intake measure that is time-efficient, and the administration of the measure immediately after exposure (Leow, 1993). The following is one item from the multiple-choice sentence completion task:

Era fundamental

a. para el comprador haber determinado el objetivo de usar la computadora.
b. que el comprador hubiese determinado el objetivo de usar la computadora.
c. el comprador haber determinado el objetivo de usar la computadora.
d. que el comprador había determinado el objetivo de usar la computadora.

A post-exposure debriefing questionnaire assured that prior knowledge and/or recognition of the target grammatical form prior to participation in the study did not contaminate the data. It provided an example of the past perfect subjunctive and asked participants if they knew/recognized this form before doing the exercises. The data of any participant answering in the affirmative was excluded from the study.

A language background questionnaire was also administered to ensure that English was a first language of all participants and that no participant had more than two years of study of another Romance language.

Procedure

The experiment took place over two sessions separated by three weeks; both sessions took place in a computer laboratory. During the first session, participants completed the pretest multiple-choice sentence completion task in which they were asked to mark the response that best completed the sentence. The instructions explicitly stated that participants would not be able to backtrack to review prior answers or questions. Participants were informed that they would have 15 minutes to complete the pretest via computer. Time on task was recorded. Participants then completed a concurrent verbal report practice activity in which they had to do a mathematical problem while thinking their thoughts aloud.

The second session began with aural exposure to the input passage. Participants used headphones to listen once to the recording. Immediately following the experimental task, they were instructed to begin recording themselves using the computer and to think their thoughts aloud. They completed the post-test multiple-choice sentence completion task on the computer; time on task was again recorded. The participants then answered the debriefing questionnaire and the language background questionnaire, also via computer.

Operationalizations and codings

Levels of awareness

Considering that the field of cognitive psychology often links awareness with the ability to verbally report a subjective experience (e.g., Allport, 1988; Carr & Curran, 1994; Leow, 1997; Schmidt, 2001; Tomlin & Villa, 1994), it is not surprising that Schmidt (2001) asserted that the most definitive evidence of noticing is a verbal report. This manner of documenting awareness is an effective way to address the learner's online processing. However, due to the inherent difficulty of providing an online, concurrent verbal report while listening to input, the current study operationalized awareness with the strongest alternative, the off-line concurrent verbal report. These reports were coded for two levels of awareness, as guided by Schmidt's noticing hypothesis (1990). While awareness at the level of noticing accounts for intake and item learning, awareness at the level of understanding is characterized by restructuring and system learning.

Table 2. Descriptors of levels of awareness

	noticing	**understanding**
Schmidt's (1990) description	for intake and item learning	restructuring and system learning, ability to analyze, compare, and test hypotheses
current study's descriptors	verbalize that s/he was choosing *hubiese* as an answer or make a direct reference to *hubiese* (not just read it), verbalize that they don't know what *hubiese* means	verbalize a (correct) rule about the subjunctive or say that a certain phrase requires the subjunctive
examples	"It was fundamental that the buyer had determined objectively that the computer… I'll go with one of the *que*'s. I don't remember what *había* is. it's imperfect. So I guess I'll go with *hubiese*." "Ok it was possible for someone to desire…it was possible that something has desired to do… I don't know what that means, *hubiese*."	"I think *era posible* would take past subjunctive um um so I'm gonna do D."

Depth of processing

Depth of processing was operationalized as instances of an attempt to make form-meaning connections found in the off-line concurrent verbal reports. Since this concept refers to the depth to which the learner goes to make a form-meaning connection, any instance in the off-line concurrent verbal reports documenting an attempted connection was coded as either low or high depth of processing. As shown in Table 3, low depth of processing included verbalizations of participants saying they did not know what the target structure meant, making non-specific reference to the target structure and translating the trigger[1] or the target[2]. High depth of processing included descriptors such as hypothesis formation and

1 Given that the target form (past perfect subjunctive) is part of a subordinate clause headed by a trigger phrase (e.g., *Era importante*) and the conjunction *que*, references to this trigger phrase and conjunction were also considered as factors in making form-meaning connections and thus were included in some descriptors in Table 3.

2 Although translation of a target structure would normally be considered having achieved a high level of processing because it shows that the form-meaning connection is complete, this is not the case in the current study. Given that the subjunctive is not explicitly expressed in English, the past perfect subjunctive and the pluperfect (past perfect) both translate to the same English verb. Therefore, the ability to translate the target structure in the current study does not demonstrate the same complete form-meaning connection that it typically would for other target structures, and therefore translation of the target is considered a low level of processing in this study.

confirmation, referring back to the text or to grammar/verbal tense, verbalizing the answer, or saying that the answer made sense.

Table 3. Descriptors of depth of processing

low level	high level
translating trigger phrase	forming/confirming a (correct) hypothesis
referring back to text (general)	referring back to specific target in text
translating target to English (without expressing mode)	referring to grammar or tense
looking for differences between current and past items	saying they choose target as an option
saying they don't know what it means	saying correct answer makes sense
general reference to *que*	
saying target is an option	
expressing a feeling or intuition	
wondering what the difference is between target items	

The current study used two measures of depth of processing: low depth of processing and high depth of processing.

Intake

In operationalizing intake, the present study took into consideration Leow's (1993) definition of intake as "an intermediate process between the exposure to input and actual language acquisition...that part of the input that has been attended to by second language learners while processing the input" (p. 334). Instead of measuring intake via a production task, which, according to Chaudron (1985), can make it difficult to determine what was truly taken in, the current study used a four-option multiple-choice recognition task. Following Leow (1993, 1995, 1997) and Rosa and O'Neill (1999), the multiple-choice recognition task avoided the complications of production tasks by only requiring the learner to choose the sentence completion option that they heard in the input. In this way, this task tested only what they had taken in from the input.

Scoring and coding

Data was drawn from the pre- and post-tests in addition to the off-line concurrent verbal reports. The pre- and post-tests were scored by the computer; one point was assigned for each correct answer and zero points for each incorrect answer for a possible of eight points per test. These scores served as the data for the intake variable. Table 4 shows the descriptive statistics for intake.

Table 4. Descriptive statistics for intake by proficiency level

	pretest M *(SD)*	posttest M *(SD)*	*n*
low proficiency	.39 (.85)	1.17 (2.07)	18
intermediate proficiency	1.17 (1.48)	2.83 (2.71)	6

The off-line concurrent verbal reports were coded separately for depth of processing and levels of awareness. One point was awarded per instance of each of the two levels of depth of processing on critical items. The same scoring procedure was used for the two levels of awareness.

The researcher transcribed and coded all off-line concurrent verbal protocols. A colleague coded 10% of the protocols; interrater reliability was 96%.

Results

An independent-samples *t*-test run on the pretest scores showed that there were no existing differences between the low proficiency group (M=.39, SD=.85) and the intermediate proficiency group (M=1.17, SD=1.48) at the time of the pretest: $t(22)=-1.61$, $p=.12$.

To measure the effects of level of L2 learner proficiency on their intake of the grammatical target form contained in aural input, the intake scores from the multiple-choice recognition pretest and posttest were submitted to a 2x2 repeated measures ANOVA. Learner Proficiency level was the between-group factor (low proficiency vs. intermediate proficiency) and Time was the within-subject factor (pretest vs. posttest). All analyses were run on the Statistical Package for the Social Sciences (SPSS, Version 19), and the alpha value was set at .05 for statistical significance.

As seen in Table 5, repeated measures ANOVA results revealed no significant main effect for Proficiency (F [1, 22]=3.73, p=.07), a significant main effect for Time (F [1, 22]=5.557, p=.03), and no significant interaction between Proficiency and Time (F [1, 22]=.74, p=.40). This indicates that participants scored significantly higher on the multiple-choice recognition posttest than on the multiple-choice recognition pretest (.58 vs. 1.58, p=.03). However, the lack of interaction between Proficiency and Time reveals that the difference between the multiple-choice recognition pretest and posttest scores for the low proficiency group was not significantly different from the scores for the intermediate proficiency group. In other words, although participants performed significantly better on the posttest than on the pretest, the higher proficiency group did not perform significantly better than the lower proficiency group across time. The effect size observed was large for Time ($\eta 2$=.20) but small for the interaction between Time and Proficiency ($\eta 2$=.03). The power also followed the same pattern: medium for Time (d=.62) and low for the interaction (d=.13).

Table 5. Repeated measures analysis of variance for main effects and interaction

source of variation	*df*	F	*p*	partial eta squared	observed power
Proficiency	1	3.73	.07	.15	.46
Time	1	5.56	.03	.20	.62
Proficiency x Time	1	.74	.40	.03	.13
error	22				

The effects of L2 learners' proficiency on depth of processing and levels of awareness of the grammatical target form were determined by submitting the data from the two depth of processing measures (low depth of processing vs. high depth of processing) and the two levels of awareness measures (awareness at the level of noticing and awareness at the level of understanding) to a one-way ANOVA with one between-subject factor (proficiency). As seen in Table 6, the effect for Proficiency was significant (F [1, 22]=2.75, p=.05). This means that there was a significant difference in mean scores between the two proficiency levels. In addition, awareness at both the level of noticing and the level of understanding were significant (F [1, 22]=9.14, p=.01 and F [1, 22]=.80, p=.01, respectively). In addition, low depth of processing was also significant (F [1, 22]=5.60, p=.03). In other words, proficiency significantly affected awareness at the level of noticing, awareness at the level of understanding, and low depth of processing. More specifically, mean scores (0.67, SD=1.08, *p*=.01 for low proficiency and 2.83, SD=2.48, *p*=.01 for intermediate proficiency) reveal that intermediate participants showed more instances of awareness at the level of noticing than did participants of low proficiency. Mean scores further show that intermediate participants demonstrated more instances of awareness at the level of understanding than did participants of low proficiency (0.33, SD=.69, *p*=.01 for low proficiency and 2.33, SD=2.88, *p*=.01 for intermediate proficiency). The mean scores (6.89, SD=3.94, *p*=.03 for low proficiency and 2.67, SD=3.20, *p*=.03 for intermediate proficiency) also demonstrate that participants of intermediate proficiency had significantly fewer instances of low depth of processing than did participants of low proficiency. Regarding effect size, 29% of the variability in scores for awareness at the level of noticing, 27% of the variability in scores for awareness at the level of understanding, and 20% of the variability in scores for low depth of processing were explained with knowledge of group membership on the independent variable. The power was .82 for awareness at the level of noticing, .77 for awareness at the level of understanding, and .62 for low depth of processing.

Table 6. ANOVA between-subject effects

dependent variable	*df*	F	*p*	*n*2	observed power
intake	1	2.51	.13	.10	.33
awareness					
noticing	1	9.14	.01	.29	.82
understanding	1	8.03	.01	.27	.77
depth of processing					
low level	1	5.60	.03	.20	.62
high level	1	2.68	.12	.11	.35
error	22				

In order to address the second research question, or whether there are any significant relationships between depth of processing at either a low or intermediate proficiency and a) levels of awareness and b) intake, raw scores from the multiple-choice recognition posttest (intake) and data from the two depth of processing measures and the two levels of awareness measures were submitted to a Pearson correlation analysis. Means are displayed in Table 7.

Table 7. Descriptive statistics for depth of processing, levels of awareness, and intake

	low proficiency[a]	intermediate proficiency[b]
depth of processing		
low	6.89 (3.94)	2.67 (3.20)
high	2.39 (2.83)	4.83 (4.12)
levels of awareness		
noticing	.67 (1.08)	2.83 (2.48)
understanding	.33 (.69)	2.33 (2.88)
intake	1.17 (2.07)	2.83 (2.71)

[a] n=18

[b] n=6

This analysis revealed a positive correlation in both the low and the intermediate proficiency groups between awareness at the level of noticing and high depth of processing (r=.72, p=.00; shared variance=52% and r=.86, p=.03; shared variance=74%, respectively). In other words, as awareness at the level of noticing increased in the low and intermediate proficiency groups, so did high depth of processing. There was also a positive correlation in the low proficiency group between high depth of processing and awareness at the level of understanding (r=.75, p=.00), showing that as high depth of processing increased, so did awareness at the level of understanding. High depth of processing accounted for 55% of the variance in awareness at the level of understanding.

Regarding intake, there were significant, positive correlations between high depth of processing and intake for both low and intermediate proficiency (r=.77, p=.00 and r=.96, p=.00, respectively), indicating that as intake as measured on the multiple-choice recognition test increased, so did high depth of processing for both proficiency levels. High depth of processing accounted for 60% of the variance in intake at the low proficiency level and 92% of the variance at the intermediate proficiency level. All correlations are displayed in Table 8.

Table 8. Correlations between depth of processing, levels of awareness, and intake

	depth of processing	
	low	**high**
	low proficiency[a]	
levels of awareness		
noticing	.21	.72**
understanding	.02	.75**
intake	.13	.77**
	intermediate proficiency[b]	
levels of awareness		
noticing	–.54	.86*
understanding	–.68	.78
intake	–.40	.96**

*p<.05

**p<.01

a n=18

b n=6

In order to show that proficiency did not play a significant role on time spent on the multiple-choice recognition pretest and posttest, time on each test was submitted to a one-way ANOVA. Results showed that the amount of time spent on each test did not differ significantly according to proficiency (p=.62 for pretest, p=.22 for posttest).

Discussion

The first research question aimed to investigate the effects of level of L2 proficiency on depth of processing, levels of awareness, and intake. Results showed that level of proficiency significantly affected low depth of processing and awareness at both the levels of noticing and understanding. Intake and the other measures of depth of processing were not significantly affected by L2 learner proficiency level. Regarding depth of processing, intermediate proficiency learners most likely do not need to process as deeply as low proficiency learners to get the same results. Only partial form-meaning connections in intermediate learners may have the same effect as complete form-meaning connections in low proficiency learners. Results also relate to findings from Gass et al. (2003) that focused attention had the greatest effect among lower proficiency L2 learners in three areas of language (lexicon, syntax, morphosyntax); the current study found more instances of low depth of processing in the low proficiency group than in the intermediate proficiency group. Mirroring the results of the current study, Gass et al. concluded that focused attention seems to take a diminished role at the higher proficiency level because these learners can figure out any challenges they come across by using their internal resources.

In addition, given that participants of intermediate proficiency showed more instances of awareness at both levels than did participants of low proficiency, it is possible that intermediate learners have more resources available to expend on awareness at both lower and higher levels. Likewise, the intermediate participants may be able to tackle more complex grammatical structures like the past perfect subjunctive because they are not held up trying to make sense of basic vocabulary and grammatical structure; it is thus easier for them to achieve awareness at the level of understanding. Low proficiency learners, on the other hand, may be too involved in figuring out basic grammar and simple vocabulary in the input to achieve higher levels of awareness of more complex grammar items.

However, while participants of intermediate proficiency did demonstrate superior awareness at the level of understanding, the non-significant difference in performance regarding intake also indicates that they might not have been cognitively ready to take in the target grammatical structure given its complexity together with the aural mode in which it was delivered. There might have been no main effect for proficiency because of the difficulty of the input: not only was the passage presented in the aural mode but also the grammatical target was complex. Both of these factors may have proved challenging for both proficiency levels. This explanation appears to be plausible if one were to compare these results with those reported in Leow (2005), who also provided the L2 input in the aural mode. Unlike the present study, in Leow's study the higher proficiency group (also intermediate) demonstrated superior prior knowledge on the pretest when compared to the lower proficiency group and maintained this superior performance on the posttest. If one were to consider also his target structure, which was the Spanish present and perfect subjunctive, arguably less complex than the current one employed in this study, namely, the imperfect subjunctive, then the non-significant difference in performance between the two levels of proficiency after only a single exposure of two minutes and twenty seconds to the experimental passage may account for this result.

The significantly fewer instances of low depth of processing in the intermediate proficiency group serve to expand the knowledge base regarding this new strand in SLA. Qi and Lapkin (2001) concluded that "while promoting noticing in a reformulation task may be important, improving the quality of the noticing may be even more important" (p. 294). While the current study only addressed depth of processing as a dependent variable and therefore cannot make definitive statements regarding its effects on intake, it can further Qi and Lapkin's conclusion by purporting that depth of processing at the intermediate proficiency level does not appear to be as important in an intake task as attaining awareness at the level of understanding. It seems plausible that once awareness at the level of understanding is achieved, depth of processing logically decreases. Although the current study does not address this facet of the data, it is interesting to note the case of a participant of intermediate proficiency. Within an off-line concurrent verbal report of 588 words, the participant achieved awareness at the level of understanding after 297 words. Before that point the participant had 11 instances of depth of processing, nine of which were low and two of which were high. After achieving awareness at the level of understanding, the participant showed only three more instances of depth of processing, all of which were at a low level. This hints that once awareness at the level of understanding is reached, high levels of depth of processing are not only unnecessary but also infrequent.

The second research question sought to address whether there were any significant relationships between depth of processing at either a low or intermediate proficiency and a) levels of awareness and b) intake. Regarding levels of awareness, results showed significant correlations in the low proficiency group between high depth of processing and both awareness at the level of noticing and the level of understanding. In the intermediate group there was a significant positive relationship between high depth of processing and awareness at the level of noticing. Furthermore, there were significant positive relationships between high depth of processing and intake at both proficiency levels.

First, the correlations at low proficiency highlight the importance of high depth of processing in learners of low proficiency. The low proficiency group seemed to depend heavily on high depth of processing to make meaning from the aural passage. Overall, it is plausible that low proficiency learners need to obtain high depth of processing to be able to make up for the high levels of awareness that they do not attain because they do not have the resources to focus on more complex grammar. These high levels of awareness have been found to be beneficial in L2 development (Leow, 1997, 2001; Martínez-Fernández, 2008; Rosa & Leow, 2004, Rosa & O'Neill, 1999; Sachs & Suh, 2007). Given the previously discussed finding that intermediate participants showed more instances of awareness at the level of understanding than did participants of low proficiency, the intermediate participants may be able to achieve higher levels of awareness with lower levels of processing. Considering the positive correlation between high depth of processing and awareness at the level of noticing, it seems that intermediate proficiency participants reaching high depth of processing do not necessarily also need to achieve awareness at the level of understanding. However, the very strong correlations between high depth of processing and intake at the intermediate level suggests that when intermediate learners do in fact attain high depth of processing, it is extremely effective in facilitating better intake. This strong correlation is not surprising considering Gass' (1988) *levels of analysis* proposal, purporting that the level of analysis of the input that a learner reaches determines whether a particular instance of comprehended input will become intake. In addition, given that Morgan-Short et al. (2012) found a positive relationship between level of processing and comprehension, it then seems logical that higher depth of processing should also be related to intake.

Limitations of the study and future research

Before making any definitive conclusions regarding the role of proficiency in depth of processing, levels of awareness, and intake, several methodological issues need to be resolved. First, although there was a total of 24 participants, the proficiency groups were not equally divided due to so many of the intermediate students already claiming knowledge of the target structure. Likewise, using a Pearson correlation analysis on small group numbers is problematic, and results need to be interpreted with caution. An increased number of participants could remedy this. Furthermore, the assumption of equal variance for the parametric statistics was less desired. In addition, there was no test of comprehension of the aural passage; future studies should include a comprehension test after the experimental exposure to ensure that participants were listening for meaning. Claims regarding depth of processing that occurred in the presence of demonstrated comprehension would be stronger if it could be supported by a comprehension score. Another limitation involves the question of the participants' developmental readiness to learn the past perfect subjunctive. Last of all, the results of the current study need to be interpreted with caution due to the inability to use online concurrent verbal reports with aural input. The consecutive nature of the off-line concurrent verbal reports left little time in between the experimental aural input presentation and the subsequent verbal report, but regardless, this method is different than that used in many of the previous studies reported earlier, and therefore, results may not be fully transferable.

Future studies need to isolate depth of processing as an independent variable in order to be able to determine the effects it has on other variables. Furthermore, given the richness of data available from verbal reports, a logical extension of the current study would examine the concept of cognitive effort, or the effort that learners put forth in making form-meaning connections, regardless of whether the connection is correct. In addition, future studies should attempt to create more fine-tuned distinctions between the descriptors of depth of processing and levels of awareness.

Conclusion

The present study was designed to address the issues of L2 learner proficiency, levels of awareness, intake, and the relatively unexplored concept of depth of processing within Schmidt's (1990, 1993, 1994, 1995) noticing hypothesis postulated for L2 learning. By using off-line concurrent verbal reports and a multiple-choice recognition test, the dependent variables of depth of processing, levels of awareness, and intake were able to be investigated as they relate to L2 development.

Depth of processing appears to play a facilitative role at the intake stage of L2 Spanish learning of the past perfect subjunctive when the input is aural; however, the results highlight the ultimate importance of awareness. The roles that these two variables play seem to depend on learner proficiency. More specifically, although the low and intermediate proficiency participants all demonstrated depth of processing, they did so to varying degrees. Intermediate participants showed more instances of awareness at the levels of noticing and understanding than did participants of low proficiency, and the intermediate proficiency group also had significantly fewer instances of low depth of processing than did participants of low proficiency. Furthermore, in the low proficiency group, there were significant positive relationships between high depth of processing and not only both levels of awareness but also intake; in the intermediate proficiency group, there were significant positive relationships between high level of processing and intake, in addition to high level of processing and awareness at the level of noticing. These findings suggest that low proficiency learners may be too involved in figuring out basic grammar and simple vocabulary in the input to be able to often achieve higher levels of awareness of more complex grammar items. However, the correlations at low proficiency highlight the importance of high depth of processing in learners of low proficiency. Intermediate learners, on the other hand, may have more resources to tackle more complex grammar and thus can employ higher levels of awareness. Because they attain higher levels of awareness more than low proficiency learners, there is not as much of a need for them to also employ high depth of processing. When they do attain a high depth of processing, however, it appears to provide a boost in regards to what they are able to take in. Consequently, the current study ultimately provides support for the beneficial role that awareness plays in Schmidt's noticing hypothesis while underscoring the potential role depth of processing may play alongside the role of awareness during the input-to-intake phase of the L2 learning process.

References

Allport, A. (1988). What concept of consciousness? In A. J. Marcel & E. Bisiach (Eds.), *Consciousness in contemporary science* (pp. 159–182). London: Clarendon Press.

Baddeley, A. D., & Wilson, B. A. (2002). Prose recall and amnesia: Implications for the structure of working memory. *Neuropsychologia, 40*, 1737–1743.

Bowles, M. A. (2010). *The think-aloud controversy in language acquisition research*. New York: Routledge.

Broadbent, D. (1958). *Perception and communication*. New York: Academic Press.

Carr, T., & Curran, T. (1994). Cognitive factors in learning about structured sequences: Applications to syntax. *Studies in Second Language Acquisition, 16*, 205–230.

Chaudron, C. (1985). Comprehension, comprehensibility, and learning in the second language classroom. *Studies in Second Language Acquisition, 7*, 216–232.

Cohen, A. (1996). Verbal reports as a source of insights into second language learner strategies. *Applied Language Learning, 7*, 5–24.

Cohen, A. (1998). *Strategies in learning and using a second language*. London: Longman.

Craik, F. I. M. (2002). Levels of processing: Past, present, and future? *Memory, 10*, 305–318.

Craik, F. I. M., & Lockhart, R. S. (1972). Levels of processing: A framework for memory research. *Journal of Verbal Learning and Verbal Behavior, 11*, 671–684.

Craik, F. I. M., & Tulving, E. (1975). Depth of processing and the retention of words in episodic memory. *Journal of Experimental Psychology: General, 104*, 268–294.

Deutsch, J. A., & Deutsch, D. (1963). Attention: Some theoretical considerations. *Psychological Review, 70*, 80–90.

Egi, T. (2007). Recasts, learners' interpretations, and L2 development. In A. Mackey (Ed.) *Conversational interaction in second language acquisition: A series of empirical studies* (pp. 249–267). Oxford: Oxford University Press.

Egi, T. (2008). Investigating stimulated recall as a cognitive measure: Reactivity and verbal reports in SLA research methodology. *Language Awareness, 17*, 212–228.

Ericsson, K., & Simon, H. (1984). *Protocol analysis*. Cambridge, MA: MIT Press.

Ericsson, K., & Simon, H. (1993). *Protocol analysis: Verbal reports as data* (2nd ed.). Cambridge, MA: MIT Press.

Faerch, C., & Kasper, G. (1987). From product to process: Introspective methods in second language research. In C. Faerch & G. Kasper (Eds.), *Introspection in second language research* (pp. 5–23). Clevedon: Multilingual Matters.

Gass. S. M. (1988). Integrating research areas: A framework for second language studies. *Applied Linguistics, 9*, 198–217.

Gass, S. M., & Mackey, A. (2000). *Stimulated recall methodology in second language research*. Mahwah, NJ: Lawrence Erlbaum Associates.

Gass, S., Svetics, I., & Lemelin, S. (2003). Differential effects of attention. *Language Learning, 53*, 497–545.

Leow, R. P. (1993). To simplify or not to simplify: A look at intake. *Studies in Second Language Acquisition, 15*, 333–355.

Leow, R. P. (1995). Modality and intake in second language acquisition. *Studies in Second Language Acquisition, 17,* 79–89.

Leow, R. P. (1997). Attention, awareness, and foreign language behavior. *Language Learning, 47,* 467–505.

Leow, R. P. (2001). Attention, awareness, and foreign language behavior. *Language Learning, 51,* Issue Supplement s1,113–155.

Leow, R. P., Hsieh, H., & Moreno, N. (2008). Attention to form and meaning revisited. *Language Learning, 58,* 665–695.

Leow, R. P., Johnson, E., & Zárate-Sández, G. (2010). Getting a grip on the slippery construct of awareness: Toward a finer-grained methodological perspective. In C. Sanz & R. Leow (Eds.), *Implicit and explicit conditions, processes, and knowledge in SLA and bilingualism* (pp. 61–72). Washington, DC: Georgetown University Press.

Litman, L., & Reber, A. S. (2005). Implicit cognition and thought. In K. J. Holyoak & R. G. Morrison (Eds.), *The Cambridge handbook of thinking and reasoning* (pp. 431–453). New York: Cambridge University Press.

Mackey, A. (2006). Feedback, noticing, and instructed second language learning. *Applied Linguistics, 27,* 405–430.

Martínez-Fernández, A. (2008). Revisiting the involvement load hypothesis: Awareness, type of task, and type of item. In M. Bowles, R. Foote, S. Perpiñán, & B. Rakesh (Eds.), *Selected proceedings of the 2007 Second Language Research Forum* (pp. 210–228). Somerville, MA: Cascadilla Proceedings Press.

McLaughlin, B. (1987). *Theories of second language learning.* London: Edward Arnold.

Morgan-Short, K., Heil, J., Botero-Moriarty, A., & Ebert, S. (2012). Allocation of attention to second language form and meaning: Issues of think alouds and depth of processing. *Studies in Second Language Acquisition, 34,* 659–685.

Qi, D., & Lapkin, S. (2001). Exploring the role of noticing in a three-stage second language writing task. *Journal of Second Language Writing, 10,* 277–303.

Robinson, P. (1995). Attention, memory, and the 'noticing' hypothesis. *Language Learning, 45,* 283–331.

Rosa, E., & Leow, R. P. (2004). Awareness, different learning conditions, and L2 development. *Applied Psycholinguistics, 25,* 269–292.

Rosa, E., & O'Neill, M. D. (1999). Explicitness, intake, and the issue of awareness. *Studies in Second Language Acquisition, 21,* 511–556.

Sachs, R., & Suh, B.-R. (2007). Textually enhanced recasts, learner awareness, and L2 outcomes in synchronous computer-mediated interactions. In A. Mackey (Ed.), *Conversational interaction in second language acquisition: A series of empirical studies* (pp. 197–227). Oxford: Oxford University Press.

Schmidt, R. W. (1990). The role of consciousness in second language learning. *Applied Linguistics, 2,* 24–52.

Schmidt, R. (1993). Awareness and second language acquisition. *Annual Review of Applied Linguistics, 13,* 206–226.

Schmidt, R. W. (1994). Deconstructing consciousness in search of useful definitions for applied linguistics. *AILA Review, 11,* 11–26.

Schmidt, R. (1995). Consciousness and foreign language learning: A tutorial on the role of attention and awareness in learning. In R. Schmidt (Ed.), *Attention and awareness in foreign language learning* (pp. 1–63). Honolulu, HI: University of Hawai'i, National Foreign Language Resource Center.

Schmidt, R. (2001). Attention. In P. Robinson (Ed.), *Cognition and second language instruction* (pp. 3–32). Cambridge: Cambridge University Press.

Shook, J. D. (1994). FL/L2 reading, grammatical information, and the input to intake phenomenon. *Applied Language Learning, 5,* 57–93.

Swain, M., & Lapkin, S. (2002). Talking it through: Two French immersion learners' response to reformulation. *International Journal of Educational Research, 37,* 285–304.

Tomlin, R. S., & Villa, V. (1994). Attention in cognitive science and second language acquisition. *Studies in Second Language Acquisition, 16,* 183–203.

Whittlesea, B. W., & Dorken, M. D. (1993). Incidentally, things in general are particularly determined: An episodic-processing account of implicit learning. *Journal of Experimental Psychology: General, 122,* 227–248.

Wickens, C. D. (1989). Attention and skilled performance. In D. H. Holding (Ed.), *Human skills* (pp. 71–105). New York: John Wiley.

NFLRC
monographs

The Effects of Aural Input Enhancement on L2 Acquisition

Minyoung Cho
The University of Hawai'i at Mānoa

Hayo Reinders
Anaheim University

Input enhancement involves attempts to direct the learner's attention to specific linguistic forms in target language input (Sharwood Smith, 1993). One way to do this is by manipulating the input in order to attract learners' attention to the target feature, for example, by underlining or bolding it or by artificially increasing its frequency in the input (an input flood). A number of studies have investigated the effects of enriched input (e.g., Jourdenais, Ota, Stauffer, Boyson, & Doughty, 1995; Reinders & Ellis, 2009; Trahey & White, 1993; White, 1998). Although there is some evidence that enriched input can affect L2 acquisition of certain grammatical features, the results are not conclusive. Furthermore, previous studies have been limited to textual input enrichment. In this chapter we investigated the effects of aural input enhancement, a type of input enhancement that to the best of our knowledge has not been reported on before. Participants in the study were given an audiobook to listen to outside of class in which passive structures had been manipulated by 1) artificially increasing the volume slightly of the target items or by 2) slowing down the speed with which the target items were read out. A control group listened to the audiobooks in their original form. The repeated-measures ANOVA analysis showed no significant effect for the manipulated input on acquiring the target form. We discuss some possible reasons for this finding.

Introduction

There now exists a considerable body of research into the effects of different types of focus on form (FoF) or attempts to direct learners' attention to form in an otherwise meaning-oriented context (see Ellis, 2009, for an overview). A distinction can be made between more or less obtrusive types of FoF; an example of the former would be the use of consciousness-

Cho, M., & Reinders, H. (2013). The effects of aural input enhancement on L2 acquisition. In J. M. Bergsleithner, S. N. Frota, & J. K. Yoshioka (Eds.), Noticing and second language acquisition: Studies in honor of Richard Schmidt (pp. 123–138). Honolulu: University of Hawai'i, National Foreign Language Resource Center.

raising (Fotos & Ellis, 1991) or input processing (VanPatten, 1996). Unobtrusive FoF includes the use of positive input enhancement as attempts to manipulate the input and direct the learner's attention to a specific linguistic form (Sharwood Smith, 1993). This can be done, for example, by underlining or bolding the target form or by artificially increasing its frequency in the input (an *input flood*). A number of studies have investigated the effects of this so-called enriched input on different aspects of language learning (Jourdenais, Ota, Stauffer, Boyson, & Doughty, 1995; Reinders & Ellis, 2009; Trahey & White, 1993; White, 1998). Although there is some evidence that enriched input can affect L2 acquisition of certain grammatical features, the results are not conclusive. In addition, previous studies have been limited to textual input enrichment, and no studies exist that we are aware of that have investigated aural manipulation. In this chapter we report on the results of a study that adopted aural input enhancement in an extensive listening activity. Participants in the study listened to an audiobook that was artificially enhanced in order to attract their attention to the target structure of the study.

Effects of input enhancement

Input enhancement

The proliferation of input enhancement research reflects the recognition of the crucial role of attention in SLA. It is clear that learners do not make use of all the input that they are exposed to, and it has been widely argued that attention is necessary for L2 learning (Leow, 1997, 1999, 2001; Robinson, 1995; Schmidt, 1990, 1993, 1994, 1995; Sharwood Smith, 1991, 1993; Tomlin & Villa, 1994) or at least that "There is no doubt that attended learning is far superior, and for all practical purposes, attention is necessary for all aspects of L2 learning" (Schmidt, 2001, p. 3). As attention can be externally manipulated (Schmidt, 1990), a number of studies have investigated ways of drawing learners' attention to formal aspects of the input in otherwise meaning-oriented activities, a technique referred to as *focus on form*. The importance of external manipulation lies in the assumption that L2 learners, according to VanPatten's (1996) input processing hypothesis, tend to prioritize meaning over form in the input. Formal aspects of the input are only processed insofar as they are crucial for understanding meaning and insofar as the learner has the cognitive resources available to pay attention to them. Therefore, without intentional attention to linguistic form, it is less likely that learners will attend to or use a particular linguistic form in the input for learning. As a result, a range of external attention-drawing techniques have been proposed, including explicit rule presentation, input flooding, and—the focus of this study—input enhancement.

Input enhancement involves the manipulation of input salience, with an attempt to direct learners' attention to a specific linguistic form in the input (Sharwood Smith, 1991, 1993). Salience refers to the ease with which learners can perceive given input. Salience of input is determined by various learner-internal, structural, and external factors. For example, learners' interlanguage development (Spada & Lightbown, 1999), inherent features in linguistic structure such as communicative value (Dulay & Burt, 1978), and external manipulation may alter the degree of salience of certain features in the input. Although the sources of input salience vary, it is of course learners themselves who must further process the input for learning (Schmidt, 1990). For this reason many studies of input enhancement have investigated whether input enhancement is effective in drawing learners' attention to form and its effect on subsequent acquisition of that form. Different external manipulations have been incorporated to increase the salience of input, including manipulation of frequency (input flood), visual salience (typographical or textual manipulation), and corrective feedback in discourse (e.g., repetition or recast).

According to Sharwood Smith (1993), input enhancement can be categorized as either positive or negative. Positive enhancement emphasises the correct form, such as through input flood and input enhancement, whereas negative enhancement incorporates the indication of errors in, for example, learners' production that can be enhanced by means of explicit instruction and/or corrective feedback. Both enhancement types are intended to trigger changes in input processing mechanisms of salient forms, but in this chapter we are concerned only with positive input enhancement. Examples of positive enhancement include manipulating textual or typographical aspects of the text (e.g., bolding, underlining, italicising, or changing the font type or size), visual enhancement (e.g., pictures), and technological enhancement (e.g., using a combination of keystrokes to type diacritics).

As discussed above, the use of external salience is susceptible to diverse learner-internal and external factors, and these, together with a number of methodological problems, have been speculated to explain some of the inconsistent results in input enhancement research (Han, Park, & Combs, 2008; Lee & Huang, 2008). These include the length of exposure to the target input (Leow, 1997), learners' prior knowledge of the language and the target items (Jourdenais et al., 1995; Leow, Egi, Nuevo, & Tsai, 2003), the nature of the target form (Wong, 2003), and its modality (Leow, 1993, 1995).

Types of input enhancement

Although a strict interpretation of input enhancement (Barcroft, 2003) accepts only a considerable alteration of input (through a change of or addition to the original input), a more liberal interpretation also includes other techniques such as technological enhancement and visual enhancement.

Technological enhancement refers to the use of technology as a means to draw learners' attention to the target object. Gascoigne's (2006) study, for example, involved participants listening to L2 input and then transcribing the input either on a computer or on paper. She hypothesized that the insertion of diacritics when typing on a computer, involving the pressing of additional keys, would force learners to pay conscious attention to the orthography. The results showed that keyboard transcription had a positive effect on recall of the target items compared with pen-and-paper transcription.

Another form of input enhancement is visual enhancement, which involves the inclusion of visual information (e.g., pictures) to highlight certain aspects of the text. Labrie's (2000) study compared beginning L2 learners' acquisition of vocabulary by comparing a web-based reading text enriched with images and sounds with a paper-based text without visual and aural aids. Labrie found, perhaps not surprisingly, that the inclusion of visual and aural information helped with vocabulary acquisition.

Finally, aural input enhancement involves the manipulation of listening materials, for example, by increasing the volume of target items in the text or by including a short pause before and/or after the target items. Although Gascoigne (2006) mentioned that an "*oral* [our emphasis] equivalent of textual enhancement" could be achieved via stress, intonation, or gestures (p. 149), we are unaware of previous studies investigating this type of input enhancement. Compared to the number of studies on written input enhancement, this lack is perhaps surprising, especially as aural enhancement may occur in natural or classroom discourse as a form of corrective feedback or recast.

Modality and aural enhancement

It is generally acknowledged that modality has a significant effect on input processing (and consequently on intake and acquisition). The separate streams hypothesis (Penny, 1980) posits that visual and audio language input are separately and independently processed without interference. L1 studies investigating differences between reading and listening have shown that listening is more taxing than reading of the same input[1] (Anderson, 1980; Danks, 1980; Rost, 1990), as learners do not have the same amount of control over the aural input as they do over written input. When reading, learners can more easily recognise different text elements, such as words, sentences, and paragraphs, and can re-read parts of the text (Rost, 1990), whereas in listening, segmentation of word boundaries or even boundaries between different word elements are not discrete, and learners need to rely on prosodic and intonational cues in the input to understand sequences of input (Anderson, 1980). L2 research has also shown that modality places constraints on the way input is processed; Johnson's (1992) and V. Murphy's (1997) studies, for instance, revealed that (adult) learners' performance on grammaticality judgement tasks was slower and less accurate in the aural mode than in the written mode. And Wong (2001) compared the ability of learners to focus on both form and meaning in aural and written modes and found that the aural mode was more challenging than the written mode.

In terms of aural enhancement, early SLA research into teacher talk has shown frequent use of speech modifications by ESL teachers. Some studies (Dahl, 1981; Håkansson, 1986; Henzl, 1979) revealed that teachers adjusted their speech rate to the level of learners' proficiency, and others (Chaudron, 1982; Wesche & Ready, 1985) reported teachers' insertion of pauses around certain aspects of their speech production to make it more comprehensible to learners. Chaudron (1982), in particular, descriptively observed native teachers' tendency to insert pauses around difficult words to make them more comprehensible to ESL learners. Other phonological, intonational, or stress characteristics have been reported to be modified by teachers (Chaudron, 1982; Henzl, 1973). Although those early studies are not generalizable due to the lack of a comparable baseline, Chaudron (1988) concludes that native teachers seem to modify their speech in certain ways to make it more comprehensible for learners. A decade later, in a study on the effects of recasts, Doughty and Varela (1998) used recasts with a rising intonation to draw learners' attention to a particular form. Because the study did not include a baseline recast (with no intonational emphasis), it is difficult to interpret the effects of intonational emphasis in recasts; however, it seems likely that such intonational emphasis has been accepted by practitioners and researchers as one possible attention-drawing technique.

No studies, to the best of our knowledge, have investigated the effects of aural manipulation in the input on drawing learners' attention to form in the experimental context. Leow's (1995) study does give us some insight, as it was a replication of an earlier study (1993) into the effects of simplified written input, type of linguistic items, and L2 experience on intake, but in the aural mode, allowing for a comparison between the two. Although the studies did not reveal modality effects of simplified input on learner intake of the target form, mode of input did seem to have an effect on learners' intake of different types of input, possibly due to the phonological salience of different morphemes. Leow emphasised the need to further investigate the effects of modality on input processing.

1 It should be noted, however, that there is also an important age effect.

Study

Participants

A total of 72 Korean learners of English participated in the study. Participants were enrolled in a compulsory freshman English course, entitled "Academic English for business majors." They were from three intact classes taught by the same instructor. Students in the classes were randomly placed into one of these classes, if they had insufficiently high scores on one of the accepted university entrance tests (e.g., TOEFL or the university entrance exam). The experiment was conducted as part of a classroom activity on extensive listening, and participants received extra points for their participation. Participants' TOEFL IBT scores ranged from 80 to 110 (out of 120) and national university entrance exam scores in English from 94 to 100 (all students had at least one of these scores), indicating that participants could be expected to be able to complete listening to an audiobook independently outside of the classroom without too much trouble. The class instructor was consulted regarding the participants' English ability to complete the task. Participants were told the purpose of the study was to look at extensive listening practice and were given information about the length of the study and its procedures.

Participants at this level might be expected to know the basic rules pertaining to passive structures, especially considering the fact that they are introduced early in formal education (e.g., compulsory English education from Grade 3) and the fact that their formation is relatively simple. Nonetheless, many previous studies have noted challenges for students in fully mastering passive forms, even at advanced levels (Hinkel, 2002). This was confirmed for the participants in this study also as shown in their pretest scores (see below).

Design

A computer-based timed grammaticality judgement test (GJT) was administered to participants as a pretest. The GJT was preceded by instructions and a practice session. Next, the three classes were randomly assigned to either one of the two experimental groups [the Pause Group (PG, *n*=24) or the Reduced Speed Group (SG, *n*=23)] or the control group (CG, *n*=25). Participants in each group were given an audio version of a graded reader (see below) to listen to. They received their respective files via the university course management system so that no other individuals except the study participants could access the audio files. Students were told they were only to use the files themselves for the purposes of the study and not to share the files with others. The two experimental groups were given artificially manipulated files, which either included short pauses around the target forms (PG) or which had the speed of the audio recording reduced for the target items (SG). The control group received the original (unaltered) audio file. Participants were asked to listen to the audio files for the purpose of enjoying the story in the book as part of their course homework. They were given one week to complete listening to the approximately 90-minute recording.

After one week participants completed a posttest GJT, which included the same items as the pretest but in a different order. A survey (see Appendix) was administered after the posttest, and this asked learners about their background in learning English, their experience in listening to the audiobook (for example, where and when they listened to it), what devices they used for listening, as well as whether they had noticed anything special about the recording (to establish whether they had noticed the input enhancement). In addition, participants were asked whether, and how often, they had listened to the book in the debriefing questionnaire. Nine participants indicated they had not listened to the audiobook or had listened to it more than once. They were removed from the dataset.

Target structure

The English passive was chosen as the target form for the study. As Hinkel (2002) points out, although the passive structure is common in English, classroom practice and instruction on passives have focused on deriving passives from active structures, making it difficult for learners to master the form on its own. Particularly in L2 production, common types of errors in passive production include the use of the intransitive verb in passive constructions and the use of the form in inappropriate contexts.

For example:

a. The accident happened.

b. *The accident was happened.

Previous studies on L2 learners' passive acquisition have revealed that even advanced L2 learners tend to overpassivitise unaccusative verbs such as *occur* and *happen* (Kim, 2003; Yip, 1995) and tend to accept ungrammatical sentences including passive structures with unaccusative verbs. Further complicating matters for learners is the fact that the agent of an action verb in an active structure tends to be phonologically suppressed and that the passive structure does not follow the *first noun principle.* VanPatten (1996, 2004) has shown that learners, regardless of their L1, tend to perceive the first noun or pronoun in a sentence as an agent, which is not the case in passive structures. These factors together make it difficult for L2 learners to recognise thematic relationships in passive sentences. Based on the level of the participants (see above), we felt the passive form was both challenging enough, while not being beyond the participants' grasp. In order not to make the tests too difficult, we included mainly simple passives, similar to those found in the audiobook. In addition, the passive structure occurred frequently in the audiobooks we considered, thus making it a good practical choice. In general, for the correct passive forms, grammatically correct simple sentences with a *by*-phrase were presented (e.g., 'The new rules were written by the head teacher'), and for the incorrect forms, the *be* verb in the passive structure was omitted (e.g., '*He injured when he fell off his bike').

Treatment

After consulting with the course instructor, the book *Frankenstein*, a level three book from the Penguin Active Reading series of graded readers was chosen. Permission was obtained from the publisher to manipulate the audio recordings for the purpose of our study[2]. The audio files were digitally manipulated with the use of the sound editing software Audacity (a freely available audio editing program) by inserting pauses of about 1.5 seconds before and after the target forms or by slowing down the playback speed of the target items. We slowed down the recording by 7–10% while not altering its pitch—so as not to make the slowed down text sound unnatural. The files were then converted to mp3 files, and students were instructed to download the files through the university course management system and listen to the audiobook through their mobile phones or any other listening device. Further, they were asked to listen to the book only once (so as to avoid adding length of exposure as an additional variable). Participants were not told about the purpose of the study, other than

2 The narrator of the story uses British English. Korean learners of English are more used to hearing American English. However, because of the relatively low level of the text and the absence of any clear regional expressions in the text, we considered this acceptable.

that it was about extensive listening. No instruction on the target structure was given during the experimental period.

Tests

A timed grammaticality judgement test (GJT) was administered as a pretest and a posttest. Both tests contained the same items but in a different order. There were 50 sentences of which 20 contained the target structure and the remaining 30 were distracters. Out of the 20 target items, 10 were grammatical and 10 were ungrammatical. Items were randomly presented. The items were similar to those found in the audiobook in terms of their complexity. Before the test, participants were instructed on how to complete the GJT and completed a number of practice items. Participants were asked to press the *enter* key on the keyboard if they thought a sentence was grammatical and the left-hand *shift* key if they thought it was ungrammatical. The keys were labelled with stickers indicating *correct* and *incorrect*. Since the tests aimed at measuring learners' implicit knowledge of the target feature, learners received only a few seconds to judge their grammaticality. They were encouraged to use their intuition, rather than to consciously apply grammar rules. The sentence presentation time differed, depending on the length of the sentence, and was based on Reinders (2009).

Although GJTs have some drawbacks (see, for example, Birdsong, 1989), the timed GJT seemed appropriate as the most likely effect of the extensive listening treatment would be the development of implicit knowledge. With regards to item consistency, a Kuder-Richardson 20 (*KR–20*) score was calculated. In the pretest the score was 0.715, and in the posttest it was 0.878, showing sufficiently high consistency.

In addition to the GJT, participants were given a comprehension test at the same time as the GJT posttest. This included six multiple-choice questions related to the main plot of the story to confirm that they had listened to the audiobook. These questions were written so as to be impossible to answer without having read the book (e.g., 'Where did Robert Walton first meet Victor Frankenstein, as he wrote in his first letter?').

Analysis

To measure performance on the pre- and post-tests, participants were given one point for each correct item and zero points for each incorrect or missing item. The score comparisons among groups included both overall GJT scores and scores on the target features. The analysis of the pretest revealed that there were no significant group differences for both scores (overall scores and passive scores), so it was assumed that the three groups were similar in terms of their knowledge of the passive structure and English grammar in general at the start of the study.

Results

In order to examine mean differences in individuals' passive knowledge improvement under different conditions of audio input, a mixed-design repeated-measures ANOVA was adopted. That is, Condition was used as a between-subject factor with three levels—the pause group (PG) vs. the reduced speed group (SG) vs. the control group (CG)—and Time was used as a within-subject factor with two levels (pretest vs. posttest). The dependent variable was learners' passive scores from the grammaticality judgement test. This analysis seemed more appropriate than a one-way ANOVA on posttest scores only because it is possible that all learners may benefit from merely listening to the audio file, regardless of the different audio input.

Table 1 shows descriptive statistics for scores on passive structures from the pretest and posttest. The mean score on the pretest for passives was 13.083 (*SD*=3.488) for the PG, 12.087 (*SD*= 2.968) for the SG, and 11.880 (*SD*=2.773) for the CG. The posttest scores seem similar across all three groups with the average scores of PG=14.208 (*SD*=3.106), SG=13.217 (*SD*=3.147), and CG=13.120 (*SD*=3.059), although overall PG (pause group) performed better in both pretest and posttest, followed by SG and CG, in that order.

Table 1. Descriptive statistics for passive structures on the pretest and posttest

	group	N	*Mean*	*SD*	*SE*
pretest	PG	24	13.083	3.488	.712
	SG	23	12.087	2.968	.619
	CG	25	11.880	2.773	.555
posttest	PG	24	14.208	3.106	.634
	SG	23	13.217	3.147	.656
	CG	25	13.120	3.059	.612

note. PG=pause group, SG=reduced speed group, CG=control group (original format)

In order to examine the main effects for Time (pretest-posttest) and Condition (treatment) and the interactions of Time by Condition, the repeated-measures ANOVA was used. As can be seen in Table 2, there was a significant Time effect in the analysis ($F(1, 69)=15.821$, $p=.00$), suggesting that learners' passive scores significantly improved from pretest to posttest. Although the proportion of variance explained by Time in the within group design was only 18.7% (partial $\eta^2=.187$), the significant result can be interpreted with substantial power (power=.975). However, in terms of the main effect for Condition, there was no significant difference in group scores ($F(2, 69)=.162$, $p=.319$, partial $\eta^2=.033$), with Condition explaining only 3.3% of the variance in the score in the between group design. The results suggest treatment differences in the three groups did not influence the amount of improvement from pretest to posttest scores on the target form. Further, no significant interaction of Time and Condition was observed ($F(1, 69)=.017$, $p=.983$, partial $\eta^2=.000$), with the interaction explaining 0.0% of the variance in the within group design. This suggests that there is no interaction effect for Time and Condition on learner scores.

Table 2. Statistics for the effects of Time, Condition, and their interaction

source of variance	*SS*	*df*	*MS*	F	*p*	partial η^2	power
within group							
Time	48.816	1	48.816	15.821	.000	.187	.975
Time*Condition	.103	2	.052	.017	.983	.000	.052
Condition							
error	212.897	69	3.085				
between group							
Condition	37.392	2	18.696	1.162	.319	.033	.247
error	1109.914	69	16.086				

Figure 1 reveals the score changes from pretest to posttest for the three groups. As the figure suggests, all groups improved from pretest to posttest (Time 1 to Time 2), implying that all groups in general improved their knowledge of the passive forms after listening to the audiobook. However, overall there is clearly no interaction between Condition and Time (i.e., score improvement).

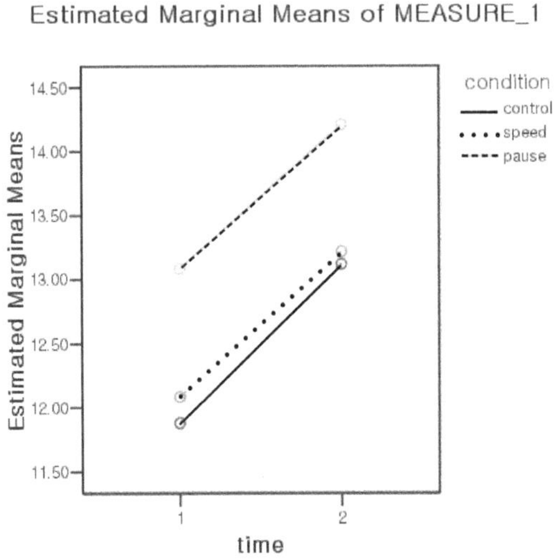

Figure 1. Plots for pretest and posttest scores for each group

To sum up, the results indicate that learners' knowledge of the passive form improved from pretest to posttest by listening to the audiobook regardless of the type of aural input they received. At the same time, the results suggest no differential effect for aural enhancement on learners' knowledge improvement of the target form. Although score improvement from pretest to posttest occurred in all three conditions with substantial power (power=.975), the findings for the effect of aural manipulation must remain tentative due to the low power (power for Condition effect=.247; power for Condition * Time effect=.052), because the lack of power may not allow us to detect any significant effects, even if such effects exist in reality.

Questionnaire

Upon completion of the posttest, participants were given a questionnaire that asked (among other questions) whether they had noticed anything special about the recordings. Approximately 70% of participants (17/24) in the pause group (PG) said they had noticed the pauses, and of those who did, about 47% (8/17) said the pauses were intended to make them concentrate on the story, two said it was to give them more time to understand the input (without mentioning the exact object of the input), and one said it was intended to encourage attention to the words that followed the pauses. Three further students said they did not know why the pauses were included. Participants in the reduced speed group (SG) did not specifically point out the slowing down of the target structure. Some also mentioned other aspects of the recording, which had not been altered by us, such as the British pronunciation, the general speed of the recording, and the length of the book. This applied to students in the control group (CG) also. None of the participants' responses indicated they had noticed that the pauses or recording speed were intended to draw their attention to the target structure, which indicated that students' attention to the target form had not reached the level of awareness. However, given that some participants mentioned that the reason for the pauses were to get them to pay attention to the recording (although none specified a form), it seems possible that the pauses may have increased learners' readiness to accept or process the subsequent input. Nonetheless, the students' responses clearly indicate the contrasts in terms of learners' recognition of the manipulation; pauses seem to be more salient than a reduction in recording speed.

Another aspect of our study was whether extensive listening can be successfully implemented as an out-of-class activity. 60% of the learners indicated they listened to the audiobook with their own portable devices such as MP3 players and mobile phones. Only 40% of participants had listened to the book on a computer. Most participants (66%) indicated that they had listened to the book in an informal setting such as on the subway or bus when commuting to and from home or before going to bed, while 25 respondents (34%) said that they had listened to it at school. The responses point to the potential of using mobile devices for encouraging out-of-class practice.

Comprehension test

Students performed well on the comprehension questions they were given at the same time as the questionnaire (*Mean*=87.04, *SD* =14.91), showing that they had indeed listened to the story and the level was suitable for them.

Discussion

This study investigated whether external manipulation of features in L2 aural input contributes to the acquisition of the passive structure. Learners were exposed to natural language input by listening to an audiobook in which the target structure was either slowed down or in which pauses were inserted around the target structure. Participants' knowledge of the form was examined by comparing their receptive knowledge on two grammatical judgment tests (GJT), administered before and after the treatment. Although participants' test scores improved from pretest to posttest (most likely as a result of completing the extensive listening as part of the treatment), there was no effect for aural enhancement. Although it is hard to directly compare the current results to previous input enhancement studies, due to the different modality, some methodological issues can be raised in discussing possible reasons for our findings.

First, it is possible that the amount of enhanced input in the current study was not sufficient for learners to construct the rule (or at least to do so to a greater extent than participants in the control group, who simply listened to the unaltered audiobook). Similarly, the period of time over which the input was presented may have been too short. Participants listened to only one fairly short audiobook and were exposed to only 65 correct exemplars of the target structures. It is possible that they would need, if not more, than at least more repeated exposure to the target structure, for example by listening to several books over an extended period (weeks, months) of time. Schmidt (1990) emphasized the importance of frequency of input, given other things being equal, along with perceptual salience in increasing the likelihood of input to be perceived as intake and further processed for learning.

Another variable is the complexity of the target structure; simple rules are more susceptible to enhancement than complex ones. Although variables determining complexity are subject to debate (e.g., Dekeyser, 1994, 1998; Robinson, 1996), some studies (Kim, 2003; Yip, 1995) have highlighted the difficulty of acquiring the passive form. Although the passive structure adopted in the current study seems simple in terms of rule formation, adaptation of the form and use of it in a sentence is relatively complex when it comes to the incorrect use of intransitive verbs in passive and double-object constructions. Robinson's studies (1995, 1996) showed that with complex rules, learners with explicit instruction are better at acquiring the form than those in implicit and incidental learning conditions. Based on this, grammar learning in sentences beyond identifying simple rule formation may not work in incidental enhanced form learning conditions as used in the current study.

Moreover, the difficulty of processing *aural* input may have had an impact. A number of studies have pointed out the challenges of processing aural input compared with written input (Anderson, 1980; Danks, 1980; V. Murphy, 1997; Rost, 1990). One of the important differences between written and aural input processing is that learners have very little control over the incoming input when listening. Therefore, participants may have been unable to benefit from the input enhancements.

Although no differential effect on learning was observed for the pause and the slowed speed groups, the results from the debriefing questionnaire showed that about 70% of learners (17/24) in the pause group had noticed the pauses, whereas none in the slowed speed group (SG) had noticed the change in speed. Future studies investigating the effects of aural input enhancement may thus wish to use pauses rather than alter the playback speed. In addition, it is interesting to consider why such recognition did not lead to acquisition. Although there was no effect for the enhanced input and participants were not aware of the enhancement's purpose to draw their attention to the target structure, it is theoretically possible that participants did in fact notice the target structure but not to the point of awareness and therefore did not engage in further processing. Williams' study (1999) showed that, especially in meaning-oriented tasks, further processing of noticed input is necessary for the underlying rules to be formulated:

> If learning distributional rules is critically dependent upon the subjects initially paying attention to relations between elements in the input, then it follows that even the simplest rules might not be learned if the subjects for some reason fail to attend to those relationships. (p. 32)

In other words, participants may have noticed the form but failed to allocate attention to related grammatical segments or at least did not make the form-meaning connections necessary to establish their underlying rules (cf. Baddeley, 1990). In addition, the lack of explicit instruction and the fact that learners were not asked to focus on the target form may have prevented them from allocating attention to the target grammar (G. Murphy & Shapiro, 1994). Also, the lack of feedback may have prevented them from attempting to generate their underlying rules (Baddeley, Gathercole, & Papagno, 1998; Williams, 1999).

To reiterate, a number of methodological issues identified in previous enhancement studies may have played a role in this study also; external input saliency cannot guarantee internal focus on the form. Although learners' attention may have been activated by the external manipulation, their attention to form may have remained at a shallow level, thus not leading to an association of the form and its underlying rule.

Nevertheless, as some students did notice the manipulation through the insertion of pauses, without having been alerted to it through instructions or examples, it seems possible to enhance learners' readiness to accept the following input (either in terms of content or grammar) through this type of enhancement. This, nonetheless, needs more robust empirical evidence.

We feel that the methodological significance of the study lies in its attempts to incorporate authentic materials in the study of focus on form/input enhancement, as well as incorporation of input enhancement in an out-of-class learning context. That is, this study tried to examine whether L2 learners can successfully allocate their attention to salient features of grammar within (purely) meaning-oriented activities in a non-pedagogical environment. Unlike many other previous input enhancement studies where learners are placed into experimental conditions where the target form is presented more frequently than in its natural context, the extensive listening task adopted in this study more closely resembles a natural language learning situation. Learners' main purpose for completing the listening activity was to understand and enjoy the story rather than to pay attention to details of the language or text. Further studies such as this may help to better understand the pedagogical potential of implementing form-focused instruction in informal language learning settings.

Conclusion

This study attempted to investigate whether aural input enhancement in extensive listening can facilitate acquisition of the passive structure. Passive structures in an audiobook were aurally enhanced, and the effect of the enhancement on learning was measured with a grammaticality judgement test. Analysis of the results showed no significant aural enhancement effect on acquisition of the target structure. The results could be attributed to the cognitive demands in processing extensive auditory input; extensive listening is a primarily meaning-oriented type of language practice, which may have made participants less likely to pay attention to language form.

However, a number of limitations prevent us from making definitive statements to explain our research findings. First, a lack of a noticing measurement in the study means we were unable to determine whether learners did not notice the form, or did notice it but did not acquire the structure as a result. Although post-treatment self-reports were used to reveal participants' noticing of the enhanced target structure, self-report can only provide limited information. Also, because participants listened to the audiobook in an uncontrolled environment, contextual factors could have had an effect. These include the time interval between finishing listening to the book and taking the test, as well as the conditions during listening (e.g., listening in silence vs. listening in a noisy environment). Finally, the modality in the treatment was different from that in the tests (listening versus reading). Our reason for using the GJT was that it would allow us to easily include a large number of target items in an easy-to-administer test of relatively short duration. In future studies, however, it will be important to reconsider this issue.

Despite these limitations, we do feel it is important to investigate extensive listening in its natural environment, and by using tools that the young adult learners in this study are most comfortable with, we feel that the study benefits from greater ecological validity (Van Lier, 1996). Laboratory conditions, although affording greater control in terms of data collection, may not be suitable if the results are to be a true indication of the potential effect of extensive listening activities. In this sense, the current study hopefully makes a small but significant contribution to contextualizing aural input enhancement research.

References

Anderson, J. (1980). *Cognitive psychology and its implications*. New York: W. H. Freeman.

Baddeley, A. (1990). *Human memory*. London: Lawrence Erlbaum Associates.

Baddeley, A., Gathercole, S., & Papagno, C. (1998). The phonological loop as a language learning device. *Psychological Review, 105*, 158–173.

Barcroft, J. (2003). Distinctiveness and bidirectional effects in input enhancement for vocabulary learning. *Applied Language Learning, 13*, 133–159.

Birdsong, D. (1989). *Metalinguistic performance and interlinguistic competence*. New York: Springer.

Chaudron, C. (1982). Vocabulary elaboration in teachers' speech to L2 learners. *Studies in Second Language Acquisition*, 4, 170–180.

Chaudron, C. (1988). *Second language classrooms: Research on teaching and learning.* New York: Cambridge University Press.

Dahl, D. (1981). The role of experience in speech modifications for second language learners. *Minnesota Papers in Linguistics and Philosophy of Language, 7*, 78–93.

Danks, J. (1980). Comprehension in listening and reading: Same or different? In J. Danks & K. Pezdek (Eds.), *Reading and understanding* (pp. 25–40). Newark, DE: International Reading Association.

DeKeyser, R. (1994). How implicit can adult second language learning be? *AILA Review, 11*, 83–96.

DeKeyser, R. (1998). Beyond focus on form: Cognitive perspectives on learning and practicing second language grammar. In C. Doughty & J. Williams (Eds.), *Focus on form in classroom SLA* (pp. 42–63). New York: Cambridge University Press.

Doughty, C., & Varela, E. (1998). Communicative focus on form. In C. Doughty & J. Williams (Eds.), *Focus on form in classroom second language acquisition* (pp. 114–138). Cambridge: Cambridge University Press.

Dulay, H. C., & Burt, M. K. (1978). Some remarks on creativity in language acquisition. In W. C. Ritchie (Ed.), *Second language acquisition research: Issues and implications* (pp. 65–89). New York: Academic Press.

Ellis, R. (2009). Implicit and explicit learning, knowledge, and instruction. In R. Ellis, S. Loewen, C. Elder, R. Erlam, J. Philp, & H. Reinders (Eds.), *Implicit and explicit knowledge in second language learning, testing, and teaching* (pp. 3–26). Bristol: Multilingual Matters.

Fotos, S., & Ellis, R. (1991). Communicating about grammar: A task-based approach. *TESOL Quarterly, 25*, 46–69.

Gascoigne, G. (2006). Toward an understanding of incidental input enhancement in computerized L2 environments. *CALICO Journal, 24*, 147–162.

Håkansson, G. (1986). Quantitative aspects of teacher talk. In G. Kasper (Ed.), *Learning, teaching, and communication in the foreign language classroom* (pp. 83–98). Aarhus, Denmark: Aarhus University Press.

Han, Z., Park, E. S., & Combs, C. (2008). Textual enhancement of input: Issues and possibilities. *Applied Linguistics, 29*, 597–618.

Henzl, V. (1973). Linguistic register of foreign language instruction. *Language Learning, 23*, 207–227.

Henzl, V. (1979). Foreigner talk in the classroom. *International Review of Applied Linguistics, 17*, 159–167.

Hinkel, E. (2002). Why English passive is difficult to teach (and learn). In E. Hinkel & S. Fotos (Eds.), *New perspectives on grammar teaching* (pp. 233–260). Mahwah, NJ: Lawrence Erlbaum Associates.

Johnson, J. (1992). Critical period effects in second language acquisition: The effect of written versus auditory materials on the assessment of grammatical competence. *Language Learning, 42*, 217–48.

Jourdenais, R., Ota, M., Stauffer, S., Boyson, B., & Doughty, C. (1995). Does textual enhancement promote noticing? A think-aloud protocol analysis. In R. Schmidt (Ed.), *Attention and awareness in foreign language learning* (pp. 183–216). Honolulu: University of Hawai'i, National Foreign Language Resource Center.

Kim, Y.-W. (2003). The acquisition of English unaccusative verbs by Korean EFL learners. *English Language Teaching, 15*, 203–221.

Labrie, G. (2000). A French vocabulary tutor for the web. *CALICO Journal, 17*, 475–499.

Lee, S., & Huang, H. (2008). Visual input enhancement and grammar learning: A meta-analytic review. *Studies in Second Language Acquisition, 30*, 307–331.

Leow, R. P. (1993). To simplify or not to simplify. *Studies in Second Language Acquisition, 15*, 333–355.

Leow, R. P. (1995). Modality and intake in second language acquisition. *Studies in Second Language Acquisition, 17*, 79–89.

Leow, R. P. (1997). The effects of input enhancement and text length on adult L2 readers' comprehension and intake in second language acquisition. *Applied Language Learning, 8*, 151–182.

Leow, R. P. (1999). Attention, awareness, and focus on form research: A critical overview. In J. F. Lee & A. Valdman (Eds.), *Form and meaning: Multiple perspectives* (pp. 69–96). Boston: Heinle & Heinle.

Leow, R. P. (2001). Do learners notice enhanced forms while interacting with the L2? An online and offline study of the role of written input enhancement in L2 reading. *Hispania, 84*, 496–509.

Leow, R. P., Egi, T., Nuevo, A., & Tsai, Y. (2003). The roles of textual enhancement and type of linguistic item in adult L2 learners' comprehension and intake. *Applied Language Learning, 13*, 1–16.

Murphy, G., & Shapiro, A. (1994). Forgetting verbatim information in discourse. *Memory and Cognition, 22*, 85–94.

Murphy, V. (1997). The effect of modality on a grammaticality judgment task. *Second Language Research, 13*, 34–65.

Penny, C. (1980). Order of report in bisensory verbal short-term memory. *Canadian Journal of Psychology, 34*, 190–95.

Reinders, H. (2009). Learner uptake and acquisition in three grammar-oriented production activities. *Language Teaching Research, 13*, 201–222.

Reinders, H., & Ellis, R. (2009). The effects of two types of positive enhanced input on intake and L2 acquisition. In R. Ellis, S. Loewen, R. Erlam, J. Philp, C. Elder, and H. Reinders (Eds.), *Implicit and explicit knowledge in a second language* (pp. 262–280). Clevedon: Multilingual Matters.

Robinson, P. (1995). Review article: Attention, memory, and the noticing hypothesis. *Language Learning, 45*, 283–331.

Robinson, P. (1996). Learning simple and complex second language rules under implicit, incidental, rule-search, and instructed conditions. *Studies in Second Language Acquisition, 18*, 27–68.

Rost, M. (1990). *Listening in language learning.* London: Longman.

Schmidt, R. (1990). The role of consciousness in second language learning. *Applied Linguistics, 11*, 129–158.

Schmidt, R. (1993). Awareness and second language acquisition. *Annual Review of Applied Linguistics, 13*, 206–226.

Schmidt, R. (1994). Deconstructing consciousness in search of useful definitions for applied linguistics. *AILA Review, 11*, 11–26.

Schmidt, R. (1995). Consciousness and foreign language learning: A tutorial on the role of attention and awareness in learning. In R. Schmidt (Ed.), *Attention and awareness in foreign language learning* (pp. 259–302). Honolulu: University of Hawai'i, National Foreign Language Resource Center.

Schmidt, R. (2001). Attention. In P. Robinson (Ed.), *Cognition and second language instruction* (pp. 3–32). Cambridge: Cambridge University Press.

Sharwood Smith, M. (1991). Speaking to many minds: On the relevance of different types of language information for the L2 learner. *Second Language Research, 7*, 118–132.

Sharwood Smith, M. (1993). Input enhancement in instructed SLA: Theoretical bases. *Studies in Second Language Acquisition, 15*, 165–179.

Spada, N., & Lightbown, P. M. (1999). Instruction, first language influence, and developmental readiness in second language acquisition. *Modern Language Journal, 83*, 1–22.

Tomlin, R., & Villa, V. (1994). Attention in cognitive science and second language acquisition. *Studies in Second Language Acquisition, 16*, 183–203.

Trahey, M., & White, L. (1993). Positive evidence and preemption in the second language classroom. *Studies in Second Language Acquisition, 15*, 181–204.

Van Lier, L. (1996). *Interaction in the language curriculum: Awareness, autonomy, and authenticity*. London: Longman.

VanPatten, B. (1996). *Input processing and grammar instruction in second language acquisition*. Norwood, NJ: Ablex.

VanPatten, B. (2004). *Processing instruction: Theory, research, and commentary*. Mahwah, NJ: Lawrence Erlbaum Associates.

Wesche, M., & Ready, D. (1985). Foreigner talk in the university classroom. In S. Gass & C. Madden (Eds.), *Input in second language acquisition* (pp. 89–114). Rowley, Mass.: Newbury House.

White, J. (1998). Getting the learners' attention: A typographical input enhancement study. In C. Doughty & J. Williams (Eds.), *Focus on form in classroom second language acquisition* (pp. 85–113). Cambridge: Cambridge University Press.

Williams, J. N. (1999). Memory, attention, and inductive learning. *Studies in Second Language Acquisition, 21*, 1–48.

Wong, W. (2001). Modality and attention to meaning and form in the input. *Studies in Second Language Acquisition, 23*, 345–368.

Wong, W. (2003). Textual enhancement and simplified input: Effects on L2 comprehension and acquisition of non-meaningful grammatical form. *Applied Language Learning, 13*, 17–45.

Yip, V. (1995). *Interlanguage and learnability: From Chinese to English*. Amsterdam: John Benjamins.

Appendix

Q1. What device did you use for the listening?

__ MP3 player

__ cell-phone

__ computer

__ other, please specify:

____

Q2. Where did you listen to the audiobook?

__ on the subway

__ on the bus

__ at home

__ in school

__ other, please specify:

____

Q3. How many times did you listen to the audiobook?

__ none

__ once

__ twice

__ more than three times

Q4. When did you finish listening to the audiobook?

__ today

__ yesterday

__ two days ago

__ three days ago

__ more than four days ago

Q5. Had you read this book before (or listened to it as an audiobook)?

__ yes

__ no

Q6. Did you notice anything unusual about the recording (quality of recording)? If so, what?

____

Q7. If you answered yes, what do you think was the purpose of the unusual recording?

____

NFLRC
monographs

Instruction in Support of Noticing: An Empirical Study of EFL in Brazil

Sylvia Nagem Frota
Federal University of Rio de Janeiro

Joara M. Bergsleithner
University of Brasília

Schmidt's (1990) noticing hypothesis, the claim that learners have to consciously notice instances of the constructions of a second language in input in order to acquire them, was initially based on his personal experiences learning Portuguese as an L2 in Brazil (Schmidt & Frota, 1986). In that study Schmidt and Frota reported several findings concerning the relationships among instruction, noticing, and learning. Although instruction itself did not guarantee acquisition, classroom instruction was nevertheless useful, both directly, in the sense that constructions taught and drilled in the language class sometimes appeared almost immediately in the learner's output, and indirectly, often serving a priming function so that structures that were taught in class were subsequently noticed when encountered in communicative input. The study reported in this chapter investigates this priming function of instruction, asking whether undergraduate English majors at a Brazilian university are more likely to notice instances of a specific target structure (pre-modified English nouns) in written input after receiving explicit instruction about such structures. After completing a short pretest to determine whether these participants were already sensitive to the occurrence of pre-modified nouns (which are common in English but rare in Portuguese), they received explicit instruction on these English structures. Recognition tests administered immediately after the treatment and again two weeks later were used to assess whether their sensitivity to the occurrence of such structures was enhanced by the treatment. The hypothesis that instruction would lead to enhanced noticing was largely supported, although limitations of the study are acknowledged and some suggestions for future research are proposed.

Frota, S. N., & Bergsleithner, J. M. (2013). Instruction in support of noticing: An empirical study of EFL in Brazil. In J. M. Bergsleithner, S. N. Frota, & J. K. Yoshioka (Eds.), *Noticing and second language acquisition: Studies in honor of Richard Schmidt* (pp. 139–150). Honolulu: University of Hawai'i, National Foreign Language Resource Center.

Introduction

Conscious and unconscious processes and the relationships between them have been controversial and hotly debated issues in the fields of second language acquisition (SLA) and second language learning (SLL) for the last two decades or so. In one influential contribution to this debate, Schmidt's noticing hypothesis (1990, 1992, 1994, 1995), the claim that learners have to consciously notice instances of the constructions of the second language in input in order to acquire them, was initially based on his personal experiences learning Portuguese as an L2 in Brazil (Schmidt & Frota, 1986). In that study, Schmidt and Frota reported several important findings from his case study that they took to be evidence that noticing is relevant to SLA/SLL, including the following:

- Classroom instruction was useful, both directly (in the sense that constructions taught and drilled in class sometimes appeared almost immediately in the learner's output) and indirectly, serving a priming function so that what was taught in class was often quickly noticed in communicative input. Instruction by itself did not guarantee acquisition (defined in this study as *productive use*), however.
- Frequency in linguistic input was also important, perhaps because this increased the probability that the learner attended to such forms and noticed them.
- Whether or not target language forms and constructions were frequently taught or appeared frequently in input, it seems that this L2 learner actually learned (and produced) them only after noticing them when processing input (i.e., when interacting with target language speakers in authentic communicative contexts).
- Noticing the gap: It was suggested that L2 learners who have started to automatize (and potentially fossilize) interlanguage errors may need to notice the difference between their current forms or competence and the forms or structures appearing in input in order to recover from error.

The noticing hypothesis is in line with most information processing theories, which typically view attention as a filter or gate that determines what information from complex input is ultimately taken in or not for further processing. For example, the noticing hypothesis shares numerous points of contact with:

- McLaughlin's (1987) information processing theory, since both theories relate learning to attention, a control construct that transfers information into focal awareness (noticing);
- Anderson's ACT* theory of cognitive architecture and skill development (1980, 1983), which claims that a new domain of knowledge (such as L2 learning) starts with declarative knowledge (propositional) that subsequently becomes procedural through practice (Ellis & Schmidt, 1997); and
- Baars' cognitive theory of consciousness (1986, 1988, 1997), which states that conscious experience is always informative.

In this view

> ...learning begins with the realization that something is to be learned, progresses through a series of stages that establish a context for understanding new material, and concludes with the new material fading out of consciousness as it becomes itself a part of the unconscious context that shapes the interpretation of future events. (Schmidt, 1990, p. 138, based on Baars, 1988)

Theories of information processing have associated consciousness with a variety of constructs such as attention, control processing, and working memory capacity. However, Schmidt (1990) claims that "all theories of consciousness specify a crucial role for consciousness in dealing with novel information, novice behavior, and learning" (p. 138). Thus, attention to input is necessary for storage and a precursor to hypothesis formation and testing (Schmidt, 2001).

Schmidt's idea is essentially about learners noticing what is in communicative input, whether it comes through interaction with native or nonnative speakers, listening, reading, or the like. Noticing in his sense of the term is not necessarily about what learners understand about a teacher's grammar instruction. However, there are probably relationships between instruction and noticing; instruction about target language constructions may make it more likely that learners will subsequently notice those constructions when they occur in input. For example, a learner who has had instruction in pre-modification of nouns may be more likely than someone who has not had such instruction to notice that the phrase *teaching experience* (rather than *experience in teaching* or some other expression) occurs in a text such as the following: "Candidates with degrees in English, Education, or TEFL/ Applied Linguistics are preferred, but candidates from all majors are welcome to apply. Some previous teaching experience is preferred." The suggestion here is that those individuals who have been exposed to such L2 features through explicit instruction may be more likely to notice their occurrence in subsequent input than someone who did not receive any explicit instruction on these aspects of the target language before encountering them in input.

Link between instruction and noticing

Several researchers (e.g., Ellis, 1994, 2001; Robinson, 1995, 1996; Swain, 1998) have argued in favor of instruction in L2 classes, providing both theoretical arguments and empirical evidence. Norris and Ortega (2000) carried out a meta-analysis of 49 studies that focused on L2 instruction in L2 classes to examine its effectiveness for L2 learning. Their findings across the comparisons of average effect sizes within these studies showed that, even though they present somewhat heterogeneous findings, they consistently point out that instructional treatments are useful for L2 learning and improvement in language development. In a later study Norris and Ortega (2003) put forward a strong rationale for investigating potential explanatory constructs (e.g., noticing) underlying instructional treatments. They state that

> where interpretations are to be made about the relationship between causal or moderating processes (noticing, comprehension, cognitive resources of memory and attention, attentional focus, language aptitude, etc.) and L2 acquisition products, behavioral evidence for such constructs will also need to be specified and associated measurement tasks selected. SLA research frequent employs dependent variable measures which only provide evidence bearing on the linguistic products of acquisition (vocabulary recognition items, grammaticality judgment tasks, elicited imitation, communicative performance, etc.). Such measures do little to inform interpretations about the independent variables to which acquisition-related behavioral patterns are ascribed; the actual construct interpretation (i.e., about the relationship between certain causes and linguistic outcomes in acquisition) will thus be underrepresented within measurement practice. (p. 729–730)

Among other empirical studies on noticing of L2 formal features, several studies have found that noticing may benefit L2 learners' accuracy in oral and/or written production. Leow (1997), for example, defined noticing as "some form of subjective awareness of new targeted linguistic forms in L2 data as revealed in learners' think-aloud protocols produced while completing a problem-solving task" (p. 474). He investigated noticing and its effects on L2 behavior in written production, finding links between awareness and both enhanced processing and accuracy in written production.

Further studies have shown that externally provided assistance or instruction of various kinds can lead to greater gains in L2 learning. For instance, Mackey (2006) used multiple measures of noticing and development in her study. The results showed that learners reported more noticing when feedback was provided. Learners who reported noticing questions were more likely to demonstrate L2 development than those who did not report anything, and learners who exhibited more noticing developed more than those who exhibited less noticing.

The findings of studies such as these support some of Schmidt's major noticing hypothesis claims, specifically that noticing benefits L2 learning and that instruction can play a role in making noticing more likely. As Schmidt (1990, 1995) has pointed out, noticing can happen when processing input either before or after instruction. The crucial point for the present study is that instruction may lead L2 learners to notice linguistic features in subsequent input that they might not otherwise notice. In our view it is especially important to investigate whether instruction might serve as a bridge and a pathfinder for noticing in subsequent input, thus supporting learners when noticing does not happen spontaneously. The main aim of this study is thus to ascertain whether instruction can lead learners to notice the targeted linguistic aspects of subsequent input, eventually promoting L2 learning and development.

Noun phrase pre-modification in the L2 English of Brazilian Portuguese L1 speakers

In a previous study Frota and Vereza (1992) analyzed the use of noun phrases in the written production of Brazilian university students majoring in English. They found that students had great difficulty with some but not all mechanisms of pre-modification. One of the possible reasons may be the fact that, in Portuguese, pre-modification is not as highly productive as it is in English and the most frequently used modification mechanism is post-modification, essentially expressed by means of an adjective, a prepositional phrase, or a relative clause, as in *um professor brilhante* (a brilliant professor), *casas de campo* (country houses), and *bigode espesso com pontas recurvas, que lembram o formato de um guidom* (handlebar moustache), respectively. The high level of structural and semantic complexity associated with pre-modification may also explain why this is such a difficult structure for speakers of Portuguese to master. The difficulty lies in establishing the underlying semantic relationship present in these types of structures in English. The relationship between the elements of a N+N phrase is implicit and not easily comprehended based on a compositional analysis of the nouns. Also, these noun phrases fluctuate between semantic transparency (e.g., *chocolate bar*, Portuguese: *barra de chocolate*) and opacity (*soap opera*, Portuguese: *novela*) and may be freely produced, once they make sense within a context (Levi, 1978). Noun phrases with a noun pre-modifier may have Portuguese corresponding structures of different types. They may be translated into a single noun (e.g., *apple tree*, Portuguese: *macieira*), compound nouns (e.g., *textbook*, Portuguese: *livro-texto*), prepositional phrases (e.g., *vanilla ice cream*, Portuguese: *sorvete de creme*), or even relative clauses (*drug deaths*, Portuguese: *mortes causadas por/em decorrência do uso de drogas*). Finally, another possible reason for this difficulty may be the fact that nouns are rarely used as modifiers in Portuguese. With this function they are only found in compound nouns as in *navio-escola* ('school ship') but always in a post-nominal position.

Interestingly enough, using adjectives as pre-modifiers did not pose any particular difficulty for learners in the Brazilian EFL context. This was not fully expected, since adjectives in Portuguese most often follow the nouns they modify, so a transfer hypothesis would predict difficulties in the adjective+noun order in English, which did not occur. In fact, this type of noun phrase (NP) seems to be efficiently incorporated into the Portuguese speaker's interlanguage early on in the learning process. By the same token, a similar lack of difficulty happens among English speakers learning Portuguese as a foreign language, who also easily reverse the order (Schmidt & Frota, 1986).

Nouns as pre-modifiers, on the other hand, represent a major source of difficulty for speakers of Brazilian Portuguese (though other pre-modifiers may also lead to difficulties) according to the findings reported by Frota and Vereza (1992). They are very frequently used in English; nouns were the second most common type of pre-modifier found in all five types of text chosen for the present study. In addition, pre-modifying nouns bring with them rather complex semantic and pragmatic issues and express a wide range of form-meaning relationships. In the written production of the EFL learners studied by Frota and Vereza, all the examples of noun+noun sequences that were found indicated that the students did not use this type of pre-modifier productively but rather relied heavily on clichéd expressions and formulaic combinations such as *birthday parties*. Given all these considerations, an attempt to raise L2 learners' awareness of the intricacies inherent in pre-modified noun constructions might lead to a better reception and production of this highly complex aspect of English.

Present study

This study investigated the relationship between instruction and subsequent noticing of the modification mechanisms of the English NP structure in input. The purpose of the instruction was to present the formal features of modification to the participants of the study, with the structure being exemplified and contextualized in texts read by these EFL learners. The primary motivation for this was to help Brazilian EFL learners better understand and overcome potential difficulties with the mechanisms of NP modification.

The purpose of the initial part of the study was to expose learners to contextualized instances of novel features of the English noun phrase and see whether these learners would notice exemplars of such structures in the text without any prior prompting. Following this first phase, as it was expected that probably some participants would not notice these NP structural features, an instructional treatment was delivered with the aim of priming them to specifically notice the target structure in subsequent input—a new text in which the same form was repeated several times. After treatment, two posttests (one immediate and the other delayed) were applied to verify whether instruction led to increased noticing.

The following research questions guided this study:

RQ1 Do EFL learners notice exemplars of the pre-modification NP structure when reading texts prior to instruction?

RQ2 Does instruction on formal features of English NPs result in sensitivity to the presence of those features in input? If so, does such sensitivity last beyond an immediate treatment effect?

In relation to these questions, the hypotheses were:

Hypothesis 1 Some participants will probably notice exemplars of the target structure in the input prior to any instruction and others will not (individual differences hypothesis).

Hypothesis 2 Instruction will enhance the participants' ability to notice and recall instances of the target structure when exposed to subsequent input.

Method

The design of this quantitative study was pre-experimental, using a single group pretest, treatment, posttest, delayed posttest design without a control group, to assess the extent to which participants noticed exemplars of the target structure (pre-modification in NPs) in written input before and after instruction.

Participants

All participants were recruited from a language and literature undergraduate course at a university in Brazil, and all were majoring in English. They were enrolled in the same English course, "The English Noun Phrase," offered in the third semester. Participants' level of proficiency in English as an L2 was controlled by administering an English proficiency test (institutional TOEFL) in order to obtain a relatively homogenous *intermediate* level population, eliminating both highly proficient participants (TOEFL>550) and low proficiency participants (TOEFL<450). After selection, a group of 27 Brazilian learners of English as an L2 participated in this study and completed all phases of the study.

Instructional treatment

The aim of the instructional treatment was to help participants notice exemplars of the target structure (pre-modification in English NPs) in subsequent input. Instruction targeted pre- and post-modification mechanisms in noun phrases and followed the principles of *form-focused instruction* (FFI) (Ellis, 2001), including pre-selection of the linguistic structures to be taught. The treatment was delivered in two sessions. It consisted of descriptions of NP modification mechanisms and exercises on the different types of NP modification.

Procedures

As mentioned above, the study design featured a pretest, an immediate posttest, and a delayed posttest two weeks later (see Appendix). Each test required the participants to read a text and then to recognize specific exemplars of NP modification (pre- or post-modification) that occurred in a text they had just read. Thus, noticing was assessed in three different research phases, in the pretest and the two posttest occasions.

Prior to the instructional treatment, all participants read a text and immediately responded to a test that asked them whether specific noun phrases had or had not occurred in the text that they had just read (*Recognition Test of Noticing*—see Appendix). The objective of this task was to see whether participants spontaneously attend to, notice, and can accurately recognize exemplars of the target structure when reading a text before any instruction. Then, participants were given the instruction on the pre- and post-modification of NPs in English. After the instructional treatment, participants read another text from the same source, on the same subject, and with a similar level of linguistic complexity and once again were required to do the same task—reading a text and then immediately saying whether specific instances of pre-modification (e.g., *course objectives*) or post-modification (e.g., *objectives of the course*) had occurred in the text they had just read.

Two weeks after the treatment, they repeated the same task, once more with another new text from the same source, on the same subject, and with a similar level of linguistic complexity. Immediately after reading the text, they again were asked to recognize whether specific instances of the target structure occurred in the text or not.

Therefore, in all phases, noticing was assessed through a Recognition Test of Noticing (see Appendix), developed by the researchers. Participants were asked to decide whether specific noun phrases were in the text they had just read (10 per text), marking "( ) yes, it was in the text" or "( ) no, it was not in the text." Each correct response was scored 1, so that total noticing scores for each text ranged from 0 to 10.

Results and discussion

An ANOVA was run to verify the differences in the results among the participants before and after the treatment by measuring the dependent variable *noticing*.

Table 1 reports the descriptive statistics for noticing. Based on the results, it seems that instruction did indeed enhance participants' sensitivity to exemplars of the target structure in subsequent input after the instruction in both the immediate and delayed posttests. These results support both Hypothesis 1 (there were individual differences in sensitivity among the participants prior to instruction) and Hypothesis 2 (instruction enhanced the participants' ability to notice instances of the target structure in input).

Table 1. Descriptive statistics for noticing

	M	*SD*	N
pretest	38.09	2.13	27
immediate	49.25	1.59	27
delayed	57.88	1.73	27

note. Scores are expressed in ratios.

The ANOVA results show statistically significant differences among the three different tested phases overall, $F(2,52)=8.991$, $p<.001$, with a medium effect size (partial eta squared=26%). The contrast between the pretest (mean of 38.09) and the immediate posttest (mean of 49.25) was not statistically significant, $F(1,27)=3.97$, $p=.057$, perhaps because of the relatively small sample size. However, the difference between the pretest and the delayed posttest was statistically significant, $F(1,27)=22.62$, $p<.001$, with a large effect size (partial eta squared=47%).

When the data was inspected at the finer individual level, the results showed some exceptions to the general trend: nine participants increased their noticing rate on the immediate posttest but demonstrated a decrease in the delayed posttest. Perhaps, in these cases, instruction was good enough to enhance sensitivity to language input temporarily but did not lead to any long-term increase in input sensitivity with respect to this structure.

Limitations and conclusion

Several limitations must be recognized. First, our interpretations are limited by the absence of a control group that would be exposed to the target structures through the tests but would not experience any instructional treatment of those structures. Including a control in the design of future research would allow us to determine the added value of instruction in supporting noticing above the benefits likely derived from sheer input exposure and test practice. In addition, we still need to test learning through additional measures to ascertain whether learning actually occurred over a longer period after instruction and exposure to the same input. Further, we feel it would be relevant in the future to apply a working memory test in order to investigate the role of working memory capacity as a moderator variable in the interaction between instruction and noticing, possibly including differences in performance on the immediate and delayed posttests. Finally, it should be acknowledged that this study investigated only the relationship between instruction and noticing, only the first step in learning from input, and did not address the relationship between noticing and actual productive use, in real communicative contexts (both verbal and written), the ultimate goal of instruction.

These limitations notwithstanding, we can say that our evidence is encouraging in support of the proposal that noticing is beneficial for maintenance of newly detected language and that instruction can serve as a bridge or a pathfinder in support of noticing in subsequent input. We hope the results of our study contribute to renewed future efforts to investigate the role of noticing and instruction in the foreign language teaching/learning process in language classes.

References

Anderson, J. R. (1980). *Cognitive psychology and its implications.* San Francisco: Freeman.

Anderson, J. R. (1983). *The architecture of cognition.* Cambridge: Harvard University Press.

Baars, B. J. (1986). What is a theory of consciousness a theory of? The search for criterial constraints on theory. *Imagination, Cognition, and Personality, 6,* 3–23.

Baars, B. J. (1988). *A cognitive theory of consciousness.* New York: Cambridge University Press.

Baars, B. J. (1997). *In the theater of consciousness: The workspace of the mind.* New York: Oxford University Press.

Ellis, N. C., & Schmidt, R. (1997). Morphology and longer distance dependencies: Laboratory research illuminating the A in SLA. *Studies in Second Language Acquisition, 19,* 145–171.

Ellis, R. (1994). *The study of second language acquisition.* Oxford: Oxford University Press.

Ellis, R. (2001). *Form-focused instruction and second language learning.* Malden, MA: Blackwell.

Frota, S. N., & Vereza, S. (1992, September). Um estudo comparativo do sintagma nominal em Inglês e em Português e suas implicações pedagógicas. Unpublished paper presented at III Congresso Brasileiro de Lingüística Aplicada, UNICAMP, Campinas, SP, Brazil.

Leow, R. P. (1997). Attention, awareness, and foreign language behavior. *Language Learning, 47,* 467–505.

Levi, J. (1978). *The syntax and semantics of complex nominals.* New York, NY: Academic Press.

Mackey, A. (2006). Feedback, noticing, and instructed second language learning. *Applied Linguistics, 27,* 405–530.

McLaughlin, B. (1987). *Theories of second-language learning.* London: Edward Arnold.

Norris, J. M., & Ortega, L. (2000). Effectiveness of L2 instruction: A research synthesis and quantitative meta-analysis. *Language Learning, 50,* 417–528.

Norris, J. M., & Ortega, L. (2003). Defining and measuring SLA. In C. J. Doughty & M. H. Long (Eds.), *The handbook of second language acquisition* (pp. 717–761). Malden, MA: Blackwell.

Reis, R. M. (2010, April 12). How to get all-important teaching experience. *The Chronicle of Higher Education.* Retrieved from http://chronicle.com/article/How-To-Get-All-Important-Te/46358/

Robinson, P. (1995). Attention, memory, and the "noticing" hypothesis. *Language Learning, 45,* 283–331.

Robinson, P. (1996). Learning simple and complex second language rules under implicit, incidental, rule-search, and instructed conditions. *Studies in Second Language Acquisition*, *18*, 26–67.

Schmidt, R. (1990). The role of consciousness in second language learning. *Applied Linguistics*, *11*, 129–158.

Schmidt, R. (1992). Psychological mechanisms underlying second language fluency. *Studies in Second Language Acquisition*, *14*, 423–41.

Schmidt, R. (1994). Implicit learning and the cognitive unconscious: Of artificial grammars and SLA. In N. Ellis (Ed.), *Implicit and explicit learning of languages* (pp. 165–209). San Diego, CA: Academic Press.

Schmidt, R. (1995). Consciousness and foreign language learning: A tutorial on attention and awareness in learning. In R. Schmidt (Ed.), *Attention and awareness in foreign language learning* (pp. 1–63). Honolulu, HI: University of Hawai'i, National Foreign Language Resource Center.

Schmidt, R. (2001). Attention. In P. Robinson (Ed.), *Cognition and second language instruction* (pp. 3–32). Cambridge: Cambridge University Press.

Schmidt, R., & Frota, S. N. (1986). Developing basic conversational ability in a second language: A case study of an adult learner of Portuguese. In R. R. Day (Ed.), *Talking to learn: Conversation in second language acquisition* (pp. 237–326). Rowley, MA: Newbury House.

Street, S. (2010, April 21). Academe's house rules. *The Chronicle of Higher Education*. Retrieved from http://chronicle.com/article/Academes-House-Rules/65163/

Swain, M. (1998). Focus on form through conscious reflection. In C. Doughty & J. Williams (Eds.), *Focus on form in classroom second language acquisition* (pp. 64–81). Cambridge: Cambridge University Press.

Appendix: Recognition test of noticing

Pretest

Text used: Reis, R. M. (2010, April 12). How to get all-important teaching experience. *The Chronicle of Higher Education*. Retrieved from http://chronicle.com/article/How-To-Get-All-Important-Te/46358/

Next to each of the following phrases, indicate which ones occurred in the passage you just read:

1. teaching skills

   __ yes, it was in the text

   __ no, it was not in the text

2. skills in teaching

   __ yes, it was in the text

   __ no, it was not in the text

3. assistantship in teaching

   __ yes, it was in the text

   __ no, it was not in the text

4. teaching assistantship

   __ yes, it was in the text

   __ no, it was not in the text

5. chemistry student

   __ yes, it was in the text

   __ no, it was not in the text

6. student in chemistry

   __ yes, it was in the text

   __ no, it was not in the text

7. experience as a graduate-student or postdoc

   __ yes, it was in the text

   __ no, it was not in the text

8. graduate-student or postdoc experience

   __ yes, it was in the text

   __ no, it was not in the text

9. portfolio of experiences and references

   __ yes, it was in the text

   __ no, it was not in the text

10. experiences and references portfolio

    __ yes, it was in the text

    __ no, it was not in the text

Immediate posttest

Text used: Reis, R. M. (2010, April 12). How to get all-important teaching experience. *The Chronicle of Higher Education*. Retrieved from http://chronicle.com/article/How-To-Get-All-Important-Te/46358/

Next to each of the following phrases, indicate which ones occurred in the passage you just read:

1. experience as a graduate-student or postdoc

   __ yes, it was in the text

   __ no, it was not in the text

2. your graduate-student or postdoc experience

   __ yes, it was in the text

   __ no, it was not in the text

3. university employee

   __ yes, it was in the text

   __ no, it was not in the text

4. employee of the university

    __ yes, it was in the text

    __ no, it was not in the text

5. course objectives

    __ yes, it was in the text

    __ no, it was not in the text

6. objectives of the course

    __ yes, it was in the text

    __ no, it was not in the text

7. laboratory experiments

    __ yes, it was in the text

    __ no, it was not in the text

8. experiments in a laboratory

    __ yes, it was in the text

    __ no, it was not in the text

9. faculty members

    __ yes, it was in the text

    __ no, it was not in the text

10. members of the faculty

    __ yes, it was in the text

    __ no, it was not in the text

Delayed posttest

Text used: Street, S. (2010, April 21). Academe's house rules. *The Chronicle of Higher Education*. Retrieved from http://chronicle.com/article/Academes-House-Rules/65163/

Next to each of the following phrases, indicate which ones occurred in the passage you just read:

1. teaching assignments

    __ yes, it was in the text

    __ no, it was not in the text

2. assignments in teaching

    __ yes, it was in the text

    __ no, it was not in the text

3. limitations in the budget

    __ yes, it was in the text

    __ no, it was not in the text

4. budget limitations

    __ yes, it was in the text

__ no, it was not in the text

5. measures of job security

   __ yes, it was in the text

   __ no, it was not in the text

6. job security measures

   __ yes, it was in the text

   __ no, it was not in the text

7. teaching positions

   __ yes, it was in the text

   __ no, it was not in the text

8. positions in teaching

   __ yes, it was in the text

   __ no, it was not in the text

9. members of the faculty

   __ yes, it was in the text

   __ no, it was not in the text

10. faculty members

   __ yes, it was in the text

   __ no, it was not in the text

Investigating Relationships Among Noticing, Working Memory Capacity, and Accuracy in L2 Oral Performance

Joara M. Bergsleithner
University of Brasília

Mailce Borges Mota
Federal University of Santa Catarina

This study investigates how noticing of L2 instances in input relates to working memory capacity (WMC) and to grammatical accuracy in L2 oral tasks. Participants were 30 Brazilian adult learners of English who were required to perform several tasks, which aimed at assessing: (a) noticing instances of formal aspects of indirect questions (the target structure), (b) WMC, and (c) grammatical accuracy of the target structure when used in oral performance. The results reveal that there is a statistically significant relationship among the noticing of formal features of the target structure, WMC, and grammatical accuracy in L2 oral performance. Together, the results can be taken as evidence that learners are more prone to noticing L2 formal aspects if they have a larger WMC and, as a consequence, are also able to perform their L2 speech more accurately.

Introduction

The role of noticing and attention has been a prominent topic of debate in the field of second language acquisition (SLA) for several decades. Schmidt's (1990) noticing hypothesis has made a huge contribution to this debate and to the second language studies literature. He proposed that L2 learners can acquire the formal aspects of language through exposure to input only if they notice (i.e., consciously register) instances of linguistic structures or rules that they encounter in the input. For Schmidt, noticing is an internal subjective experience that can arise spontaneously whenever one is exposed to novel input (Bergsleithner, 2007, 2009; Schmidt, 1990, 1995), but it can also be facilitated by instruction. For example, instruction about the formal features of language can serve as

Bergsleithner, J. M., & Mota, M. B. (2013). Investigating relationships among noticing, working memory capacity, and accuracy in L2 oral performance. In J. M. Bergsleithner, S. N. Frota, & J. K. Yoshioka (Eds.), *Noticing and second language acquisition: Studies in honor of Richard Schmidt* (pp. 151–167). Honolulu: University of Hawai'i, National Foreign Language Resource Center.

a priming function that makes learners more sensitive to properties of input (Schmidt & Frota, 1986), and instruction can facilitate noticing more generally whenever teachers, texts, or instructional tasks help learners to pay attention to aspects of language that they are unlikely to notice on their own.

Another link between noticing and instruction is related to the construct of *noticing-the-gap* (Schmidt & Frota, 1986). L2 learners can become aware of gaps in their language abilities when they make comparisons between their own output and what they encounter in input and detect mismatches (Ellis, 1994; Gass, 1988, 1997; Schmidt, 2001; Schmidt & Frota, 1986; Swain, 1993, 1995, 1998). Other researchers propose that noticing and awareness of L2 formal aspects may arise directly within instruction (Ellis, 1990, 1994, 1999, 2001; Robinson, 1996a, 1997, 2002; Skehan, 1996)—the focus of the study described in this chapter.

The other related issue in the investigation of noticing regards its measurement. Although this psychological construct seems to be difficult to assess (because the measures of noticing, attention, or awareness might overlap), a number of studies have examined different methods of assessing noticing, such as think-aloud protocols, diaries, eye-tracking, uptake, and stimulated recall. In this study, noticing was accessed (and assessed) by means of uptake, referring to what learners claim to learn from a particular lesson focused on a specific grammar topic (Loewen, 2004). In this sense uptake can be considered evidence of noticing, a report of what learners noticed or paid attention to during a teacher's instruction. Furthermore, it also shows learners' awareness and reflection upon what they are studying, and it could be related to the recall of what has been noticed since it requires verbalizable or reportable knowledge of the focus of instruction (Slimani, 1989, 1992).

Aiming at investigating the relationship between noticing and working memory capacity (WMC), researchers have uncovered interesting findings. Robinson (1995a, 1995b, 1996a, 1996b, 1997, 2001, 2002, 2003) found that noticing and WMC are closely related, and WMC may constrain noticing. Mackey, Philp, Fujii, Egi, and Tatsumi (2002) also found that WMC and noticing (in this case, the noticing of interactional feedback) were related but pointed out that noticing is not related to WMC alone but also to other factors such as "grammatical sensitivity and field independence, as well as socio-psychological factors" (p. 202). Other researchers have shown that grammatical sensitivity is closely related to WMC (Harrington, 1992; Harrington & Sawyer, 1992) but, again, that other factors besides grammatical sensitivity may also constrain noticing, such as lack of familiarity with the task, lack of motivation to do the task, anxiety when being recorded in language labs, and/or a general lack of interest in the formal aspects of language (Bergsleithner, 2007).

The cognitive construct of WMC in the current study concerns: (a) the system or mechanism responsible for storage and processing of information during performance of complex cognitive tasks (Baddeley, 1986; Baddeley & Hitch, 1974; Daneman, 1991; Daneman & Green, 1986; Harrington, 1992; Harrington & Sawyer, 1992); (b) "the relative capacity to intake and integrate information in immediate, online processing" (Harrington, 1992, p. 123); (c) "the mechanism of retrieval and maintenance of information during cognitive processing" (Watanabe & Bergsleithner, 2006, p. 47); and (d) "the cognitive construct responsible for the storage and processing of information and for the processes of recall and maintenance of the information acquired" (Bergsleithner, 2007, p. 38).

In order to understand how noticing and WMC might affect individuals' L2 learning and L2 oral performance, one must first understand how these cognitive constructs trigger individual differences among humans when dealing with grammatical accuracy. Some researchers have shown that individuals can be distinguished with regard to several cognitive constructs such as noticing and WMC (Robinson, 1995a, 1995b, 1997; Schmidt, 2012; Skehan, 1989, 1998). Several studies have revealed that individuals with a larger WMC (higher spans/higher processors) demonstrate better performance on complex cognitive tasks, since they efficiently allocate attentional cognitive resources demanded by the task. In contrast, lower WMC span learners seem to allocate these resources in a less efficient way (Bergsleithner, 2007, 2010; Daneman & Green, 1986; Fortkamp, 1999, 2000; Miyake & Friedman, 1998; Miyake & Shah, 1999; Mota, 2003, 2009).

Other researchers' findings have shown that noticing could be related to WMC and indeed may impact L2 oral performance (Bergsleithner, 2007; Fortkamp, 1999, 2000; Mota, 2003, 2009), and some studies show that WMC is closely related to the performance of L2 oral production (Bergsleithner, 2007; Fortkamp, 1999, 2000; Mota, 2003, 2009; Payne & Ross, 2005; Payne & Whitney, 2002; Weissheimer, 2007; Weissheimer & Mota, 2011). Together, the results of the above studies can be taken as at least indirect evidence that noticing exemplars of L2 formal aspects in L2 oral performance may be related to individuals' WMC.

Study

This study aimed at investigating the relationship among noticing, WMC, and accuracy of indirect questions—the target form—in L2 oral performance. Accuracy mirrors grammatical correctness and individuals' effort to control their attentional resources to avoid errors (Bergsleithner, 2007; Ellis, 2005; Ortega, 2003; Skehan, 1998).

The central hypothesis of this investigation is that individuals who notice more instances of formal L2 features will have better recall of what has been noticed and will more efficiently develop their oral performance if they have a larger WMC, in contrast to those with a smaller WMC. In order to guide this experimental study, the following five research questions (RQ) were posed, followed by their research hypotheses (RH):

RQ1 Are there relationships among individual differences in the noticing of L2 forms, WMC, and L2 oral performance?

RH1 There will be statistically significant relationships among individual differences in the noticing of L2 features, WMC, and L2 oral performance. Individuals with a larger WMC, as measured by the Speaking Span Test (SST), will notice more L2 formal aspects of the target structure and demonstrate more accuracy in performing L2 oral tasks using that target structure, while individuals with a smaller WMC will notice less and will be less accurate in using the target structure when performing oral tasks.

RQ2 Is noticing related to WMC?

RH2 There will be a statistically significant relationship between noticing and WMC. Individuals with a larger WMC will notice more L2 formal aspects when receiving L2 linguistic input and have more ability to recall what has been noticed.

RQ3 Is WMC related to L2 oral performance?

RH3 There will be a statistically significant relationship between WMC and L2 oral performance. Individuals with a larger WMC will demonstrate better accuracy in the performance of L2 oral tasks.

RQ4 Is noticing related to L2 oral performance?

RH4 There will be a statistically significant relationship between noticing and oral performance. Individuals who notice more will demonstrate better performance with the target structure in the L2 oral tasks on the two posttests.

RQ5 Is accuracy in oral performance of the target structure—indirect questions (i.e., embedded questions)—statistically different between pretest and posttest phases? If so, is this difference related to noticing and/or WMC?

RH5 There will be a statistically significant difference in accuracy in the oral performance of the target structure between the pretest and posttests and an improvement in accuracy in the performance of the target structure. This difference in the accuracy of oral performance in the three test conditions (one pretest phase and two posttest phases) will be related to noticing and/or WMC. However, some weakening of accuracy in the oral performance of the target structure in the delayed posttest is expected.

Method

Participants

Thirty adult native speakers of Brazilian Portuguese who were learning English as a foreign language (EFL) were the participants of the present study. They ranged from 18 to 43 years old, with a mean age of 25 years old. Seventeen were male and 13 were female, and they were enrolled at a university in the south of Brazil. They were studying lesson 2 of the book adopted for their course, *New Interchange 2* (Richards, Hull, & Proctor, 2002). Participant selection was done through a two-minute picture description task in order to verify the participants' grammatical accuracy level to obtain a more homogenous group. Then, the participants' speech samples were transcribed and later judged by four raters with regard to accuracy but not fluency or complexity. They judged the participants' accuracy on a scale of 0 to 5, following a rating scale adapted from the FCE Speaking Test Assessment Scales (Cambridge Examination) by Iwashita, McNamara, and Elder (2001) and from the RSA test by Hughes (1989). Out of 50 participants in the selection process, 18 were excluded due to their very high or very low level of proficiency.

Materials and tasks for data collection

The experiment consisted of five tasks. One task aimed at assessing noticing through an oral protocol (Bergsleithner, 2007, based on Robinson, 1995a, 1997), the other aimed at assessing WMC through the SST (Daneman, 1991; Daneman & Green, 1986; Fortkamp, 1999, 2000), and the other three oral tasks aimed at assessing grammatical accuracy[1] through the participants' oral performance of twelve *indirect questions*, with six questions each generated from two different pictures. The grammatical structure chosen for this study was part of the syllabus of the course in which the participants were engaged.

Pretest phase

The pretest phase was conducted through the performance of an L2 oral production task by 32 participants. First, they were instructed in Portuguese to look at a picture of a map and make six questions using indirect questions about the map, and secondly, they were required to make six indirect questions for another picture in which people were performing various actions. Out of 32 participants, two demonstrated previous knowledge of the target form and were eliminated, leaving 30 participants who took part in the study.

1 In this study *grammatical accuracy* was assessed in the utterances by analyzing the target structure only in order to avoid assessing complexity as well.

Treatment and procedure for the treatment

An instructional treatment on indirect questions was given to facilitate noticing. The kind of treatment was form-focused instruction[2], as proposed by Ellis (2001). The participants were taught some specific formal aspects of indirect questions (embedded questions)[3] that were part of the course syllabus. This structure seems to be more complex than others and demands more cognitive effort from learners, distinguishing, thus, higher from lower processors.

First, implicit instruction on the target form had as the initial aim to call learners' attention to the target form. Secondly, they were asked about the situations in which indirect rather than direct questions are more properly used. Finally, the target structure was explicitly shown to help them notice the modifications in the position of the verb when comparing the structure of direct and indirect questions, the use and position of auxiliary verbs, and the main verbs in both kinds of questions.

Posttest phases

Two posttests were carried out in this study: an immediate posttest (the same day of treatment) and a delayed posttest (two weeks after treatment), both consisting of an oral protocol and the performance of an L2 oral task.

Oral protocol

The oral protocol aimed at assessing the learners' noticing of instances of the indirect questions structure, which they had been taught. Robinson's (1995a) framework (whether learners notice any rules, look for rules, and verbalize rules) was used as a guide to elaborate the questions for the oral protocol as well as to analyze the learners' answers. One more item (whether they could remember the target grammar structure which they had been taught and whether they could explain how such target grammar structure was organized in indirect questions) and an oral task (to orally perform two questions by using the target structure) were added to the oral protocol (see Appendix A). The questions were administered in the language lab, and the oral protocol was administered in Portuguese in order to facilitate the participants' understanding of the questions.

Although Robinson's framework was followed in this study, as in Bergsleithner (2007), the latter acknowledged that *looking for rules* is a weak measure of noticing for two reasons. First of all, looking for rules is a statement about what one does when speaking (i.e., producing utterances, possibly with the help of explicit knowledge) not about how one learns or gets that knowledge. Secondly, looking for rules is not the same as finding them. Thus, if someone answers "yes" to this question in the oral protocol, it does not guarantee that this person has necessarily noticed anything. Therefore, in order to see if looking for rules made any difference in the outcome, the participants' noticing was scored in the following two ways: (a) Noticing 1, in which Robinson's second question (Did you look for rules?) was not included, and (b) Noticing 2, in which Robinson's second question was included to score the measure of noticing.

Oral tasks

Immediately after the oral protocol, a new recording was made at the language lab, right after the instructional treatment, in order to verify whether the participants noticed

2 "The term *form-focused instruction* (FFI) is used to refer to any planned or incidental instruction activity that is intended to induce language learners to pay attention to linguistic form" (Ellis, 2001, p. 1).

3 Embedded questions require a complex language process from the participants, that is, to elaborate a question embedded into the other (Bergsleithner, 2007).

instances of the target structure they had been instructed in and whether they could orally perform the target structure. A new map and a new picture were selected for the participants to use with the structure in order to minimize the effects of task repetition in oral performance, as proposed by Bygate (2001) and Skehan (1996).

The delayed posttest was conducted two weeks after the treatment. A new recording was collected with the same task conducted in the language lab, however with different pictures. This final language lab recording aimed at verifying whether the participants could (a) notice indirect questions during treatment, (b) perform indirect questions in a delayed phase, and (c) sustain grammatical accuracy in performing indirect questions two weeks after treatment.

Variables assessed

Noticing assessment

Noticing was measured by means of the oral protocol, which elicited the participants' uptake. This indirect measure of noticing was assessed by recalling the formal features of the target form, which participants were supposed to notice through instruction, called here the recalling of noticing (Bergsleithner, 2007) or retrospective accounts (Ericsson & Simon, 1980, 1993). Noticing, thus, was indirectly measured *off-line*[4] by means of uptake in the oral protocol, immediately after the instructional treatment (see Appendix B).

Working memory capacity assessment

The Speaking Span Test was applied to assess individuals' WMC. This test was first proposed for L1 studies (Daneman, 1991; Daneman & Green, 1986) and then adapted for L2 studies (Fortkamp, 1999, 2000). In this study it aims at assessing individuals' WMC in L2 speech production and consists of 60 unrelated nouns, organized in sets of two to six words. Each word in bold was individually presented for one second in the center of a computer screen and required the participants to read it aloud. At the end of each set, two to six question marks appeared respectively in the middle of the screen to inform the participants that the set had finished. The number of question marks indicated the number of words presented in each set. Participants were asked to produce a sentence aloud for each word presented containing the words in their original form and order of presentation to be considerate accurate—1 point each (Fortkamp, 1999, 2000).

Accuracy assessment in the three oral tasks

Some parameters for scoring the participants' oral performance were established with the help of a native speaker of American English, who also assisted in judging the accuracy of the participants in the SST scores. They were used to judge whether the indirect questions performed by the participants, by means of elicitation of L2 oral production tasks, were accurate or not. The parameters were divided into three different general categories: (1) target errors for the sentences, which were considered inaccurate concerning the target structure; (2) sentence errors that were not scored as indirect question errors; and (3) accurate sentences that correctly contained the target structure (see Appendix C for all three categories). All accurate indirect questions (taking the target structure into account only) were scored—1 point each.

Results and discussion

Table 1 below indicates that in the three oral performance (OP) tasks (here called *tests*), there was a sizeable difference in the mean learner performance between OP1 and OP2, and OP1 and OP3, that is, before and after treatment. However, as can be seen in Table 1, there is a similarity in the mean performance between OP2 and OP3, both tests after treatment, although the first was immediate and the second delayed.

4 The term *off-line* is considered throughout this study as an instant after input.

Besides the oral performance test data, the descriptive statistics in Table 1 include the two scores for the measures of WMC (WM-strict and WM-lenient) and the two scores obtained for noticing 1 (N1) and noticing 2 (N2) through the oral protocol. The correlations between the scores of these variables are shown in Table 2, which displays the results for working memory capacity and noticing.

Table 1. Descriptive statistics for oral performance scores, working memory capacity, and noticing (*N*=30)

	min.	max.	M	*SD*
OP1	0	3	0.97	1.12
OP2	1	12	7.27	2.79
OP3	0	12	7.17	3.35
WM-strict	5	34	18.50	5.93
WM-lenient	6	35	19.46	6.08
N1	2	9	6.40	2.04
N2	2	10	7.50	2.31

As shown in Table 1, while OP1 shows a mean performance of 0.97 and a standard deviation (*SD*) of 1.12, these scores are minimal, demonstrating only a small change. However, performances in OP2 and OP3 show a considerable difference in the mean scores of participants, OP2 with a mean of 7.27 and a *SD* of 2.79 and OP3 with a mean of 7.17 and a *SD* of 3.35. These results indicate that there was a change in the mean scores of this test from the pretest to the posttests. There was also greater score variability in performance within the group on later administrations. Despite this variability it can be seen that there was an overall difference between performance with the target structure before and after treatment. This finding suggests that there was noticing of instances of formal aspects of the target structure and some language development, since participants could accurately produce oral sentences using the structure.

Moving on to Table 2, correlational findings are displayed among the measures of all variables: (a) oral performance (grammatical accuracy in oral performance); (b) working memory capacity; and (c) noticing. Pearson correlations were calculated among the two measures of working memory (WM-strict and WM-lenient), the two measures of noticing (N1 and N2), and oral performance scores on the three testing occasions (OP1, OP2, OP3). A two-tailed alpha decision level of $p<.05$ was set for all inferential decisions of statistical significance for the correlations.

Table 2. Correlations between oral performance scores, working memory capacity, and noticing

	OP1	OP2	OP3	WM-strict	WM-lenient	N1	N2
WM-strict	.15	.61*	.64*	–	–	–	–
WM-lenient	.17	.61*	.63*	.99*	–	–	–
N1	.26	.60*	.70*	.41*	.42*	–	–
N2	.38*	.59*	.72*	.42*	.43*	.95*	–

* *p*<. 05, two-tailed.

Several findings are apparent in Table 2. First, for these correlational comparisons, the choice of strict versus lenient WM measures makes little difference. The two measures are very highly correlated (r=.99), and correlations with the oral tests change by only a few decimal points, if at all, based on the strict versus lenient WMC scoring. Second, the choice of N1 versus N2 as the measure of noticing does not make much difference for comparisons with measures of WMC, nor for comparisons with either the immediate posttest or the delayed posttest. However, there is a larger difference between the N1 and N2 correlations with the pretest (r=.26 versus r=.38, respectively). Notice also that, although there is some degree of relationship between N and WMC, it is not particularly strong (around r=.42), suggesting that these two measures are tapping distinct constructs (Robinson, 1995b, 2003).

Moving on to the immediate posttests, where noticing and WMC would be presumed to exhibit some kind of influence (if they are indeed related to oral test performance), there is a clear, if moderate, relationship between both the noticing and WMC variables and oral test performance, ranging almost imperceptibly for each between r=.59 to r=.61. Perhaps of most interest, moving to the delayed test, the strength of relationships increases for both the noticing and WMC variables. However, a much larger increase is apparent for noticing (for N1, from r=.60 on the posttest to r=.70 on the delayed test). These findings suggest that, while both noticing and WMC are moderately related to immediate test performance (and by extension, perhaps, to the learning that was required to perform well), noticing is slightly more strongly related to sustained performance on the delayed test.

Inferential statistics: Oral performance results

The above findings suggest apparent patterns in participants' oral performance before and after treatment. However, in order to examine the statistical reliability of apparent observed differences between the three testing occasions (see Table 2), one repeated measures analysis of variance (ANOVA) was performed with pretest, immediate posttest, and delayed posttest as the three levels of the within-subjects variable. The alpha level was set at p<.05 for the inferential decision of statistical significance.

As reported in Table 3, the differences between OP1 and OP2, and OP1 and OP3 are all statistically significant since they show a considerable progress in the mean performance regarding the scores of grammatical accuracy in the sentences produced by the participants, while using the specific target structure in the three testing occasions. In Table 3 an overall statistically significant effect was found for *test*, Wilks' lambda F(2, 28)=86.09, p<.00. A high eta-squared effect size (0.86) indicated that *test* accounted for a large proportion of the overall difference between the three sets of scores (i.e., overall, there was considerable magnitude of difference between the testing occasions).

Table 3. Overall statistical effect observed for test

value	F	hypothesis *DF*	*df*	error *df*	sig.	partial eta squared
Wilks' lambda	.14	86.09	2	28	<.00	.86

From the overall statistically significant effect for *test*, subsequent pairwise comparisons were also conducted between each of the three pairs of tests (OP1, OP2, OP3). Statistically significant differences were found between the pretest and the immediate posttest (p<.00), and between the pretest and the delayed posttest (p<.00), but not between the two posttests (p=.77). Apparently, the learners changed in substantially and statistically trustworthy degrees from the pretest to the posttest, but there was little perceptible change from immediate to delayed posttest. As follows, Table 4 shows the pairwise comparisons among the three testing occasions.

Table 4. Pairwise comparisons among the three testing occasions

					95% confidence interval for difference	
(I) test	(J) test	mean difference (I–J)	std. error	sig.	lower bound	upper bound
OP 3	OP 1	6.20(*)	.59	.00	4.71	7.7
OP 2	OP 1	6.30(*)	.47	.00	5.10	7.50
OP 3	OP2	.1	.33	1	–.75	.95

* The mean difference is significant at the .05 level.

In response to the first research question, the above findings suggest that there are statistically significant relationships among noticing of L2 formal features, WMC, and L2 oral performance. Based on these findings, Hypothesis 1, which predicts a relationship among the three variables, was supported because most of the higher span participants when compared to the lower span participants seem to be better at noticing instances of the target structure. Moreover, the higher span participants orally performed indirect questions more accurately. In contrast, most of the lower span participants could neither notice nor orally produce language using the target structure with the same accurate performance as the higher processors. However, there were two exceptions among the higher spans learners. One person did not notice instances of the target structure nor could accurately produce it. This person informed us that he had lived a year abroad in the United States. Because of that, he is probably more willing to learn languages within interactional settings with native speakers, rather than through classroom instruction. He is possibly more inclined to notice online L2 formal aspects during conversational interaction. Therefore, his ability to recall and retrieve the target structure might have been influenced by the task in the lab as well as by the method of instructional treatment. The second person could notice instances of the target structure, but he could not orally produce it nor accurately perform the oral tasks on the three testing occasions. Unknown psychological factors (Mackey et al., 2002) may have constrained noticing or accurate oral performance. Additionally, perhaps his lack of familiarity with the task in the language lab or perhaps even lack of interest in learning the specific target structure or any other grammatical structures influenced his performance (Bergsleithner, 2007).

Moving on to the second question of whether noticing is related to working memory capacity, results show that noticing is closely related to WMC. Hypothesis 2 predicts that there is a relationship between noticing and WMC, as measured by the SST. The results related to this hypothesis can be seen in Table 2, and they seem to be supported since there is a statistical relationship between these two cognitive variables, although they tap different constructs (Robinson, 1995b, 2003). The results reveal that the higher spans noticed more exemplars of the target structure, while the lower spans noticed fewer instances of it, indicating that WMC constrains noticing and supporting Robinson's (1997, 2001, 2002) suggestions. Besides the WMC limit, other factors could have constrained noticing for the lower span learners in this study, such as grammatical sensitivity, thus corroborating Harrington (1992) and Harrington and Sawyer's (1992) findings that WMC is closely related to grammatical sensitivity. Other factors may constrain noticing such as: (a) the lack of familiarity with the task, since the task was carried out at the language lab; (b) the lack of motivation in doing the task as well as in participating in the research; (c) the degree of the participants' anxiety about being recorded; and (d) the lack of interest in knowing the target structure or any other grammar structures (Bergsleithner, 2007, p. 112).

As regards the third and fourth questions of whether WMC is related to oral performance and noticing is related to oral performance, results reveal that both cognitive constructs seem to be related to oral performance on the three different testing occasions. The correlation coefficients suggest that there are indeed relationships, and the strength of these relationships changes from one test to the next. Thus, Hypotheses 3 and 4, which predicted that individuals with a larger WMC would demonstrate better accuracy in performance of L2 oral tasks, and those who notice more L2 formal aspects would demonstrate better performance with the target structure in the L2 oral tasks in both posttests after instruction, seem to be supported. The results reveal that there was some weakening of accuracy in oral performance of the target structure in the delayed posttest compared to the immediate posttest, due to the difficulty of maintaining the target structure, which is related to the constraints of WMC and noticing. However, maintenance of the target rule occurred and was sustained for two weeks. This suggests that noticing occurred in input during the treatment, and then, it was indirectly recalled two weeks later. Such effort involved in maintenance must have probably occurred because of noticing, which made learners aware of the target structure and also contributed to the process of recalling the structure by means of uptake. Even though Loewen (2004) has advocated that "noticing/learning" is possible without the production of uptake, the participants' utterances (although not as accurate as they should be) offered some reasons to believe that noticing occurred and that learners were indeed engaged in learning.

Most participants were able to verbalize the target structure and give examples after treatment. Once more, in general, higher span learners performed more accurately than those who had lower spans. This implies that accuracy is maintained in the oral performance tasks due to noticing, as well as supported by the mechanisms of recall and retrieval included in models of WMC (Bergsleithner, 2007; Fortkamp, 1999, 2000; Mota, 2003, 2009). In addition, WMC played a crucial role in the process of recall of noticing, especially when participants had to use the target structure in the delayed posttest. Furthermore, task repetition appears to have played a role in participants' maintenance and retrieval of the target structure after two weeks (Bygate, 2001). The occurrence of noticing was the main reason for maintenance, although task repetition probably contributed to recall and to the participants' maintenance of the target structure for a longer period of time (Bygate, 2001; Skehan, 1996).

Last but not least, in response to the fifth question of whether (a) changes happen with instructional treatment; (b) accuracy in oral performance seems to be better after treatment; and (c) immediate differences after treatment last, the results suggest that there was a statistically significant improvement in grammatical accuracy scores between tests. Specifically, there was a significant difference between tests 1 and 2, and tests 1 and 3, while the difference between tests 2 and 3 was not statistically significant because grammatical accuracy remained relatively constant in both tests. This finding in the mean learner performance between OP2 and OP3 consistently indicates maintenance of accuracy scores for two weeks after treatment. Thus, Hypothesis 5 was supported since grammatical accuracy in the performance of oral tasks was present in the posttest phases, after the treatment condition, and also because the participants could verbalize the target structure as well as maintain it for two weeks. Such verbalization was obtained by means of uptake in the oral protocol by recalling noticing. That does not imply, however, that if a speaker does not successfully produce uptake, the linguistic form was not noticed in input. Such results might be interpreted as an indication that other factors may be related to this failure, such as: (a) the language processing between input and output in language development; (b) the level of cognitive processing the participants had to engage in; and (c) the cognitive individual differences that the participants bring to the process of acquiring a second language (Bergsleithner, 2007, p. 129).

Conclusions

The objective of this study was to investigate the relationships among noticing, working memory capacity, and accuracy in L2 oral performance. The present study findings support Schmidt's and Robinson's suggestions that noticing is closely related to and may be constrained by working memory capacity (Robinson, 1995a, 1995b, 1996b, 1997, 2001, 2002, 2003; Schmidt, 1990, 1995, 2001, 2012). Moreover, the results corroborate previous researchers' findings that WMC correlates with accuracy in L2 oral production (Bergsleithner, 2007; Fortkamp, 1999, 2000; Mota, 2003, 2009; Payne & Ross, 2005; Payne & Whitney, 2002; Weissheimer, 2007; Weissheimer & Mota, 2011).

The findings also resonate with other researchers' (Ellis, 1993, 1994, 1999, 2001; Robinson, 1995a, 1995b, 1997, 2001, 2002, 2003; Skehan, 1996) suggestions that noticing instances of L2 forms in the course of instruction might facilitate L2 learning, enhance grammatical accuracy in L2 oral production, and improve language development (Bergsleithner, 2007; Robinson, 1995a, 1995b, 1996a, 1996b, 2001) and also that grammatical sensitivity is closely related to working memory capacity (Bergsleithner, 2007, 2010; Harrington, 1992; Harrington & Sawyer, 1992). These findings reveal that individual differences in WMC are closely related to grammatical accuracy in L2 oral performance.

Moreover, some improvement in oral task performance, especially of some lower spans, probably occurred because of the instructional treatment and task repetition on the three test occasions (Bygate, 2001; Skehan, 1996). Initially, task repetition was avoided by shifting the pictures of the maps and the other pictures several times; however, later on, it was detected that this issue could not be avoided by only changing pictures each time. In other words, the pictures were different, but the oral task was exactly the same for the three tests. Hence, task repetition might be beneficial to L2 oral performance since the frequency and practice of input in the same task may contribute to noticing (Ellis & Schmidt, 1997), to the recalling of noticing, and to language maintenance (Bergsleithner, 2007, 2010).

Concerning pedagogy, the above results may inform L2 language teachers' reflections on how to: (a) design different tasks to call learners' attention to L2 linguistic formal aspects, (b) provide learners with opportunities to notice formal aspects in input, (c) make learners aware of what they are learning, and (d) give instructional treatments, since it might benefit L2 learners, contributing to both L2 development and performance in L2 oral tasks.

The present study has several limitations. Due to the limited number of participants, it was not possible to do a regression analysis in order to see which variable predicted learning better. Further research should replicate this study in order to validate whether it is noticing or WMC that is the best accuracy predictor in oral performance. Second, WMC was not assessed in L1, only in L2. Future research should assess WMC in L1 to make sure L2 language proficiency has not distorted WMC scores. The other limitation of this study was that it investigated noticing only through instructional treatment. Further research is needed to detect noticing in other contexts such as in online occasions through interaction in input and interactional feedback, as well as with different kinds of instruction within implicit and explicit teaching. Our interpretations were also limited by the absence of a control group, which should be included in the design of a future study to compare the two groups and verify the importance of instruction. In order to assess maintenance over a longer period of time, future research should apply two or more delayed posttests, for example, one two weeks after treatment and the other at least a month after treatment to verify the results in a longitudinal period of time. Further studies should replicate this study by assessing other aspects of participants' speech such as fluency, complexity, and/or lexical density as well.

To conclude, the current study can be taken as contributing to a better understanding of how learners' individual differences constrain their performance when dealing with complex cognitive tasks such as L2 speech. Together, the results can be taken as evidence that learners were more prone to noticing L2 instances of the target structure in the current study if they were higher span learners and also that these learners performed more accurately during L2 oral tasks.

References

Baddeley, A. D. (1986). *Working memory*. Oxford: Clarendon Press.

Baddeley, A. D., & Hitch, G. (1974). Working memory. In G. H. Bower (Ed.), *The psychology of learning and motivation* (pp. 47–89). New York: Academic Press.

Bergsleithner, J. M. (2007). *Working memory capacity, noticing, and L2 speech production*. Unpublished doctoral dissertation, Universidade Federal de Santa Catarina, Florianópolis, Brazil.

Bergsleithner, J. M. (2009). Mas afinal, o que é a noticing hypothesis? *Interdisciplinar: Revista de Estudos em Língua e Literatura*, 9, 101–106.

Bergsleithner, J. M. (2010). Working memory capacity and L2 writing performance. *Ciências & Cognição,15*(2), 002–020. Retrieved from http://www.cienciasecognicao.org.

Bygate, M. (2001). Effects of task repetition on the structure and control of oral language. In M. Bygate, P. Skehan, & M. Swain (Eds.), *Researching pedagogic tasks: Second language learning, teaching, and testing* (pp. 23–48). London: Longman.

Daneman, M. (1991). Working memory as a predictor of verbal fluency. *Journal of Psycholinguistic Research, 20*, 445–464.

Daneman, M., & Green, I. (1986). Individual differences in comprehending and producing words in context. *Journal of Memory and Language, 25*, 1–18.

Ellis, N. C., & Schmidt, R. (1997). Morphology and longer distance dependencies: Laboratory research illuminating the A in SLA. *Studies in Second Language Acquisition, 19*, 145–171.

Ellis, R. (1990). *Instructed second language acquisition*. Oxford: Basil Blackwell.

Ellis, R. (1993). The structural syllabus and second language acquisition. *TESOL Quarterly, 27*, 91–112.

Ellis, R. (1994). *The study of second language acquisition*. Oxford: Oxford University Press.

Ellis, R. (1999). Theoretical perspectives on interaction and language learning. In R. Ellis (Ed.), *Learning a second language through interaction* (pp. 3–33). Philadelphia, PA: John Benjamins.

Ellis, R. (2001). Investigating form-focused instruction. *Language Learning, 51*, 1–46.

Ellis, R. (2005). Planning and task-based performance: Theory and research. In R. Ellis (Ed.), *Planning and task performance in a second language* (pp. 3–34). Amsterdam: John Benjamins.

Ericsson, K., & Simon, H. (1980). Verbal reports as data. *Psychological Review, 87,* 215–251.

Ericsson, K., & Simon, H. (1993). *Protocol analysis: Verbal reports as data* (2nd ed.). Cambridge, MA: MIT Press.

Fortkamp, M. B. M. (1999). Working memory capacity and aspects of L2 speech production. *Communication and Cognition, 32,* 259–296.

Fortkamp, M. B. M. (2000). *Working memory capacity and L2 speech production: An exploratory study.* Unpublished doctoral dissertation, Universidade Federal de Santa Catarina, Florianópolis, Brazil.

Gass, S. M. (1988). Integrating research areas: A framework for second language studies. *Applied Linguistics,* 9, 198–217.

Gass, S. M. (1997). *Input, interaction, and the second language learner.* Mahwah, NJ: Erlbaum.

Harrington, M. (1992). Working memory capacity as a constraint on L2 development. In R. J. Harris (Ed.), *Cognitive processing in bilinguals* (pp. 123–135). Amsterdam: Elsevier.

Harrington, M., & Sawyer, M. (1992). L2 working memory capacity and L2 reading skill. *Studies in Second Language Acquisition, 14,* 25–38.

Hughes, A. (1989). *Testing for language teachers.* Cambridge and New York: Cambridge University Press.

Iwashita, N., McNamara, T., & Elder, C. (2001). Can we predict task difficulty in an oral proficiency test? Exploring the potential of an information processing approach to task design. *Language Learning, 21,* 401–436.

Loewen, S. (2004). Uptake in incidental focus on form in meaning-focused ESL lessons. *Language Learning, 54,* 153–188.

Mackey, A., Philp, J., Fujii, A., Egi, T., & Tatsumi, T. (2002). Individual differences in working memory, noticing of interactional feedback, and L2 development. In P. Robinson (Ed.), *Individual differences and instructed language learning* (pp. 181–208). Philadelphia, PA: John Benjamins.

Miyake, A., & Friedman, N. P. (1998). Individual differences in second language proficiency: Working memory as language aptitude. In A. F. Healy & L. E. Bourne, Jr. (Eds.), *Foreign language learning: Psycholinguistic studies on training and retention* (pp. 339–364). Mahwah, NJ: Lawrence Erbaum.

Miyake, A., & Shah, P. (1999). *Models of working memory: Mechanisms of active maintenance and executive control.* Cambridge: Cambridge University Press.

Mota, M. B. (2003). Working memory capacity and fluency, accuracy, complexity, and lexical density in L2 speech. *Fragmentos, 24* (Florianópolis/jan-jun/ 2003), 69–104.

Mota, M. B. (2009). Individual differences in working memory capacity and the development of L2 speech production. *Issues in Applied Linguistics, 17,* 34–52.

Ortega, L. (2003). Syntactic complexity measures and their relationship to L2 proficiency: A research synthesis of college-level L2 writing. *Applied Linguistics, 24,* 492–518.

Payne, J. S., & Ross, B. M. (2005). Synchronous CMC, working memory, and L2 oral proficiency development. *Language Learning & Technology,* 9(3), 35–54.

Payne, J. S., & Whitney, P. J. (2002). Developing L2 oral proficiency through synchronous CMC: Output, working memory, and interlanguage development. *CALICO Journal, 20,* 7–32.

Richards, J., Hull, J., & Proctor, S. (2002). *Interchange* book series. New York: Cambridge University Press.

Robinson, P. (1995a). Aptitude, awareness, and the fundamental similarity of implicit and explicit second language learning. In R. Schmidt (Ed.), *Attention and awareness in foreign language learning* (pp. 303–357). Honolulu: University of Hawai'i, National Foreign Language Resource Center.

Robinson, P. (1995b). Attention, memory, and the "noticing" hypothesis. *Language Learning, 45*, 283–331.

Robinson, P. (1996a). Learning simple and complex second language rules under implicit, incidental, rule-search, and instructed conditions. *Studies in Second Language Acquisition, 18*, 27–67.

Robinson, P. (1996b). *Consciousness, rules, and instructed second language acquisition.* New York: Peter Lang.

Robinson, P. (1997). Generalizability and automaticity of second language learning under implicit, incidental, enhanced, and instructed conditions. *Studies in Second Language Acquisition, 19*, 223–247.

Robinson, P. (2001). *Cognition and second language instruction.* Cambridge: Cambridge University Press.

Robinson, P. (2002). Effects of individual differences in intelligence, aptitude, and working memory on adult incidental SLA: A replication and extension of Reber, Walker, and Hernstadt (1991). In P. Robinson (Ed.), *Individual differences in instructed language learning* (pp. 211–266). Amsterdam/Philadelphia: John Benjamins.

Robinson, P. (2003). Attention and memory during SLA. In C. J. Doughty & M. H. Long (Eds.), *The handbook of second language acquisition* (pp. 631–678). Malden, MA: Blackwell.

Schmidt, R. (1990). The role of consciousness in second language learning. *Applied Linguistics, 11*, 129–158.

Schmidt, R. (1995). Consciousness and foreign language learning: A tutorial on attention and awareness in learning. In R. Schmidt (Ed.), *Attention and awareness in foreign language learning* (pp. 1–63). Honolulu, HI: University of Hawai'i, National Foreign Language Resource Center.

Schmidt, R. (2001). Attention. In P. Robinson (Ed.), *Cognition and second language instruction* (pp. 3–32). Cambridge: Cambridge University Press.

Schmidt, R. (2012). Attention, awareness, and individual differences in language learning. In W. M. Chan, K. N. Chin, S. Bhatt, & I. Walker (Eds.), *Perspectives on individual characteristics and foreign language education* (pp. 27–50). Boston, MA: Mouton de Gruyter.

Schmidt, R., & Frota, S. (1986). Developing basic conversational ability in a second language: A case study of an adult learner of Portuguese. In R. R. Day (Ed.), *Talking to learn: Conversation in second language acquisition* (pp. 237–326). Rowley, MA: Newbury House.

Skehan, P. A. (1989). *Individual differences in second-language learning.* London: Edward Arnold.

Skehan, P. A. (1996). A framework for the implementation of task-based instruction. *Applied Linguistics, 17*, 38–62. Oxford: Oxford University Press.

Skehan, P. A. (1998). *A cognitive approach to language learning.* Oxford: Oxford University Press.

Slimani, A. (1989). The role of topicalization in classroom language learning. *System, 17,* 223–234.

Slimani, A. (1992). Evaluation of classroom interaction. In C. Anderson & A. Beretta (Eds.), *Evaluating second language education* (pp. 197–221). Cambridge: Cambridge University Press.

Swain, M. (1993). The output hypothesis: Just speaking and writing aren't enough. *The Canadian Modern Language Review, 50,* 158–164.

Swain, M. (1995). Three functions of output in second language learning. In G. Cook & B. Seidlhofer (Eds.), *Principle and practice in applied linguistics* (pp. 125–144). Oxford: Oxford University Press.

Swain, M. (1998). Focus on form through conscious reflection. In C. Doughty & J. Williams (Eds.), *Focus on form in classroom second language acquisition* (pp. 64–81). Cambridge: Cambridge University Press.

Watanabe, Y., & Bergsleithner, J. M. (2006). A research synthesis of L2 working memory measurements. In Z. Madden-Wood & K. Ueki (Eds.), *Proceedings 2006: Selected papers from the Tenth College-wide Conference for Students in Languages, Linguistics, and Literature* (pp. 47–60). Honolulu, HI: University of Hawai'i, National Foreign Language Resource Center.

Weissheimer, J. (2007). *Working memory capacity and the development of L2 speech production.* Unpublished doctoral dissertation, Universidade Federal de Santa Catarina, Florianópolis, Brazil.

Weissheimer, J., & Mota, M. B. (2011). Working memory capacity and lexical density in L2 speech production. *Organon (UFRGS), 51,* 267–287.

Appendix A: Oral protocol (adapted by Bergsleithner, 2007, from Robinson, 1995a)

1. Do you notice grammatical rules when the teacher explains?

   ( ) yes ( ) no ( ) sometimes

2. Do you look for rules before speaking?

   ( ) yes ( ) no ( ) sometimes

3. Do you remember the rule the teacher explained today?

   ( ) yes ( ) no ( ) sometimes

4. Can you verbalize the target rule? Talk about the rule.

5. Give two examples using the rule.

Appendix B: Assessment of noticing (Bergsleithner, 2007)

Scores ranged from 0 to 9 for Noticing 1 (N1) or from 0 to 11 for Noticing 2 (N2).

1. Do you notice any rules when the teacher explains?

   0—no

   1—sometimes

   2—yes

2. Do you look for rules before speaking?

   0—no

   1—sometimes

   2—yes

3. Do you remember the rule the teacher explained today?

   0—no

   1—yes

4. Can you verbalize the target rule? Talk about the rule.

   0—cannot verbalize the target structure

   1—yes, but limited understanding

   2—yes, seem to understand

5. Give two examples using the rule.

   a. 0 (zero)—no example

      1—example, but not really correct

      2—good example

   b. 0 (zero)—no example

      1—example, but not really correct

      2—good example

Appendix C: Parameters to assess the participants' accuracy in the performance of indirect questions in the three oral production tasks (adapted from Bergsleithner, 2007)

Scores ranged from 0 to 12 for the grammatical accuracy in the target structure.

Target errors for the sentences

1. Repetition of the verb *to be* in the middle and at the end of a sentence, e.g., *Can you tell me what's the bill is?*
2. When the grammatical construction or organization of the sentence is totally wrong or incomprehensible, e.g., *Could you tell stand up in the table and stop shout?*
3. When the structure of the sentence retains the form of a direct question, e.g., *Could you tell me where's the Central Park?*
4. When the structure of the sentence retains the form of a direct question as well as problems of verb agreement, e.g., *Can you tell me where are 2nd Street?*
5. Problems of subject and verb agreement, when part of the indirect question structure, e.g., *Could you tell me how many peoples in the restaurant is?*
6. When important words in the target structure are missing, e.g., *Could you tell who ate that fish?* (instead of *Could you tell me*)
7. Substitution of *have* for *be* in indirect questions, e.g., *Could you tell me what has in that soup?*
8. Verb tense errors in indirect questions, such as use of the simple present instead of the present continuous, e.g., *Do you know what the couple talks?* (instead of *is talking about*)

9. Relative pronoun errors in indirect questions, e.g., *Could you tell me what the manager was?*
10. When a sentence is incomplete, missing an important word, e.g., *Could you tell me how much there is?*
11. Missing subject, e.g., *Could you tell me please what kind of soup is?* (*this* is missing)
12. Auxiliary *be* omission, e.g., *Could you tell me what the waitress serving?*
13. Interrogative pronoun omission, e.g., *Do you know the Bakerly Street is?* (*where* is missing)
14. Passivization of unaccusative verbs in indirect questions, e.g., *Do you know what is happened?*
15. Direct questions e.g., *Can you help me to find the Central Park?* when the task required an indirect question.

Sentence errors that were not scored as indirect question errors

1. Article errors, e.g., *Could you tell me where Hudson River is?*
2. Inadequate lexicon
   2.1. Preposition use, e.g., *Could you tell me who is in the phone?* (*in* instead of *on*)
   2.2. Word choice that does not interfere with the meaning or coherence of the whole sentence, e.g., *Could you tell me what the woman is calling?*
3. Missing words that are not part of the target structure, e.g., *Could you tell me Northern Boulevard is near this Stain Way?* (*if* is missing)
4. Noun morphology problems, including singular/plural, count/non-count errors, e.g., *Do you know if there are much people in the restaurant?*
5. Reduplicative pronouns in indirect questions, e.g., *Could you tell me what it is going on?* (Not counted as an error because this was not included in the instruction)
6. Verb tense errors that don't interfere with the indirect-question structure, e.g., *Can you tell me what she lunch?* (instead of *lunched on*)
7. Relative pronoun errors that don't interfere with the target structure or overall coherence, e.g, *Could you tell me what the woman is calling?* (instead of *who* or *why*)
8. Missing words that are not part of the target structure and do not interfere with the meaning of the whole sentence, e.g., *Could you tell me who is the person she is talking?* (*talking to* or *about*)
9. Participle and gerund errors that don't interfere with the target structure, e.g., *Can you tell me why she is so exciting?* (instead of *excited*)

Accurate sentences that correctly contained the target structure

Examples:

Do you know/Could you tell me what time the restaurant closes?

Do you know what the waiter is doing?

Do you happen to know how long the Park Evis is?

NFLRC monographs

Nurturing Noticing

Peter Skehan
University of Auckland/St. Mary's University College

This chapter[1] discusses the relationship between task-based instruction and the concept of noticing. First of all, noticing is related to stages of second language development. A broad distinction is made between stages concerned with development and change in the language system and then growth of control or expertise. In this second area a distinction is made between control over the system (i.e., development of procedural knowledge) and development of nativelikeness. The chapter then discusses task-based approaches and analyses how task choice and also task conditions can be related to noticing and how noticing can be related to the stages of development and control/nativelikeness. It is argued that attentional capacity and also selective attention within task performance have an important role to play in whether noticing is enhanced and capitalised upon. The final section explores the potential for post-task pedagogic activity to nurture noticing. It is argued that the most significant function of tasks is to make noticing more likely to occur, but that noticing in itself has to be nurtured carefully if it is to be enduring in its impact. A variety of ways in which this nurturing can take place through post-task activity are discussed.

Introduction

The literature on a task-based approach to language acquisition has grown enormously in the last three decades, as researchers have explored how the use of tasks can have an impact on second language performance and development. This line of inquiry has tried to establish how choices as to which task or task-type to use and what conditions operate when a task is used have systematic effects (Samuda & Bygate, 2008; Skehan, 1998). This endeavour has been, in no small measure, directed to offering a more grounded version of how a

1 The author would like to thank the editors of this volume and Dick Schmidt himself for the invitation to contribute. The author would also like to thank two anonymous reviewers, whose comments have strengthened the article considerably.

Skehan, P. (2013). Nurturing noticing. In J. M. Bergsleithner, S. N. Frota, & J. K. Yoshioka (Eds.), *Noticing and second language acquisition: Studies in honor of Richard Schmidt* (pp. 169–180). Honolulu: University of Hawai'i, National Foreign Language Resource Center.

communicative approach to language teaching can be justified, through research studies which provide generalisations about task performance (Skehan, 2011).

Using tasks, though, is not without pitfalls. One of the problems that has been identified is the danger that learners focus so much on getting a task done, and on expressing meanings, that they do not pay sufficient attention to form. The use of communication strategies and the acceptability, within communication, of elliptical forms as well as some error means that tasks can be completed without form needing to be primary. Learners may become skilled at transacting tasks but not necessarily better in developing an underlying interlanguage system or in controlling such a system. In response to this perceived difficulty, within task-based approaches a focus-on-form approach is often promoted, such that pedagogic devices are used to make it more likely that form will not be forgotten. Unadorned task-based approaches, as it were, are then moderated in some way to ensure that form retains some level of focus, and so there is potential for change, growth, and greater accuracy.

One way such a focus-on-form can occur is when noticing is promoted. In such a case, as the chapters in this volume make clear, something in the input which is received, or in the output that the speaker is trying to produce, causes attention to be heightened and focussed, as something which was previously ground now becomes figure. Regarding input, Dick Schmidt (Schmidt, 1990, 1995; Schmidt & Frota, 1986), for example, himself provides the example of pronoun forms (varying in formality and number) in Brazilian Portuguese. These were copiously available to him but unobtrusive in input. But at one point, for whatever reason, they stood out and were noticed, thereby potentially becoming the basis for change and development, as Schmidt's journals (Schmidt & Frota, 1986) and performance made clear. Regarding output, a speaker, in trying to say something, may realise that there is a gap in their interlanguage. This means they have a function or meaning that they want to express but notice that the means of doing so is lacking. In the former case we have input noticing, and the latter, output noticing. As chapters in this volume make clear, this is the necessary precursor to development and change in the interlanguage system. The insight that noticing is important then becomes the stimulus for asking how noticing, a form of focus-on-form, can be made more likely.

Still at the preliminary stage in this chapter, we need to cover one more issue. This is that noticing is a precursor to something, and we need to be more precise in characterising what that something might be. Skehan (2002, 2011) suggests the following sequence:

- noticing
- organising, integrating
- extending, restructuring
- avoiding error
- making salient
- automatising, proceduralising
- lexicalising

In other words, noticing is the vital starting point for other things to happen. This may be building a system on the basis of what has been noticed or of fitting what has been noticed into an existing system. In these cases *noticing* something simply adds to an existing interlanguage system. But it may be that something is noticed which challenges an existing system and pushes the learner to reorganise that system. In both these cases, though, the focus is on the language system—its size and its organisation. But more is needed than that, and the remaining stages are all concerned, to some degree, with control over that system and its usability. *Avoiding error* concerns the way facility with the language system develops and examines how performance conditions and amount of time pressure influence accuracy. In this case the interlanguage system is not challenged, but its use for language production focusses on slow carefulness. In parallel with this there is the issue of *salience and repertoire creation*. Learners may know much more language than they use, and what they don't use, at any particular time, may be more ambitious than what they do use. They may rely on careful, well-worn if less advanced language. Part of the study of development then has to be how lower salience items come to be used more routinely. Control, though, goes further than this and also requires some degree of *proceduralisation* (Ullmann, 2005), such that not only can language be produced in supportive circumstances, it can also be produced when conditions are more demanding and with relatively little (if any) conscious effort. In this case the process of language production does not consume attention and operates automatically. Then finally, and beyond proceduralisation, there is the possibility of *lexicalising* chunks of what is said, so that these function as prefabricated wholes and consume even less processing capacity to use (Wray, 2008). Where such lexicalisations are part of the currency of a speech community, one also has nativelike idiomaticity.

Although several distinct stages are outlined above, there is also a more organised way of looking at what happens. First, there is a concern for language-as-system. *Organising, integrating* suggests that something new has been noticed, and that this can be added to a system to make it larger but without challenging the system. *Extending, integrating* is also concerned with language-as-system, but here what is noticed is assumed to have implications not for simple increases in size, but for some reorganisation of the system as what has been noticed is seen to have implications for a need to change the system (e.g., as what was seen to be one pattern is now realised to be two distinct patterns). Second, there is the wider issue of control, as what is initially apprehended (and which can be handled only under unrealistically supportive undemanding conditions) comes to be used under more realistic conditions. At a first level, this might be to avoid error, (even though things are done slowly), as potential problems are realised and potential errors are avoided. Whatever pattern (or rule) has been noticed comes to be operated more correctly. But beyond this is a wider challenge. It is not only to produce language under supportive conditions slowly, but more ambitiously to do so more quickly and without excessive attention being required. In other words, the goal is to produce language in a fairly automatic manner, in real time, at a speed which resembles that of the native speaker and with pausing and fluency disruption which also approximates native language speech. What starts as declarative, in this view, becomes, with time, procedural. (Although, of course, it should be pointed out that alternative accounts exist, e.g., Paradis, 2009, of the relationship between declarative and procedural systems, which propose that there is no interface between the two systems.)

Third, there is yet another dimension involved here, one that might be termed *nativelikeness* (Pawley & Syder, 1983). Broadly, this is concerned with second language speakers making native-speaker-like choices. At a simpler level this is concerned with salience, with the way second language speakers learn to realise when to use what they have learned, as they do not simply develop more complex interlanguage systems but also acquire the ability to mobilise these systems when appropriate (even though, possibly, less elaborate but less nativelike alternatives exist). Learning to use more complex modality (e.g., *may, might*) rather than relying excessively on a restricted range of forms (e.g., *maybe, it is possible*) might exemplify this. More ambitiously, though, there is the challenge to have available a repertoire of nativelike forms which can be deployed as memorised wholes, as prefabricated chunks, either in their entirety or as patterns which enable slot-and-filler variation. In this way nativelike fluency can be achieved (Schmidt, 1992; Segalowitz, 2010), where language is used on the basis of memory and exemplar even though constructed, rule-governed alternatives exist (Skehan, 1996). The memorised choices (of forms in native language currency) enable easier processing, familiarity for interlocutors, and much greater nativelikeness. We can represent this analysis in the form of a diagram:

Noticing

⇓

Language as System

(organising, integrating)
(extending, restructuring)

Control

error avoidance
proceduralisation

Nativelikeness

repertoire creation, salience
lexicalisation

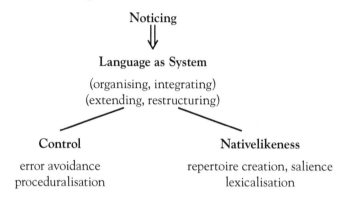

Figure 1. Noticing and sequences of acquisition

The diagram simply provides a visual representation of the ideas from the preceding discussion. The starting points are the same—noticing, followed by a focus on the language system. But then, conceptually, there is a divergence. One set of processes is concerned with achieving control over an emerging system, with development reflecting control under supportive and attention-demanding conditions and the avoidance of mistakes, first of all, followed by developing automaticity, robustness in the face of diverse conditions, and lower attentional demands, on the other. But distinct from this is a concern for choice amongst possible means of expression. At a lower level this choice is between alternative means of saying broadly the same thing, but where development consists of choosing a more ambitious (and perhaps more nativelike) means of expression. At a higher level, the choice is towards using an exemplar-based system rather than a rule-governed system or perhaps the capacity to switch between the two. In this way the speaker can focus on the flexibility and openness of the rule-based system or the efficiency and speed of the lexicalised exemplar-based choice, where this is available.

To finish this section, we need to return to noticing. So far we have discussed noticing-in-input and noticing-in-output. In a sense, relating these to Figure 1, *classic* noticing would impact on the language-as-system stage, whether through organising/integrating or through extending/restructuring. But it is important to say that noticing is relevant for other stages too. Noticing error, for example, is fundamentally concerned with monitoring in speech production (Levelt, 1989). It then becomes vital in achieving the early stages of control. As confidence grows in noticing errors when they occur, so there is hope that higher levels of control can be attained. Noticing is also significant in making language salient and creating a repertoire. Here what needs to be noticed is that there are alternative means of expression available and that relying on a functional but limited repertoire is inadequate. The noticing needs to be of possibilities within what one *could* do but usually doesn't. And a major influence here could be noticing in native-language input, as previously unimagined alternatives are apprehended.

Obviously here the final stages of proceduralisation and lexicalisation are least affected by noticing. They are concerned with automaticity and ease of processing, and so awareness of other possibilities is not the major issue. In any case, we turn next to a different perspective. We assume that noticing is important, and we explore how such noticing can be nurtured in a particular pedagogic context—the use of tasks in language learning.

Noticing and tasks

We have seen that noticing is the first stage in a complex sequence. It is not sufficient, but it is necessary to enable the remaining stages to function effectively. What the remainder of this chapter will do is explore how tasks can be chosen, implemented, and supported to facilitate the sequence that is implied in Figure 1, including the initial noticing. In doing this, three general areas will be discussed. These are *task choice*, where the issues concern task design and what we know about how different tasks predispose different sorts of performances; *task conditions*, where we explore alternatives for the implementation of a given task which may have consequences for the likelihood of effective noticing; and *post-task work*, where the concern is largely on exploiting and not losing the potential of any noticing which may have occurred during task performance. The perspective is psycholinguistic, and so the sort of real-world relationship central to other task researchers (e.g., Long & Norris, 2000) is somewhat downplayed.

Task choice

At the outset, it is worth saying that noticing during ongoing task performance is not easy. If one assumes that the focus is likely to be on meaning and that communication pressures are likely to be demanding of attention, then noticing is going to be something of a luxury. But it is possible, if (a) a task provides attentional scope to enable noticing to happen, and/or (b) something in the task performance draws attention towards some interesting aspect of form.

There are two issues here: task difficulty and task orientation. With the first, one is only concerned with the impact task difficulty may have in reducing the amount of attention left over that might be available for noticing. Other things being equal, it is assumed that easier tasks will lead to more *surplus* attention being available and so greater potential for noticing to occur. So if a task generates potential for insight about the language, either as noticing something from one's interlocutor's contribution or some shortcoming in one's own performance, easier tasks are likely to make this more probable to occur.

Task orientation reflects the way the research literature has begun to offer generalisations about tasks which are more likely to be form-oriented. This comes in two flavours: form-general and form-specific tasks. With form-general tasks, features such as structured tasks, or tasks based on familiar or concrete operations, or tasks which are flexible and permit some negotiation on the part of the speaker (and do not contain so many obligatory elements) lead to less error (Skehan, 2011). One assumes that such tasks, since they seem to catalyse a concern for form, might also lead speakers to pay attention to language and therefore notice. But this may not always work, in that a concern for form-as-accuracy may suggest conservatism in what is said and a lack of openness. This is, at the very least, an open, empirical question and one which would be promising for research.

But there are also proposals for tasks which predispose the use of particular forms. Essentially this goes back to Loschky and Bley-Vroman's (1993) proposals regarding predictions of the use of specific structures in tasks that tasks can be natural, probable, or necessary for the use of specific language. Robinson, Cadierno, and Shirai (2009), more recently, as part of the cognition hypothesis, has proposed how particular tasks can lead to particular language forms being more likely to be used. On such occasions one assumes that clever task design, which focusses on particular areas, can make noticing more likely to occur. Samuda (2001), similarly, argues that the use of relative clauses can be facilitated in this way, and so noticing in such a targeted area, while not certain, will be more likely.

Task conditions

A small diversion is in order at the beginning of this section. This relates to what is noticed when production is involved (as opposed to noticing in input). The issue connects to the distinction in task performance between accuracy and complexity (Skehan & Foster, 1997). In the former case, noticing is likely to focus on error, as monitoring of ongoing performance detects an error and tries to do something about it, either by self-correcting before production or by immediate self-repair and reformulation. In this case, in terms of Figure 1, the speaker is trying to do things to achieve greater control and, ultimately, a more automatic basis for speech. But where the noticing concerns complexity, it is likely that the focus is on either extending what can be said or alternatively on identifying an alternative form of speech, for whatever reason. With extension, the noticing is likely to be a noticing-the-gap, where the Conceptualiser stage of speech production (Levelt, 1999) outputs a pre-verbal message so that the second language speaker has requirements which the interlanguage system or the second language mental lexicon cannot currently meet. In this case the speaker might find another means of expression to handle the omission in resources. But alternatively, the gap which is noticed then becomes the stimulus to find out how it can be resolved. So the noticing is the first stage, and this generates the potential for a second stage which is the basis for development, extension, or restructuring. The noticing might also lead the speaker not to self-correct or to realise that a means of expression is lacking, but instead to activate existing knowledge but knowledge which was not initially activated. In this case we are dealing with repertoire creation, as perhaps a more elementary and limiting form is replaced by a more complex, demanding form. To sum up, noticing is a general process, and one has to then explore what sort of thing has been noticed. The interest then changes to exploring how different task conditions might have different effects, different tendencies, to lead to a range of beneficial consequences. The distinctions implied in this paragraph then become relevant for understanding how task conditions might exert their effects.

Pre-task phase

The major pre-task activity which has been explored in a task-based approach is pre-task or strategic planning (Ellis, 2005). Typically, and following Crookes (1989), second language speakers are given time, usually ten minutes, to prepare for the task to come. The powerful generalisation which emerges from this research across a wide range of studies is that complexity and fluency are raised, with medium to large effect sizes being typical. Accuracy is also raised but not as dependably and with smaller effect sizes. These findings lead one to consider how noticing might fit into this pattern of results.

It would seem that planning time opportunities often link with Levelt's Conceptualiser stage, as the time is used to build ideas which then, during speech, have to be handled by the Formulator stage. In a sense here, when the ideas are built, the forms of language which will then clothe these ideas are secondary and follow from what needs to be said to match the thinking that has taken place. In other words, the planning opportunities push learners to try to say things which are at the limit of their interlanguage systems (or even beyond). They are therefore sensitised to what they would like to say but may lack the means of doing so. They are induced, that is, to notice a gap and perhaps use planning time to handle this problem, in a way, perhaps, which primes the language which will be used later. They may also be prepared to look for means of expression afterwards on the (frequent) occasions when the available planning time only serves to identify what is lacking in current resources. So planning, in this view, has an important role in pushing learners to the limits of their competence in the second language and to preparing the ground for them, through what they have noticed, to make subsequent progress. (This, of course, depends a lot on the extent to which there are opportunities to revisit what they have wanted to say, a point which we return to in the next main section.)

During-task phase

There are many factors which come into play here, such as whether additional information is introduced, mid-task (Skehan & Foster, 2005), or the participant structure of the task varies through numbers of participants or distribution of roles and information (Pica, Kanady, & Falodun, 1993). But we will focus on two issues which are of relevance to noticing: the time pressures within the task and the opportunities for feedback. Ellis (2005) has distinguished between pre-task planning and online planning, linking the former to complexity and fluency effects and the latter to accuracy effects. He argues that slower speech production conditions, i.e., greater online planning opportunities, enable a greater degree of monitoring and therefore, a concern for error-avoidance and accuracy. Wang (2009) and Skehan, Bei, Li, and Wang (2012) argue that the best conditions are, in fact, a combination of pre-task and online planning, but this does not change the central insight here—less demanding processing conditions are associated with more accuracy. In such conditions the implications for noticing seem more towards monitoring and error-detection. The noticing is not of anything new but rather of the way control needs to be developed. In this way, more effective noticing can contribute to the process of proceduralisation, as learners become more able to use language in real time. The noticing helps learners to avoid and weaken unhelpful paths and instead predisposes them to the use of rule-governed language.

The other during-task feature that links with noticing is feedback. There are many studies and reviews which argue for the effectiveness of feedback and especially recasts. The extensive literature on feedback which arises out of communication (Mackey, 2008) proposes that moves such as clarification requests, confirmation checks, comprehension checks, and most especially recasts (and subsequent uptake) are strong contributors to interlanguage development. Here the focus will only be on feedback linked to noticing. Where noticing is concerned, such feedback is likely to push the speaker/learner to have pause for thought. The feedback, while not interrupting communication much, is still a signal that something is not right or at least not clear, and so within ongoing communication, attention is drawn to form. When recasting occurs, the correct form is being modelled (with the proviso that the recasted version has to be recognised as providing just such a model version). Self-generated noticing (of something in input or of a gap) has, simultaneously, the advantage of being *inner driven*, and so reflects readiness, and the disadvantage that external stimuli, which might push the learner in new directions, are not so prominent. Feedback and recasting have the advantages that they can respond to areas of development that the learner is ready for, but they can also, if communication-problem driven, inject new influences into development and change. Anyway, the consequence of this is that it is relevant to explore which tasks are more likely to generate feedback and recasting, since such tasks are more likely to direct attention, mid-task, to some aspect of form which may then be noticed. There is the proviso that for the feedback to work, it has to be recognised as feedback and reacted to. A second proviso, which will be returned to later, is that the feedback is more than ephemeral and in some way has to be built upon and consolidated. There is the danger, in other words, that feedback may not be processed deeply, as the pressures of ongoing communication predominate.

Post-task stage

The following section in this chapter is also concerned with the post-task stage with tasks, so it is important to distinguish between what will be covered here and then what will be covered later. In this section, the focus is on the impact of the post-task stage on task performance itself. So although we are exploring post-task activities (whose nature will become clearer in a moment), their relevance is for actual performance, i.e., what the speaker was doing before the post-task! The next section which follows is concerned with post-task activities in their own terms, so to speak, where these activities themselves are the key, irrespective of earlier task performance.

Essentially what we are concerned with in this section are post-task activities which are meant to change the way the earlier task was done. Examples of this are requiring participants to re-do a task publicly after the original task was done (Skehan & Foster, 1997) or alternatively requiring speakers to transcribe some of their recorded performance (Foster & Skehan, in press). In each case, it is the *anticipation* of the subsequent post-task, while the task is being done, that is hypothesised to have an influence on performance. Skehan and Foster (1997) used the former condition, a public performance, to try to direct attention towards accuracy, reasoning that foreknowledge of this public performance would raise the relevance of pedagogic norms, and so lead learners to direct attention to avoiding error. They were successful but only with one of the three tasks involved (a decision-making task but not a personal information exchange task or a narrative). Foster and Skehan (in press) used a post-task transcription condition and report accuracy effects for each of the two tasks they used in this study, a decision-making and a narrative, with large effect sizes in each case. This finding has subsequently been confirmed by Li (2010). The original predictions in this research were that post-task conditions would selectively raise accuracy only, as was found in Skehan and Foster (1997). But this later study (Foster & Skehan, in press) also showed a strong effect of the post-task transcription condition on language complexity. Further, there was no significant correlation in performance between accuracy and complexity, suggesting that post-task transcription induced some speakers to take a more conservative approach and focus on accuracy, while others were more risk-taking and focussed on complexifying what they said (even if this caused accuracy to suffer). It seems that for the same person to simultaneously focus attention on accuracy and complexity was difficult.

What these studies have shown, most broadly, is that a post-task condition can change the way attention is allocated while a task is being done, particularly towards a greater concern for form. In that respect, it is important that the initial hypothesis, that a post-task condition would selectively influence only accuracy, now has to be broadened to encompass other aspects of form, including structural (Foster and Skehan, in press) and lexical (Li, 2010) complexity. To put this another way, one can draw the conclusion from these studies that a post-task condition, in addition to inducing a concern for form, is also creating conditions favourable to noticing occurring. In other words, what seems to happen is that a concern for form is heightened, either to achieve a greater level of complexity or to avoid error. Attention is being directed, to some degree, to the form of language. This, in turn, is likely to push speakers to notice something, whether this is how to select a more complex manner of saying something or to pre-empt possible error. As a result, there is potential for interlanguage change which would not otherwise occur.

Noticing and post-task pedagogic activity

The sequence outlined at the beginning of this chapter is relevant here. It proposed that noticing is the initial stage of the several stages that are needed if effective language development is to proceed. The next group of stages concern the way an initial insight about the target language is nurtured, developed, complexified, and integrated into a larger system. Then there are stages concerned either with the proceduralisation of a newly developed area of the interlanguage system, or with the selection of more nativelike forms (where other forms might be available and might get the job done), and with the development of more nativelike, lexicalised, and idiomatic forms. The chapter then explored how a task-based approach to instruction might link to noticing through task choices and task conditions. Based on this, we can consider how the use of tasks, and noticing, can set the scene for subsequent effective post-task instructional options.

The central insights here are (a) tasks enable salient language which is relevant for the learner to emerge and be noticed and (b) they therefore clarify what language would be most useful for the learner to work on afterwards. So noticing and tasks share the potential to guide learning in the direction relevant to the learner, rather than have the learner following agendas set by others, e.g., coursebook writers. In this view the key for both noticing and tasks is what happens afterwards, so to speak. To notice something or to have a task push the learner to new insights is obviously a good thing. But it is not enough. To convert the initial inroad into substantial progress, more things need to happen.

It is the phase after a task has been done which best exploits what has emerged in that task. Bear in mind that if one uses a Willis and Willis (2007) approach to methodology, within the Task Cycle there will have already been a sequence of Task>Planning>Re-do Extension Task, and this may have already provided learners with relevant "quick fixes." So when we get to the post-task phase proper, things can be more ambitious. The remainder of the chapter will examine the sorts of things which can emerge during the task phase and also how they can be responded to.

So the first possibility here is that some language has been made salient through a task, as when something new needs to be formulated and it is realised that the resources are not present, or perhaps some language has been used by another student and noticed, or even has been suggested by the teacher or another student through feedback. Such language might be tentative, and so the first stage has to be some sort of consolidation. There could be revision or the generation of more examples. More substantially, what is noticed may be part of a system, but the system and the new item's place in it may not be clear (Organisation, Integration). Encountering a new pronoun, or a new irregular verb form, or a new conjunction could all exemplify this. More challengingly, the newly noticed form may challenge an existing system and so could trigger wider change (Extending, Restructuring). In these cases the point, in English, where it is realised that the simple past has both regular and irregular forms could be an example of this, as could insights on differences between past continuous and simple past. The teacher needs to build upon what might otherwise be an evanescent insight, since otherwise the noticing may not lead to what used to be termed *one-trial learning* and its potential would not be realised. So an important consequence of this analysis is that there is a need that some record is kept of what happened during the task which can then become the basis for subsequent action. This could be students trained to note aspects of language. It could be the result of designated students being responsible for paying attention to language used by others. It could be the circulating teacher who eavesdrops (but doesn't interfere) and so can note what things are being focussed on. Or it could be some sort of record, such as the unobtrusive recordings made for the transcription studies mentioned earlier.

The vital point is that input drawn from any of these sources could be the basis for teacher post-task activity. The assumption here is that more extended teacherly work is essential. There will be a need to widen the treatment of an insight derived from the earlier task, and this may even require some exercise-based work to clarify a distinction. So, for example, a contrast between two tenses may require not simply an account but also examples for and problem solving by learners. Or a treatment of modality might involve a wider account of different ways realising how modality is expressed. When noticing leads to a possibility of restructuring, the post-task work may have to become even more extensive and could be the starting point for a lot of classroom time devoted to a particular point. More ambitiously, the teacher could use metalinguistic work to try to systematise what has been noticed, with this being particularly important in cases of restructuring where a system has to be dismantled before it can be reassembled. Metalinguistic treatment (White & Ranta, 2002) may be the most effective way of achieving this. In general, the purpose for the teacher here is to achieve focussed and possibly circumscribed reactive clarity which takes the point that has been noticed and capitalises upon the opportunities this noticing has provided.

Noticing, though, does not always have to be of something new. Returning to Figure 1, there are times when what is noticed, perhaps through monitoring, is error, and so the challenge becomes one of using the post-task phase to deal with errors that have been noticed. The errors, in general, are taken to be evidence of a lack of control over some part of a system. The need therefore is for consolidation or practice, where the purpose of the post-task phase becomes one of gaining control over some area which is currently undependable in operation. It is assumed here that what is involved is an error rather than a lapse. Learners of English, for example, may be fundamentally clear about the difference between tenses, e.g., present perfect, simple past, past progressive, but nonetheless make mistakes too often. If these were an issue that emerged during a task performance, a teacher may decide to focus on this area and do exercises which require decision making about (possibly decontextualised) examples of use of these tenses. Alternatively, if lexical confusion emerged in a task, e.g., use of the verb *explain*, then that too could become the basis for focussed work, with semantic and syntactic focus.

Figure 1 also explores how development in a language means becoming more nativelike in the choices one makes when one is speaking and proposes that at a lower level this involves choosing from a number of alternative means of expression the one that is perhaps more complex (and so avoiding using simple forms excessively) or simply more "done" (creating a repertoire). At a more advanced level we have nativelikeness achieved through lexicalisation.

Noticing is clearly relevant in these cases too. The noticing is of choices available and the realisation that there are alternative expressions to say more or less the same thing. It is also relevant that some of these choices may be more desirable than others, either because they push the learner to use perhaps less controlled forms or because they sound more like the thing a native speaker would say. If this sort of noticing occurs, the post-task response has to be slightly different. It may emphasise form-meaning pairings and may push the teacher to incorporate consciousness-raising activities to sensitise learners for the future to the choices available. Or it might draw in corpus and concordance work to bring out for learners subtle differences in meaning achieved by different forms. This might extend to sociolinguistically-oriented explication, as learners are shown how different choices that they might make could lead to different levels of appropriateness and inappropriateness.

Conclusion

The purpose of this chapter has been first, to show how wide-ranging the concept of noticing is, and second, to bring out how naturally it links with a task-based approach to instruction. The focus on the concept itself has tried to show how there are different areas for noticing and that each is important in the wider sequence of second language development. The links with a task-based approach show how tasks need to promote noticing. More widely, though, the central point that has been argued is that noticing has to be the starting point for the process of acquisition and that more needs to happen if the initial noticing is to be nurtured and develop into acquisition. The post-task phase seems to be the key as to how this will come about.

References

Crookes, G. (1989). Planning and interlanguage variation. *Studies in Second Language Acquisition, 11*, 367–383.

Ellis, R. (Ed.). (2005). *Planning and task performance in a second language*. Amsterdam: John Benjamins Publishing Company.

Foster, P., & Skehan, P. (in press). Anticipating a post-task activity: The effects on accuracy, complexity, and fluency of L2 language performance. *Canadian Modern Language Journal*.

Levelt, W. J. (1989). *Speaking: From intention to articulation*. Cambridge: Cambridge University Press.

Levelt, W. J. (1999). Language production: A blueprint of the speaker. In C. Brown & P. Hagoort (Eds.), *Neurocognition of language* (pp. 83–122) Oxford: Oxford University Press.

Li, Q. C. (2010). *Focus on form in task-based language teaching—Exploring the effects of post-task activities and task practice on learners' oral performance*. Unpublished doctoral dissertation, Chinese University of Hong Kong, Hong Kong.

Long, M. H., & Norris, J. M. (2000). Task-based language teaching and assessment. In M. Byram (Ed.), *Encyclopedia of language teaching* (pp. 597–603). London: Routledge.

Loschky, L., & Bley-Vroman, R. (1993). Grammar and task-based methodology. In G. Crookes & S. Gass (Eds.), *Tasks and language learning: Integrating theory and practice* (pp. 123–167). Clevedon, Avon: Multilingual Matters.

Mackey, A. (2008). *Conversational interaction in second language acquisition*. Oxford: Oxford University Press.

Paradis, M. (2009). *Declarative and procedural determinants of second languages*. Amsterdam/ Philadelphia: John Benjamins.

Pawley, A., & Syder, F. (1983). Two puzzles for linguistic theory: Nativelike selection and nativelike fluency. In J. C. Richards & R. W. Schmidt (Eds.), *Language and communication* (pp. 191–225). London: Longman.

Pica, T., Kanagy, R., & Falodun, J. (1993). Choosing and using communicative tasks for second language instruction. In G. Crookes & S. Gass (Eds.), *Tasks and language learning: Integrating theory and practice* (pp. 9–34). Clevedon, Avon: Multilingual Matters.

Robinson, P., Cadierno, T., & Shirai, Y. (2009). Time and motion: Measuring the effects of the conceptual demands of tasks on second language speech production. *Applied Linguistics, 30*, 533–554.

Samuda, V. (2001). Guiding relationships between form and meaning during task performance: The role of the teacher. In M. Bygate, P. Skehan, & M. Swain (Eds.),

Researching pedagogic tasks: Second language learning, teaching, and testing (pp. 119–140). London: Longman.

Samuda, V., & Bygate, M. (2008). *Tasks in second language learning.* London: Palgrave Macmillan.

Schmidt, R. (1990). The role of consciousness in second language learning. *Applied Linguistics, 11*, 17–46.

Schmidt, R. (1992). Psychological mechanisms underlying fluency. *Studies in Second Language Acquisition, 14*, 357–383.

Schmidt, R. (1995). Consciousness and foreign language learning: A tutorial on the role of attention and awareness in learning. In R. Schmidt (Ed.), *Attention and awareness in foreign language learning* (pp. 1–63). Honolulu, Hawai'i: University of Hawai'i, National Foreign Language Resource Center.

Schmidt, R., & Frota, S. (1986). Developing basic conversational ability in a second language: A case study of an adult learner. In R. R. Day (Ed.), *Talking to learn* (pp. 237–326). Rowley, Mass.: Newbury House.

Segalowitz, N. (2010). *Cognitive bases of second language fluency*. London: Routledge.

Skehan, P. (1996). A framework for the implementation of task based instruction. *Applied Linguistics, 17*, 38–62.

Skehan, P. (1998). *A cognitive approach to language learning.* Oxford: Oxford University Press.

Skehan, P. (2002). Theorising and updating aptitude. In P. Robinson (Ed.), *Individual differences and instructed second language learning* (pp. 69–93). Amsterdam: John Benjamins.

Skehan, P. (2011). *Researching tasks: Performance, assessment, pedagogy*. Shanghai: Shanghai Foreign Language Education Press.

Skehan, P., & Foster, P. (1997). Task type and task processing conditions as influences on foreign language performance. *Language Teaching Research, 1*, 185–211.

Skehan, P., & Foster, P. (2005). Strategic and on-line planning: The influence of surprise information and task time on second language performance. In R. Ellis (Ed.), *Planning and task performance in a second language* (pp. 193–216). Amsterdam: John Benjamins Publishing Company.

Skehan, P., Bei, X., Li, Q., & Wang, Z. (2012). The task is not enough: Processing approaches to task-based performance. *Language Teaching Research, 16*, 170–187.

Ullmann, M. (2005). A cognitive neuroscience perspective on second language learning: The declarative-procedural model. In C. Sanz (Ed.), *Mind and context in adult second language acquisition: Methods, theory, practice* (pp. 141–178). Washington, DC.: Georgetown University Press.

Wang, Z. (2009). *Modelling speech production and performance: Evidence from five types of planning and two task structures.* Unpublished doctoral dissertation, Chinese University of Hong Kong, Hong Kong.

White, J., & Ranta, L. (2002). Examining the interface between metalinguistic task performance and oral production in a second language. *Language Awareness, 11*, 259–290.

Willis, D., & Willis, J. (2007). *Doing task-based teaching.* Oxford: Oxford University Press.

Wray, A. (2008). *Formulaic language: Pushing the boundaries.* Oxford: Oxford University Press.

Part Three:
Keeping a Close Eye on Noticing

NFLRC
monographs

What Do Eye Movements Tell Us About Awareness? A Triangulation of Eye-Movement Data, Verbal Reports, and Vocabulary Learning Scores

Aline Godfroid
Jens Schmidtke
Michigan State University

Common wisdom suggests that paying attention is an effective way to acquire new information. In the area of second language acquisition (SLA), Schmidt argued that attention facilitates learning because it leads to noticing, which he defined as the conscious registration of some surface element of language (Schmidt, 1995, 2012). This study triangulates distinct measures of attention and awareness—namely, eye-movement recordings and verbal reports—to elucidate the differential contributions of these two mechanisms to receptive vocabulary learning. Advanced EFL learners read 20 English paragraphs embedded with 12 novel pseudowords for meaning, while an eye-tracker recorded their eye movements. Participants' ability to recognize the pseudowords in context was tested on a surprise posttest. After that, each participant took part in a post-task interview that measured her conscious recollection of reading each of the 12 target words. Results showed that both a participant's total fixation time on the pseudoword and her recollection of reading the word predicted word recognition. Furthermore, words for which participants reported autonoetic *awareness (i.e., retrieval of an episodic memory) were fixated significantly longer than words with reported* noetic *awareness (i.e., a sense of familiarity) or no awareness. When both fixation times and awareness levels were entered into a single regression model, the awareness codings sufficed to predict word recognition scores. These findings suggest that attention (looking at a word) induced awareness (encoding the* what, where, *or* when *of a processing episode), which was itself a strong predictor of vocabulary learning.*

The noticing hypothesis (Schmidt, 1990, 1994, 1995, 2001, 2012) has been highly influential in the second language acquisition (SLA) research of the past 20 years as evidenced, for

Godfroid, A., & Schmidtke, J. (2013). What do eye movements tell us about awareness? A triangulation of eye-movement data, verbal reports, and vocabulary learning scores. In J. M. Bergsleithner, S. N. Frota, & J. K. Yoshioka (Eds.), *Noticing and second language acquisition: Studies in honor of Richard Schmidt* (pp. 183–205). Honolulu: University of Hawai'i, National Foreign Language Resource Center.

example, by over 2,000 citations of the 1990 paper on Google Scholar. At a general level, it has fuelled SLA researchers' interest in cognitive processes in SLA—most notably, attention and awareness—and has incited part of the SLA community to delve into the psychological literature on these topics. The influence of the noticing hypothesis also shows in scholars' sustained efforts to refine its theoretical foundations (Godfroid, Boers, & Housen, in press; Godfroid, Housen, & Boers, 2010; Truscott & Sharwood Smith, 2011). This study continues the latter line of research.

The process of *noticing*, which is hypothesized to be necessary for adult second-language (L2) learning (Schmidt, 1990), is comprised of two psychological mechanisms: focal attention and a low level of awareness (e.g., Robinson, 1995, 2003; Schmidt, 1995, 2001). Many SLA researchers have investigated noticing by focusing on a single constituent process, either awareness or attention. We combined distinct measures of attention and awareness in a mixed-method approach to test the extent to which these two measures coincide as predictors of learning and, thereby, lend indirect evidence to the existence of a mediating construct, noticing. Our results suggest that attention and awareness may be closely related but that, due to the different nature of the data collected to measure each mechanism, a mixed-method approach will afford a richer perspective on L2 learners' cognitive processes than any single measure could.

Noticing as attention and awareness

The noticing hypothesis, put in its simplest form, states that learning can only take place if new linguistic structures are noticed in the input, whereby noticing is defined as "the conscious registration of attended specific instances of language" (Schmidt, 2012, p. 32) or "the conscious registration of the occurrence of some event" (Schmidt, 1995, p. 29). In its strongest form, the hypothesis claims that noticing is a "necessary and sufficient condition for the conversion of input to intake" (Schmidt, 1990, p. 129). Schmidt's original hypothesis was a reaction against Krashen's (1981, 1983, 1985) ideas about subconscious language learning driven by simple exposure to comprehensible language input. Thus, Schmidt's hypothesis must be viewed as an attempt to underscore the importance of focused attention to linguistic form in adult SLA (see also Truscott & Sharwood Smith, 2011, p. 502).

Central to the noticing hypothesis are the psychological constructs of attention and awareness. Learners have to attend to features in the input to notice them, and, according to Schmidt, attending to features is virtually the same as being aware of them: "A low level of awareness, called here 'noticing,' is nearly isomorphic with attention and seems to be associated with all learning" (Schmidt, 1995, p. 1) and "focal attention and awareness are essentially isomorphic" (Schmidt, 1995, p. 20). As the review below indicates, second-language researchers appear to subscribe to this view, as, to the best of our knowledge, no SLA study to date has attempted to disentangle attention and awareness empirically or conceptually.

Operationalization of the constructs of attention and awareness in SLA

Attention in SLA

The role of attention in learning a second language had captivated SLA researchers years before Schmidt's first publication of the noticing hypothesis. Sharwood Smith (1981, 1991), for example, discussed *input enhancement* (originally dubbed *consciousness raising*; Sharwood Smith, 1981[1]), a technique that consists of highlighting (e.g., bolding or underlining) certain words or structures in a text that the teacher or researcher

1 In the later publication, Sharwood Smith (1991) preferred the term *input enhancement* to avoid the terminological and conceptual issues surrounding the term *consciousness*.

wants learners to focus on. The function of input enhancement is to make the chosen target features more salient to learners in hopes that learners will notice them. In this sense, input enhancement is primarily a manipulation of stimulus-driven or bottom-up attention (Corbetta & Shulman, 2002) as opposed to top-down allocation of attention initiated by the learner. It is, of course, not guaranteed that this manipulation will draw the learner's attention to the stimulus (Sharwood Smith, 1991, p. 120–22) or that the stimulus-driven attention, if any, will be complemented or enhanced by a learner's top-down attention. Nevertheless, the idea of input enhancement has been taken up in many SLA studies yielding mixed results (see Han, Park, & Combs, 2008; Lee & Huang, 2008, for meta-analyses).

One study that looked at the effect of enhanced vs. unenhanced input is Gass, Svetics, and Lemelin (2003). The authors argued that enhanced input, operationalized in this study by underlining target structures, can be beneficial for learning, because highlighting certain language features may help language learners focus their limited-capacity attention on relevant aspects of the text. Thirty-four college students of Italian were randomly assigned to either a [+focused attention] or a [–focused attention] condition. The former group made significantly more progress from pre- to post-test than the latter, revealing a positive effect of enhanced over unenhanced input. Gass et al. (2003) concluded that "focused attention does seem to be a powerful mechanism for learning" (p. 526). At the same time, though, the authors noted that "there is no claim that [their] experimental procedure unequivocally results in attention's being focused in one condition and not in the other" (p. 508) and recommend adding a stimulated recall procedure for future research. Thus an inherent limitation of this kind of research is that inferences about learners' attention can only be made indirectly by comparing pretest to posttest scores.

An important step forward in this respect was Winke (2013), who measured attention online by means of eye-tracking technology. The author tested 55 intermediate ESL learners on their correct use of passive constructions before and after reading a text flooded with sentences in the passive voice. Half of the participants read the text with textual enhancements of the passives (underlining and coloring) and the other half read it without any enhancements. Winke's eye-movement data revealed that the participants in the [+enhancement] condition looked at the passives longer than those in the [–enhancement] condition did. However, participants in both groups showed only small improvements on a passive form correction test, and their gain scores did not differ significantly from each other. Thus it appears that "noticing" the colored and underlined passive forms did not contribute to form learning in this study, perhaps because the learners did not go beyond the registration of the physical appearance of the passive verbs. More generally, eye tracking can only tell us what participants looked at but not what their internal thought processes were—for instance, whether they really noticed the passive constructions or only their textual layout. Therefore, as we argue in this chapter, combining a measure of attention (eye tracking) with a measure of awareness might provide us with a more complete picture of learners' cognitive processes in SLA. In the next section we review two ways in which awareness has been operationalized and measured in SLA research.

Awareness in SLA

Studies on awareness in SLA have made extensive use of verbal reports, either concurrent or retrospective. This approach capitalizes on the fact that *reportability* is a key property of awareness (Baars, 2003; Weiskrantz, 1997) or, in Schmidt's (2001) words, the assumption that "nothing can be verbally reported other than the current contents of awareness" (p. 20).

Concurrent verbal reports are known colloquially as think-aloud protocols. They consist of a participant saying out loud, in real time, the thoughts that he or she has while carrying out a particular task. Think-aloud protocols gained momentum in the field of SLA following Leow's (1997, 2000) influential studies. Leow (1997, 2000) added a think-aloud procedure to a traditional pretest, treatment, posttest design. The treatment was designed to induce learners' awareness of certain target forms and thereby trigger noticing, which was operationalized as "making a verbal or written correction to the targeted form" (Leow, 1997, p. 474). After coding the verbal protocols for awareness, Leow found a positive association between levels of awareness (Leow, 1997) or between unawareness vs. awareness (Leow, 2000) and learning gains observed on immediate and delayed posttests. This led Leow to conclude that awareness is facilitative of SLA (Leow, 1997) or even necessary (Leow, 2000).

An exclusive reliance on think-aloud protocols, however, may not warrant the strong conclusion drawn by Leow (2000), given that a lack of verbal report need not imply a lack of awareness. Because participants do not verbalize everything they are aware of (Allport, 1988; Jourdenais, 2001; Robinson, Mackey, Gass, & Schmidt, 2012; Rosa & O'Neill, 1999; Sachs & Polio, 2007), a number of participants who are reportedly unaware may, in fact, have a low-level awareness of the target form that they fail to render in their verbal protocols. The extent to which verbal protocols yield an exhaustive record of learners' conscious experiences is known as their completeness (Ericsson & Simon, 1993, chapter 3). Research on completeness has been overshadowed thus far by research on reactivity (i.e., the question of whether concurrent verbalizations change one's thought processes; Bowles, 2010; Fox, Ericsson, & Best, 2011); nonetheless, the completeness issue seems just as important, especially if evidence is to be inferred from the absence of a given piece of information from a verbal report.

The question of whether learning a second language, or certain second-language features, is possible without awareness remains a debated issue in the field of SLA (e.g., Truscott, 1998; Truscott & Sharwood Smith, 2011). Williams (2004, 2005) reported data from two studies showing that learning without awareness might be possible. In an improved version of his 2004 study design, Williams (2005) presented participants with four novel articles combined with existing English words. Participants were told that the articles indicated the distance of the referent to the subject of the sentence: *gi* and *ro* for 'near' and *ul* and *ne* for 'far'. Participants were not told, however, that within each distance category, the choice of article was determined by the animacy of the accompanying noun (*gi* and *ul* for inanimates, *ro* and *ne* for animates). During a learning phase, participants were asked to make judgments about an object's distance from the subject based on the article. Later, participants were given new and old, animate and inanimate nouns along with two article choices, the one for animate and the one for inanimate objects. Results showed that participants were able to choose the correct article above chance even when they did not report awareness of the underlying animacy rule during a post-task interview.

An extension of Williams (2005), Hama and Leow (2010) did not replicate Williams's findings of unaware (i.e., implicit) learning (see also Faretta-Stutenberg & Morgan-Short, 2011). An important part of Hama and Leow's (2010) argument centered on the time when participants' awareness of the underlying rule is measured best: online, at the "stage of encoding the incoming information" (p. 466) or off-line, at the "stage of retrieval of stored knowledge of the construct" (ibid.). Hama and Leow (2010) added think-alouds (as a measure of awareness at the time of encoding) to Williams's original exit questionnaire (a measure of awareness at the time of retrieval). They found a small number of mismatches, namely three, where a participant made reference to animacy at one time of measurement but not the other. While Hama and Leow's triangulation of two types of verbal report corroborates the construct validity of either measure as an index of awareness, it does not provide compelling evidence for the superiority of think-alouds over retrospective reports (see also Leung & Williams, 2011, p. 37; Leung & Williams, 2012, p. 638). In particular, unlike Williams's (2005) participants (who had performed the training task in silence), the unaware, verbalizing participants in Hama and Leow showed no significant memory for article–noun combinations, even for "old" items that they had encountered six times during the training phase. This raises the question of whether the think-aloud requirement prevented participants from rehearsing the article–noun pairs subvocally and thereby interfered with their encoding of the processed information in a more durable memory format (e.g., Baddeley, 2007; Craik & Lockhart, 1972; Craik & Tulving, 1975; Gathercole, 2006).

In another extension of Williams's (2004, 2005) research, Leung and Williams (2011, 2012) did report further evidence for unaware learning. The major methodological improvement of these studies, compared to Williams (2004, 2005), was that the learning of the target rule was no longer evaluated by means of posttests, but online, from participants' reaction times (RTs) to increasing numbers of article–noun exemplars. Participants were once again introduced to a set of four novel articles, governed by two semantic dimensions (e.g., distance and animacy), with only one dimension being made explicit to them. They saw two pictures on a screen and heard a sentence containing a novel article plus a noun that referred to one of the entities on the screen. Their task was to respond to the named entity as fast as possible. Learning was measured "by reaction time slowdowns in a block of trials in which some regularity [was] violated" (Leung & Williams, 2012, p. 654), in particular where the mapping between the article and the "hidden" semantic property was reversed (e.g., the word *bull* appeared with the article for inanimate objects). Leung and Williams (2012, Experiment 1) indeed observed slower responses on violation trials for participants who later reported to be unaware of the animacy rule. They took this as evidence for implicit learning. In addition, the authors compared RTs of aware and unaware participants, as established by post-experiment interviews. Only the aware participants who could report the correct form-meaning mapping showed evidence in their RT behavior of correctly anticipating the target object before they actually heard it (very fast button presses). Thus, the RTs served as a cross-validation of participants' verbal reports.

When comparing Williams (2005) and Leung and Williams (2011, 2012) to Hama and Leow (2010), there seems to be a trade-off between memory decay in the case of retrospective verbal reports and the additional task demands of concurrent verbal reports. Furthermore, either type of verbal report is prone to be incomplete (see above). We believe that triangulating some type of verbal report with eye-movement data may reduce potential omission issues because, unlike verbalizations, participants' eye movements during processing never stop and never stop being recorded. In this sense, eye tracking provides a complete record of participants' cognitive processing. Unfortunately, eye tracking and think-aloud protocols can only be combined in a between-subjects design, because the requirement to voice one's thoughts increases time on task (Bowles, 2010) and will thus distort the durations of any eye movements made in the process. In this study, we found it important to collect attention and awareness data *for the same participants* (i.e., within subjects) and therefore we used retrospective, rather than concurrent, verbal reports.

Attention and awareness in vocabulary learning

The studies reviewed above all deal with the acquisition of some aspect of grammar: either verb morphology (Leow, 1997, 2000; see also Godfroid & Uggen, 2013) or form-meaning connections in articles (Faretta-Stutenberg & Morgan-Short, 2011; Hama & Leow, 2010; Leung & Williams, 2011, 2012; Williams, 2004, 2005). One might argue that grammar learning involves the learning of abstract rules that cannot possibly be noticed in the input (Truscott, 1998) and that vocabulary learning, the focus of the current study, is very different because it does not involve rules. However, from a usage-based perspective, all learning is initially item based. Linguistic rules are not innate but emerge gradually as abstract knowledge schemata over the piecemeal accumulation of instances in memory (Abbot-Smith & Tomasello, 2006; Ellis, 2002a; Goldberg, 2003). Individual items or exemplars have to be noticed in Schmidt's (2012) sense (cf. Ellis, 2002a, 2002b) whereas it is usually assumed that the abstraction of regularities can occur without the individual being aware of this process (Williams, 2005). However, an individual can become aware of an underlying linguistic regularity, in which case this knowledge would equal awareness at the level of understanding (Schmidt, 1990, 1995, 2012). In Leow (1997, 2000), for example, participants did not have to generalize the target structure to previously unseen verbs but were only tested on the verb forms that were in the crossword puzzle. In contrast, Williams (2004, 2005) also tested new article–noun combinations, for which participants arguably had to have abstracted the animacy rule to perform above chance. Some participants showed awareness at the level of understanding—those who could report the animacy rule—and others awareness at the level of noticing.

Clearly attention to the form and context of a word is necessary to make form-meaning connections, but the question is whether this is a conscious process. Ellis (1994) maintains that vocabulary acquisition involves both conscious and unconscious processes: "Recognition and production aspects of vocabulary learning rely on unconscious processes, whereas meaning and mediational aspects of vocabulary heavily involve explicit, conscious learning processes" (p. 39). In this view, reading a word may leave a memory trace of the orthographic representation of that word without any conscious processes, but inferring its meaning is a conscious process.

An alternative view is that learning new words might involve an unconscious statistical learning mechanism where the meaning of a word is abstracted over multiple encounters with the word from the contexts where the word occurred. For example, Smith and Yu (2008) showed how infants as young as 12 months can infer the referents of novel words presented in ambiguous contexts over multiple trials. In this study children saw two novel objects, A and B, and heard two novel words, for example, *bossa* and *gasser*. On another trial, children saw objects B and C and heard *gasser* and *manu*. Thus the probability of *gasser* referring to object B was higher than that of *gasser* referring to objects A or C. After a learning phase of less than four minutes involving six novel objects and words, children were shown two objects and heard a word associated with one of the objects while their eye gazes were recorded. They looked at the "right" object significantly longer than at the distractor, thus showing that they were able to learn the associations between the words and their referents over multiple trials despite their ambiguity. Although Smith and Yu (2008) did not address the issue of consciousness in their article, it seems reasonable to assume that 12-month-olds are not yet conscious of their learning in the sense of explicit learning.[2] Further evidence for the assumption that word learning can occur implicitly comes from studies investigating people with amnesia. Williams (2005, p. 274) cites three amnesia studies presenting evidence of implicit vocabulary learning in people that had impaired explicit memory. Thus it seems that consciousness, or awareness, might not be necessary for learning

2 Yu and Smith (2007) demonstrated that adults were also able to learn via cross-situational statistics although with the difference that participants were instructed to learn the words and their referents, which likely led to more conscious processing.

new words, not when it comes to the recognition of a word and possibly not when it comes to mapping form and meaning either.

In addition, there might be alternative ways to characterize awareness in vocabulary learning besides the distinction between noticing and understanding. Tulving (1983, 2002), among others, proposed the existence of two different explicit memory systems, *semantic* memory and *episodic* memory. Encoding in or retrieval from semantic memory (i.e., memory for facts) involves *noetic* consciousness, which is the state of knowing (consciously) that something happened. On the other hand, access to episodic memory is hypothesized to rely on *autonoetic* consciousness, which is the conscious recollection of the *what*, *where*, and *when* of past experiences[3]. To illustrate the reality of this psychological construct, Tulving (2002) gives the example of K. C., a patient with amnesia. After an accident at age 30, his semantic memory for events prior to the accident remained largely intact but his episodic memory was severely impaired. He could still remember detailed facts such as that his parents had a summer cottage and where it was on a map, but he did not have any memory of personal experiences. The difference between noetic and autonoetic awareness can also be seen in classic memory experiments in which participants are asked to remember lists of words (for a review see Yonelinas, 2002). Participants might remember that a certain word was on the list (noetic consciousness or familiarity) or they might remember the experience of reading the word on the list (autonoetic consciousness or recollection). This is known as the remember-know paradigm (Tulving, 1985). As we will discuss later, we found some evidence for this distinction with respect to incidental vocabulary acquisition in the data we present here.

Operationalization of attention and awareness in the present study

Attention

We operationalized attention in the present study as the time a participant spent fixating a novel word, when other word properties (e.g., length, predictability, part of speech) were held constant. The relationship between eye gaze data and attention is well established in reading research (e.g., Rayner, 2009). More recently, attempts have been made to relate the noticing construct to eye gaze during reading (Godfroid et al., 2010; Godfroid et al., in press; Godfroid & Uggen, 2013; Smith, 2010; Winke, 2013).

Although they did not frame their research in terms of attention, two studies measuring reading times have reported an association between eye fixation durations and vocabulary learning. Williams and Morris (2004) did an eye-tracking study on the effects of word familiarity on word-based reading times. Their second experiment included one novel-word condition in which the participants, English native speakers, read sentences that contained an English-like pseudoword followed by a highly constraining context: for example, *Jim said the BOSER was killed for its fur* (capitalization ours). After the reading task, an unannounced vocabulary posttest assessed the participants' receptive knowledge of the novel word meanings by means of a two-option synonym test. Williams and Morris (2004) found that readers tended to spend *less* initial processing time (shorter gaze duration) on novel words whose meaning they later identified correctly but *more* time rereading them (as indexed by second pass time).

Brusnighan and Folk (2012) examined the roles of contextual and morphological information in native English speakers' compound processing. Their second experiment

3 According to Tulving (2002), episodic memory is what allows us to travel back in time in our minds and re-experience past events.

was a self-paced reading task in which participants read novel compounds embedded in informative sentence frames. Similar to Williams and Morris's (2004) study, participants subsequently took a receptive knowledge test on the novel word meanings with two answer choices per item. Mean accuracy was over 90%, suggesting the participants may have become aware of the presence of the novel words in the sentences and, hence, of the purpose of the experiment. (They were informed at the beginning that there would be two parts to the experiment, only not what the second part would be.) Nonetheless, Brusnighan and Folk (2012) demonstrated that sentences whose targets were correctly defined on the posttest were read significantly more slowly than sentences with target words whose meaning later was not identified correctly.

Awareness

We originally operationalized awareness in the present study as a participant's ability to remember reading a particular novel word as reported in a post-task interview. In the interview, which followed the vocabulary posttest, the first author showed the items from the posttest one by one and asked the participant if she remembered what she had answered and whether she remembered reading the word. A trial was initially coded as [+aware] if a participant indicated that she remembered reading a word and as [–aware] in all other cases. This procedure resulted in 75% agreement between two raters, the second author and a research assistant. We noticed, however, that many of the disputed cases were trials for which a participant indicated that she had seen the word before but was unable to remember the context in which the word had appeared. This finding reminded us of the literature on episodic memory (see the discussion of Tulving, 2002, in the previous section) and, in particular, of the distinction between remembering and knowing. As a result, we opted for a more detailed coding scheme of the verbal reports that comprised three categories:

1. The participant does not consciously remember the target word, which results in a coding of [–awareness].[4] In this case the participant might attribute a correct choice on the posttest to intuition, feel, or guessing.
2. The participant remembers that the word was somewhere in the texts she read (sense of familiarity or noetic awareness).
3. The participant remembers reading the word in a particular sentence (recollection or autonoetic awareness).

Note that we use the term *recall* in this study to refer to participants' recollection of seeing or processing the target word in the readings (i.e., to operationalize awareness) whereas *recognition* is used to denote participants' correct identification of the target word on the vocabulary posttest (i.e., it is our measure of receptive word learning).

The operationalizations of attention and awareness are independent of one another in this study although it is reasonable to assume that in practice the two mechanisms will often co-occur; that is, participants who can recall the experience of reading a certain word likely also paid more attention to that particular word during reading.

Our research questions then were as follows:

4 We use the labels *no awareness* and *unaware* as shorthand for "no verbal report of awareness." We acknowledge that the absence of a verbal signaling of awareness does not necessarily imply that there was no awareness (see section Awareness in SLA).

RQ1 Do advanced EFL learners' eye fixation durations on novel words during reading predict their recognition of these words in an unannounced, immediate vocabulary posttest?

RQ2 Does advanced EFL learners' recall of reading a novel word in a text predict their subsequent recognition of that word?

RQ3 Do advanced EFL learners look longer at those words for which they subsequently report awareness?

RQ4 Are eye fixation durations and retrospective verbal reports equally good predictors of subsequent word recognition?

Methods

Participants

Twenty-nine female, advanced EFL learners (L1: Dutch) participated in this study. All of them were second or third-year English language majors (age range: 19–28) at the same Belgian university and were proficient in English. They had started to learn English as a foreign language from age 13 onwards in secondary school in Belgium. Their English proficiency level was at the B2 (upper intermediate) or C1 (lower advanced) levels of the Council of Europe's (2001) *Common European Framework* (CEF). All participants had either normal or corrected-to-normal eyesight.

Materials

Participants read 20 English paragraphs, of which 12 were critical to the experiment. All the paragraphs were pretested on a group of first-year English language majors at the same university to ensure that most words would be known to the present, more advanced sample of students. Thus, the participants encountered the novel words in contexts with mostly familiar words that could help them infer the meaning of the novel targets. Each participant read the experimental paragraphs in one of four conditions that were identical except for the target word. For example, for the paragraph with the target word *average* a participant would read either: (i) *average* (control condition); (ii) *canimat;* (iii) *canimat or average;* or (iv) *average or canimat* (see Appendix A for the full sample paragraph).[5] Condition was varied within subjects, such that each participant read three different paragraphs per condition, good for a total of 12 critical paragraphs. The assignment of a given paragraph to a given condition was counterbalanced between subjects according to a Latin square design.

Target-word retention was measured through an unannounced vocabulary posttest. On this test, participants saw the original sentence in which the target had appeared, along with 18 possible answers for the missing word. Appendix B contains an example. The majority of the distractors were novel words that participants had read in a different paragraph. Some others were novel words that had not appeared before, and two or three items were known English words. As there were 18 answer options, the probability of guessing the correct word by chance was low.

Procedure

All participants were tested individually. They were instructed to read the 20 paragraphs for meaning while an eye tracker, the EyeLink II, recorded their eye movements. Next, they took the unannounced vocabulary posttest. Finally, they took part in an interview with the

5 For an analysis of the effects of contextual cues on attention and vocabulary recognition, see Godfroid et al. (in press).

researcher in Dutch. In the interview the researcher showed the participant the vocabulary posttest items again, one by one, and asked the participant whether she remembered what she had answered. If she did not, the correct response was provided. Then the researcher asked the participant if she could remember reading the word (see Figure 1). If she did, the researcher asked her what she had thought. The participants were not informed that most of the target words were artificial until a debriefing session that took place a few months after the experiment. To judge by their interview protocols, none of the participants debunked the pseudowords in the texts.

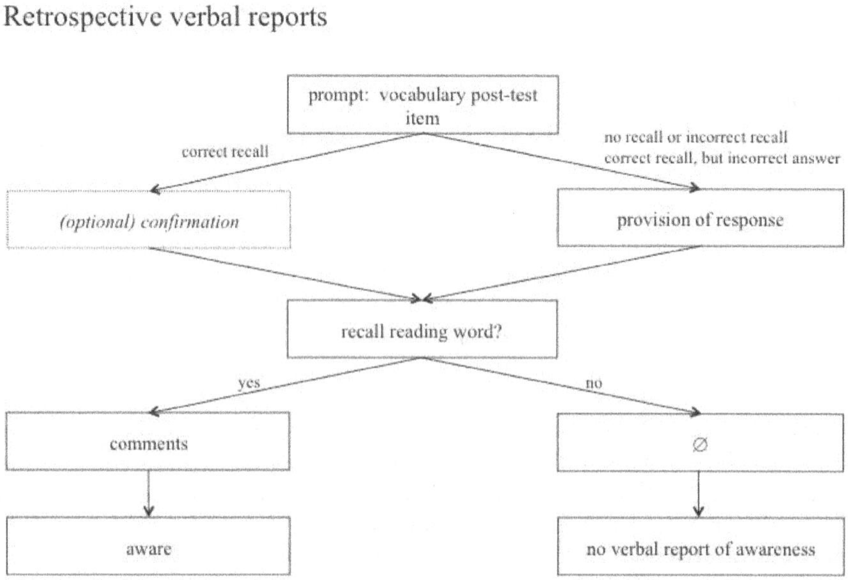

Figure 1. The interview procedure (with the original, binary coding scheme for awareness)

Analysis

All retrospective verbal reports were transcribed verbatim and translated into English. Then two raters independently coded each experimental item as +awareness or –awareness based on whether the participant indicated that she could remember reading the word or not. This procedure resulted in 75% simple percent agreement. Because many cases that resulted in disagreement could not easily be classified as one or the other, we decided that dividing the +awareness category into two distinct categories might capture the data better (see Operationalization of Awareness above). After recoding the data with the three-tiered system, interrater reliability rose to 86%, which appears to confirm our decision to opt for a more fine-grained coding scheme. The remaining cases of disagreement were discussed until we reached consensus. This resulted in the following 2 (± recognition) by 3 (autonoetic/noetic/no awareness) cross-tabulation of possible outcomes (Table 1):

Table 1. Percentage of words that participants recognized and did not recognize on the posttest as a function of awareness

	recognition on posttest	no recognition on posttest	total
autonoetic awareness	8.0% (21)	4.2% (11)	12.3% (32)
noetic awareness	5.7% (15)	13.0% (34)	18.8% (49)
no awareness	6.9% (18)	60.5% (158)	67.4% (176)
total	20.7% (54)	77.8% (203)	98.5% (257)

note. Percentages refer to the total number of pseudowords. Four words were coded as missing values with regard to awareness.

The following interview excerpts, translated from Dutch, illustrate the six possible classifications. Note that recognition refers to recognition of the correct word on the posttest. "P" is participant and "R" is researcher.

[+recognition, autonoetic awareness] : target is *lurgled*:

P5 Yes, "lu-, lu-, lu-".

R "Lurgled," yes.

P5 I do not know. That word stuck because it was a word that I also found funny.

R Yes.

P5 I do not know why, but that's... I paid special attention to it when I read it, like "oh, such a cool word."

[–recognition, autonoetic awareness] : target is *evidoses*:

R Sentence 4?

P5 I think I picked "eliphor" or "evidoses," it was with an "e." It was one of the two.

R Yes.

P5 I do not know which one.

R What do you think?

P5 I do not remember what I picked, but it was one of those two. I think I picked "evidoses."

R You picked "eliphor."

P5 Ah "eliphor" yes. [Laughs]

(...)

R Do you remember—

P5 —I remember, I remember that it was with an "e," I paid attention to that. I do not know exactly why I now [inaudible] but...I know it was something with an "e."

[+recognition, noetic awareness] : target is *staveners*:

R Sentence 20?

P7 Yes, I did not remember this one well, either... I picked "staveners."

R Hm.

P7 Yes... [hesitant] [laughs]. I do not know. I could not specifically recall it, but... yes, somehow I was thinking "it could be."

[–recognition, noetic awareness] : target is *staveners*:

R (…) Here it's "staveners."

P14 Yes.

R Does it ring a bell?

P14 Yes, it looks familiar, but [inaudible], well many of those words I do not know huh, so...

[+recognition, no awareness] : target is *canimat*:

R Sentence 9?

P8 3, "wricety?" No, cannot be. No...

R You also answered this one correctly (…). 18, "canimat."

P8 [Laughs] That was a guess.

R A guess? Based on how the word looks or, or...?

P8 Maybe unconsciously that I could remember, I do not know. [Laughs]

[–recognition, no awareness] : target is *redaster*:

R And when I say this, does it, does it ring a bell, do you say "Ah yes, that's true?"

P1 No, no.

To measure attention, we used the total amount of time that a participant fixated a pseudoword during reading, which consists of the duration of the first eye fixation plus any subsequent fixations made on the target word. We addressed the research questions by means of mixed-model regression analyses with random intercepts for subjects and words (Baayen, Davidson, & Bates, 2008). Including a random intercept for subjects allows for individual differences in reading times, while the hierarchical structure of the model pulls outlying observations towards the grand mean. Overall model fit was assessed by means of marginal and conditional R^2 (see Nakagawa & Schielzeth, 2012). Marginal R^2 shows the variance explained by the fixed factors (i.e., fixation time and/or awareness level) whereas conditional R^2 measures the variance explained by both the fixed and the random factors (i.e., subjects and words).

Results

RQ1: Attention predicts word recognition

In general, the vocabulary posttest proved a difficult task. Participants recognized an average of 2.1 out of nine words (SD=1.42). To see whether more attention paid to a word increased the probability of recognizing that word on the posttest, we ran a logistic mixed model with (posttest) recognition as binary outcome variable and fixation times as a continuous predictor variable. We centered fixation times around the y-axis to improve model fit. Two outlying observations (<1% of the data) that were larger than mean+3 *SD*s were given a value of mean+3 *SD*s to obtain more precise regression coefficient estimates.

Results showed a positive effect of fixation times on recognition, b=0.79, 95% CI=[0.13, 1.44],[6] p=.018, marginal R^2=4.7, conditional R^2=22.8. For example, an increase in fixation

6 Confidence intervals were calculated using the *sim* function of the arm package in R (see Gelman & Hill, 2007).

time on a target word from 1 *SD* below the mean (i.e., 150 msec) to 1 *SD* above the mean (i.e., 1348 msec) was associated with an 11.2% increase in the probability of recognizing the word on the test, a change from 12.6% to 23.8% (see Figure 2).

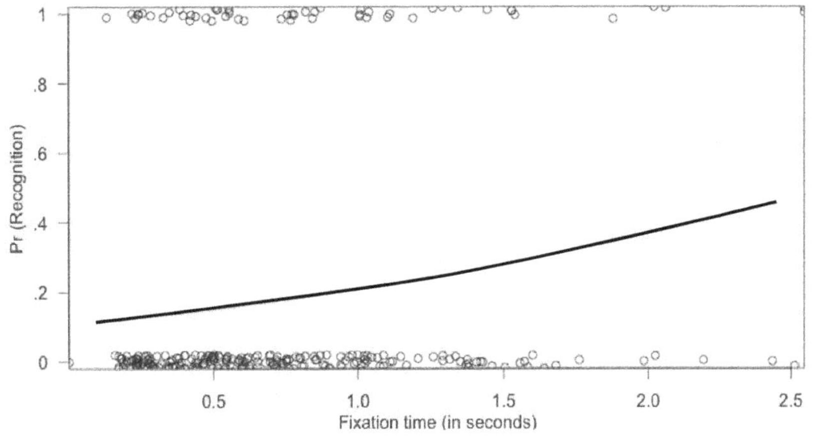

Figure 2. The probability of recognizing a target word on the posttest as a function of fixation time. Each circle indicates one observation. The mean was at 0.749 sec and 1 standard deviation corresponded to 0.599 sec.

RQ2: Awareness predicts word recognition

When we entered awareness as a three-level factor with no awareness as the reference category, there was a significant, positive effect for both noetic, b=1.50, 95% CI=[0.64, 2.35], p=.001, and autonoetic awareness, b=3.18, 95% CI=[2.20, 4.20], p<.001, marginal R^2=22.5, conditional R^2=39.7. Thus, when a participant reported noetic or autonoetic awareness of a target word in the interview, the likelihood was 26.8% or 66.5%, respectively, that she could identify that word correctly on the posttest.

RQ3: Autonoetic awareness is associated with more attention

Next we investigated the relationship between how long a participant looked at a word during reading and the level of awareness she subsequently reported for it. To this end, we ran a mixed-effects model with fixation times as the outcome variable and awareness as the predictor variable. The mean fixation time for words in the baseline condition (i.e., no awareness) was 703 msec (95% CI=[582, 827]). Words for which participants reported noetic awareness tended to be processed by an extra 31 msec (95% CI=[–135, 212]), but this effect was not reliable. The effect of autonoetic awareness, on the other hand, was highly reliable. On average, participants tended to look at a word 306 msec (95% CI=[108, 510]) longer when they subsequently reported autonoetic awareness of that word.

RQ4: Awareness alone suffices to predict word recognition

Finally we were interested in whether attention and awareness make differential contributions to receptive word learning, and so we entered both the fixation times and the awareness codings into the same model. We found that the estimates for awareness remained virtually unchanged (see Results for RQ2) but that the effect for fixation time was now only marginally significant, b=0.61, 95% CI=[–0.09, 1.30], p=.083, marginal R^2=25.3, conditional R^2=42.1. The previous analysis revealed an association between fixation times and reported awareness level, which points to the possibility of multicollinearity.[7] However, fixation times and awareness levels correlated only weakly (Spearman correlation, ρ=.14, p=.03) and the variance inflation factor (VIF), which is a formal measure of multicollinearity, did not exceed 1.2. Therefore, we believe that multicollinearity may not be the reason why attention and learning are less strongly related in this model. Rather, there might be insufficient variance in the data (due to the low accuracy rates on the vocabulary posttest) for attention to have an effect above and beyond awareness (see Table 1). Model comparisons further confirmed that the model including fixation times and awareness did not fit the data better than a model with only awareness, $\chi^2(1)$=1.97, p=.160. Nonetheless, the rising slopes in Figure 3 reveal a trend for total processing time to be positively related with word recognition.

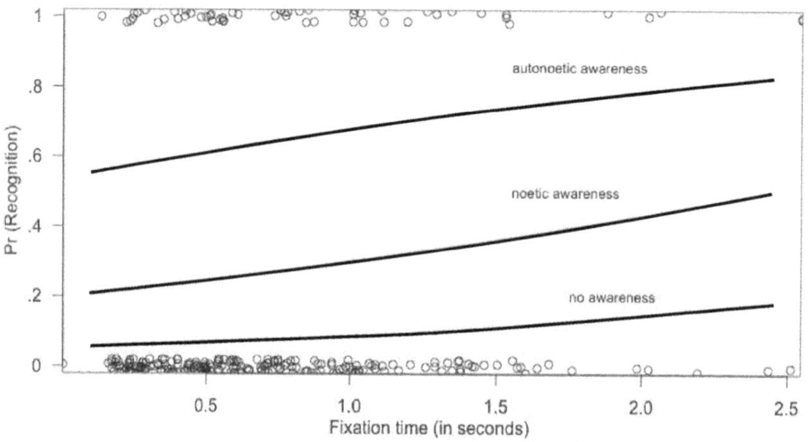

Figure 3. Probability of recognizing a word as a function of awareness and fixation times. Each circle represents one observation.

Discussion

The aim of this project was to refine existing operationalizations of the noticing construct by employing distinct measures for each of its constituent processes. In particular, we triangulated eye fixation durations, as a measure of attention, and retrospective verbal reports, as an index of awareness, with vocabulary posttest data to assess the relative contributions of each cognitive mechanism to learning. Our results supported the notion that attention and awareness are facilitative of incidental vocabulary learning and are themselves intimately related. We found that attention enabled access to awareness (cf. Baars, 1988, 1997, 2002; Cowan, 1988, 1995; Dehaene & Changeux, 2004; Dehaene, Changeux, Naccache, Sackur, & Sergent, 2006; Dehaene & Naccache, 2001; James, 1890; Koch, 2004; Posner, 1994; Schmidt, 2001; Styles, 2006; *inter alia*), which was itself a strong predictor of vocabulary learning.

Beneficial effects of attention on language learning

Logan (1988) postulated that "encoding into memory is an obligatory, unavoidable consequence of attention" (p. 493). As attention is itself a complex, multicomponential phenomenon, there is no simple explanation for why attention is crucial for memory. Knudsen (2007) described how top-down components of attention (i.e., working memory

7 Multicollinearity occurs when two predictors in a regression model are strongly correlated, which may result in inaccurate coefficient estimates (Baayen, 2008, p. 198).

and sensitivity control) direct bias signals to selected neural circuits, which increases their responsiveness and results in a higher-quality input for processing. Dehaene and Naccache (2001) similarly state that top-down attention to an incoming stimulus amplifies the extent of processing through "increased cerebral activation in attended areas and a transient increase in their efficiency" (p. 14). This phenomenon, dubbed *attentional amplification*, is essentially a neurobiological account of the attentional spotlight (e.g., Baars, 1988, 1997; Crick, 1993; Posner, Snyder, & Davidson, 1980)—the idea that "attention can be likened to a spotlight that enhances the efficiency of detection of events within its beam" (Posner et al., 1980, p. 172). Research from different disciplines therefore supports the notion that attention increases the depth and efficiency of processing of selected information, which improves memory for this information.

The present study examined the same topic from an applied linguistics perspective by measuring L2 learners' eye fixation durations for novel words during reading and relating these fixation durations to novel-word recognition (research question 1). It built on previous reading research with English native speakers that has shown a positive relation between reading times and word learning (Brusnighan & Folk, 2012; Williams & Morris, 2004). The ecological validity of the present study, however, may be higher than that of the former two, as it employed short reading texts instead of isolated sentences. Furthermore, our claims about the relationship between attention and word learning derive from word-based reading measures (total time on the pseudoword), a feature we share with Williams and Morris's (2004) eye-tracking study but not with Brusnighan and Folk's (2012) self-paced reading experiment, given that the latter analyzed total sentence reading times.

Beneficial effects of awareness on language learning

Just like participants' eye fixation durations were predictive of word learning, so was their awareness of having seen the word before, particularly if that awareness involved specific details of the original processing episode (research question 2). We noted in the literature review that awareness of a lexical item may be somewhat different than awareness of a grammatical item. Specifically, it is unclear what awareness at the level of understanding would entail in the realm of vocabulary learning. Although the lexicon also has a system level (in that individual words combine to form multiword units, collocations, etc.), it seems doubtful that individuals can develop a conscious understanding of the "rules" behind these multiword units, similar to the way they could verbalize a rule for the occurrence of the *–s* ending in English verbs. On the other hand, the early stages of grammar learning are likely to be lexically based, as they may consist of storing many different individual exemplars or items (Ellis, 2002a; Godfroid & Uggen, 2013). In this regard, the findings of the present vocabulary study may be relevant to the initial steps in L2 grammar learning also.

A key finding of this study was that, rather than the traditional distinction between noticing and understanding, the distinction between noetic awareness and autonoetic awareness was helpful in accounting for the data. We asked participants whether they remembered reading a target word on the assumption that this prompt would help them access the conscious thought processes (if any) they had had when reading the lexical target in the text. During data coding, however, it became clear that this question had elicited a number of responses that were difficult to categorize in a binary system. In particular, in about 20% of the cases, participants responded that they knew the particular word was somewhere in the texts they had read. It seemed familiar to them, but they could not remember the actual experience of reading the word. The distinction between a "feeling of knowing" a word versus the ability to re-experience the original event is what, in Tulving's (1983, 2002) framework, separates noetic awareness from autonoetic awareness (see also Baars & Gage, 2010, pp. 325–329).

Yonelinas (2002), who uses the terms recollection and familiarity instead of autonoetic and noetic awareness, noted that "recollection is particularly well suited to support learning of novel associations, and familiarity is only expected to support novel learning under very limited conditions" (pp. 446–447). One reason why autonoetic awareness may be important for forming new associations is that it requires hippocampal activity (e.g., Eldridge, Knowlton, Furmanski, Bookheimer, & Engel, 2000; Yonelinas, Otten, Shaw, & Rugg, 2005). The hippocampus, a limbic system structure in the medial temporal lobe, plays a central role in the formation and consolidation of explicit memories, of which episodic memories are a subset. Ellis (2002b) notes that "the hippocampal system subserves rapid explicit memory, one-off learning, [and] the establishment of new conjunctions of arbitrarily different elements" (p. 300). He links these mechanisms to the process of noticing. Given that learning a new word minimally requires making a new form-meaning connection that is largely arbitrary, hippocampal activity and the ensuing autonoetic awareness may assist in binding feature representations that were until then unrelated.

On the other hand, the vocabulary posttest format, which involved word recognition in context, may also explain why a sense of familiarity with the word was helpful but not sufficient for identifying the correct word. Participants had to be able to link a target word to its original context in order to discriminate successfully between the distractors, most of which were pseudowords they had also encountered in the texts. These findings, then, may explain why autonoetic awareness was associated with a higher proportion of word learning than noetic awareness.

What do eye-movement data reveal about awareness?

Research question 3 concerned the relationship between eye fixation times and awareness, an area that seems to be underexplored in psychology and SLA (but see Bohan & Sanford, 2008). We found a significant, positive association between the total amount of time a participant spent reading a pseudoword and her reported awareness of the pseudoword. In particular, autonoetic awareness was associated with an average of 306 ms extra total processing time on the pseudoword, relative to pseudowords for which participants reported no awareness. In contrast, the distinction between noetic awareness and unawareness could not be predicted based on a participant's total time for the corresponding pseudoword. These findings, then, lend independent support to the identification of a subset (12.3%) of trials with autonoetic awareness in our experiment, in which participants engaged in a highly subjective manner with the novel word in the text, such that they could later recall specific details of the processing event. Given that autonoetic awareness was associated with significantly longer total times than noetic awareness, autonoetic awareness arguably represents a higher level, or richer quality, of awareness than noetic awareness (also see previous section).

Because the fixation durations predicted the awareness levels, it is perhaps not surprising that when both factors were entered into a single regression model, the fixation durations were no longer significantly associated with the word-recognition scores (research question 4). This raises the question of whether levels of awareness alone might suffice to account for the initial stages of incidental vocabulary learning through reading. In our view, there are two reasons why such a conclusion is premature. Firstly, the off-line measure of awareness in this study (i.e., recall of word processing) is conceptually similar to the measure of receptive word learning (i.e., word recognition), which may have biased the results in favor of an association between these two phenomena. Nonetheless, the trials with autonoetic or noetic awareness yet no word recognition (4.2 and 13.0% of the data, respectively) suggest that retrieving a processing episode is not the same as retrieving the information that was potentially encoded during this processing episode (see Table 1). Indeed, we believe that these 45 cases of [+awareness, –recognition], which mostly involve partial word knowledge or lexical retrieval errors, are important and noteworthy observations in this study.

A second potentially biasing factor in this project is that both the interviewer and the interviewee knew whether the interviewee had identified the correct word on the test by the time she was asked if she could recall reading that word. A blinded procedure, whereby neither party knows how the interviewee did on the knowledge part of the experiment, could eliminate any observer- or subject-expectancy effects that may have resulted from the present design. Alternatively, one could abandon the within-subjects design with online eye tracking and off-line verbal reports and collect both data types online for different participant groups. Godfroid & Spino (2013) did just that, collecting think-aloud data for a between-subjects extension of this study.

Regardless of when one chooses to collect the verbal reports, we believe the eye-movement data are an integral part of this research, as they provide more fine-grained, low-level information about the reading process. They also show what type of cognitive processing went on at times when participants did not report anything. In this study, awareness was operationalized as a categorical variable with three levels: no verbal report of awareness, noetic awareness, and autonoetic awareness. While other classification systems are common (e.g., perception–noticing–understanding), awareness is typically conceived of as having only a limited number of levels or states (i.e., as a categorical variable; Cowan, 1995, p. 200). In contrast, attention is normally operationalized as a continuous variable, which reflects the view that one can pay differing amounts of attention to a stimulus. Eye fixation durations are a case in point, as they can take any value from 0 to some unspecified, upper limit. It stands to reason, then, that discarding the attention data (i.e., the eye fixation durations) would entail an enormous loss of information, as processing would effectively be reduced to one of a limited number of possible states. Rather, we believe that the attention data support and enrich the awareness analysis by showing that the different qualities of awareness identified in our verbal reports correspond to different amounts of processing and can, therefore, be ordered hierarchically, as awareness levels.

Conclusion

This study is an attempt at improved construct specification and measurement (cf. Norris & Ortega, 2003) of noticing, a process that is hypothesized to be essential to the early stages of L2 learning (Schmidt, 1990). In particular, we triangulated data from two independent sources, eye movements and verbal reports, to examine the extent to which attention and awareness jointly operate in the umbrella construct of noticing. In so doing, we empirically addressed Schmidt's claim that "a low level of awareness, called here 'noticing', is nearly isomorphic with attention, and seems to be associated with all learning" (Schmidt, 1995, p. 1). We also extended Hama and Leow's (2010) mixed-method design with two types of verbal report to one type of verbal report and a completely different measure, namely eye tracking.

Overall, our results support Schmidt's idea that attention and awareness are closely related at the behavioral level (see also James, 1890; Koch, 2004; Posner, 1994; Wyart & Tallon-Baudry, 2008). We found that advanced learners' attention to novel words during leisure reading was positively related to their subsequent word recognition, as was their awareness of these words during reading. Furthermore, eye fixation durations significantly differentiated between higher-level (autonoetic) awareness and lower-level (noetic) awareness or unawareness. The strong, positive relationship between autonoetic awareness and word learning suggests that language learners' subjective engagement with novel material (e.g., by invoking sound patterns, meaning associations, or personal experiences) may be especially facilitative of vocabulary learning (cf., Boers & Lindstromberg, 2009; Schmitt, 2008). Language learners bring their selves to the task. They are not mechanistic information processors but individuals carrying a potential for autobiographical experiences, which, if tapped, may strengthen and enhance their language learning in important ways.

Additional mixed-method studies are needed to examine whether attention and awareness are still as closely related when using a slightly different design. We are currently analyzing concurrent verbal reports that were collected for a between-subjects extension of this study. Alternatively, one could ask half of the eye-tracking group to do retrospective verbal reports and the other half to take a posttest. This design has the advantage of keeping most comparisons within subjects (attention–awareness; attention–learning) while limiting the repeated exposure to the target forms. The present study is only a first step in what will hopefully become a long journey.

References

Abbot-Smith, K., & Tomasello, M. (2006). Exemplar-learning and schematization in a usage-based account of syntactic acquisition. *The Linguistic Review, 23*, 275–290.

Allport, D. A. (1988). What concept of consciousness? In A. J. Marcel & E. Bisiach (Eds.), *Consciousness in contemporary science* (pp. 159–182). London: Clarendon Press.

Baars, B. J. (1988). *A cognitive theory of consciousness.* New York: Cambridge University Press.

Baars, B. J. (1997). *In the theater of consciousness: The workspace of the mind.* New York: Oxford University Press.

Baars, B. J. (2002). The conscious access hypothesis: Origins and recent evidence. *Trends in Cognitive Sciences, 6*, 47–52.

Baars, B. J. (2003). Introduction: Treating consciousness as a variable: The fading taboo. In B. J. Baars, W. P. Banks, & J. Newman (Eds.), *Essential sources in the scientific study of consciousness* (pp. 1–10). Cambridge, MA: MIT Press.

Baars, B. J., & Gage, N. M. (2010). *Cognition, brain, and consciousness: Introduction to cognitive neuroscience.* London: Elsevier Academic Press.

Baayen, R. H. (2008). *Analyzing linguistic data: A practical introduction to statistics.* Cambridge: Cambridge University Press.

Baayen, R. H., Davidson, D. J., & Bates, D. M. (2008). Mixed-effects modeling with crossed random effects for subjects and items. *Journal of Memory and Language, 59*, 390–412.

Baddeley, A. D. (2007). *Working memory, thought, and action.* Oxford: Oxford University Press.

Boers, F., & Lindstromberg, S. (2009). *Optimizing a lexical approach to instructed second language acquisition.* Basingstoke, UK: Palgrave Macmillan.

Bohan, J., & Sanford, A. J. (2008). Semantic anomalies at the borderline of consciousness: An eye-tracking investigation. *The Quarterly Journal of Experimental Psychology, 61*, 232–239.

Bowles, M. A. (2010). *The think-aloud controversy in second language research.* New York/London: Routledge.

Brusnighan, S. M., & Folk, J. R. (2012). Combining contextual and morphemic cues is beneficial during incidental vocabulary acquisition: Compound word processing. *Reading Research Quarterly, 47,* 172–190.

Corbetta, M., & Shulman, G. L. (2002). Control of goal-directed and stimulus-driven attention in the brain. *Nature Reviews Neuroscience, 3,* 201–15.

Council of Europe. (2001). *Common European Framework of Reference for Languages: Learning, teaching, assessment.* New York: Cambridge University Press.

Cowan, N. (1988). Evolving conceptions of memory storage, selective attention, and their mutual constraints within the human information-processing system. *Psychological Bulletin, 104,* 163–191.

Cowan, N. (1995). *Attention and memory: An integrated framework.* Oxford: Oxford University Press.

Craik, F. I. M., & Lockhart, R. S. (1972). Levels of processing: A framework for memory research. *Journal of Verbal Learning and Verbal Behavior, 11,* 671–684.

Craik, F. I. M., & Tulving, E. (1975). Depth of processing and the retention of words in episodic memory. *Journal of Experimental Psychology: General, 104,* 268–294.

Crick, F. (1993). *The astonishing hypothesis: The scientific search for the soul.* New York: Scribner's.

Dehaene, S., & Changeux, J. (2004). Neural mechanisms for access to consciousness. In M. S. Gazzaniga (Ed.), *The cognitive neurosciences III* (pp. 1145–1158). Cambridge, MA: MIT Press.

Dehaene, S., Changeux, J., Naccache, L., Sackur, J., & Sergent, C. (2006). Conscious, preconscious, and subliminal processing: A testable taxonomy. *Trends in Cognitive Sciences, 10,* 204–211.

Dehaene, S., & Naccache, L. (2001). Towards a cognitive neuroscience of consciousness: Basic evidence and a workspace framework. *Cognition, 79,* 1–37.

Eldridge, L. L., Knowlton, B. J., Furmanski, C. S., Bookheimer, S. Y., & Engel, S. A. (2000). Remembering episodes: A selective role for the hippocampus during retrieval. *Nature Neuroscience, 3,* 1149–1152.

Ellis, N. C. (1994). Consciousness in second language learning: Psychological perspectives on the role of conscious processes in vocabulary acquisition. *AILA Review, 11,* 37–56.

Ellis, N. C. (2002a). Frequency effects in language processing: A review with implications for theories of implicit and explicit language acquisition. *Studies in Second Language Acquisition, 24,* 143–188.

Ellis, N. C. (2002b). Reflections on frequency effects in language processing. *Studies in Second Language Acquisition, 24,* 297–339.

Ericsson, K. A., & Simon, H. A. (1993). *Protocol analysis: Verbal reports as data* (rev. ed.). Cambridge, MA: MIT Press.

Faretta-Stutenberg, M., & Morgan-Short, K. (2011). Learning without awareness reconsidered: A replication of Williams (2005). In G. Granena, J. Koeth, S. Lee-Ellis, A. Lukyanchenko, G. Prieto Botana, & E. Rhoades (Eds.), *Selected proceedings of the 2010 Second Language Research Forum: Reconsidering SLA research, dimensions, and directions* (pp. 18–28). Somerville, MA: Cascadilla Proceedings Project.

Fox, M. C., Ericsson, K. A., & Best, R. (2011). Do procedures for verbal reporting of thinking have to be reactive? A meta-analysis and recommendations for best reporting methods. *Psychological Bulletin, 137,* 316–344.

Gass, S., Svetics, I., & Lemelin, S. (2003). Differential effects of attention. *Language Learning, 53*, 497–545.

Gathercole, S. E. (2006). Nonword repetition and word learning: The nature of the relationship. *Applied Psycholinguistics, 27*, 513–543.

Gelman, A., & Hill, J. (2007). *Data analysis using regression and multilevel/hierarchical models.* New York, NY: Cambridge University Press.

Godfroid, A., Boers, F., & Housen, A. (in press). An eye for words: Gauging the role of attention in incidental L2 vocabulary acquisition by means of eye tracking. *Studies in Second Language Acquisition, 35*(3).

Godfroid, A., Housen, A., & Boers, F. (2010). A procedure for testing the noticing hypothesis in the context of vocabulary acquisition. In M. Pütz & L. Sicola (Eds.), *Inside the learner's mind: Cognitive processing and second language acquisition* (pp. 169–197). Amsterdam / Philadelphia: John Benjamins.

Godfroid, A., & Spino, L. (2013, March). *Timing is of the essence: Disentangling the roles of attention and awareness in L2 vocabulary learning.* Paper presented at the American Association for Applied Linguistics Conference, Dallas, TX.

Godfroid, A., & Uggen, M. S. (2013). Attention to irregular verbs by beginning learners of German—An eye movement study. *Studies in Second Language Acquisition, 35*, 291–322.

Goldberg, A. E. (2003). Constructions: A new theoretical approach to language. *Trends in Cognitive Sciences, 7*, 219–224.

Hama, M., & Leow, R. P. (2010). Learning without awareness revisited. *Studies in Second Language Acquisition, 32*, 465–491.

Han, Z., Park, E. S., & Combs, C. (2008). Textual enhancement of input: Issues and possibilities. *Applied Linguistics, 29*, 597–618.

James, W. (1890). *The principles of psychology.* New York: Henry Holt.

Jourdenais, R. (2001). Cognition, instruction, and protocol analysis. In P. Robinson (Ed.), *Cognition and second language instruction* (pp. 354–375). Cambridge: Cambridge University Press.

Knudsen, E. I. (2007). Fundamental components of attention. *Annual Review of Neuroscience, 30*, 57–78.

Koch, C. (2004). *The quest for consciousness: A neurobiological approach.* Englewood, CO: Roberts and Company Publishers.

Krashen, S. D. (1981). *Second language acquisition and second language learning.* Oxford: Pergamon.

Krashen, S. D. (1983). Newmark's "ignorance hypothesis" and current second language acquisition theory. In S. Gass & L. Selinker (Eds.), *Language transfer in language learning* (pp. 135–153). Rowley, MA: Newbury House.

Krashen, S. D. (1985). *The input hypothesis: Issues and implications.* London: Longman.

Lee, S.-K., & Huang, H.-T. (2008). Visual input enhancement and grammar learning: A meta-analytic review. *Studies in Second Language Acquisition, 30*, 307–331.

Leow, R. P. (1997). Attention, awareness, and foreign language behavior. *Language Learning, 47*, 467–505.

Leow, R. P. (2000). A study of the role of awareness in foreign language behavior. *Studies in Second Language Acquisition, 22*, 557–584.

Leung, J. H. C., & Williams, J. N. (2011). The implicit learning of mappings between forms and contextually derived meanings. *Studies in Second Language Acquisition, 33*, 33–55.

Leung, J. H. C., & Williams, J. N. (2012). Constraints on implicit learning of grammatical form-meaning connections. *Language Learning, 62*, 634–662.

Logan, G. D. (1988). Toward an instance theory of automatization. *Psychological Review, 95*, 492–527.

Millard, R. (2007, April 29). The joy of text. *Times*. Retrieved from http://women.timesonline.co.uk/tol/life_and_style/women/relationships/article1720309.ece.

Nakagawa, S., & Schielzeth, H. (2012). A general and simple method for obtaining R2 from generalized linear mixed-effects models. *Methods in Ecology and Evolution*. Article first published online: 3 DEC 2012DOI: 10.1111/j.2041–210x.2012.00261.x

Norris, J. M., & Ortega, L. (2003). Defining and measuring SLA. In C. J. Doughty & M. H. Long (Eds.), *The handbook of second language acquisition* (pp. 717–761). New York: Blackwell.

Posner, M. I. (1994). Attention: The mechanisms of consciousness. *Proceedings of the National Academy of Sciences USA, 91*, 7398–7403.

Posner, M. I., Snyder, C. R. R., & Davidson, B. J. (1980). Attention and the detection of signals. *Journal of Experimental Psychology: General, 109*, 160–174.

Rayner, K. (2009). Eye-movements and attention in reading, scene perception, and visual search. *The Quarterly Journal of Experimental Psychology, 62*, 1457–1506.

Robinson, P. (1995). Attention, memory, and the "noticing" hypotheses. *Language Learning, 45*, 283–331.

Robinson, P. (2003). Attention and memory during SLA. In C. J. Doughty & M. H. Long (Eds.), *The handbook of second language acquisition* (pp. 631–678). New York: Blackwell.

Robinson, P., Mackey, A., Gass, S. M., & Schmidt, R. W. (2012). Attention and awareness in second language acquisition. In S. M. Gass & A. Mackey (Eds.), *The Routledge handbook of second language acquisition* (pp. 247–267). New York: Routledge.

Rosa, E., & O'Neill, M. D. (1999). Explicitness, intake, and the issue of awareness. Another piece to the puzzle. *Studies in Second Language Acquisition, 21*, 511–556.

Sachs, R., & Polio, C. (2007). Learners' uses of two types of written feedback on an L2 writing revision task. *Studies in Second Language Acquisition, 29*, 67–100.

Schmidt, R. W. (1990). The role of consciousness in second language learning. *Applied Linguistics, 11*, 129–158.

Schmidt, R. W. (1994). Deconstructing consciousness in search of useful definitions for applied linguistics. *AILA Review, 11*, 11–26.

Schmidt, R. W. (1995). Consciousness and foreign language learning: A tutorial on the role of attention and awareness in learning. In R. W. Schmidt (Ed.), *Attention and awareness in foreign language learning* (pp. 1–63). Honolulu, HI: University of Hawai'i, National Foreign Language Resource Center.

Schmidt, R. W. (2001). Attention. In P. Robinson (Ed.), *Cognition and second language instruction* (pp. 3–32). Cambridge: Cambridge University Press.

Schmidt, R. (2012). Attention, awareness, and individual differences in language learning. In W. M. Chan, K. N. Chin, S. Bhatt, & I. Walker (Eds.), *Perspectives on individual characteristics and foreign language education* (pp. 27–50). Boston, MA: Mouton de Gruyter.

Schmitt, N. (2008). Instructed second language vocabulary learning. *Language Teaching Research, 12*, 329–363.

Sharwood Smith, M. (1981). Consciousness raising and the second language learner. *Applied Linguistics, 2*, 159–168.

Sharwood Smith, M. (1991). Speaking to many minds: On the relevance of different types of language information for the L2 learner. *Second Language Research, 7*, 118–132.

Smith, B. (2010). Employing eye-tracking technology in researching the effectiveness of recasts in CMC. In F. M. Hult (Ed.), *Directions and prospects for educational linguistics* (pp. 79–97). New York: Springer Verlag.

Smith, L., & Yu, C. (2008). Infants rapidly learn word-referent mappings via cross-situational statistics. *Cognition, 106*, 1558–68.

Styles, E. A. (2006). *The psychology of attention*. Hove, UK: Psychology Press.

Truscott, J. (1998). Noticing in second language acquisition: A critical review. *Second Language Research, 14*, 103–135.

Truscott, J., & Sharwood Smith, M. (2011). Input, intake, and consciousness. *Studies in Second Language Acquisition, 33*, 497–528.

Tulving, E. (1983). *Elements of episodic memory*. Oxford: Clarendon Press.

Tulving, E. (1985). Memory and consciousness. *Canadian Psychology, 26*, 1–12.

Tulving, E. (2002). Episodic memory: From mind to brain. *Annual Review of Psychology, 53*, 1–25.

Weiskrantz, L. (1997). *Consciousness lost and found: A neuropsychological exploration*. New York: Oxford University Press.

Williams, J. N. (2004). Implicit learning of form-meaning connections. In B. VanPatten, J. Williams, S. Rott, & M. Overstreet (Eds.), *Form meaning-connections in second language acquisition* (pp. 203–218). Mahwah, NJ: Lawrence Erlbaum Associates.

Williams, J. N. (2005). Learning without awareness. *Studies in Second Language Acquisition, 27*, 269–304.

Williams, R., & Morris, R. (2004). Eye movements, word familiarity, and vocabulary acquisition. *European Journal of Cognitive Psychology, 16*, 312–339.

Winke, P. M. (2013). The effects of input enhancement on grammar learning and comprehension: A modified replication of Lee, 2007, with eye-movement data. *Studies in Second Language Acquisition, 35*, 323–352.

Wyart, V., & Tallon-Baudry, C. (2008). Neural dissociation between visual awareness and spatial attention. *The Journal of Neuroscience, 28*, 2667–79.

Yonelinas, A. P. (2002). The nature of recollection and familiarity: A review of 30 years of research. *Journal of Memory and Language, 46*, 441–517.

Yonelinas, A. P., Otten, L. J., Shaw, K. N., & Rugg, M. D. (2005). Separating the brain regions involved in recollection and familiarity in recognition memory. *Journal of Neuroscience, 25*, 3002–3008.

Yu, C., & Smith, L. B. (2007). Rapid word learning under uncertainty via cross-situational statistics. *Psychological Science, 18*, 414–20.

Appendix A: Example of an experimental paragraph

Each participant read this paragraph in only one of the four conditions. Target words were not capitalized in the text that participants read.

A survey last week reported that one in five women have so little time with their partners that they spend more time sending them text messages than in old-fashioned face-to-face conversation. Apparently men and women now have a(n) AVERAGE / CANIMAT / CANIMAT OR AVERAGE / AVERAGE OR CANIMAT / *of only 10 minutes a day in which to talk to one another, nine minutes of which are usually taken up talking about the children, tax bills, or what to put in the microwave. That explains why text messages (sent via mobile phone or email) have risen to become key components in the typical adult relationship.*

95 words, adapted from Millard (2007)

Appendix B: Example of a vocabulary posttest item

This item represents condition ii, in which a participant read the paragraph with the target word *canimat* occurring by itself. For conditions iii and iv, the central part of the sentence prompt read .... *or average* and *average or* ...., respectively.

1. lurgled	7. staveners	13. redaster
2. offspring	8. prantenon	14. cumblery
3. dooters	9. listeners	15. quirkology
4. comfilment	10. broadcaster	16. hypergenity
5. dilactives	11. jurdistemy	17. paniplines
6. scrandivist	12. canimat	18. evidoses

Apparently men and women now have a(n) .... of only 10 minutes a day in which to talk to one another, nine minutes of which are usually taken up talking about the children, tax bills, or what to put in the microwave.

NFLRC monographs

Observing Noticing While Reading in L2

Daphnée Simard
Denis Foucambert
Université du Québec à Montréal

In the present study,[1] *the effect of textual enhancement (TE) on noticing was investigated taking into account three individual differences, i.e., attentional capacity, reading skills in L1 and in L2, and individual sensitivity to TE. Noticing was measured through eye movements and answers to a retrospective questionnaire. Results showed that TE induced more noticing as measured by eye movements than the unenhanced control condition. Results also showed that only attentional capacity was significantly linked to noticing and that attentional capacity was in interaction with the language in which TE was presented to the participants (L1 or L2). More specifically, participants with a lower attentional capacity fixated longer on the enhanced condition presented in their L2. Finally, the off-line measure of noticing was not in interaction with any of the online measures of noticing or individual differences.*

Introduction

According to Schmidt, awareness at the level of noticing is necessary for second language acquisition (SLA) to take place (1990, 1993a, 1993b, 1995, 2012). In this perspective it is *noticing*, defined as "the conscious registration of the occurrence of some event" (Schmidt, 1990, p. 139), that allows input to be converted into intake (Schmidt, 1993a, p. 209). This is also known as the *noticing hypothesis* (Schmidt, 1990, 2001, 2012). Intake is then available for further processing. There is a substantial amount of empirical evidence demonstrating that increased awareness at the level of noticing results in more learning (e.g., Huot, 1995; Jourdenais, Ota, Stauffer, Boyson, & Doughty, 1995; Leow, 1997, 1998, 2001; Rosa & Leow, 2004; Rosa & O'Neil, 1999; Schmidt & Frota, 1986).

1 We wish to thank Francis Bédard and Michael Zuniga who assisted us during various phases of the project. A special thanks also goes to Leslie Redmond for her help with the text. We also wish to thank the students who took part in the study. Finally, we thank the anonymous reviewers for their insightful comments.

Simard, D., & Foucambert, D. (2013). Observing noticing while reading in L2. In J. M. Bergsleithner, S. N. Frota, & J. K. Yoshioka (Eds.), *Noticing and second language acquisition: Studies in honor of Richard Schmidt* (pp. 207–226). Honolulu: University of Hawai'i, National Foreign Language Resource Center.

In order to investigate the role played by noticing in SLA, researchers have used, among others, external means of increasing the perceptual saliency of language features in the input (Overstreet, 2007, p. 85). It is maintained that when specific features of the language input are salient, learners are more likely to select them for intake (e.g., Gass, 1991; Schmidt, 1993a, 1993b, 1995, 2001; Sharwood Smith, 1981, 1991, 1993; VanPatten, 1990, 1996). As Ellis and Laporte (1997) noted, "instruction can usefully increase the salience of target language forms in input, thus making them more likely to be noticed" (p. 71).

One way to increase the perceptual salience of grammatical features is the use of typographical cues (e.g., Alanen, 1995; Jourdenais, 2001; Lee, 2007; Leow, 2001; Overstreet, 1998; Shook, 1994; Simard, 2002, 2009; Wong, 2003). Typographical cues can take different forms among which, italics, underlining, bold, change of fonts, or size of letters can be used alone or in combination (e.g., using bold and underlining at the same time) (Simard, 2009). Their use in texts creates an *isolation effect* (von Restorff, 1933, also known as a von Restorff effect), according to which an isolated item among a series of items will be better retained or learnt than the average of the non-isolated items (Wallace, 1965). Three types of modification lead to the isolation of an item in a homogenous list. One of them is what Wallace (1965) refers to as *addition* (translated from von Restorff, 1933). According to Wallace, an example of addition would be the use of a red word in a list of words written in black.

Findings from studies on the use of typographical cues, also called textual enhancement studies (hereafter TE) in SLA, show substantial variation (Cho, 2010; Han, Park, & Combs, 2008; Izumi, 2003; Lee, 2007; Lee & Huang, 2008; Simard, 2002, 2009). While some authors observed a positive effect of the presence of typographical cues on intake (Cho, 2010; Doughty, 1991; Simard, 2009), others saw none (Alanen, 1995; Izumi, 2002; M. Song, 2007; White, 1998; Wong 2001, 2003; see Lee & Huang, 2008, and Simard, 2002, for detailed reviews). These conflicting results make it impossible to draw a strong conclusion with regard to the contribution of TE to SLA. Differences in research designs across studies, which prevent direct comparisons of their results, can certainly explain this situation (Lee & Huang, 2008; Simard, 2002, 2009).

One of these differences corresponds to the measurement instruments used. The choice of the correct measure of noticing still presents a challenge. As Smith (2010) emphasizes, "there does not seem to be a consensus in L2 literature on the best way to measure it" (p. 82).

Two different types of measures have been used in studies investigating noticing: off-line and online measures. In *off-line measures*, the measurement of noticing is done after administering the task devised to elicit it (e.g., debriefing questionnaires), whereas in *online measures*, the measure is taken in real time during the task devised to elicit noticing (e.g., verbal reports) (Leow, 2006). Online measures of noticing are considered to be superior to off-line ones since "they allow more direct access to learners' ongoing internal processes and minimize possible memory loss" (S. Song, 2007, p. 5).

Another related issue in the investigation of noticing is the influence online measures might have on language processing (see Bowles, 2010a, 2010b, and Jourdenais, 2001, for a detailed discussion on the topic). According to Chaudron (1983, 1985a, 1985b), measurement instruments influence the way input is processed by the participants. It is possible to believe that a non-intrusive online means of observation, such as the observation of eye movements, would allow for a more accurate measure of noticing (Godfroid, Housen, & Boers, 2010).

In this regard, many consider that eye movements constitute an essential indicator of information intake (e.g., Juola, Bouwhuis, Cooper, & Warner, 1991; Theeuwes, 1993) and cognitive processing while reading for comprehension (e.g., Rayner, 1998). Since the middle of the 1970s, scholarly texts on eye movement while reading have been particularly numerous (e.g., Kennedy, Murray, & Boissiere, 2004; Radach & Kennedy, 2004; Rayner & Juhasz, 2004; Reichle, Rayner, & Pollatsek, 2003; Vitu, Kapoula, Lancelin, & Lavigne, 2004). Among these online observation techniques of reading processes, eye tracking represents an ecological and minimally intrusive method (van der Schoot, Vasbinder, Tako, & van Lieshout, 2008).

To our knowledge, three studies in SLA have used the eye-tracker to measure noticing. Godfroid, Housen, and Boers (2010) investigated the use of the eye-tracker to measure noticing in the context of vocabulary acquisition among nine (N=9) young adult ESL learners. The authors combined an online measure of noticing (the eye-tracker) to an off-line one (stimulated recall) and used a multiple-choice recognition test to measure vocabulary acquisition. They also used a reading comprehension test to make sure the participants actually paid attention to the meaning of the text. They concluded that the eye-tracker is a suitable measure of noticing since they observed "plenty of instances where one can tell by sight that the target word received notably more attention than the other words on the screen" (p. 183).

Smith (2010) also investigated the use of the eye-tracker to measure noticing. He verified whether recasts in computer-mediated communication were noticed through eye movement among eight (N=8) young adult learners of English. More specifically, Smith verified whether the participants noticed the recasts that were provided to them in a chat environment. *Intensive recasts* (as opposed to naturally-occurring and "isolated recasts") were provided by the researcher in the next possible turn of interaction. The participants viewed one of three versions of a short silent clip. They had to retell the story in order for the researcher to be able to choose which among the three versions they viewed. Every time the participants made an error, they were immediately corrected. According to the author, 60% of all recasts were noted since they were fixated on them for 500 ms or longer. Smith concluded that the eye-tracker provides a good indication of noticing. No inferential statistics were run on the data due to the limited sample size (p. 94).

The third study specifically looked at the effect of TE on noticing as measured by eye movement. In their study Loewen and Inceoglu (2013) investigated the effect of TE and *lexical glossing*, consisting of definitions and/or translations of targeted words inserted in texts (p. 9), on the noticing of Spanish preterit and imperfect forms and the learning of lexical items. The targeted items were enhanced with colours (imperfect in red and preterit in green on a blue screen), and the five glossed lexical items appeared in a word bank located at the bottom part of each slide. The authors used eye movements to operationalize noticing of the targeted items and a series of tests for the measurement of learning. Thirty college-level participants (N=30) enrolled in a second semester course in Spanish were randomly assigned to one of two groups: enhanced (n=15) and unenhanced (n=15) groups. A control group composed of sixteen (N=16) native speakers of Spanish also participated in the study. Eight read the enhanced text and the other eight, the unenhanced text. Results show that the participants in the enhanced group noticed the targeted items. However, there was no statistical difference between the two groups (enhanced and unenhanced). Additionally, there was no difference between the two groups for the learning of the targeted items as measured by the tests.

One recent study in L1 also observed the effect of TE on the readers' attention through eye movement. Chi, Gumbrecht, and Hong (2007) compared underlining keywords to

ScentHighlighting, i.e., "which automatically highlights both keywords and sentences that are conceptually related to a set of search keywords" (p. 591). Their six participants (N=6) were instructed to read 12 factual questions and then to provide answers from the information presented in the text. The authors concluded that highlighting key words in a text presented on a computer produces an isolation effect, which then leads the participants to pay attention to the enhanced elements (p. 590). Interestingly, their results also reveal possible effects of individual differences in text processing.

In light of what was presented above, the observation of eye movements to investigate noticing in SLA is promising as it has shown to provide "useful insights into the amount of attention that is given to a targeted structure" (Loewen & Inceoglu, 2013). Along with the obvious need for more data obtained from this type of online paradigm, there is also a need for the investigation of individual differences in studies examining the impact of TE on noticing. According to Schmidt (2012), individual differences should be taken into account when studying noticing, since some L2 learners seem to notice more than others. Additionally, Sachs and Suh (2007) mention that "textual enhancement has a place in the learning process which is mediated by individual differences in cognitive abilities and propensities" (p. 219).

Therefore, in the present study we investigated noticing measured through eye movement in a TE study context taking into account three individual differences. Firstly, considering that TE is used to induce language-feature noticing and that the capacity to pay attention to target features might vary from one individual to another (e.g., Mackey, Philp, Egi, Fujii, & Tatsumi, 2002), it is possible to think that attentional capacity interacts with the intake produced by the participants. In that respect, Trofimovich, Ammar, and Gatbonton (2007) observed a link between their participants' attentional capacity and the way they paid attention to the target language features. Therefore, a measure of attentional capacity was added to our study's experimental design.

Next, since prior studies conducted in L1 offer results indicating interactions between the level of reading comprehension and the processing of TE (Beck, 1984; Bernard, 1990), a reading skills measure in both L1 and L2 was added to the study.

Finally, in addition to these two individual difference variables, it is possible to think that individual sensitivity to typographical cues might have an effect on the way TE is noticed by the participants. In their conclusion Chi et al. (2007) highlighted the effect of individual differences in text processing. Accordingly, a control of the participants' sensitivity to the presence of TE in their L1 was used.

To our knowledge such measures of individual differences have never been taken into account in previous L2 TE studies.

Methodology

Participants

Twenty students enrolled in a French immersion program at the university level participated in this study. They were all undergraduates from English-speaking provinces in Canada, and they attended intermediate French level classes. There were originally 14 females and six males, and their mean age was 24.1 (minimum 21, maximum 32). Unfortunately, data from two participants were lost: one due to mechanical problems and the other as all of this participant's fixation times were two standard deviations away from the other subjects' mean times ($>M+2SD$).

Language features

According to Cho (2010), TE works better when the enhanced language features have a relatively higher communicative value (p. 73). *Communicative value* corresponds to the degree of contribution of a particular language feature to the understanding of a sentence's referential meaning (VanPatten, 1996). This degree of contribution is determined by the semantic value and redundancy of information a language feature carries in a sentence. For instance, a language feature of high communicative value would be semantically rich and non redundant (e.g.,—*ing*), whereas a language feature of low communicative value would be redundant but still have some semantic value (e.g., past tense markers, if they co-occur with lexical temporal indications) (VanPatten, 2000, p. 298). A language feature of no communicative value would have no semantic value (e.g., gender agreement markers on adjectives) (VanPatten, 2000, p. 298). For the present study, we chose to enhance complex relative pronouns.

According to Keenan and Comrie (1977), relative clause formation can be placed in an implicative hierarchy (Accessibility Hierarchy). From a cross-linguistic examination of fifty languages, they defined the accessibility to relativization, which states that the relativization of noun phrases in the subject position is more accessible than in the direct object position, which is in turn more accessible than in indirect object, oblique, possessor, and comparative positions respectively (see Keenan & Comrie, 1977, p. 66, for more detail). Language forms that are more accessible are believed to be more easily learnt (see Keenan, 1972) or processed (e.g., Traxler, Morris, & Seely, 2002).

In the online measure of noticing (explained below), we only used oblique relatives (prepositional complement) as in "*Blunt from whom we had almost not heard a word*" (Christie, 1926) in both the French and English versions.

Noticing measures

Two different types of instruments were used to measure noticing: an online measure and an off-line one.

Online measure of noticing. The online measure corresponds to the observation of eye movement during a reading task. We used FaceLab v4.6 (2008) to do so. FaceLab not only allows for the recording of the participant's eye movement but also for each eye-gaze fixation time. This system is known to be simple to use and non-intrusive. Essentially, it works with two digital infrared cameras and is piloted by GazeTrackerTM v8 (2008), which allows the preparation of experiments and a dynamic and synchronised recording of data. Data is taken every 16 ms (60 Hz). A flat screen (376,3 mm by 301,1 mm) with a resolution of 1280 X 1024 pixels was used. The participants were 80 cm away from the screen.

In order to obtain the data from the eye-tracker, the participants had to read parts of Agatha Christie's (1926, 1927) "The Murder of Roger Ackroyd" (see Appendix A). The text was presented by alternating from one page in French to one page in English (using the published translation in French). To control for language sequence, the participants were randomly assigned to one of the two different conditions: one starting with French and the other one with English. Each text contained 20 occurrences of the complex relative pronouns (five per page) which were enhanced by **<u>underlined and bolded</u>** font.

Each page contained about 350 words (in font 12, Times New Roman) and was immediately followed by a multiple-choice comprehension question in the language in which the page was written in order to verify that the participants were engaged in reading comprehension.

We ensured that the enhanced language features were located in the same zones in the texts in French and English (Appendix B). The texts were balanced according to usual parameters (e.g., word frequency, sentence complexity) (Cobb, n.d.).

Off-line measure of noticing. The second measurement of noticing was a verbal report from the participants. They were asked to tell the experimenter whether they had noticed anything while reading and if yes, to explain what it was. The participants' answers were collected individually immediately after the experimental task by research assistants.

Individual difference measures

The following section describes the instruments used to measure the individual variables selected in the present study.

Trail Making Test. We used the *Trail Making Test* integrated into the *Halstead–Reitan Neuropsychological Test Battery* (Reitan, 1958) in order to get a measure of the participants' attentional capacity. This is one of the most commonly used cognitive tests (Rabin, Barr, & Burton, 2005) and permits the measurement of visual search and attention-shift capacity (Arbuthnott & Frank, 2000; Atkinson & Ryan, 2008). The test is composed of two parts. Each part contains 25 circles randomly distributed over a sheet of paper. For Part A, the participants must draw a line to connect the circles that are numbered from 1 to 25 in ascending order. For Part B, the participants do the same type of exercise, however this time when connecting the circles (containing numbers from 1 to 13, and letters from A to L), they must alternate between numbers and letters (i.e., 1-A–2-B–3-C, etc.). Both parts must be completed as fast as the participants can.

Reading skills. Our participants' reading skills were measured in their L1 and L2 using a task targeting reading skills (comprehension and speed). We developed a software program for our study in order to capture exact reading times for each condition (English L1 and French L2) (Foucambert, 2000, 2003, 2007). We used other extracts taken from Agatha Christie's (1926, 1927) book *The Murder of Roger Ackroyd.* The participants read a 550 word long extract and then answered five multiple-choice comprehension questions. They did it in both French and English, and the sequence was also counterbalanced. Reading speed for each participant in each language was recorded along with the reading comprehension score. Reading comprehension was measured at different levels (e.g., explicit information presented in the text, inferences).

Sensitivity to TE in L1. Finally, in order to get a measure of our participants' sensitivity to TE, we used the data obtained from the online noticing task in English (participants' L1).

Procedure

The participants were recruited at the university, and each participant was met individually in a quiet room. The administration of the task took about 45 minutes and was done in the following order: 1) personal questionnaire, 2) the attention measure (TMT), 3) the online noticing measure in L1 and L2 (according to a randomly assigned order), 4) the debriefing questionnaire which allowed to identify the participants as aware or unaware of the presence of TE in the texts (off-line measure of noticing), and finally, 5) the reading skills measure in L1 and L2 (in a randomly assigned order).

For the TMT, the participants received the instructions and then did a training session before each part. Their performance time was noted separately (for Part A and for Part B).

For the online noticing measure, prior to the task itself, the participants had a training session using the same protocol with a different book by Agatha Christie (1934a, 1934b),

Murder on the Orient Express. The training session also served as a means to calibrate the apparatus. The calibration was done for each of the participants. To do so, the participants had to put on the head-mounted eye-tracker. During the calibration the participants were asked to follow a moving blue dot with their eyes. Then, they were given the instruction to read the text presented on the screen and to press enter when they were done. They were told that after reading the page, they would have to answer a multiple-choice question. They were also told that the text would alternate between their first and second languages.

In order to measure reading skills, the participants were instructed that they would have to read two texts presented on a computer screen, one in English and one in French, and that after reading each page, they had to press « enter ». A multiple-choice comprehension question they would have to answer would then appear on the screen. One training item was presented to them.

For participating in the study, the participants received a ticket to go see any movie showing in a movie theatre featuring French-speaking movies and financial compensation of ten dollars.

Data coding and analysis

For the online noticing measure, the unit of analysis corresponds to fixations in *lookzones*, which are defined as frames containing one word before the target and one word after. We decided to observe a window of n–1, n, and n+1 words for two reasons. Firstly, our targets are high-frequency short words, and past studies have repeatedly shown that they are often skipped (Carpenter & Just, 1983; Just & Carpenter, 1980; Rayner & Well, 1996). Secondly, when reading alphabetic languages, the area from which readers can obtain information extends 3–4 letters to the left of fixation (corresponding to word n–1) and 14 letters to the right (corresponding to words n and n+1) (McConkie & Rayner, 1975).

In the experimental condition, the lookzones targeted the enhanced linguistic features, i.e., relative pronouns. In the control conditions, the lookzones targeted conjunctions, which were not enhanced. This allowed us to compare the durations of the fixations on enhanced and unenhanced language material. We chose conjunctions since they are as frequent in the texts as the relative pronouns, are about the same length, and are located in the same spots in the texts in both French and English. We considered that they carried approximately the same level of communicative value as the relative pronouns, since they have a high semantic value and are not redundant.

We examined three standard reading time measures (Rayner, 1998) for the relevant lookzones in a sentence: (1) total reading time (the sum of all fixations on a word, including regressions to the word), (2) first-fixation duration (the duration of the first fixation on the word) and (3) regression duration (the duration of the fixations when the reader returns to the lookzone). Fixations of less than 80 ms were not considered for analysis. Because of the nature of our study, gaze duration was not examined (the sum of all of the fixations on a word prior to moving to another word) in order to focus on our third specific measure (regression duration) which is of more interest in studies pertaining to attention. According to Dussias (2010), regression duration has been interpreted "as a sensitive measure of immediate anomaly detection, given that readers often respond to processing difficulties by regressing to earlier portions of the sentence" (p. 153). These anomaly detections could be induced by the presence of TE.

For the TMT, the participants' performance time on both parts were used to group them into three categories according to their scores (categorical scoring). Participants with a score ≥ third quartile were categorized in the higher attention group, those with a score ≤ first quartile were categorized in the lower attention group, and those between these two boundaries were categorized in the average attention group.

As for the reading task, each correct answer (reading comprehension questions) was given one point for a maximum score of five. The reading time was also recorded. Then, in order to get a general reading skills measure, the four variables from the reading tasks (French and English) with a factor analysis were summarized to create categories. The two comprehension scores (French and English) and the two reading speed measures (French and English) were entered as active variables in a factor analysis, using a principal components analysis with varimax rotation (Kaiser, 1958). An examination of the eigenvalues (Kaiser's criterion, 1960, and Cattell's method, 1966) and cumulative percentage of variance explained by the four successive dimensions tend to show the presence of only one general factor that synthesizes the global reading skills of our participants. This classic size-effect (Hotelling, 1933; Lebart, Morineau, & Piron, 1997) represents a general reading skills ability: the subject's position on factor 1 was saved as the reading skills value. This observation is in line with previous studies demonstrating a link between reading skills in L1 and in L2, particularly among proficient readers (e.g., Bernhardt & Kamil, 1995; Sarig, 1987). The general reading skills measure was categorized the same way the TMT measure was categorized (low=≤ first quartile; high ≥ third quartile; average between first and third quartile).

Results

Firstly, the descriptive statistics for the examined variables will be presented. Table 1 shows the results for fixation time according to the independent variables. These independent variables are *Off-line Noticing* (i.e., being aware or unaware of the presence of TE), *Reading Skills* (i.e., low, average, or good readers), and *Attentional Capacity* (i.e., low, average, or high attentional capacity).

In general, fixation durations are always longer in the experimental (enhanced) condition than in the control condition. However, two exceptions can be observed, that is, between the experimental and control conditions in French L2 for *Reading Skills* and for *Attentional Capacity*. Additionally, fixation durations are always longer in L2 than in L1, independently of the variables. The most striking differences, whether between L1 and L2 or between enhanced and unenhanced, are observed in the regression fixation durations.

Three successive mixed between-within subjects ANOVAs were conducted, with *Online Noticing* (i.e., enhanced or unenhanced condition) and *Language* (i.e., texts in English L1 or French L2) as within-subjects variables and *Off-line Noticing, Reading Skills,* and *Attentional Capacity* as between-subjects variables. We first verified the assumptions required by this kind of statistical analysis: normality of DVs (with Kolmogorov-Smirnov tests—all ns; skewness<1), homogeneity of variance (with Levens's test—all ns), and homogeneity of intercorrelations (by Box's M tests—all ns). Unless otherwise noted, only significant effects are reported, and any main effects or interactions that are not mentioned did not reach significance. The results are presented in Table 2.

Table 1. Fixation duration means (standard deviations) as a function of the variables

			enhanced						unenhanced					
			L2 French			L1 English			L2 French			L1 English		
		N	TTR	FFD	RFD	TTR	FFD	RFD	TTR	FFD	RFD	TTR	FFD	RFD
off-line noticing														
	Y	13	1067 (310)	288 (81)	967 (377)	715 (250)	221 (48)	684 (215)	930 (283)	265 (78)	870 (332)	565 (232)	204 (61)	470 (181)
	N	5	1150 (333)	305 (79)	980 (212)	835 (336)	221 (52)	776 (456)	1020 (322)	330 (82)	920 (357)	669 (237)	219 (85)	535 (164)
reading skills														
	LR	4	1152 (303)	280 (18)	942 (291)	697 (360)	204 (50)	692 (562)	943 (226)	361 (82)	778 (232)	568 (265)	177 (108)	426 (181)
	GR	5	973 (352)	286 (112)	819 (330)	687 (272)	225 (50)	647 (206)	815 (259)	272 (94)	739 (258)	581 (302)	235 (70)	533 (198)
	AR	9	1128 (307)	301 (81)	1067 (353)	805 (252)	226 (50)	752 (183)	1038 (322)	254 (58)	1011 (374)	613 (202)	208 (39)	491 (171)
attention														
	H	5	1075 (337)	294 (91)	875 (287)	782 (254)	230 (43)	638 (291)	882 (150)	304 (55)	835 (224)	637 (291)	225 (83)	501 (222)
	A	8	923 (197)	281 (81)	792 (177)	749 (339)	214 (44)	767 (378)	889 (375)	265 (102)	775 (353)	565 (243)	220 (66)	499 (163)
	L	5	1373 (260)	311 (75)	1351 (281)	713 (209)	224 (65)	689 (86)	1133 (169)	292 (79)	1106 (320)	598 (188)	174 (44)	458 (175)
total		18	1090 (309)	292 (78)	970 (333)	748 (271)	221 (48)	710 (289)	955 (288)	283 (82)	883 (329)	594 (231)	208 (66)	488 (174)

note. Total Reading Time (TTR), First Fixation Duration (FFD) and Regression Fixation Duration (RFD) in Enhanced and Unenhanced Lookzones in L2 and L1 reading as a function of off-line noticing, reading skills, and attention levels. Low Readers (LR), Good Readers (GR), and Average Readers (AR). High Attentional Capacity (H), Average (A), and Low (L). Values of means (and standard deviations) are in milliseconds.

Table 2. Main effects and interaction for online noticing and language by fixation durations

effect	*df*	total time		first fixation		regression fixation	
		F	*p*	F	*p*	F	*p*
intercept	1	225.57	0.00	407.03	0.00	236.08	0.00
off-line noticing	1	1.55	0.24	1.22	0.29	1.11	0.31
reading skills	2	1.02	0.39	0.01	0.99	1.31	0.31
attentional capacity	2	1.65	0.23	0.35	0.71	2.10	0.16
error	12						
online noticing	1	9.45	0.01	0.00	0.96	5.77	0.03
online noticing x off-line noticing	1	0.01	0.91	0.15	0.70	0.02	0.88
online noticing x reading skills	2	0.11	0.90	0.51	0.61	0.21	0.82
online noticing x attentional capacity	2	0.35	0.71	0.17	0.85	0.42	0.67
error	12						
language	1	33.25	0.00	39.87	0.00	31.24	0.00
languagex off-line noticing	1	0.00	0.96	0.88	0.37	0.09	0.77
language x reading skills	2	0.49	0.63	2.79	0.10	2.11	0.16
languagex attentional capacity	2	3.70	0.06	1.82	0.20	8.20	0.01
error	12						
online noticing x language	1	0.07	0.79	0.66	0.43	0.63	0.44
online noticing x language x off-line noticing	1	0.00	0.96	0.03	0.86	0.03	0.87
online noticing x language x reading skills	2	0.31	0.74	1.97	0.18	0.19	0.83
online noticing x language x attentional capacity	2	0.73	0.50	0.51	0.61	0.44	0.65
error	12						

note. Language (lang); attentional capacity (attention); reading skills (reading skills).

First, for total time, we can observe an effect of *Online Noticing*, $F(1, 12)=9.45$, $p<0.01$, $\eta^{p}_{2}=0.44$. The enhanced condition showed an increase of 145ms (without mention of language). *Language* is associated with an important increase of times when participants read in French L2 (+351ms), $F(1, 12)=33.25$, $p<0.001$, $\eta^{p}_{2}=0.73$. It should be noted that the effect sizes reported are large (Cohen, 1988). No other main effect approaches significance, and only the interaction between *Language* and *Attentional Capacity* is close to significance $F(2, 12)=3.69$, $p<0.06$.

Figure 1 illustrates this aspect: we can see that the participants with a lower attentional capacity show a higher total reading time in L2.

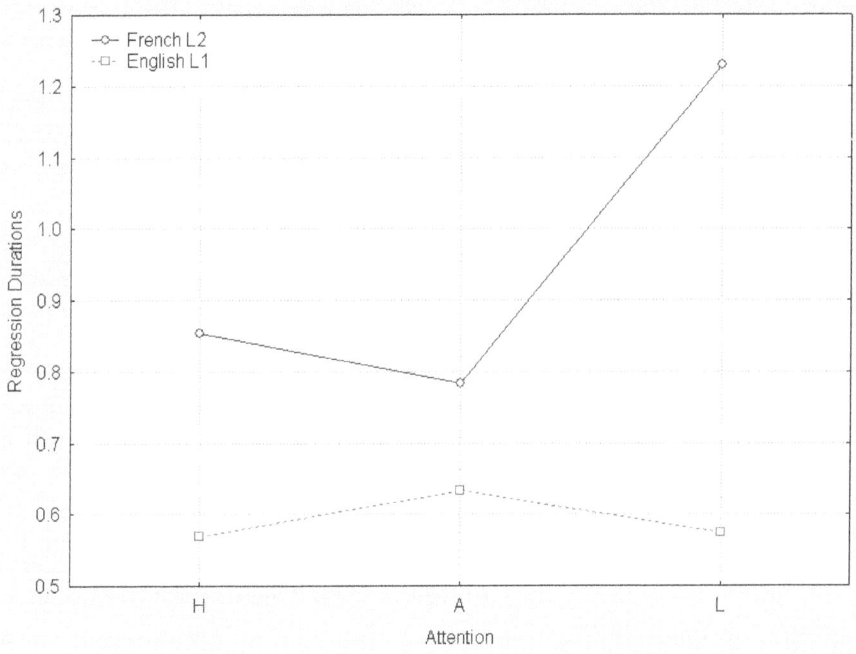

Figure 1. Regression durations as a function of attention and language

Secondly, the results for regression fixations follow the same pattern as those for total time and actually explain them. Regressions on lookzones are longer (+153ms) on enhanced materials—*Online Noticing* , $F(1, 12)=5.77$, $p<0.03$, $\eta^{p}_{2}=0.33$, and *Language* (in which the text is presented) is again associated with an important increase in times when participants read French L2 texts (+327ms), $F(1, 12)=31.24$, $p<0.001$, $\eta^{p}_{2}=0.75$. The interaction between *Language* and *Attentional Capacity* this time reaches significance $F(2, 12)=8.20$, $p<0.006$, $\eta^{p}_{2}=0.58$. Again, all the effect sizes reported are large (Cohen, 1988).

The post hoc tests (Bonferroni's test) revealed that the participants with lower attentional capacity spent significantly more time on the enhanced target lookzones when they were reading French L2 texts than all other conditions (e.g., higher attentional capacity reading in French L2, higher attentional capacity reading in English L1) (all $ps<0.05$).

Discussion

In the present study we investigated noticing in a TE study context taking into account three individual differences: attentional capacity, reading skills in L1 and L2, and individual sensitivity to TE. Noticing was measured through eye movements and the answers provided in a retrospective questionnaire.

Our results first show that our participants fixated significantly longer on the enhanced experimental condition than the unenhanced control one. This indicates that using bold print and underlining is a good way to increase the salience of the targeted language features. This is in line with Chi et al. (2007) who also observed that their participants fixated longer on underlined key words in L1. It also indirectly lends support to L2 studies that observed the effect of TE on noticing (measured by means other than eye movements). This alludes to the work of Cho (2010), Doughty (1991), and Simard (2009).

As for Loewen and Inceoglu (2013), although their results showed that the participants in their study fixated on the enhanced linguistic items, they emphasized that there was no statistical difference between the enhanced and unenhanced control groups. Despite the similarities between their study design and ours (similar task to collect online data and similar participants), some differences (notably the TE format, the type of control condition, and the targeted linguistic features) may explain the discrepancy between the results obtained in both studies.

One explanation might lie in the difference in the TE format used in their study and ours. They used green and red on a blue screen. It is possible that the contrast between the script and the screen was not high enough to induce an isolation or von Restorff effect. Underlining, in particular, has been shown to attract attention in previous TE studies (i.e., Chi et al., 2007; Simard, 2009). Another possible explanation is that in our study we were unable to have enough participants to create the same type of control group as in Loewen and Inceoglu (2013). In their study 15 participants were exposed to a text without any form of TE. In our study, for the sake of size effect, we thought it was better to expose the 18 participants we had to one text containing two types of lookzones: experimental and control ones. This procedure also allowed us to use repeated measures, which is known to increase the power of the analysis (Howell, 2004). Loewen and Inceoglu (2013) actually mention their results "may be due in part to the small sample size and high standard deviations."

It can also be argued that the difference in communicative value between the linguistic features they used and those used in our study could explain the results. We enhanced complex relative pronouns, which we believe carry a high communicative value. In their study Loewen and Inceoglu (2013) enhanced the Spanish preterit and imperfect. Although past tense markers are considered of low communicative value in general (see VanPatten, 2000), this value remains dependent on the other indications of past (e.g., temporal expressions) found in the text. In order to present the targeted linguistic features, they used *Little Red Riding Hood.* It is possible that the nature of the text, starting with *once upon a time,* contributed to lowering the communicative value of the targeted language features, even though the aspectual distinction between the preterit and imperfect is not found anywhere else in the text besides in the verbs themselves. It would be very interesting in future research to experimentally investigate the effect of linguistic features' communicative value on eye movements.

As expected, of the three fixation durations examined in the present study, regression fixations carried the effect. As mentioned earlier, regression fixations are interpreted as a sensitive measure of detection of anomalies in a text (Dussias, 2010). We had hypothesized that this detection "of anomalies" could be related to the presence of TE. This was confirmed by our results. Viewed in this light, our results lend support to the assumption that eye movements provide an accurate measure of noticing (e.g., Godfroid et al., 2010;

Loewen & Inceoglu, 2013; Smith 2010). More specifically, we would hypothesize that regression fixations constitute the finest measure of noticing. This of course requires further investigation.

Additionally, there was no effect of first fixation durations in our results (for both L1 and L2), indicating that noticing requires some delay after the first passage over the enhanced zone. We would argue that this first passage over the enhanced language features corresponds to *preliminary intake* (Chaudron, 1985a, p. 2). According to Chaudron, preliminary intake is derived from input in the initial stages of perception. Intake, in this view, is not a single event or product, it is rather:

> a complex phenomenon of information processing that involves several stages, roughly characterized as (1) the initial stages of perception of input, (2) the subsequent stages of recoding and encoding of the semantic (communicated) information into long term-memory, and (3) the series of stages by which the learners fully integrate and incorporate the linguistic information in their developing grammars. (p. 2)

In this perspective the product of noticing, defined at the beginning of this article as the "conscious registration of the occurrence of some event," would then correspond to a subsequent type of intake, one that requires a somewhat deeper form of processing. The fact that this behaviour is observed in both L1 and L2 conditions means that it is representative of a general underlying cognitive process.

Our results also indicate a strong effect of language: the participants took longer to read in their L2 than in their L1. This was expected, as readers generally take longer to read in L2 than in L1 (e.g., Thomas & Healy, 2012).

Turning now to the individual differences measured in the present study, our results first indicate that the fixation durations of enhanced target items are associated with the subjects' attentional capacity. This lends support to Sachs and Suh's (2007) assumption that individual differences intervene in the learning process in TE studies. Our results also show an interaction between the language in which the enhanced targeted linguistic features are presented and the participants' attentional capacity. This is particularly visible in the regression fixation duration. Our results show that when reading in their L2, for the participants with lower attentional capacity, their fixation durations were significantly longer. This result also supports Schmidt's (2012) assumption that individual differences come into play in noticing and that some learners are "better noticers" than others. We would argue that for participants with lower attentional capacity, the effort to "detect anomalies," i.e., the presence of TE, is greater (see Dussias, 2010).

With regards to reading skills, the second individual difference measured in our study, our results show that they have no effect on the fixation durations of enhanced target items. We expected reading skills to be associated with the noticing of enhanced language features. Recall that we used a composite measure of comprehension and speed in both L1 and L2 to create our reading comprehension indicator. It could be that only one of these indicators interacts with noticing in TE conditions. In our study the use of a composite measure served to limit the number of variables since we had a rather small number of participants. This merits further research.

Finally, our third individual difference, i.e., individual sensitivity to the presence of TE as measured by the noticing task in English L1, did not seem to play an important role since the results revealed no interaction between the language in which TE was presented and any of the noticing measures. Globally, our results indicate that independently of the language in which the condition is presented to the participants and the level of reading comprehension, the same behaviour is observed. This again supports the hypothesis that it is indicative of lower level cognitive processes.

We believe that particular attention in the study of the effect of TE on noticing should be devoted to the role played by other individual differences. In our study, we observed that attentional capacity profiles are in interaction with the online measures of noticing. Nevertheless, other individual differences have been mentioned to potentially interact with noticing, namely language aptitude (e.g., Schmidt, 2012). This was first observed in Sawyer and Ranta (2001) who advanced the hypothesis of a link between language aptitude and noticing and called for more work exploring the relationship between these two.

Finally, as for the retrospective measure of noticing, it is worth mentioning that it was not associated with any of the online measures of noticing, indicating a lack of relation between the two constructs. Although off-line measures such as a retrospective questionnaire have been commonly used to measure noticing in SLA, the data they provide "may not reflect truly what learners became aware of while exposed to the input" (Leow, 2006, p. 128).

Conclusion

Noticing is without a doubt a very important construct in SLA, and it has been for many years. Many researchers adopt the position that without noticing, acquisition cannot take place or at least that noticing facilitates SLA. In the present study we looked at one way of promoting noticing, i.e., TE and took into account three individual differences: attentional capacity, reading skills in L1 and in L2, and individual sensitivity to TE. We measured the effect of TE on noticing through eye movement and a retrospective questionnaire. Our results showed that TE induced more noticing that the unenhanced control condition. Our results also showed that of the three individual differences investigated in the present study, only attentional capacity was significantly linked to noticing. Furthermore, it was shown that attentional capacity was in interaction with the language in which TE was presented to the participant (L1 or L2). Finally, our results demonstrated that the off-line measure of noticing was not in interaction with any online measure of noticing or individual differences.

References

Alanen, R. (1995). Input enhancement and rule presentation in second language acquisition. In R. Schmidt (Ed.), *Attention and awareness in foreign language acquisition* (pp. 259–302). Honolulu, HI: University of Hawai'i, National Foreign Language Resource Center.

Arbuthnott, K., & Frank, J. (2000). Trail Making Test, part B as a measure of executive control: Validation using a set-switching paradigm. *Journal of Clinical and Experimental Neuropsychology, 22*, 518–528.

Atkinson, T. M., & Ryan, J. P. (2008). The use of variants of the Trail Making Test in serial assessment: A construct validity study. *Journal of Psycho-educational Assessment, 26*, 42–53.

Beck, C. R. (1984). Visual cueing strategies: Pictorial, textual, and combinational effects. *Educational Communication and Technology Journal, 32*, 207–216.

Bernard, R. M. (1990). Effects of processing instructions on the usefulness of a graphic organizer and structural cueing in text. *Instructional Science, 19*, 207–217.

Bernhardt, E. B., & Kamil, M. L. (1995). Interpreting relationships between L1 and L2 reading: Consolidating the linguistic threshold and the linguistic interdependence hypotheses. *Applied Linguistics, 16*, 15–34.

Bowles, M. (2010a). *The think-aloud controversy in second language research*. New York: Routledge.

Bowles, M. (2010b). Concurrent verbal reports in second language acquisition research. *Annual Review of Applied Linguistics, 30*, 111–127.

Carpenter, P. A., & Just, M. A. (1983). What your eyes do while your mind is reading. In K. Rayner (Ed.), *Eye movements in reading: Perceptual and language processes* (pp. 275–307). New York: Academic.

Chaudron, C. (1983). Simplification of input: Topic reinstatements and their effects on L2 learners' recognition and recall. *TESOL Quarterly, 17*, 437–458.

Chaudron, C. (1985a). Intake: On models and methods for discovering learners' processing of input. *Studies in Second Language Acquisition, 7*, 1–14.

Chaudron, C. (1985b). A method for examining the input/intake distinction. In S. Gass & C. Madden (Eds.), *Input in second language acquisition* (pp. 285–300). Rowley, MA.: Newbury House.

Cattell, R. B. (1966). The scree test for the number of factors. *Multivariate Behavioral Research, 1*, 245–276.

Chi, E. H., Gumbrecht, M., & Hong, L. (2007). Visual foraging of highlighted text: An eye-tracking study. In J. Jacko (Ed.), *Human-computer interaction, Part III, HCII 2007, LNCS 4552* (pp. 589–598). Berlin: Springer-Verlag.

Cho, M. Y. (2010). The effects of input enhancement and written recall on noticing and acquisition. *Innovations in Language Learning and Teaching, 4*, 71–87.

Christie, A. (1926). *The murder of Roger Ackroyd*. London: Collins.

Christie, A. (1927). *Le meurtre de Roger Ackroyd* (traduit par Miriam Dou-Despates). Paris: Librairies des Champs Elysées.

Christie, A. (1934a). *Murder on the Orient Express*. London: Collins.

Christie, A. (1934b). *Le crime de l'Orient Express* (traduit par Louis Postif). Paris: Librairies des Champs Elysées.

Cobb, T. (n.d.). *The compleat lexical tutor for data-driven learning on the web* [Software]. Available from http://lextutor.ca/

Cohen, J. (1988). *Statistical power analysis for the behavioral sciences* (2nd ed.). New Jersey: Lawrence Erlbaum.

Doughty, C. (1991). Second language instruction does make a difference: Evidence from an empirical study of SL relativization. *Studies in Second Language Acquisition, 13*, 431–469.

Dussias, P. E. (2010). Uses of eyetracking data in second language sentence processing research. *Annual Review of Applied Linguistics, 30*, 149–166.

Ellis, N. C., & Laporte, N. (1997). Contexts of acquisition: Effects of formal instruction and naturalistic exposure on second language acquisition. In A. de Groot & J. Kroll (Eds.), *Tutorials in bilingualism: Psycholinguistic perspectives* (pp. 53–83). Mahwah, NJ: Lawrence Erlbaum Associates.

FaceLab 4 user manual (2008). Australia: Canberra.

Foucambert, D. (2000). Les effets d'une année d'entraînement à la lecture avec un logiciel éducatif : résultats en classe de sixième de collège. *Revue française de pédagogie, 133*, 63–73.

Foucambert, D. (2003). *Syntaxe, vision parafovéale et processus de lecture. Contribution du modèle structural à la pédagogie* [Syntax, parafoveal vision, and the reading process.

Contribution of the structural model to pedagogy]. Unpublished doctoral dissertation, Université Grenoble 2, France.

Foucambert, D. (2007). *Quand la syntaxe guide la compréhension en lecture: Premières approches issues du modèle structural de lecture.* Paper presented at the 15th European Conference on Reading, Humboldt University, Berlin.

Gass, S. M. (1991). Grammar instruction, selective attention, and learning process. In R. Philipson, E. Kellerman, L. Selinker, M. Sharwood Smith, & M. Swain (Eds.), *Foreign/second language pedagogy research* (pp. 134–141). Clevedon, England: Multilingual Matters.

GazeTracker Software Guide, v8 (2008). Eye Response Technologies Inc.

Godfroid, A., Housen, A., & Boers, F. (2010). A procedure for testing the noticing hypothesis in the context of vocabulary acquisition. In M. Putz & L. Sicola (Eds.), *Cognitive processing in second language acquisition: Inside the learner`s mind* (pp. 169–197). Amsterdam: John Benjamins.

Han, Z.-H., Park, E. S., & Combs, C. (2008). Textual enhancement of input: Issues and possibilities. *Applied Linguistics, 29*, 597–618.

Hotelling, H. (1933). Analysis of a complex of statistical variables into principal components. *Journal of Educational Psychology, 24*, 498–520.

Howell, D. C. (2004). *Fundamental statistics for the social sciences* (5th ed.). Belmont, CA: Brooks/Cole.

Huot, D. (1995). Observer l'attention: Quelques résultats d'une étude de cas. In R. Schmidt (Ed.), *Attention and awareness in foreign language acquisition* (pp. 85–126). Honolulu, HI: University of Hawai'i, National Foreign Language Resource Center.

Izumi, S. (2002). Output, input enhancement, and the noticing hypothesis. *Studies in Second Language Acquisition, 24*, 541–577.

Izumi, S. (2003). Visual input enhancement as focus on form. *Sophia Linguistica, 51*, 1–30.

Jourdenais, R. (2001). Cognition, instruction, and protocol analysis. In P. Robinson (Ed.), *Cognition and second language instruction* (pp. 354–375). Cambridge: Cambridge University Press.

Jourdenais, R., Ota, M., Stauffer, S., Boyson, B., & Doughty, C. (1995). Does textual enhancement promote noticing? A think-aloud protocol analysis. In R. Schmidt (Ed.), *Attention and awareness in second language learning* (pp. 183–216). Honolulu, HI: University of Hawai'i, National Foreign Language Resource Center.

Juola, J. F., Bouwhuis, D. G., Cooper, E. E., & Warner, C. B. (1991). Control of attention around the fovea. *Journal of Experimental Psychology—Human Perception and Performance, 17*, 125–141.

Just, M. A., & Carpenter, P. A. (1980). A theory of reading: From eye fixations to comprehension. *Psychological Review, 87*, 329–354.

Kaiser, H. F. (1958). The varimax criterion for analytic rotation in factor analysis. *Psychometrika, 23*, 187–200.

Kaiser, H. F. (1960). The application of electronic computers to factor analysis. *Educational and Psychological Measurement, 20*, 141–151.

Keenan, E. (1972). On semantically based grammar. *Linguistic Inquiry, 3*, 413–461.

Keenan, E., & Comrie, B. (1977). Noun phrase accessibility and universal grammar. *Linguistic Inquiry, 8*, 63–99.

Kennedy, A., Murray, W. S., & Boissiere, C. (2004). Parafoveal pragmatics revisited. *European Journal of Cognitive Psychology, 16*, 128–153.

Lebart, L., Morineau, A., & Piron, M. (1997). *Statistique exploratoire multidimensionnelle.* Paris: Dunod.

Lee, S. K. (2007). Effects of textual enhancement and topic familiarity on Korean EFL students' reading comprehension and learning of passive voice. *Language Learning, 57*, 87–118.

Lee, S. K., & Huang, H. T. (2008). Visual input enhancement and grammar learning: A meta-analytic review. *Studies in Second Language Acquisition, 30*, 307–331.

Leow, R. P. (1997). Attention, awareness, and foreign language behavior. *Language Learning, 47*, 465–505.

Leow, R. P. (1998). Toward operationalizing the process of attention in SLA: Evidence for Tomlin and Villa's (1994) fine-grained analysis. *Applied Psycholinguistics, 19*, 133–159.

Leow, R. P. (2001). Do learners notice enhanced forms while interacting with the L2?: An on-line and off-line study of the role of written input enhancement in L2 reading. *Hispania, 84*, 496–509.

Leow, R. P. (2006). The role of awareness in L2 development: Theory, research, and pedagogy. *Indonesian Journal of English Language Teaching, 2*, 125–139.

Loewen, S., & Inceoglu, S. (2013). *Tracking focus on form in Spanish L2 reading.* Manuscript submitted for publication.

Mackey, A., Philp, J., Egi, T., Fujii, A., & Tatsumi, T. (2002). Individual differences in working memory, noticing of interactional feedback, and L2 development. In P. Robinson (Ed.), *Individual differences and instructed language learning* (pp. 181–209). Philadelphia: John Benjamins.

McConkie, G. W., & Rayner, K. (1975). The span of the effective stimulus during a fixation in reading. *Perception and Psychophysics, 17*, 578–586.

Overstreet, M. (1998). Text enhancement and content familiarity: The focus of learner attention. *Spanish Applied Linguistics, 2*, 229–258.

Overstreet, M. (2007). Saliency in second language listening and reading. In C. Gascoigne (Ed.), *Assessing the impact of input enhancement in second language education: Evolution in theory, research, and practice* (pp. 71–88). Stillwater, OK: New Forum Press Inc.

Rabin, L. A., Barr, W. B., & Burton, L. A. (2005). Assessment practices of clinical neuropsychologists in the United States and Canada: A survey of INS, NAN, and APA Division 40 members. *Archives of Clinical Neuropsychology, 20*, 33–65.

Radach, R., & Kennedy, A. (2004). Theoretical perspectives on eye movements in reading: Past controversies, current issues, and an agenda for future research. *European Journal of Cognitive Psychology, 16*, 3–26.

Rayner, K. (1998). Eye movements in reading and information processing: 20 years of research. *Psychological Bulletin, 124*, 372–422.

Rayner, K., & Juhasz, B. J. (2004). Eye movements in reading: Old questions and new directions. *European Journal of Cognitive Psychology, 16*, 340–352.

Rayner, K., & Well, A. D. (1996). Effect of contextual constraint on eye movements in reading: A further examination. *Psychonomic Bulletin and Review, 3*, 504–509.

Reichle, E. D., Rayner, K., & Pollatsek, A. (2003). The E-Z Reader model of eye movement control in reading: Comparisons to other models. *Behavioral and Brain Sciences, 26*, 445–526.

Reitan, R. (1958). Validity of the Trail Making Test as an indication of organic brain damage. *Perceptual and Motor Skills, 8*, 271–276.

Rosa, E. E., & Leow, R. P. (2004). Awareness, different learning conditions, and L2 development. *Applied Psycholinguistics, 25*, 269–292.

Rosa, E. E., & O'Neill, M. (1999). Explicitness, intake, and the issue of awareness: Another piece to the puzzle. *Studies in Second Language Acquisition, 21*, 511–556.

Sachs, R., & Suh, B.-R. (2007). Textually enhanced recasts, learner awareness, and L2 outcomes in synchronous computer-mediated interaction. In A. Mackey (Ed.), *Conversational interaction and second language acquisition: A series of empirical studies* (pp. 197–227). Oxford: Oxford University Press.

Sarig, G. (1987). High-level reading in the first and in the foreign language: Some comparative process data. In J. Devine, P. Carrell, & D. E. Eskey (Eds.), *Research in reading in English as a second language* (pp. 105–120). Washington, D.C.: TESOL.

Sawyer, M., & Ranta, L. (2001). Aptitude, individual differences, and L2 instruction. In P. Robinson (Ed.), *Cognition and second language instruction* (pp. 319–353). Cambridge: Cambridge University Press.

Schmidt, R. (1990). The role of consciousness in second language learning. *Applied Linguistics, 11*, 129–158.

Schmidt, R. (1993a). Consciousness, learning, and interlanguage pragmatics. In G. Kasper & S. Blum-Kulka (Ed.), *Interlanguage pragmatics* (pp. 21–42). Oxford: Oxford University Press.

Schmidt, R. (1993b). Awareness and second language acquisition. *Annual Review of Applied Linguistics, 13*, 206–226.

Schmidt, R. (1995). Consciousness and foreign language learning: A tutorial on attention and awareness in learning. In R. Schmidt (Ed.), *Attention and awareness in foreign language learning* (pp. 1–63). Honolulu, HI: University of Hawai'i, National Foreign Language Resource Center.

Schmidt, R. (2001). Attention. In P. Robinson (Ed.), *Cognition and second language instruction* (pp. 3–32). New York: Cambridge University Press.

Schmidt, R. (2012). Attention, awareness, and individual differences in language learning. In W. M. Chan, K. N. Chin, S. K. Bhatt, & I. Walker (Eds.), *Perspectives on individual characteristics and foreign language education* (pp. 27–50). Boston/Berlin: De Gruyter Mouton.

Schmidt, R., & Frota, S. (1986). Developing basic conversational ability in a second language: A case study of an adult learner of Portuguese. In R. R. Day (Ed.), *Talking to learn: Conversation in second language acquisition* (pp. 237–326). Rowley, MA: Newbury House.

Sharwood Smith, M. (1981). Consciousness-raising and the second language learner. *Applied Linguistics, 2*, 159–168.

Sharwood Smith, M. (1991). Speaking to many minds: On the relevance of different types of language information for the L2 learner. *Second Language Research, 7*, 118–132.

Sharwood Smith, M. (1993). Input enhancement in instructed SLA: Theoretical bases. *Studies in Second Language Acquisition, 15*, 165–179.

Shook, D. J. (1994). FL/L2 reading, grammatical information, and the input to intake phenomenon. *Applied Language Learning, 5*, 57–93.

Simard, D. (2002). La mise en évidence textuelle: d'où venons-nous et où allons-nous? *Canadian Modern Language Review, 59*, 236–263.

Simard, D. (2009). Differential effects of textual enhancement formats on intake. *System: An International Journal of Educational Technology and Applied Linguistics, 37*, 124–135.

Smith, B. (2010). Employing eye-tracking technology in researching the effectiveness of recasts in CMC. In F. M. Hult (Ed.), *Directions and prospects for educational linguistics* (pp. 79–97). New York: Springer.

Song, M. (2007). Getting learners' attention: Typographical input enhancement, output, and their combined effects. *English Teaching, 62*, 193–215.

Song, S. (2007). Beginning ESL learners' noticing of morphological and syntactic changes in recasts. *Working Papers in TESOL & Applied Linguistics, 7*, 1–25.

Theeuwes, J. (1993). Visual selective attention: A theoretical analysis. *Acta Psychologica, 83*, 93–154.

Thomas, H. K., & Healy, A. F. (2012). A comparison of rereading benefits in first and second language reading. *Language Learning, 62*, 198–235.

Traxler, M. J., Morris, R. K., & Seely, R. E. (2002). Processing subject and object relative clauses: Evidence from eye movements. *Journal of Memory and Language, 47*, 69–90.

Trofimovich, P., Ammar, A., & Gatbonton, E. (2007). How effective are recasts? The role of attention, memory, and analytical ability. In A. Mackey (Ed.), *Conversational interaction in second language acquisition: A series of empirical studies* (pp. 171–195). Oxford University Press.

van der Schoot, M., Vasbinder, A. L., Tako, M. H., & van Lieshout, E. C. D. M. (2008). The role of two reading strategies in text comprehension: An eye fixation study in primary school children. *Journal of Research in Reading, 31*, 203–223.

VanPatten, B. (1990). Attending to form and content in the input: An experiment in consciousness. *Studies in Second Language Acquisition, 12*, 287–301.

VanPatten, B. (1996). *Input processing and grammar instruction: Theory and research.* Norwood, NJ: Ablex.

VanPatten, B. (2000). Thirty years of input or intake, the neglected sibling. In B. Swierzbin, F. Morris, M. E. Anderson, C. A. Klee, & E. Tarone (Eds.), *Social and cognitive factors in second language acquisition* (pp. 287–311). Somerville, MA: Cascadilla Press.

Vitu, F., Kapoula, Z., Lancelin, D., & Lavigne, F. (2004). Eye movements in reading isolated words: Evidence for strong biases towards the center of the screen. *Vision Research, 44*, 321–338.

von Restorff, H. (1933). Über die Virkung von Bereichsbildungen im Spurenfeld. *Psychologie Forschung, 18*, 299–342.

Wallace, W. P. (1965). Review of historical, empirical, and theoretical status of the von Restorff phenomenon. *Psychological Bulletin, 63*, 410–424.

White, J. (1998). Getting the learners' attention: A typographical input enhancement study. In C. Doughty & J. Williams (Eds.), *Focus on form in second language classroom acquisition* (pp. 91–128). Cambridge: Cambridge University Press.

Wong, W. (2001). Modality and attention to meaning and form in the input. *Studies in Second Language Acquisition, 23*, 345–368.

Wong, W. (2003). Textual enhancement and simplified input: Effects on L2 comprehension and acquisition of non-meaningful grammatical form. *Applied Language Learning, 13*, 17–45.

Appendix A: Sample text from the noticing task

Text in English:

'Excuse me, sir, did the person **with whom** you spoke on the telephone use my name?'

I'll give you the exact words **with which** he addressed me. "Is that Dr Sheppard? Parker, the butler at Fernly, speaking. Will you please come at once, sir. Mr Ackroyd has been murdered."

Parker, **with whom** I was talking, stared at me blankly.

Translation in French:

'Excusez-moi, monsieur, la personne **avec laquelle** vous avez parlé au téléphone a-t-elle utilisé mon nom ? '

'Je vais vous répéter les mots **avec lesquels** elle m'a parlé : «Dr Sheppard ? Ici Parker, le maître d'hôtel de Fernly. Voudriez-vous venir tout de suite, docteur ? Mr Ackroyd a été assassiné.» '

Parker, **avec qui** je parlais, me dévisagea totalement déconcerté.

Appendix B: Comprehension questions in English

1. Whose life was saved by the General?
   a) The Lieutenant
   b) Hercule Poirot
   c) Wagon lit conductor
2. Which of the following sentences could be found after the text.
   a) The conductor outstretched his hand in a suggestive way.
   b) He was a ridiculously-looking little man.
   c) Poirot was moved by such attention.
3. What groups of words are found in the text?
   a) Train, coal, fast, anxious
   b) Stranger, relaxed, conversation, conductor
   c) Moustache, luggage, pillow, Turkey
4. The General was a good man.
   a) True
   b) False
   c) It is not mentioned in the story.
5. Why did Mary Debenham get up?
   a) Because she heard men speaking French.
   b) Because she could not sleep.
   c) Because she wanted to look around.

NFLRC
monographs

Coming Eye-to-Eye with Noticing

Patti Spinner
Susan Gass
Michigan State University

Jennifer Behney
Youngstown State University

An important issue in the SLA literature is the role of attention and noticing in learning. This study investigates noticing of morphophonology and syntax in an attempt to understand what precisely learners attend to as they sort out issues of gender agreement. This study uses eye-tracking methodology to investigate the extent to which 20 second-semester English-speaking learners of Italian notice syntactic and/or morphophonological information when determining appropriate gender marking on adjectives. Learners completed a forced-choice task in which they selected the appropriate form of predicate adjectives. We measured eye fixations on the article and on the noun ending as learners made decisions about gender marking. Results showed that there was equal attention paid to nouns and articles: learners looked equally at nouns and articles, which suggests that they are able to use both kinds of cues to determine noun gender. This was the case even in those instances in which noun endings did not provide needed information or with unfamiliar (pseudo) nouns which lack any gender specification in the learners' lexicons. This finding supports the notion that learners actively look for relevant information regarding gender wherever they can find it.

Introduction

One of the authors of this paper—Susan Gass—recalls giving a talk at the University of Hawai'i in 1987 in which she briefly brought up the issue of attention. Dick Schmidt asked an astute question that immediately pinpointed a crucial issue regarding attention and its mandatory role in learning. His question was whether attention was subconscious or whether it could be (or even had to be) conscious. At that point, Schmidt was deep into his

Spinner, P., Gass, S., & Behney, J. (2013). Coming eye-to-eye with noticing. In J. M. Bergsleithner, S. N. Frota, & J. K. Yoshioka (Eds.), *Noticing and second language acquisition: Studies in honor of Richard Schmidt* (pp. 227–246). Honolulu: University of Hawai'i, National Foreign Language Resource Center.

thinking about attention, noticing, and awareness, areas which were to become crucial to our understanding of the nature of second language learning.

The prominence of the role of noticing and attention in SLA research is due in large part to the work and thinking of Richard Schmidt. His earliest publication on this topic and one that has been particularly influential came as a result of his study of Portuguese in Brazil (Schmidt & Frota, 1986) where he recognized that a crucial part of his learning involved noticing a gap between his second language production and the target language input. In that early article Schmidt and Frota took the *noticing-the-gap* argument (originally conceptualized by Krashen [1983] as a subconscious process) and claimed that "...a second language learner will begin to acquire the target like form if and only if it is present in comprehended input and 'noticed' in the normal sense of the word, that is, consciously" (p. 311). Schmidt first operationalized noticing as a written entry in his diary, which attested to the noticing of a form or lexical item, coupled with later production of that item. This conceptualization of noticing as conscious rather than subconscious was an important contribution and represented a shift in the thinking at that time.

These initial observations led Schmidt over the next few years to propose the *noticing hypothesis,* which states that the first step of acquisition is the learner's noticing of a particular language feature (see Schmidt, 1990, 1994, 1995, 2001), thus integrating the concepts of attention and awareness. In his 1990 article he makes a strong case for "the requirement of noticing" (p. 149), stating further that "subliminal learning is impossible" (p. 149). Schmidt's notion of noticing also fit clearly into a prevailing view of child language learning which emphasized children's attention to language. For example, Slobin (1985, p. 1164) states "...the only linguistic material that can figure in language-making are stretches of speech that attract the child's *attention* to a sufficient degree to be noticed and held in memory" (emphasis in original).

In the years since Schmidt's early publications, numerous positions have been taken with regard to the roles of attention, awareness, and noticing in SLA (see Robinson, Mackey, Gass, & Schmidt, 2012 for an overview as well as Gass, 1988; Robinson, 1995, 1996; Schmidt, 1993a, b, c, 1994, 1995, 2001; Tomlin & Villa, 1994; Truscott, 1998, to name a few). In fact, Schmidt himself has modified and clarified his position to some extent. Specifically, he suggested that the role of *attention* is one of facilitation rather than a necessary condition for language acquisition. However, *noticing* is a necessary and sufficient condition for learning or, in more technical terms, for "conversion of input to intake" (1990, p 129).

Unfortunately, in all of these approaches over the years, the terms *noticing, attention*, and *awareness* have been fraught with difficulty, with a frequent lack of precision in their use (see the cogent review of these terms and concepts by Godfroid, Boers, & Housen, in press). Some studies have focused on noticing as attention, some on noticing as awareness, and some on noticing as both. One of the reasons for this difficulty centers on the empirical evidence for noticing: How do we know if something has been noticed? In this paper our working definition of noticing is operationalized through eye-movements. We return to this below.

Depending on the research questions being asked, there are various approaches to the question of determining what has been noticed. The main techniques that have been used are: 1) diary studies; 2) verbalizations, for example, stimulated recall or think-aloud tasks; 3) language-focused methods; and 4) psycholinguistic methods—in particular eye-tracking, the focus of the experiment described in this paper.

Diary studies—analyses of written records of an individual's thoughts while learning—have had a long history in SLA research (see Bailey, 1983; Schumann & Schumann, 1977). They can be records of experiences in a classroom setting (Bailey, 1983) or in an immersion context (Kinginger, 2004, 2008; Schumann & Schumann, 1977). In the case of Schmidt's own diaries, they are records of a variety of specific instances of language learning. It is from these entries that the noticing hypothesis was formed. An example from his diary (Schmidt & Frota, 1986, p. 281) reflects this:

(1) Journal entry, week 22

> I just said to N *o que è que você quer*, but quickly [*kekseker*]. Previously I would have just said *o que*. N didn't blink, so I guess I got it right, except now I wonder if it should have been *quiser*. I can't believe that what I notice isn't crucial for what I can do.

Schmidt and Frota (p. 281) conclude from this:

> It seems, then, that if R was to learn and use a particular type of verbal form, it was not enough for it to have been taught and drilled in class. It was also not enough for the form to occur in input, but R had to *notice* the form in the input. As indicated by [the entry in (1)], R subjectively felt as he was going through the learning process that conscious awareness of what was present in the input was causal. [emphasis added]

It is the pairing of thoughts about language and language production that is the hallmark of this strand of research.

Diary studies are not the only example of first-person reports used to empirically investigate the concept of noticing. Stimulated recall (see Gass & Mackey, 2000, for a description) and self-reports, including note-taking, are common techniques used to measure noticing. Stimulated recall investigates what learners are thinking about at the time of producing language. In a stimulated recall study, data consist of thoughts regarding a prior language task. The original task is often a video—or audio-taped interactive activity; alternatively, the learner may produce a written text. After completion of the language task, the recording or the written text is used to stimulate a learner's thinking about the original time of language production. An example from Mackey, Gass, and McDonough (2000) is given in (2). In this example, the NNS is describing a picture. She mispronounces a word, is corrected with a clarification request, and recognizes the correction, as is made clear through her recall of the event (even though she does not make the correction).

(2) An example of feedback with correction

NNS: *Vincino la tavolo è. (the correct form is *vicino*)
'Near the table is'

INT: Vicino?
'Near?'

NNS: La, lu tavolo.
'The ? table.'

Recall: I was thinking . . . when she said *vicino* I was thinking, OK, did I pronounce that right there?

However, in example (3) an ESL learner does not notice that there is a correction about her morphology and is not able to make a change in her production.

(3) Morphosyntactic feedback (perceived as semantic feedback)

NNS: So one man feed for the birds.

NS: So one man's feeding the birds?

NNS The birds.

Recall: When I saw the picture I thought this is a park and I tried to describe.

In these examples, inferences can be made through their comments after the interaction about what learners did or did not notice.

Another mechanism used to determine attention/awareness/noticing is concurrent verbalizations (also referred to as *think-aloud* data; see Bowles, 2010). In these studies (e.g., Hama & Leow, 2010; Sachs & Polio, 2007) participants report out loud what they are thinking as they are doing a task. For example, Leow (1997, 2000) asked participants to think out loud as they were doing a crossword puzzle with a focus on Spanish past tense forms and took their comments to reflect instances of awareness.

Godfroid et al. (in press) argue that both think-aloud and stimulated recall methodologies can measure awareness but not necessarily attention, because "the number of attended information pieces to which a subject can give verbal expression is constrained by the demands of the primary task, in particular by the amount of information overall that the subject needs to keep in mind in order to complete the primary task successfully." On the other hand, studies that use less intrusive measures, such as underlining or note-taking (Hanaoka, 2007; Izumi, 2002; Izumi & Bigelow, 2000; Uggen, 2012) may be better suited to measure attention because fewer resources are drawn away into reporting (although in some instances awareness is implicated as well).

Language-focused methods involve an examination of actual production. For example, by looking at self-corrections or pauses (filled or unfilled) in oral production, we are able to infer through lexical or grammatical searches that the speaker is aware of a problem (either an error in the case of self-correction or a knowledge gap in the case of pauses). Similarly, when there are corrections of ungrammatical forms in written data, one can infer that the individual has noticed a problem area. Of course, these are only inferences and do not provide direct evidence of noticing because lengthy pauses may indicate *inter alia* that the speaker's mind has wandered and not that there is a particular lexical or grammatical gap.

All of these techniques have provided insight into the role of awareness and attention. However, Godfroid et al. (in press) make the argument that the most reliable measures for determining noticing are "*on-line* process-oriented techniques" (emphasis in original) such as eye-tracking, because they avoid the pitfalls associated with the previous approaches while providing rich data about learner behaviour. In particular, eye-trackers measure and record precise eye movements, generally while learners are reading text on a computer screen. The measurements generally include eye fixations, which include where and for how long each learner looks at parts of the text, as well as eye movements (saccades) to different areas of the screen. Godfroid et al. explain that eye-tracking research is considered particularly valuable because it is likely that eye fixations and movements are a reflection of what is happening in the mind. (See Reichle, Pollatsek, & Rayner [2006] on the "eye-mind" link.) As Godfroid et al. put it: "Under this assumption, overt attention (as manifested by the exact eye location) and covert attention (mental focus) are tightly linked, and cognitive processing is considered a major determinant of when and where the eyes move during complex task performance, such as reading (Just & Carpenter, 1980; Rayner, 2007)." Thus eye-tracking methodology is ideal for investigating attention as a component of noticing.[1]

1 A review of the cognitive psychology literature on eye-tracking is beyond the scope of this paper. The reader is referred to Roberts and Siyanova-Chanturia (2013) as well as the eye-tracking studies in *SSLA, Volume 35 (2)*, 2013.

Study

The current study deals with what L2 learners attend to when required to mark agreement. In particular, we examine the marking of gender agreement by English-speaking L2 learners of Italian. Grammatical gender has been the subject of a great deal of interest; numerous articles from a variety of perspectives have emerged in recent years (Alarcón, 2011; Bell, 2009; Bordag & Pechmann, 2007, 2008; Carroll, 1999; Dussias, Valdés Kroff, Guzzardo Tamargo, & Gerfen, 2013; Foucart & Frenck-Mestre, 2011; Franceschina, 2005; Lew-Williams & Fernald, 2010; Sagarra & Herschensohn, 2010, 2011). Many of these studies have focused on whether or not L2 learners can acquire gender successfully and what aspects of the input make acquisition easier or more difficult.

It is clear that learners make a large number of errors in marking L2 gender. Some of these errors appear to be lexical, in that learners fail to assign a gender to a noun (Spinner & Juffs, 2008). Other errors appear to be agreement errors, in which learners mark agreeing elements such as adjectives or determiners with the wrong form, even if they know the gender of the noun (Franceschina, 2005).

Both lexical and agreement errors appear to occur more frequently with certain nouns than with others. In particular, L2 learners tend to be more accurate at marking gender with nouns that have clear morphophonological cues to their gender than with nouns that do not. For example, in Spanish, *-o* is a typical ending for masculine nouns, such as *hermano* 'brother' and *zapato* 'shoe,' and *-a* is a typical ending for feminine nouns, such as *hermana* 'sister' and *casa* 'house.' Learners are more successful at marking gender with Spanish nouns ending in *-o* or *-a* than with nouns ending in other vowels or consonants. This finding is robust and has held with a variety of methodologies (Alarcón, 2006, 2009; Cain, Weber-Olsen, & Smith, 1987; Fernández-García, 1999; Finnemann, 1992; Franceschina, 2005; Schlig, 2003).

On the other hand, some researchers have argued that at least a part of L2 learners' gender marking errors may stem from the fact that they are insensitive to morphosyntactic agreement markers, including gender markers (e.g., Guillelmon & Grosjean, 2001; Lew-Williams & Fernald, 2010). That is, learners do not use the gender agreement information marked on agreeing elements such as adjectives and determiners to determine gender or to process it accurately. For instance, Lew-Williams and Fernald (2010) used an eye-tracker to investigate whether native speakers and L2 learners of Spanish used grammatical gender agreement to orient to a target picture. When native speakers heard the gender-marked article *la* (feminine) or *el* (masculine), they oriented to a picture with the corresponding gender more quickly. However, nonnative speakers of Spanish did not.

Thus, the current research shows, at least to some extent, that learners are sensitive to morphophonological cues to gender, such as word endings, but not sensitive to morphosyntactic cues to gender, such as agreement marking on adjectives and determiners. One possible explanation for this difference is that learners focus on gender information on nouns (which is in fact the location of the interpretable gender feature, in Generative terms [Carstens, 2000]) but do not focus on agreement information.

This particular issue has not yet been investigated in research on learner attention and awareness. In fact, there are only a handful of studies investigating second language learners' attention to and awareness of grammatical gender. These studies have primarily used think-aloud or stimulated recall methodology to investigate diverse issues. For example, Bell and Collins (2009) used a think-aloud protocol to measure learners' awareness of noun endings as cues to gender in French, finding that learners who reported awareness of the noun endings had no advantage in a judgment task. Zyzik (2009) also used a think-aloud protocol to measure the attention of English-speaking learners of Spanish to inflectional and derivational endings on words that are cues to grammatical class. She found that learners attend more frequently to grammatical endings (such as gender markers) than they do to semantic or external cues to grammatical class. Finally, Gass and Alvarez Torres (2005) investigated whether learners' attention to grammatical gender agreement and the copular verb *estar* would be enhanced by presenting input on the grammatical features before the learners had a chance to interact with their peers in communicative discussion or afterwards. Presenting input first resulted in greater gains on a posttest.

The current study takes a different approach. We use eye-tracking methodology to investigate the issue of noticing with respect to grammatical gender. Specifically, with eye-tracking data we can investigate learners' noticing of noun endings and agreement markers as cues to gender.

Grammatical gender in Italian

This study focuses on morphosyntactic and morphophonological cues to the grammatical gender of nouns. In Italian the morphosyntactic cues to gender are agreement marking on determiners and adjectives, as shown in (4) and (5).

(4) Il gatto nero

The [masc] cat [masc] black [masc]
'the black cat'

(5) La stella rossa

The [fem] star [fem] red [fem]
'the red star'

For example, in (4), the article *il* 'the' and the adjective *nero* 'black' demonstrate masculine agreement marking because of their association with the masculine noun *gatto* 'cat.' In (5), the article *la* and the adjective *rossa* 'red' demonstrate feminine agreement marking because of their association with the feminine noun *stella* 'star.' The agreement marking on articles and adjectives are morphosyntactic indicators of the gender of the associated nouns. Plural nouns demonstrate similar agreement but will not be dealt with in this paper.

Morphophonological cues in Italian are noun endings (word markers, in Harris's 1985 analysis of Spanish) that are associated with either masculine or feminine gender. Similar to Spanish, Italian nouns ending in *-o* tend to be masculine, while nouns ending in *-a* tend to be feminine. For example, *tavolo* 'table' and *gatto* 'cat' are masculine, while *sedia* 'chair' and *casa* 'house' are feminine. Nouns with these particular noun endings are *transparent*, in that the morphophonological cue to gender is straightforward. However, as in Spanish, there are also nouns that do not fit this pattern, the so-called *opaque* nouns. These nouns end in either a consonant (generally words of foreign origin, such as *bar, sport*) or a vowel other than *-o* and *-a* and thus provide no morphophonological cue to gender. Opaque nouns may be either masculine or feminine. For example, *nome* 'name' and *pesce* 'fish' are masculine, and *notte* 'night' and *carne* 'meat' are feminine.[2]

It should be noted that because not all nouns are marked with clear cues to gender, a learner who is uncertain of a noun's gender will find agreement markers on determiners and adjectives to be a far more reliable cue. However, whether they are able to employ this

2 Franck, Vigliocco, Anton-Mendez, Collina, and Frauenfelder (2008) state that 80% of nouns in Italian are transparent. 17% of masculine nouns are opaque, and 19% of feminine nouns are opaque.

information during processing is still unclear. Whether a learner is actually aware of this process is not measured by an eye-tracker. Therefore, we operationalize noticing as fixations on various language elements and assume that these movements reflect the attention of the learner, with or without conscious awareness of what she or he is attending to and why.

Research questions

The present study investigates the extent to which L2 learners of Italian notice morphosyntactic and/or morphophonologial cues when attempting to determine noun gender and mark agreement on adjectives.

This question has two parts:

RQ1 Do learners' eye movements indicate more reading time on morphosyntactic cues (articles) or morphophonological cues (noun endings) to gender?

RQ2 Do learners' eye movements to morphosyntactic or morphophonological cues vary according to the following properties of the noun:

- transparency (transparent or opaque)
- familiarity (familiar or pseudo)
- gender (masculine or feminine)?

Our prediction is that learners will look longer at noun endings than articles, reflecting the possibility that they attend more to morphophonological than morphosyntactic cues. With regard to other characteristics of nouns, we first predict that learners will look longer and more often at opaque noun endings than at transparent noun endings. This prediction is based on the reasoning that learners will search for useful information regarding the gender of the noun on the noun itself; that search will take longer (and ultimately fail) if the noun is opaque. Presumably, learners will then need to spend additional time looking at the articles associated with these nouns to determine the gender of the noun. Second, we predict that learners will look longer and more often at unfamiliar (pseudo) nouns and their associated articles, because the learners must try to locate the unfamiliar noun in the mental lexicon (even though they presumably are unable to do so). Our final prediction relates to masculine versus feminine nouns. We predict that looking time will be lower for masculine nouns because of the status of masculine as a default gender in many Romance languages (White, Valenzuela, Kozlowska-MacGregor, & Leung, 2004).

Method

Participants

Twenty-five individuals participated in this study[3] of whom 20 were kept for analysis. One native speaker of Portuguese and four participants from fourth semester Italian were removed from the participant pool in order to keep the population as uniform as possible. This left only native speakers of English enrolled in second-semester university Italian courses. All of these speakers had studied second languages (e.g., Spanish, French, or Italian) in elementary, middle, and/or high school. We also had five native speakers who served as a rudimentary control group, although the results will not be reported here.

In Table 1 we provide information regarding the participants.

3 Some of these results have previously appeared in Spinner, Gass, and Behney (2013), where the design is reviewed and compared to more traditional eye-tracker designs.

Table 1. Participants

N	M age	N males	previously studied languages	number of participants
20	20.15	8	Spanish	12
			French	6
			Italian	4
			Latin	1
			German	1

Materials

The experimental materials included eight masculine transparent nouns, eight masculine opaque nouns, eight feminine transparent nouns, and eight feminine opaque nouns. To ensure to the greatest extent possible that the participants were familiar with the nouns in the *familiar* category, a list of nouns was selected from the students' textbook (Merlonghi, Merlonghi, Tursi, & O'Connor, 2006). A group of students similar to those used in the current study ranked the vocabulary in terms of familiarity from 1 to 3, 3 being the most familiar. From these rankings, we selected those that were most familiar (average 2.73 rating). They were controlled across conditions for familiarity, $F(7, 63)=1.49$, $p=.19$. Nouns were also controlled across gender and transparency conditions for number of syllables (2 or 3), $F(7, 63)=.095$, $p=.998$.

In addition to these 32 familiar nouns, 32 pseudo nouns were included. Loosely following Stark and McClelland (2000), we created the pseudo nouns by placing syllables from different nouns together (e.g., *fiume* 'river' and *paese* 'country' were used to form the pseudoword *fiuse*). These 64 nouns were presented in both singular and plural (only singular results are reported here) for a total of 128 slides. (See Appendix A for a list of the nouns used in this study.)

The adjectives that learners marked for gender were taken from the first eight chapters in the first-year Italian textbook. All adjectives had transparent endings; no adjectives with opaque endings (e.g., *verde* 'green') were included. (See Appendix B.)

Apparatus

An Eye Link 1000 eye-tracker with a desktop mount was used for this experiment. (See sr-research.com/mount_desktop.html for a picture of the desktop mount.) Only movements from the right eye were recorded, although viewing was binocular. The eye-tracker was interfaced with a Hewlett-Packard computer with a 20-inch high-resolution CRT color monitor. Participants were seated approximately 80 centimeters from the screen. The experiments were written with Experiment Builder software (SR Research Ltd). Sentences appeared in black upper and lowercase letters on a light gray background.

Design

Because readers frequently skip over short (2–3 letter) words (Frenck-Mestre, 2005, p. 179), the words were printed in a large font (Calibri 44 pt.) on three separate lines. This allowed us to capture the eye movements of the participants to articles, which, at least for singular nouns, are only two letters long. The sentences appeared on the left-hand side of the screen with the article appearing on the first line and the noun appearing on the second line. This allowed us to clearly distinguish whether participants were fixating on the article or the noun. The adjective choices appeared on the right-hand side of the screen. (See Figure 1, which translates as 'Besides, the meat is too fatty.') Learners were instructed to read each sentence and then to click on the appropriate adjective choice. The choices varied as to number and gender.

In order to compensate for the likelihood that the participants would favor the top left side of the screen when reading, we added adverbs of varying length to the beginnings of the sentences so that the items of interest would not appear at the top left. Additionally, to prevent participants from becoming accustomed to seeing each lexical item in a certain place, which might lead to strategies for eye movements, we added a prenominal adjective (e.g., *grande*, 'big') to half of the slides; of these, half of the adjectives were on the first line and half on the second. This made the placement of items less predictable. Figure 2 provides an example of a slide in which *grande* was used (translation: 'Tonight, the loud noise is really bothersome').

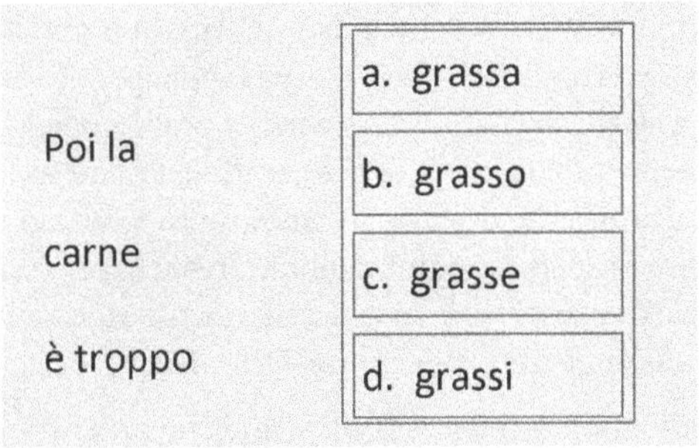

Figure 1. Screen layout for eye-tracking experiment

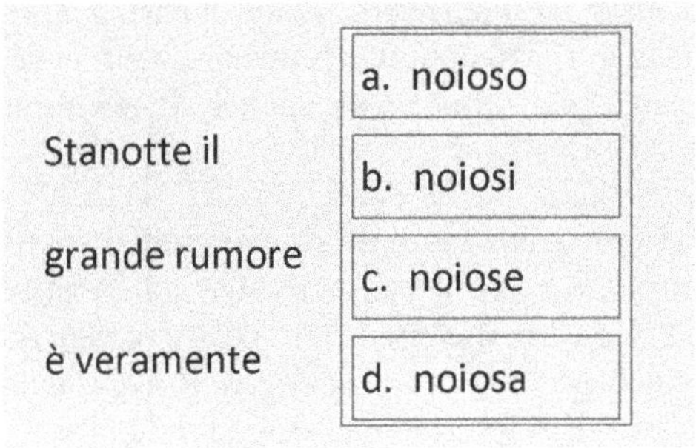

Figure 2. Screen layout using the adjective *grande*

We delineated three separate interest areas. One was around the article on the first line. It extended both to the left and the right by approximately a centimeter in order to capture eye movements to that area that did not fall directly on the article but nearby enough to perceive it. A second interest area was around the noun on the second line (with a similar extension), and a third was around the adjective choices on the right. The interest areas are shown in Figure 3 (translation: 'Besides, the big cat is really sly').

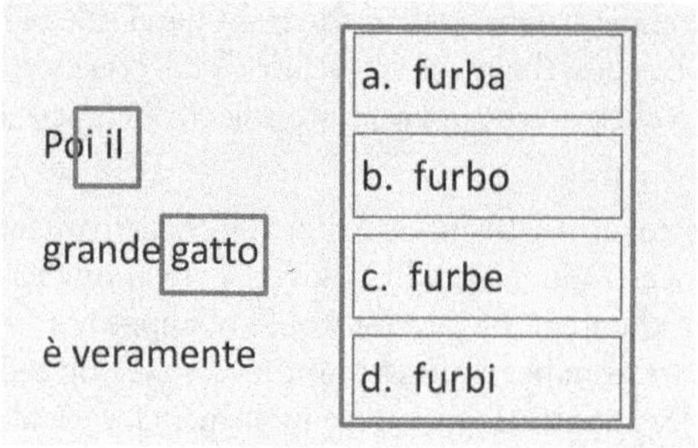

Figure 3. Interest area placement

Procedure

A background questionnaire, which included information about learners' previous language study (Italian and other languages), their native language, the age at which they began to study Italian, travel to Italy, and self-assessment of proficiency, was first completed. The participants were then seated in front of the eye-tracker and were instructed to place their foreheads and chins against the desktop mount and to focus on the fixation target when it appeared on the screen. A nine-point calibration accuracy test was then given. For the actual experiment, participants were instructed to read each sentence and then to click with the mouse on the word (adjective choice) that they felt best completed the sentence.[4]

The 128 slides were divided into three blocks, and the order of the three blocks and of the slides within the blocks were randomized for each participant. Breaks were given after each block, at which point another nine-point calibration accuracy test was given. Participants read the sentences silently at their own pace; the program advanced to the next slide when the participants clicked on their adjective choice. If participants did not click on one of the adjective choices, the item timed out after 10 seconds and moved on to the next slide. The entire task for most participants took approximately 15–18 minutes.

Data analysis

To respond to our research questions, only accurate responses to items containing singular nouns are included in these data analyses, although comparative data from inaccurate responses are brought in during the discussion. Learners were 86.9% accurate (SD=18.0) on singular nouns. We calculated the fixations on two interest areas on each slide: an interest area around the article and an interest area around the noun.

Results

We conducted our analysis using a linear mixed model. This model is used for two reasons: first, because the assumption of independence of samples required for ANOVA was not met; and second, because we needed to account for the variance that is introduced by the varying length of the nouns and articles used in the study. A linear mixed model contains not only the fixed effects factor but also the random effects of participant and of word length. The model therefore takes into account the variance added by the potential correlations between the repeated measurements of the same participant (as a participant is measured in terms of how

4 We are aware of the fact that metalinguistic knowledge may or may not be brought into the picture. And, in fact, the learners may be aware of what they are doing. We are not making a distinction in this paper between low-level noticing and higher-level noticing that may include awareness. We are grateful to an anonymous reviewer for this clarification.

long he/she looks at the article and the noun on each of the slides and the times spent by the same participant might be correlated) and the variance that is added by the varying lengths of the words (as time spent on words of the same length might be correlated). In other words, this model allows for the comparison of learners' eye movements to nouns and articles, despite the difference in size of the words; the length of each lexical item is included in the model.

The first measure of learners' attention to nouns versus articles is Total Dwell Time, that is, the amount of time learners spent looking at each type of cue. The analysis demonstrated that participants spent the same amount of time looking at nouns and articles, $b=-365.86$, $t(4.05)=-1.53$, $p=.199$. This finding held for all conditions, based on an analysis with marginal means comparisons with Sidak adjustments for multiple comparisons. That is, participants spent the same amount of time looking at masculine nouns and masculine articles (mean difference=280.44, $SE=233.48$, $p=.301$) and the same amount of time looking at feminine nouns and feminine articles (mean difference=234.85, $SE=234.24$, $p=.376$). Similarly, participants spent the same amount of time looking at transparent nouns and at articles appearing with transparent nouns (mean difference=247.37, $SE=233.49$, $p=.353$) and the same amount of time on opaque nouns and on articles appearing with opaque nouns (mean difference=267.91, $SE=234.09$, $p=.320$). Finally, they spent the same amount of time looking at pseudo nouns as at articles appearing with pseudo nouns (mean difference=378.38, $SE=233.73$, $p=.186$) and at familiar nouns as at articles appearing with familiar nouns (mean difference=136.91, $SE=233.79$, $p=.592$).

Differences between the conditions emerge when comparing separately the amount of time learners spent looking at nouns or articles. First, learners looked longer at both articles and nouns in the opaque condition than in the transparent condition, $b=-121.51$, $t(2169.43)=-2.71$, $p=.007$ (articles: mean difference=100.98, $SE=43.76$, $p=.021$; nouns: mean difference=121.52, $SE=44.79$, $p=.007$). Second, learners looked longer at nouns in the pseudo condition than in the familiar condition, $b=-224.54$, $t(2165.72)=-5.12$, $p< .0005$ (mean difference=224.54, $SE=43.87$, $p=.00$); however, they did not look longer at articles in the pseudo condition than in the familiar condition, (mean difference=16.93, $SE=43.02$, $p=.694$). Finally, there was no difference in the amount of time learners looked at articles or nouns with masculine or feminine nouns, $b=14.37$, $t(1993.38)=.31$, $p=.755$ (articles: mean difference=31.21, $SE=43.11$, $p=.469$; nouns: mean difference=14.37, $SE=46.01$, $p=.755$). These results can be seen in Figure 4.

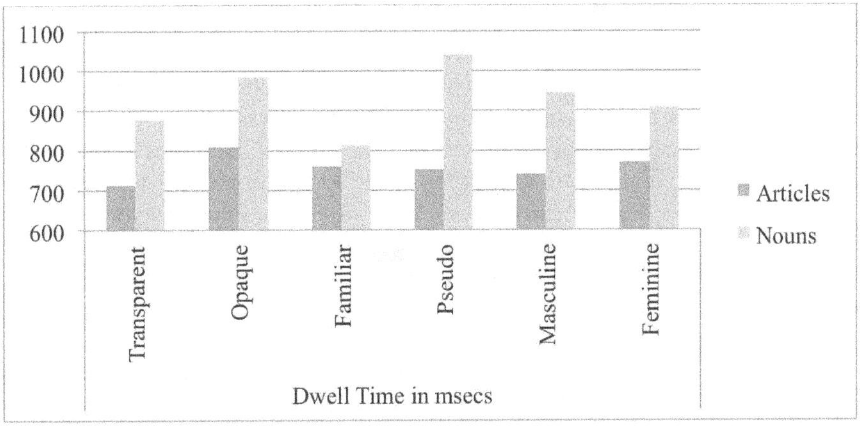

Figure 4. Mean total dwell times on articles and nouns in experimental conditions

Discussion

Research questions on the L2 acquisition of gender

We first address the research questions, reproduced below.

> **RQ1** Do learners' eye movements indicate more reading time on morphosyntactic cues (articles) or morphophonological cues (noun endings) to gender?

The linear mixed model analysis demonstrated that learners spent an equal amount of time on nouns and articles during the gender-assignment task. This finding was contrary to our prediction; recall that some previous research has suggested that learners are not sensitive to morphosyntactic information, such as determiner and adjective agreement, in online tasks. If viewing time on grammatical elements reflects learners' attention, as Godfroid et al. (in press) suggest, then we can conclude that these learners do in fact attend to both morphophonological cues and morphosyntactic cues when conducting a gender-assignment task such as the one in the present study. Not only that, but they focus on the particular aspects of the input that are useful in any given situation. For instance, when the noun ending fails to provide sufficient information about the gender of the noun (as is the case with opaque nouns), learners focus longer on articles, which provide more information about gender.

Since attending to forms is viewed as a first step towards acquiring them (see Gass, 1997; Robinson et al., 2012), we suggest that these learners are at least able to take that first step towards acquiring gender assignment and agreement, based on their attention to both morphosyntactic and morphophonological information (and indeed perhaps they have progressed further than this given their overall correctness of responses). What this study was able to show was that attention can be directed to either morphosyntactic or morphophonological information. Whether learners can ultimately process gender in the same way as native speakers is a separate, but interesting, question that goes beyond the scope of this paper.

The second research question is reproduced below.

> **RQ2** Do learners' eye movements to morphosyntactic or morphophonological cues vary according to the following properties of the noun:
>
> - transparency (transparent or opaque)
> - familiarity (familiar or pseudo)
> - gender (masculine or feminine)?

The results of the experiment indicate that learners pay attention to different aspects of the input under different conditions. First, transparency plays a role; learners spent more time looking at both nouns and articles when the noun was opaque. This finding supports our predictions. Learners may have a strategy of searching the nouns for cues to gender; however, failing to find one, they must rely solely on the article to determine the gender of the noun (if they are not able to access it swiftly through their prior knowledge). This search-and-search again process requires more attention than does determining gender from a straightforwardly transparent noun. Second, learners looked longer at pseudo nouns than familiar nouns. This finding is also as we predicted, because learners presumably must spend more time searching their mental lexicons to find a match for a pseudo word (a match that is of course not available). This search requires additional attention to complete. However, contrary to our predictions, learners did not spend more time on feminine nouns and articles than masculine nouns and articles. That is, there was no clear indication of the use of a masculine default in this case.

Inaccurate responses

In order to explore these results more thoroughly and specifically to determine whether learners' errors on gender marking were due to differences in their focus of attention, we conducted an ad hoc analysis of the inaccurate data, which represented 14% of the original collected data (175 items). As a preliminary step, we examined the types of nouns that learners had the most difficulty with. First, learners were more frequently inaccurate with nouns with opaque endings than those with transparent endings; across participants, 139 items containing opaque nouns were incorrect versus 36 items containing transparent nouns. This finding supports our understanding that learners computed gender online, at least part of the time. That is, they were not able to directly access the gender of the noun from the lexical item but rather determined the gender (or at least confirmed it) by using the available input as they completed the task. If learners were able to swiftly and effectively access the gender directly from the lexical item, they would presumably not need to use the noun ending to determine gender and would be equally accurate on both kinds of nouns.

Second, in terms of familiarity of the nouns, there was no difference in learners' accuracy. Learners were incorrect on 85 items containing familiar nouns and on 90 items containing pseudo nouns. Recall that learners do spend longer looking at pseudo nouns than familiar nouns when they are accurate in gender marking. This fact could indicate that they are able to access stored knowledge of gender at least part of the time, since it may take them longer to compute the gender of a noun which does not have a gender previously associated with it. However, it is not clear whether the fact that they spend longer on pseudo nouns is due to an increased need to determine gender online or simply surprise at encountering an unfamiliar word and an effort to locate it in the lexicon. In fact, the finding that the difference between pseudo and familiar nouns is not associated with a difference in accuracy may provide further evidence that learners are not always able to access their previously stored knowledge of gender, since it would be expected that learners would be more accurate when they have this additional information at hand during the task. That is, we would expect that learners would be more accurate on nouns for which they already know the gender.

Third, participants were somewhat less accurate on feminine nouns than masculine nouns; across participants 100 items that were incorrect contained feminine nouns whereas only 75 of the incorrect items were masculine. This result may be due to learners' use of a masculine default. Note that previous studies have indicated that masculine serves as a default for learners acquiring languages similar to Italian (see White et al. for findings on Spanish). That is, learners mark feminine nouns as feminine in the lexicon but leave masculine nouns unmarked for gender. If that is the case, nouns that are indeterminate as to their gender will be assigned masculine gender rather than feminine, leading to higher accuracy on masculine nouns.

The results regarding accurate and inaccurate responses are displayed in Table 2.

Table 2. Accurate and inaccurate responses in experimental conditions

	masculine	feminine	transparent	opaque	familiar	pseudo
accurate	540	565	604	501	555	550
inaccurate	100	75	36	139	85	90

We also computed overall gaze times on nouns and articles for the inaccurate data, with the same analysis that was used for the accurate data, the linear mixed model. As with the accurate responses, the results indicated that the amount of time participants spent looking at the noun as compared to the article was not a significant factor in the Total Dwell Time, $b=-690.58$, $t(2.60)=-2.54$, $p=.098$. This was true in all of the conditions; marginal means comparisons revealed that participants did not look significantly longer at masculine articles than masculine nouns (mean difference=545.05 ms, $SE=246.34$, $p=.168$) nor significantly longer at feminine nouns than feminine articles (mean difference=604.76 ms, $SE=262.86$, $p=.135$). Participants did not look longer at transparent nouns than at articles appearing with transparent nouns (mean difference=545.57 ms, $SE=290.29$, $p=.141$) nor at opaque nouns than at articles appearing with opaque nouns (mean difference=595.34 ms, $SE=230.15$, $p=.174$). Finally, they did not look longer at pseudo nouns than at articles appearing with pseudo nouns (mean difference=640.29 ms, $SE=254.89$, $p=.125$) nor at familiar nouns than at articles appearing with familiar nouns (mean difference=509.52 ms, $SE=251.96$, $p=.181$).

Thus it is not the case that learners' attention to nouns versus articles influenced accuracy on this task. This is true despite the fact that a strategy of attending only to articles would be the most efficient and effective way to complete the task. However, the learners do not appear to have taken this approach; rather, they use whatever information is available to mark gender on the adjective. Note that in general they are also successful in this endeavor, since inaccurate responses are only a small portion of the total.

Finally, we examined the overall gaze times on nouns in the various conditions when learners were inaccurate at marking gender. In this case there were some differences between accurate and inaccurate responses. First, noun transparency was not a significant factor, in that learners did not look significantly longer at articles or at nouns in the opaque condition than in the transparent condition, $b=-46.43$, $t(330.76)=.27$, $p=.785$ (articles: mean difference=87.31 ms, $SE=167.74$, $p=.603$; nouns: mean difference=46.44 ms, $SE= 330.76$, $p=.785$). Noun familiarity was also not a significant factor for either articles or nouns. Learners did not look significantly longer at articles or at nouns in the pseudo condition than in the familiar condition, $b=-56.84$, $t(299.33)=-.43$, $p=.670$ (articles: mean difference=73.93 ms, $SE=130.53$, $p=.571$; nouns: mean difference=56.84 ms, $SE=133.34$, $p=.670$). However, there was a difference between the overall amount of time that the learners looked at masculine and feminine nouns and at masculine and feminine articles on inaccurate items, $b=-312.69$, $t(130.75)=-2.14$, $p=.034$. Specifically, the gaze times were longer on both articles (marginally significant) and nouns when the noun was feminine than when it was masculine (articles: mean difference=252.98 ms, $SE=135.79$, $p=.063$; nouns: mean difference=312.69 ms, $SE=145.88$, $p=.034$). These results are demonstrated in table form in Table 3, alongside the results of the same tests with accurate responses.

Table 3. Results of accurate and inaccurate responses in experimental conditions

	noun transparency	noun familiarity	noun gender
accurate responses			
nouns	opaque>transparent	pseudo>familiar	masculine=feminine
articles	opaque>transparent	pseudo=familiar	masculine=feminine
inaccurate responses			
nouns	opaque=transparent	pseudo=familiar	feminine>masculine
articles	opaque=transparent	pseudo=familiar	feminine>masculine

There are several notable findings in the contrasts between these accurate and inaccurate results. First, note that when learners are accurate, they spend longer looking at opaque nouns and articles than transparent nouns and articles. We reasoned that this was because it took longer for learners to determine gender when there was less available information on the noun regarding gender; learners examined the noun for gender cues but ultimately needed to use the article to determine gender. However, when learners were inaccurate, the data did not demonstrate this difference. This result might reflect a failure of the learners to use the available information appropriately; that is, when learners do not avail themselves of the information on articles in the case of opaque nouns, they fail to mark the gender agreement accurately on the adjective.

Second, learners demonstrate no difference in dwell times on pseudo and familiar nouns when they are inaccurate, while they spend longer on pseudo nouns when they are accurate. This may reflect the fact that some learners may not have a gender stored for nouns, even if they are familiar. If the learner does not have a gender assigned to the noun in the lexicon (or simply fails to recognize the noun), then there is no difference between the response on that noun and pseudo nouns. These nouns are all "pseudo" in the sense of lacking a stored gender, and accuracy is generally poorer when there is less information available to determine the appropriate gender marking.

Finally, learners had longer dwell times on feminine nouns than masculine nouns when they were inaccurate. This result suggests the use of a masculine default and is particularly interesting in light of the fact that no difference was found between masculine and feminine nouns when learners were accurate. We reason that this difference is due to the fact that learners rely more heavily on a default gender when they are uncertain of the gender of the noun (and thus more inaccurate at marking gender on adjectives). An alternate explanation reverses the causation: that is, when learners rely too heavily on a default, they are more often inaccurate. There is no way to determine with these data whether one of these explanations is more appropriate, but further research could explore this area more thoroughly.

Overall, the findings on inaccurate responses support the viewpoint that learners generally use all available morphosyntactic and morphophonological cues, as well as their own stored knowledge of gender, to successfully mark gender in this task. In fact, in general learners are quite successful at determining the gender of the noun and marking gender on an agreeing element appropriately, as they are 86% successful. On the other hand, on the occasions when they fail to use these available cues or when they rely more on a default, they tend to be more inaccurate. It is important to note here that our scope was limited in that we deal only with noticing as indicated by dwell times; we are not making further claims about acquisition based on these data.

Conclusion

In this study we examined whether learners attend to both morphosyntactic information regarding the gender of nouns (articles) and morphophonological information regarding the gender of nouns (noun endings) when completing a task requiring them to mark appropriate gender marking on adjectives. We used an eye-tracker to measure learners' noticing of these cues. We found that learners attended equally to nouns and articles, which suggests that they are able to use both kinds of cues to determine noun gender. Additionally, the learners tended to spend longer looking at nouns and articles in conditions that were more challenging in that they did not provide cues at the expected sites: opaque nouns, which lack noun ending cues, and unfamiliar nouns, which lack any gender specification in the learners' lexicons. This finding supports the notion that learners actively look for relevant information regarding gender wherever they can find it. On the other hand, an analysis of data with inaccurate responses suggested that when learners did not make use of the available information regarding gender, they tended to be inaccurate in their marking of adjectives. However, this was not the usual case; in general, the learners in this study were highly successful at marking gender on adjectives.

In summary, our results demonstrate that the L2 learners were wise and eclectic in their attention to the input when marking gender on adjectives. While previous studies have demonstrated that L2 learners are insensitive to certain cues to gender (particularly morphosyntactic cues) when measured by other highly sensitive psycholinguistic methodologies, we argue that learners do attend to all available sources of information, at least when they have the time and opportunity to do so.

References

Alarcón, I. V. (2006). *The second language acquisition of Spanish gender agreement: The effects of linguistic variables on accuracy*. Munich: Lincom Europa.

Alarcón, I. V. (2009). The processing of gender agreement in L1 and L2 Spanish: Evidence from reaction time data. *Hispania, 92*, 814–828.

Alarcón, I. V. (2011). Spanish gender agreement under complete and incomplete acquisition: Early and late bilinguals' linguistic behavior within the noun phrase. *Bilingualism: Language and Cognition, 14*, 332–350.

Bailey, K. M. (1983). Competitiveness and anxiety in adult second language learning: Looking at and through the diary studies. In H. W. Seliger & M. H. Long (Eds.), *Classroom oriented research in second language acquisition* (pp. 67–103). Rowley, MA: Newbury House.

Bell, P. (2009). Le cadeau or la cadeau? The role of aptitude in learner awareness of gender distinctions in French. *The Canadian Modern Language Review/La revue canadienne des langues vivantes, 65*, 615–643.

Bell, P., & Collins, L. (2009). "It's vocabulary"/"It's gender": Learner awareness and incidental learning. *Language Awareness, 18*, 277–293.

Bordag, D., & Pechmann, T. (2007). Factors influencing L2 gender processing. *Bilingualism: Language and Cognition, 10*, 299–314.

Bordag, D., & Pechmann, T. (2008). Grammatical gender in speech production: Evidence from Czech. *Journal of Psycholinguistic Research, 37*, 69–85.

Bowles, M. (2010). *The think-aloud controversy in second language research*. New York: Routledge.

Cain, J., Weber-Olsen, M., & Smith, R. (1987). Acquisition strategies in a first and second language: Are they the same? *Journal of Child Language, 14*, 333–352.

Carroll, S. (1999). Input and SLA: Adults' sensitivity to different sorts of cues to French gender. *Language Learning, 49*, 37–92.

Carstens, V. (2000). Concord in minimalist theory. *Linguistic Inquiry, 31*, 319–355.

Dussias, P., Valdés Kroff, J., Guzzardo Tamargo, R., & Gerfen, C. (2013). When gender and looking go hand in hand: Grammatical gender processing in L2 Spanish. *Studies in Second Language Acquisition, 35*, 353–387.

Fernández-García, M. (1999). Patterns of gender agreement in the speech of second language learners. In J. Gutiérrez-Rexach & F. Martínez-Gil (Eds.), *Advances in Hispanic linguistics: Papers from the 2nd Hispanic Linguistics Symposium* (pp. 3–15). Somerville, MA: Cascadilla Press.

Finnemann, M. D. (1992). Learning agreement in the noun phrase: The strategies of three first-year Spanish students. *International Review of Applied Linguistics in Teaching, 30,* 121–136.

Foucart, A., & Frenck-Mestre, C. (2011). Grammatical gender processing in L2: Electrophysiological evidence of the effect of L1-L2 syntactic similarity. *Bilingualism: Language and Cognition, 14,* 379–399.

Franceschina, F. (2005). *Fossilized second language grammars: The acquisition of grammatical gender.* Philadelphia: John Benjamins.

Franck, J., Vigliocco, G., Anton-Mendez, I., Collina, S., & Frauenfelder, U. (2008). The interplay of syntax and form in sentence production: A cross-linguistic study of form effects on agreement. *Language and Cognitive Processes, 23,* 329–374.

Frenck-Mestre, C. (2005). Eye-movement recording as a tool for studying syntactic processing in a second language: A review of methodologies and experimental findings. *Second Language Research, 21,* 175–198.

Gass, S. (1988). Integrating research areas: A framework for second language studies. *Applied Linguistics, 9,* 198–217.

Gass, S. (1997). *Input, interaction, and the second language learner.* Mahwah, NJ: Lawrence Erlbaum Associates.

Gass, S., & Alvarez-Torres, M. (2005). Attention when? An investigation of the ordering effect of input and interaction. *Studies in Second Language Acquisition, 27,* 1–31.

Gass, S., & Mackey, A. (2000). *Stimulated recall methodology in second language research.* Mahwah, NJ: Lawrence Erlbaum Associates.

Godfroid, A., Boers, F., & Housen, A. (in press). An eye for words: Gauging the role of attention in L2 vocabulary acquisition by means of eye-tracking. *Studies in Second Language Acquisition.*

Guillelmon, D., & Grosjean, F. (2001). The gender marking effect in spoken word recognition: The case of bilinguals. *Memory and Cognition, 29,* 503–511.

Hama, M., & Leow, R. (2010). Learning without awareness revisited: Extending Williams (2005). *Studies in Second Language Acquisition, 32,* 465–491.

Hanaoka, O. (2007). Output, noticing, and learning: An investigation into the role of spontaneous attention to form in a four-stage writing task. *Language Teaching Research, 11,* 459–479.

Harris, J. W. (1985). Spanish word markers. In F. H. Nuessel Jr. (Ed.), *Current issues in Hispanic phonology and morphology* (pp. 34–54). Bloomington, IN: Indiana Linguistics Club.

Izumi, S. (2002). Output, input enhancement, and the noticing hypothesis: An experimental study on ESL revitalization. *Studies in Second Language Acquisition, 24,* 541–577.

Izumi, S., & Bigelow, M. (2000). Does output promote noticing in second language acquisition? *TESOL Quarterly, 34,* 239–278.

Just, M. A., & Carpenter, P. A. (1980). A theory of reading: From eye fixations to comprehension. *Psychological Review, 87,* 329–354.

Kinginger, C. (2004). Alice doesn't live here anymore: Foreign language learning as identity (re)construction. In A. Pavlenko & A. Blackledge (Eds.), *Negotiation of identities in multilingual contexts* (pp. 219–242). Clevedon, UK: Multilingual Matters.

Kinginger, C. (2008). Language learning in SA: Case studies of Americans in France. *The Modern Language Journal, 92(Supplement* s1), 1–124.

Krashen, S. D. (1983). Newmark's 'ignorance hypothesis' and current second language acquisition theory. In S. Gass & L. Selinker (Eds.), *Language transfer in language learning* (pp. 135–152). Rowley, MA: Newbury House.

Leow, R. P. (1997). Attention, awareness, and foreign language behavior. *Language Learning, 47,* 467–505.

Leow, R. P. (2000). A study of the role of awareness in foreign language behavior. *Studies in Second Language Acquisition, 22,* 557–584.

Lew-Williams, C., & Fernald, A. (2010). Real-time processing of gender-marked articles by native and non-native Spanish speakers. *Journal of Memory and Language, 63,* 447–464.

Mackey, A., Gass, S., & McDonough, K. (2000). Learners' perceptions about feedback. *Studies in Second Language Acquisition, 22,* 471–497.

Merlonghi, F., Merlonghi, F., Tursi, F., & O'Connor, B. (2006). *Oggi in Italia: A first course in Italian* (8th ed.). Boston, MA: Wadsworth, Cengage Learning.

Rayner, K. (2007, July). *Attention and eye movements in reading, scene perception, and visual search.* Bartlett lecture to the Experimental Psychology Society, Edinburgh.

Reichle, E. D., Pollatsek, A., & Rayner, K. (2006). E-Z Reader: A cognitive-control, serial-attention model of eye movement behaviour during reading. *Cognitive Systems Research, 7,* 4–22.

Roberts, L., & Siyanova-Chanturia, A. (in press). Using eye-tracking to investigate topics in L2 acquisition and L2 processing. *Studies in Second Language Acquisition, 35,* 213–235.

Robinson, P. (1995). Attention, memory, and the "noticing" hypothesis. *Language Learning, 45,* 283–331.

Robinson, P. (1996). *Consciousness, rules, and instructed second language acquisition.* New York: Peter Lang.

Robinson, P., Mackey, A., Gass, S., & Schmidt, R. (2012). Attention and awareness in second language acquisition. In S. Gass & A. Mackey (Eds.), *Routledge handbook of second language acquisition* (pp. 247–267). New York: Routledge.

Sachs, R., & Polio, C. (2007). Learners' uses of two types of written feedback on an L2 writing revision task. *Studies in Second Language Acquisition, 29,* 67–100.

Sagarra, N., & Herschensohn, J. (2010). The role of proficiency and working memory in gender and number agreement processing in L1 and L2 Spanish. *Lingua, 20,* 2022–2039.

Sagarra, N., & Herschensohn, J. (2011). Proficiency and animacy effects on L2 gender agreement processes during comprehension. *Language Learning, 61,* 80–116.

Schlig, C. (2003). Analysis of agreement errors made by third year students. *Hispania,* 86, 312–319.

Schmidt, R. (1990). The role of consciousness in second language learning. *Applied Linguistics, 11,* 129–158.

Schmidt, R. (1993a). Awareness and second language acquisition. *Annual Review of Applied Linguistics, 13,* 206–226.

Schmidt, R. (1993b). Consciousness, learning, and interlanguage pragmatics. In G. Kasper & S. Blum–Kulka (Eds.), *Interlanguage pragmatics* (pp. 21–42). New York: Oxford University Press.

Schmidt, R. (1993c). *Consciousness in second language learning: Introduction*. Paper presented at the meeting of AILA Tenth World Congress of Applied Linguistics, Amsterdam.

Schmidt, R. (1994). Implicit learning and the cognitive unconscious: Of artificial grammars and SLA. In N. Ellis (Ed.), *Implicit and explicit learning of languages* (pp. 165–209). London: Academic Press.

Schmidt, R. (1995). Consciousness and foreign language learning: A tutorial on the role of attention and awareness in learning. In R. Schmidt (Ed.), *Attention and awareness in foreign language learning* (pp. 1–64). Honolulu, HI: University of Hawai'i, National Foreign Language Resource Center.

Schmidt, R. (2001). Attention. In P. Robinson (Ed.), *Cognition and second language instruction* (pp. 3–32). Cambridge, UK: Cambridge University Press.

Schmidt, R., & Frota, S. (1986). Developing basic conversational ability in a second language: A case study of an adult learner of Portuguese. In R. R. Day (Ed.), *Talking to learn: Conversation in second language acquisition* (pp. 237–326). Rowley, MA: Newbury House.

Schumann, F. E., & Schumann, J. H. (1977). Diary of a language learner: An introspective study of second language learning. In H. D. Brown, C. A. Yorio, & R. H. Crymes (Eds.), *On TESOL '77, teaching and learning English as a second language: Trends in research and practice* (pp. 241–249). Washington, DC: TESOL.

Slobin, D. (1985). Crosslinguistic evidence for the language-making capacity. In D. I. Slobin (Ed.), *The crosslinguistic study of language acquisition* (Volume 2) (pp. 1157–1249). Hillsdale, NJ: Lawrence Erlbaum Associates.

Spinner, P., Gass, S., & Behney, J. (2013). Ecological validity in eye-tracking: An empirical study. *Studies in Second Language Acquisition, 35*, 389–415.

Spinner, P., & Juffs, A. (2008). L2 grammatical gender errors: Seeking the source of the problem. *International Review of Applied Linguistics, 46*, 315–348.

Stark, C. E. L., & McClelland, J. L. (2000). Repetition priming of words, pseudowords, and nonwords. *Journal of Experimental Psychology: Learning, Memory, and Cognition, 26*, 945–972.

Tomlin, R. S., & Villa, V. (1994). Attention in cognitive science and second language acquisition. *Studies in Second Language Acquisition, 16*, 183–203.

Truscott, J. (1998). Noticing in second language acquisition: A critical review. *Second Language Research, 14*, 103–135.

Uggen, M. (2012). Re-investigating the noticing function of output. *Language Learning, 62*, 506–540.

White, L., Valenzuela, E., Kozlowska-MacGregor, M., & Leung, Y. I. (2004). Gender and number agreement in nonnative Spanish. *Applied Psycholinguistics, 25*, 105–133.

Zyzik, E. (2009). Noun, verb, or adjective? L2 learners' sensitivity to cues to word class. *Language Awareness, 18*, 147–164.

Appendix A: Nouns

familiar				pseudo			
masculine		feminine		masculine		feminine	
trans.	**opaq.**	**trans.**	**opaq.**	**trans.**	**opaq.**	**trans.**	**opaq.**
quaderno	giornale	festa	vocale	giolo	nore	cuvira	pante
libro	bicchiere	sera	carne	vorno	pecale	vercita	catente
volo	nome	spiaggia	legge	merceggio	biale	cadia	nonte
viaggio	paese	casa	gente	vicato	macchiesce	riduna	stacale
formaggio	mare	mattina	notte	gago	fiuse	seltina	lorne
mercato	pesce	rivista	stagione	forderno	runase	spitira	racane
lago	fiume	chiesa	ragione	quamaro	giormose	fiesa	vogione
gatto	rumore	cucina	canzone	liggio	mame	sesa	gete

Appendix B: Adjectives

masculine				feminine			
piccolo	buono	straniero	alto	favolosa	fredda	brutta	vicina
rosso	povero	vecchio	magro	bella	grassa	prossima	meravigliosa
pieno	fresco	diverso	basso	affollata	vera	cattiva	impegnata
sicuro	furbo	ricco	noioso	gialla	intera	brava	antipatica

Part Four:
Beyond Noticing

NFLRC
monographs

Implicit and Explicit Knowledge of Form-Meaning Connections: Evidence From Subjective Measures of Awareness

Patrick Rebuschat
Lancaster University

Phillip Hamrick
Rebecca Sachs
Kate Riestenberg
Nicole Ziegler
Georgetown University

Two recent studies on the possibility of learning form-meaning connections without awareness (Hama & Leow, 2010; Williams, 2005) reached contradictory conclusions. This conceptual replication and extension clarifies the differences in their results by adding subjective measures of awareness, namely confidence ratings and source attributions (Rebuschat, 2008). Experimental participants were exposed to sentences of a semi-artificial language consisting of English words and four artificial determiners (gi, ro, ul, ne). Participants were told the determiners encoded distance (near/far) but were not told about a hidden regularity involving animacy. Trained control subjects were exposed to the same sentences and instructions, but determiner animacy was randomized. On a posttest with new sentences, participants had to choose determiners from two options differing only in animacy. In addition, they also had to indicate the basis of each test response (guess, intuition, memory, rule) and their confidence (on a 4-point scale), allowing us to assess the conscious or unconscious status of their structural knowledge (of content) and judgment knowledge (knowing that they knew). Our results showed that the experimental group significantly outperformed the trained controls in terms of overall accuracy. The analysis of the subjective measures of awareness further showed that, while participants were aware of having acquired knowledge, they were at least partially unaware of what knowledge they had acquired. In other words, incidental exposure had resulted in the acquisition of both conscious

Rebuschat, P., Hamrick, P., Sachs, R., Riestenberg, K., & Ziegler, N. (2013). Implicit and explicit knowledge of form-meaning connections: Evidence from subjective measures of awareness. In J. M. Bergsleithner, S. N. Frota, & J. K. Yoshioka (Eds.), *Noticing and second language acquisition: Studies in honor of Richard Schmidt* (pp. 249–269). Honolulu: University of Hawai'i, National Foreign Language Resource Center.

(explicit) and unconscious (implicit) knowledge. These results are consistent with previous studies using subjective measures to investigate the implicit and explicit learning of novel words (e.g., Hamrick & Rebuschat, 2012, in press) and L2 syntax (e.g., Rebuschat, 2008; Rebuschat & Williams, 2012). The results also demonstrate the benefit of employing subjective measures of awareness and of utilizing trained control groups.

Introduction

Implicit learning, essentially the process of acquiring unconscious (implicit) knowledge, is a fundamental aspect of human cognition (see Perruchet, 2008; Reber, 1993; Shanks, 2005, for overviews). Many essential skills, including language comprehension and production, social interaction, music perception, and intuitive decision making, are largely dependent on implicit knowledge (Berry & Dienes, 1993; Dienes, 2012; Reber, 1993). The term *implicit learning* was first employed by Arthur Reber (1967) to describe a process during which participants derive knowledge from a complex, rule-governed stimulus domain without intending to and without becoming aware of the knowledge they have acquired. The term *explicit learning* is usually applied to a mode of learning that usually occurs under conditions in which participants are instructed to actively look for patterns; that is, learning is intentional, a process which tends to result in conscious (explicit) knowledge (though see footnote 3).

The field of Second Language Acquisition (SLA) has a long-standing interest in the topic of implicit and explicit learning (see DeKeyser, 2003, and Williams, 2009, for reviews). One of the central questions concerns the possibility of second language (L2) learning without awareness, and Richard Schmidt's seminal publications have had a profound impact, both in terms of theoretical debates (e.g., Robinson, 1995, 2003; Schmidt, 1990, 1993, 1994, 1995, 2001; Tomlin & Villa, 1994) and empirical inquiry (e.g., Faretta-Stutenberg & Morgan-Short, 2011; Hama & Leow, 2010; Leow, 1997, 1998, 2000; Leung & Williams, 2011a, 2011b; Rosa & Leow, 2004; Rosa & O'Neill, 1999; Sachs & Suh, 2007; Williams, 2004, 2005). Schmidt (1995, p. 29) distinguishes two levels of awareness. Awareness at the level of noticing refers to the "conscious registration of an event," whereas awareness at the level of understanding refers to the "recognition of a general principle, rule or pattern." Registering instances of the morpheme *-ed* (*walked, jumped, played*, etc.) in a text would be an example of noticing. Recognizing that *-ed* indicates the past tense or, further, recognizing that there is a very productive rule underlying these instances (*add an -ed to produce the regular past tense*) would be awareness at the level of understanding. According to Schmidt (1990, 1993, 1994, 1995, 2001), only awareness at the level of noticing is required for initial processing of novel input: Noticing is "the necessary and sufficient condition for the conversion of input into intake" (Schmidt, 1993, p. 209).

Schmidt's proposals have been highly influential in SLA research, and the view that awareness is important (if not essential) for learning to take place has received empirical support from a series of studies (e.g., Leow, 1997, 1998, 2000; Rosa & Leow, 2004; Rosa & O'Neill, 1999). For example, Leow (2000) investigated the relationship between awareness (or the lack thereof) and L2 learners' subsequent recognition and written production of morphological forms (irregular 3rd-person singular and plural preterit forms of stem-changing *-ir* verbs). L2 learners of Spanish completed an ingenious crossword-puzzle task that made the target feature available to participants. They were then tested to see whether learning took place. Importantly, participants were instructed to think aloud while completing the experimental tasks. Leow (2000, pp. 564–565) used these concurrent verbal reports to classify participants into aware and unaware groups: "Any participant who provided a report of being aware of the targeted forms or some form of metalinguistic description of the underlying rule would be assigned to the aware group; participants failing to fulfill the criteria would be assigned to the unaware group." The results indicated that only learners who were aware of the target forms improved from pretest to posttest; learners who were unaware of the target forms did not improve at all. Based on these findings, Leow (2000) suggested that awareness plays a crucial role in L2 acquisition by making input available for subsequent processing. Leow's observation has received support from a series of studies using the same think-aloud methodology (Leow, 1997, 1998; Rosa & Leow, 2004; Rosa & O'Neill, 1999). It seems well established that higher levels of awareness are generally associated with greater demonstrations of learning (Hamrick & Rebuschat, 2012; Rebuschat & Williams, 2012; Rosa & Leow, 2004; Rosa & O'Neill, 1999; Sachs & Suh, 2007).

While it is generally accepted that attention and awareness play an important role in learning (see Leow & Bowles, 2005; Robinson, 2003; Schmidt, 2001, for reviews), the assumption that low levels of awareness of linguistic phenomena are necessary for their acquisition has been challenged in recent years. In a widely cited study, Williams (2005) examined the acquisition of an artificial determiner system in a meaning-oriented task. Participants were exposed to four new determiners (*gi*, *ro*, *ul*, and *ne*) which encoded both distance (near vs. far) and animacy (animate vs. inanimate). At the beginning, participants were told that the determiners functioned like English determiners, except that they also encoded distance; for example, *gi* and *ro* were used for near objects, while *ul* and *ne* were used for far objects.[1] Participants were not informed that the artificial determiners also encoded animacy: *gi* and *ul* were used with animate objects, whereas *ro* and *ne* were used with inanimate ones. The role of animacy in determiner usage thus served as a hidden regularity.

Participants were exposed to the semi-artificial language under incidental learning conditions; that is, they did not know they were going to be tested. In the training phase, participants were instructed to listen to each training sentence (e.g., "I spent an hour polishing *ro* table before the dinner party") to indicate whether the novel determiner used in the sentence meant *near* or *far*, to repeat the sentence verbatim, and to form a mental image of the general situation described by the picture. The testing phase consisted of two parts. In the first part, participants read part of a novel sentence such as "The lady spent many hours sewing..." and then had to select the appropriate segment to complete it from two options which matched in their distance values and differed only according to animacy, e.g., "... *gi* cushions / *ro* cushions." Participants were then interviewed to gauge their awareness of the animacy regularity. In the second part, those participants who were still unaware of the relevance of the animacy feature were given the same test sentences but this time with the instruction to discover the rules that determined the choice of determiners. They were then interviewed again to assess the conscious or unconscious status of any acquired knowledge.

Williams (2005) found that, after the first part of the test, 80% of participants reported to be unaware of the relevance of animacy in determiner usage, despite performing at 61% accuracy (significantly above chance) in the sentence completion task. After the rule discovery task, 50% of participants were still unaware of the rule, yet their accuracy was still significantly above chance (58%). The results were interpreted as demonstrating that participants can acquire form-meaning connections without becoming aware of what those connections are. In other words, learning without awareness was taken to be possible.

1 In Williams (2005), half the participants were told that *gi* and *ro* were used for near objects and *ne* and *ul* for distant ones, while the other half were told the opposite.

Williams (2005) was recently the target of an important extension study. Hama and Leow (2010) adapted the methodology of Williams (2005) to assess whether learning without awareness is, in fact, possible. According to Hama and Leow, the discrepancy between Leow (2000) and Williams (2005) can be explained by methodological differences. While the former study employed think-aloud protocols to assess awareness during the training and testing phases (in addition to probe questions after each phase, e.g., "Did you notice anything interesting about the verbs?"), the latter study relied on retrospective verbal reports. As a consequence, Leow (2000) investigated the role of awareness at the time of encoding, whereas Williams (2005) examined whether exposure had resulted in conscious or unconscious knowledge. In other words, Leow (2000) focused on the process of learning while Williams (2005) focused on the product. Hama and Leow's (2010) replication of Williams (2005) modified the original design by adding think-aloud protocols to the experimental tasks, i.e., participants were prompted to verbalize their thoughts while performing the tasks. They also included a production task and changed the forced-choice test to include four options instead of two. Finally, they also kept all of the tasks in the auditory modality, in contrast to Williams (2005), who had used the auditory modality for training and the written modality for testing.

Forty-three native speakers of English were exposed to the artificial determiner system employed by Williams (2005) by means of the same exposure task. Afterwards, participants were asked to perform the two tests (multiple choice recognition, production). The recorded verbal reports were transcribed and coded as *understanding*, *noticing*, or *no report* (see Rosa & O'Neill, 1999). A verbal report was coded as *noticing* when some aspect of animacy was mentioned or commented upon, *understanding* when correct rules related to animacy were mentioned, or *no report* when the report did not fall under the coding categories of noticing or understanding. Hama and Leow (2010) found no evidence for awareness of animacy during the training phase. However, the think-aloud protocols for the test phase clearly provided evidence for awareness at the level of noticing and at the level of understanding. Based on the data, nine participants were classified as aware of the hidden regularity and 34 as unaware. Further analyses indicated a significant learning effect in the aware group on both tests but no learning effect in the unaware group; that is, learning was restricted to those participants who became aware of the hidden regularity. Hama and Leow (2010) concluded that there was no evidence for learning without awareness. These results are supported by another extension study, Faretta-Stutenberg and Morgan-Short (2011).

Despite measuring awareness at different stages of the learning process, the methodologies employed by Williams (2005) and Leow (2000; Hama & Leow, 2010) share a basic limitation: They both rely on verbalization (or lack thereof) to disentangle implicit and explicit processes (Leow) and knowledge (Williams). In the case of concurrent reports (think-aloud protocols), it is assumed that learning proceeds without awareness if participants do not verbalize relevant features of the target system while engaged in either the training task or the test task. As Schmidt (2001, p. 20) writes, "the clearest evidence that something has exceeded the subjective threshold and been consciously perceived or noticed is concurrent verbal report."[2] In the case of retrospective reports, it is assumed that knowledge is unconscious when participants show an effect of training (e.g., above-chance performance on a grammaticality judgment task), despite being unable to describe the knowledge that

2 Schmidt (2001) is not arguing here that verbalization is an exhaustive index of awareness. He is merely highlighting that, when participants do verbalize knowledge, one can be confident that this knowledge is consciously represented. Studies of awareness and learning, however, sometimes appear to assume that if something is not verbalized, then it has not been noticed, which does not follow from Schmidt's (2001) observation.

underlies their performance. In both cases these assumptions are probably not warranted. For example, awareness may happen more quickly than concurrent verbalization allows expression of, given that "subjective awareness is fleeting and cannot be completely recorded" (Schmidt, 1995, p. 28). In retrospective verbalization, awareness may have decayed in memory by the time participants are asked to report on it. In addition, participants might fail to report knowledge simply because they lack confidence or do not realize that the knowledge is relevant. When participants are given the option of not responding during retrospective or concurrent verbal reports, then conscious knowledge, though present, may simply not be detected. Erdelyi and Becker (1974, cited in Dienes & Berry, 1997) also report that participants who are unable to verbalize knowledge on their first attempt are often able to do so when prompted again at a later point in time. Verbal reports might thus not be sensitive enough to capture all of the relevant conscious knowledge.

While lack of verbalization does not provide strong evidence for learning without awareness (in the case of think-alouds) or implicit knowledge (in the case of retrospective reports), it is important to note that the presence of verbalization does not automatically mean that all learning in the experiment involved awareness or that only explicit knowledge was acquired. Both procedures lack exclusivity in the sense that they might be contaminated by unconscious knowledge (Reingold & Merikle, 1990). When think-aloud data indicates that participants were aware of a given complex L2 phenomenon, this does not necessarily mean that other aspects of the same phenomenon have not been acquired without awareness. In addition, one needs to ask what processes contributed to participants suddenly becoming aware of a feature in the first place, with implicit processing (e.g., in the form of associative or statistical learning) a possible candidate in this case. Likewise, when participants verbalize knowledge at the end of the experiment, this does not mean that participants only acquired conscious knowledge. In fact, recent research (Hamrick & Rebuschat, 2012, in press; Rebuschat, 2008; Rebuschat & Williams, 2012, 2013; Tagarelli, Borges Mota, & Rebuschat, 2011) suggests that, even under incidental learning conditions, participants are quite likely to acquire both implicit and explicit knowledge.[3]

The present study is the third extension of Williams (2005), after Hama and Leow (2010) and Faretta-Stutenberg and Morgan-Short (2011). Our primary objective is to contribute to the debate on awareness and language learning by illustrating the usefulness of a measure of awareness that does not rely on verbalization. Before discussing the details of our experiment, we briefly introduce the subjective measures of awareness we employed in order to assess the conscious status of learners' knowledge in our study. For a more comprehensive review, see Rebuschat (2013).

Subjective measures of awareness

Dienes (2004, 2012) advocated the use of subjective measures in order to assess whether the knowledge acquired during Artificial Grammar Learning (AGL) tasks is conscious or unconscious. One way of dissociating conscious and unconscious knowledge is to collect confidence ratings and source attributions (e.g., Dienes & Scott, 2005). This can be done, for example, by asking participants to perform a grammaticality judgment task and to indicate, for each judgment, how confident they were in their decision (e.g., guess, somewhat confident, very confident) and what their decision was based on (e.g., guess, intuition,

3 Using subjective measures of awareness, these studies indicate that participants acquire both conscious (explicit) and unconscious (implicit) knowledge as a result of exposure and that the type of knowledge seems to depend on the learning context. Under incidental conditions, participants develop primarily unconscious knowledge, while under intentional conditions, they develop primarily conscious knowledge.

memory, rule knowledge). Knowledge can be considered unconscious if participants believe they are guessing when their classification performance is, in fact, significantly above chance. Dienes, Altmann, Kwan, and Goode (1995) called this the *guessing criterion*. Knowledge can also be considered unconscious if participants' confidence is unrelated to their accuracy. This criterion, introduced by Chan (1992), was labeled the *zero correlation criterion* by Dienes et al. Several studies have shown that performance on standard AGL tasks can result in unconscious knowledge according to these criteria (e.g., Dienes et al., 1995).

Dienes (2004) suggested that, when participants are exposed to letter sequences in an AGL experiment, they learn about the structure of the sequences. This *structural* knowledge can consist, for example, of knowledge of whole exemplars, knowledge of fragments, or knowledge of rules (e.g., *A letter sequence can start with an M or a V*). In the testing phase, participants use their structural knowledge to construct a different type of knowledge, namely whether the test items share the same underlying structure as the training items (e.g., *MRVXX has the same structure as the training sequences*). Dienes labeled this *judgment* knowledge. Both forms of knowledge can be conscious or unconscious. For example, a structural representation such as *An R can be repeated several times* is conscious only if it is explicitly represented, that is, if there is a higher-order thought such as *I know/think/believe that an R can be repeated several times* (Rosenthal, 2005). Likewise, judgment knowledge is conscious only if there is a corresponding higher-order thought (e.g., *I know/think/believe that MRVXX has the same structure as the training sequences*).

Dienes and Scott (2005) assume that conscious structural knowledge leads to conscious judgment knowledge. However, if structural knowledge is unconscious, judgment knowledge could still be either conscious or unconscious. This explains why, in the case of natural language, people can be very confident in their grammaticality judgments without knowing why. Here, structural (linguistic) knowledge is unconscious while judgment knowledge is conscious. The phenomenology in this case is that of intuition, that is, knowing that a judgment is correct but not knowing why. If, on the other hand, both structural and judgment knowledge are unconscious, the phenomenology is that of guessing. In both cases (guessing and intuition), the structural knowledge acquired during training is unconscious. The experiment below exemplifies how subjective measures can be employed to investigate whether incidental exposure to a new determiner system can result in unconscious knowledge in adult learners.

Methods

The present study had two objectives. The first objective was to confirm that adult learners can acquire novel form-meaning mappings incidentally as a result of exposure in a meaning-oriented task and that they are able to generalize this knowledge to novel stimuli. The second, more important objective was to illustrate the usefulness of subjective measures of awareness and to compare the latter to the information gained via retrospective reports.

Participants

Thirty undergraduate students at Georgetown University participated in the study (18 women, 12 men; M_{age}=20) and were either assigned to the experimental group (*n*=15) or the trained control group (*n*=15). A *trained* control condition was used following recent calls for more robust procedures to ascertain learning (e.g., Hamrick, 2012, 2013; Reber & Perruchet, 2003). Trained control groups receive training conditions that are identical to experimental groups but with the relevant independent variables randomized and balanced, rather than removed altogether. The logic behind this procedure stems from the notion that all participants have unforeseen response biases in test phases based on their prior knowledge (Reber & Perruchet, 2003). These biases are "noise" that influences test performance beyond what is learned during training. The use of trained controls ensures that such noise can be identified and accounted for, allowing the effects of the independent variable(s) to be isolated.

All participants were native speakers of English. Twelve participants reported having an additional native language; these included Farsi, French, German, Korean, Mandarin, and Spanish. Twenty-seven participants had studied a foreign language, including Spanish (18), French (12), German (7), Arabic (4), Korean (4), Latin (4), Italian (3), Mandarin (3), Russian (2), Catalan (1), Japanese (1), and Portuguese (1). Only three participants said they did not know any foreign languages. Experimental and control groups did not differ significantly with regard to age, gender, number of linguistics courses taken, number of foreign languages studied, or university year, all $p>.05$. Eleven participants were pursuing degrees in linguistics (seven in the experimental group and four in the control group). Participants who were enrolled in a linguistics course were offered 5% extra credit on a homework assignment in that course for their participation.

Materials

The artificial determiner system used in this experiment was taken from Williams (2004, 2005) (see also Faretta-Stutenberg & Morgan-Short, 2011; Hama & Leow, 2010). The system consists of four artificial determiners (*gi*, *ro*, *ul*, and *ne*) which encode both distance (near vs. far) and animacy (animate vs. inanimate). The determiners *gi* and *ro* precede nouns that refer to objects that are near, while *ul* and *ne* are used for nouns that refer to distant objects. In addition, *gi* and *ul* are employed to refer to animate entities (natural, living, moving things), whereas *ro* and *ne* are used with inanimate ones (man-made, non-living, stationary things). As in the previous studies, participants were trained explicitly on the near/far distinction but were not told of the regularity involving animacy. The training and test sentences employed in the current experiment are available in the IRIS digital repository (www.iris-database.org). The form-meaning mappings are illustrated in Table 1.

Table 1. Artificial determiner system used in the present study

	near	**far**
animate	*gi*	*ul*
inanimate	*ro*	*ne*

Training items

The noun phrases (NPs) used in the exposure phase for the experimental group can be found in Table 2. As in Williams (2005, Experiment 2), the training set included 12 animate and 12 inanimate nouns, each of which was presented in both its singular and its plural form. There were thus 48 items in total (24 singular, 24 plural). Each noun, in both singular and plural forms, only appeared with one determiner (e.g., *gi bear* and *gi bears*). This was done to ensure that participants who demonstrated improvement would be doing so on the basis of their learning of form-meaning connections (e.g., that *gi* is used with animate nouns) as opposed to, perhaps, form-form associations between determiners (e.g., that any noun that takes *gi* [near] also takes *ul* [far]).

Table 2. Noun phrases (48) employed in the exposure phase of the experimental group

animate		inanimate	
near	**far**	**near**	**far**
gi bear(s)	*ul* bee(s)	*ro* box(es)	*ne* book(s)
gi cow(s)	*ul* bird(s)	*ro* cup(s)	*ne* clock(s)
gi dog(s)	*ul* cat(s)	*ro* picture(s)	*ne* cushion(s)
gi lion(s)	*ul* fly (flies)	*ro* sofa(s)	*ne* plate(s)
gi pig(s)	*ul* monkey(s)	*ro* table(s)	*ne* stool(s)
gi rat(s)	*ul* snake(s)	*ro* television(s)	*ne* vase(s)

note. The nouns appeared in both singular and plural forms.

The training set was subdivided into two sets, with six NPs of each type (near/animate, near/inanimate, far/animate, far/inanimate) per set. The same determiner-noun combinations were used in Set 1 and Set 2, but they differed in terms of grammatical number. That is, if a given noun appeared in its singular form in Set 1, then the same noun appeared in the plural in Set 2, and vice versa. Each set (and therefore each sentence) was repeated three times during training so that subjects were exposed to a total of 144 items, the same number as in Williams (2005). The sets were presented in alternating order (Set 1, Set 2, Set 1, Set 2, Set 1, Set 2), and the ordering of the sentences within each set was randomized on each iteration. Some new sentences also had to be created so that nouns could be trained in both their singular and plural forms.

In order to allow for the inclusion of a trained control group, an additional set of training materials was developed. The 48 sentences for the trained controls were identical to those of the experimental participants except that the animacy regularity was removed by changing which determiners were used with which nouns in such a way that none of the determiners was reliably associated with a particular animacy value. That is, each determiner was used half of the time with animate nouns and half the time with inanimate nouns. Since all participants were pre-trained explicitly on distance, the near/far meanings of the determiners were maintained. Care was also taken to ensure that each determiner appeared half the time with a singular noun and half the time with a plural noun. Table 3 contains the items used during the exposure phase for the trained control group.

Table 3. Noun phrases (48) employed in the exposure phase of the trained controls

animate		inanimate	
near	**far**	**near**	**far**
gi bear *gi* bears	*ul* bee *ne* bees	*gi* pictures *ro* picture	*ul* cushions *ne* cushion
ro rat *ro* rats	*ul* bird *ne* birds	*gi* sofa *ro* sofas	*ul* clocks *ne* clock
gi dog *gi* dogs	*ul* cat *ne* cats	*gi* boxes *ro* box	*ul* stool *ne* stools

ro pig *ro* pigs	*ul* flies *ne* fly	*gi* cups *ro* cup	*ul* vases *ne* vase
gi lion *gi* lions	*ul* monkeys *ne* monkey	*ro* tables *ro* table	*ul* books *ne* book
ro cow *ro* cows	*ul* snake *ne* snakes	*gi* television *gi* televisions	*ul* plate *ne* plates

Test items

The testing set, which was the same for both groups, contained completely new sentence contexts, none of which had appeared during the training. The sentences were designed to test three types of NPs: *trained*, *partially-trained*, and *new*. For the experimental group, the trained NPs had already occurred in exactly the same form in the exposure phase (e.g., *gi bears*). In the case of the partially-trained NPs, the determiner and the noun had occurred during training but not in this specific configuration. For example, if *ro picture* (the near picture) had occurred in training, then either the singular or plural version of the noun *picture* was presented in a far context, requiring *ne*, on the test. Finally, the new NPs were items in which the noun had not occurred at all during the exposure phase (e.g., *gi rabbit*). It is important to note that Williams (2004, 2005), Hama and Leow (2010), and Faretta-Stutenberg and Morgan-Short (2011) only featured two types of test items, namely trained and partially-trained (which they call "generalization"). In contrast to the present experiment, their studies did not contain true generalization items.

Table 4. Noun phrases employed in the testing phase

	animate		**inanimate**	
	near	**far**	**near**	**far**
trained	*gi* rats	*ul* bees	*ro* cups	*ne* cushions
trained	*gi* cow	*ul* flies	*ro* television	*ne* clocks
trained	*gi* dog	*ul* cat	*ro* sofa	*ne* book
partially-trained	*gi* monkeys	*ul* bears	*ro* plates	*ne* pictures
partially-trained	*gi* snakes	*ul* lion	*ro* stools	*ne* table
partially-trained	*gi* bird	*ul* pig	*ro* vase	*ne* box
new	*gi* elephants	*ul* camels	*ro* desks	*ne* candles
new	*gi* hamster	*ul* horses	*ro* spoons	*ne* lamp
new	*gi* rabbit	*ul* turtle	*ro* phone	*ne* towel

note. Trained items were noun phrases repeated from training. Partially-trained items feature nouns that occurred during training but with a different determiner. New items feature nouns that did not occur during training.

There were 36 test items—novel sentences taken mostly from Williams (2005) and Hama and Leow (2010)—with six of each type (*trained*, *partially-trained*, and *new*) for each animacy class.[4] Plurality and distance values were balanced within each test-item type so that, for example, the six trained animate items included three singular and three plural NPs as well as three near and three far NPs, taking care not to confound plurality and distance.

4 Some of the sentences from Williams (2005) were modified to follow North American English as opposed to British English.

The trained and partially-trained items were the same as the ones used by Williams (2005), with the exception of the noun *rat*, which we included instead of *mouse* in order to avoid irregular plurals. Most of the new NPs in the current study contain nouns taken from Hama and Leow (2010), plus four new nouns (*hamster, camel, towel, desk*), which we added for counterbalancing purposes (and to test generalization ability). Table 4 displays the NPs used in the testing phase.

Procedure

The experiment consisted of (i) informed consent, (ii) vocabulary pre-training, (iii) a training phase, (iv) a testing phase, and (v) debriefing. Participants met individually with one of the researchers in a quiet laboratory setting. The training and assessment tasks were run on Apple iMac computers and delivered via Cedrus SuperLab Pro (version 4.0.7b). Participants were also audio-recorded while performing the tasks (by means of a handheld digital recorder placed on the table) to ensure that they had followed the instructions. The experiment concluded with a debriefing session during which participants completed a post-exposure interview (retrospective verbal report) with one of the authors and a background questionnaire. The entire session took approximately one hour.

Vocabulary pre-training

As in Williams (2005) and Hama and Leow (2010), a vocabulary pre-training activity introduced participants to the four novel determiners and their English translations. The activity was administered via Microsoft PowerPoint. Participants were told that they were going to learn four new words (*gi, ro, ne, ul*) and were presented with a list of the words and their respective distance values in English (*gi* and *ro*=near, *ne* and *ul*=far). Participants then completed two practice tasks that exposed them to 12 written repetitions of each novel word. In the first task, participants saw the four determiners and their English translations on the screen, but question marks appeared for one of the determiners (e.g., *ne*=far, *??*=far, *gi*=near, *ro*=near). They were instructed to say aloud the missing determiner (in the example, *ul*). Afterwards, they pressed a mouse button and the missing determiner would appear; that is, they received feedback. In the second task, participants were presented with one of the artificial determiners on the screen. Their task this time was to say aloud the English translation of the novel word. After saying the word, participants clicked on the screen, and the correct translation would appear. Presentation order was randomized and repeated five times for each determiner. The remaining four exposures occurred during the instructions and examples provided for each portion of the pre-training exercise.

Participants were encouraged to complete the vocabulary pre-training at their own pace and more than once if they desired and were informed that the pre-training would be immediately followed by a short test to evaluate whether they had successfully learned the four novel words. One participant in the control group and two in the experimental group chose to repeat the pre-training once. The quiz was administered using the online survey and testing website *ClassMarker* (www.classmarker.com). Participants were required to score 90% or higher on the quiz in order to move on to the training phase, and all were able to do this on their first attempt.

Training phase

Experimental participants and trained controls were provided with written instructions, explaining the general purpose of the experiment. These were based on the instructions provided by Williams (2005, pp. 281–282) with only minor changes. Participants were informed that the four artificial determiners functioned like the English word *the*, except that they also encoded distance: *gi* and *ro* were used for near objects, while *ul* and *ne* were used for far objects. Importantly, participants were not informed that *gi* and *ul* were used with animate objects, whereas *ro* and *ne* were used with inanimate ones. A sample sentence (*The little boy patted gi tiger in the zoo*), which did not recur during the training task, illustrated how the determiners could be used in a sentence context.

Participants were then told that they would be presented with written sentences that included the new words they had learned during the pre-training phase and that their task was to read the sentence aloud and then indicate, as quickly and accurately as possible, whether the novel word meant *near* or *far* by pressing the corresponding key (marked with a sticker) on the computer's keyboard. (Note that, unlike Williams, 2005, and Hama and Leow, 2010, the training sentences were presented visually on the screen, not auditorily.) After each decision they were also asked to repeat the novel word together with its noun (*gi tiger*, in the example above), while simultaneously forming a mental image of the situation. For example, in the sample sentence, participants were encouraged to imagine a boy patting a tiger that was close to him. Forming a mental image of the sentence context, including the relationship between the novel word and the following noun, encouraged participants to process the meanings of the words and the overall situation described in the sentence. This was emphasized as an important aspect of the experiment by the researcher administering the treatment. Trained control participants received the same instructions and procedure. The only difference was that the determiners they saw were randomized and counterbalanced so that no determiner ever reliably indicated animacy. All participants completed a short practice session with four sentences that were not repeated in the training phase.

Testing phase

After the exposure phase, participants were visually presented with 36 completely new sentences. For each test item, the computer displayed a sentence context (e.g., *The boy patted ___ tiger in the zoo*) with two choices of artificial determiners (e.g., *gi* and *ro*) located in the bottom left and right corners of the screen. Importantly, these options always matched in their distance values (*gi* and *ro* can both refer to near entities) while differing in their animacy values, which means that participants could no longer respond only according to the distance information they had been explicitly taught during the vocabulary pre-training phase (and which they had been instructed to focus on while processing the sentences of the training phase). The participants were instructed to read through the entire sentence and to "choose the word that seems more familiar, better, or more appropriate," based on what they had done so far. They could enter their choice by pressing a corresponding key on the keyboard. As in Williams (2005), there were two response options. (Hama and Leow, 2010, provided participants with four options.)

After selecting which word best filled the blank, participants were also asked to indicate how confident they were in their decision and what the basis of their decision was. These confidence ratings and source attributions, respectively, served as subjective measures of awareness. Participants could indicate their levels of confidence by selecting one of four response options for each item: *complete guess*, *somewhat confident*, *very confident*, or *absolute certainty*. Participants were instructed to select the *complete guess* category only if they had no confidence whatsoever in their classification decision and truly believed to be guessing. If they had some degree of confidence, they were asked to select the *somewhat confident* or the *very confident* categories instead. If they were 100% certain that their classification was correct, then they were instructed to select the *absolute certainty* category. In the case of the source attributions, participants were asked to select one of four response options: *guess*, *intuition*, *memory*, or *rule knowledge*. Participants were instructed to use the *guess* category only when decisions were based on real guesses; that is, they might as well have flipped a coin. The *intuition* category was to be selected if participants had a gut feeling that they were right but did not know why. The *memory* category was to be selected when judgments were based on the recollection of items from the earlier part of the experiment. Finally, the *rule knowledge* category was to be selected following decisions that were based on a rule that participants would be able to report at the end of the experiment. All participants were provided with these instructions before starting the testing phase. (Note that we had only one test phase, in contrast to Williams, 2005, who featured two.) Participants completed a short practice session with four sentences that were not repeated in the test phase.

The 36 test sentences were presented in the same order for all participants. As in Williams (2005), they were arranged so that participants would not be able to make animacy comparisons across adjacent items with the same distance values. For example, test items targeting far animate NPs (e.g., *ul bees*) were never followed by far inanimate NPs (e.g., *ne clocks*). Because our study featured three types of test items (as opposed to two in Hama & Leow, 2010, and Williams, 2005), we could not use exactly the same item ordering as that employed by Williams (2005). However, we did follow his ordering on the more abstract level of plurality, distance, and animacy features.

Debriefing session

Following the testing phase, all participants completed a short interview with one of the researchers. Participants were first asked what criteria they had used to make their choices. If they made any references to living/nonliving, moves/doesn't-move, or a similar distinction, they were asked at what point they had become aware of this difference. The participants were then asked whether they had ever indicated rule knowledge as a basis for their decisions. If so, they were asked to describe what they had been thinking and why they had selected the *rule knowledge* category. If they had not indicated rule knowledge as a source, they were prompted to share any other ways in which they had made their choices, whether on the basis of intuition or other sources. If, up to this point in the interview, participants had not mentioned anything related to animacy or had not reported indicating rule knowledge as a basis for their decisions, they were informed that there was a rule and were asked to speculate about what the rule might have been. If animacy was still not mentioned, the researcher explained the system, and then asked participants if they had considered the possible relevance of animacy at any point during the training or assessment task.

In addition to the retrospective verbal reports, participants also completed a brief questionnaire asking for their age, field of study, previous experience in linguistics courses, native language(s), and foreign languages studied. Where applicable, participants provided additional information regarding their foreign language background, including contexts of instruction, levels of formal schooling, length of study, and self-reported proficiency.

Results

As in Williams (2005), performance on the two-alternative forced-choice (2AFC) task served as the measure of learning. The confidence ratings, source attributions, and retrospective verbal reports were used to determine to what extent participants were aware of having acquired knowledge and whether the acquired knowledge was conscious or not. It is worth remembering that Williams (2005) only relied on retrospective verbal reports.

Performance on the two-alternative forced-choice (2AFC) task

Overall performance of experimental and control groups

The analysis of the test data showed that the experimental group identified 74.8% (*SD*=28.3%) of the test items correctly and the trained control group 49.3% (*SD*=9.6%). Levene's statistic showed that variances were not homogeneous. The adjusted independent sample *t*-test indicated that the experimental participants significantly outperformed the trained controls, $t(17.16)=3.31$, $p<.05$. Further analysis showed that the experimental group performed significantly above chance on this task, $t(14)=3.39$, $p<.05$, while the controls scored at chance, $p>.05$. That is, the training phase produced a clear overall learning effect in the experimental participants but not a clear overall learning effect in the trained controls.

As described above, eleven participants (seven experimental, four control) were pursuing a degree in linguistics (major or minor). Given the potential impact of this background on performance in the experiment (see Williams, 2004, 2005), we decided to compare these students to those who were not studying for a degree in linguistics. The analysis showed that, in the experimental group, the non-linguistics students identified 79.3% (*SD*=18%) of the test items correctly and linguistics students 69.4% (*SD*=37.8%). In the control group, the non-linguistics students performed at 51% (*SD*=10.2%) and the linguistics students at 46% (*SD*=8.4%). Our analysis showed that there were no significant differences in performance between linguistics participants and non-linguistics participants, either in the experimental group, $t(13)=.66$, $p>.05$, or the control group, $t(13)=.87$, $p>.05$.

Performance of experimental and control groups across different test-item types

The experimental group correctly identified 78.3% (*SD*=9.5%) of the trained NPs, 73.3% (*SD*=7.5%) of the partially-trained NPs, and 72.8% (*SD*=10%) of the new NPs. The trained controls correctly identified only 41.1% (*SD*=17.3%) of the trained NPs, 52.2% (*SD*=13.3%) of the partially-trained NPs, and 54.4% (*SD*=5.6%) of the new NPs. The experimental group performed significantly above chance on trained NPs, which had already occurred in the exposure phase (though in different sentence contexts), $t(11)=10.35$, $p<.001$, as well as on partially-trained NPs, whose noun had occurred with a different determiner during training, $t(11)=10.74$, $p<.001$, and also on new (generalization) NPs, which had not occurred during training at all, $t(11)=7.86$, $p<.001$. The trained controls performed significantly above chance on new NPs, $t(11)=2.76$, $p<.05$, but not on trained or partially-trained NPs, $p>.05$.

A 2x3 mixed ANOVA with Group (2 levels: Experimental, Control) as the between-subjects variable and Test-Item Type (3 levels: trained, partially-trained, new) as the within-subjects variable revealed no effect of Test-Item Type, but there was a significant main effect of Group, $F(1, 22)=97.89$, $p<.001$, $\eta_p^2=.82$, and a significant Group*Test-Item Type interaction, $F(2, 44)=4.87$, $p<.05$, $\eta_p^2=.18$. To follow up on the significant interaction effect, we performed additional ANOVAs comparing the groups (Experimental, Control) on each type of test item. These revealed that the experimental group was significantly more accurate than the control group on all three test-item types: trained, $F(1, 23)=42.90$, $p<.001$, partially-trained, $F(1, 23)=22.95$, $p<.001$, and new (corrected with Welch's *F*), $F_W(1, 17.18)=17.18$, $p<.001$. We also performed repeated-measures ANOVAs to establish if there were differences within each group across the test-item types (trained, partially-trained, new). In the experimental group, there was no significant effect of Test-Item Type, $F(2, 22)=1.40$, $p>.05$, which shows that, in this group, participants performed similarly across the types of test items. However, in the control group, performance did differ significantly across test-item types, $F(2, 22)=3.48$, $p<.05$, $\eta_p^2=.24$. Contrasts showed there was a significant difference between trained and new items, $F(1, 11)=8.25$, $p<.05$, $\eta_p^2=.43$, but no significant difference between trained and partially-trained items, $F(1, 11)=2.57$, $p>.05$, or between partially-trained and new items, $F(1, 11)=.27$, $p>.05$. Figure 1 illustrates the performance of the two groups across the three types of test items.

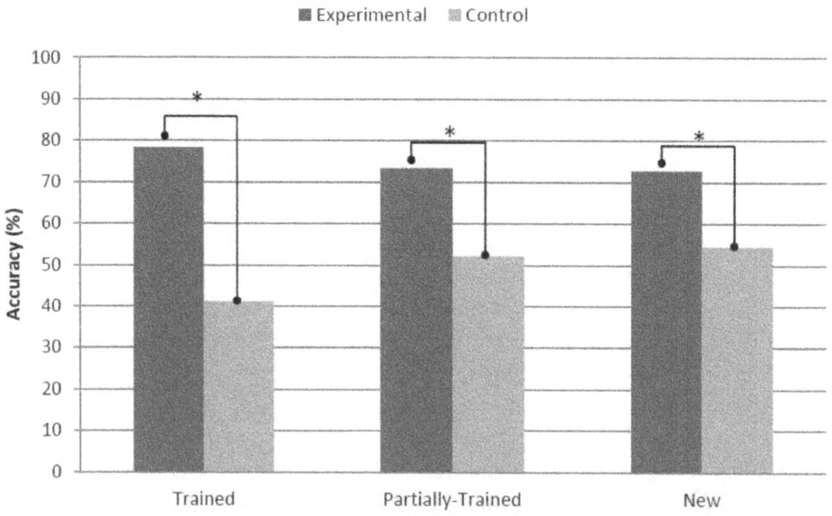

Figure 1. Test performance of experimental and control participants on trained, partially-trained, and new items

Retrospective verbal reports

The following analyses focus on the experimental group, given that there was no overall learning effect in the trained controls. The verbal report data from two experimental participants was not available for analysis due to technical failure. The analysis of the remaining data showed that nine participants were able to verbalize at least some knowledge regarding the animacy regularity. In the analyses below, these participants will be referred to as the *aware group*. The four remaining experimental participants expressed no awareness of the animacy regularity. These will be referred to as the *unaware group*. Below we report the performance of both groups on the 2AFC task.

Overall performance of aware and unaware experimental participants on the 2AFC task

The aware group identified 79.6% (SD=31.6%) of the test items correctly and the unaware group 53.5% (SD=10.7%). Aware participants performed significantly above chance, $t(8)=2.82$, $p<.05$, while unaware participants were indistinguishable from chance, $p>.05$. A t-test showed that aware participants did not significantly outperform unaware participants, $p>.05$. However, this result is likely an uninteresting effect of the small number of participants in the unaware group (n=4). The analysis of the retrospective verbal reports suggests that learning in this experiment was restricted to those participants who were able to verbalize at least some knowledge related to the hidden animacy regularity. In contrast to Williams (2005), the verbal reports thus provide no evidence of unconscious knowledge in the experimental group (though see below).

Performance of aware and unaware participants across different test items

The aware group identified correctly 82.4% (SD=11%) of the trained items, 79.6% (SD=6.4%) of the partially-trained items, and 76.9% (SD=11%) of the new items. In all cases, these scores were significantly above chance, *ps*<.001. The unaware group identified correctly 64.6% (*SD*=41.9%) of the trained items, 54.2% (*SD*=33.4%) of the partially-trained items, and 56.3% (*SD*=35.6%) of the new items. However, none of the scores were significantly above chance, *ps*>.05. Further analysis indicated that aware participants significantly outperformed unaware participants on partially-trained items, $t(11.81)=2.59$, $p<.05$, but there were no significant differences between groups on trained items or new items. Again, this is probably due to the small sample size of the unaware group, coupled with large standard deviations. Figure 2 illustrates the performance of the aware and unaware groups across the three types of items.

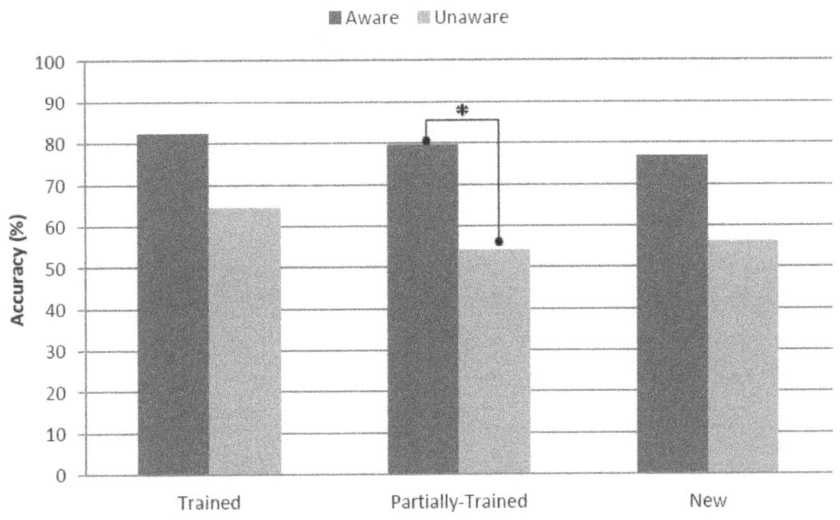

Figure 2. Test performance of aware and unaware participants on trained, partially-trained, and new items

Subjective measures

The following analyses of the subjective measures focus on the experimental group, given that we did not find an overall learning effect in the trained controls.

Confidence ratings

As shown in Table 5, in terms of proportion, experimental participants tended to select the *absolute certainty* category most frequently and the *complete guess* category least frequently. In terms of accuracy, the analysis indicated that experimental participants were most accurate when reporting to be very confident in their decisions and less accurate when reporting to be absolutely certain or somewhat confident. Accuracy was lowest for those grammaticality decisions in which participants had no confidence whatsoever and reported to be truly guessing. Experimental participants scored significantly above chance when reporting to be somewhat confident, very confident, and absolutely certain, *ps*<.05. However, when participants reported to be guessing, performance was indistinguishable from chance, $p>.05$, indicating that the guessing criterion for unconscious judgment knowledge was not satisfied. The fact that participants were more accurate when reporting higher levels of confidence (82.6% and 74.4%, respectively) also suggests the existence of conscious judgment knowledge. In other words, the confidence ratings suggest that participants in the experimental group were aware of having acquired some knowledge during the training phase. Table 5 summarizes the findings.

Table 5. Accuracy and proportion of responses (%) across confidence ratings

	complete guess	somewhat confident	very confident	absolute certainty
accuracy	50	72.6*	82.6*	74.4*
proportion	6	23	34	36

note. Significance from chance: * $p<.001$.

Source attributions

As shown in Table 6, in terms of proportion, experimental participants most frequently believed their classification decisions to be based on rule knowledge, followed by memory and intuition. The *guess* category was selected least frequently. In terms of accuracy, experimental participants scored highest when reporting to have relied on memory, followed by the *intuition* and *rule knowledge* categories. Participants were least accurate when basing decisions on guesses. Further analysis showed that participants performed significantly above chance across the four categories, $ps<.05$. The fact that participants performed significantly above chance when basing their decisions on guessing or intuition suggests that at least some of the acquired structural knowledge was unconscious. Table 6 summarizes the findings.

Table 6. Accuracy and proportion of responses (%) across source attributions

	guess	intuition	memory	rule
accuracy	66.7*	75.4**	84.1**	74.4**
proportion	7	24	21	48

note. Significance from chance: *$p<.05$, **$p<.001$

Discussion

The results of the experiment confirm that adult learners are able to establish novel form-meaning connections under incidental learning conditions without the benefit of feedback and after a relatively brief exposure period. As described above, the present study employed three types of test items (*trained* NPs, *partially-trained* NPs, and *new* NPs), in contrast to Williams (2005), Hama and Leow (2010), and Faretta-Stutenberg and Morgan-Short (2011), who did not include true generalization items. Experimental participants performed significantly above chance across all test-item types, including new items, indicating that they were able to generalize their knowledge and that exposure to the artificial determiner system resulted in a knowledge base that is, at least partially, abstract.[5]

The analysis of the retrospective verbal reports showed that 70% of participants were able to verbalize some knowledge regarding the hidden animacy regularity. Further analysis showed that only these aware participants were actually performing significantly above chance in the testing phase, with unaware participants ($n=4$) performing at chance. The evidence from the verbal reports thus indicates that learning in the experiment was restricted to those experimental participants who had acquired explicit knowledge. In other words, while

5 One could argue, of course, that exposure did not result in abstract knowledge but that abstraction occurred during the test phase, when participants compared stored exemplars to the test items. Grammaticality judgments would then be based on "abstract analogy" (Brooks & Vokey, 1991; Vokey & Higham, 2005).

learning in the experiments occurred under incidental conditions, participants developed explicit knowledge, some of which they could verbalize in the form of partial or complete metalinguistic rules. At the least, participants were aware of having acquired some form of knowledge, even if they had difficulty verbalizing it. These observations are consistent with Hama and Leow's (2010) findings.

Interestingly, the subjective measures of awareness (confidence ratings and source attributions) show that the picture is more complex than this. The analysis of the confidence ratings showed that experimental participants scored significantly above chance when reporting to be somewhat confident, very confident, or absolutely certain in their classification decision but only at chance when reporting no confidence whatsoever in the accuracy of a judgment. This suggests that the experimental group had acquired conscious judgment knowledge; that is, they had a sense of having acquired knowledge and of relying on this knowledge in the testing phase. The analysis of the source attributions showed that experimental participants performed significantly above chance across the four response categories, including responses based on guessing or intuition. When basing decisions on implicit categories (guess, intuition), participants were accurate in 71% of judgments. This finding indicates the presence of at least some unconscious structural knowledge, which is consistent with Williams (2005). Given that participants also performed significantly above chance when basing decisions on more explicit categories (memory or rule, with a combined accuracy of 80%), it seems that participants acquired both conscious and unconscious structural knowledge as a result of exposure. Taken together, the subjective measures thus indicate that, while participants were aware of having acquired knowledge, they were at least partially unaware of what knowledge they had acquired. These results are consistent with previous studies using subjective measures to investigate the implicit and explicit learning of novel words (e.g., Hamrick & Rebuschat, 2012, in press) and L2 syntax (e.g., Rebuschat, 2008; Rebuschat & Williams, 2012).

From a methodological perspective, the experiment confirms that sole reliance on retrospective verbal reports (as in Williams, 2004, 2005) is clearly insufficient for the study of implicit and explicit learning, as Williams (2005, 2009) clearly acknowledges. The analysis of our verbal reports showed that most participants were able to describe the rules of the artificial determiner system and that learning was apparently restricted to these aware participants. If we had not included more sensitive measures of awareness in the form of confidence ratings and source attributions, we might have erroneously concluded that exposure to the artificial system resulted exclusively in explicit knowledge. We propose that future explorations of implicit and explicit language learning could benefit from the inclusion of more sensitive ways of detecting implicit and explicit knowledge. Our research suggests that subjective measures could play a useful role, though it is clear that these are not the only solution and that subjective measures have their own methodological difficulties (see Rebuschat, 2013, for a comprehensive discussion).

The experiment also extends previous work using trained control participants (Hamrick, 2012, 2013; Hamrick & Sachs, 2013). In the first SLA study to use this procedure, Hamrick (2012, 2013) incidentally exposed participants to semi-artificial sentences with either probabilistic syntactic structures (experimental condition) or randomized syntactic structures (trained control condition). The training sentences in the experimental condition contained transitional probabilities between categories of 67% and 33% (e.g., the probability that an NP was followed by a PP was 67%). In the control condition, the same training sentences were presented, but the syntax was randomized and all of the transitional probabilities were balanced at 25%. Thus, trained control sentences contained no probabilistic cues to syntactic structure. Interestingly, in the surprise grammaticality judgment task following exposure, trained controls outperformed experimental participants on one of the three syntactic target structures. Thus, the trained controls, who unlike the experimental group were not exposed to and therefore could not have learned the probabilistic structure, displayed a clear bias toward endorsing one of the syntactic structures. Such findings raise issues of what counts as a valid baseline for learning, especially considering other studies that show that controls may perform significantly below chance (e.g., Rebuschat & Williams, 2012). In the present study, the trained control group did not perform significantly above chance in terms of overall accuracy, though they did perform above chance on new items, which confirms again that the validity of 50% as a baseline should not simply be assumed.

Conclusion

The main objective of this study was to contribute to the ongoing debate on the implicit and explicit learning of languages by focusing on a central methodological issue, namely how to detect implicit and explicit knowledge (Ellis, 2005). Our extension of Williams (2005) confirmed that learners are able to establish novel form-meaning connections under incidental learning conditions (see also Faretta-Stutenberg & Morgan-Short, 2011; Hama & Leow, 2010; Leung & Williams, 2011a, 2011b). Importantly, our study also showed that incidental exposure can result in both implicit and explicit knowledge of language, which helps to shed light on the conflicting results obtained by Williams (2005) and Hama and Leow (2010). Williams (2005) might have underestimated the extent to which participants acquired explicit knowledge, given that his study relied on a relatively insensitive measure of awareness (retrospective verbal reports). On the other hand, Hama and Leow (2010) might have overestimated the role of explicit knowledge, given that they were unable to assess whether there was also implicit knowledge present in their aware participants.

There are outstanding issues that our study, due to the nature of its design, was unable to address. For example, it is uncertain *when* participants developed conscious knowledge. Participants could have become aware of the hidden regularity either during the training phase or during the test phase, when they were suddenly forced to make a choice between options differing only in their animacy values and when they were prompted with requests for source attributions that suggested that their responses might have been based on a rule. The think-aloud protocols of Hama and Leow (2010) suggest that their participants became aware during the test phase, as do the comments of several of our participants in their retrospective verbal reports. If this is the case, then it could well be that the acquired knowledge was implicit until it was required for the test phase, the nature of which could then have led participants to become aware of the target feature.

More research is also necessary to establish how the acquired knowledge is represented. Participants in our study are likely to have acquired abstract knowledge, given their performance on generalization items. However, it is not clear what the nature of this knowledge is (patterns, chunks, etc.). If participants had acquired the hidden animacy rule, their performance on those classifications attributed to (relevant) rule knowledge should have been significantly higher (close to 100%). Our results showed that they actually were slightly less accurate on judgments based on rule knowledge (74.4%) when compared to those based on intuition (75.4%) or memory (84.1%).[6] Finally, both of our measures of awareness assessed the conscious and unconscious status of the acquired knowledge; like Williams (2005), we focused on the *product* of learning and not on the *process* of learning (see Hama & Leow, 2010). For

6 When reporting to be using rule knowledge, some participants may have relied on *micro-rules*, that is, a partial but representative subset of the rules employed to generate the stimuli (Dulany, Carlson, & Dewey, 1984; Reber, 1993).

this reason, we are unable to say much about the role of noticing in our study, though given that most experimental participants were able to verbalize some knowledge, it seems clear that noticing is likely to have played a role. The inclusion of a variety of awareness measures, ranging from off-line tasks such as retrospective verbal reports and subjective measures to online tasks such as think-aloud protocols, is likely to be necessary to move the discussion forward (see Rebuschat, Hamrick, Sachs, Riestenberg, and Ziegler, 2013).

References

Berry, D. C., & Dienes, Z. (1993). *Implicit learning: Theoretical and empirical issues*. Hove, UK: Lawrence Erlbaum.

Brooks, R. L., & Vokey, R. J. (1991). Abstract analogies and abstracted grammars: Comments on Reber (1989) and Mathews et al. (1989). *Journal of Experimental Psychology: Learning, Memory, and Cognition, 120*, 316–323.

Chan, C. (1992). *Implicit cognitive processes: Theoretical issues and applications in computer systems design*. Unpublished DPhil thesis, University of Oxford, UK.

DeKeyser, R. (2003). Implicit and explicit learning. In C. J. Doughty & M. H. Long (Eds.), *Handbook of second language acquisition* (pp. 313–348). Oxford: Blackwell.

Dienes, Z. (2004). Assumptions of subjective measures of unconscious mental states: Higher order thoughts and bias. *Journal of Consciousness Studies, 11*, 25–45.

Dienes, Z. (2012). Conscious versus unconscious learning of structure. In P. Rebuschat & J. N. Williams (Eds.), *Statistical learning and language acquisition* (pp. 337–364). Berlin: Mouton de Gruyter.

Dienes, Z., Altmann, G., Kwan, L., & Goode, A. (1995). Unconscious knowledge of artificial grammars is applied strategically. *Journal of Experimental Psychology: Learning, Memory, and Cognition, 21*, 1322–1338.

Dienes, Z., & Berry, D. C. (1997). Implicit learning: Below the subjective threshold. *Psychonomic Bulletin and Review, 4*, 3–23.

Dienes, Z., & Scott, R. (2005). Measuring unconscious knowledge: Distinguishing structural knowledge and judgment knowledge. *Psychological Research, 69*, 338–351.

Dulany, D. E., Carlson, R., & Dewey, G. (1984). A case of syntactical learning and judgement: How concrete and how abstract? *Journal of Experimental Psychology: Learning, Memory, and Cognition, 113*, 541–555.

Ellis, R. (2005). Measuring implicit and explicit knowledge of a second language: A psychometric study. *Studies in Second Language Acquisition, 27*, 141–172.

Erdelyi, M., & Becker, J. (1974). Hypermnesia for pictures: Incremental memory for pictures but not words in multiple recall trials. *Cognitive Psychology*, 6, 159–171.

Faretta-Stutenberg, M., & Morgan-Short, K. (2011). Learning without awareness reconsidered: A replication of Williams (2005). In G. Granena, J. Koeth, S. Lee-Ellis, A. Lukyanchenko, G. Prieto Botana, & E. Rhoades (Eds.), *Selected proceedings of the 2010 Second Language Research Forum* (pp. 18–28). Somerville, MA: Cascadilla Proceedings Project.

Hama, M., & Leow, R. P. (2010). Learning without awareness revisited: Extending Williams (2005). *Studies in Second Language Acquisition, 32*, 465–491.

Hamrick, P. (2012, October). *Associative learning supports early phases of adult L2 syntactic development: Behavioral and computational evidence*. Poster presented at the Second Language Research Forum, Pittsburgh, PA.

Hamrick, P. (2013). *Development of conscious knowledge during early incidental learning of L2 syntax*. Doctoral dissertation, Georgetown University, Washington, DC.

Hamrick, P., & Rebuschat, P. (2012). How implicit is statistical learning? In P. Rebuschat & J. N. Williams (Eds.), *Statistical learning and language acquisition* (pp. 365–382). Berlin: Mouton de Gruyter.

Hamrick, P., & Rebuschat, P. (in press). Frequency effects, learning conditions, and the development of implicit and explicit lexical knowledge. In J. Connor-Linton & L. Amoroso (Eds.), *Measured language: Quantitative approaches to acquisition, assessment, processing, and variation*. Washington, DC: Georgetown University Press.

Hamrick, P., & Sachs, R. (2013). *The need for appropriately trained control groups in applied linguistics research*. Manuscript in preparation.

Leow, R. P. (1997). Attention, awareness, and foreign language behavior. *Language Learning, 47*, 467–505.

Leow, R. P. (1998). Toward operationalizing the process of attention in SLA: Evidence for Tomlin and Villa's (1994) fine-grained analysis of attention. *Applied Psycholinguistics, 19*, 133–159.

Leow, R. P. (2000). A study of the role of awareness in foreign language behavior: Aware versus unaware learners. *Studies in Second Language Acquisition, 22*, 557–584.

Leow, R. P., & Bowles, M. (2005). Attention and awareness in SLA. In C. Sanz (Ed.), *Mind and context in adult second language acquisition* (pp. 179–203). Washington, DC: Georgetown University Press.

Leung, J. H. C., & Williams, J. N. (2011a). Constraints on implicit learning of grammatical form-meaning connections. *Language Learning, 62*, 634–662.

Leung, J. H. C., & Williams, J. N. (2011b). The implicit learning of mappings between forms and contextually-derived meanings. *Studies in Second Language Acquisition, 33*, 33–55.

Perruchet, P. (2008). Implicit learning. In J. Byrne (Ed.), *Learning and memory: A comprehensive reference* (Vol. 2: Cognitive psychology of memory, pp. 597–621). Oxford: Elsevier.

Reber, A. S. (1967). Implicit learning of artificial grammars. *Journal of Verbal Learning and Verbal Behavior, 6*, 317–327.

Reber, A. S. (1993). *Implicit learning and tacit knowledge: An essay on the cognitive unconscious*. Oxford: Oxford University Press.

Reber, R., & Perruchet, P. (2003). The use of control groups in artificial grammar learning. *The Quarterly Journal of Experimental Psychology, 56A*, 97–115.

Rebuschat, P. (2008). *Implicit learning of natural language syntax*. Unpublished PhD dissertation, University of Cambridge, UK.

Rebuschat, P. (2013). Measuring implicit and explicit knowledge in second language research. *Language Learning, 63*, 595–626. doi:10.1111/lang.12010

Rebuschat, P., Hamrick, P., Sachs, R., Riestenberg, K., & Ziegler, N. (2013). *Awareness, reactivity, and subjective measures*. Manuscript in preparation.

Rebuschat, P., & Williams, J. N. (2012). Implicit and explicit knowledge in second language acquisition. *Applied Psycholinguistics, 33*, 829–856.

Rebuschat, P., & Williams, J. N. (2013). *Explicit learning and the development of implicit L2 knowledge*. Manuscript in preparation.

Reingold, E. M., & Merikle, P. M. (1990). On the inter-relatedness of theory and measurement in the study of unconscious processes. *Mind & Language, 5*, 10–28.

Robinson, P. (1995). Attention, memory, and the 'noticing' hypothesis. *Language Learning, 45*, 283–331.

Robinson, P. (2003). Attention and memory during SLA. In C. J. Doughty & M. H. Long (Eds.), *Handbook of second language acquisition* (pp. 630–678). Oxford: Blackwell.

Rosa, E., & Leow, R. P. (2004). Awareness, different learning conditions, and L2 development. *Applied Psycholinguistics, 25*, 269–292.

Rosa, E., & O'Neill, M. D. (1999). Explicitness, intake, and the issue of awareness. *Studies in Second Language Acquisition, 21*, 511–556.

Rosenthal, D. M. (2005). *Consciousness and mind.* Oxford: Oxford University Press.

Sachs, R., & Suh, B.-R. (2007). Textually enhanced recasts, learner awareness, and L2 outcomes in synchronous computer-mediated interaction. In A. Mackey (Ed.), *Conversational interaction and second language acquisition: A series of empirical studies* (pp. 197–227). Oxford: Oxford University Press.

Schmidt, R. (1990). The role of consciousness in second language learning. *Applied Linguistics, 11*, 129–158.

Schmidt, R. (1993). Awareness and second language acquisition. *Annual Review of Applied Linguistics, 13*, 206–226.

Schmidt, R. (1994). Deconstructing consciousness in search of useful definitions for applied linguistics. *AILA Review, 11*, 11–26.

Schmidt, R. (1995). Consciousness and foreign language learning: A tutorial on attention and awareness in learning. In R. Schmidt (Ed.), *Attention and awareness in foreign language learning* (pp. 1–63). Honolulu, HI: University of Hawai'i, National Foreign Language Resource Center.

Schmidt, R. (2001). Attention. In P. Robinson (Ed.), *Cognition and second language instruction* (pp. 3–32). Cambridge: Cambridge University Press.

Shanks, D. R. (2005). Implicit learning. In K. Lambert & R. Goldstone (Eds.), *Handbook of cognition* (pp. 202–220). London: Sage.

Tagarelli, K., Borges Mota, M., & Rebuschat, P. (2011). The role of working memory in implicit and explicit language learning. In L. Carlson, C. Hölscher, & T. Shipley (Eds.), *Proceedings of the 33rd Annual Conference of the Cognitive Science Society* (pp. 2061–2066). Austin, TX: Cognitive Science Society.

Tomlin, R. S., & Villa, V. (1994). Attention in cognitive science and second language acquisition. *Studies in Second Language Acquisition, 16*, 183–203.

Vokey, J. R., & Higham, P. A. (2005). Abstract analogies and positive transfer in artificial grammar learning. *Canadian Journal of Experimental Psychology, 59*, 54–61.

Williams, J. N. (2004). Implicit learning of form-meaning connections. In B. VanPatten, J. Williams, S. Rott, & M. Overstreet (Eds.), *Form-meaning connections in second language acquisition* (pp. 203–218). Mahwah, NJ: Lawrence Erlbaum.

Williams, J. N. (2005). Learning without awareness. *Studies in Second Language Acquisition, 27*, 269–304.

Williams, J. N. (2009). Implicit learning in second language acquisition. In W. C. Ritchie & T. K. Bhatia (Eds.), *The new handbook of second language acquisition* (pp. 319–353). Bingley, UK: Emerald Press.

NFLRC
monographs

Implicit Second Language Learning and Individual Differences

Daniel O. Jackson
University of Hawai'i at Mānoa

The purpose of this chapter is twofold. It reviews the literature on learning second languages in the absence of awareness, and it explores evidence concerning the potential roles of cognitive, experiential, and other differences in such learning. The first section presents a narrative review of 19 empirical reports on implicit second language learning, focusing on the linguistic features claimed to be learnable without awareness. In the second section, theoretical links between implicit learning and attention are outlined, and individual difference variables, including general intelligence, language experience, working memory, and personality, among others, are considered in terms of their possible roles in implicit learning. The conclusion draws the above strands together, based on Schmidt's recent commentary on noticing, awareness, and individual differences.

Introduction

Beginning in the late 1960s, Arthur Reber pioneered a research program in psychology that established *implicit learning* as an unconscious process resulting in abstract knowledge (1967, 1989, 1993; see Pothos, 2007, for an overview of theoretical accounts of the knowledge resulting from such learning). In the field of second language learning, implicit learning is postulated to occur when learners acquire abstract phonological, morphological, syntactic, or other rules in a second language (L2) without awareness (Schmidt, 1990, 1994a, 1994b, 1995, 2001; for further discussion, see DeKeyser, 2003; Hulstijn, 2005; Williams, 2009). This chapter first provides an overview of evidence for implicit learning based on laboratory studies, focusing on the types of linguistic knowledge that can be learned implicitly. It then examines the potential role of individual differences in learning without awareness from the perspective of research in second language acquisition and cognitive psychology. This review proposes that, following Schmidt (2012), if individual differences influence noticing, we should also expect to find a role for individual differences in implicit learning.

Jackson, D. O. (2013). Implicit second language learning and individual differences. In J. M. Bergsleithner, S. N. Frota, & J. K. Yoshioka (Eds.), *Noticing and second language acquisition: Studies in honor of Richard Schmidt* (pp. 271–287). Honolulu: University of Hawai'i, National Foreign Language Resource Center.

Implicit learning in SLA

Theoretical underpinnings: Early research

Three early studies laid a conceptual foundation for research on implicit learning in SLA. First, Nation and McLaughlin (1986) used two artificial grammars from Reber and Allen (1978) to test monolinguals, bilinguals, and multilinguals under implicit and explicit learning conditions. These two grammars consisted of "semantic-free" letter strings governed by a system of rules argued to be too complex to decode explicitly (Reber, 1993, p. 29). In the implicit condition, which came first in Nation and McLaughlin's study, the instructions to participants were "intentionally nebulous; they were simply asked to pay close attention" (p. 46). The study found that the multilingual group outperformed the other two groups, scoring just above 70% correct on grammaticality judgments of test strings under both implicit and explicit conditions. Nation and McLaughlin therefore suggested that experience plays a role in how learners process novel language stimuli (for further discussion, see McLaughlin & Nayak, 1989). Next, Hulstijn (1989) conducted two experiments with Dutch-speaking groups: L1 speakers studied a semi-artificial version of their mother tongue, and L2 speakers learned advanced subordinate clause structures in Dutch. On the basis of evidence from cued recall and timed copying tests, Hulstijn concluded that, "for implicit and incidental learning of structural elements to take place, attention to form at input encoding is a sufficient condition" (p. 72). Later, a study by Ellis (1993) focused on soft mutation rules for initial consonants in Welsh (e.g., *Bangor* becomes *o Fangor*). Instructional conditions included rule plus instance, rule, and random groups, with the latter considered implicit or "naturalistic." Ellis reported, among other results, that implicit learners' accurate judgments steadily increased for old and new well-formed examples, though they performed poorly on ungrammatical items. In general, however, the rule groups outperformed the implicit group (p. 312).

Taken together, these early studies suggest that implicit L2 learning may be: (a) prone to individual differences in foreign language experience; (b) linked to attention to form or *noticing*, the object of which is "elements of the surface structure of utterances in the input" (Schmidt, 2001, p. 5); and (c) accumulated slowly. These issues resonate throughout the body of research that follows.

Comparisons of implicit versus other learning conditions

Building on these early experiments, a widely cited study by DeKeyser (1995, see also 1994a, 1994b) was motivated by pedagogical concerns over the learnability of rules under varying conditions of exposure. DeKeyser employed an artificial language exhibiting both categorical rules and prototypical patterns, hypothesizing that the former would be better learned under explicit conditions, while the latter would be better learned under implicit conditions. Both treatments involved multiple training sessions in which the explicit group was provided with written rule explanations. DeKeyser's first hypothesis was confirmed: Explicit learners performed better than those in the implicit group on the production test of categorical rules. While there was some evidence for the second hypothesis (better learning of prototypical patterns in the implicit group), this could not be confirmed statistically.

Alanen (1995) was likewise concerned with the impact of providing explicit, metalinguistic information on learning outcomes. Thirty-six participants studied Finnish locative suffixes and consonant changes in two sessions. During these sessions verbal reports were collected to gauge whether participants noticed the target structures. Participants in explicit conditions performed better on a sentence completion test than those in implicit conditions.

Furthermore, participants' comments on the structures correlated with performance. Alanen concluded that these results supported Schmidt's (1990) hypothesis that noticing benefits acquisition.

In a string of reports based on his 1994 doctoral dissertation, Robinson (1995a, 1996, 1997a) took up the issues of rule complexity, awareness, and instructional conditions. Here, the implicit condition was compared to incidental, rule-search, and instructed conditions. Participants were 104 English learners who performed grammaticality judgment tasks in order to assess learning of rules governing fronted adverbial clauses and pseudo-clefts of location. Each group trained on 40 sentences, with procedures varying by condition. Learners in the implicit condition saw the sentences and indicated whether two words appeared next to each other. The study showed a main effect for condition, with no interaction between rule complexity and condition. Those in the instructed condition scored highest for both rules. There were also significant differences in the extent to which participants looked for rules across the four conditions, with fewer participants looking for rules in the implicit condition. Lastly, concerning self-reported noticing, those who could verbalize the rules scored higher than those who could not. As above, this suggests an advantage for participants who are aware of rules, regardless of condition.

A later study by Robinson (1997b) used the same training conditions, but employed artificial verbs based on English, to explore the question of whether learning is memory-based or driven by rule abstraction. Sixty native Japanese speakers participated. The implicit, incidental, rule-search, and instructed groups again saw 40 sentences, this time containing pseudo-verbs approximating dative alternation rules in English (e.g., "Peter pelled the English teacher an excellent paper," p. 232). Accuracy and reaction times (RTs) for trained and new (grammatical and ungrammatical) items were assessed by means of a grammaticality judgment task. Interestingly, both accuracy and RTs for trained items were equivalent across the four conditions. Even still, instructed learners gave significantly more accurate responses to new, ungrammatical items, and there was also some support for better performance by instructed learners on new, grammatical items. Robinson argued that, for all groups, "rule-based knowledge...and implicit memory-based knowledge interact in decision-making" (p. 242).

In another study, de Graaff (1997) contrasted learning outcomes under implicit versus explicit treatments. There were 27 learners in each group who received ten lessons on a modified version of Esperanto. The target features were simple and complex morphological structures, including plural and imperative markers and placement rules for negatives and objects. A four-part proficiency test was used to assess learning. Learners receiving explicit rule explanations did better than those in the implicit group; however, unlike DeKeyser's (1995) study, little support was found for the hypothesis that the learning of specific rules and features would vary by condition.

A recurring observation in the studies discussed so far has been the superior performance of learners characterized as having some degree of awareness, by means of either group assignment into experimental conditions or self-report of awareness. While there is some evidence suggesting that rule complexity interacts with implicit and explicit learning, the advantage is generally in favor of explicit L2 learning. Implicit L2 learning may not extend beyond instances to which learners are exposed and may thus be based on associative memory rather than abstract generalization (Robinson, 1997b, p. 242; see Ortega, 2009, pp. 100–102, for discussion). Finally, as these studies focused on the effects of assigning learners to different conditions, they share one obvious caveat: implicit *conditions* in no way guarantee implicit *learning*.

Measuring the implicitness of learning

Recent studies have attempted to deal directly with the problems of measuring implicit knowledge[1]. In 2012, Rebuschat and Williams published a report describing the implicit learning of syntax. Their study made use of several rules related to verb placement in German sentences. These rules were interspersed within sentences using lexical items from English (the participants' L1). Thus, meaningful stimuli could be constructed (e.g., "*Today bought John the newspaper in the supermarket*," p. 9). Participants listened to training items and indicated whether or not they were plausible. Then, during testing, they supplied grammaticality judgments along with binary confidence ratings (Experiment 1). A second experiment varied the training phase and added source attributions as a further measure of awareness. Confidence ratings and source attributions are approaches to measuring implicit learning recommended by Dienes (e.g., Dienes & Scott, 2005; Dienes, 2012). They require participants to judge test items, and then indicate confidence in their judgments (in terms of a percentage or scale descriptor such as *somewhat confident, very confident*), and/or state the basis for their judgments: rule knowledge, intuition, memory, or guessing. Rebuschat and Williams used both these measures as signposts of unconscious learning, by analyzing scores according to the participants' attested confidence and source identifications. Regarding confidence ratings, two metrics were applied to evaluate the relationship between accuracy and confidence, the combination of which has been used to assess implicit learning (for discussion, see Rebuschat & Williams, 2012, as well as Dienes, Altmann, Kwan, & Goode, 1995). With regard to the source attribution data, in Experiment 2, Rebuschat and Williams noted an accuracy rate of 59% when participants attributed their knowledge to intuition. Because this was significantly above chance, it suggests that accurate performance can be based on intuition. The authors took this as evidence of implicit learning.

Tagarelli, Borges-Mota, and Rebuschat (2011) employed the same semi-artificial language based on German verb placement rules as in Rebuschat and Williams (2012). This time, participants were asked to listen to 120 sentences and either judge their plausibility (incidental condition) or search for underlying rules (explicit condition). Measures of grammaticality judgment, confidence ratings, and source attributions were used. Both groups scored above chance on the judgment task, though the explicit group performed better. Furthermore, again using data from source attributions, the authors showed that both groups scored above chance even when they claimed intuition as the basis for their grammaticality judgments. Specifically, when attributing responses to intuition, the implicit group scored 61%, and the explicit group scored 64%. Here again, they argued that this constitutes evidence of unconscious grammatical knowledge.

Other studies as well have employed source attributions and confidence ratings, providing further evidence upon which to assess the value of such methodological innovations. In one recent example, researchers combined verbal reports, confidence ratings, and an inclusion/exclusion task in order to assess L1 Cantonese speakers' awareness of Spanish word stress rules after training (Chan & Leung, 2012).

---

1 Two standards have been proposed to evaluate awareness tests (Shanks & St. John, 1994, p. 373). The first of these is the information criterion, or the requirement for measures to elicit information responsible for learning. The second is the sensitivity criterion, which requires that tests exhaustively measure knowledge pertaining to learning (see Robinson, Mackey, Gass, & Schmidt, 2012, for discussion). Bearing these criteria in mind, studies have attempted to offer evidence for implicit learning, as described in this section.

Implicit learning of form-meaning mappings

Recent work also reflects a specific focus on the unaware learning of associations between form and meaning when participants are engaged in comprehending semi-artificial L2 systems. Williams (2004) reported on two such experiments. In the first of these, 37 participants learned an artificial language, based on Italian, which coded nouns for definiteness and animacy. Seven of the participants gained awareness of the role of animacy during training and were excluded from further analyses. The remaining participants scored 61% on generalization items—this rose to 71% for participants who spoke an L1 marking grammatical gender. Both figures were above chance. In Williams' second experiment, 17 participants were exposed to an artificial language consisting of four determiners marking nouns for distance and animacy. Participants were taught that the articles *gi* and *ro* meant 'near' and *ul* and *ne* meant 'far.' Unbeknownst to them, *gi* and *ul* accompanied living things, and *ro* and *ne* were used for non-living things. This time, none of the participants became aware during the training phase, scores on an initial test of generalization items did not differ from chance, and evidence for implicit learning of animacy was scant.

Shortly thereafter, Williams (2005) achieved results shedding more light on the nature of implicit learning in two additional experiments building on Experiment 2 above. In contrast, in these experiments the learning task was simplified, the number of noun tokens was increased, and sentences (not phrases) were presented in training. The system of determiners was the same, however. In Experiment 1, 41 individuals received instruction on the distance factor and proceeded to listen to and repeat sentences across 144 learning trials. Eight reported awareness of animacy during the test phase. Among unaware participants, performance was above chance on all item types. In Experiment 2, revised materials were used with 24 participants. Seven of these individuals indicated awareness. Mean scores of the 17 unaware participants were significantly above chance for both novel and trained items.

Later, Hama and Leow (2010) conducted a study extending Williams (2005), using concurrent verbal reports (i.e., think-aloud protocols) to measure awareness. They also increased the number of multiple-choice test options (from two to four), employed a production test, conducted training and testing phases in the same spoken modality, and screened participants who had a linguistics background. In short, none of the 34 included participants became aware of, or learned, the relevance of animacy. These results raise the possibility that the verbal reasoning required of participants during the think-alouds may have interfered with learning. The issue of whether concurrent verbalization is *reactive*, that is, the extent to which it increases task demands and alters mental processing, is a matter of considerable debate in the SLA literature (Bowles, 2010; Leow & Bowles, 2005). Another replication of Williams (2005), by Faretta-Stutenberg and Morgan-Short (2011), also found limited evidence of implicit learning.

Leung and Williams (2011) considered the possibility that implicit learning is limited to those features that can be lexically derived (e.g., *gi* and *ul* are always associated with nouns denoting living things). They therefore set out to investigate whether implicit learning is possible when these determiners are correlated instead with the thematic role of the noun. The sentence stimuli they created used *gi* and *ul* to mark agents and *ro* and *ne* to mark patients (with *gi* and *ro* used for adults and *ul* and *ne* for children). Importantly, word order was flexible, so that it was not a cue to thematic role. The procedure involved an adapted version of the contextual cueing paradigm (Chun, 2000; Jiang & Chun, 2003). On each trial, participants (a) described a picture, (b) listened to a sentence containing the artificial thematic role markers, (c) clicked a left or right mouse button to identify the agent in the picture, and (d) reformulated the sentence in English. When participants unknowingly reached the violation block (i.e., the series of trials in which the artificial system was violated), the form-meaning mappings were reversed, although the task remained the same. Five participants (out of 25) displayed awareness in a subsequent debriefing. As for the remaining participants, the authors reported a significant increase in reaction times on the violation block items, when compared to the items in the control block. In view of these findings, Leung and Williams argued that implicit learning mechanisms enable detection of correlations between form and contextually-derived meanings based on events.

Leung and Williams (2012) described two more studies adapting the contextual cueing paradigm to investigate implicit L2 learning. As in their previous study, they looked at the issue of precisely which meaning distinctions can be learned under implicit conditions of exposure. Experiment 1 used the artificial determiners from Williams (2005) to encode animacy and distance, whereas Experiment 2 used them to encode relative size and distance, on the assumption that relative size is not a grammaticalized concept and thus would not interact with language processing as strongly as animacy (Leung & Williams, 2012, p. 639). In Experiment 1, 13 participants became aware. The violation effect for the unaware participants was –68 ms, while for aware participants it was –232 ms. In both cases, these effects reached significance. In the second experiment, 26 participants were studied and six of them became aware. This time, neither group showed a significant violation effect. In their discussion the authors attempted to explain the different results of Experiments 1 and 2 in terms of the activation rate for animacy versus the computation of relative size.

Two additional reports also speak to the issue of learning form-meaning mappings without awareness. First, Chen et al. (2011) utilized source attributions and verbal reports to demonstrate gains in unconscious knowledge of form-meaning pairings in a conceptual replication of Williams (2005) using modified Chinese characters (Experiments 1 and 2), also showing that a linguistically-irrelevant feature was not learned this way (Experiment 3). Second, Guo et al. (2011) explored the development of implicit knowledge of semantic prosody (e.g., the typical usage of the verb *cause* with negative consequences) by Chinese learners of English in an experiment using pseudowords, this time pairing confidence ratings and source attributions. Both papers expand the range of linguistic features investigated with important implications.

In summary, Williams' initial null findings as well as Hama and Leow's unsuccessful replication demonstrate that learning without awareness may be highly sensitive to experimental conditions and/or testing methods. Nonetheless, based on subsequent results, Williams has stated that, "at least for some individuals, it is possible to learn form-meaning connections without awareness of what those connections are" (2005, p. 293). Also, the studies by Rebuschat and Williams (2012) and Tagarelli, Borges-Mota, and Rebuschat (2011) showed some evidence of implicit learning, as demonstrated by above chance judgments of syntactic patterns learned under limited exposure conditions, when participants claimed intuition as the basis of these judgments. Finally, by using reaction time as a methodology, Leung and Williams (2011, 2012) showed implicit learning based on behaviors that reflect cognitive processes arguably beyond participants' conscious control (for discussion, see Norris & Ortega, 2003, p. 730). Given these recent findings, a gradual consensus is emerging that implicit learning of L2 constructions appears to be possible for certain features and for certain individuals (Schmidt, 2012; Williams, 2009).

Table 1 lists the linguistic features of L2 systems targeted in the 19 reports just reviewed. To recap, the kinds of L2 features that participants have learned implicitly mainly covered morphology and syntax[2].

Table 1. Overview of the linguistic features in the studies reviewed

study	classification	language(s)	target linguistic feature(s)
Nation & McLaughlin (1986)	artificial	N/A	letter strings based on a finite-state grammar
Hulstijn (1989)	Indo-European	Dutch	semi-artificial Dutch & subordinate clauses
Ellis (1993)	Indo-European	Welsh	consonant mutation rules
DeKeyser (1995)	artificial	Implexan	plural, gender, & object suffixes
Alanen (1995)	Uralic, Finnic	Finnish	locative suffixes & consonant changes
Robinson (1995a)	Indo-European	English	fronted adverbials & pseudo clefts
Robinson (1997b)	semi-artificial	English	artificial verbs exhibiting dative alternation
de Graaff (1997)	semi-artificial	Esperanto	plurals, imperative, & negation
Williams (2004)	semi-artificial	Italian/English	determiners for animacy
Williams (2005)	semi-artificial	English	determiners for animacy
Hama & Leow (2010)	semi-artificial	English	determiners for animacy
Chen et al. (2011)	semi-artificial	Chinese	determiners for animacy/relative size
Guo et al. (2011)	semi-artificial	English	semantic prosody
Faretta-Stutenberg & Morgan-Short (2011)	semi-artificial	English	determiners for animacy
Leung & Williams (2011)	semi-artificial	English	determiners for thematic role
Rebuschat & Williams (2012)	semi-artificial	English/German	German verb placement
Tagarelli, Borges-Mota, & Rebuschat (2011)	semi-artificial	English/German	German verb placement
Leung & Williams (2012)	semi-artificial	English	determiners for animacy/ relative size
Chan & Leung (2012)	Indo-European	Spanish	word stress rules

2 Related studies have investigated word segmentation and other phenomena within the framework of statistical learning (Aslin & Newport, 2009). In fact, the mechanisms underlying implicit and statistical learning have been argued to be similar (Perruchet & Pacton, 2006). For an account of how statistical learning may impact adult SLA, see Onnis (2012).

Individual differences in implicit learning

Having reviewed empirical evidence for learning without awareness, I now turn to the issue of individual differences (IDs) in implicit learning (for a comprehensive review of the role of IDs in language learning, see Dörnyei, 2005). Intelligence, language learning experience, working memory, and personality are examined in depth, and additional candidate variables from the literature in cognitive psychology are then described. Before this, however, I will review some theoretical assumptions that may support a case for the role of IDs in implicit second language learning.

First, there is broad agreement that implicit learning relies on attention (Hsiao & Reber, 1998; Shanks, 2003). Most researchers further assume that attention and working memory are interdependent, although various positions have been advanced on the precise relationship between these two constructs (for commentary, see Baddeley, 2007; Cowan, 2008; Engle, 2002; Kane, Conway, Bleckley, & Engle, 2001; and in SLA, Robinson, 1995b, 2003). Thus, in principle, the mechanisms assumed to underlie implicit learning and noticing are alike. Assuming that adult L2 learning draws on existing language knowledge and general problem-solving mechanisms (Bley-Vroman, 1990), then such learning may proceed on the basis of fundamentally similar—and individually varying—processes, whether accompanied by awareness or not (see Robinson, 1997a, 2007). A related argument is that implicit cognitive processes showing IDs (e.g., priming) may predict learning (Woltz, 2003). In these ways theory has challenged the notion of implicit processes as less variable than explicit processes (Reber, 1993). Evidence is also amassing to support a reassessment of this claim.

Intelligence

Reber has consistently stated that implicit learning should show less variability than explicit learning on measures such as intelligence (for discussion in SLA contexts, see Winter & Reber, 1994; Reber, 2011). Yet, when Robinson replicated the study upon which this claim is based (Reber, Walkenfeld, & Hernstadt, 1991), the results were not entirely consistent. Robinson (2002, 2005, 2010) reported on three experiments to investigate the generalizability of findings from the literature on artificial grammar learning to L2 learner populations and to the learning of a foreign language, in this case, Samoan, under incidental conditions. The participants were 54 undergraduates at a university in Japan. The first two experiments were replications focused on the learning of letter strings. Experiment 1 replicated Reber et al. (1991). Reber and colleagues had based their study on the premise that, because implicit learning systems phylogenetically pre-date conscious functioning, they should show less variance than explicit systems and correlate less strongly with standard measures of cognitive ability (Reber, 1993; Reber & Allen, 2000). Based on a group of 20 participants, they demonstrated both of these outcomes, offering higher correlations between IQ and an explicit series-solution task (r=.69) than an implicit artificial grammar learning (AGL) task (r=.25) as supporting evidence. The replication by Robinson, which used an experimental group of 37 participants, indeed found less variance in scores on the implicit AGL task than on the explicit problem-solving task. In this same experiment, however, Robinson unexpectedly found a negative correlation between implicit learning and intelligence, as measured by an IQ test, which he attributed to high-IQ participants' unsuccessful attempts to process the letter strings analytically.

In a related study, Gebauer and Mackintosh (2007) administered AGL, serial reaction time (SRT), and process control tasks to 605 participants under implicit and explicit conditions, reporting a greater number of significant correlations on measures of intelligence and memory when learning was explicit. Again, these tasks did not involve learning form-meaning connections but rather letter strings.

Language learning experience

Looking back on the literature on implicit SLA, one other variable seems likely to be an influence. That is, participants who know two or more languages have performed better under implicit learning conditions (Nation & McLaughlin, 1986; Williams, 2005). Although language knowledge is not traditionally considered to be an ID variable in SLA (because it accrues over time), researchers accept that it may show an influence on implicit learning. The advantages here may be in terms of general processing abilities, or they may come from positive transfer, as those having knowledge of languages with grammatical features resembling the target stimuli may perform better. Although at present these influences are not often clearly separated in the research, nor are they well understood, Schmidt, discussing Williams' research, recently suggested that, "prior experience in language learning may play a role in implicit learning" (2012, p. 36).

Working memory

Much research and theorizing has positioned working memory (WM) as an important variable operating at many levels of L2 learning and use (for recent reviews, see Juffs & Harrington, 2011; Williams, 2012). In their investigation, Tagarelli et al. (2011) employed two separate working memory tasks (i.e., letter-number ordering and operation span). This study was unique in that it tested Reber's (1993) claim that implicit learning is less influenced by IDs using meaningful stimuli—unlike those used in Reber et al.'s (1991) study and Robinson's (2005) replication. Note here that working memory (but not IQ) correlated with performance in the third experiment reported in Robinson (2005), which examined the influence of IDs on learning Samoan under incidental conditions. Tagarelli et al. found support for the notion that IDs in working memory influence learning under explicit, rule-search conditions. This group (n=26) showed a significant correlation of r=0.47, indicating 22% shared variance between the grammaticality judgment task and the letter-number ordering task. The authors found no significant correlations, however, for the incidental group.

In contrast, a recent study by Misyak and Christiansen (2012) reported moderate correlations between a digit span task and measures of adjacent (r=0.46) and non-adjacent (r=0.53) statistical learning with a group of 30 participants. Bo, Jennett, and Seidler (2011) also supported the view that WM and implicit learning are related, uncovering significant correlations between the rate of performance change during implicit learning in an SRT task and visuospatial WM (r=– 0.65) as well as verbal WM (r=– 0.53), based on 21 participants. These findings are interesting in light of Ellis' (2005) discussion, which posited a role for WM in the implicit and explicit learning of form, as well as a role for WM plus awareness in connecting meaningful events during learning (p. 335). Also relevant are recent empirical demonstrations suggesting that WM can operate outside of conscious awareness (Hassin, Bargh, Engell, & McCulloch, 2009).

Personality

An array of studies outside the SLA field has investigated personality factors, often based on the well-known Five Factor Model of personality (or, Big Five), which includes: openness to experience, conscientiousness, extraversion, agreeableness, and neuroticism (McCrae & Costa, 2003). Woolhouse and Bayne (2000) reported a positive association between implicit learning scores and scores on the sensing-intuition scale of the Myers-Briggs Type

Inventory (Myers, McCaulley, Quenk, & Hammer, 1998). Norman, Price, and Duff (2006) found some support for a positive relationship between openness to feelings on the NEO PI-R (Costa & McCrae, 1992) and performance under certain conditions in an SRT task, though conscientiousness was unrelated to performance (see also Norman, Price, Duff, & Mentzoni, 2007). A study by Wilson and Hamlin (2007) also reported a positive relationship between extraversion on a personality measure and implicit sequence learning in a card task. As described by McCrae and Costa, openness to feelings is a facet of openness that involves strongly experiencing ones' own feelings and valuing this experience, while extraversion is a domain composed of the six facets of warmth, gregariousness, assertiveness, activity, excitement seeking, and positive emotions (2003, p. 49).

More recently, Kaufman et al. (2010) employed an SRT task with two recurring sequences in order to investigate relationships between implicit learning and a wide range of ID measures. Their findings suggest that there may be an ability for implicit learning that is positively related to cognitive factors (i.e., verbal reasoning and processing speed) and personality variables. Several key personality factors here relate to those measured by BFAS (Big Five Aspect Scales) openness; NEO Personality Inventory aesthetics, which taps an appreciation for art and beauty; as well as to MBTI Intuition, a measure of individuals' concentration on possibilities and patterns instead of details. Kaufman et al. report significant correlations between these variables and implicit learning, based on data from approximately 150 participants, which were as high as r=0.29 for BFAS openness. Furthermore, implicit learning was negatively correlated with (lack of) premeditation (r=–0.23), where premeditation "refers to the tendency to think and reflect on the consequences of an act before engaging in that act" (Whiteside & Lynam, 2001, p. 685).

Pretz, Totz, and Kaufman (2010) similarly found correlations between, on the one hand, probabilistic sequence learning and artificial grammar learning, and, on the other, rational ability, a subscale on the rational-experiential inventory (Pacini & Epstein, 1999), but again, the shared variance was small (4% and 6%, respectively). Rational ability is linked to a self-reported "high level of ability to think logically and analytically" (Pacini & Epstein, 1999, p. 974). This study also experimentally manipulated participants' mood and found a relation between positive and negative mood conditions and learning in the SRT task. The authors conclude that even though IDs appear relatively less influential in implicit learning, meaningful differences do exist.

Other candidate variables

Implicit learning research in SLA has yet to confirm the role of a number of other candidate variables. In an early report, McLaughlin and Nayak (1989) described an unpublished study by Nayak, Hansen, Krueger, and McLaughlin (1987) in which multilingual participants exposed to an artificial grammar were found more likely to apply mnemonic *learning strategies* in a memory condition (though multilinguals and monolinguals did not differ in the extent to which they learned the artificial language system). Additionally, a series of experiments by Eitam and colleagues (Eitam, Hassin, & Schul, 2008; Eitam, Schul, & Hassin, 2009) have manipulated the goal relevance of stimuli in artificial grammar learning, linking implicit learning to participants' *motivational states*. Finally, there has been recent work based on Nisbett's (2003) provocative suggestion that Asians and Westerners prefer different *thinking styles*. Kiyokawa, Dienes, Tanaka, Yamada, and Crowe (2012) conducted four experiments using stimuli which presented AGL sequences simultaneously in global and local patterns, finding that Japanese participants outperformed English participants on global strings. Interestingly, this advantage was removed when participants were instructed to focus on one or the other pattern (Experiment 3), suggesting that such preferences are malleable. The attribution method (see above) was used to assess qualitative differences in learning outcomes with respect to awareness.

Table 2 summarizes IDs variables hypothesized to potentially influence implicit L2 learning, including those that have only been dealt with outside of the field. In sum, the territory in SLA appears largely uncharted at present, though promising, as well. Looking ahead, an important rebuttal to any claim of IDs in implicit L2 learning involves the measurement of awareness: construct specification and methodological rigor are, of course, prerequisites to uncovering the role of learner factors in this area. The first half of this chapter revealed a growing sensitivity to this issue as well as increasing sophistication in L2 research on awareness.

Table 2. Individual difference variables potentially related to implicit L2 learning

positively related	negatively related
intuition	intelligence
extraversion	(lack of) premeditation
language learning experience	
learning strategy use	
motivation/goal relevance	
openness to aesthetics	
openness to experience	
openness to feelings	
processing speed	
rational ability	
verbal reasoning	
working memory	

Conclusion

The first section of this chapter presented an up-to-date review of research on implicit learning, or learning in the absence of self-reported awareness. Target linguistic forms argued to be learnable in this fashion included morphology and syntax, among others. Implicit learning studies contend that learning without awareness is possible but do not purport to show evidence of learning without attention. Having examined the past and present of implicit L2 learning research, the latter section then considered the role of IDs. Intelligence, language experience, and working memory are several variables that may exert influence on attentional processing in the absence of awareness. However, the spectrum of IDs is much broader, and a number of other variables may also warrant investigation, including those subsumed under the label personality.

This chapter has surveyed empirical findings and offered speculation on imminent directions for L2 research. In closing, it should be noted that there are a number of alternate perspectives on the two areas reviewed here (see, e.g., Frankish & Evans, 2009; Reber, 1993; Reber & Allen, 2000; Reber, Walkenfeld, & Hernstadt, 1991; Robinson, 2002, 2005, 2010). Presently, little is known about the role of IDs in implicit L2 learning. Therefore, further research with a range of linguistic constructions and learner types will be necessary before implications can be stated. In general, however, additional findings may benefit the areas of language pedagogy and SLA theory.

Insofar as this relates to noticing, it is useful to remember that "individual differences are an important part of the story, and both inclinations and abilities affect who notices what" (Schmidt, 2012, p. 44). If implicit learning is taken to be a process of unconscious generalization across *noticed* instances, then factors affecting noticing should also influence implicit learning. Perhaps the influence arises from combinations of interacting variables, from those that induce noticing of surface features of the input to those that trigger semantic processing and the development of form-meaning connections. The second language field does not yet have a complete answer to the question of whether the IDs that influence implicit and explicit learning are the same or different, but we are making progress toward a more detailed understanding. As described throughout this book, Richard Schmidt's profound insight serves as a guide.

References

Alanen, R. (1995). Input enhancement and rule presentation in second language acquisition. In R. Schmidt (Ed.), *Attention and awareness in foreign language learning* (pp. 259–302). Honolulu, HI: University of Hawai'i, National Foreign Language Resource Center.

Aslin, R. N., & Newport, E. L. (2009). What statistical learning can and can't tell us about language acquisition. In J. Colombo, P. McCardle, & L. Freund (Eds.), *Infant pathways to language: Methods, models, and research disorders* (pp. 15–29). New York, NY: Lawrence Erlbaum.

Baddeley, A. D. (2007). *Working memory, thought, and action.* Oxford, UK: Oxford University Press.

Bley-Vroman, R. (1990). The logical problem of foreign language learning. *Linguistic Analysis, 20,* 3–49.

Bo, J., Jennett, S., & Seidler, R. D. (2011). Working memory capacity correlates with implicit serial reaction time task performance. *Experimental Brain Research, 214,* 73–81.

Bowles, M. A. (2010). *The think-aloud controversy in second language research.* New York, NY: Routledge.

Chan, R., & Leung, J. (2012). Implicit learning of L2 word stress rules. In N. Miyake, D. Peebles, & R. P. Cooper (Eds.), *Proceedings of the 34th Annual Conference of the Cognitive Science Society* (pp. 192–197). Austin, TX: Cognitive Science Society.

Chen, W., Guo, X., Tang, J., Zhu, L., Yang, Z., & Dienes, Z. (2011). Unconscious structural knowledge of form-meaning connections. *Consciousness and Cognition, 20,* 1751–1760.

Chun, M. M. (2000). Contextual cueing of visual attention. *Trends in Cognitive Sciences, 4,* 170–178.

Costa, P. T., & McCrae, R. R. (1992). *Revised NEO Personality Inventory (NEO-PI-R) and NEO Five-Factor Inventory (NEO-FFI).* Professional Manual. Odessa, FL: Psychological Assessment Resources.

Cowan, N. (2008). What are the differences between long-term, short-term, and working memory? In W. S. Sossin, J.-C. Lacaille, V. F. Castellucci, & S. Belleville (Eds.), *Progress in brain research* (pp. 323–338). Amsterdam, Netherlands: Elsevier.

de Graaff, R. (1997). The *Experanto* experiment: Effects of explicit instruction on second language acquisition. *Studies in Second Language Acquisition, 19,* 249–276.

DeKeyser, R. M. (1994a). Implicit and explicit learning of L2 grammar: A pilot study. *TESOL Quarterly, 28,* 188–194.

DeKeyser, R. M. (1994b). How implicit can adult second language learning be? *AILA Review, 11,* 83–96.

DeKeyser, R. M. (1995). Learning second language grammar rules: An experiment with a miniature linguistic system. *Studies in Second Language Acquisition, 17*, 379–410.

DeKeyser, R. M. (2003). Implicit and explicit learning. In C. J. Doughty & M. H. Long (Eds.), *The handbook of second language acquisition* (pp. 313–348). Malden, MA: Blackwell.

Dienes, Z. (2012). Conscious versus unconscious learning of structure. In P. Rebuschat & J. N. Williams (Eds.), *Statistical learning and language acquisition* (pp. 337–364). Berlin: Mouton de Gruyter.

Dienes, Z., Altmann, G. T. M., Kwan, L., & Goode, A. (1995). Unconscious knowledge of artificial grammars is applied strategically. *Journal of Experimental Psychology: Learning, Memory, and Cognition, 21*, 1322–1338.

Dienes, Z., & Scott, R. (2005). Measuring unconscious knowledge: Distinguishing structural knowledge and judgment knowledge. *Psychological Research, 69*, 338–351.

Dörnyei, Z. (2005). *The psychology of the language learner: Individual differences in second language acquisition*. Mahwah, NJ: Lawrence Erlbaum.

Eitam, B., Hassin, R. R., & Schul, Y. (2008). Nonconscious goal pursuit in novel environments: The case of implicit learning. *Psychological Science, 19*, 261–267.

Eitam, B., Schul, Y., & Hassin, R. R. (2009). Goal relevance and artificial grammar learning. *The Quarterly Journal of Experimental Psychology, 62*, 228–238.

Ellis, N. C. (1993). Rules and instances in foreign language learning: Interactions of explicit and implicit knowledge. *European Journal of Cognitive Psychology, 5*, 289–318.

Ellis, N. C. (2005). At the interface: Dynamic interactions of explicit and implicit language knowledge. *Studies in Second Language Acquisition, 27*, 305–352.

Engle, R. W. (2002). Working memory capacity as executive attention. *Current Directions in Psychological Science, 11*, 19–23.

Faretta-Stutenberg, M., & Morgan-Short, K. (2011). Learning without awareness reconsidered: A replication of Williams (2005). In G. Granena, J. Koeth, S. Lee-Ellis, A. Lukyanchenko, G. Prieto Botana, & E. Rhoades (Eds.), *Selected proceedings of the 2010 Second Language Research Forum* (pp. 18–28). Somerville, MA: Cascadilla Proceedings Project.

Frankish, K., & Evans, J. S. B. T. (2009). The duality of mind: An historical perspective. In J. S. B. T. Evans & K. Frankish (Eds.), *In two minds: Dual processes and beyond* (pp. 1–28). Oxford, UK: Oxford University Press.

Gebauer, G. F., & Mackintosh, N. J. (2007). Psychometric intelligence dissociates implicit and explicit learning. *Journal of Experimental Psychology: Learning, Memory, and Cognition, 33*, 34–54.

Guo, X., Zheng, L., Zhu, L., Yang, Z., Chen, C., Zhang, L., Ma, W., & Dienes, Z. (2011). Acquisition of conscious and unconscious knowledge of semantic prosody. *Consciousness and Cognition, 20*, 417–425.

Hama, M., & Leow, R. P. (2010). Learning without awareness revisited. *Studies in Second Language Acquisition, 32*, 465–491.

Hassin, R. R., Bargh, J. A., Engell, A. D., & McCulloch, K. C. (2009). Implicit working memory. *Consciousness and Cognition, 18*, 665–678.

Hsiao, A. T., & Reber, A. S. (1998). The role of attention in implicit sequence learning. In M. A. Stadler & P. A. Frensch (Eds.), *Handbook of implicit learning* (pp. 471–494). Thousand Oaks, CA: Sage.

Hulstijn, J. (1989). Implicit and incidental second language learning: Experiments in the processing of natural and partly artificial input. In H.-W. Dechert & M. Raupach (Eds.), *Interlingual processes* (pp. 49–73). Tübingen, Germany: Gunter Narr Verlag.

Hulstijn, J. (2005). Theoretical and empirical issues in the study of implicit and explicit second-language learning. *Studies in Second Language Acquisition, 27*, 129–140.

Jiang, Y., & Chun, M. M. (2003). Contextual cueing: Reciprocal influences between attention and implicit learning. In L. Jiménez (Ed.), *Attention and implicit learning* (pp. 277–296). Amsterdam, Netherlands: John Benjamins.

Juffs, A., & Harrington, M. (2011). Aspects of working memory in L2 learning. *Language Teaching, 44*, 137–166.

Kane, M. J., Conway, A. R. A., Bleckley, M. K., & Engle, R. W. (2001). A controlled-attention view of working-memory capacity. *Journal of Experimental Psychology: General, 130*, 169–183.

Kaufman, S. B., DeYoung, C. G., Gray, J. R., Jiménez, L., Brown, J., & Mackintosh, N. (2010). Implicit learning as an ability. *Cognition, 116*, 321–340.

Kiyokawa, S., Dienes, Z., Tanaka, D., Yamada, A., & Crowe, L. (2012). Cross cultural differences in unconscious knowledge. *Cognition, 124*, 16–24.

Leow, R. P., & Bowles, M. A. (2005). Reactivity and type of verbal report in SLA research methodology. *Studies in Second Language Acquisition, 27*, 415–440.

Leung, J. H. C., & Williams, J. N. (2011). The implicit learning of mappings between forms and contextually derived meanings. *Studies in Second Language Acquisition, 33*, 33–55.

Leung, J. H. C., & Williams, J. N. (2012). Constraints on implicit learning of grammatical form-meaning connections. *Language Learning, 62*, 634–662.

McCrae, R. R., & Costa, P. T. (2003). *Personality in adulthood: A five-factor theory perspective.* New York, NY: Guilford Press.

McLaughlin, B., & Nayak, N. (1989). Processing a new language: Does knowing other languages make a difference? In H.-W. Dechert & M. Raupach (Eds.), *Interlingual processes* (pp. 5–16). Tübingen, Germany: Gunter Narr Verlag.

Misyak, J. B., & Christiansen, M. H. (2012). Statistical learning and language: An individual differences study. *Language Learning, 62*, 302–331.

Myers, I., McCaulley, M. H., Quenk, N. L., & Hammer, A. L. (1998). *Manual: A guide to the development and use of the Myers-Briggs Type Indicator, 2nd ed.* Palo Alto, CA: Consulting Psychologists Press.

Nation, R., & McLaughlin, B. (1986). Novices and experts: An information processing approach to the "good language learner" problem. *Applied Psycholinguistics, 7*, 41–56.

Nayak, N., Hansen, N., Krueger, N., & McLaughlin, B. (1987). *Language-learning strategies in monolingual and multilingual subjects.* Unpublished manuscript, University of California, Santa Cruz, Santa Cruz, CA.

Nisbett, R. E. (2003). *The geography of thought: How Asians and Westerners think differently... and why.* New York, NY: The Free Press.

Norman, E., Price, M. C., & Duff, S. C. (2006). Fringe consciousness in sequence learning: The influence of individual differences. *Consciousness and Cognition, 15*, 723–760.

Norman, E., Price, M. C., Duff, S. C., & Mentzoni, R. A. (2007). Gradations of awareness in a modified sequence learning task. *Consciousness and Cognition, 16*, 809–837.

Norris, J., & Ortega, L. (2003). Defining and measuring SLA. In C. J. Doughty & M. H. Long (Eds.), *The handbook of second language acquisition* (pp. 717–761). Malden, MA: Blackwell.

Onnis, L. (2012). The potential contribution of statistical learning to second language acquisition. In P. Rebuschat & J. N. Williams (Eds.), *Statistical learning and language acquisition* (pp. 203–235). Berlin: Mouton de Gruyter.

Ortega, L. (2009). *Understanding second language acquisition*. London, UK: Hodder Education.

Pacini, R., & Epstein, S. (1999). The relation of rational and experiential information processing styles to personality, basic beliefs, and the ratio-bias phenomenon. *Personality Processes and Individual Differences, 76*, 972–987.

Perruchet, P., & Pacton, S. (2006). Implicit learning and statistical learning: One phenomenon, two approaches. *Trends in Cognitive Sciences, 10*, 233–238.

Pothos, E. M. (2007). Theories of artificial grammar learning. *Psychological Bulletin, 133*, 227–244.

Pretz, J. E., Totz, K. S., & Kaufman, S. B. (2010). The effects of mood, cognitive style, and cognitive ability on implicit learning. *Learning and Individual Differences, 20*, 215–219.

Reber, A. S. (1967). Implicit learning of artificial grammars. *Journal of Learning and Verbal Behavior, 6*, 855–863.

Reber, A. S. (1989). Implicit learning and tacit knowledge. *Journal of Experimental Psychology: General, 118*, 219–235.

Reber, A. S. (1993). *Implicit learning and tacit knowledge: An essay on the cognitive unconscious*. Oxford, UK: Oxford University Press.

Reber, A. S. (2011). An epitaph for grammar: An abridged history. In C. Sanz & R. P. Leow (Eds.), *Implicit and explicit language learning: Conditions, processes, and knowledge in SLA and bilingualism* (pp. 23–34). Washington, DC: Georgetown University Press.

Reber, A. S., & Allen, R. (1978). Analogic and abstraction strategies in syntactic grammar learning: A functionalist interpretation. *Cognition, 6*, 189–221.

Reber, A. S., & Allen, R. (2000). Individual differences in implicit learning: Implications for the evolution of consciousness. In R. G. Kunzendorf & B. Wallace (Eds.), *Individual differences in conscious experience* (pp. 227–247). Philadelphia, PA: John Benjamins.

Reber, A. S., Walkenfeld, F. F., & Hernstadt, R. (1991). Implicit and explicit learning: Individual differences and IQ. *Journal of Experimental Psychology: Learning, Memory, and Cognition, 17*, 888–896.

Rebuschat, P., & Williams, J. (2012). Implicit and explicit knowledge in second language acquisition. *Applied Psycholinguistics, 33*, 829–856.

Robinson, P. (1994). *Learning simple and complex second language rules under implicit, incidental, rule-search, and instructed conditions*. Unpublished doctoral dissertation, University of Hawai'i, Honolulu, HI.

Robinson, P. (1995a). Aptitude, awareness, and the fundamental similarity of implicit and explicit second language learning. In R. Schmidt (Ed.), *Attention and awareness in foreign language learning* (pp. 303–357). Honolulu, HI: University of Hawai'i, National Foreign Language Resource Center.

Robinson, P. (1995b). Attention, memory, and the "noticing" hypothesis. *Language Learning, 45*, 283–331.

Robinson, P. (1996). Learning simple and complex second language rules under implicit, incidental, rule-search, and instructed conditions. *Studies in Second Language Acquisition, 18*, 27–67.

Robinson, P. (1997a). Individual differences and the fundamental similarity of implicit and explicit adult second language learning. *Language Learning, 47*, 45–99.

Robinson, P. (1997b). Generalizability and automaticity of second language learning under implicit, incidental, enhanced, and instructed conditions. *Studies in Second Language Acquisition, 19*, 223–247.

Robinson, P. (2002). Effects of individual differences in intelligence, aptitude, and working memory on adult incidental SLA: A replication and extension of Reber, Walkenfeld, and Hernstadt (1991). In P. Robinson (Ed.), *Individual differences and instructed language learning* (pp. 211–266). Amsterdam, Netherlands: John Benjamins.

Robinson, P. (2003). Attention and memory during SLA. In C. J. Doughty & M. H. Long (Eds.), *The handbook of second language acquisition* (pp. 631–678). Malden, MA: Blackwell.

Robinson, P. (2005). Cognitive abilities, chunk-strength, and frequency effects in implicit artificial grammar and incidental L2 learning: Replications of Reber, Walkenfeld, and Hernstadt (1991) and Knowlton and Squire (1996) and their relevance for SLA. *Studies in Second Language Acquisition, 27*, 235–268.

Robinson, P. (2007). Aptitudes, abilities, contexts, and practice. In R. M. DeKeyser (Ed.), *Practice in a second language: Perspectives from applied linguistics and psychology* (pp. 256–286). Cambridge, UK: Cambridge University Press.

Robinson, P. (2010). Implicit artificial grammar and incidental natural second language learning: How comparable are they? *Language Learning, 60*, 245–263.

Robinson, P., Mackey, A., Gass, S. M., & Schmidt, R. (2012). Attention and awareness in second language acquisition. In S. M. Gass & A. Mackey (Eds.), *The Routledge handbook of second language acquisition* (pp. 247–267). New York, NY: Routledge.

Schmidt, R. W. (1990). The role of consciousness in second language learning. *Applied Linguistics, 11*, 129–158.

Schmidt, R. (1994a). Deconstructing consciousness in search of useful definitions for applied linguistics. *AILA Review, 11*, 11–26.

Schmidt, R. (1994b). Implicit learning and the cognitive unconscious: Of artificial grammars and SLA. In N. C. Ellis (Ed.), *Implicit and explicit learning of languages* (pp. 165–209). London, UK: Academic Press.

Schmidt, R. (1995). Consciousness in foreign language learning: A tutorial on the role of attention and awareness in learning. In R. Schmidt (Ed.), *Attention and awareness in foreign language learning* (pp. 1–63). Honolulu, HI: University of Hawai'i, National Foreign Language Resource Center.

Schmidt, R. (2001). Attention. In P. Robinson (Ed.), *Cognition and second language instruction* (pp. 3–32). New York, NY: Cambridge University Press.

Schmidt, R. (2012). Attention, awareness, and individual differences in language learning. In W. M. Chan, K. N. Chin, S. Bhatt, & I. Walker (Eds.), *Perspectives on individual characteristics and foreign language education* (pp. 27–50). Boston, MA: Mouton de Gruyter.

Shanks, D. R. (2003). Attention and awareness in "implicit" sequence learning. In L. Jiménez (Ed.), *Attention and implicit learning* (pp. 11–42). Amsterdam/Philadelphia: John Benjamins.

Shanks, D. R., & St. John, M. F. (1994). Characteristics of dissociable human learning systems. *Behavioral and Brain Sciences, 17,* 367–447.

Tagarelli, K. M., Borges-Mota, M., & Rebuschat, P. (2011). The role of working memory in implicit and explicit language learning. In L. Carlson, C. Hölscher, & T. Shipley (Eds.), *Proceedings of the 33rd Annual Conference of the Cognitive Science Society* (pp. 2061–2066). Austin, TX: Cognitive Science Society.

Whiteside, S. P., & Lynam, D. R. (2001). The Five Factor Model and impulsivity: Using a structural model of personality to understand impulsivity. *Personality and Individual Differences, 30,* 669–689.

Williams, J. N. (2004). Implicit learning of form-meaning connections. In B. VanPatten, J. Williams, S. Rott, & M. Overstreet (Eds.), *Form-meaning connections in second language acquisition* (pp. 203–218). Mahwah, NJ: Lawrence Erlbaum.

Williams, J. N. (2005). Learning without awareness. *Studies in Second Language Acquisition, 27,* 269–304.

Williams, J. N. (2009). Implicit learning in second language acquisition. In W. C. Ritchie & T. K. Bhatia (Eds.), *The new handbook of second language acquisition* (pp. 319–353). Bingley, UK: Emerald Group Publishing Limited.

Williams, J. N. (2012). Working memory and SLA. In S. M. Gass & A. Mackey (Eds.), *The Routledge handbook of second language acquisition* (pp. 427–441). New York, NY: Routledge.

Wilson, S., & Hamlin, I. (2007). Implicit learning in a card prediction task. *European Journal of Parapsychology, 22,* 3–29.

Winter, B., & Reber, A. (1994). Implicit learning and the acquisition of natural languages. In N. C. Ellis (Ed.), *Implicit and explicit learning of languages* (pp. 115–145). San Diego, CA: Academic Press.

Woltz, D. J. (2003). Implicit cognitive processes as aptitudes for learning. *Educational Psychologist, 38,* 95–104.

Woolhouse, L. S., & Bayne, R. (2000). Personality and the use of intuition: Individual differences in strategy and performance on an implicit learning task. *European Journal of Personality, 14,* 157–169.

NFLRC monographs

A Cognitive Neuroscientific Approach to Studying the Role of Awareness in L2 Learning

Lester C. Loschky
Kansas State University

Michael Harrington
University of Queensland, Australia

Schmidt (1990, 1995) proposed a seminal theory of the role of awareness in second language (L2) learning, distinguishing two levels of awareness, noticing, argued to be necessary for L2 learning, and understanding, which was not. This theory has framed subsequent debate on the role of awareness in L2 learning, and the phrase noticing the gap has entered the common lexicon of L2 researchers. However, while Schmidt's distinction suggests hypotheses that are in principle testable, in practice, thorny difficulties have impeded progress. Theoretical difficulties arise in drawing the line between noticing and understanding, and methodological problems relate to the use of verbal protocols as the measure of understanding. Verbal protocols have created difficulties because measuring understanding depends on both how articulate the learner is and what the rater's definition of understanding is. We concur with Truscott and Sharwood Smith (2011) that one cannot non-arbitrarily distinguish between noticing and understanding and suggest that progress can be made by combining both under the heading of awareness. We also suggest that a better approach to measuring awareness is to use the cognitive neurophysiological approach of measuring event-related potentials (ERPs) while learners perform grammaticality judgment tasks (GJTs), together with behavioral measures of GJT sensitivity. If that approach is combined with provision of explicit or implicit feedback on each trial, one can observe differential awareness and differential learning within a single experiment. We briefly review recent studies that have investigated online L2 processing of grammatical violations using ERPs and shown evidence for both conscious and unconscious processing of such violations, as well as ERP studies of learners' online conscious and unconscious processing of their own response errors.

Loschky, L. C., & Harrington, M. (2013). A cognitive neuroscientific approach to studying the role of awareness in L2 learning. In J. M. Bergsleithner, S. N. Frota, & J. K. Yoshioka (Eds.), *Noticing and second language acquisition: Studies in honor of Richard Schmidt* (pp. 289–307). Honolulu: University of Hawai'i, National Foreign Language Resource Center.

By using the above methods, we believe it is possible to trace the trajectory of both implicit and explicit learning, to determine the role of awareness in L2 learning. However, based on the available evidence, we conclude that awareness is not necessary but is clearly facilitative of L2 learning.

Introduction

Schmidt's (e.g., Schmidt, 1990, 1995) theory of the role of awareness in second language (L2) learning has raised a number of critically important questions. Until recently, many of these questions have remained unanswered due in large part to limitations in research methodology and instrumentation. This has changed with recent advances in cognitive neuroscience in which neural and behavioral measures are providing an increasingly fine-grained picture of implicit learning processes, allowing researchers to move beyond more traditional research methods. With these changes we believe it is useful to revisit Schmidt's original awareness account and consider its viability in terms of what we are learning about the cognitive neuroscience of L2 learning.

Input is the primary stuff on which language acquisition works. At the heart of SLA theory is understanding the cognitive and linguistic mechanisms responsible for extracting from input that information used in acquisition, namely *intake* (Carroll, 2000). A key element in our understanding of how input gets converted to intake is the role played by *awareness*, or *consciousness*. The two terms are used in different contexts and for different purposes but both refer to the same phenomenon and will be used interchangeably here. A central issue concerns whether it is possible to learn an L2 without awareness. The issue of learning without awareness, or *implicit learning*, has long been debated in cognitive psychology. A key question has been whether abstract principles, such as the sequential regularities embodied in artificial grammars, can be learned implicitly, with research published that both supports (Frensch & Rünger, 2003; Nissen & Bullemer, 1987; Reber & Squire, 1998) and challenges the notion (Perruchet & Vintner, 2002; Shanks, 2003; Wilkinson & Shanks, 2004). The ongoing and vigorous debate in SLA over the possibility of implicit learning and the limits of awareness in learning has been heavily influenced by the seminal work of Schmidt. The broader research question that this chapter addresses concerns the role of conscious awareness, or what Schmidt termed *awareness at the level of understanding*, in learning L2 grammatical structures, and the roles of implicit and explicit error feedback in that process.

Schmidt was one of the first SLA researchers to systematically address the relationship between awareness and L2 learning (Schmidt, 1990, 1995; Schmidt & Frota, 1986). Schmidt proposed two levels of awareness when processing language, according to whether noticing or understanding is involved. Noticing was defined as the "conscious registration of the occurrence of some event," while understanding was the "recognition of a general principle, rule or pattern" (Schmidt, 1995, p. 29). Noticing was posited to be a necessary condition for the conversion of input into intake; that is, learning is not possible without it, while understanding was not. Although both levels were assumed to involve conscious awareness, they differ markedly in how that awareness was conceptualized and how it could be empirically observed. Both will be briefly described here.

Awareness at the level of noticing: The need for focal attention

According to Schmidt, noticing is the *conscious registration* of specific attended features of the target language. What does this conscious registration entail? Williams (2005) invokes Cowan's (1999) model of working memory as a framework for characterizing attention and memory (see also Robinson, 1995). In Cowan's model of working memory, representations are activated by external stimuli or internally generated associations. These activations dissipate quickly unless they receive focal attention, which serves to increase the activation level of a limited number of the representations. The attended-to representations remain active longer, are often of higher quality, and become available to a wider range of information processes than would otherwise be the case. Focal attention processes are partly voluntary but are also controlled by an attentional orienting system that automatically directs attention to unexpected stimuli. Thus the representations can be a novel combination of existing objects or a novel combination of features making up a novel object (Daheane & Naccache, 2001; Williams, 2005). For Cowan (1999, p. 89) focal attention is synonymous with conscious awareness (but see Koch and Tsuchiya, 2007, who have forcefully argued for the logical and empirical independence of consciousness and attention) and necessary for language use.

Focal attention also plays a key role in Schmidt's definition of noticing, which is generally understood as necessary for learning (Schmidt, 1995; Hama & Leow, 2010; Williams, 2005), though recently Schmidt seems to suggest that noticing may be best understood as having a graded, facilitative effect (Schmidt, 2001). The outcome of a single noticing event is an episodic, instance-based representation of a specific form-meaning link. These instances are the basis for the generalizations from which language rules emerge. The way in which these generalizations emerge is beyond the noticing account proper and most likely involves significant implicit learning (Hulstijn, 2005; Schmidt, 1995). It is the process of generalization, of rule-learning in general, that has come to be associated with noticing. The terms *noticing* and *noticing the gap* have entered into common usage by L2 researchers and teachers alike and are used in ways that ignore the original distinction Schmidt made between noticing, on the one hand, and the rule-learning process that can be reflected in metalinguistic awareness in the form of understanding, on the other (Egi, 2004; Izumi & Bigelow, 2000; Leow, 1997; Mackey, 2006; Nicholas, Lightbown, & Spada, 2001; Philp, 2003; Qi & Lapkin, 2001). More broadly, the term *noticing* has taken on the more general meaning of involving some sort of focus on form (Nassaji & Fotos, 2004; Ortega, 2009). Thus, among the wide and varied contributions that Dick Schmidt has made to the SLA and applied linguistics literature, the noticing account is arguably his most lasting legacy, but in a manner that bears only minimal resemblance to the original proposal.

The strong claim that noticing is necessary for learning provides a categorical prediction that is in principle open to disconfirmation. However, to date the noticing construct has resisted empirical validation or even attempts to test it. Studies that have discussed the proposal at length (e.g., Leow, 1997) only address it in theoretical terms. The strong claim about noticing is regarding the conditions needed for learning novel form-function mappings. But this is not a simple issue. As Truscott and Sharwood Smith (2011) note, the most problematic aspect of the noticing account concerns *what* is noticed, namely what constitutes an "event" or, for that matter, "an aspect of the stimuli" (Gass, 1988) or "features" (Robinson, 1995). The upper bound of a noticing event consists of general principles, rules, and patterns—the stuff that Schmidt considers to be the *understanding* that emerges from the noticing process. The lower bound might be simple perceptual recognition processes, for example that what is being heard is a human language, or is spoken by a young female, or that it is Brazilian Portuguese, etc. However, it is clear that Schmidt's concept of noticing means more than just a simple detection of perceptual aspects of the current input. Instead, what is being registered must have something to do with formal linguistic knowledge of the input. This could be, for example, that the perceived utterance is a noun, or a modifier, or a grammatical affix like English *-s* (Schmidt, 1995). Noticing requires the form be processed in such a way that it is consciously registered (i.e., recognized) but without involving recognition of any rules or patterns (which would then be called *understanding*). And this is presumably only in the case of noticing a morphosyntactic form. Learning meaning/semantics is another matter entirely and one that seems to be ignored in the theory of noticing (see Truscott & Sharwood Smith, 2011, pp. 14–15). However, as Truscott and Sharwood Smith (2011) note, it is hard to imagine a case of noticing something morphosyntactic that involves no understanding of the rules or patterns of the language. And we should add that such understanding would relate to both the target L2 as well as the learner's native or other existing languages. Noticing that the perceived object is a noun implies an understanding of *nouniness* and the language structure in which it exists.

Given these issues, it is understandable that researchers interested in the role of awareness in L2 learning have ignored noticing and focused instead on the role of awareness at the level of understanding. But this leaves open the question as to whether the noticing account is testable. Is it possible to operationalize noticing in a way that in principle separates noticing from understanding such that unambiguous evidence for its role in learning can be established? Truscott and Sharwood Smith suggest that it is not, that the distinction between noticing and understanding is "probably impossible to operationalize in any nonarbitrary way" (Truscott & Sharwood Smith, 2011, p. 37). Likewise, as discussed above, setting the lower bound of noticing seems equally arbitrary. For example, Leow (1997) operationally defined noticing as "*some form of subjective awareness* of new targeted linguistic forms in L2 data as revealed in learners' think aloud protocols" [emphasis added] (p. 474). While we laud this attempt at operationally defining this elusive construct, we feel that any such operational definitions necessarily depend on 1) how articulate the learner is, 2) the researcher's interpretation of the learner's verbalization, and 3) where the researcher decides the lower bound is. Thus, operationally defining noticing and distinguishing it from understanding become inherently subjective and noisy.

Awareness at the level of understanding

Awareness in Schmidt's account also plays a role in learning at the metalinguistic level at which the learner consciously recognizes rules or patterns in the input. Awareness at the level of understanding often (but not always) involves explicit learning and thus plays a facilitative but not necessary role in learning. Implicit learning is also assumed to play an important role (Schmidt, 1995, 2001). From the time Schmidt's original proposal appeared, researchers have been interested in showing whether, and to what degree, awareness at the level of understanding is needed in L2 learning. The problem has been approached from two perspectives. Experimental research has sought evidence for the role of understanding using implicit learning designs. In these studies learners are trained on a task involving materials that embody abstract grammatical rules unrelated to the task and then given a posttest to assess if the rules can be used correctly (DeKeyser, 1995; Hama & Leow, 2010; Robinson, 1995; Williams, 2005). Metalinguistic self-report responses are also elicited to assess if the learner was aware of what was learned. Evidence that participants can perform above chance at test, without being able to provide any kind of verbal report as to the nature of the rule or pattern, is taken as evidence that learning without awareness is possible (DeKeyser, 1995; Hama & Leow, 2010; Robinson, 1995; Williams, 2005). For example, Williams (2005) reported a statistically significant learning effect in a posttest for participants who otherwise indicated no awareness of any underlying regularities for modifier-noun combinations in an artificial language learning task. Alternatively, above-chance performance on posttests only by participants who are also able to verbalize to some degree knowledge of an underlying rule or pattern is taken as evidence that learning without understanding is impossible (Hama & Leow, 2010; Leow, 2000). Both approaches rely crucially on verbal self-report. The verbal reports can be obtained *off-line*, elicited as part of the posttest as done by Williams (2005), or they can be collected *online* in the form of verbal reports while the participant is undergoing training, as in Hama and Leow (2010). Verbal self-reports can be informative, but the methodology also has significant limitations as a window on underlying cognitive processes as discussed above.

Interactionist researchers have been interested in understanding as it relates to the recognition, uptake, and integration of recasts in interactional feedback (Gass & Varonis, 1994; Izumi & Bigelow, 2000; Long, Inagaki, & Ortega, 1998; Mackey, 2006; Mackey & Philp, 1998; Nicholas et al., 2001; Philp, 2003). However, as indicated above, some of the latter (e.g., Mackey, 2006; Mackey & Philp, 1998; Philp, 2003) use the term *noticing* for what could also be taken to mean *understanding*. A now substantial research literature has established that recast behavior is pervasive in NS-NNS interactions, but the role of understanding in the uptake of recasts by learners, as well as the effect of recast behavior on learning outcomes, is highly variable (Mackey & Goo, 2007). As is the case for the experimental research, evidence for understanding has come from verbal self-report.

The varying and sometimes conflicting evidence from the experimental and interactionist research as to the role of understanding in L2 rule learning reflects both conceptual and methodological limitations. At a conceptual level is the fact that, as we have discussed above, it is difficult to draw a line between *noticing* and *understanding*. This then leads to methodological complications in separating the two. In particular, verbal self-reports provide only limited evidence of learner sensitivity to grammatical patterns and regularities. Given that even highly trained linguists often cannot agree as to what a correct statement of a grammatical rule is, it seems that reportability of a rule may be a poor measure of understanding by learners. Taken together, these conceptual and methodological limitations lead us to suggest dropping Schmidt's distinction between *noticing* and *understanding*. Given that noticing was defined as "conscious registration of the occurrence of some event" and understanding was defined as the "[conscious] recognition of a general principle, rule or pattern" (Schmidt, 1995, p. 29), if we drop any attempt to distinguish between noticing and understanding, we are left with the role of consciousness, or *awareness* in learning, namely the limits of implicit learning. Truscott and Sharwood Smith (2011) note that the noticing construct has had no counterpart in the implicit learning literature (p. 12), despite attempting to account for the same problem of how abstract knowledge can be acquired without awareness of some kind. The lack of progress to date in providing empirical evidence for noticing may simply reflect the fact that it doesn't exist.

Recent work in experimental cognitive neuroscience has sought to establish if and how awareness contributes to L2 learning outcomes at a neurobehavioral level (Morgan-Short, Sanz, Steinhauer, & Ullman, 2010; Tanner, McLaughlin, Herschensohn, & Osterhout, 2012). Evidence from event-related brain potentials (ERPs) is being used to test the claim that L2 grammar learning can take place outside the awareness of the individual, such that it does not rely on verbal self-report (Davidson & Indefrey, 2008; McLaughlin et al., 2010; Tokowicz & MacWhinney, 2005), though as we will see, some sort of overt behavior of the learner is still required to substantiate claims about awareness.

An important element in this research is the systematic manipulation of feedback and the measurement of error processes as a window on the role of awareness in learning.

Roles of implicit and explicit feedback in learning

There is compelling evidence that negative feedback, of both the explicit and implicit types, facilitates L2 grammar learning. Tomasello and Herron (1989) found that negative feedback on elicited L1–L2 transfer errors, using the garden path technique, produced better learning at three retention intervals (from 1 to 17 days) than simply explaining what errors to avoid. Likewise, Carroll, Roberge, and Swain (1992) and Carroll and Swain (1993) found that four different feedback conditions, ranging from implicit (telling learners they were wrong or asking if they were sure) to explicit (with grammatical explanations) all produced superior learning of the dative alternation in English compared to a no-feedback control condition, but that explicit feedback was most effective. Finally, Rosa and Leow (2004) compared the effects of several types of explicit feedback (with grammatical explanations) with the effects of an implicit feedback condition (only reporting if a response was incorrect) and found that all feedback produced better long-term learning of several Spanish "contrary-to-fact" past constructions than simply reading (processing) the sentences without feedback. Again, however, the explicit feedback was most effective in producing learning. The facilitative impact of negative feedback on L2 grammar learning evident in these studies has been more broadly established in meta-analyses that have shown the superiority of providing negative feedback over less explicit (Norris & Ortega, 2000) or no error-focused feedback (Russell & Spada, 2006). Furthermore, the theoretical mechanism of feedback on learning has generally been thought of in terms of comparing the learner's current L2 representations with those in the input, based on the feedback (Carroll & Swain, 1993; Rosa & Leow, 2004; Tomasello & Herron, 1989). Thus, feedback is assumed to help convert input into intake at some level of awareness.

Cognitive neuroscientific evidence for awareness

The relationship between awareness and learning is complex, and evidence for both learner awareness and learning outcomes may be expected to be as well. Likewise, evidence for the effect of the one on the other is sensitive to a range of developmental, linguistic, cognitive, and task factors. As such, the tools used to date provide only a coarse-grained view of the underlying processes. While the use of *online* measures as represented in the concurrent verbal report technique provide the required focus on the underlying cognitive processes, more sophisticated tools are now available that will allow a more rigorous, millisecond-scale investigation of this domain. We will focus here on the use of event-related potentials (ERPs), which are a class of neurophysiological indices that hold significant promise for examining the potential role of awareness in learning. As we will discuss, ERPs can be used to both gauge the degree to which an L2 learner consciously or unconsciously detects a specific grammatical violation in real time (Rossi, Gugler, Friederici, & Hahne, 2006; Tokowicz & MacWhinney, 2005) and the degree to which the learner is aware of having committed an error in real time (Endrass,

Reuter, & Kathmann, 2007; Ganushchak & Schiller, 2009; Gehring, Goss, Coles, Meyer, & Donchin, 1993).

ERPs provide online indicators of linguistic processing on a millisecond time scale. ERPs are electroencephalogram (EEG) signals (brain waves) that have been averaged over trials sharing the same experimental conditions and time-locked (i.e., matched) to specific events (e.g., stimulus or response onset). Specific ERPs have been shown to be reliably associated with specific processing functions. Of particular interest here, three ERP waveforms, the LAN, the N400, and the P600, have been shown to be associated with syntactic processing. The LAN is an early left anterior negatively deflected waveform that peaks roughly 300 ms after stimulus presentation, the N400 is a negatively deflected waveform that peaks at roughly 400 ms after stimulus presentation, and the P600 is a positively deflected waveform that peaks roughly 600 ms after stimulus presentation. The LAN appears to be automatic and is associated with detecting morphosyntactic violations (Rossi et al., 2006), though it is not always found, even in native speakers (Tanner et al., 2012). The N400 is also relatively automatic and is generally associated with semantic processing difficulty (Kutas & Hillyard, 1983; West & Holcomb, 2002) but is also associated with morphosyntactic processing difficulty in less linguistically proficient individuals (McLaughlin et al., 2010; Moreno, Rodríguez-Fornells, & Laine, 2008; Tanner et al., 2012). The P600 is more controlled and is associated with syntactic processing difficulty, such as when encountering an ungrammatical constituent in a sentence (Davidson & Indefrey, 2008; McLaughlin et al., 2010; Rossi et al., 2006).

A cross-sectional study by Rossi and colleagues showed that the LAN and P600 indicated developmental changes in L2 learners of German and Italian (Rossi et al., 2006). See Figure 1 for results for German learners. Specifically, when encountering ungrammatical items in a grammaticality judgment task (GJT), low-proficiency L2 learners did not produce the LAN and produced delayed P600s as shown on the right side of the figure, whereas both the high-proficiency learners on the left and native speakers, not shown, produced similar LANs and P600s. These ERP results were also consistent with the grammaticality judgments, which were less accurate for the beginning L2 learners than the advanced learners and native speakers. Thus, ERPs provide an online measure of L2 learners' awareness of grammatical violations prior to making any overt response. In sum, these ERPs are evidence of the purest sort of grammatical competence in the L2 that one can hope to measure, are objectively measurable, and do not require introspection. As a caution, though, it should also be noted that individual differences in L2 ERP performance between L2 learners and relative to the L1 baseline can be considerable (Morgan-Short et al., 2010; Tanner et al., 2012). Specifically, it has been shown repeatedly that L2 learners who are initially learning that an L2 structure is ungrammatical will often show an N400 to it but that with time, as their learning progresses, they switch to showing a P600 (McLaughlin et al., 2010; Tanner et al., 2012). This transition, then, between N400 to P600 to L2 grammatical violations is a measure of learning. But if the ERPs of learners showing N400s are averaged with learners showing P600s, the result will mask both patterns (Tanner et al., 2012). This potential problem requires careful attention when interpreting ERP outcomes.

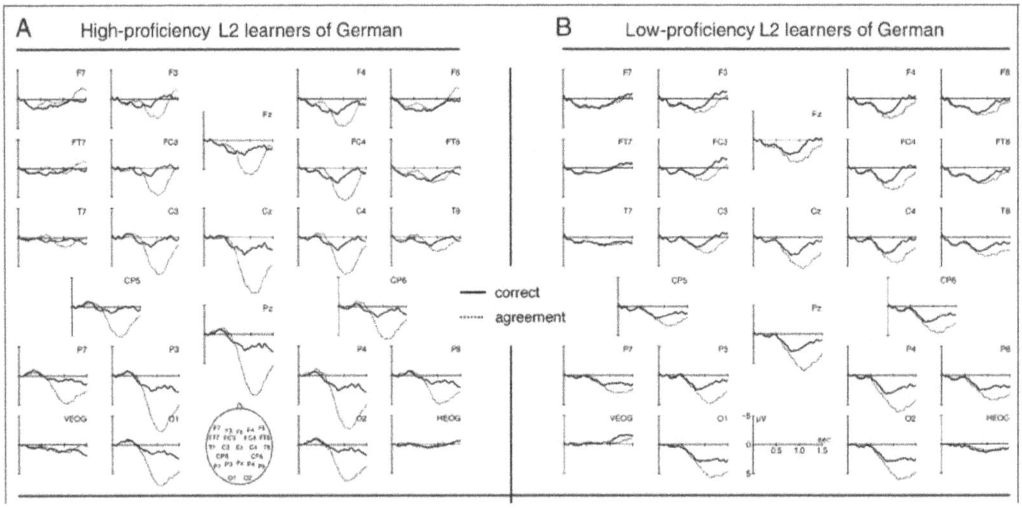

Figure 1. Adapted from Rossi et al. (2006).[1] Grand average ERPs at 25 electrode locations for (A) 16 high-proficiency learners and (B) 19 low-proficiency learners of German in a grammaticality judgment task. ERPs are shown for sentences having incorrect agreement (*agreement*) versus sentences that are correct (*correct*), with waveforms relative to verb onset (0 msec) up to 1500 msec later. The 25 electrode locations include F(frontal), C (central), T (temporal), P (parietal), and O (occipital) locations, each with numbered subscripts. In this figure, negative voltage is plotted upward.

The Rossi et al. (2006) study showed cross-sectionally that ERPs were related to the accuracy results of a GJT. Their findings are consistent with other studies, both cross-sectional (Tanner et al., 2012) and longitudinal (McLaughlin et al., 2010; Morgan-Short et al., 2010; Osterhout, McLaughlin, Pitkänen, Frenck-Mestre, & Molinaro, 2006) showing that L2 learners' P600 amplitudes are highly correlated with their GJT sensitivity. This suggests, then, that the P600 may be an online measure of L2 learners' awareness of grammatical violations.

Given the above results, the skeptical reader might ask why one should go to the trouble of measuring ERPs if they tell us little more than the GJT task itself, except perhaps indicating which particular word is ungrammatical (based on the time-locked ERP response to it)? Put another way, it would seem far simpler and cheaper to simply ask L2 learners to, say, circle the ungrammatical words in each test sentence, in addition to making the standard binary grammaticality judgment. However, not all ERP studies of L2 learners carrying out a GJT have shown ERPs to correlate with conscious behavioral measures. Tokowicz and MacWhinney (2005) and McLaughlin, Osterhout, and Kim (2004) both found ERPs showing implicit knowledge of the L2, which the learners were unable to demonstrate explicitly. Specifically, the studies found P600s in response to morphosyntactic violations (Tokowicz & MacWhinney, 2005) or P400s in response to lexical violations (McLaughlin et al., 2004), which were not reflected in sensitivity on a grammaticality judgment task or a word/non-word judgment task respectively. Thus, assuming

1 Rossi, S., Gugler, M. F., Friederici, A. D., & Hahne, A. (2006). The impact of proficiency on syntactic second-language processing of German and Italian: Evidence from event related potentials. *Journal of Cognitive Neuroscience, 18*, 2030–2048. MIT Press Journals. Reprinted by permission of MIT Press Journals. © 2006 Massachusetts Institute of Technology.

that sensitivity in the GJT and word/non-word tasks reflected learners' conscious awareness, the ERPs indicated implicit knowledge of which learners were unaware.[2]

Therefore, using ERPs together with behavioral responses (such as sensitivity in a GJT) allow us to distinguish four logically possible combinations of L2 grammatical violation processing and awareness, as shown in Table 1. Note that one combination would not plausibly occur: (–) Processing of violation and (+) Awareness—a learner could not plausibly be aware of the violation upon reading it without processing the violation as such. However, the other three logical possibilities are of great interest. As discussed above, there is clear evidence of processing of L2 violations, as shown by ERPs, both with and without awareness, as indicated by L2 judgment task sensitivity or the lack thereof. And, of course, prior to any learning of the L2 structures, there is a lack of either processing of the violation as such and naturally no awareness of it as being a violation. This serves as a critically important baseline condition to compare the other two combinations of interest.

Table 1. Combinations of L2 violation processing and violation awareness, and associated outcomes for ERPs and L2 judgment task sensitivity (with example references)

	(+) awareness of violation	**(–) awareness of violation**
(+) processing of violation	(+) ERPs & (+) L2 JT sensitivity (McLaughlin et al., 2010; Morgan-Short et al., 2010; Rossi et al., 2006; Tanner et al., 2012)	(+) ERPs & (–) L2 JT sensitivity (McLaughlin et al., 2004; Tokowicz & MacWhinney, 2005)
(–) processing of violation	*(–) ERPs & (+) L2 JT sensitivity (*This would not plausibly occur)	(–) ERPs & (–) L2 JT sensitivity (Davidson & Indefrey, 2008; McLaughlin et al., 2004; McLaughlin et al., 2010)

note. (+)=present; (–)=absent; ERPs=event–related potentials to an L2 violation; L2 JT=L2 judgment task (e.g., grammaticality judgment, or word/non–word judgment)

ERPs can also be associated with processing of one's own performance errors in, for example, a GJT (Davidson & Indefrey, 2008). We argue that awareness of one's GJT performance errors should indicate awareness in Schmidt's terms. Specifically, knowing that one's GJT response was an error implies that a) one has a representation of the target language structure in question; b) one has a representation of the structure in the stimulus sentence about which one made a grammaticality judgment, and c) in the case of a "miss" in the grammaticality judgment (i.e., a response of "grammatical" when one should have responded "ungrammatical"), one has consciously detected a difference between the two, just after making a response.

Of particular importance are two well-known ERPs—the error-related negativity (Ne) (Gehring et al., 1993) and the error positivity (Pe) (Nieuwenhuis, Ridderinkhof, Blom, Band, & Kok, 2001). The Ne has been intensively studied over the last two decades and is known to be produced roughly 80–100 ms after an error has been committed, to increase in amplitude as a greater emphasis is put on task accuracy, and to be associated with efforts at error recovery (Gehring et al., 1993). However, more recent research has shown that while many errors are associated with the Ne, only errors for which the subject shows awareness

2 An even stronger argument along these lines would be to aggregate the ERP data not only on whether the L2 structure was grammatical or not, but also based on whether the grammaticality judgment responses were correct or not. If the same native-like P600s were found on ungrammatical sentence trials that were responded to as "ungrammatical" or "grammatical," it would most clearly show the disconnect between implicit processing and awareness (Tanner et al., 2012).

produce the Pe (e.g., Endrass et al., 2007; Nieuwenhuis et al., 2001). In particular, the late Pe, which occurs ~600 ms after the response, is most clearly associated with error awareness (e.g., by making a second response indicating that their first response was an error) and subsequent error compensation (i.e., self-correcting) (Endrass et al., 2007). Thus, the Ne and Pe together allow us to distinguish between unconscious and conscious error processing.

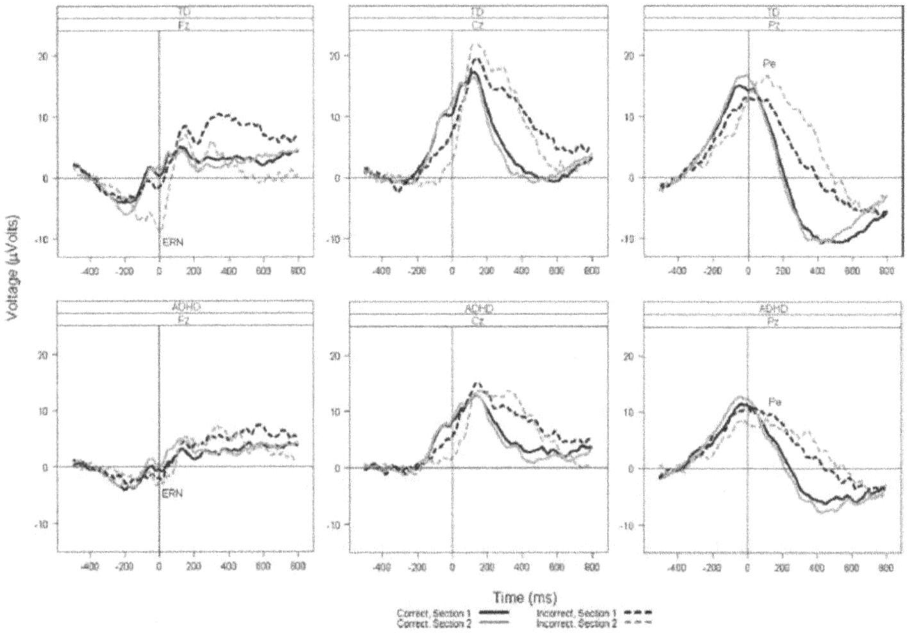

Response-locked ERPs. ERP waveforms time locked to the response (0 ms) are depicted at Fz, Cz and Pz for the informative condition. For both the first and second sections of the task separate waveforms are shown for correct and incorrect responses.

Figure 2. Adapted from Groen et al. (2008).[3] Grand average ERPs, for correct and incorrect responses in a probabilistic learning task, both early in learning (Section 1) and later in learning (Section 2), by typically developing children (TD) and children with unmedicated ADHD. Waveforms are relative to the time of response (0 ms) and range from –400 msec before to 800 msec after. Waveforms are plotted for three electrode locations, Fz (frontal), Cz (central), and Pz (parietal). "ERN" is another name for Ne, and "Pe" is Pe. In this figure, negative voltage is plotted downward.

Other research by Groen and colleagues has compared the roles of individual differences in attentional capabilities and the effects of learning on error awareness as indicated by the Ne and Pe (Groen et al., 2008). Their study compared children with unmedicated ADHD with typically developing children and found that those with unmedicated ADHD showed a trend toward smaller Ne waveforms and significantly smaller Pe waveforms, indicating a clear lack of explicit awareness of their errors (compare the 1st and 2nd rows of Figure 2). Of critical importance for the study of learning, Groen et al. had the children perform a probabilistic learning task

3 Reprinted from *Clinical Neurophysiology, 119*, Groen, Y., Wijers, A. A., Mulder, L. J. M., Waggeveld, B., Minderaa, R. B., & Althaus, M., Error and feedback processing in children with ADHD and children with autistic spectrum disorder: An EEG event-related potential study. Copyright (2008), with permission from Elsevier.

and showed that the typically developing children learned more and showed larger Ne and Pe waveforms, indicating greater awareness of their response errors, as learning progressed. This is shown in Figure 2 by a comparison of the gray broken lines for errors in section 2 with the black broken lines for errors in section 1, particularly in the left column for the Pz electrode location, which is over parietal areas, and is known to produce stronger Pe waveforms (Endrass, Klawohn, Preuss, & Kathmann, 2012; Endrass et al., 2007). Conversely, the children with unmedicated ADHD learned less and showed less development of awareness of when they committed response errors, as shown by the corresponding comparisons in the bottom row of Figure 2.

These results are important for our current discussion for several reasons. First, they show that a person's assumed attentional capabilities are positively correlated with their degree of awareness of their response errors (as indicated by the amplitude of their Pe). Second, such awareness seems to be correlated with how much is learned. Third, at a methodological level, the results provide a neurophysiological correlate of online learning in terms of increasing amplitude of the Pe when errors are made. And, indeed, studies with L2 learners have found large Ne waveforms when making L2 speech errors (Ganushchak & Schiller, 2009) or L2 GJT errors (Davidson & Indefrey, 2008).

In sum, by measuring the above ERPs, we can track L2 learners' moment-by-moment implicit and explicit processing of L2 structural violations (i.e., with and without awareness) and their implicit and explicit processing of their own performance errors (i.e., with and without awareness). In doing so, we can provide a profile of developing L2 structural knowledge and learners' awareness. Specifically, such ERP data indicate whether there is movement of the learners' interlanguage towards the target language, even when the learner is not yet aware of it. Likewise, we can determine whether this movement includes intermediate steps in which the learner's error responses are initially not processed as such, when the learner knows nothing of the structure, but gradually change to being implicitly processed, and then explicitly processed (with awareness).

GJT data is particularly suited to this undertaking. The ability to focus on the processing of target linguistic features while performing a discrete yes/no judgment task provides the degree of task control needed for collecting and interpreting ERP results. Although the sensitivity of binary GJT responses to gradient grammatical rules has been questioned (e.g., Schütze, 1996), the fact remains that most structures lend themselves to categorical judgments as to whether a sentence is grammatical or ungrammatical. Furthermore, recent evidence suggests a close correspondence in performance between binary and gradient grammaticality judgments across sentences that differ in the degree of agreement among native speakers (e.g., Bader & Haussler, 2010). While acknowledging the potential limitations, we also believe the GJT provides an important window on linguistic processing.

Key questions for further research

Recent developments in the cognitive neuroscience of L2 learning offer better methods and evidence for investigating whether awareness is necessary or only facilitative of L2 learning. Such studies provide rigorous, implicit, online, neurophysiological measures of L2 structural processing and learning. Together with standard behavioral measures of sensitivity to such structures and learning, one can address the following research questions:

- Is it possible to learn L2 grammatical structures without awareness?
- Does awareness facilitate learning L2 grammatical structures?
- How does implicit and explicit error feedback influence awareness of L2 grammatical structures and L2 learning?

How do we research awareness? Online processing and post-processing performance

Let us consider the minimal experimental design that one would need to address the research questions above. One would need to examine learning within a short time frame such that one could see the processes of turning input into intake as they unfold in real time. A good way to do this would be to use both behavior in a GJT and one's implicit measures of awareness via ERPs as dependent measures. Such a study would likely use a pretest/posttest design, with experimental treatment in the middle, to measure learning. In order to quickly examine learning, one could provide feedback to the GJT on every trial during the experimental treatment, thus allowing the learner to compare their representations of the target language rules/patterns with those in the input. The feedback could be either explicit or implicit (a la Rosa & Leow, 2004). We would expect that learning would vary as a function of the type of feedback, with explicit feedback producing quicker learning. Ideally, feedback would be given via an automated computer-assisted instruction program (e.g., Rosa & Leow, 2004) in order to ensure that it is given in exactly the same ways to all participants.

A spread of proficiency levels is also important. One would ideally include subjects from three levels: lower L2 proficiency, higher L2 proficiency, and a native speaker control group. Having the two L2 proficiency levels would allow one to see if the effects of the feedback were stronger for one proficiency level than another. However, with sufficient pilot testing, one could eliminate one or the other proficiency level. The native speaker control group would be absolutely necessary, however, to provide baseline data to compare with the L2 learners and would only take the pretest and posttest, or, assuming that performance would be at ceiling, could take the test only once.

The dependent variables would include the accuracy of the grammaticality judgment responses, as well as the reaction times for the responses (because when people are aware they have committed an error, their responses tend to be slower on the following trial than when they are unaware of having committed an error) (Endrass et al., 2007). Importantly, EEG data would be collected throughout the experiment, including the pretest and posttest. One would analyze this data in terms of ERPs that are time-locked to two specific events: 1) the onset of the ungrammatical word in each GJT sentence and 2) the subject's manual response ("grammatical" or "ungrammatical") for that sentence. The logical outcomes for the responses and ERPs to grammatical and ungrammatical stimuli are set out in the tree diagram shown in Figure 3.

Of particular interest would be the ERPs and responses to ungrammatical stimuli (the right half of the tree diagram in Figure 3). For the first event, the onset of the first ungrammatical word, one could determine whether or not the subject shows the LAN, N400, or P600 ERPs, indicating whether the ungrammaticality has been processed and to what level (since N400s indicate shallow processing of an ungrammatical item) (McLaughlin et al., 2010). As discussed in Table 1, at the earliest stage before learning anything about the L2 structure, learners should show no processing of an L2 violation (e.g., no P600) nor any awareness of it as a violation (e.g., no sensitivity in the GJT). Furthermore, after learning, they should show both processing of the violation (e.g., a strong P600) and awareness of it (sensitivity in the GJT). The interesting question is how often one finds cases of implicit, unaware processing of the violation (i.e., a strong P600 but no sensitivity in the GJT). In addition, one can ask whether implicit processing of the violation is optionally an intermediate stage of learning that occurs prior to full awareness. Additionally, we could ask how the provision of implicit versus explicit feedback influences the implicit versus explicit processing of the violations.

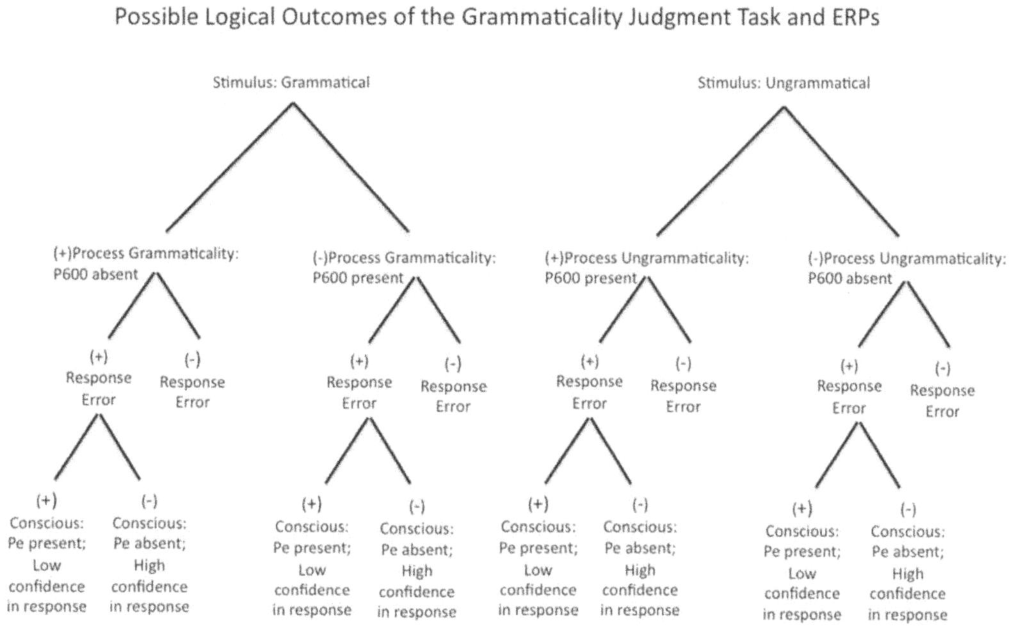

Figure 3. Possible logical outcomes for grammatical and ungrammatical sentences in a grammaticality judgment task. Outcomes include ERPs and overt responses. (+)=present, (–)=absent. P600=the P600 ERP waveform, associated with processing of syntactic violations. Pe=the Pe ERP waveform, associated with consciousness of oneself having committed an error.

For the second event, the subject's overt response ("grammatical" or "ungrammatical"), one could determine whether the subject shows either an Ne or Pe when making a GJT error. To help identify the Pe, we would also have learners rate their confidence in each grammaticality judgment. There are three logical possibilities for what we might observe: 1) neither an Ne nor a Pe, indicating no processing of the error; 2) an Ne but no Pe, indicating implicit processing of the error, without awareness; or 3) both an Ne and a Pe, indicating full awareness of having committed an error. (Note that all of this is prior to receiving feedback on the response.) As with the online ERP responses to the L2 violation discussed above, a key question is whether implicit processing of one's response errors (Ne without Pe) is an optional intermediate stage of learning that occurs prior to full awareness of one's errors (Ne and Pe). Alternatively, the learning progression could bypass the implicit error processing stage. One hypothesis is that when given only implicit error feedback, error processing progresses more slowly and includes the intermediate implicit error processing stage, whereas when given explicit error feedback, learners may jump straight from no processing of their response errors (neither Ne nor Pe) to full awareness of them (showing both an Ne and Pe). Finally, an interesting question is whether those learners who show robust Pe waveforms to their own errors, namely awareness of their errors, learn more quickly and make fewer errors than those learners who show only the Ne, indicating implicit, unaware error processing.

Davidson and Indefrey (2008) embodies key elements of our ideal study, though with some important differences, especially with regard to the feedback condition. In their study they found rapid learning of a target grammatical structure (in L2 German by L1 Dutch speakers). At pretest they showed neither sensitivity in the GJT nor a P600 (or LAN) to the ungrammatical items. However, over the course of the single session experiment, they showed learning (increased sensitivity in the GJT) and the development of a P600 to the ungrammatical items. Thus, learning was shown, and it was associated with conscious processing of the grammatical violations. In addition, they found no Ne or Pe responses to the learners' errors at pretest but strong Ne- and Pe-like waveforms during training, and to a lesser degree, during the posttest a week later. The error-related waveforms were found to be strongest for those who showed the greatest increase in sensitivity in the GJT. Furthermore, this relationship remained after a regression analysis had accounted for learners' L2 proficiency. This result is important because it suggests that increased processing of one's errors was associated with increased learning. However, because it was a correlational finding, we do not know the direction of causation (i.e., whether increased processing of one's errors caused greater learning or whether greater learning caused greater processing of one's errors or if a third factor caused both).

The Davidson and Indefrey (2008) experiment is an excellent example of the type of study we believe is needed to investigate the role of awareness in L2 learning. Nevertheless, there were several aspects of the study that limit the conclusions that can be drawn concerning the nature of the learning outcomes observed. There was no evidence of unconscious learning, since the increases in both the P600 and Ne were associated with increases in GJT sensitivity. As such, the Davidson and Indefrey (2008) study provides evidence of awareness being positively associated with L2 learning but does not rule out the potential role of unconscious learning. Specifically, just because a study shows no evidence of unconscious learning does not prove that unconscious learning is impossible. (Absence of evidence is not evidence of absence.) Indeed, we have already cited ERP evidence of implicit learning—processing of violations without accompanying conscious GJT sensitivity (McLaughlin et al., 2004; Tokowicz & MacWhinney, 2005)—namely, learning without awareness. Furthermore, those studies only add to the available literature showing implicit learning. Schmidt's (1990, 1995) theory posits that understanding is not necessary and admits implicit learning as an example of learning without understanding. However, if we also accept Truscott and Sharwood Smith's (2011) argument that we cannot meaningfully distinguish between noticing and understanding, then we may conclude that awareness is not necessary for L2 learning. This is consistent with the evidence shown by McLaughlin et al. (2004) and Tokowicz and MacWhinney (2005).

Thus, the data from Davidson and Indefrey (2008) can be said to most clearly support the facilitative role of awareness in error processing, particularly as indicated by the fact that the Ne and Pe were strongly positively correlated with increases in GJT sensitivity. However, even here, the data is naggingly equivocal. Specifically, Davidson and Indefrey's (2008) Pe, which is associated with conscious processing of one's errors, was abnormally early, occurring roughly 150 ms after an erroneous response, whereas the Pe usually occurs at roughly 600 ms after the error. Indeed, it is the later Pe that is most closely associated with consciousness (Endrass et al., 2007). The lack of a clear Pe means that learners' error processing waveforms in Davidson and Indefrey's (2008) study cannot be definitively associated with awareness of errors. Interestingly, Ganuschak et al. (2009) also failed to report Pe waveforms in their study of L2 ERPs to speech errors but did report strong Ne waveforms. Whether normal Pe waveforms are found in L2 learners is clearly an issue that begs for careful investigation in further such studies.

As noted earlier, Davidson and Indefrey (2008) did not manipulate the type of feedback (explicit vs. implicit) that was provided. This might have produced differential levels of awareness of both violations and learner response errors, and differential learning outcomes.

The behavioral data thus far suggest that explicit feedback is more effective for learning than implicit feedback (Carroll & Swain, 1993; Rosa & Leow, 2004). This suggests at least a facilitative role for awareness for L2 learning, on the assumption that explicit error negative feedback engages the learner's awareness. Nevertheless, L2 learning studies combining both types of error feedback with ERP recordings are needed to more precisely determine the relationships between a) the two types of feedback, b) learners' conscious error processing (Pe & Ne) and unconscious error processing (Ne without Pe), and c) learners' gains in GJT sensitivity (i.e., turning input into intake).

Finally, future research along the lines suggested here should benefit from doing trial-level analyses of their ERP data using multi-level modeling (Zayas, Greenwald, & Osterhout, 2011). Such analyses would allow one to determine the effects of, say, P600 amplitude on a given trial on subsequent GJT accuracy, or the effect of Pe amplitude on a given trial on trial accuracy on the following trial. In this way we can begin to truly understand the role of awareness on single trials on L2 learning.

Summary and conclusion

We have sketched out a line of research that we believe can answer important questions raised by Schmidt's theory of the role of awareness in L2 learning that have not yet been adequately addressed. Specifically, by measuring changes in L2 learners' ERPs over the course of many trials, both during the processing of target grammatical structures and immediately after making response errors, it is possible to determine the degree to which L2 learning occurs without conscious awareness within the time frame of a single experiment. Similarly, one can also determine the degree to which explicit feedback, conscious awareness of grammaticality, and conscious awareness of one's response errors facilitate L2 learning. Importantly, such questions are now beginning to be addressed using robust physiological measures capable of showing both conscious and unconscious processing of input and one's responses to it (Davidson, 2010).

So where does this leave Schmidt's original formulations? As we note, it is probably impossible to distinguish between noticing and understanding as originally proposed, largely due to difficulties in conceptualizing and operationalizing each relative to the other. Schmidt has previously argued that awareness at the level of noticing is necessary for learning, while awareness at the level of understanding is not, because of the role that implicit (unaware) learning can play in our conscious understanding. However, consistent with more recent discussions by Schmidt (2012), it seems to us that awareness, at whichever level one wants to define it, is best understood as *facilitative* of learning. It seems that the effect of awareness on learning operates more in terms of a continuum (more or less learning) than a dichotomy (no or some learning).

In our discussion of an approach to studying the relationship between awareness and L2 learning, we have deliberately left out specific details such as the target L2, the particular grammatical structures to be tested, etc. Such details are of course critical to the success of any such study. However, our purpose in this paper is to draw attention to what we believe is a useful approach to studying the role of awareness in L2 learning and the logic behind it. Indeed, in the words of Greenwald (2012), "there is nothing so theoretical as a good method." That is, in science it is often the case that long-standing theoretical debates are only settled when an appropriate method is developed to test between competing hypotheses. We believe that the methods discussed here will be able to do just that with regard to the debate on the role of awareness in L2 learning—a debate that Dick Schmidt has played a seminal role in shaping.

References

Bader, M., & Haussler, J. (2010). Toward a model of grammaticality judgments. *Journal of Linguistics, 46*, 273–330.

Carroll, S. (2000). *Input and evidence: The raw material of second language acquisition.* Amsterdam: John Benjamin.

Carroll, S., Roberge, Y., & Swain, M. (1992). The role of feedback in adult second language acquisition: Error correction and morphological generalization. *Applied Psycholinguistics, 13*, 173–189.

Carroll, S., & Swain, M. (1993). Explicit and implicit negative feedback: An empirical study of the learning of linguistic generalizations. *Studies in Second Language Acquisition, 15*, 357–386.

Cowan, N. (1999). An embedded-processes model of working memory. In A. Miyake & P. Shah (Eds.), *Models of working memory: Mechanisms of active maintenance and executive control* (pp. 62–102). New York: Cambridge University Press.

Daheane, S., & Naccache, L. (2001). Toward a cognitive neuroscience of consciousness: Basic evidence and a workspace framework. *Cognition, 79*, 1–37.

Davidson, D. J. (2010). Short-term grammatical plasticity in adult language learners. *Language Learning, 60*, 109–122. doi: 10.1111/j.1467–9922.2010.00603.x

Davidson, D. J., & Indefrey, P. (2008). An event-related potential study on changes of violation and error responses during morphosyntactic learning. *Journal of Cognitive Neuroscience, 21*, 433–446. doi: 10.1162/jocn.2008.21031

DeKeyser, R. M. (1995). Learning second language grammar rules: An experiment with a miniature language system. *Studies in Second Language Acquisition, 17*, 379–410.

Egi, T. (2004). Verbal reports, noticing, and SLA research. *Language Awareness, 13*, 243–264.

Endrass, T., Klawohn, J., Preuss, J., & Kathmann, N. (2012). Temporospatial dissociation of Pe subcomponents for perceived and unperceived errors. [Original Research]. *Frontiers in Human Neuroscience, 6*. doi: 10.3389/fnhum.2012.00178

Endrass, T., Reuter, B., & Kathmann, N. (2007). ERP correlates of conscious error recognition: Aware and unaware errors in an antisaccade task. *European Journal of Neuroscience, 26*, 1714–1720. doi: 10.1111/j.1460–9568.2007.05785.x

Frensch, A. A., & Rünger, D. (2003). Implicit learning. *Current Directions In Psychological Science, 12*, 13–18.

Ganushchak, L. Y., & Schiller, N. O. (2009). Speaking one's second language under time pressure: An ERP study on verbal self-monitoring in German–Dutch bilinguals. *Psychophysiology, 46*, 410–419. doi: 10.1111/j.1469–8986.2008.00774.x

Gass, S. (1988). Integrating research areas: A framework of second language studies. *Applied Linguistics, 9*, 187–217.

Gass, S., & Varonis, E. M. (1994). Input, interaction, and second language production. *Studies in Second Language Acquisition, 16*, 283–302.

Gehring, W. J., Goss, B., Coles, M. G. H., Meyer, D. E., & Donchin, E. (1993). A neural system for error detection and compensation. *Psychological Science, 4*, 385–390. doi: 10.1111/j.1467–9280.1993.tb00586.x

Greenwald, A. G. (2012). There is nothing so theoretical as a good method. *Perspectives on Psychological Science, 7*, 99–108. doi: 10.1177/1745691611434210

Groen, Y., Wijers, A. A., Mulder, L. J. M., Waggeveld, B., Minderaa, R. B., & Althaus, M. (2008). Error and feedback processing in children with ADHD and children with autistic spectrum disorder: An EEG event-related potential study. *Clinical Neurophysiology, 119*, 2476–2493.

Hama, M., & Leow, R. P. (2010). Learning without awareness revisited. *Studies in Second Language Acquisition, 32*, 465–491.

Hulstijn, J. H. (2005). Theoretical and empirical issues in the study of implicit and explicit second-language learning. *Studies in Second Language Acquisition, 27*, 129–140.

Izumi, S., & Bigelow, M. (2000). Does output produce noticing and second language acquisition. *TESOL Quarterly, 34*, 239–278.

Koch, C., & Tsuchiya, N. (2007). Attention and consciousness: Two distinct brain processes. *Trends in Cognitive Sciences, 11*, 16–22. doi: 10.1016/j.tics.2006.10.012

Kutas, M., & Hillyard, S. (1983). Event-related brain potentials to grammatical errors and semantic anomalies. *Memory & Cognition, 11*, 539–550. doi: 10.3758/bf03196991

Leow, R. P. (1997). Attention, awareness, and foreign language behavior. *Language Learning, 47*, 467–505.

Leow, R. P. (2000). A study of the role of awareness in foreign language behavior: Aware versus unaware learners. *Studies in Second Language Acquisition, 22*, 557–584.

Long, M. H., Inagaki, S., & Ortega, L. (1998). The role of implicit negative feedback in SLA: Models and recasts in Japanese and Spanish. *Modern Language Journal, 82*, 357–371.

Mackey, A. (2006). Feedback, noticing, and instructed second language learning. *Applied Linguistics, 27*, 405–430. doi: 10.1093/applin/ami051

Mackey, A., & Goo, J. M. (2007). Interaction research in SLA: A meta-analysis and research synthesis. In A. Mackey (Ed.), *Input, interaction, and corrective feedback in L2 learning* (pp. 379–452). New York: Oxford University Press.

Mackey, A., & Philp, J. (1998). Conversational interaction and second language development: Recasts, responses, and red herrings? *Modern Language Journal, 82*, 338–356.

McLaughlin, J., Osterhout, L., & Kim, A. (2004). Neural correlates of second-language word learning: Minimal instruction produces rapid change. *Nature Neuroscience, 7*, 703–704.

McLaughlin, J., Tanner, D., Pitkänen, I., Frenck-Mestre, C., Inoue, K., Valentine, G., & Osterhout, L. (2010). Brain potentials reveal discrete stages of L2 grammatical learning. *Language Learning, 60*, 123–150. doi: 10.1111/j.1467–9922.2010.00604.x

Moreno, E. M., Rodríguez-Fornells, A., & Laine, M. (2008). Event-related potentials (ERPs) in the study of bilingual language processing. *Journal of Neurolinguistics, 21*, 477–508. doi: 10.1016/j.jneuroling.2008.01.003

Morgan-Short, K., Sanz, C., Steinhauer, K., & Ullman, M. T. (2010). Second language acquisition of gender agreement in explicit and implicit training conditions: An event related potentials study. *Language Learning, 60*, 154–193.

Nassaji, H., & Fotos, S. (2004). Current developments in research on the teaching of grammar. *Annual Review of Applied Linguistics, 24*, 126–145.

Nicholas, H., Lightbown, P. M., & Spada, N. (2001). Recasts as feedback to language learning. *Language Learning, 51*, 719–758.

Nieuwenhuis, S., Ridderinkhof, K. R., Blom, J., Band, G. P. H., & Kok, A. (2001). Error-related brain potentials are differentially related to awareness of response errors:

Evidence from an antisaccade task. *Psychophysiology, 38*, 752–760. doi: 10.1111/1469–8986.3850752

Nissen, N., & Bullemer, P. (1987). Attentional requirements of learning: Evidence from performance measures. *Cognitive Psychology, 19*, 1–32.

Norris, J. M., & Ortega, L. (2000). Effectiveness of L2 instruction: A research synthesis. *Language Learning, 50*, 417–528.

Ortega, L. (2009). *Understanding second language acquisition*. London: Hoder Education.

Osterhout, L., McLaughlin, J., Pitkänen, I., Frenck-Mestre, C., & Molinaro, N. (2006). Novice learners, longitudinal designs, and event-related potentials: A means for exploring the neurocognition of second language processing. *Language Learning, 56*, 199–230.

Perruchet, P., & Vintner, A. (2002). The self-organizing consciousness. *Behavioral and Brain Sciences, 25*, 297–388.

Philp, J. (2003). Constraints on 'noticing the gap': Nonnative speakers' noticing of recasts in NS-NNS interactions. *Studies in Second Language Acquisition, 25*, 99–126.

Qi, D. S., & Lapkin, S. (2001). Exploring the role of noticing in a three-stage second language writing task. *Journal of Second Language Writing, 10*, 277–303.

Reber, R., & Squire, L. (1998). Encapsulation of implicit and explicit memory in sequence learning. *Journal of Cognitive Neuroscience, 10*, 248–263.

Robinson, P. (1995). Attention, memory, and the noticing hypothesis. *Language Learning, 45*, 283–331.

Rosa, E. M., & Leow, R. P. (2004). Computerized task-based exposure, explicitness, type of feedback, and Spanish L2 development. *The Modern Language Journal, 88*, 196–215.

Rossi, S., Gugler, M. F., Friederici, A. D., & Hahne, A. (2006). The impact of proficiency on syntactic second-language processing of German and Italian: Evidence from event-related potentials. *Journal of Cognitive Neuroscience, 18*, 2030–2048. doi: 10.1162/jocn.2006.18.12.2030

Russell, J., & Spada, N. (2006). The effectiveness of corrective feedback for the acquisition of L2 grammar: A meta-analysis of the research. In J. M. Norris & L. Ortega (Eds.), *Synthesizing research on learning and teaching* (pp. 133–166). Amsterdam: John Benjamins.

Schmidt, R. W. (1990). The role of consciousness in second language learning. *Applied Linguistics, 11*, 129–158. doi: 10.1093/applin/11.2.129

Schmidt, R. W. (1995). Consciousness and foreign language learning: A tutorial on the role of attention and awareness in learning. In R. Schmidt (Ed.), *Attention and awareness in foreign language learning* (pp. 1–63). Honolulu, Hawai'i: University of Hawai'i, National Foreign Language Resource Center.

Schmidt, R. W. (2001). Attention. In P. Robinson (Ed.), *Cognition and second language instruction* (pp. 3–32). New York: Cambridge University Press.

Schmidt, R. (2012). Attention, awareness, and individual differences in language learning. In W. M. Chan, K. N. Chin, S. Bhatt, & I. Walker (Eds.), *Perspectives on individual characteristics and foreign language education* (pp. 27–50). Boston, MA: Mouton de Gruyter.

Schmidt, R. W., & Frota, S. N. (1986). Developing basic conversational ability in a second language: A case study of an adult learner of Portuguese. In R. R. Day (Ed.), *Talking to learn: Conversation in second language acquisition* (pp. 237–326). Rowley, MA: Newbury House.

Schütze, C. T. (1996). *The empirical base of linguistics*. Chicago: University of Chicago Press.

Shanks, D. R. (2003). Attention and awareness in "implicit" sequence learning. In L. Jiménez (Ed.), *Attention and implicit learning* (pp. 11–42). Amsterdam: John Benjamins.

Tanner, D., McLaughlin, J., Herschensohn, J., & Osterhout, L. (2012). Individual differences reveal stages of L2 grammatical acquisition: ERP evidence. *Bilingualism: Language and Cognition*, FirstView Article published online 16 August 2012, 1–16. doi: 10.1017/S1366728912000302

Tokowicz, N., & MacWhinney, B. (2005). Implicit and explicit measures of sensitivity to violations in second language grammar. *Studies in Second Language Acquisition, 27*, 173–204.

Tomasello, M., & Herron, C. (1989). Feedback for language transfer errors: The garden path technique. *Studies in Second Language Acquisition, 11*, 385–395. doi: doi:10.1017/S0272263100008408

Truscott, J., & Sharwood Smith, M. (2011). Input, intake, and consciousness: The quest for a theoretical foundation. *Studies in Second Language Acquisition, 33*, 497–598.

West, W. C., & Holcomb, P. J. (2002). Event-related potentials during discourse-level semantic integration of complex pictures. *Cognitive Brain Research, 13*, 363–375. doi: 10.1016/s0926-6410(01)00129-x

Wilkinson, L., & Shanks, D. R. (2004). Intentional control and implicit sequence learning. *Journal of Experimental Psychology: Learning, Memory, and Cognition, 30*, 354–369.

Williams, J. N. (2005). Learning without awareness. *Studies in Second Language Acquisition, 27*, 269–304.

Zayas, V., Greenwald, A. G., & Osterhout, L. (2011). Unintentional covert motor activations predict behavioral effects: Multilevel modeling of trial-level electrophysiological motor activations. *Psychophysiology, 48*, 208–217. doi: 10.1111/j.1469–8986.2010.01055.x

NFLRC monographs

The Task at Hand: Noticing as a Mind–Body–World Phenomenon

Christine M. Jacknick
Borough of Manhattan Community College

Scott Thornbury
The New School

As originally conceptualised, noticing in SLA is essentially a cognitive process, implicating the learner's conscious and limited attentional resources. On the other hand, a sociocognitive perspective recognises that language use and learning "have both a social and cognitive dimension which interact" (Batstone, 2010). This relationship is a dynamic one, as learners continuously adapt to and align themselves with the (socio–cultural–linguistic) environment. Hence, noticing is not simply the unidirectional focusing of cognitive faculties on external phenomena; rather, it is adaptive, reciprocal, and motivated. The present study aims to locate and describe noticing as an externalized and collaborative focusing of attention, mediated through speech, gesture, and proxemics and argues for a more situationally-embedded and socially-constructed conceptualization of cognitive processes like noticing.

Introduction

As originally conceptualised and subsequently refined (e.g., Schmidt, 1990; Schmidt & Frota, 1986), the construct of *noticing* is firmly situated within a cognitivist account of second language acquisition, i.e., one which takes as axiomatic the belief that, as Long and Richards (2001) put it,

> second language acquisition is first and foremost a mental process—one that occurs in a behavioural and social context, to be sure, but fundamentally a matter of acquiring a new knowledge system. Cognition and cognitive factors, therefore, are central to any account of how and why SLA works, or so often fails. (p. vii)

Jacknick, C. M., & Thornbury, S. (2013). The task at hand: Noticing as a mind–body–world phenomenon. In J. M. Bergsleithner, S. N. Frota, & J. K. Yoshioka (Eds.), *Noticing and second language acquisition: Studies in honor of Richard Schmidt* (pp. 309–329). Honolulu: University of Hawai'i, National Foreign Language Resource Center.

Noticing, then, plays a determining role in any cognitivist model of SLA and, if not sufficient, is arguably necessary: "no noticing, no acquisition," as Ellis (1995, p. 89) succinctly puts it. Likewise, Gass (1997), in propounding what has come to be known as the input–interaction–output (IIO) model of second language acquisition (Block, 2003), argues that "the input–interaction view must take the position that noticing is crucial. In negotiation the learner is focusing on linguistic form, and that focus, or specific attention paid to linguistic form, is the first step toward grammar change" (p. 101).

By the same token, failure to notice linguistic forms in the input can, according to this model, result in the kind of premature stabilization of the developing interlanguage system that Schmidt (1983) documented in an earlier, equally seminal, case-study. Input-related factors that might help trigger noticing include phonological salience, frequency in the input, and previous encounters with the items in question (a *priming* effect). Since incidental exposure alone may be insufficient to drive acquisition, the noticing hypothesis supports the case for formal instruction. As Schmidt (2001) argues, "instructional practices that focus learners' attention on things that they are less likely to attend to or notice on their own also have a solid justification" (p. 29).

Noticing, then, is firmly entrenched, not only in the theoretical domain but also in the literature on second language instruction (see, for example, Batstone, 1996; Thornbury, 1997). The premise that the learner's attention needs to be manipulated in some overt way has been used to vindicate a range of instructional interventions such as input flooding (Williams & Evans, 1998), input enhancement (Sharwood Smith, 1993), the *garden path* treatment (Tomasello & Herron, 1988), *pushed* output (Swain, 1985), negative feedback, and a focus on form (Doughty & Williams, 1998).

Nevertheless, all these interventions, aimed as they are at bringing to conscious awareness preselected features of the linguistic environment, are predicated on a view of learners as "limited capacity processors of information" (Schmidt, 1990, p. 135) and, by extension, as somewhat disembodied, de-contextualised, and asocial. This view, in turn, is associated with a computational metaphor for the mind, as if—as Pinker (1997) disarmingly puts it—the mind were "the on-board computer of a robot made of tissue" (p. 92). While acknowledging that the mind-computer is not immune to the influence of the 'tissue' (noticing, after all, is dependent on sensory organs), nor to the effects of the external context (the notion of input presupposes some kind of external source, while interaction assumes the presence of an interlocutor), proponents of a cognitivist model are resistant to the idea that contextual factors are anything other than peripheral and certainly do not merit incorporation into the theoretical model (Long, 1997). However, as Block (2003) observes, in documenting what he calls *the social turn* in second language acquisition research, "there is... a growing number of scholars who subscribe to the view that mental processes are as social as they are individual and external as they are internal" (p. 93). One such scholar is van Lier (1996), who has long argued that "we need to move away from viewing language learning (or any learning, for that matter) in terms of the input/output metaphor (or, more generally, from an information-processing perspective)" (p. 50). This metaphor, he claims, promotes "a causal, and rather mechanistic, perspective on learning in which the establishment of intersubjectivity and reciprocity, and the social nature of language and cognition, are ignored" (*ibid.*).

Accordingly, alternative models of cognition—and, by extension, of learning—foreground social, cultural, contextual, and somatic factors, a development that has been largely driven by the increasing popularization of sociocognitive accounts of language learning (e.g., Batstone, 2010), which in turn share common ground with sociocultural learning theory

(Lantolf, 2000; Lantolf & Thorne, 2006) as well as with theories of language socialization (Kramsch, 2002), of identity formation (Kramsch, 2009; Norton, 2000), and of ecology, insofar as this relates to language learning and use (van Lier, 2004). What these various schools of thought share is an allegiance to a contextually-sensitive and socially-situated view of learning, where language acquisition is no longer regarded as a purely internal and cognitive process, subject primarily to the effect of noticed input, but one which has a social dimension as well. The net effect of these new social perspectives is the view that, in Ortega's (2009) words, "additional language learning is not only shaped by the social context in which it happens; it is bound inextricably to such context" (p. 217).

Some scholars go further and suggest that mind and context are more than just bound. Rather, they interpenetrate one another. Thus, Foster and Ohta (2005) argue,

> These [social] approaches view mind as distributed and learning as something intermental, embedded in social interaction. This means that individuals and environments mutually constitute one another and persons are not considered to be separable from the environments and interactions through which language development occurs. In this view, knowledge is not owned solely by the learner, but is also a property of social settings and the interface between person and social context. (p. 403)

More recently, theories of situated cognition (e.g., Clark, 2011; Robbins & Aydede, 2009) are now re-drawing the nature and extent of the mind–context interface, claiming that "the boundaries of cognitive systems lie *outside* the envelope of individual organisms, encompassing features of the physical and social environment [emphasis added]" (Robbins & Aydede, 2009, p. 8). This view derives from the observation that many cognitive processes, such as computation, memorization, and even conversation, typically involve a productive loop between the biological brain and external environmental structures, whether physical, social, or technological, creating an interdependent 'coupled system.' In this sense, cognition—rather than being purely internal—is *extended,* that is to say "continuous with processes in the environment" (Clark, 2011, p. 223).

Applied to our own field, this conceptualization of the mind extending into its social context has, in turn, prompted a reconsideration of the way that such cognitive processes as noticing and attention are described and framed. For example, Tarone (2010) foregrounds the determining role that the social context plays, arguing that

> whether the focus of attention is on language form or language meaning...the core underlying social variable that causes attention to be directed to one or another linguistic variant is the people present in a social setting—the *audience*—and most powerfully, the interlocutor. (p. 55)

According to this more situated view of cognition, noticing is not simply the unidirectional focusing of cognitive faculties on external phenomena; rather, it is adaptive, reciprocal, and motivated: "We devote attentional resources to something not because it exists, but because it is potentially important for our survival and prosperity. [. . .] What really matters to a person—what is *adaptive*—is what gets attended" [emphasis in original] (Atkinson, 2010a, p. 35).

Gesture

This ecological and embodied view of the mind as contiguous with, and contingent upon, social and environmental processes has accelerated an interest in the role of gesture as a mediator and embodiment of cognition. As Streeck (2009) notes, "gestures. . .occupy a unique position in human behaviour: they are bodily actions, but they are also cognitive actions" (p. 171). Because gestures are the main focus of the present study, a typology of the form that gestures take, as well as a discussion of their role in both communication and cognition, is therefore in order. Gesture studies (see McCafferty & Stam, 2008, for a review) owe much to the comprehensive work of Kendon (1990, 2004) and McNeill (1992, 2005), and our study follows McNeill's (1992) claim that gesture and language function as a single, coupled multidimensional meaning-making system. While many types of gesture have been identified, this study will include three types in particular: beat, iconic, and metaphoric gestures, each of which will be described in turn below.

Typography of gesture

Beat gestures, quick movements "at the meta-level of discourse" (Stam & McCafferty, 2008, p. 8), are some of the most familiar, given their presence in formal speeches and other prepared talk. They do, however, also occur in spontaneous talk. While their form may differ (head nods, chin movements, hand/arm movements), McNeill (1992) notes that there are only two possible *movement phases*: up/down or in/out from the body. Beats have been argued to be a "manifestation of inner speech" by Lantolf and Thorne (2006), as well as an indication that a speaker is "monitoring...production" (p. 96). In a study of language learners performing a picture narration task, McCafferty (1998) found that "subjects were found to use beats when struggling with expression in the L2, in a sense 'highlighting' linguistic difficulties, gesturally" (p. 93). In this study, beats are employed by both teacher and students and are argued to serve the purpose of monitoring speech by self or others.

Both iconic and metaphoric gestures are representational, though they differ in what they represent. Iconic gestures display an action and/or the manner of the action itself. In the case of displaying the action, iconic gestures generally serve a co-expressive function, duplicating information also found in speech (McNeill, 1992). Thus, a speaker might say, "He got smacked right on the head" while hitting his forehead with his right hand. In this case the action is the same in the gesture and the speech. However, there is also complementarity, in that the gesture conveys where on the head the smack landed (the forehead) and possibly what did the smacking (a hand). Metaphoric gestures differ from iconic gestures in that the representation is of an abstract concept. For example, a speaker might say, "He went on and on" while moving her right hand in a circle away from her body, signaling the continuous nature of the action. While some have claimed that representational gestures are related to lexical retrieval (Gullberg, 1998; Hadar & Butterworth, 1997), others argue that iconic gesture is not the only type that occurs with lexical trouble (Beattie & Coughlan, 1998), and thus there is no clear one-to-one correspondence between gesture type and function.

Functions of gesture

The terms beat, metaphoric, and iconic are ways of talking about types of gesture with relation to meaning, but an understanding of how gesture functions in language learning requires contextualization of gesture within the surrounding discourse. Researchers have identified a number of functions of gesture, including the observation that speakers gesture when they are having difficulties in speech production or when searching for lexical items. This self-regulatory function accounts for the fact that gesturing seems to occur even when there is no explicit communicative need for it, such as when speaking on the phone or to oneself. Moreover, as Clark (2011) notes, gesturing increases with task difficulty and "when reasoning about a problem rather than merely describing the problem" (p. 123). This cognitive function of gesture would seem to be significantly implicated in learning.

This underscores the fact that gesture seems to facilitate thinking and, by extension, learning. As Lantolf and Thorne (2006) put it, gestures are "material carriers of thinking" (p. 95): they serve a self-regulatory function by means of which speakers manage their internal thought processes. Gesture can thus be seen as a way of externalizing thought and/or language in order to stimulate the process of internalization. Gullberg (2008) hypothesises that, by gesturing, "speakers unload cognition onto an external representation, thereby liberating processing resources which can be re-assigned to memorization, planning, or other working-memory intense operations" (p. 293). As evidence, Gullberg cites studies that show that "children who receive gestural input with vocabulary explanations retain significantly more items than those who do not. Importantly, children who also reproduce the gestures themselves perform even better than children who do not even if they have had gestural input" (p. 292).

Within a sociocultural theory of mind, regulation of thought progresses from object to other to self, with the 'other' in this case representing "an expert or more capable peer" (Lantolf & Thorne, 2006, p. 290). An individual may be able to convey meaning through gesture that they are not yet capable of encoding in speech. Indeed, Platt and Brooks (2008) note that when gestures are co-deployed with speech, "they constitute a form of other-to-self regulation that in turn leads to internalization" (p. 81). Gestures deployed in interaction have *bidirectional regulatory potential* (Negueruela, Lantolf, Jordan, & Gelabert, 2004); they allow speakers to communicate with interlocutors and help speakers transform thought into speech. The gestures used by learners in this study are indeed argued to serve both functions. They allow learners to make clear that they are saying what they intend to communicate, and they provide learners with an externalized, materialized way of gaining control over the L2 form. This, in turn, accounts for the fact that, as Gullberg (2008) observes, "L2 learners produce more gestures when speaking the L2 than when speaking their L1" (p. 288).

But, as well as conferring to learners some control of their own communicative resources, gestures may also play an important part in the process of acquisition itself. In our study we pay particular attention to the way that the gestures of one learner are imitated and transformed by another. The reproduction and imitation of gestures as a means of appropriating unfamiliar concepts is integral to a sociocultural view of learning. Vygotsky (1978) argues that the formation of concepts moves from the interpersonal to the intrapersonal plane, and thus, imitation of gesture can be seen to serve the important function of allowing the learner to appropriate a sign/symbol from the repertoire of their interlocutor and simultaneously to adapt the gesture as their own. Importantly, Vygotsky (1962, 1978) notes that imitation is only possible when the imitated sign/symbol is within the learner's zone of proximal development, i.e., the difference between what a learner can do on their own and what they can accomplish with the assistance of a more capable peer. Thus, instances of learner imitation show the learner within the "active and interactive process" of development (Newman & Holzman, 1993, p. 15), stretching beyond their individual capability by imitating the gesture of a co-participant. Imitation can serve as "an important mechanism for the internalization of socially constructed forms of mediation" (DaSilva Iddings & Jang, 2008, p. 572); language development can then occur through internalization as learners imitate and appropriate the meaning-making behavior (e.g., gesture) of others.

One person, then, may imitate the gesture of another in terms of manner (i.e., type of gesture) or form (e.g., in the case of iconic gestures). Imitative gestures have been discussed by McCafferty (2002, 2004, 2008) with particular attention to language learner gesture. In his examination of learner gesture in dyadic interaction with a native speaker, McCafferty (2002) found that both participants imitated each other's gestures. He went on to argue that this back-and-forth imitation creates a dynamic learning environment in which novices are more involved than they would be if they were only mimicking the expert (i.e., teacher or native speaker). In our study, students imitate teacher gestures, but they are also found to imitate gestures initially produced by their peers, co-constructing a rich, involving environment for learning.

Gesture, along with other paralinguistic features, such as posture and gaze, can also provide a form of scaffolding in which the learner's attentional resources can be supported and orchestrated. Goodwin (2007), for example, demonstrates how a father, in order to direct and focus his daughter's attention on aspects of her homework, uses stance and gesture to create an *ecological huddle* (Goffman, 1972) and concludes that "in face-to-face human interaction parties organise their bodies in concert with each other in ways that establish a public, shared focus of visual and cognitive attention" (Goodwin, 2007, p. 69). Proxemics, as well as beat gestures and eye gaze, are argued to promote this kind of *shared focus* among the teacher and learners in this data. Along similar lines Atkinson (2010b) proposes what he calls *the alignment principle*: "Learning is more discovering how to align with the world than extracting knowledge from it" (p. 610). To demonstrate how this might be realised in practice, he traces, in minute detail, the interaction a Japanese schoolgirl has with her aunt, an English teacher, as they work through a homework exercise together: an intricate meshing of language, gesture, gaze, and laughter, inseparable from the experience of learning itself. As Atkinson (2011) writes elsewhere, "cognition is a node in an ecological network comprising mind-body-world—it is part of a *relationship*" [emphasis in original] (p. 143). This relationship is a dynamic one, as the user/learner continuously adapts to, and aligns him- or herself with, the (socio–cultural–linguistic) environment.

Gestures in teaching and learning

The alignment principles helps explain why a teacher's own body language can play an important role in offering the learner "legitimate peripheral participation" (Lave & Wenger, 1991) in the target learning community. Quinlisk (2008), for example, refers to "a huge body of research that associates teachers' non-verbal immediacy cues with increases in affective, cognitive, and behavioural learning outcomes in various settings" (p. 39). While supporting evidence from second language classrooms is scant, Sime (2008) reports a study of SL learners' perceptions of teachers' gestures, which, among other findings, suggests that, in one classroom at least,

> a developed sense of intersubjectivity seems to exist, where both learners and teacher share a common set of gestural meanings that are regularly deployed during interaction. This seems to facilitate communication and give learners a sense of stability: they know what to expect after an answer and how to make sure that their input is right or valued. (p. 74)

The way that stance and gesture serve to align learners *with each other* has also been documented. Platt and Brooks (2008), for example, show how pairs of learners engaged in task-based learning activities use gesture, posture, and gaze in order to "aid cognition, facilitate interaction, and help to create a sense of shared social, symbolic, visible, and mental space" (p. 69). Similarly, MacArthur and Littlemore (2008) observed learners working on a vocabulary task and found that gesture often accompanied the collaborative work involved in working out the meanings of words. Gesture, then, may play an important role in language acquisition in general, and, specifically, in the way that it facilitates noticing.

Nevertheless, most studies on the nature of L2 gestures have focused on the way that the differences between a learner's gesture use in their first and second languages indicate differences in cognitive structures. While some research has also examined gesture as it relates to second language development, notably McCafferty's (2002, 2004) case studies of a non-native speaker of English in interaction with a native speaker, the nature and function of naturally-occurring gesture in the ESL classroom has received little attention. Moreover, the vast majority of studies have been experimental in nature, providing participants with a visual or verbal prompt, thus leaving naturally-occurring gesture in everyday classroom talk largely unexamined. Teacher gestures have begun to receive more attention (cf. Faraco & Kida, 2008; Sime, 2008), and Tabensky (2008) provides an in-depth look at the occurrence of gesture in expository planned discourse in the classroom (e.g., student presentations). In one of the only conversation-analytic examinations of language learner gesture in the classroom, Olsher (2008) analyzes language learner gesture in small group discussions, arguing that learner use of gesture in the repair turn may provide enhanced input due to its multimodal nature.

The current study continues this line of research, addressing Quinlisk's (2008) and Stam's (2008) calls for more research on gesture in L2 classrooms. By bringing the focus of inquiry back into the everyday classroom interactions of learners, this study begins from an ecological perspective in which the learner's interactions are argued to "not just facilitate learning, they *are* learning [emphasis in original]" (van Lier, 2000, p. 246). In particular, rather than examining language learner use of gesture in an experimental context, this study examines gestures produced by learners in the classroom, during unplanned, spontaneous talk-in-interaction, demonstrating how gesture can be used as a tool for learning. We build on prior investigations of the role of gesture in language learner development by examining how gesture functions in whole-class activity involving learners and the teacher as they talk through a grammatical concept in their advanced ESL classroom. Specifically, and consistent with this volume's concern for noticing, we examine the role that gesture plays in co-constructing learning opportunities both by embodying abstract concepts and by focussing visual and cognitive attention, thereby aligning the participants to the task (literally) at hand. Situating the research within the context of the language learning classroom allows for the examination of gesture as it is used in real-time in the classroom in pursuit of language learning.

Method

This study examines spontaneous gesture as it naturally occurs in the course of ESL classroom talk. The participants in the larger study from which this excerpt comes (Jacknick, 2009) include the students enrolled in the highest-level advanced adult ESL course in a community language program in the northeastern United States and their instructor, a 24-year-old Korean-American female graduate student in TESOL at the end of her first year of study. The teacher was solicited for participation in the research project, and the students in her randomly-assigned class were also asked to participate (all consented). All classes in the five-week semester were video- and audio-recorded, and content logs were created for all recordings. Given the focus of the original study, all instances of student-initiated participation were transcribed following conversation analytic methods. While the class was a diverse group linguistically and culturally, two students are the focus of the excerpt under analysis: Nobu, a Japanese man in his 40s, and Rodrigo, a Mexican man in his 20s (pseudonyms are used for all participants).

Following the framework of conversation analysis, data consist of video and audio recordings of classes and the transcripts created. The initial stage of analysis involved a review of all video recordings, including multiple camera angles for each class session. The excerpt under analysis was chosen because of the salience of the gestures used during the discussion and represents a single-case analysis. Hutchby and Wooffitt (1998) argue that single-case analyses allow the analyst to focus on "one apparently trivial fragment of naturally occurring interaction" in order to offer "interesting and sociologically relevant results" (p. 123). This type of fine-grained analysis of a short sequence of classroom interaction belongs to the research tradition known as *microethnography*, in which social interaction is analysed "in slow motion" (Streeck, 2008, p. 202): "It pays particular attention to the *sequential* production of gestures, utterances, and acts" (*Ibid.*, emphasis in original). By examining one interaction in which gesture features prominently, this article aims to extend prior research on language learner gesture by showing learner gestures as they occur naturally in the classroom and argues for the importance of gesture as a mediational tool for language learning.

Analysis

In this analysis, gesture is examined in terms of two key features: imitation and redundancy. In particular, the gestures of two students, Nobu and Rodrigo, and the teacher are analyzed in order to demonstrate how advanced learners of English use gesture for both intra-personal and inter-personal purposes to gain control over a target form and how nonverbal aspects of interaction (i.e., gesture, gaze, and proxemics) contribute to the creation of a shared pedagogical and interactional focus (Goodwin, 2007). A brief background of the lesson is provided below, followed by a discussion of the focal gestures.

Background

The focal excerpt in this analysis comes early in the semester during just the fifth meeting of the class. In this lesson the teacher asked students to comment on the difference in meaning between two pairs of sentences she had written on the board: "Sarah quit going to school/ Sarah quit to go to school" and "Jane tried to sing/Jane tried singing." These were the third and fourth pairs of infinitive/gerund sentences the class had discussed, and this activity came after 30 minutes of class time devoted to the gerund/infinitive grammar topic. A nominated student was unable to adequately explain the meaning difference between the "Sarah quit" sentences, so the teacher asked the students to discuss it in pairs. Once back in a large-group discussion, she again elicited interpretations of the meaning difference. In Excerpt 1 below, a focal student, Rodrigo, is shown to be unable to articulate the meaning of "Sarah quit to go to school."

Excerpt 1: Rodrigo's interpretation of "Sarah quit to go to school."

1 T: {This one.}
points to the first sentence
2 She quit? (.) to go to school.
3 {(1.8) *T has back to board, looking straight at class.*}
4 Rod: S[he, re-] {uh} refused the idea to start, to go
5 Nobu: [She] *nods to give the turn to Rodrigo*
6 Rod: to school.
7 {(1.2) *T cocks her head and looks up*}
8 T: {OK,}
quick nod

Rodrigo's response in lines 4 and 6, *She, re—uh refused the idea to start, to go to school*, demonstrates that his understanding of the meaning in the second sentence was inaccurate, or at the least incomplete. Either way, the claim can be made that Rodrigo was unable to articulate the meaning difference in English at this point in the lesson, whether or not he had some understanding of it. The teacher's response to Rodrigo's utterance was marked as dispreferred by the 1.2 second pause in line 7, as well as her nonverbal response of cocking her head and looking up (as if she had to think about it). While this nonverbal response may be seen as simple consideration of his interpretation, at a minimum, it is clear that Rodrigo's answer was not an expected response and so required additional consideration by the teacher. The teacher nodded along with her OK in line 8, possibly indicating that Rodrigo could continue to hold the floor. However, Rodrigo did not substantively return to the class discussion until 8 minutes later, where Excerpt 2 begins. This excerpt is provided in its entirety here for clarity, and individual gestures will be discussed further below.

Excerpt 2: Rodrigo demonstrates understanding

214 Nobu: Yeah, I have a:: ↑similar {example,}
T moves toward Nobu

215 T: {OK,}
still moving to Nobu, holding right wrist with left hand, continues throughout

216 Nobu: "I: {stopped (.) to (.) smoke"}
T continues to moves closer to Nobu, nods with each syllable

217 {and "I stopped? [smoking.]"}
T nods with each syllable

218 Rod: [°smoking°]

219 Nobu: It's like, "quit."

220 T: Right, °yeah. It is.°

221 Nobu: So if you say, if eh, {"I stopped to, smoke,"} means I
beats with pen with each word

222 {stopped,} (1.0) and then
right hand open, palm facing body, beat down

223 {smoked.}
right hand open, palm facing body, index and middle finger close, hand moves toward face and back quickly three times

224 T: Right.=

225 Rod: ={Yeah.}
nods

226 Nobu: But, >"I stopped smoking,"<it's uh, I stopped, you know,

227 T: Smoking.=

228 Nobu: ={smoking.=}
right hand open, palm facing body, index and middle finger close, hand moves toward face and back quickly once

229 T: ={yeah.}=
gaze to Nobu & nodding

230 Nobu: =I don't-

231 Rod: Like "I quit" {the second one.}
T turns to board and back again

232 Nobu: >Yeah ye[ah.<]

233 Rod: [Like], >no no,<you were smoking? is like I stopped

234 smoking?=

235 T: =mm-hmm,=

236 Rod: ={I decided not} to smoke.=
left hand open, palm facing down, hand moves away from body and back twice

237 T: =mm-[hmm,]

238 Rod: [any] [more]

239 Nobu: [yeah.]

240 Rod: In the first one {you were walking?}=
index and middle finger of right hand pointed downward, moving like legs in trajectory away from the body

241 T: =mm-hmm?=

242 Rod: =and then you {stopped,}
both hands open, palms down, fingers pointed toward each other, beat downward

243 and then you,=

244 Nobu: =stopped to [light] and then,

245 Rod: [{light}]
index and middle finger of left hand miming holding a cigarette, right hand miming holding a lighter, thumb moving to "light"

246 (0.6)

247 Rod: yeah.=

248 Nobu: =you do. Yeah.

249 T: Yeah, well that's a good example.

In this excerpt the teacher verbally participated minimally, with backchannels such as *mm-hmm* or *Yeah*, though her nonverbal behaviors are argued not only to provide interactional space for the new, learner-introduced example, but to create a sense of shared focus on it. In lines 214–216, she slowly moves closer to Nobu as he declares that he has *a new example*. This movement, along with Nobu's speech, seems to focus the attention of the other students on Nobu as he delivers the example—as the teacher moves closer to him, more and more students turn their eye gaze towards him as well. In addition, in lines 216–217, the teacher nods along with each syllable of Nobu's example, producing up/down beat gestures, argued here to demonstrate her close monitoring of his production. Verbally, the teacher participates minimally, with confirming responses (*right, yeah*) in lines 220, 224, and 229, though she declines to take a longer turn at talk at any of these points. Through all these lines, her eye gaze is continuously directed towards Nobu, until Rodrigo takes a substantive turn in 231, at which her eye gaze shifts to him. She briefly looks at the board when Rodrigo refers to the original sentences written there but then returns her eye gaze to him for the duration of his explanation. This continuous eye gaze, along with her proxemics (standing directly in front of Nobu and Rodrigo), serves to preserve the sense of shared focus on the examples. In the lines that follow, Rodrigo, who was unable to articulate the meaning difference in Excerpt 1, is now seen co-constructing the example with Nobu, building on the original by putting it in his own words and emphasizing the gestures accompanying the example.

The presence of a rich, involving environment for learning can be seen both by the teacher's provision of interactional space and by the co-construction of meaning by Nobu and Rodrigo throughout. Rodrigo's involvement early on in the example is seen in line 218 when he simultaneously produces the form *smoking* with Nobu, anticipating his example, as well as in line 225 when he confirms, along with the teacher, Nobu's intended meaning. Likewise, Nobu joins in during Rodrigo's explanation, confirming Rodrigo's claims uttering *Yeah* in line 232 and 239. In addition, Nobu is attending to Rodrigo's example closely enough that he can anticipate and overlap his utterance in line 244 and simultaneously produce *light* with him, likely because Nobu can see the beginning of Rodrigo's iconic gesture for a lighter. Taken together, the participation of Rodrigo and Nobu in each other's explanations points to an interactional environment in which learners are carefully attending to each other's contributions and in which the teacher has given them the space to build on these contributions—a rich, involving environment for learning.

The discussion here involving Rodrigo, Nobu, and the teacher may be considered an example of Swain's (2000) *collaborative dialogue*—"dialogue in which speakers are engaged in problem solving and knowledge building" (p. 102). Rodrigo in particular seems to be engaged in *verbalization* of the grammatical concept, which Swain (2000) argues "focuses attention [and] externalizes hypotheses" (p. 108). By building on Nobu's example and connecting it explicitly to the prior examples, Rodrigo is, as Swain puts it, "objectif[ying] thought" (p. 104). Importantly, we argue that this mediation is not verbal alone; the creation of a language object for scrutiny is accomplished in a multimodal fashion, including gesture, gaze, and proxemics.

Imitation

McCafferty (2002) argues that imitation represents a *transformational process* (p. 199), because imitation on the interpersonal level leads to internalization. In addition, we argue that imitation can also be seen as an embodiment of cognitive noticing: by imitating the gestures of another, Rodrigo demonstrates that this is where his attention has been focused. In this case, Nobu introduces several gestures along with his new example of *smoking*, and Rodrigo is seen to imitate these gestures while simultaneously making them his own. In particular, this section will focus on Nobu's metaphoric gesture for *stop* and his iconic gesture for *smoked/smoking*.

In the focal excerpt, Nobu initially introduces his new example without gestures, though the teacher nods in beats with his delivery. These beats by the teacher indicate that she is closely monitoring Nobu's speech (Lantolf & Thorne, 2006). Such attention by the teacher may direct others' attention to it as well; Rodrigo demonstrates this noticing by anticipating Nobu's *smoking* and co-producing it. Once Nobu moves to explain his example, he begins to employ gesture along with his explanation. He beats in line 221 (in imitation of the teacher previously in line 216) along with the repetition of *I stopped to smoke*, and these beats (the teacher's head nods and Nobu's beats with his pen) show that the participants are closely monitoring speech. Then, when Nobu's explanation becomes more explicit, so do his gestures. Lines 221–223 are reproduced below with visuals illustrating the co-occurrence of speech and gesture.

221 Nobu: So if you say, if eh, {"I stopped to, smoke,"} means I
beats with pen with each word

222 {stopped,} (1.0) and then
right hand open, palm facing body, beat down

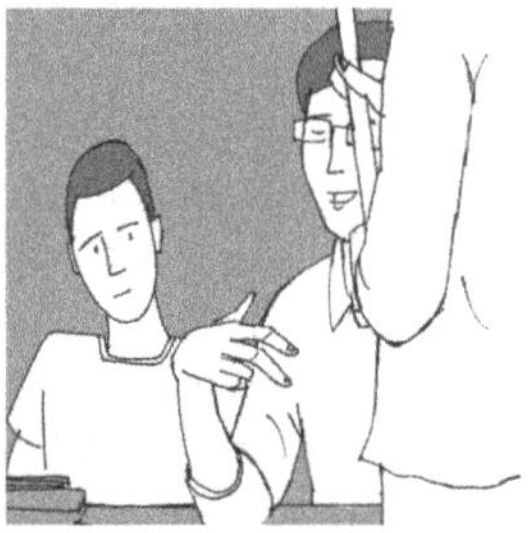

223 {smoked.}
right hand open, palm facing body, index and middle finger close, hand moves toward face and back quickly three times

Nobu's gestures become more pronounced as he begins to break down the meaning of the sentence with *means* in line 221. He produces a metaphoric gesture along with *stopped* in line 222, beating down once with his right hand open, palm facing his body. The one-second pause following this co-occurrence of the gesture and speech for *stopped* also serves to emphasize his meaning. Nobu is likely producing this metaphoric gesture to emphasize his meaning (rather than to clarify), as it is improbable he is unsure of the meaning of *stopped*. Given that the earlier examples included a verb that does not lend itself to gesture (*quit*), Nobu here is taking advantage of the affordance of gesture inherent in *stop*.

Nobu continues with his explanation, saying that once the person *stopped*, *then* they *smoked* (lines 222–223). Nobu produces an iconic gesture along with *smoked*, miming smoking a cigarette in his right hand, with the index and middle finger close but not touching, in effect miming dragging on a cigarette three times. He produces a similar gesture during his explanation of the other sentence in lines 226–228 when he says that it means *I stopped, you know, smoking*, his gesture for smoking in synchrony with his utterance of the word *smoking*. The teacher acknowledges Nobu's example and explanation with *yeah* in line 229, and although it appears Nobu was going to continue in line 230, he cut off abruptly, and then Rodrigo came in with an explicit reference to the focal sentences of the lesson (the "Sarah quit" sentences) in line 231.

Rodrigo produces a more elaborate explanation of Nobu's example, saying that "I stopped smoking" means *I decided not to smoke anymore*. He then further explains the other sentence in the pair in a similar fashion, shown below in more detail.

240 Rod: In the first one {you were walking?}=
index and middle finger of right hand pointed downward, moving like legs in trajectory away from the body

241 T: =mm-hmm?=

242 Rod: =and then you {stopped,}
both hands open, palms down, fingers pointed toward each other, beat downward

243 and then you,=

244 Nobu: =stopped to [light] and <u>then</u>,

245 Rod: [{light}]
index and middle finger of left hand miming holding a cigarette, right hand miming holding a lighter, thumb moving to "light"

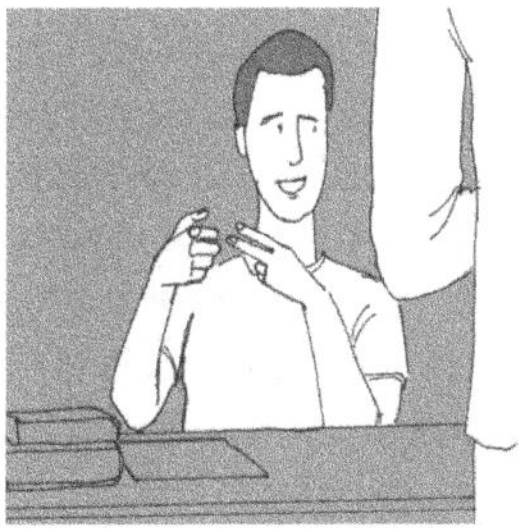

In particular, Rodrigo's gestures in lines 242 (*stopped*) and 245 (*light*) are argued to be partial imitations in figure or manner of Nobu's earlier gestures for *stop* and *smoked/smoking.* In the case of *stop*, Rodrigo imitates the manner of Nobu's gesture, with an emphatic beat down, though he uses both hands palms down, where Nobu used one hand, palm facing his body. In the case of smoking, the miming aspect (form) is present in both, but Rodrigo changes which hand is holding the cigarette (he is left-handed), and adds the element of the lighter to the mime. Rodrigo's imitation of Nobu's gestures in both form and manner demonstrate his careful attention to Nobu's introduction of the example.

Gestures have long been noted to be idiosyncratic (McNeill, 1992), so this variation may simply be the result of individual variance; however, it may also be argued that Rodrigo's imitations with variation are examples of the transformational nature of imitation. That is, by appropriating gestures that Nobu had originally produced and altering them in his own way, Rodrigo is utilizing gesture as a materialization (Stam & McCafferty, 2008) of the L2 form in the process of internalizing that form.

Redundancy

Goldin-Meadow (2003) has argued that when there is redundancy between gestures and co-occurring speech, the function of the gesture may be to "emphasize, highlight, or draw attention to that information" (p. 104), i.e., cause noticing. However, it has also been argued by Negueruela et al. (2004) that redundancy shows the use of gesture for intra-personal purposes, i.e., self-regulation. The examples to follow represent new redundant gestures Rodrigo introduced to the explanation (i.e., they were not produced earlier by Nobu), and the purposes of redundancy will be discussed in each case.

The first redundant gesture to be discussed is Rodrigo's metaphoric gesture for *not* in line 236, reproduced below.

236 Rod: ={I decided not} to smoke.=
left hand open, palm facing down, hand moves away from body and back twice

The meaning imparted by waving a hand in this manner is clearly redundant of the meaning of *not*, so why is it that Rodrigo produces this gesture? In Nobu's smoking example, a clear distinction is to be made between the sentence in which the speaker smokes and the sentence in which the speaker used to but no longer smokes. In this way the presence of *not* is critical to an understanding of the grammatical distinction. Thus, following Goldin-Meadow's (2003) claim, Rodrigo's production of the redundant gesture along with *not* in line 236 is argued to serve as emphasis. This emphasis is crucial for Rodrigo's explanation, as well as to demonstrate (to the teacher, the class, himself) that he understands the distinction, particularly given his inability to articulate it earlier.

The next gesture among redundant examples, Rodrigo's iconic gesture for walking, is shown below.

240 Rod: In the first one {you were walking?}=
index and middle finger of right hand pointed downward, moving like legs in trajectory away from the body

While the redundancy involved with *not* serves the importance of underscoring the grammatical and meaning differences, Rodrigo's use of an iconic gesture along with *walking*

represents an instance where emphasis is not required in order to make the distinction between the two sentences. Both his gesture for walking and the co-occurring speech may simply serve to provide further context for the example. However, they may also show the use of gesture for intrapersonal purposes.

Kita (2000) argues that because representational gestures also occur in the absence of interlocutors (e.g., on the telephone), they may serve a cognitive function. The cognitive function of gestures relates not only to the relationship between thought and gesture, but particularly to the idea that use of gesture "lightens the cognitive load" (Goldin-Meadow, 2003, p. 159). With regard to the first claim, McNeill and Duncan (2000) argue that gesture provides "an enhanced window onto thinking" (p. 142), because to gesture is to make thought concrete, in the same way that writing or speaking makes thought concrete. Thus, redundancy in gesture may serve to highlight or make salient some aspect of the talk. The claim that gesture lightens the cognitive load relates primarily to the modes of cognition represented in speech and gesture, linear and imagistic, respectively.[1] In effect, gesture allows a speaker to encode meaning in different ways (Goldin-Meadow, 2003; Goldin-Meadow, Nussbaum, Kelly, & Wagner, 2001; Gullberg, 2008; McNeill, 2005), freeing up cognitive space or energy to be devoted to other tasks. As an advanced speaker of English, Rodrigo does not need to internalize the meaning of *walking*, and so this gesture does not seem to be an instance of materialization. Rather, we argue that the use of an iconic gesture in this instance shows Rodrigo lightening his own cognitive load.

These excerpts show two learners utilizing gesture in their discussion of a grammatical concept, though in different ways. Nobu seemed to grasp the difference earlier in the lesson, and used his gestures to complement his speech as he explained the new example. Rodrigo demonstrated his lack of understanding earlier and then imitated and appropriated Nobu's gestures and added his own redundant gestures on his path to demonstrating understanding. These examples show that while Rodrigo had been unable to articulate the meaning difference earlier in the activity, after attending to (i.e., noticing) Nobu's example, he made the link back to the original sentences and explained the meaning difference using this new example. This segment illustrates the sociocultural concept of the zone of proximal development (Vygotsky, 1978): the gap between what Rodrigo was able to do alone in the beginning of the activity and what he was able to do later with the assistance of a more capable peer demonstrates not just his actual level of development but also his potential level of development.

In sum, this segment illustrates the way that, by means of *collaborative dialogue*, learners jointly verbalize a process of problem-solving, resulting in the construction of new knowledge. As Swain (2000) explains, "verbalization...serves several functions. For both speaker and hearer, it focuses attention; it externalizes hypotheses, tests them, and supplies possible solutions, and it mediates their implementation of such strategic behaviour as planning and evaluating" (p. 108). But, more than that, as our example shows, verbalizing works 'hand in hand' with *visualizing*, specifically the use of both imitative and redundant gestures that help focus attention, serve to illustrate the emergent concepts, and assist in their appropriation.

---

1 Speech is considered to be linear, given phrase structure rules, while gesture is imagistic because the hands and/or arms are used to represent ideas in a physical and visual way.

Discussion

This analysis of language learner gesture in the ESL classroom has important implications, both theoretical and practical. On a very basic level, these excerpts show the value of student participation and underscore the need for teachers to provide interactional space (Jacknick, 2011; Oyler, 1996). If the teacher had controlled the discussion more tightly, Nobu's new example might not have been introduced, and the learners' confusion might have persisted. Moreover, because this teacher provided her students the interactional space to work through a new example, Rodrigo was able to display his ability to explain the difference in meaning. Thus, these excerpts also highlight an example of van Lier's (2000) concept of affordances for learning, in which the teacher's minimal participation at this juncture allows further discussion among the students "so that access is available and engagement is encouraged" (p. 253). In his (2005) call for a shift in focus to *learning opportunities* from teaching points, Allwright argues that awareness of how learners affect the classroom agenda (and teachers by allowing interactional space) is necessary in order to understand how to improve teaching and learning practice.

Taking this argument a step further, the teacher's allowance of interactional space, as well as Nobu's new example, both support "the creation of potential contexts of acquisition" (Gullberg, 2008, p. 205). The new example sentences allow for the use of gesture in a way the originals did not, and this difference may account for Rodrigo's newfound ability to understand and explain the meaning of both sets of sentences.

More specifically, this analysis highlights how gesture functions in the ESL classroom, addressing an important gap in classroom discourse research as well as bringing gesture studies into the everyday classroom. In doing so, the study also argues for a more situationally embedded and socially constructed conceptualisation of such cognitive processes as noticing.

As we have argued, the sociocultural turn in SLA and TESOL makes a strong case for the situated and multimodal nature of learning, where cognition is not confined to the physical brain, but insists that, as Churchill, Okada, Nishino, and Atkinson (2010) put it, "brains are in bodies, bodies are in the world, and meaningful action in these worlds is in large part socially constructed and conducted" (p. 237). One way in which 'bodies are in the world' is the way they employ gesture. As Streeck (2009) puts it, "the actions and the play of our hands are a form of thinking, because thinking is an activity that involves the entire person" (p. 38). This analysis shows the important role gesture plays in both in the ESL classroom. Interaction is multimodal, and participants are constantly attending to nonverbal behaviors like eye gaze and gesture; researchers and teachers likewise need to attend to such important features of interaction. If studies of interaction in the ESL classroom continue to focus only on the verbal modality, a large part of the story is being left untold. As Atkinson (2002) puts it, "If language is in the world at the same time as it is in the head, then we need to account for its integrated existence, rather than adopt positions that reduce the life—the humanity—out of language" (p. 537).

Finally, the study asserts the value of ecological validity in SLA research, and takes a tentative step in that direction by examining the use of gesture in naturally-occurring classroom discussion, and demonstrates how learners use gesture to communicate, to focus attention, and to regulate their own learning. These results highlight the limitations inherent in a conception of SLA as a purely cognitive phenomenon, divorced from its social context. As Tarone (2010) argues, "social context does not just affect the L2 input that interlocutors provide learners. It also affects the way L2 learners themselves behave in negotiating meaning or focusing on L2 form" (p. 57). This underscores the need to examine second language learning processes in everyday social contexts.

One of these language learning processes is the construct of noticing, originally construed as an essentially internal mental process, but here re-envisaged as an externalized and collaborative focusing of attention, mediated through speech, gesture, and proxemics—the *visualization* as well as the verbalization of cognitive structures. Further research, including the use of stimulated recall, for instance, will need to demonstrate the contribution that gesturing, including the imitation of the gestures of one's interlocutors, plays in the bringing to conscious awareness features of the target language. But we would claim that our study is suggestive and points the way towards potentially fruitful lines of inquiry.

Acknowledgement

Special thanks to Piet Luethi for the illustrations.

References

Allwright, D. (2005). From teaching points to learning opportunities and beyond. *TESOL Quarterly*, *39*, 9–31.

Atkinson, D. (2002). Toward a sociocognitive approach to second language acquisition. *The Modern Language Journal*, *86*, 525–545.

Atkinson, D. (2010a). What sociocognition can mean for SLA. In R. Batstone (Ed.), *Sociocognitive perspectives on language use and language learning* (pp. 24–39). Oxford: Oxford University Press.

Atkinson, D. (2010b). Extended, embodied cognition and second language acquisition. *Applied Linguistics*, *31*, 599–622.

Atkinson, D. (2011). A sociocognitive approach to second language acquisition: How mind, body, and world work together in learning additional languages. In D. Atkinson (Ed.), *Alternative approaches to second language acquisition* (pp. 143–166). New York: Routledge.

Batstone, R. (1996). Key concepts in ELT: Noticing. *ELT Journal*, *50*, 273.

Batstone, R. (Ed.) (2010). *Sociocognitive perspectives on language use and language learning.* Oxford: Oxford University Press.

Beattie, G., & Coughlan, J. (1998). Do iconic gestures have a functional role in lexical access? An experimental study on the effects of repeating a verbal message on gesture production. *Semiotica*, *119*, 221–249.

Block, D. (2003). *The social turn in second language acquisition*. Edinburgh: Edinburgh University Press.

Churchill, E., Okada, H., Nishino, T., & Atkinson, D. (2010). Symbiotic gesture and the sociocognitive visibility of grammar in second language acquisition. *The Modern Language Journal*, *94*, 234–253.

Clark, A. (2011). *Supersizing the mind: Embodiment, action, and cognitive extension*. Oxford: Oxford University Press.

DaSilva Iddings, A. C., & Jang, E. Y. (2008). The mediational role of classroom practices during the silent period: New immigrant children learning the English language in the mainstream classroom. *TESOL Quarterly*, *42*, 567–590.

Doughty, C., and Williams, J. (Eds.) (1998). *Focus on form in classroom second language acquisition*. Cambridge: Cambridge University Press.

Ellis, R. (1995). Interpretation tasks for grammar teaching. *TESOL Quarterly*, *29*, 87–106.

Faraco, M., & Kida, T. (2008). Gesture and the negotiation of meaning in a second language classroom. In S. G. McCafferty & G. Stam (Eds.), *Gesture: Second language acquisition and classroom research* (pp. 280–297). New York: Routledge.

Foster, P., & Ohta, A. S. (2005). Negotiation for meaning and peer assistance in second language classrooms. *Applied Linguistics, 26*, 402–430.

Gass, S. M. (1997). *Input, interaction, and the second language learner.* New York: Routledge.

Goffman, E. (1972 [1964]). The neglected situation. In P. P. Giglioli (Ed.), *Language and social context* (pp. 61–66). Baltimore: Penguin (original publication *American Anthropologist*, 66, 133–136).

Goldin-Meadow, S. (2003). *Hearing gesture: How our hands help us think.* Cambridge, MA: The Belknap Press of Harvard University Press.

Goldin-Meadow, S., Nussbaum, H., Kelly, S. D., & Wagner, S. (2001). Explaining math: Gesturing lightens the load. *Psychological Science, 12*, 516–522.

Goodwin, C. (2007). Participation, stance, and affect in the organization of activities. *Discourse & Society, 18*, 53–73.

Gullberg, M. (1998). *Gesture as a communication strategy in second language discourse.* Lund: Lund University Press.

Gullberg, M. (2008). A helping hand? Gesture, L2 learners, and grammar. In S. G. McCafferty & G. Stam (Eds.), *Gesture: Second language acquisition and classroom research* (pp. 185–210). New York: Routledge.

Hadar, U., & Butterworth, B. (1997). Iconic gestures, imagery, and word retrieval in speech. *Semiotica, 115*, 147–172.

Hutchby, I., & Wooffitt, R. (1998). *Conversation analysis: Principles, practices, and applications.* Malden, MA: Blackwell.

Jacknick, C. M. (2009). *A conversation-analytic account of student-initiated participation in an ESL classroom.* Unpublished doctoral dissertation, Teachers College, Columbia University, New York.

Jacknick, C. M. (2011). Breaking in is hard to do: How students negotiate classroom activity shifts. *Classroom Discourse, 2*, 20–38.

Kendon, A. (1990). *Conducting interaction: Patterns of behavior in focused encounters.* Cambridge, UK: Cambridge University Press.

Kendon, A. (2004). *Gesture: Visible action as utterance.* Cambridge, UK: Cambridge University Press.

Kita, S. (2000). How representational gestures help speaking. In D. McNeill (Ed.), *Language and gesture* (pp. 162–185). Cambridge, UK: Cambridge University Press.

Kramsch, C. (Ed.) (2002). *Language acquisition and language socialization: Ecological perspectives.* London: Continuum.

Kramsch, C. (2009). *The multilingual subject.* Oxford: Oxford University Press.

Lantolf, J. P. (Ed.) (2000). *Sociocultural theory and second language learning.* New York: Oxford University Press.

Lantolf, J. P., & Thorne, S. L. (2006). *Sociocultural theory and the genesis of second language development.* New York: Oxford University Press.

Lave, J., & Wenger, E. (1991). *Situated learning: Legitimate peripheral participation.* New York: Cambridge University Press.

Long, M. H. (1997). Construct validity in SLA research: A response to Firth and Wagner. *The Modern Language Journal, 81*, 318–323.

Long, M. H., & Richards, J. C. (2001). Series editors' preface. In P. Robinson (Ed.), *Cognition and second language instruction* (p. vii). Cambridge: Cambridge University Press.

MacArthur, F., & Littlemore, J. (2008). A discovery approach to figurative language learning with the use of corpora. In F. Boers & S. Lindstromberg (Eds.), *Cognitive linguistic approaches to teaching vocabulary and phraseology* (pp. 159–188). Boston: Walter De Gruyter.

McCafferty, S. G. (1998). Nonverbal expression and L2 private speech. *Applied Linguistics, 19*, 73–96.

McCafferty, S. G. (2002). Gesture and creating zones of proximal development for second language learning. *The Modern Language Journal, 86*, 192–203.

McCafferty, S. G. (2004). Space for cognition: Gesture and second language learning. *International Journal of Applied Linguistics, 14*, 148–165.

McCafferty, S. G. (2008). Material foundations for second language acquisition: Gesture, metaphor, and internalization. In S. G. McCafferty & G. Stam (Eds.), *Gesture: Second language acquisition and classroom research* (pp. 47–65). New York: Routledge.

McCafferty, S. G., & Stam, G. (2008). *Gesture: Second language acquisition and classroom research*. New York: Routledge.

McNeill, D. (1992). *Hand and mind: What gestures reveal about thought*. Chicago: University of Chicago Press.

McNeill, D. (2005). *Gesture & thought*. Chicago: University of Chicago Press.

McNeill, D., & Duncan, S. D. (2000). Growth points in thinking-for-speaking. In D. McNeill (Ed.), *Gesture & thought* (pp. 141–161). Chicago: University of Chicago Press.

Negueruela, E., Lantolf, J. P., Jordan, S. R., & Gelabert, J. (2004). The "private function" of gesture in second language speaking activity: A study of motion verbs and gesturing in English and Spanish. *International Journal of Applied Linguistics, 14*, 113–147.

Newman, F., & Holzman, L. (1993). *Lev Vygotsky: Revolutionary scientist*. New York: Routledge.

Norton, B. (2000). *Identity and language learning: Gender, ethnicity, and educational change*. Harlow: Longman.

Olsher, D. (2008). Gesturally-enhanced repeats in the repair turn: Communication strategy or cognitive language-learning tool? In S. G. McCafferty & G. Stam (Eds.), *Gesture: Second language acquisition and classroom research* (pp. 109–130). New York: Routledge.

Ortega, L. (2009). *Understanding second language acquisition*. London: Hodder Education.

Oyler, C. (1996). *Making room for students: Sharing teacher authority in Room 104*. New York: Teachers College Press.

Pinker, S. (1997). *How the mind works*. London: Penguin.

Platt, E., & Brooks, F. B. (2008). Embodiment as self-regulation in L2 task performance. In S. G. McCafferty & G. Stam (Eds.), *Gesture: Second language acquisition and classroom research* (pp. 66–87). New York: Routledge.

Quinlisk, C. C. (2008). Nonverbal communication, gesture, and second language classrooms: A review. In S. G. McCafferty & G. Stam (Eds.), *Gesture: Second language acquisition and classroom research* (pp. 25–44). New York: Routledge.

Robbins, P., & Aydede, M. (Eds.) (2009). *The Cambridge handbook of situated cognition.* Cambridge: Cambridge University Press.

Schmidt, R. (1983). Interaction, acculturation, and the acquisition of communicative competence. In N. Wolfson & E. Judd (Eds.), *Sociolinguistics and second language acquisition* (pp. 137–174). Rowley, MA: Newbury House.

Schmidt, R. (1990). The role of consciousness in second language learning. *Applied Linguistics, 11*, 129–58.

Schmidt, R. (2001). Attention. In P. Robinson (Ed.), *Cognition and second language instruction* (pp. 3–32). Cambridge: Cambridge University Press.

Schmidt, R., & Frota, S. N. (1986). Developing basic conversational ability in a second language: A case study of the adult learner of Portuguese. In R. R. Day (Ed.), *Talking to learn: Conversation in second language acquisition* (pp. 237–326). Rowley, MA: Newbury House.

Sharwood Smith, M. (1993). Input enhancement in instructed SLA: Theoretical bases. *Studies in Second Language Acquisition, 15*, 165–179.

Sime, D. (2008). "Because of her gesture, it's very easy to understand"—Learners' perceptions of teachers' gestures in the foreign language class. In S. G. McCafferty & G. Stam (Eds.), *Gesture: Second language acquisition and classroom research* (pp. 259–279). New York: Routledge.

Stam, G. (2008). What gestures reveal about second language acquisition. In S. G. McCafferty & G. Stam (Eds.), *Gesture: Second language acquisition and classroom research* (pp. 231–255). New York: Routledge.

Stam, G., & McCafferty, S. G. (2008). Gesture studies and second language acquisition: A review. In S. G. McCafferty & G. Stam (Eds.), *Gesture: Second language acquisition and classroom research* (pp. 3–24). New York: Routledge.

Streeck, J. (2008). Laborious intersubjectivity: Attentional struggle and embodied communication in an auto-shop. In I. Wachsmuth, M. Lenzen, & G. Knoblick (Eds.), *Embodied communication in humans and machines* (pp. 201–228). Oxford: Oxford University Press.

Streeck, J. (2009). *Gesturecraft: The manu-facture of meaning.* Amsterdam: John Benjamins.

Swain, M. (1985). Communicative competence: Some roles of comprehensible input and comprehensible output in its development. In S. M. Gass & C. G. Madden (Eds.), *Input in second language acquisition* (pp. 235–253). Rowley, MA: Newbury House Publishers, Inc.

Swain, M. (2000). The output hypothesis and beyond: Mediating acquisition through collaborative dialogue. In J. P. Lantolf (Ed.), *Sociocultural theory and second language learning* (pp. 97–114). New York: Oxford University Press.

Tabensky, A. (2008). Expository discourse in a second language classroom: How learners use gesture. In S. G. McCafferty & G. Stam (Eds.), *Gesture: Second language acquisition and classroom research* (pp. 298–320). New York: Routledge.

Tarone, E. (2010). Social context and cognition in SLA: A variationist perspective. In R. Batstone (Ed.), *Sociocognitive perspectives on language use and language learning* (pp. 54–72). Oxford: Oxford University Press.

Thornbury, S. (1997). Reformulation and reconstruction: Tasks that promote "noticing." *ELT Journal, 51*, 326–335.

Tomasello, M., & Herron, C. (1988). Down the garden path: Inducing and correcting overgeneralization errors in the foreign language classroom. *Applied Psycholinguistics*, 9, 237–246.

van Lier, L. (1996). *Interaction in the language curriculum: Awareness, autonomy, and authenticity*. London: Longman.

van Lier, L. (2000). From input to affordance: Social-interactive learning from an ecological perspective. In J. P. Lantolf (Ed.), *Sociocultural theory and second language learning* (pp. 245–259). New York: Oxford University Press.

van Lier, L. (2004). *The ecology and semiotics of language learning: A sociocultural perspective*. Boston: Kluwer Academic Publishers.

Vygostky, L. (1962). *Thought and language*. Cambridge, MA: The Massachusetts Institute of Technology.

Vygotsky, L. (1978). *Mind in society: The development of higher psychological processes*. Cambridge, MA: Harvard University Press.

Williams, J., & Evans, J. (1998). What kind of focus and on which forms? In C. Doughty & J. Williams (Eds.), *Focus on form in classroom second language acquisition* (pp. 139–155). Cambridge: Cambridge University Press.

NFLRC monographs

Noticing and Mediation: A Sociocultural Perspective

Riikka Alanen
University of Jyväskylä

The role of consciousness in human activity has preoccupied a great number of scholars in philosophy, psychology and education, including the Russian psychologist Lev Vygotsky. In cognitively oriented applied linguistics, the role of consciousness in second language learning has likewise been hotly debated. Schmidt's proposal in 1990 that some form of conscious noticing is necessary for second language acquisition to take place offered researchers a new way of approaching the issue. It also created a great deal of controversy and scrutiny of the key construct: what exactly is noticing? Does it have a role at all in implicit second language learning or is it mainly relevant for metalinguistic knowledge as Truscott (1998) claimed?

In this article I will approach the notion of noticing from a neo-Vygotskian sociocultural perspective, focusing on what noticing might be and how it is linked to the powerful, all-pervasive mechanism of mediation in Vygotskian tradition. Finally, I will critically examine the current state of research, which is dominated by the need to separate the implicit from the explicit, the unconscious and the conscious in the study of second language acquisition processes. On the one hand, scientific rigor demands such a division. On the other hand, it may result in a skewed view of the processes of language use and learning: language users / learners are fundamentally conscious, intentional agents in whose actions, including the use and learning of other languages, the conscious and the unconscious are always intertwined.

Watson: "You see everything."
Holmes: "I see no more than you, but I have trained myself to notice what I see."

—Sir Arthur Conan Doyle, "The Adventure of the Blanched Soldier" (1927)

Alanen, R. (2013). Noticing and mediation: A sociocultural perspective. In J. M. Bergsleithner, S. N. Frota, & J. K. Yoshioka (Eds.), *Noticing and second language acquisition: Studies in honor of Richard Schmidt* (pp. 331–341). Honolulu: University of Hawai'i, National Foreign Language Resource Center.

Introduction: The noticing hypothesis

A great number of misunderstandings, disputes, and controversies in applied linguistics, like in any other field of science and scholarship for that matter, arise from the use of terms open for interpretation. Consciousness is one such term, and as we shall see, attention, noticing, and the noticing hypothesis are too. The issue of whether and what kind of processes in second language learning are conscious or unconscious has been hotly contested since Stephen Krashen proposed that learning was conscious, acquisition unconscious, and, to quote Rudyard Kipling, "never the twain shall meet." Why it became such a contentious issue was, perhaps unsurprisingly, related to language teaching. Of what use was teaching grammar to L2 learners—usually through written tasks—if real acquisition took place unconsciously?

Richard Schmidt, then a professor in the prestigious Second Language Studies doctoral program / English as a Second Language master's program at the University of Hawai'i, set about correcting the situation by writing a groundbreaking paper "The role of consciousness in second language learning," which was published in *Applied Linguistics* in 1990. In the article he outlined the different meanings given to the term *consciousness* and their relevance to the study of second language learning. In short, he went on to distinguish between three different senses of the term: "consciousness as awareness, consciousness as intention, and consciousness as knowledge" (1990, p. 131). More specifically, he was interested in the role of consciousness in L2 input processing. L2 input, that is, exposure to a second language, was necessary for input turning into intake, i.e., L2 language learning to take place. In terms of usage-based theories of language acquisition, in order to learn a language, you have to use it.

Schmidt's interest in whether learners had to be conscious of various elements of language input in order to learn them arose from his own experiences while learning Portuguese in Brazil in the 1980s (Schmidt & Frota, 1986). During his stay, he noted that he only learned, that is, was capable of starting to use in his own speech, such features of Portuguese he had paid conscious attention to, had noticed. This experience led him to study the role of consciousness, noticing, and eventually, attention in second language learning (Schmidt, 1990, 1993, 1995, 2001, 2012).

The noticing hypothesis—that "input does not become intake for language learning unless it is noticed, that is, consciously registered" (Schmidt, 2012, p. 27)—was first formulated by Schmidt in 1990. As Schmidt (1990) noted, various terms have been used in psychological and second language research literature to refer to the same construct, including focal awareness, episodic awareness, and apperceived input (p. 132). Noticing refers to a private, subjective experience, which can be operationally defined as availability for verbal report. Schmidt was careful to note that failure to report something is not the same thing as failure to notice and that there are experiences (e.g., features of regional accent) that are difficult to describe in words.

Drawing on research literature in cognitive psychology and information processing theories, Schmidt distinguished between three levels of awareness he considered crucial for his discussion: perception, noticing (focal awareness), and understanding. Noticing in the sense of focal awareness was located somewhere between the levels of perception and understanding; the latter for Schmidt implied reflection on the objects of consciousness in an effort to comprehend their significance. As Schmidt points out, "[P]roblem solving belongs to this level of consciousness as do metacognitions (awareness of awareness) of all types" (1990, p. 132–133).

In his 2001 discussion of attention, Schmidt further refined noticing as a "subjective correlate of attention" (p. 5). His intention was to separate *noticing* from *metalinguistic awareness* as clearly as possible, by assuming that the objects of attention and noticing are "elements of the surface structure of utterances in the input—instances of language, rather than any abstract rules or principles of which such instances may be exemplars" (p. 5). He goes on to state that

> Although statements about learners 'noticing [i.e., becoming aware of] the structural regularities of a language' are perfectly fine in ordinary language, these imply comparisons across instances and metalinguistic reflection (thinking about what has been attended and noticed, forming hypotheses, and so forth), much more than is implied by the restricted sense of noticing used here. (Schmidt, 2001, p. 5)

By reframing the concept of noticing in terms of attention, Schmidt sought to counter a type of criticism leveled at the noticing hypothesis—that noticing equals metalinguistic awareness (Truscott, 1998). Since its conception the noticing hypothesis had become part of the perennial debate about teaching grammar: is it necessary to teach grammar explicitly to L2 learners? The noticing hypothesis was seen to provide support to the advocates of any kind of grammar teaching, form-focused instruction in particular, to claims that L2 grammar can only be learned with conscious awareness of grammatical details (Truscott, 1998, p. 104).

Does the noticing hypothesis then require awareness of rules? For Schmidt, awareness of rules is a prototypical case of understanding (as Truscott notes); therefore, it falls outside his own, more restricted use of the term, which is comparable to "apperception" (Gass, 1988), "detection within selective attention" (Tomlin & Villa, 1994), and "detection plus rehearsal in short term memory" (Robinson, 1995) (Schmidt, 2001, p. 5). However, early on in the 1990s, when the idea of noticing first caught fire, other, more comprehensive interpretations very soon arose, many of them advocating some type of focus on form (e.g., Ellis, 1993; Fotos, 1994). As Schmidt (1995) admits, it is difficult to make an empirical distinction between noticing without understanding and noticing with understanding (which would mean that there is no way to prove or disprove the noticing hypothesis, i.e., it cannot be falsified). Truscott's solution was a total separation of (conscious) noticing from language acquisition; thus, he felt it was necessary to reformulate the noticing hypothesis, stating that "the acquisition of metalinguistic knowledge is tied to (conscious) noticing; development of competence is not" (p. 124). But was Truscott right? And, within the framework adopted in this paper, does it matter?

Truscott was careful to direct his criticism to "(conscious)" noticing. He also makes it very clear that he only discusses noticing as it relates to the development of competence in the Chomskyan sense of (unconscious) knowledge of language, i.e., syntactic competence. By making a distinction between the conscious and the unconscious, Truscott follows mainstream contemporary cognitive psychology in making a clear separation between the two systems, although mainly, one suspects, on linguistic grounds. What is at issue here is of course, again, the interface between the two systems, a debate by no means limited to SLA: what we are talking about are different conceptions about human cognition and consciousness and how they relate to each other.

Following Baars (1988, 1996), Schmidt (2001) considers (selective) attention as the mechanism responsible for access to awareness. In psychology, attention has been variously defined as alertness, orientation, or control (e.g., Allport, 1993). Schmidt starts his extensive discussion of attention in second language learning by first going back to William James and Wilhelm Wundt, some of the founding figures of modern psychology, to the idea that individual learners can choose the focus of their attention. Such attention is called voluntary. As Schmidt notes, there also exists more passive attention known as involuntary attention: "Involuntary attention is data driven, elicited bottom-up. Voluntary attention is top-down in the sense that attention is directed to outside events by inner intentions" (Schmidt, 2001, p. 14). Attention, then, in its various guises, seems to have been attributed features from two rather different systems, the conscious and the unconscious. Drawing on an extensive review of past research on attention, Allport suggests that there is not, and can never be, one uniform, monolithic mechanism that can be called 'attention' (1993, p. 203).

Most modern theories of attention choose to focus on specific functions of attention (like selection) or separate it into various subsystems. In reviewing the modern-day cognitive neuroscience and information processing approaches to attention and consciousness, Schmidt draws on Baars's (1988, 1996) global workspace theory of consciousness. In Baar's model, selection is a type of gatekeeping mechanism between the unlimited-capacity (i.e., unconscious) and the limited-capacity (i.e., conscious) portions of the information processing system, a kind of access-point to consciousness. Tomlin and Villa (1994) drew on Michael Posner's influential research on attention in order to clarify the role of attention in SLA. Like Posner, they distinguished between three mechanisms or subsystems of attention at work in second language acquisition: alertness, orientation, and detection. For Tomlin and Villa, detection, the cognitive registration of stimuli, is the necessary and sufficient condition for further processing and learning.

Thus, for Tomlin and Villa, registration did not necessarily imply consciousness. As Schmidt points out, it is in fact necessary to distinguish between "detection without awareness (i.e., 'registration') and detection within focal attention accompanied by awareness (conscious perception, or 'noticing')" for noticing to be considered a viable, empirically verifiable construct (2001, p. 18). Leow (1998), who further refined Schmidt's view of noticing on the basis of Tomlin and Villa's research, proposed an agenda for empirical research in noticing. This led to further controversy; see Simard and Wong (2001) and Leow (2002). Schmidt (2001), too, notes that it might be possible to operationalize the distinction between non-conscious registration and conscious perception within focal attention, at least in some experimental settings.

It is at this stage that I turn to sociocultural approaches to the development of human behavior. In what follows, I will consider some of the notions within sociocultural theory of mind to examine how noticing in the restricted sense defined by Schmidt could be conceptualized within the framework for research based on the ideas of the Russian psychologist Lev Vygotsky and his modern interpreters.

Noticing and mediation

Lev Vygotsky (1896–1934) was highly intrigued by the origins and development of higher mental functions, that is, to Vygotsky, the human mind. Like many of his contemporaries in the West in the early 1900s—George Herbert Mead, James Baldwin, and Pierre Janet, among many others—he searched for the origin of mind outside the individual mind, in the social and the cultural (Valsiner & van der Veer, 2000). Vygotsky's search for answers eventually led him to a sophisticated understanding of the relationship between thinking and speech—his most famous work is *Thinking and speech*, published first in Russian in 1934, and in 1962, 1986, and 1987 in English in different translations.

In some ways Vygotsky, too, was concerned exactly with the same issues that are current in contemporary psychology and cognitive neuroscience today and for which Schmidt, Tomlin and Villa, and Leow have tried to find answers: how are lower mental functions—processes independent of consciousness and learning such as sensory functions and involuntary attention—related to higher mental functions such as problem solving and voluntary attention? How is awareness as attention related to awareness as understanding? As it is likely that attention as a unitary, uniform construct really does not exist, Schmidt's solution was to go deeper into the various mechanisms that constitute the notion, and focus on one particular aspect, that of detection. Noticing, therefore, is the conscious registration of detection.

To Vygotsky, the mind was a system of higher mental functions, and consciousness was its organizing feature. By higher mental functions Vygotsky meant things like voluntary attention, verbal thinking, creative imagination, concept formation, and logical memory (Vygotsky, 1997, pp. 7, 17). To Vygotsky, the most salient and characteristic feature of consciousness was selection and control. Very early on in his thinking, he noted that not only did human beings have an awareness of the object they perceive, they also had a potential awareness of their own perception of the object. Vygotsky called this phenomenon doubled experience, "experience of experience"; in other words, people had reflexive awareness of their own mental states (Vygotsky, 1999). As Bakhurst (2007) notes, in *Thinking and speech*, Vygotsky's view of the relation of mind and meaning led him to a sophisticated conclusion: "Mental phenomena take as their objects meaningful states of affairs in the world or representations thereof and any mental state can itself become the object of another: my thought can become the object of attention, reasoning, memory, volition, and so forth" (p. 55).

Even though metacognition as a term was not used by Vygotsky himself, much of what is understood by metacognition in contemporary psychology falls under the notion of consciousness in Vygotsky's writings (e.g., Bråten, 1991a, 1991b, 1992). Within the Vygotskian framework, however, it is, in a way, pointless to try to distinguish involuntary attention from voluntary attention, or cognition from metacognition, in the sense that there is no inherent virtue in trying to discover "pure," unadulterated, unconscious cognitive processes. After all, it is consciousness that makes us human, and in Vygotskian thinking, consciousness in itself is a worthy object of study. In Schmidt's words, Vygotsky was undoubtedly talking about consciousness as awareness and understanding.

That, for Vygostky, conscious experience was the focal point of research does not imply, however, that he did not distinguish between lower and higher mental functions. In fact, there was a crucial difference: for Vygotsky, the singular characteristic of higher mental functions—including voluntary attention—is that they are mediated. To reframe the issue in terms of noticing, if we consciously register that we have detected a stimulus, let's say a linguistic feature in the surrounding speech, then that conscious registration is not direct, it is mediated. The question is: mediated by what?

According to Vygotsky, "[...] voluntary attention is a process of the turning inward of mediated attention" (1997, p. 161). During a child's cognitive development, higher mental functions such as voluntary attention—as opposed to natural, "primitive" attention—emerge through a process called *mediation*. Instead of a direct connection between the subject and object of action, the relationship between the two is mediated. For example, when a human being uses a physical tool such as hammer to pound a nail into the wall, we might say that his action is mediated by a physical tool. In addition to such obviously material tools, there are other means that human beings use to mediate their action, language in particular being probably the most influential of them.

But how does attention become mediated? Vygotsky (1997) described a series of experiments in which a child was presented with two cups, each covered with a lid marked with a piece of paper in a lighter or darker shade of gray. A nut was always placed by the experimenter under the cup covered with a darker shade of paper. The task of the child was to choose the cup with a nut inside. No verbal instructions were given to the child. A child of five was unable to detect the rule governing the placement of the nut after 49 experiments. At this point the experimenter placed the nut into the cup and pointed to the darker colored paper attached to the lid and then pointed to the light gray piece of paper attached to the lid of the empty cup. By the 51st experiment, the child won. Significantly, though, he was first unable to give the correct verbal explanation for his win. It was only a couple of wins later that he was not only able to transfer his reasoning to cups covered with a dark gray and black piece of paper but also consistently give the correct verbal explanation "the nut is where it is darker." (p. 164).

The experiment was based on a similar experiment carried out by the famous German psychologist Wolfgang Köhler on chimpanzees (Köhler, 1927). Köhler believed that for the chimpanzees, gesturing toward the stimulus was critical for the correct selection. Vygotsky also concluded that the roots of voluntary attention are in the function of pointing. Later Vygotsky repeated the experiment with another child that had observed the first experiment and thus had seen the pointing gestures and heard the first child's explanations. Although the second child was more successful than the first child, he too required further instruction—pointing—from the experimenter. Vygotsky goes on to expand the role of pointing to speech:

> At first, the adult directs the attention of the child with words creating as if additional pointers—arrows—to the things around the child and creates from the words potent stimuli-instructions. Then the child begins to participate actively in the instructions and himself begins to use a word or a sound as a means of indicating, that is, turning the attention of the adults to an object that interests him. (Vygotsky, 1997, p. 168)

According to Vygotsky, it is the actions and words of adults that guide the child's focus of attention. The child learns to direct her attention to the features of the task relevant for its successful completion. How she is capable of doing it was much later elaborated on by Michael Tomasello, another developmental psychologist studying the development of primates and human children.

Tomasello describes in his 2003 book *Constructing a language: A usage-based theory of language acquisition* the processes necessary for language acquisition to take place. The first of these is intention-reading (theory of mind), which include such things as the ability to share attention with other persons to objects and events of mutual interest, to follow the attention and gesturing of other persons, as well as the ability to culturally or imitatively learn the intentional actions of others. The second set of processes involves pattern-finding (categorization), e.g., the ability to form perceptual and conceptual categories and create analogies (pp. 3–4). Language structure gradually emerges from language use: "[W]hen human beings use symbols to communicate with one another, stringing them together in sequences, patterns of use emerge and become consolidated into grammatical constructions" (p. 5).

Tomasello (2003) sidesteps the thorny issue of what attention is at this point by focusing on how (joint) attention manifests itself. As he notes, the human species has a genetic predisposition to joint attention. According to Tomasello (2003), at around 9–12 months of age, human infants begin to, for example, follow the gaze of adults and imitate the way adults act on objects. "These behaviors are not dyadic—between child and adult (or child and object)—but rather they are triadic in the sense that they involve infants coordinating their interactions with both objects and people, resulting in a referential triangle of child, adult, and the object or event to which they share attention" (p. 21). Like human infants, second or foreign language learners, too, learn to direct their attention to particular features of language. But how conscious are they of the processes and mechanisms that drive their attention?

A noted developmental and cultural psychologist James Wertsch (2007, p. 180) has discussed the sometimes contradictory notion of mediation in Vygotsky's writings. In his view Vygotsky seems to use the concepts of mediation and mediational means in two rather different senses. For example, in describing a series of psychological experiments, Vygotsky talks about what Wertsch calls explicit mediation. In these experiments mediation is explicit in that individuals quite openly and intentionally introduce mediational means or signs into an ongoing stream of activity and because such means or signs are obviously material and nontransitory in nature. As Wertsch notes, explicit mediation, how people make use of cultural tools (e.g., technological tools) in remembering and action, for example, continues to be a topic of study in contemporary psychology and cognitive science.

In contrast, implicit mediation is not so obvious and far more difficult to detect. Language, or social and inner speech which Vygotsky preferred as constructs, is a prime example of implicit mediation of human consciousness. Language, in its many guises, is far more transparent and harder to detect, and since it is often an integral part of communicative acts, there is no need to introduce it artificially. According to Wertsch, one of the properties of implicit mediation is that it

> involves signs, especially natural language, whose primary function is communication. In contrast to the case for explicit mediation, these signs are not purposefully introduced into human action, and they do not initially emerge for the purpose of organizing it. (Wertsch, 2007, p. 180)

For Wertsch, then, it seems that intentionality is the characteristic feature that most effectively differentiates implicit mediation from explicit mediation. Difficulty of detection (most likely in the sense of conscious registration, or noticing introduced by Schmidt) seems to be a secondary feature, as it is relative, not absolute.

The role of language in implicit mediation highlights the complexity of issues involved in second or foreign language learning. In L2 learning, language is both the object of learning and the most important mediational means that regulates the learning process. Such regulation takes place at a number of levels, including the level of intentional goal-setting—what the learner decides to do with language. Language most likely also mediates the process of conscious registration—but what kind of language?

According to Vygotsky, inner speech is the tool used extensively by human beings in verbal thinking. It emerges from the social, external speech through the process of internalization (or rather, interiorization) whereby the speech used by others to regulate a child's activities first becomes private speech (somewhat comparable to Piaget's egocentric speech in its outward appearance) and then gradually internalized, giving birth to the inner speech. Inner speech is not like social speech in structure but much more fragmentary in nature (e.g., de Guerrero, 2005; Wertsch, 1985).

In recent years cognitive psychologists such as Alan Baddeley and Akira Miyake have associated inner speech with executive control and working memory, giving it a supporting function in task switching (Baddeley, Chincotta, & Adlam, 2001; Emerson & Miyake, 2003; Miyake, Emerson, Padilla, & Ahn, 2004). This is reminiscent of what was suggested earlier by Robinson (1995) that noticing might be defined as "detection plus rehearsal in short term memory."

The philosopher Peter Carruthers—known for the originator of the massive modularity of mind approach to human cognition—has also proposed a way to include the notion of mediation through language in human cognitive functioning (not all his views are necessarily compatible with those who lean more toward a unitary view of cognition or with some of the tenets in neo-Vygotskian thinking, see e.g., de Guerrero, 2005, p. 6, for an overview). According to Carruthers (2008), most contemporary mainstream research in human cognitive functioning presuppose the existence of two systems: System 1, which is a collection of different systems that are fast and unconscious, operating in parallel with one another, and System 2, which is slow, serial, conscious, and subject to cross-cultural and individual variation. Instead of having evolved separately, one on top of the other, Carruthers proposes that System 2 gradually evolved from System 1, through the custom of mental rehearsal of action schemata. As no overt action takes place, visual and other images of the action are "globally broadcast" (here Carruthers refers to Baars) back to System 1, instead, resulting in consciousness of said action. That System 2 seems slow and effortful is because its operation involves several cycles of operation of System 1. And because System 2 is action based, it can be influenced, for example, through advice and guidance from other human beings, beliefs, mental rehearsal, or reflection. It is at this stage that language interacts with human thought processes.

It seems to me, then, that it might be quite plausible to suggest that noticing as the conscious registration of linguistic elements can be viewed as an instantiation or reflex of mediation. Mediation can be accomplished by any number of means, inner speech being one of them, but other elements in the environment may play a role as well (gaze, gestures such as pointing, etc.). Whatever mechanism it is that drives the process of guidance or mediation, the end result is that the learner becomes subjectively aware that she had noticed a feature in the stream of speech that had previously escaped her attention. After being noticed, it may very well be that that particular feature itself may take on a mediating role in any further activity. It may be, though, that in order for that to happen, the learner must develop an awareness of regular rule-like patterns. Significantly, however, the learner is now in the position to regulate her own learning.

Conclusion

The goal of L2 learning is for the L2 user / learner to be able to master the L2 to the extent she is capable of using it on her own, that is, to achieve self-regulation. Self-regulation is a well-studied phenomenon in developmental psychology involving a research tradition rather different from the study of attention. Both Jean Piaget and Lev Vygotsky devoted whole series of experiments to its study, as have a number of notable psychologists during the past decades. What is at issue is, of course, attention as control. In short, self-regulation refers to the processes whereby individuals control their attention and behavior (Berk & Winsler, 1995; Posner & Rothbart, 1998); it may include self-generated thoughts, feelings, and behaviors that are oriented to attaining goals (Zimmerman, 2000).

Voluntary attention is an important part of its development. For Vygotsky, other forms of regulation included object-regulation and other-regulation. The child's actions may at first be regulated by objects in the immediate environment; for example, colorful building blocks or other toys in the child's immediate environment may first draw her attention directly. But very early on, as described much later by e.g., Tomasello, other people begin to regulate the child's actions in relation to objects. The key to such actions is joint attention. For human beings, primary means for carrying out other-regulatory functions is dialogic interaction. Initially, L2 users / learners require a lot of help from interlocutors. Eventually, they begin to take over a larger portion of the responsibility for strategic functions, until self-regulation, or independent strategic functioning, is achieved.

During the past two decades, an increasing number of studies in cognitive psychology have focused on executive attention as a system for the voluntary control of action (Posner & Rothbart, 1998; Rueda, Posner, & Rothbart, 2005). Such studies are trying to integrate both research traditions with hopes of showing how training attention could extend to greater cognitive or emotional regulation. Such research may have implications for L2 learning and the study of noticing as well. From the Vygotskian point of view, knowledge about self-regulation is statable and verbalizable (Bråten, 1991b). Thus, knowledge about cognition and control of cognition are inseparable aspects of higher forms of mental functioning. "... [T]he child's conscious awareness of a cognitive process, his ability to perceive it as a process of a certain kind, such as memory, also enables him to control or regulate this very process." (Bråten, 1991b, p. 315). From such perspective it is rather pointless to argue whether a phenomenon such as noticing falls within the domain of cognition or metacognition.

In sum, noticing is not only a private, subjective experience, it is a private, subjective experience of an event or act of conscious registration which plays an important part both in the development of self-regulation and during self-regulatory activities. In this chapter it is proposed that, as such, noticing can be regarded as a reflex of mediation. If this is the case, its study has interesting implications for the study of mediation as well, in particular implicit mediation involved in language use.

References

Allport, A. (1993). Attention and control: Have we been asking the wrong questions? A critical review of 25 years. In D. E. Meyer & S. Kornblum (Eds.), *Attention and performance XIV. Synergies in experimental psychology, artificial intelligence, and cognitive neuroscience* (pp. 183–218). Cambridge, MA: The MIT Press.

Baars, B. J. (1988). *A cognitive theory of consciousness.* New York: Cambridge University Press.

Baars, B. J. (1996). *In the theater of consciousness.* New York: Oxford University Press.

Baddeley, A. D., Chincotta, D., & Adlam, A. (2001). Working memory and the control of action: Evidence from task switching. *Journal of Experimental Psychology: General, 130*, 641–657.

Bakhurst, D. (2007). Vygotsky's demons. In H. Daniels, M. Cole, & J. V. Wertsch (Eds.), *The Cambridge companion to Vygotsky* (pp. 50–76). Cambridge: Cambridge University Press.

Berk, L. E., & Winsler, A. (1995). *Scaffolding children's learning: Vygotsky and early childhood education.* Washington, DC: National Association for the Education of Young Children.

Bråten, I. (1991a). Vygotsky as precursor to metacognitive theory: I. The concept of metacognition and its roots. *Scandinavian Journal of Educational Research, 35*, 179–192.

Bråten, I. (1991b). Vygotsky as precursor to metacognitive theory: II. Vygotsky as metacognitivist. *Scandinavian Journal of Educational Research, 35*, 305–320.

Bråten, I. (1992). Vygotsky as precursor to metacognitive theory: III. Recent metacognitive research within a Vygotskian framework. The concept of metacognition and its roots. *Scandinavian Journal of Educational Research, 36*, 3–18.

Carruthers, P. (2008). Language in cognition. In E. Margolis, R. Samuels, and S. Stich (Eds.), *The Oxford handbook of philosophy of cognitive science* (pp. 382–401). Oxford: Oxford University Press.

Conan Doyle, A. (1927). *The case-book of Sherlock Holmes*. London: John Murray.

de Guerrero, M. C. M. (2005). *Inner speech—L2: Thinking words in a second language*. Berlin: Springer.

Ellis, R. (1993). The structural syllabus and second language acquisition. *TESOL Quarterly 27*, 91–113.

Emerson, M. J., & Miyake, A. (2003). The role of inner speech in task switching: A dual-task investigation. *Journal of Memory and Language*, *48*, 148–168.

Fotos, S. N. (1994). Integrating grammar instruction and communicative language use through grammar consciousness-raising tasks. *TESOL Quarterly*, *28*, 323–51.

Gass, S. (1988). Integrating research areas: A framework for second language studies. *Applied Linguistics*, *9*, 198–217.

Köhler, W. (1927). *The mentality of apes*. New York: Vintage Books.

Leow, R. P. (1998). Toward operationalizing the process of attention in second language acquisition: Evidence for Tomlin and Villa's (1994) fine-grained analysis of attention. *Applied Psycholinguistics*, *19*, 133–159.

Leow, R. P. (2002). Models, attention, and awareness in SLA: A response to Simard and Wong's "Alertness, orientation, and detection: The conceptualization of attentional functions in SLA." *Studies in Second Language Acquisition*, *24*, 113–119.

Miyake, A., Emerson, M. J., Padilla, F., & Ahn, J. (2004). Inner speech as a retrieval aid for task goals: The effects of cue type and articulatory suppression. *Acta Psychologia*, *115*, 123–142.

Posner, M. I., & Rothbart, M. K. (1998). Attention, self-regulation, and consciousness. *Philosophical Transactions of the Royal Society of London, B*, *353*, 1915–1927.

Rueda, M. R., Posner, M. I., & Rothbart, M. K. (2005). The development of executive attention: Contributions to the emergence of self-regulation. *Developmental Neuropsychology*, *28*, 573–594.

Robinson, P. (1995). Aptitude, awareness, and the fundamental similiary of implicit and explicit second language learning. In R. Schmidt (Ed.), *Attention and awareness in foreign language learning* (pp. 303–357). Honolulu, HI: University of Hawai'i, National Foreign Language Resource Center.

Schmidt, R. W. (1990). The role of consciousness in second language learning. *Applied Linguistics*, *11*, 129–158.

Schmidt, R. W. (1993). Awareness and second language acquisition. *Annual Review of Applied Linguistics*, *13*, 206–226.

Schmidt, R. W. (1995). Consciousness and foreign language learning: A tutorial on the role of attention and awareness in learning. In R. Schmidt (Ed.), *Attention and awareness in foreign language learning* (pp. 1–63). Honolulu, HI: University of Hawai'i, National Foreign Language Resource Center.

Schmidt, R. W. (2001). Attention. In P. Robinson (Ed.), *Cognition and second language instruction* (pp. 3–32). Cambridge: Cambridge University Press.

Schmidt, R. (2012). Attention, awareness, and individual differences in language learning. In W. M. Chan, K. N. Chin, S. Bhatt, & I. Walker (Eds.), *Perspectives on individual characteristics and foreign language education* (pp. 27–50). Boston, MA: Mouton de Gruyter.

Schmidt, R. W., & Frota, S. N. (1986). Developing basic conversational ability in a second language: A case study of an adult learner of Portuguese. In R. R. Day (Ed.), *Talking to learn: Conversation in second language acquisition* (pp. 237–326). Rowley, MA: Newbury House.

Simard, D., & Wong, W. (2001). Alertness, orientation, and detection. The conceptualization of attentional functions in SLA. *Studies in Second Language Acquisition 23*, 103–124.

Tomasello, M. (2003). *Constructing a language: A usage-based theory of language acquistion.* Cambridge, MA: Harvard University Press.

Tomlin, R. S., & Villa, V. (1994). Attention in cognitive science and second language acquisition. *Studies in Second Language Acquisition, 16*, 183–203.

Truscott, J. (1998). Noticing in second language acquisition: A critical review. *Second Language Research, 14*, 103–135.

Valsiner, J., & van der Veer, R. (2000). *The social mind: Construction of the idea.* Cambridge: Cambridge University Press.

Vygotsky, L. S. (1987). *The collected works of L. S. Vygotsky.* Volume 1. *Problems of general psychology, including the volume Thinking and Speech.* Edited by R. W. Rieber & A. S. Carton. Translation by Norris Minick. New York: Plenum Press.

Vygotsky, L. S. (1997). *The collected works of L. S. Vygotsky.* Volume 4. *The history of the development of higher mental functions.* Edited by R. W. Rieber. Translation by Marie J. Hall. New York: Plenum Press.

Vygotsky, L. S. (1999). Consciousness as a problem in the psychology of behavior. In N. Veresov (Ed.), *Undiscovered Vygotsky: Etudes on the pre-history of cultural-historical psychology* (European Studies in the History of Science and Ideas. Vol. 8) (pp. 251–281). Frankfurt: Peter Lang.

Wertsch, J. V. (1985). *Vygotsky and the social formation of the mind.* Cambridge, MA: Harvard University Press.

Wertsch, J. V. (2007). Mediation. In H. Daniels, M. Cole, & J. V. Wertsch (Eds.), *The Cambridge companion to Vygotsky* (pp. 178–192). Cambridge: Cambridge University Press.

Zimmerman, B. J. (2000). Attainment of self-regulation: A social cognitive perspective. In M. Boekaerts, P. R. Pintrich, & M. Zeidner (Eds.), *Handbook of self-regulation* (pp. 13–39). San Diego, CA: Academic Press.

About the Contributors

Editors

Joara Martin Bergsleithner is a professor in the Department of Foreign Languages and Translation in the Institute of Letters at the University of Brasília, Brazil, where she teaches English and SLA. Her research interests are in the areas of noticing, attention, working memory, L2 oral production, second language acquisition, and different kinds of instructional strategies (e.g., explicit, implicit, focus on form, form-focused instruction, task-based instruction). Her published work includes articles, book chapters, and books on issues in second language learning and teaching. In 2005–06, she was a visiting scholar at the National Foreign Language Resource Center at the University of Hawai'i at Mānoa, where Dick Schmidt was her PhD co-advisor.

Sylvia Nagem Frota is an associate professor in the Department of English and German Studies at the Federal University of Rio de Janeiro, Brazil, where she teaches English and applied linguistics. She has a PhD in Language and Communication. Her research interests include the role of noticing in SLA and the teaching of grammar and EFL/ESL pedagogy. Her main published works are "*Developing basic conversational ability in a second language: A case study of an adult learner of Portuguese*," co-authored with Dick Schmidt, "*The development and validation of a Portuguese version of the Motivated Strategies for Learning Questionnaire*," co-authored with J. D. Brown and M. Cunha, and "*The complex noun phrase and EFL learner's production.*"

Jim Kei Yoshioka is program coordinator at the National Foreign Language Resource Center and events coordinator for the College of Languages, Linguistics, & Literature at the University of Hawai'i at Mānoa, where he also received his MA in English as a Second Language. His specialty is organizing professional development events for language researchers and educators, including international conferences and symposia (e.g., ICLDC, AAAL, SLRF, PacSLRF, etc.), national NFLRC summer institutes, and local workshops and lectures. His professional interests include event planning, pre-service job preparation, materials development, writing pedagogy and assessment, and sociolinguistics. He is very grateful for the over 12 years that Dick Schmidt was a fantastic and supportive director at the NFLRC and wishes him a well-deserved and fun retirement.

Authors

Rebecca J. Adams is the associate director of training for the Center for Faculty Excellence at Northcentral University. Her research focuses on peer interaction in language classrooms. Her research has recently been published in *Language Learning*, *TESOL Quarterly*, and *The Modern Language Journal*.

Riikka Alanen is professor of foreign language education in the Department of Teacher Education of the University of Jyväskylä, Finland. She received an MA in ESL from the University of Hawaiʻi at Mānoa in 1992. Professor Schmidt was her thesis supervisor. Her current research interests include L2 learning and teaching as mediated activity and the role of consciousness and agency in the learning process. She is particularly interested in the role of mediating artifacts, including beliefs about SLA and talk about tasks and texts (spoken and written) in the learning activity, and the way individual agency emerges and is shared by the participants in the learning activity.

Jennifer Behney is an assistant professor of Italian and second language acquisition in the Department of Foreign Languages and Literatures at Youngstown State University. She has a PhD in Second Language Studies from Michigan State University. Her research interests include grammatical gender acquisition; facilitation and inhibition in spoken word recognition; eye-tracking and gender agreement marking; L2 syntactic priming; working memory, inhibition, and interaction; and dialect/minority language preservation. Her work has appeared in *Studies in Second Language Acquisition*, as well as in several edited volumes on SLA.

Anne M. Calderón (ABD) is a PhD student in the Department of Spanish and Portuguese at Georgetown University and holds BA and MA degrees from the University of Illinois at Urbana-Champaign. Specializing in applied linguistics, her work focuses mainly on second language acquisition (SLA) and psycholinguistics. Her dissertation further investigates depth of processing, along with level of intake and type of linguistic item. In addition to research, Anne greatly enjoys teaching and working with undergraduate students.

Minyoung Cho is a PhD student at the University of Hawaiʻi at Mānoa. Her research interests lie in second language acquisition, with particular focus on the role of individual differences in L2 learning and task-based language learning and teaching. Her recent work involves the role of learner motivation in L2 task performance and language development.

Takako Egi received a PhD in linguistics from Georgetown University. She is the director of Japanese language instruction at the University of Kentucky. Her research interests include corrective feedback, attention and awareness, and verbal protocols. Her research has recently been published in *Studies in Second Language Acquisition*, *The Modern Language Journal*, and *System*.

Rod Ellis is currently professor in the Department of Applied Language Studies and Linguistics, University of Auckland, where he teaches postgraduate courses on second language acquisition, individual differences in language learning, and task-based teaching. He is also a professor in the MA in TESOL program in Anaheim University and a visiting professor at Shanghai International Studies University (SISU) as part of China's Chang Jiang Scholars Program. His published work includes articles and books on second language acquisition, language teaching, and teacher education. He is also currently editor of the journal *Language Teaching Research.*

Denis Foucambert is professor of psycholinguistics at the Université du Québec à Montréal. His research focuses on the syntactic processes during reading as well as the observation of writing processes in textual genetics and psycholinguistic frameworks.

Susan Gass is University Distinguished Professor in the Department of Linguistics, Germanic, Slavic, Asian, and African Languages at Michigan State University where she directs the English Language Center and the Second Language Studies Program. She has published widely in the field of second language acquisition including the recent fourth edition of *Second language acquisition: An introductory course* (with Jennifer Behney and Luke Plonsky) published by Routledge. She is the 1985 (with Evangeline Varonis) and 2012 (with Luke Plonsky) recipient of the Paul Pimsleur MLJ-ACTFL Award for Research in Foreign Language Education. Other awards include the Distinguished Faculty Award at Michigan State University and the American Association for Applied Linguistics award for Distinguished Service and Scholarship. She has served as president of the American Association for Applied Linguistics and the International Association of Applied Linguistics.

Aline Godfroid is an assistant professor in the second language studies program at Michigan State University. Her research focuses on cognitive processes in second language acquisition, in particular on the roles of attention and awareness in adult language learning. She teaches courses on psycholinguistics, vocabulary acquisition, and quantitative research methodology.

Phillip Hamrick is a PhD candidate in the Department of Linguistics at Georgetown University, where he focuses on the cognitive mechanisms of second language acquisition. His dissertation examines the incidental development of awareness and declarative memory in early phases of second language syntactic development. He has also published papers on behavioral and computational properties of L2 learning mechanisms, especially those relating to implicit/explicit learning, statistical learning, and associative learning. More recently, his work has focused on the use of trained control groups in SLA research.

Michael Harrington is a senior lecturer in second language acquisition at the University of Queensland, Australia. His research interests are in second language memory, lexical and sentence processing, and assessment. He completed an MA in Hawai'i in the mid-1980s. Dick's work on the psychological mechanisms underlying second language development continues to motivate and inform his research. He also remembers Dick giving great parties.

Shinichi Izumi is a professor at Sophia University, Tokyo, Japan, where he teaches in the BA program in English language studies and the MA and the PhD programs in applied linguistics and TESOL. He received his PhD in applied linguistics from Georgetown University. His principal research interest is in instructed second/foreign language acquisition—content-based instruction, task-based instruction, focus on form, and content and language integrated learning, in particular—and teacher education.

Christine M. Jacknick, an assistant professor at Borough of Manhattan Community College at the City University of New York, is a discourse analyst utilizing conversation analysis to examine discursive practices in the language classroom, highlighting the collaborative nature of talk and identifying the exercise of agency and power through interactional practices. Her research emphasizes the pairing of rigorous, line-by-line discourse analysis with larger social theories, underscoring the relevance of interactional practices to the classroom realities of teachers and students. Her interests also include cross-institutional analysis of interactional practices and micro-analysis of second language development.

Daniel O. Jackson (MS Ed. TESOL, University of Pennsylvania) is a PhD student in the Department of Second Language Studies at the University of Hawai'i at Mānoa, specializing in task-based instruction and cognitive-interactionist approaches to SLA. He is presently conducting his dissertation research under the supervision of Dr. Richard Schmidt.

Ronald P. Leow is professor of applied linguistics and director of Spanish language instruction in the Department of Spanish and Portuguese at Georgetown University. His areas of expertise include language curriculum development, teacher education, SLA, psycholinguistics, attention and awareness in language learning, and research methodology. Professor Leow has published extensively in prestigious journals, which include *Studies in Second Language Acquisition*, *Language Learning*, *Applied Psycholinguistics*, and *The Modern Language Journal*.

Lester C. Loschky is an associate professor of psychology at Kansas State University. His areas of research include visual cognition, attention, comprehension, and second language acquisition. In the late 1980s, he was a student of Dick Schmidt's, who served on his Master's thesis committee and first introduced him to the study of working memory and attention. For lighting this fire in his mind and for Dick's gracious teaching and friendship, he will always be grateful.

Nadia Mifka-Profozic has taught French, ESOL, and English writing for academic purposes in New Zealand and Croatia. She holds a MTESOL and a PhD in language teaching and learning from the University of Auckland. Her main research interests include second language acquisition, learner individual differences, and task-based learning and teaching. She is currently teaching in Croatia.

Mailce Borges Mota is an associate professor in the Department of Foreign Languages and Literatures at the Federal University of Santa Catarina, Brazil. Her research interests include the acquisition of inflectional morphology in Brazilian Portuguese, working memory, eye-tracking, and ERPs. Her work has appeared in various edited volumes on SLA and psycholinguistics.

Ana-María Nuevo holds a PhD in linguistics from Georgetown University. She teaches second language acquisition at American University in Washington, DC, and George Mason University in Fairfax, Virginia. Her research interests include interactionist and social approaches to second language learning.

Patrick Rebuschat is a lecturer in second language acquisition and bilingualism at Lancaster University, UK. He obtained a PhD from the University of Cambridge in 2008 with a dissertation on the implicit learning of natural language syntax. Prior to moving to Lancaster, he spent three years teaching at Georgetown University and two years at Bangor University in North Wales. His research focuses on second language cognition, implicit and explicit learning, and language and music. He is the editor of

Implicit and explicit learning of languages (John Benjamins, 2013) and the co-editor of *Statistical learning and language acquisition* (Mouton de Gruyter, 2012) and *Language and music as cognitive systems* (Oxford University Press, 2011).

Hayo Reinders (www.innovationinteaching.org) is TESOL professor and director of the doctoral program at Anaheim University in the United States and visiting professor at Chulalongkorn University in Thailand. He is also editor-in-chief of *Innovation in Language Learning and Teaching.* Hayo's interests are in technology in education, learner autonomy, and out-of-class learning, and he is a speaker on these subjects for the Royal Society of New Zealand. His most recent books are on teacher autonomy, teaching methodologies, and second language acquisition, and he edits a book series on *New Language Learning and Teaching Environments* for Palgrave Macmillan.

Kate Riestenberg is a PhD student in general linguistics at Georgetown University. Her major areas of interest include language acquisition and development, acquisition theory, and language typology. She is especially interested in the acquisition of understudied and endangered languages. Her most recent work investigates thinking for speaking among second language speakers of English in Uganda. Kate also has experience in language testing and teaching English as a foreign language. Kate holds a BA in Hispanic linguistics from The Ohio State University.

Rebecca Sachs is a visiting assistant professor in the Department of Linguistics at Georgetown University. She holds a Master's in TESOL from Michigan State University and a PhD in linguistics from Georgetown. Much of her research involves exploring adult language learners' awareness of linguistic phenomena and uses of feedback in relation to both internal factors (e.g., age, working memory, metalinguistic knowledge, motivation) and external factors (e.g., task complexity, type of feedback, implicit vs. explicit learning conditions), with the ultimate goal of optimizing learning opportunities according to the profiles of individual students. Many of her studies also assess the veridicality and reactivity of awareness measures with the goal of advancing research methods in the field of SLA. Her work has appeared in edited collections and in journals such as *Language Learning, Computer Assisted Language Learning,* and *Studies in Second Language Acquisition.*

Jens Schmidtke is a doctoral student in second language studies at Michigan State University. He received his BA from the University of Bochum, Germany, and his MA from the University of Connecticut. His research interests lie in psycholinguistics and bilingualism.

Daphnée Simard is professor of second language acquisition at the Université du Québec à Montréal. Her research investigates the relationship between attentional processes, metalinguistic reflection, and second language acquisition.

Peter Skehan now splits his time between part-time posts at the University of Auckland and St. Mary's University College, Twickenham. Previously he taught at universities in the U.K. and Hong Kong. He is interested in second language acquisition, especially task-based performance and language aptitude. He has published extensively in each of these areas, such as *Individual differences in second language learning* and *A cognitive approach to language learning.* Most recently, a collection of his publications has appeared as *Researching tasks: Performance, assessment, and pedagogy* (2011) with Shanghai Foreign Language Education Press.

Patti Spinner is an assistant professor of second language studies in the Department of Linguistics, Germanic, Slavic, Asian and African Languages at Michigan

State University. Her research takes a formal perspective on the acquisition of morphosyntax, especially features such as gender and number. Recent work has examined the acquisition of gender in German, Italian, and Swahili. Her work has appeared in *Studies in Second Language Acquisition*, *Second Language Research*, *Applied Linguistics*, and the *International Review of Applied Linguistics*.

Scott Thornbury is the curriculum coordinator on the MA TESOL program at The New School in New York. His previous experience includes teaching and teacher training in Egypt, UK, Spain, and in his native New Zealand, and he is a frequent presenter at international conferences. His writing credits include several award-winning books for teachers on language and methodology, as well as a number of journal articles and book chapters on such diverse subjects as voice-setting phonology, corpus linguistics, speaking instruction, and embodied learning.

John N. Williams graduated in psychology at the University of Durham, U.K., and then went on to do doctoral research at the Medical Research Council Cognition and Brain Sciences Unit, Cambridge, receiving a PhD from the University of Cambridge for work on semantic processing during spoken language comprehension. He spent two years as a post-doctoral researcher at the University of Padua, Italy, working on semantic access and word recognition, and worked as an English language assistant at the University of Florence for one year before taking up his present post in the Department of Theoretical and Applied Linguistics (formerly Research Centre for English and Applied Linguistics), University of Cambridge. His current main research interests are in the cognitive mechanisms of second language learning and second language lexical and syntactic processing.

Nicole Ziegler recently completed a PhD in applied linguistics at Georgetown University and is now an assistant professor in the Department of Second Language Studies at the University of Hawaiʻi at Mānoa. Her research focuses on adult and child instructed second language acquisition, interaction, and the role of technology and corpus linguistics in second language development and instruction.

Pragmatics & Language Learning

Gabriele Kasper, series editor

Pragmatics & Language Learning ("PLL"), a refereed series sponsored by the National Foreign Language Resource Center, publishes selected papers from the International Pragmatics & Language Learning conference under the editorship of the conference hosts and the series editor. Check the NFLRC website for upcoming PLL conferences and PLL volumes.

PRAGMATICS AND LANGUAGE LEARNING VOLUME 13

Tim Greer, Donna Tatsuki, & Carsten Roever (Editors), 2013

Pragmatics & Language Learning Volume 13 examines the organization of second language and multilingual speakers' talk and pragmatic knowledge across a range of naturalistic and experimental activities. Based on data collected among ESL and EFL learners from a variety of backgrounds, the contributions explore the nexus of pragmatic knowledge, interaction, and L2 learning outside and inside of educational settings.

292pp., ISBN 978–0–9835816–4–2 $30.

PRAGMATICS AND LANGUAGE LEARNING VOLUME 12

Gabriele Kasper, Hanh thi Nguyen, Dina R. Yoshimi, & Jim K. Yoshioka (Editors), 2010

This volume examines the organization of second language and multilingual speakers' talk and pragmatic knowledge across a range of naturalistic and experimental activities. Based on data collected on Danish, English, Hawai'i Creole, Indonesian, and Japanese as target languages, the contributions explore the nexus of pragmatic knowledge, interaction, and L2 learning outside and inside of educational settings.

364pp., ISBN 978–09800459–6–3 $30.

PRAGMATICS AND LANGUAGE LEARNING VOLUME 11

Kathleen Bardovi-Harlig, César Félix-Brasdefer, & Alwiya S. Omar (Editors), 2006

This volume features cutting-edge theoretical and empirical research on pragmatics and language learning among a wide variety of learners in diverse learning contexts from a variety of language backgrounds and target languages (English, German, Japanese, Kiswahili, Persian, and Spanish). This collection of papers from researchers around the world includes critical appraisals on the role of formulas in interlanguage pragmatics, and speech-act research from a conversation analytic perspective. Empirical studies examine learner data using innovative methods of analysis and investigate issues in pragmatic development and the instruction of pragmatics.

430pp., ISBN 978–0–8248–3137–0 $30.

NFLRC Monographs

Monographs of the National Foreign Language Resource Center present the findings of recent work in applied linguistics that is of relevance to language teaching and learning (with a focus on the less commonly taught languages of Asia and the Pacific) and are of particular interest to foreign language educators, applied linguists, and researchers. Prior to 2006, these monographs were published as "SLTCC Technical Reports."

NEW PERSPECTIVES ON JAPANESE LANGUAGE LEARNING, LINGUISTICS, AND CULTURE

KIMI KONDO-BROWN, YOSHIKO SAITO-ABBOTT, SHINGO SATSUTANI, MICHIO TSUTSUI, & ANN WEHMEYER (EDITORS), 2013

This volume is a collection of selected refereed papers presented at the Association of Teachers of Japanese Annual Spring Conference held at the University of Hawai'i at Mānoa in March of 2011. It not only covers several important topics on teaching and learning spoken and written Japanese and culture in and beyond classroom settings but also includes research investigating certain linguistics items from new perspectives.

208pp., ISBN 978–0–9835816–3–5 $25.

DEVELOPING, USING, AND ANALYZING RUBRICS IN LANGUAGE ASSESSMENT WITH CASE STUDIES IN ASIAN AND PACIFIC LANGUAGES

JAMES DEAN BROWN (EDITOR), 2012

Rubrics are essential tools for all language teachers in this age of communicative and task-based teaching and assessment—tools that allow us to efficiently communicate to our students what we are looking for in the productive language abilities of speaking and writing and then effectively assess those abilities when the time comes for grading students, giving them feedback, placing them into new courses, and so forth. This book provides a wide array of ideas, suggestions, and examples (mostly from Māori, Hawaiian, and Japanese language assessment projects) to help language educators effectively develop, use, revise, analyze, and report on rubric-based assessments.

212pp., ISBN 978–0–9835816–1–1 $25.

RESEARCH AMONG LEARNERS OF CHINESE AS A FOREIGN LANGUAGE

MICHAEL E. EVERSON & HELEN H. SHEN (EDITORS), 2010

Cutting-edge in its approach and international in its authorship, this fourth monograph in a series sponsored by the Chinese Language Teachers Association features eight research studies that explore a variety of themes, topics, and perspectives important to a variety of stakeholders in the Chinese language learning community. Employing a wide range of research methodologies, the volume provides data from actual Chinese language learners and will be of value to both theoreticians and practitioners alike. *[in English & Chinese]*

180pp., ISBN 978–0–9800459–4–9 $20.

MANCHU: A TEXTBOOK FOR READING DOCUMENTS (SECOND EDITION)

Gertraude Roth Li, 2010

This book offers students a tool to gain a basic grounding in the Manchu language. The reading selections provided in this volume represent various types of documents, ranging from examples of the very earliest Manchu writing (17th century) to samples of contemporary Sibe (Xibo), a language that may be considered a modern version of Manchu. Since Manchu courses are only rarely taught at universities anywhere, this second edition includes audio recordings to assist students with the pronunciation of the texts.

418pp., ISBN 978–0–9800459–5–6 $36.

TOWARD USEFUL PROGRAM EVALUATION IN COLLEGE FOREIGN LANGUAGE EDUCATION

John M. Norris, John McE. Davis, Castle Sinicrope, & Yukiko Watanabe (Editors), 2009

This volume reports on innovative, useful evaluation work conducted within U.S. college foreign language programs. An introductory chapter scopes out the territory, reporting key findings from research into the concerns, impetuses, and uses for evaluation that FL educators identify. Seven chapters then highlight examples of evaluations conducted in diverse language programs and institutional contexts. Each case is reported by program-internal educators, who walk readers through critical steps, from identifying evaluation uses, users, and questions, to designing methods, interpreting findings, and taking actions. A concluding chapter reflects on the emerging roles for FL program evaluation and articulates an agenda for integrating evaluation into language education practice.

240pp., ISBN 978–0–9800459–3–2 $30.

SECOND LANGUAGE TEACHING AND LEARNING IN THE NET GENERATION

Raquel Oxford & Jeffrey Oxford (Editors), 2009

Today's young people—the Net Generation—have grown up with technology all around them. However, teachers cannot assume that students' familiarity with technology in general transfers successfully to pedagogical settings. This volume examines various technologies and offers concrete advice on how each can be successfully implemented in the second language curriculum.

240pp., ISBN 978–0–9800459–2–5 $30.

CASE STUDIES IN FOREIGN LANGUAGE PLACEMENT: PRACTICES AND POSSIBILITIES

Thom Hudson & Martyn Clark (Editors), 2008

Although most language programs make placement decisions on the basis of placement tests, there is surprisingly little published about different contexts and systems of placement testing. The present volume contains case studies of placement programs in foreign language programs at the tertiary level across the United States. The different programs span the spectrum from large programs servicing hundreds of students annually to small language programs with very few students. The contributions to this volume address such issues as how the size of the program, presence or absence of heritage learners, and population changes affect language placement decisions.

201pp., ISBN 0–9800459–0–8 $20.

CHINESE AS A HERITAGE LANGUAGE: FOSTERING ROOTED WORLD CITIZENRY

Agnes Weiyun He & Yun Xiao (Editors), 2008

Thirty-two scholars examine the sociocultural, cognitive-linguistic, and educational-institutional trajectories along which Chinese as a Heritage Language may be acquired, maintained, and developed. They draw upon developmental psychology, functional linguistics, linguistic and cultural anthropology, discourse analysis, orthography analysis, reading research, second language acquisition, and bilingualism. This volume aims to lay a foundation for theories, models, and master scripts to be discussed, debated, and developed, and to stimulate research and enhance teaching both within and beyond Chinese language education.

280pp., ISBN 978–0–8248–3286–5 $20.

PERSPECTIVES ON TEACHING CONNECTED SPEECH TO SECOND LANGUAGE SPEAKERS

James Dean Brown & Kimi Kondo-Brown (Editors), 2006

This book is a collection of fourteen articles on connected speech of interest to teachers, researchers, and materials developers in both ESL/EFL (ten chapters focus on connected speech in English) and Japanese (four chapters focus on Japanese connected speech). The fourteen chapters are divided up into five sections:

- What do we know so far about teaching connected speech?
- Does connected speech instruction work?
- How should connected speech be taught in English?
- How should connected speech be taught in Japanese?
- How should connected speech be tested?

290pp., ISBN 978–0–8248–3136–3 $20.

CORPUS LINGUISTICS FOR KOREAN LANGUAGE LEARNING AND TEACHING

Robert Bley-Vroman & Hyunsook Ko (Editors), 2006

Dramatic advances in personal-computer technology have given language teachers access to vast quantities of machine-readable text, which can be analyzed with a view toward improving the basis of language instruction. Corpus linguistics provides analytic techniques and practical tools for studying language in use. This volume provides both an introductory framework for the use of corpus linguistics for language teaching and examples of its application for Korean teaching and learning. The collected papers cover topics in Korean syntax, lexicon, and discourse, and second language acquisition research, always with a focus on application in the classroom. An overview of Korean corpus linguistics tools and available Korean corpora are also included.

265pp., ISBN 0–8248–3062–8 $25.

NEW TECHNOLOGIES AND LANGUAGE LEARNING: CASES IN THE LESS COMMONLY TAUGHT LANGUAGES

Carol Anne Spreen (Editor), 2002

In recent years, the National Security Education Program (NSEP) has supported an increasing number of programs for teaching languages using different technological media. This compilation of case study initiatives funded through the NSEP Institutional Grants Program presents a range of technology-based options for language programming that will help universities make more informed decisions about teaching less commonly taught languages. The eight chapters describe how different types of technologies are used to support language programs (i.e., Web, ITV, and audio- or video-based materials), discuss identifiable trends in e-language learning, and explore how technology addresses issues of equity, diversity, and opportunity. This book offers many lessons learned and decisions made as technology changes and learning needs become more complex.

188pp., ISBN 0–8248–2634–5 $25.

AN INVESTIGATION OF SECOND LANGUAGE TASK-BASED PERFORMANCE ASSESSMENTS

James Dean Brown, Thom Hudson, John M. Norris, & William Bonk, 2002

This volume describes the creation of performance assessment instruments and their validation (based on work started in a previous monograph). It begins by explaining the test and rating scale development processes and the administration of the resulting three seven-task tests to 90 university-level EFL and ESL students. The results are examined in terms of (a) the effects of test revision; (b) comparisons among the task-dependent, task-independent, and self-rating scales; and (c) reliability and validity issues.

240pp., ISBN 0–8248–2633–7 $25.

MOTIVATION AND SECOND LANGUAGE ACQUISITION

Zoltán Dörnyei & Richard Schmidt (Editors), 2001

This volume—the second in this series concerned with motivation and foreign language learning—includes papers presented in a state-of-the-art colloquium on L2 motivation at the American Association for Applied Linguistics (Vancouver, 2000) and a number of specially commissioned studies. The 20 chapters, written by some of the best known researchers in the field, cover a wide range of theoretical and research methodological issues, and also offer empirical results (both qualitative and quantitative) concerning the learning of many different languages (Arabic, Chinese, English, Filipino, French, German, Hindi, Italian, Japanese, Russian, and Spanish) in a broad range of learning contexts (Bahrain, Brazil, Canada, Egypt, Finland, Hungary, Ireland, Israel, Japan, Spain, and the U.S.).

520pp., ISBN 0–8248–2458–X $30.

A FOCUS ON LANGUAGE TEST DEVELOPMENT: EXPANDING THE LANGUAGE PROFICIENCY CONSTRUCT ACROSS A VARIETY OF TESTS

Thom Hudson & James Dean Brown (Editors), 2001

This volume presents eight research studies that introduce a variety of novel, nontraditional forms of second and foreign language assessment. To the extent possible, the studies also show the entire test development process, warts and all. These language testing projects not only demonstrate many of the types of problems that test developers run into in the real world but also afford the reader unique insights into the language test development process.

230pp., ISBN 0–8248–2351–6 $20.

STUDIES ON KOREAN IN COMMUNITY SCHOOLS

Dong-Jae Lee, Sookeun Cho, Miseon Lee, Minsun Song, & William O'Grady (Editors), 2000

The papers in this volume focus on language teaching and learning in Korean community schools. Drawing on innovative experimental work and research in linguistics, education, and psychology, the contributors address issues of importance to teachers, administrators, and parents. Topics covered include childhood bilingualism, Korean grammar, language acquisition, children's literature, and language teaching methodology. [in Korean]

256pp., ISBN 0–8248–2352–4 $20.

A COMMUNICATIVE FRAMEWORK FOR INTRODUCTORY JAPANESE LANGUAGE CURRICULA

Washington State Japanese Language Curriculum Guidelines Committee, 2000

In recent years, the number of schools offering Japanese nationwide has increased dramatically. Because of the tremendous popularity of the Japanese language and the shortage of teachers, quite a few untrained, nonnative and native teachers are in the classrooms and are expected to teach several levels of Japanese. These guidelines are intended to assist individual teachers and professional associations throughout the United States in designing Japanese language curricula. They are meant to serve as a framework from which language teaching can be expanded and are intended to allow teachers to enhance and strengthen the quality of Japanese language instruction.

168pp., ISBN 0–8248–2350–8 $20.

FOREIGN LANGUAGE TEACHING AND MINORITY LANGUAGE EDUCATION

KATHRYN A. DAVIS (EDITOR), 1999

This volume seeks to examine the potential for building relationships among foreign language, bilingual, and ESL programs towards fostering bilingualism. Part I of the volume examines the sociopolitical contexts for language partnerships, including:

- obstacles to developing bilingualism;
- implications of acculturation, identity, and language issues for linguistic minorities; and
- the potential for developing partnerships across primary, secondary, and tertiary institutions.

Part II of the volume provides research findings on the Foreign Language Partnership Project, designed to capitalize on the resources of immigrant students to enhance foreign language learning.

152pp., ISBN 0–8248–2067–3 $20.

DESIGNING SECOND LANGUAGE PERFORMANCE ASSESSMENTS

JOHN M. NORRIS, JAMES DEAN BROWN, THOM HUDSON, & JIM YOSHIOKA, 1998, 2000

This technical report focuses on the decision-making potential provided by second language performance assessments. The authors first situate performance assessment within a broader discussion of alternatives in language assessment and in educational assessment in general. They then discuss issues in performance assessment design, implementation, reliability, and validity. Finally, they present a prototype framework for second language performance assessment based on the integration of theoretical underpinnings and research findings from the task-based language teaching literature, the language testing literature, and the educational measurement literature. The authors outline test and item specifications, and they present numerous examples of prototypical language tasks. They also propose a research agenda focusing on the operationalization of second language performance assessments.

248pp., ISBN 0–8248–2109–2 $20.

SECOND LANGUAGE DEVELOPMENT IN WRITING: MEASURES OF FLUENCY, ACCURACY, AND COMPLEXITY

KATE WOLFE-QUINTERO, SHUNJI INAGAKI, & HAE-YOUNG KIM, 1998, 2002

In this book, the authors analyze and compare the ways that fluency, accuracy, grammatical complexity, and lexical complexity have been measured in studies of language development in second language writing. More than 100 developmental measures are examined, with detailed comparisons of the results across the studies that have used each measure. The authors discuss the theoretical foundations for each type of developmental measure, and they consider the relationship between developmental measures and various types of proficiency measures. They also examine criteria for determining which developmental measures are the most successful and suggest which measures are the most promising for continuing work on language development.

208pp., ISBN 0–8248–2069–X $20.

THE DEVELOPMENT OF A LEXICAL TONE PHONOLOGY IN AMERICAN ADULT LEARNERS OF STANDARD MANDARIN CHINESE

Sylvia Henel Sun, 1998

The study reported is based on an assessment of three decades of research on the SLA of Mandarin tone. It investigates whether differences in learners' tone perception and production are related to differences in the effects of certain linguistic, task, and learner factors. The learners of focus are American students of Mandarin in Beijing, China. Their performances on two perception and three production tasks are analyzed through a host of variables and methods of quantification.

328pp., ISBN 0–8248–2068–1 $20.

NEW TRENDS AND ISSUES IN TEACHING JAPANESE LANGUAGE AND CULTURE

Haruko M. Cook, Kyoko Hijirida, & Mildred Tahara (Editors), 1997

In recent years, Japanese has become the fourth most commonly taught foreign language at the college level in the United States. As the number of students who study Japanese has increased, the teaching of Japanese as a foreign language has been established as an important academic field of study. This technical report includes nine contributions to the advancement of this field, encompassing the following five important issues:

- Literature and literature teaching
- Technology in the language classroom
- Orthography
- Testing
- Grammatical versus pragmatic approaches to language teaching

164pp., ISBN 0–8248–2067–3 $20.

SIX MEASURES OF JSL PRAGMATICS

Sayoko Okada Yamashita, 1996

This book investigates differences among tests that can be used to measure the cross-cultural pragmatic ability of English-speaking learners of Japanese. Building on the work of Hudson, Detmer, and Brown (Technical Reports #2 and #7 in this series), the author modified six test types that she used to gather data from North American learners of Japanese. She found numerous problems with the multiple-choice discourse completion test but reported that the other five tests all proved highly reliable and reasonably valid. Practical issues involved in creating and using such language tests are discussed from a variety of perspectives.

213pp., ISBN 0–8248–1914–4 $15.

LANGUAGE LEARNING STRATEGIES AROUND THE WORLD: CROSS-CULTURAL PERSPECTIVES

Rebecca L. Oxford (Editor), 1996, 1997, 2002

Language learning strategies are the specific steps students take to improve their progress in learning a second or foreign language. Optimizing learning strategies improves language performance. This groundbreaking book presents new information about cultural influences on the use of language learning strategies. It also shows innovative ways to assess students' strategy use and remarkable techniques for helping students improve their choice of strategies, with the goal of peak language learning.

166pp., ISBN 0–8248–1910–1 $20.

TELECOLLABORATION IN FOREIGN LANGUAGE LEARNING: PROCEEDINGS OF THE HAWAI'I SYMPOSIUM

MARK WARSCHAUER (EDITOR), 1996

The Symposium on Local & Global Electronic Networking in Foreign Language Learning & Research, part of the National Foreign Language Resource Center's 1995 Summer Institute on Technology & the Human Factor in Foreign Language Education, included presentations of papers and hands-on workshops conducted by Symposium participants to facilitate the sharing of resources, ideas, and information about all aspects of electronic networking for foreign language teaching and research, including electronic discussion and conferencing, international cultural exchanges, real-time communication and simulations, research and resource retrieval via the Internet, and research using networks. This collection presents a sampling of those presentations.

252pp., ISBN 0–8248–1867–9 $20.

LANGUAGE LEARNING MOTIVATION: PATHWAYS TO THE NEW CENTURY

REBECCA L. OXFORD (EDITOR), 1996

This volume chronicles a revolution in our thinking about what makes students want to learn languages and what causes them to persist in that difficult and rewarding adventure. Topics in this book include the internal structures of and external connections with foreign language motivation; exploring adult language learning motivation, self-efficacy, and anxiety; comparing the motivations and learning strategies of students of Japanese and Spanish; and enhancing the theory of language learning motivation from many psychological and social perspectives.

218pp., ISBN 0–8248–1849–0 $20.

LINGUISTICS & LANGUAGE TEACHING: PROCEEDINGS OF THE SIXTH JOINT LSH-HATESL CONFERENCE

CYNTHIA REVES, CAROLINE STEELE, & CATHY S. P. WONG (EDITORS), 1996

Technical Report #10 contains 18 articles revolving around the following three topics:

- Linguistic issues—These six papers discuss various linguistic issues: ideophones, syllabic nasals, linguistic areas, computation, tonal melody classification, and wh-words.
- Sociolinguistics—Sociolinguistic phenomena in Swahili, signing, Hawaiian, and Japanese are discussed in four of the papers.
- Language teaching and learning—These eight papers cover prosodic modification, note taking, planning in oral production, oral testing, language policy, L2 essay organization, access to dative alternation rules, and child noun phrase structure development.

364pp., ISBN 0–8248–1851–2 $20.

ATTENTION & AWARENESS IN FOREIGN LANGUAGE LEARNING

RICHARD SCHMIDT (EDITOR), 1995

Issues related to the role of attention and awareness in learning lie at the heart of many theoretical and practical controversies in the foreign language field. This collection of papers presents research into the learning of Spanish, Japanese, Finnish, Hawaiian, and English as a second language (with additional comments and examples from French, German, and miniature artificial languages) that bear on these crucial questions for foreign language pedagogy.

394pp., ISBN 0–8248–1794–X $20.

VIRTUAL CONNECTIONS: ONLINE ACTIVITIES AND PROJECTS FOR NETWORKING LANGUAGE LEARNERS

MARK WARSCHAUER (EDITOR), 1995, 1996

Computer networking has created dramatic new possibilities for connecting language learners in a single classroom or across the globe. This collection of activities and projects makes use of email, the internet, computer conferencing, and other forms of computer-mediated communication for the foreign and second language classroom at any level of instruction. Teachers from around the world submitted the activities compiled in this volume—activities that they have used successfully in their own classrooms.

417pp., ISBN 0–8248–1793–1 $30.

DEVELOPING PROTOTYPIC MEASURES OF CROSS-CULTURAL PRAGMATICS

THOM HUDSON, EMILY DETMER, & J. D. BROWN, 1995

Although the study of cross-cultural pragmatics has gained importance in applied linguistics, there are no standard forms of assessment that might make research comparable across studies and languages. The present volume describes the process through which six forms of cross-cultural assessment were developed for second language learners of English. The models may be used for second language learners of other languages. The six forms of assessment involve two forms each of indirect discourse completion tests, oral language production, and self-assessment. The procedures involve the assessment of requests, apologies, and refusals.

198pp., ISBN 0–8248–1763–X $15.

THE ROLE OF PHONOLOGICAL CODING IN READING KANJI

SACHIKO MATSUNAGA, 1995

In this technical report, the author reports the results of a study that she conducted on phonological coding in reading kanji using an eye-movement monitor, and draws some pedagogical implications. In addition, she reviews current literature on the different schools of thought regarding instruction in reading kanji and its role in the teaching of nonalphabetic written languages like Japanese.

64pp., ISBN 0–8248–1734–6 $10.

PRAGMATICS OF CHINESE AS NATIVE AND TARGET LANGUAGE

GABRIELE KASPER (EDITOR), 1995

This technical report includes six contributions to the study of the pragmatics of Mandarin Chinese:

- A report of an interview study conducted with nonnative speakers of Chinese; and
- Five data-based studies on the performance of different speech acts by native speakers of Mandarin—requesting, refusing, complaining, giving bad news, disagreeing, and complimenting.

312pp., ISBN 0–8248–1733–8 $20.

A BIBLIOGRAPHY OF PEDAGOGY AND RESEARCH IN INTERPRETATION AND TRANSLATION

ETILVIA ARJONA, 1993

This technical report includes four types of bibliographic information on translation and interpretation studies:

- Research efforts across disciplinary boundaries—cognitive psychology, neurolinguistics, psycholinguistics, sociolinguistics, computational linguistics, measurement, aptitude testing, language policy, decision-making, theses, and dissertations;
- Training information covering program design, curriculum studies, instruction, and school administration;
- Instructional information detailing course syllabi, methodology, models, available textbooks; and
- Testing information about aptitude, selection, and diagnostic tests.

115pp., ISBN 0–8248–1572–6 $10.

PRAGMATICS OF JAPANESE AS NATIVE AND TARGET LANGUAGE

GABRIELE KASPER (EDITOR), 1992, 1996

This technical report includes three contributions to the study of the pragmatics of Japanese:

- A bibliography on speech-act performance, discourse management, and other pragmatic and sociolinguistic features of Japanese;
- A study on introspective methods in examining Japanese learners' performance of refusals; and
- A longitudinal investigation of the acquisition of the particle *ne* by nonnative speakers of Japanese.

125pp., ISBN 0–8248–1462–2 $10.

A FRAMEWORK FOR TESTING CROSS-CULTURAL PRAGMATICS

THOM HUDSON, EMILY DETMER, & J. D. BROWN, 1992

This technical report presents a framework for developing methods that assess cross-cultural pragmatic ability. Although the framework has been designed for Japanese and American cross-cultural contrasts, it can serve as a generic approach that can be applied to other language contrasts. The focus is on the variables of social distance, relative power, and the degree of imposition within the speech acts of requests, refusals, and apologies. Evaluation of performance is based on recognition of the speech act, amount of speech, forms or formulae used, directness, formality, and politeness.

51pp., ISBN 0–8248–1463–0 $10.

RESEARCH METHODS IN INTERLANGUAGE PRAGMATICS

GABRIELE KASPER & MERETE DAHL, 1991

This technical report reviews the methods of data collection employed in 39 studies of interlanguage pragmatics, defined narrowly as the investigation of nonnative speakers' comprehension and production of speech acts, and the acquisition of L2-related speech-act knowledge. Data collection instruments are distinguished according to the degree to which they constrain informants' responses, and whether they tap speech-act perception/comprehension or production. A main focus of discussion is the validity of different types of data, in particular their adequacy to approximate authentic performance of linguistic action.

51pp., ISBN 0–8248–1419–3 $10.

CPSIA information can be obtained
at www.ICGtesting.com
Printed in the USA
FFHW011303150119
50188685-55139FF